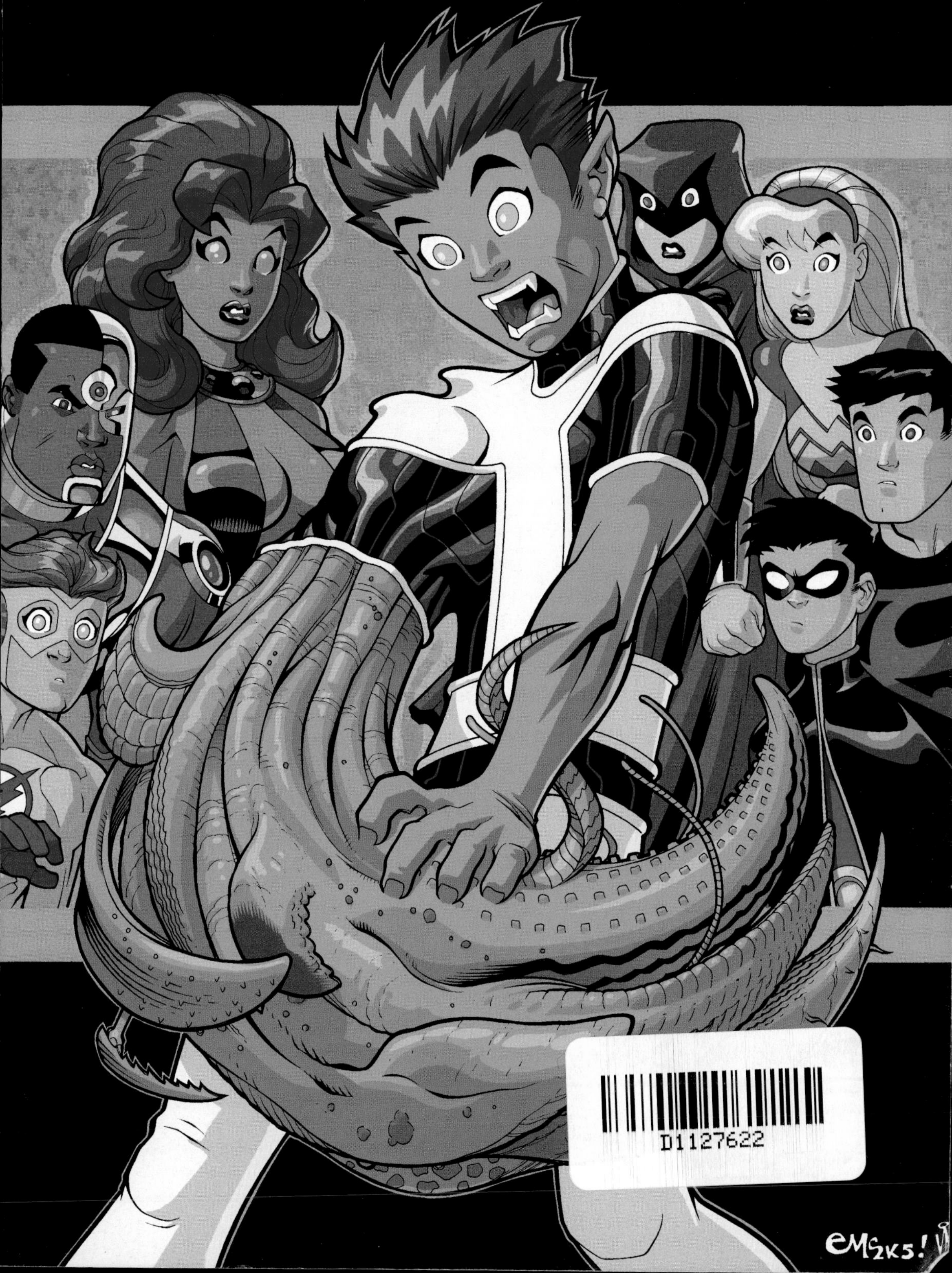

BEAST BOY: PASSENGER 15B

GEOFF JOHNS
BEN RAAB
Writers

JUSTINIANO
Penciller

CHRIS IVY
Inker

JASON WRIGHT
Colorist

BILL OAKLEY
Letterer

ED McGUINNESS & DEXTER VINES
Cover Artists

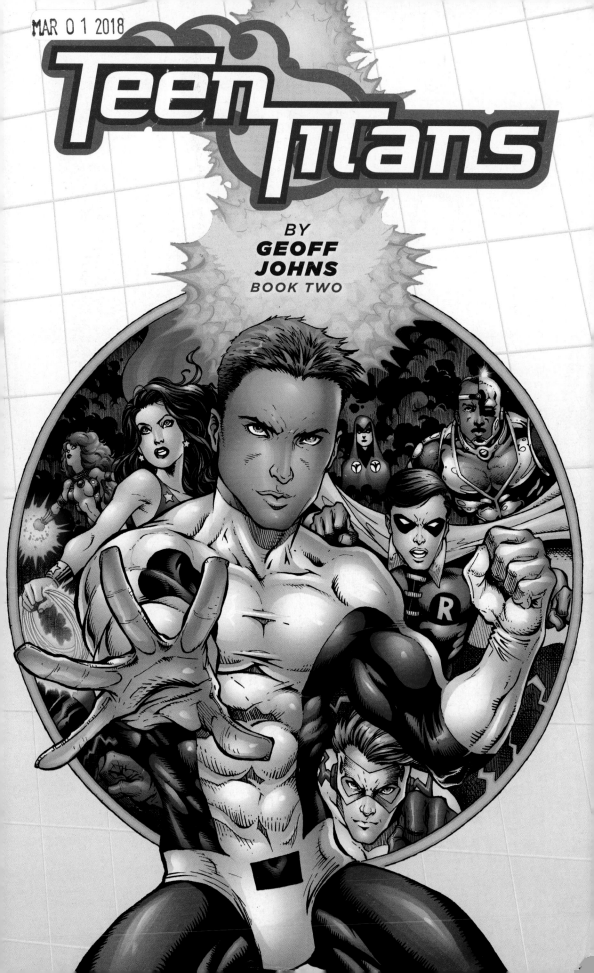

Teen Titans

BY **GEOFF JOHNS**
BOOK TWO

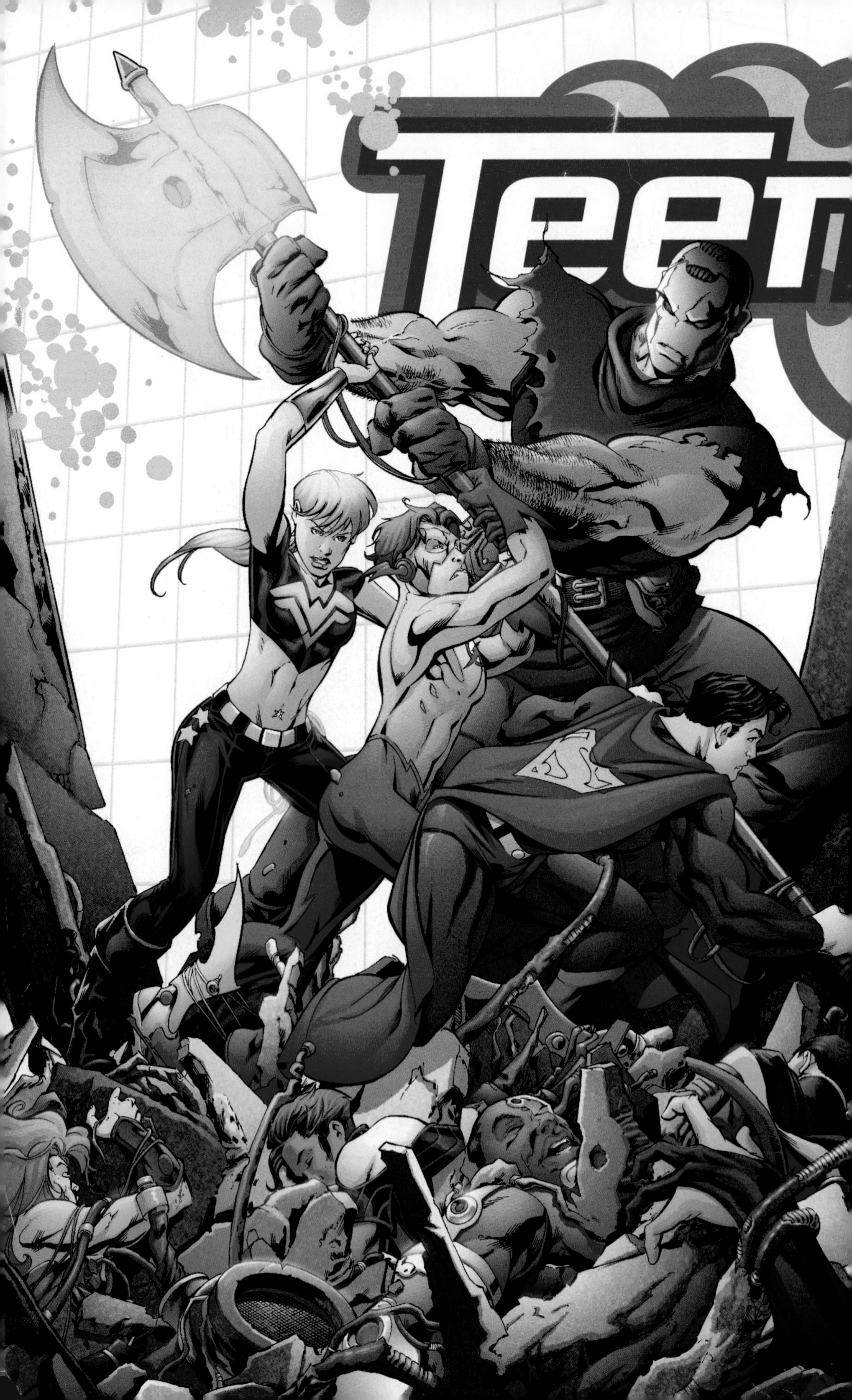

TITANS

BY **GEOFF JOHNS**
BOOK TWO

GEOFF JOHNS
BEN RAAB   **MARK WAID**
WRITERS

MIKE McKONE
TOM GRUMMETT   **JUSTINIANO**
JOE PRADO   **IVAN REIS**
PENCILLERS

CHRIS IVY
MARLO ALQUIZA   **MARC CAMPOS**
LARY STUCKER
INKERS

JEROMY COX
SNO-CONE
JASON WRIGHT
COLORISTS

COMICRAFT
ROB LEIGH
BILL OAKLEY
LETTERERS

PHIL JIMENEZ, ANDY LANNING, AND TANYA & RICHARD HORIE
COLLECTION COVER ARTISTS

BEAST BOY CREATED BY **ARNOLD DRAKE**

SUPERBOY CREATED BY **JERRY SIEGEL**
BY SPECIAL ARRANGEMENT WITH THE JERRY SIEGEL FAMILY

NIGHTWING CREATED BY **MARV WOLFMAN** AND **GEORGE PÉREZ**

BATMAN CREATED BY **BOB KANE** WITH **BILL FINGER**

MIKE CARLIN   EDDIE BERGANZA
Editors – Original Series

MAUREEN McTIGUE   TOM PALMER JR.
Associate Editors – Original Series

JEANINE SCHAEFER
Assistant Editor – Original Series

JEB WOODARD
Group Editor – Collected Editions

BETSY GOLDEN
Editor – Collected Edition

STEVE COOK
Design Director – Books

CURTIS KING JR.
Publication Design

BOB HARRAS
Senior VP – Editor-in-Chief, DC Comics

PAT McCALLUM
Executive Editor, DC Comics

DIANE NELSON
President

DAN DiDIO
Publisher

JIM LEE
Publisher

GEOFF JOHNS
President & Chief Creative Officer

AMIT DESAI
Executive VP – Business & Marketing
Strategy, Direct to Consumer
& Global Franchise Management

SAM ADES Senior
VP & General Manager, Digital Services

BOBBIE CHASE
VP & Executive Editor, Young Reader
& Talent Development

MARK CHIARELLO
Senior VP – Art, Design
& Collected Editions

JOHN CUNNINGHAM
Senior VP – Sales & Trade Marketing

ANNE DePIES
Senior VP – Business Strategy, Finance &
Administration

DON FALLETTI
VP – Manufacturing Operations

LAWRENCE GANEM
VP – Editorial Administration & Talent
Relations

ALISON GILL
Senior VP – Manufacturing & Operations

HANK KANALZ
Senior VP – Editorial Strategy &
Administration

JAY KOGAN
VP – Legal Affairs

JACK MAHAN
VP – Business Affairs

NICK J. NAPOLITANO
VP – Manufacturing Administration

EDDIE SCANNELL
VP – Consumer Marketing

COURTNEY SIMMONS
Senior VP – Publicity & Communications

JIM (SKI) SOKOLOWSKI
VP – Comic Book Specialty Sales & Trade
Marketing

NANCY SPEARS
VP – Mass, Book, Digital Sales & Trade
Marketing

MICHELE R. WELLS
VP – Content Strategy

FSC
www.fsc.org

MIX
Paper from
responsible sources
FSC® C016956

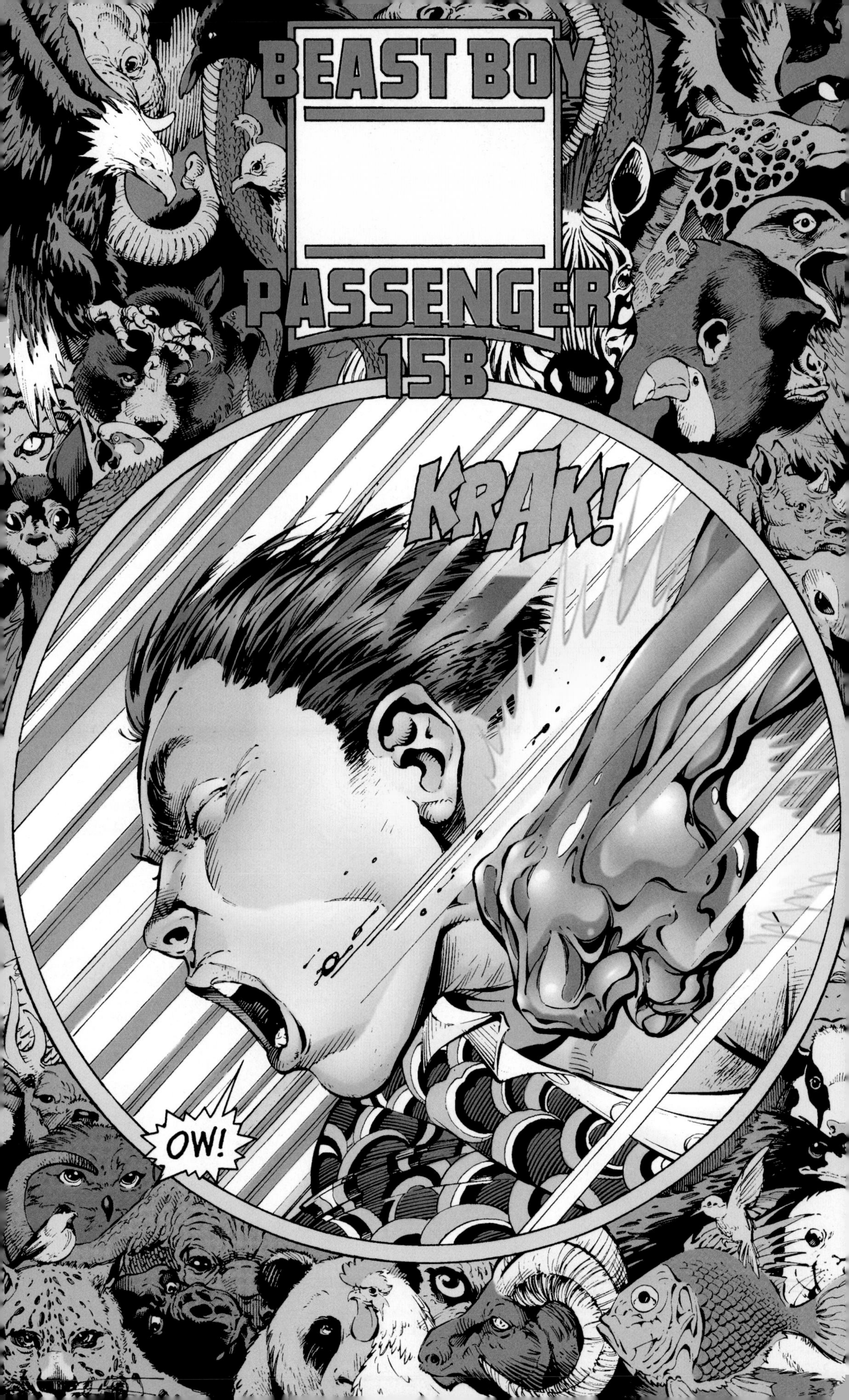

BEAST BOY
PASSENGER 15B
KRAK!
OW!

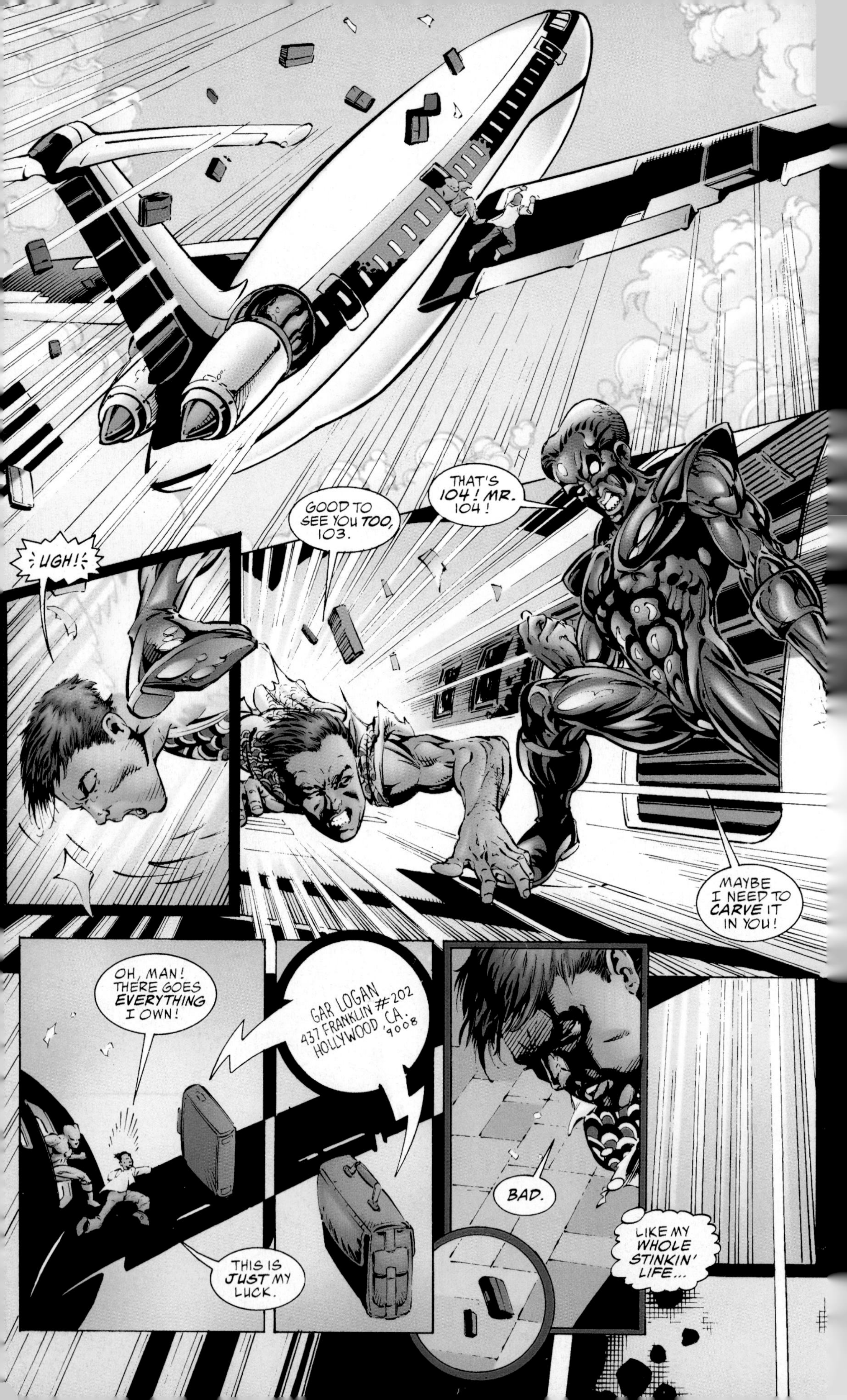
GOOD TO SEE YOU TOO, 103.
THAT'S 104! MR. 104!
UGH!
MAYBE I NEED TO CARVE IT IN YOU!
OH, MAN! THERE GOES EVERYTHING I OWN!
THIS IS JUST MY LUCK.
GAR LOGAN 437 FRANKLIN #202 HOLLYWOOD, CA. 9008
BAD.
LIKE MY WHOLE STINKIN' LIFE...

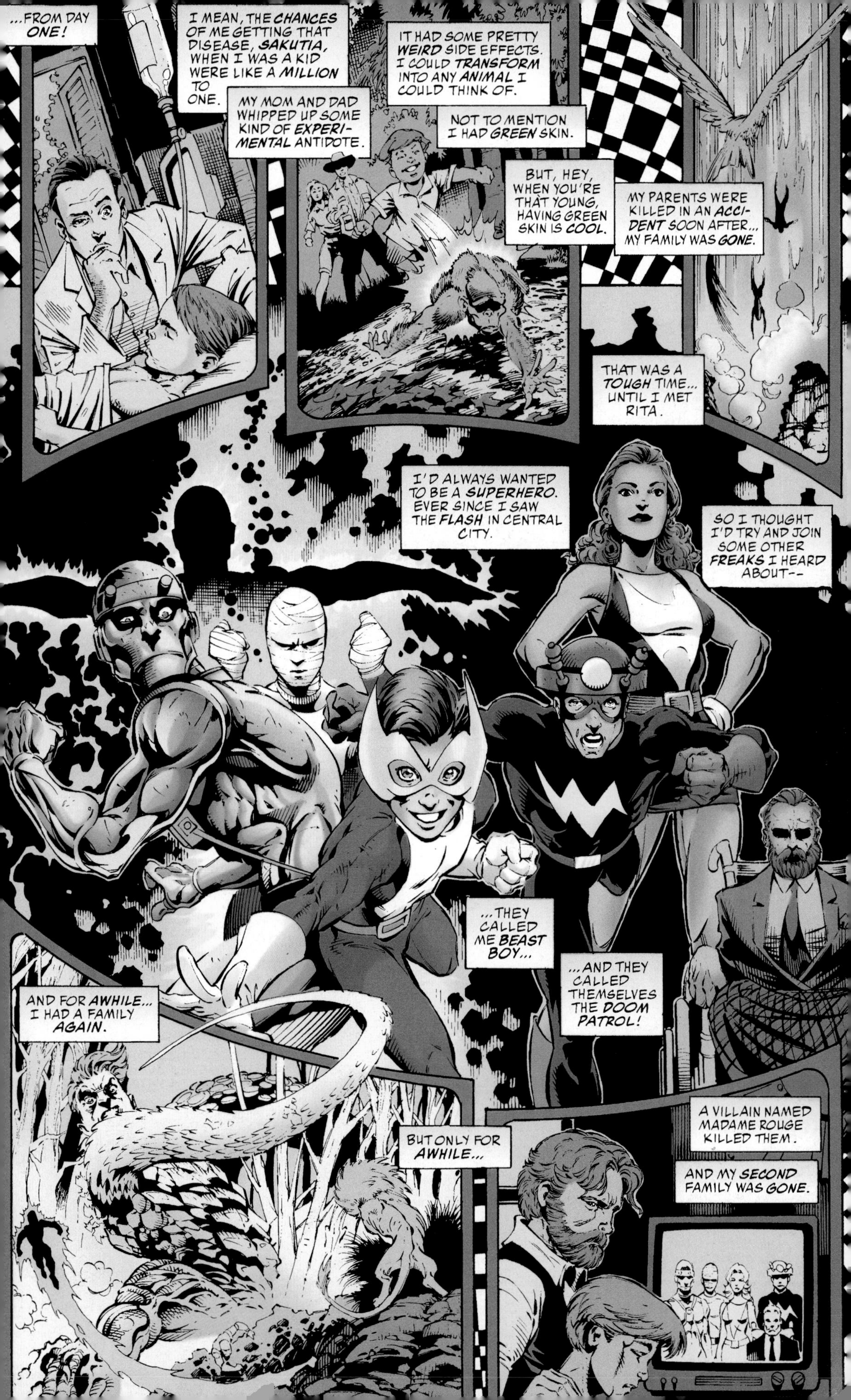
...FROM DAY ONE!
I MEAN, THE CHANCES OF ME GETTING THAT DISEASE, SAKUTIA, WHEN I WAS A KID WERE LIKE A MILLION TO ONE.
MY MOM AND DAD WHIPPED UP SOME KIND OF EXPERIMENTAL ANTIDOTE.
IT HAD SOME PRETTY WEIRD SIDE EFFECTS. I COULD TRANSFORM INTO ANY ANIMAL I COULD THINK OF.
NOT TO MENTION I HAD GREEN SKIN.
BUT, HEY, WHEN YOU'RE THAT YOUNG, HAVING GREEN SKIN IS COOL.
MY PARENTS WERE KILLED IN AN ACCIDENT SOON AFTER... MY FAMILY WAS GONE.
THAT WAS A TOUGH TIME... UNTIL I MET RITA.
I'D ALWAYS WANTED TO BE A SUPERHERO. EVER SINCE I SAW THE FLASH IN CENTRAL CITY.
SO I THOUGHT I'D TRY AND JOIN SOME OTHER FREAKS I HEARD ABOUT--
...THEY CALLED ME BEAST BOY...
...AND THEY CALLED THEMSELVES THE DOOM PATROL!
AND FOR AWHILE... I HAD A FAMILY AGAIN.
BUT ONLY FOR AWHILE...
A VILLAIN NAMED MADAME ROUGE KILLED THEM.
AND MY SECOND FAMILY WAS GONE.

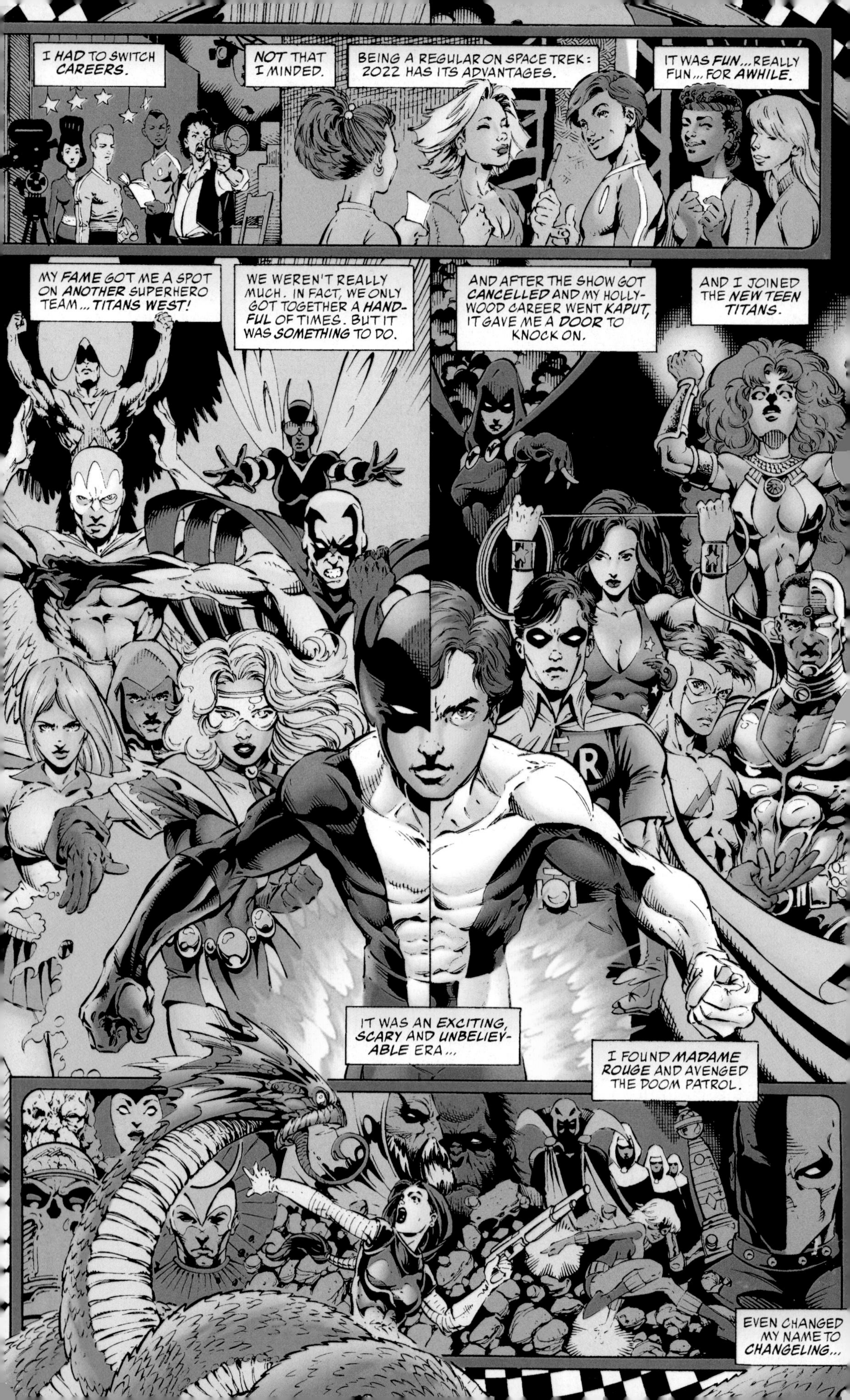

I HAD TO SWITCH CAREERS.
NOT THAT I MINDED.
BEING A REGULAR ON SPACE TREK: 2022 HAS ITS ADVANTAGES.
IT WAS FUN... REALLY FUN... FOR AWHILE.
MY FAME GOT ME A SPOT ON ANOTHER SUPERHERO TEAM... TITANS WEST!
WE WEREN'T REALLY MUCH. IN FACT, WE ONLY GOT TOGETHER A HANDFUL OF TIMES. BUT IT WAS SOMETHING TO DO.
AND AFTER THE SHOW GOT CANCELLED AND MY HOLLYWOOD CAREER WENT KAPUT, IT GAVE ME A DOOR TO KNOCK ON.
AND I JOINED THE NEW TEEN TITANS.
IT WAS AN EXCITING, SCARY AND UNBELIEVABLE ERA...
I FOUND MADAME ROUGE AND AVENGED THE DOOM PATROL.
EVEN CHANGED MY NAME TO CHANGELING...

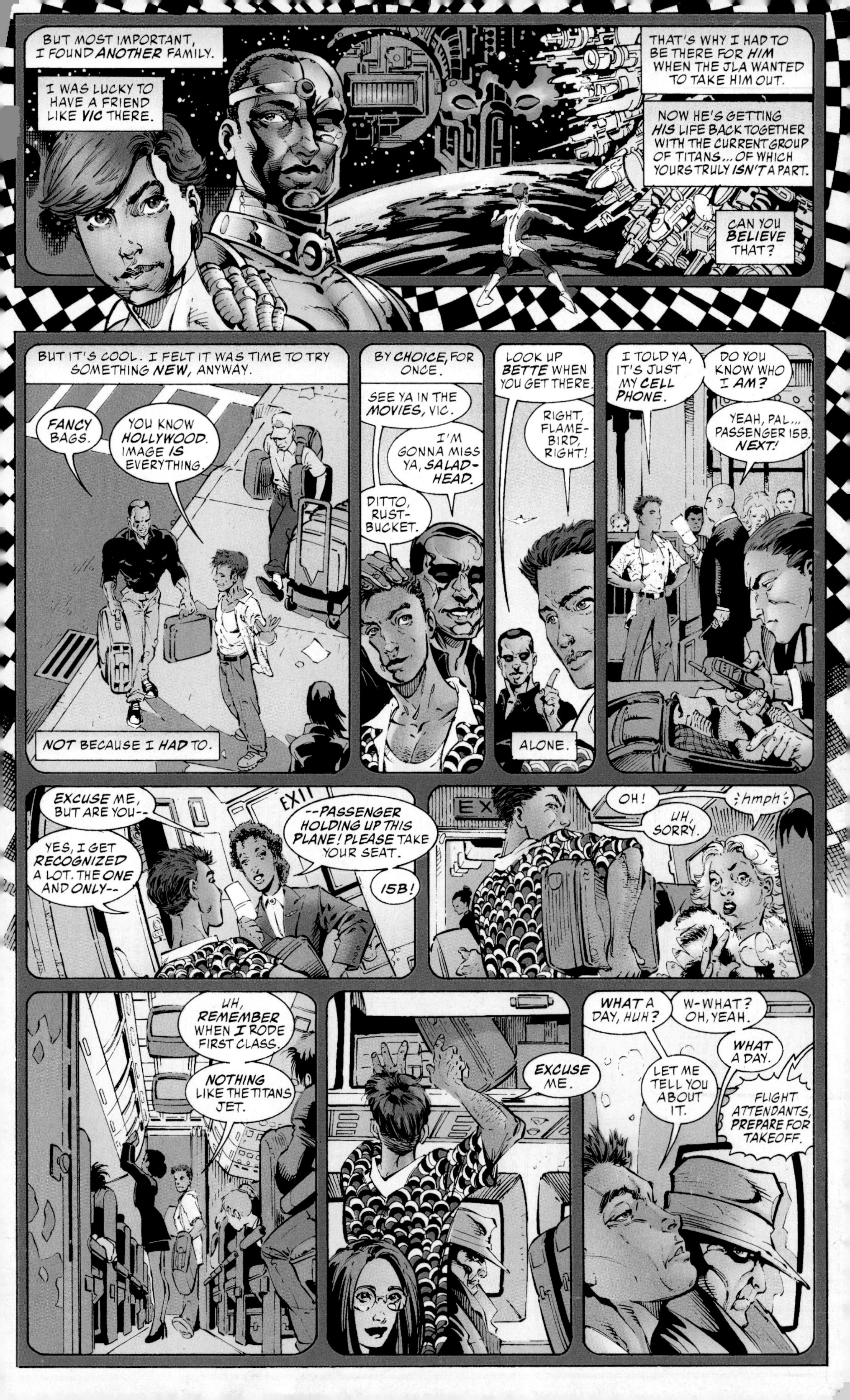

BUT MOST IMPORTANT, I FOUND ANOTHER FAMILY.
I WAS LUCKY TO HAVE A FRIEND LIKE VIC THERE.
THAT'S WHY I HAD TO BE THERE FOR HIM WHEN THE JLA WANTED TO TAKE HIM OUT.
NOW HE'S GETTING HIS LIFE BACK TOGETHER WITH THE CURRENT GROUP OF TITANS... OF WHICH YOURS TRULY ISN'T A PART.
CAN YOU BELIEVE THAT?
BUT IT'S COOL. I FELT IT WAS TIME TO TRY SOMETHING NEW, ANYWAY.
FANCY BAGS.
YOU KNOW HOLLYWOOD. IMAGE IS EVERYTHING.
NOT BECAUSE I HAD TO.
BY CHOICE, FOR ONCE.
SEE YA IN THE MOVIES, VIC.
I'M GONNA MISS YA, SALAD-HEAD.
DITTO, RUST-BUCKET.
LOOK UP BETTE WHEN YOU GET THERE.
RIGHT, FLAME-BIRD, RIGHT!
ALONE.
I TOLD YA, IT'S JUST MY CELL PHONE.
DO YOU KNOW WHO I AM?
YEAH, PAL... PASSENGER 15B. NEXT!
EXCUSE ME, BUT ARE YOU--
YES, I GET RECOGNIZED A LOT. THE ONE AND ONLY--
--PASSENGER HOLDING UP THIS PLANE! PLEASE TAKE YOUR SEAT.
15B!
EXIT
OH!
UH, SORRY.
;hmph;
UH, REMEMBER WHEN I RODE FIRST CLASS.
NOTHING LIKE THE TITANS JET.
EXCUSE ME.
WHAT A DAY, HUH?
W-WHAT? OH, YEAH.
WHAT A DAY.
LET ME TELL YOU ABOUT IT.
FLIGHT ATTENDANTS, PREPARE FOR TAKEOFF.

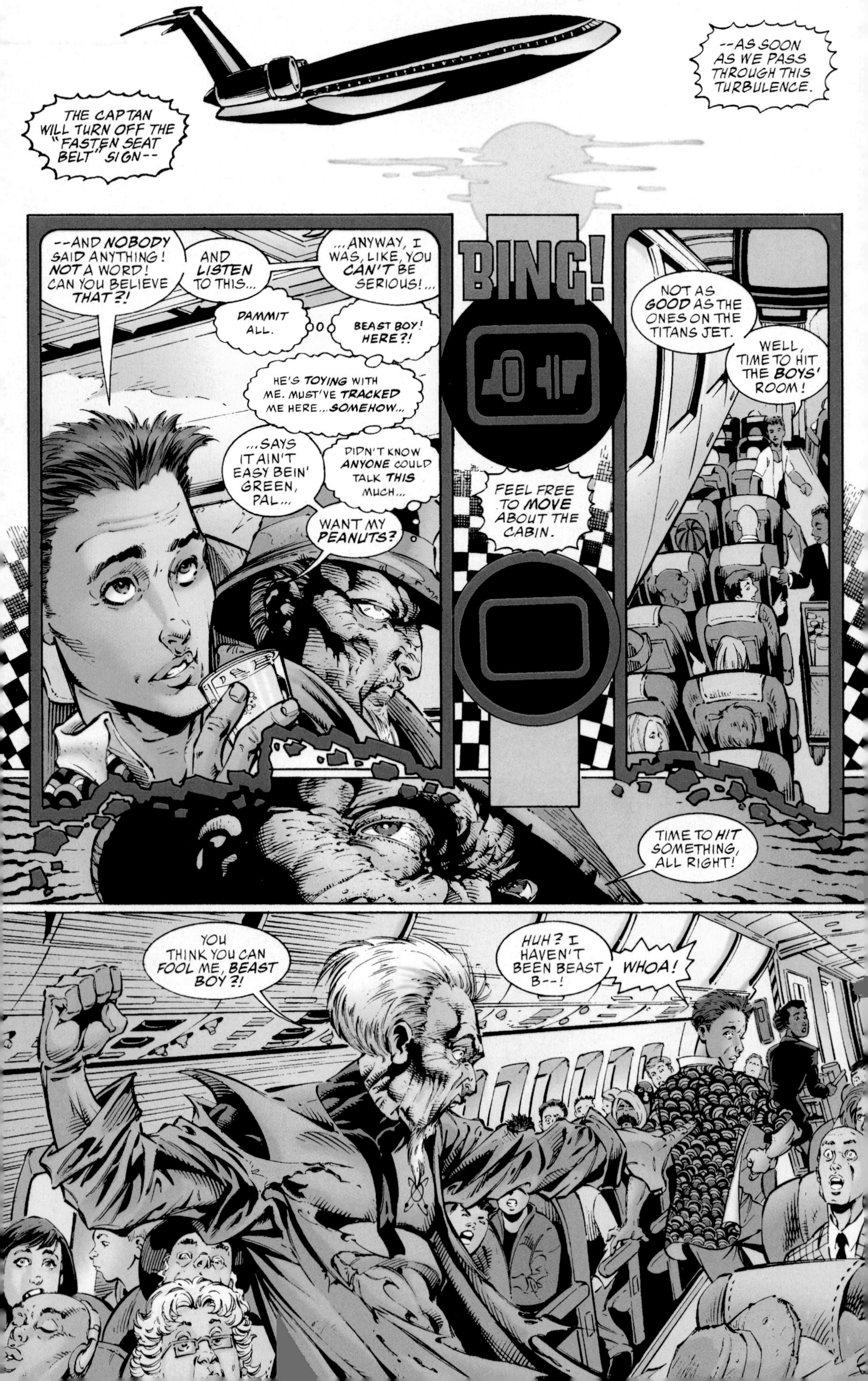
THE CAPTAN WILL TURN OFF THE "FASTEN SEAT BELT" SIGN--
--AS SOON AS WE PASS THROUGH THIS TURBULENCE.
--AND NOBODY SAID ANYTHING! NOT A WORD! CAN YOU BELIEVE THAT?!
AND LISTEN TO THIS...
...ANYWAY, I WAS, LIKE, YOU CAN'T BE SERIOUS!...
DAMMIT ALL.
BEAST BOY! HERE?!
HE'S TOYING WITH ME. MUST'VE TRACKED ME HERE...SOMEHOW...
...SAYS IT AIN'T EASY BEIN' GREEN, PAL...
DIDN'T KNOW ANYONE COULD TALK THIS MUCH...
WANT MY PEANUTS?
BING!
FEEL FREE TO MOVE ABOUT THE CABIN.
NOT AS GOOD AS THE ONES ON THE TITANS JET.
WELL, TIME TO HIT THE BOYS' ROOM!
TIME TO HIT SOMETHING, ALL RIGHT!
YOU THINK YOU CAN FOOL ME, BEAST BOY?!
HUH? I HAVEN'T BEEN BEAST B--!
WHOA!

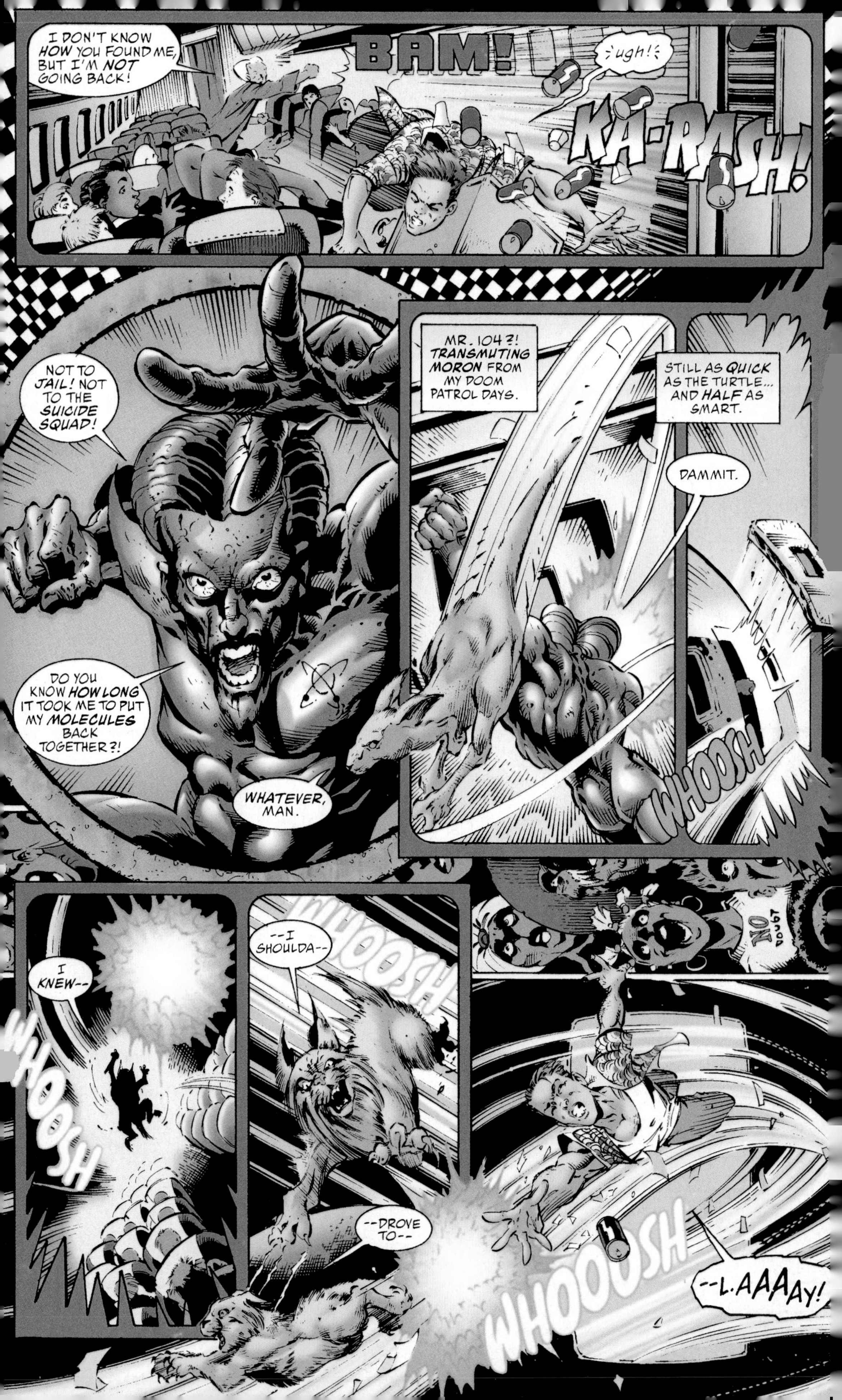
I DON'T KNOW HOW YOU FOUND ME, BUT I'M NOT GOING BACK!
BAM!
ugh!
KA-RASH!
NOT TO JAIL! NOT TO THE SUICIDE SQUAD!
DO YOU KNOW HOW LONG IT TOOK ME TO PUT MY MOLECULES BACK TOGETHER?!
WHATEVER, MAN.
MR. 104?! TRANSMUTING MORON FROM MY DOOM PATROL DAYS.
STILL AS QUICK AS THE TURTLE... AND HALF AS SMART.
DAMMIT.
WHOOSH
I KNEW--
WHOOSH
--I SHOULDA--
WHOOSH
NO DOUBT
--DROVE TO--
WHOOOSH
--L.AAAAY!

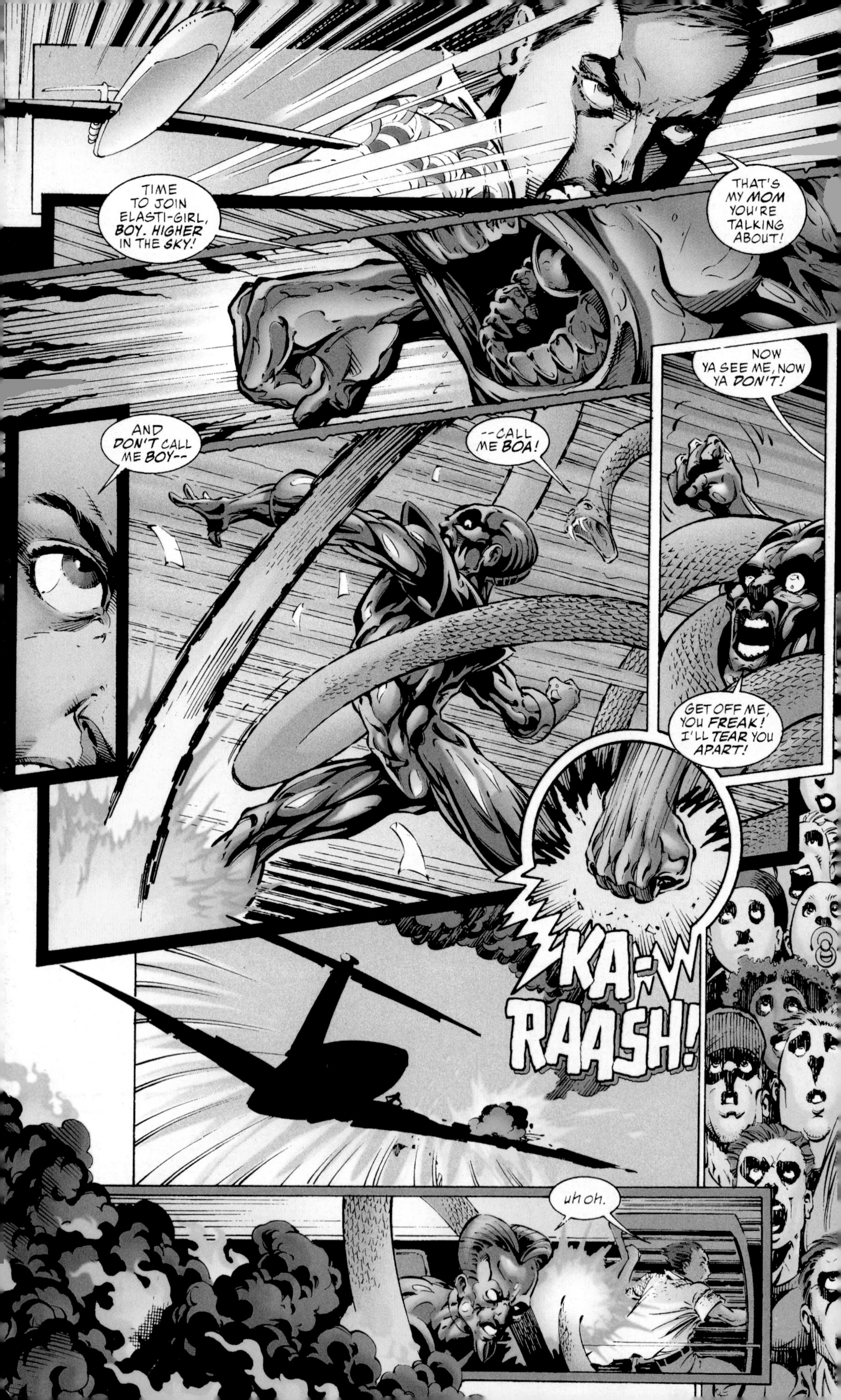
TIME TO JOIN ELASTI-GIRL, BOY. HIGHER IN THE SKY!
THAT'S MY MOM YOU'RE TALKING ABOUT!
AND DON'T CALL ME BOY--
--CALL ME BOA!
NOW YA SEE ME, NOW YA DON'T!
GET OFF ME, YOU FREAK! I'LL TEAR YOU APART!
KA-RAASH!
uh oh.

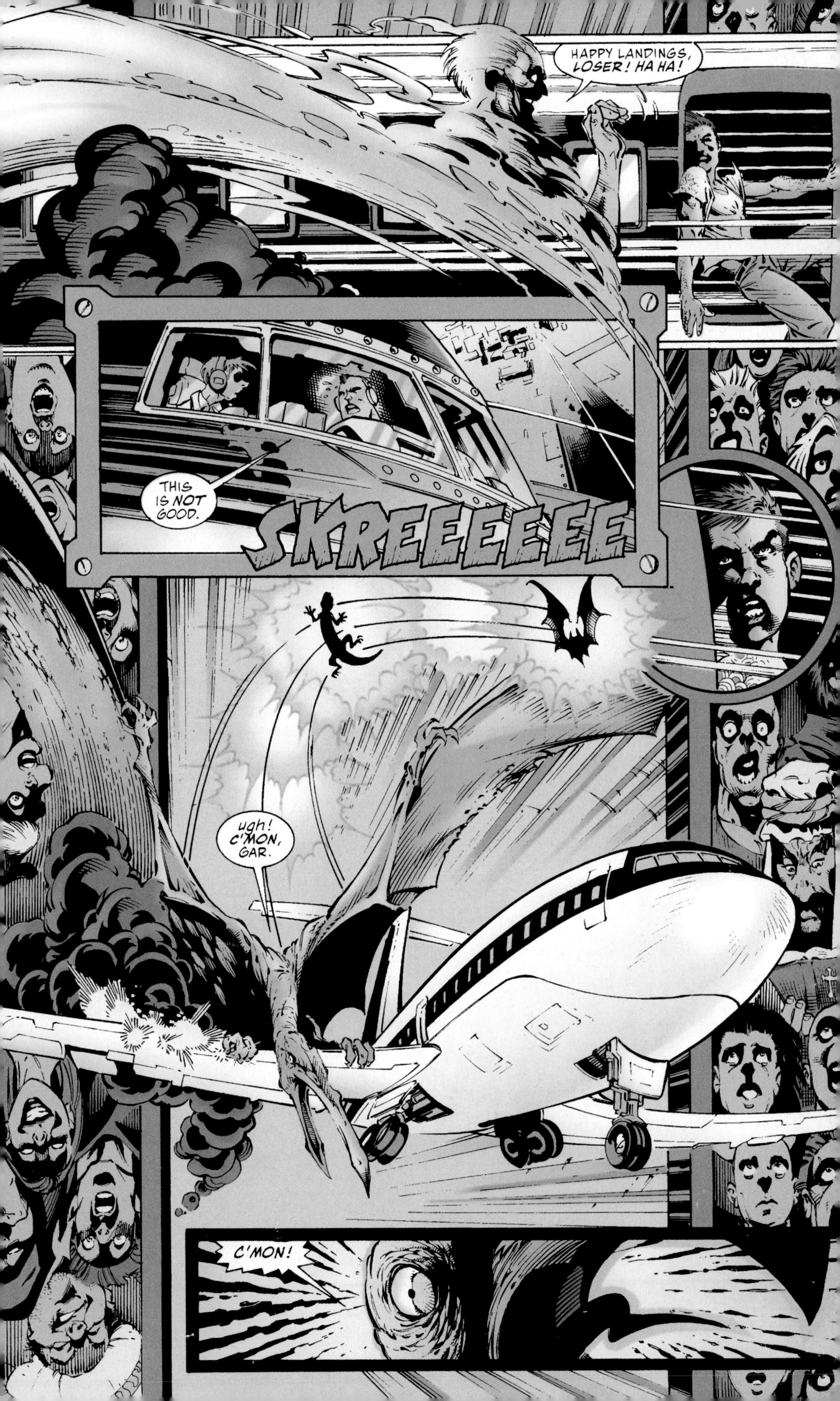

HAPPY LANDINGS, LOSER! HA HA!
THIS IS NOT GOOD.
SKREEEEEEE
ugh! C'MON, GAR.
C'MON!

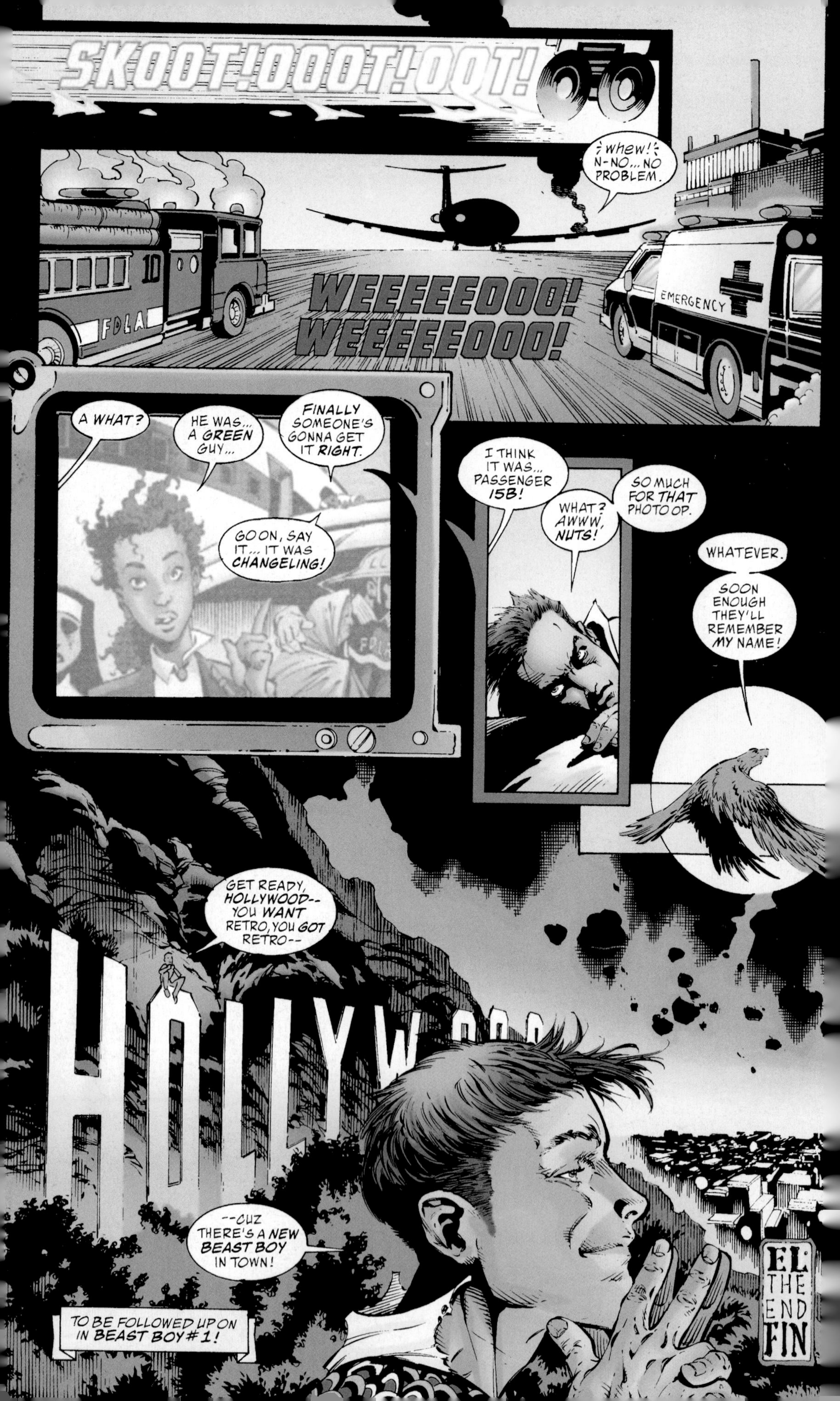
SKOOT!OOOT!OOT!
whew! N-NO... NO PROBLEM.
WEEEEEOOO! WEEEEEOOO!
EMERGENCY
FDLA
A WHAT?
HE WAS... A GREEN GUY...
FINALLY SOMEONE'S GONNA GET IT RIGHT.
GO ON, SAY IT... IT WAS CHANGELING!
I THINK IT WAS... PASSENGER 15B!
WHAT? AWWW, NUTS!
SO MUCH FOR THAT PHOTO OP.
WHATEVER.
SOON ENOUGH THEY'LL REMEMBER MY NAME!
GET READY, HOLLYWOOD-- YOU WANT RETRO, YOU GOT RETRO--
--CUZ THERE'S A NEW BEAST BOY IN TOWN!
TO BE FOLLOWED UP ON IN BEAST BOY #1!
EL THE END FIN

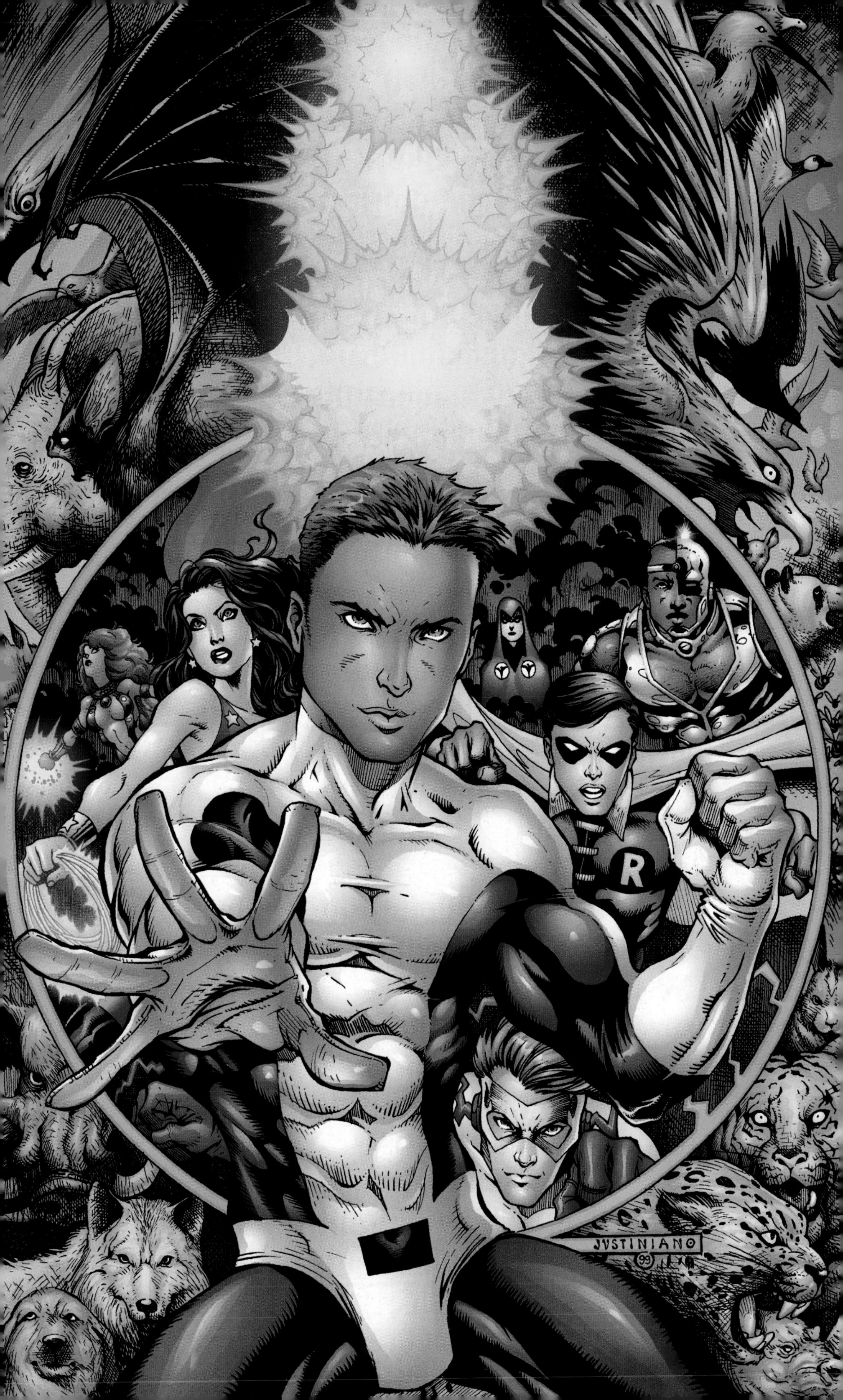
JUSTINIANO
99

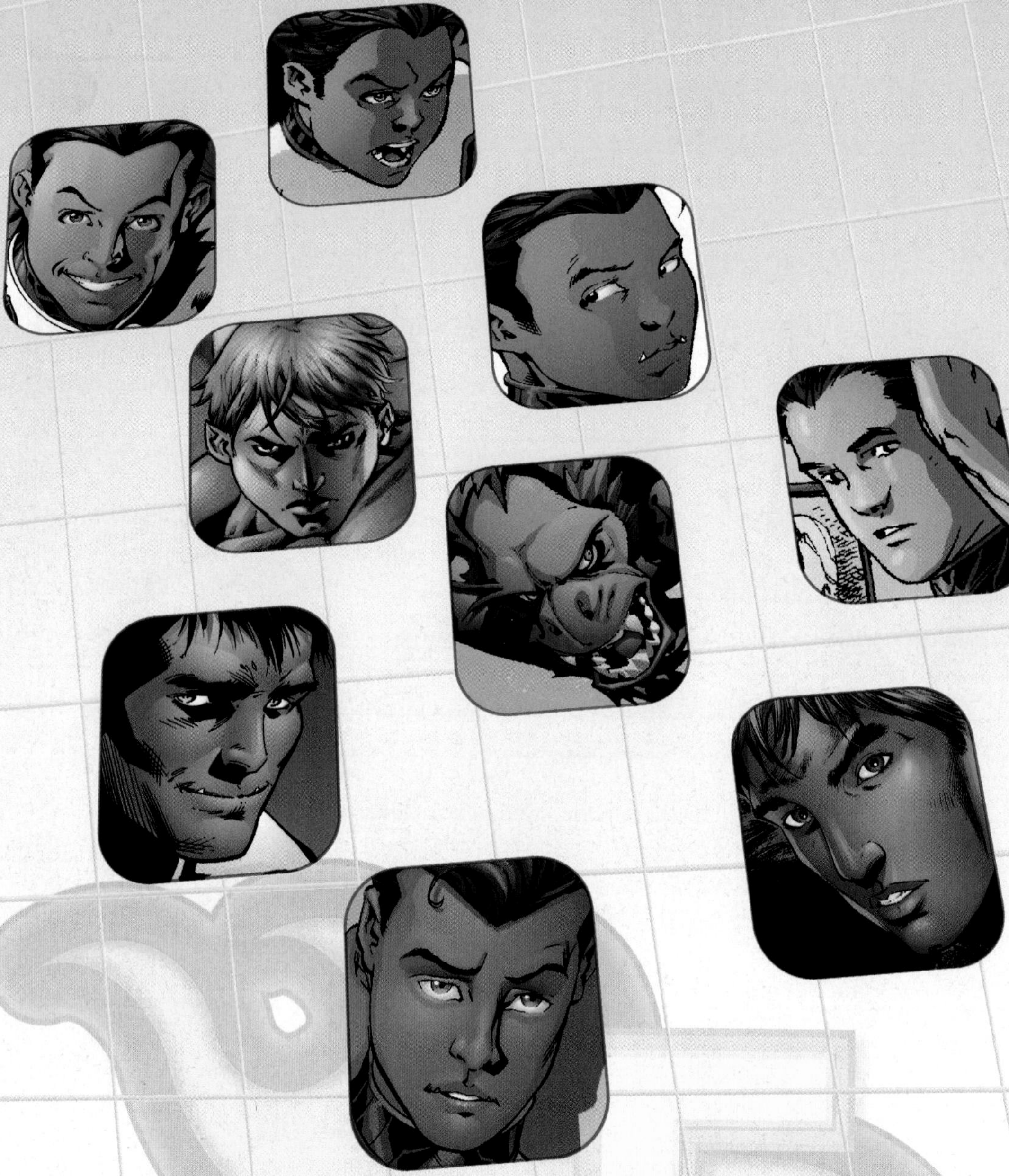

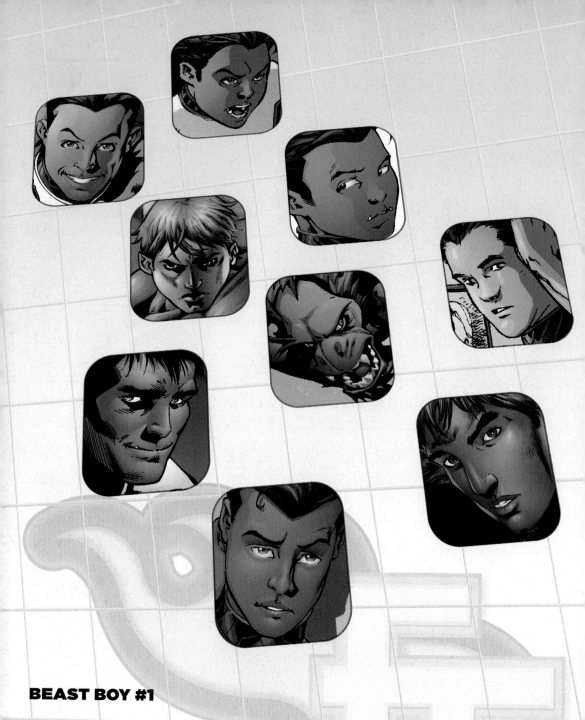

BEAST BOY #1

GEOFF JOHNS
BEN RAAB
Writers

JUSTINIANO
Penciller

CHRIS IVY
Inker

JASON WRIGHT
Colorist

COMICRAFT
Letterer

JUSTINIANO and TANYA & RICHARD HORIE
Cover Artists

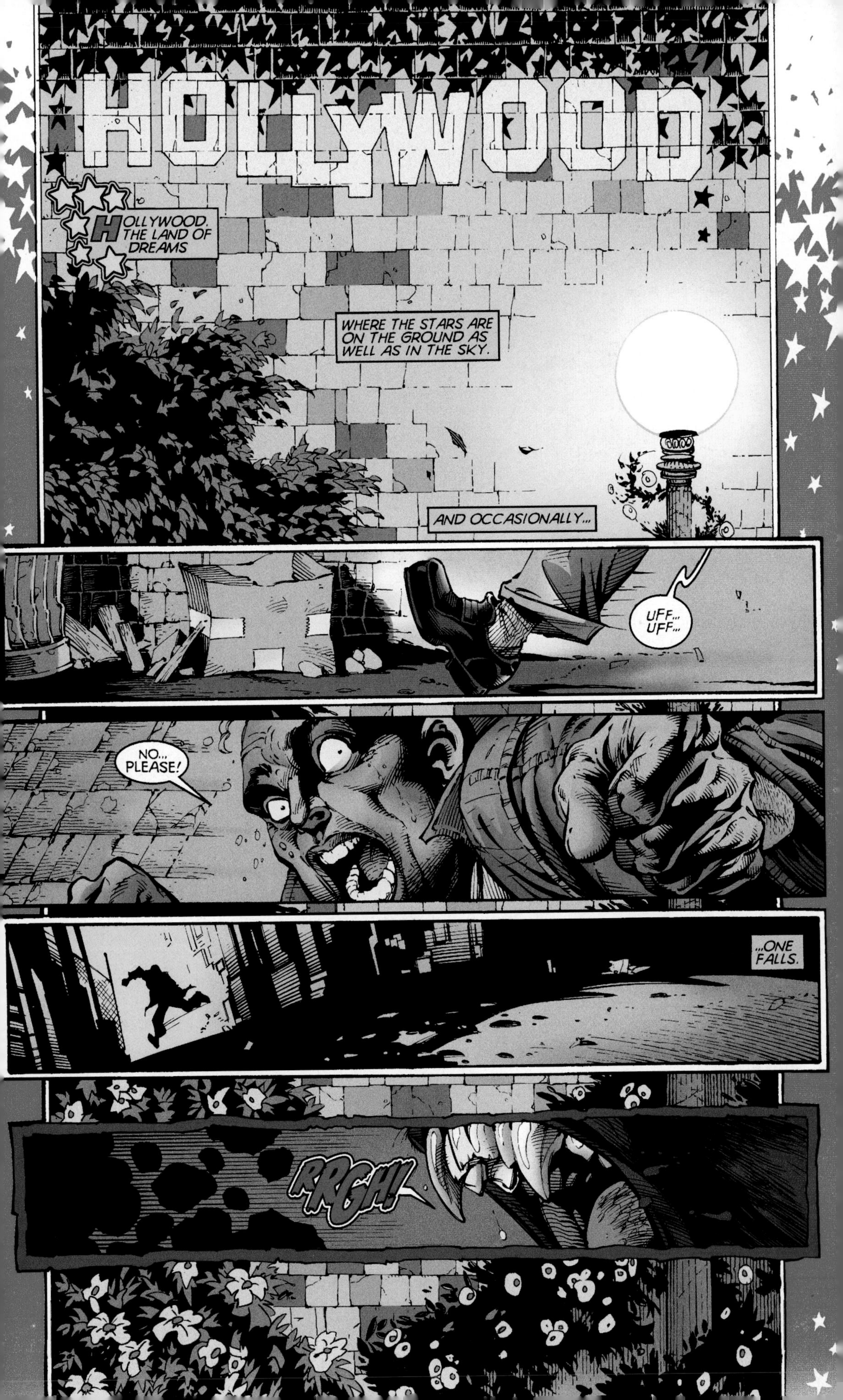
HOLLYWOOD
HOLLYWOOD. THE LAND OF DREAMS
WHERE THE STARS ARE ON THE GROUND AS WELL AS IN THE SKY.
AND OCCASIONALLY...
UFF... UFF...
NO... PLEASE!
...ONE FALLS.
RRGH!

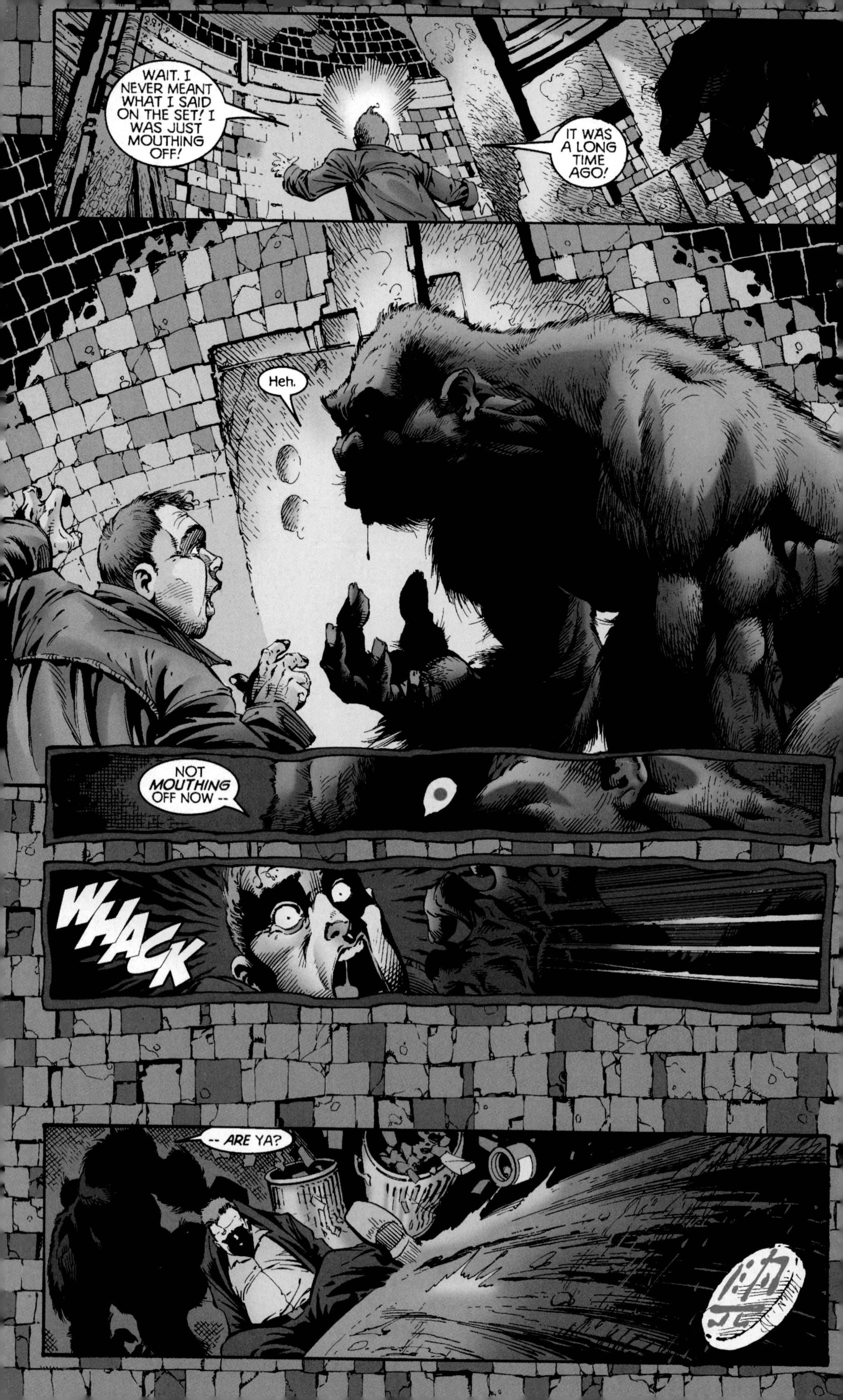
WAIT. I NEVER MEANT WHAT I SAID ON THE SET! I WAS JUST MOUTHING OFF!
IT WAS A LONG TIME AGO!
Heh.
NOT *MOUTHING* OFF NOW --
WHACK
-- *ARE* YA?

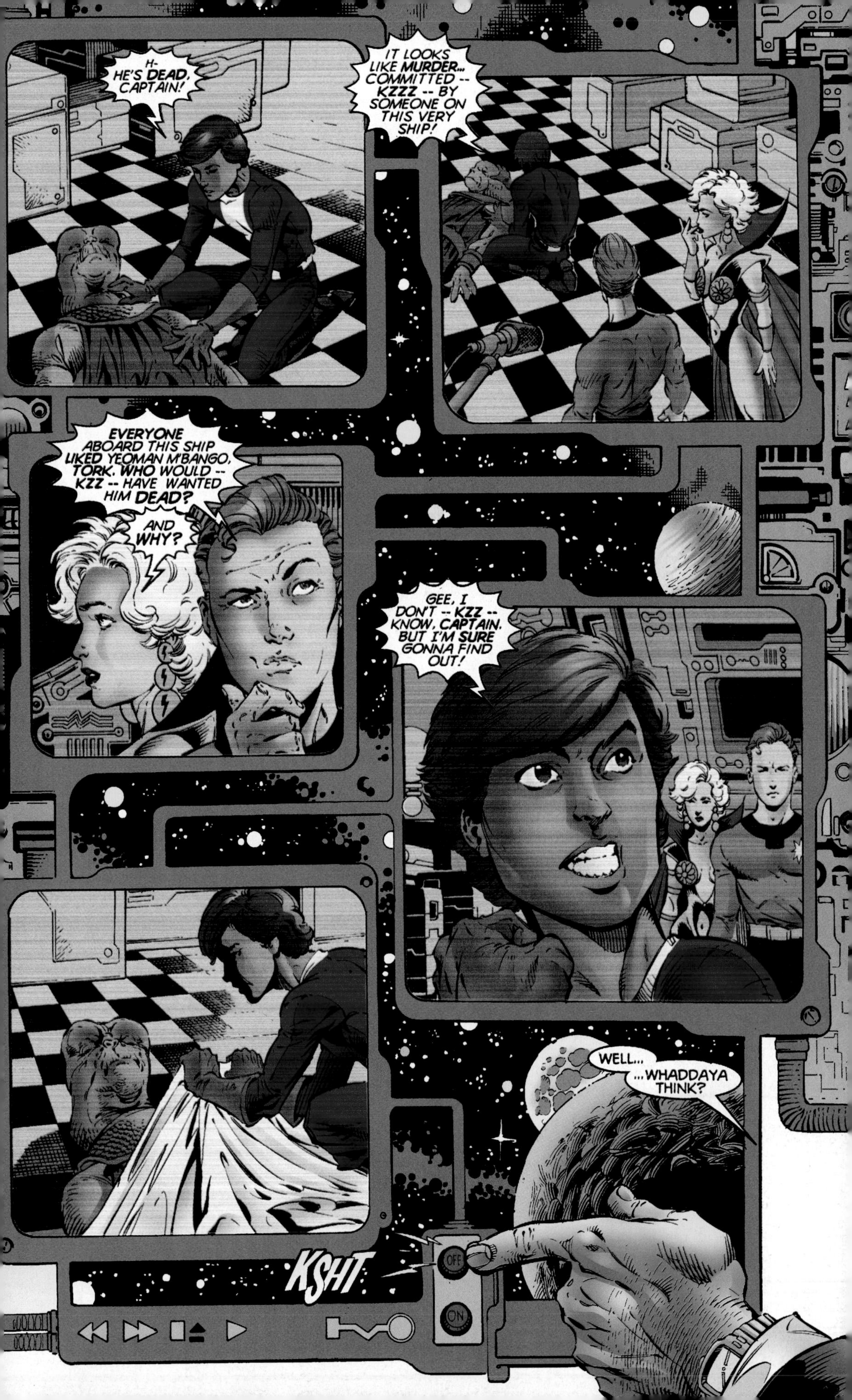
H-
HE'S DEAD, CAPTAIN!
IT LOOKS LIKE MURDER... COMMITTED -- KZZZ -- BY SOMEONE ON THIS VERY SHIP!
EVERYONE ABOARD THIS SHIP LIKED YEOMAN M'BANGO, TORK. WHO WOULD -- KZZ -- HAVE WANTED HIM DEAD?
AND WHY?
GEE, I DON'T -- KZZ -- KNOW, CAPTAIN. BUT I'M SURE GONNA FIND OUT!
WELL...
...WHADDAYA THINK?
KSHT
OFF
ON

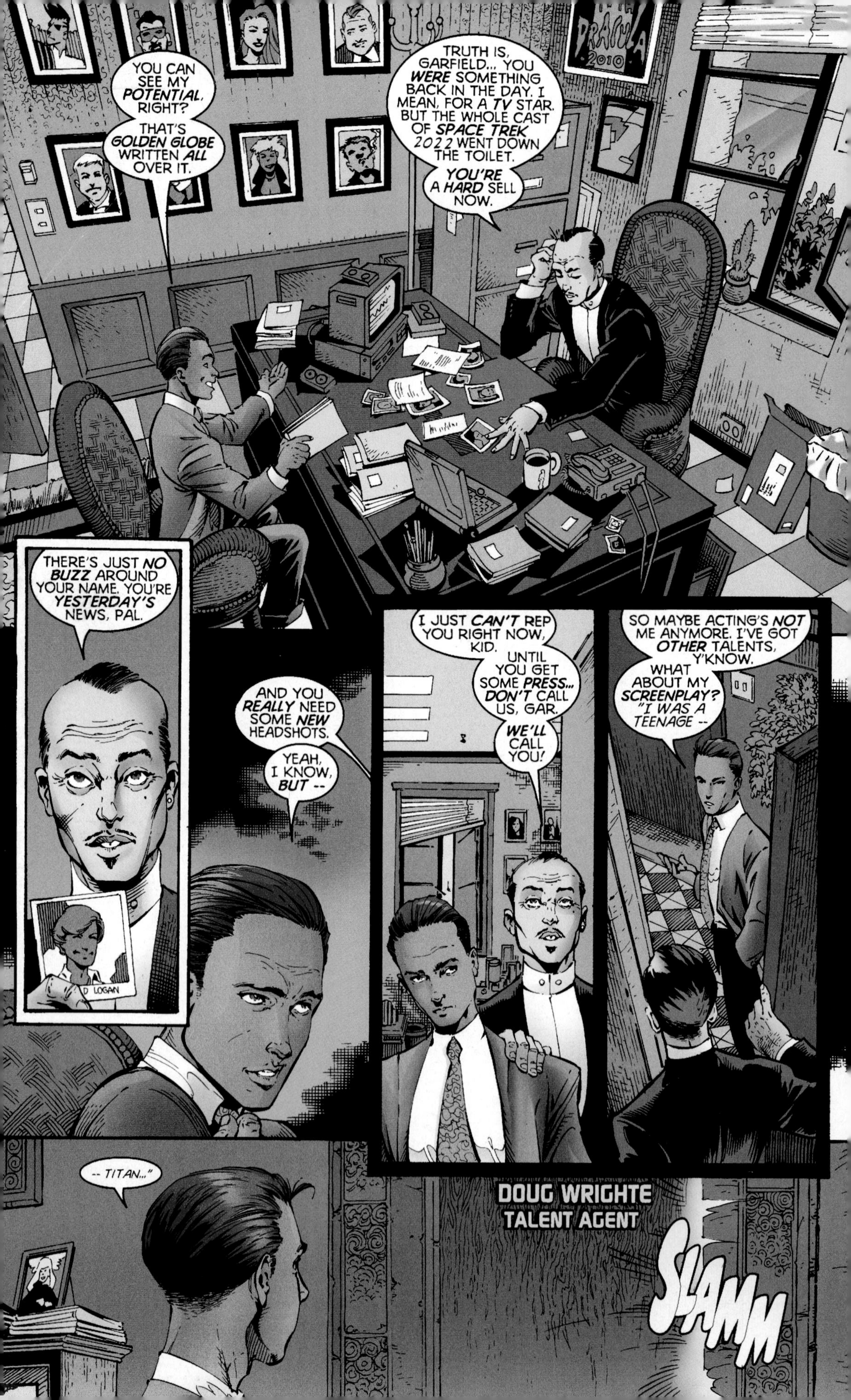
YOU CAN SEE MY POTENTIAL, RIGHT?
THAT'S GOLDEN GLOBE WRITTEN ALL OVER IT.
TRUTH IS, GARFIELD... YOU WERE SOMETHING BACK IN THE DAY. I MEAN, FOR A TV STAR. BUT THE WHOLE CAST OF SPACE TREK 2022 WENT DOWN THE TOILET.
YOU'RE A HARD SELL NOW.
DRACULA 2010
THERE'S JUST NO BUZZ AROUND YOUR NAME. YOU'RE YESTERDAY'S NEWS, PAL.
D LOGAN
AND YOU REALLY NEED SOME NEW HEADSHOTS.
YEAH, I KNOW, BUT --
I JUST CAN'T REP YOU RIGHT NOW, KID.
UNTIL YOU GET SOME PRESS... DON'T CALL US, GAR.
WE'LL CALL YOU!
SO MAYBE ACTING'S NOT ME ANYMORE. I'VE GOT OTHER TALENTS, Y'KNOW.
WHAT ABOUT MY SCREENPLAY? "I WAS A TEENAGE --
-- TITAN..."
DOUG WRIGHTE
TALENT AGENT
SLAMM

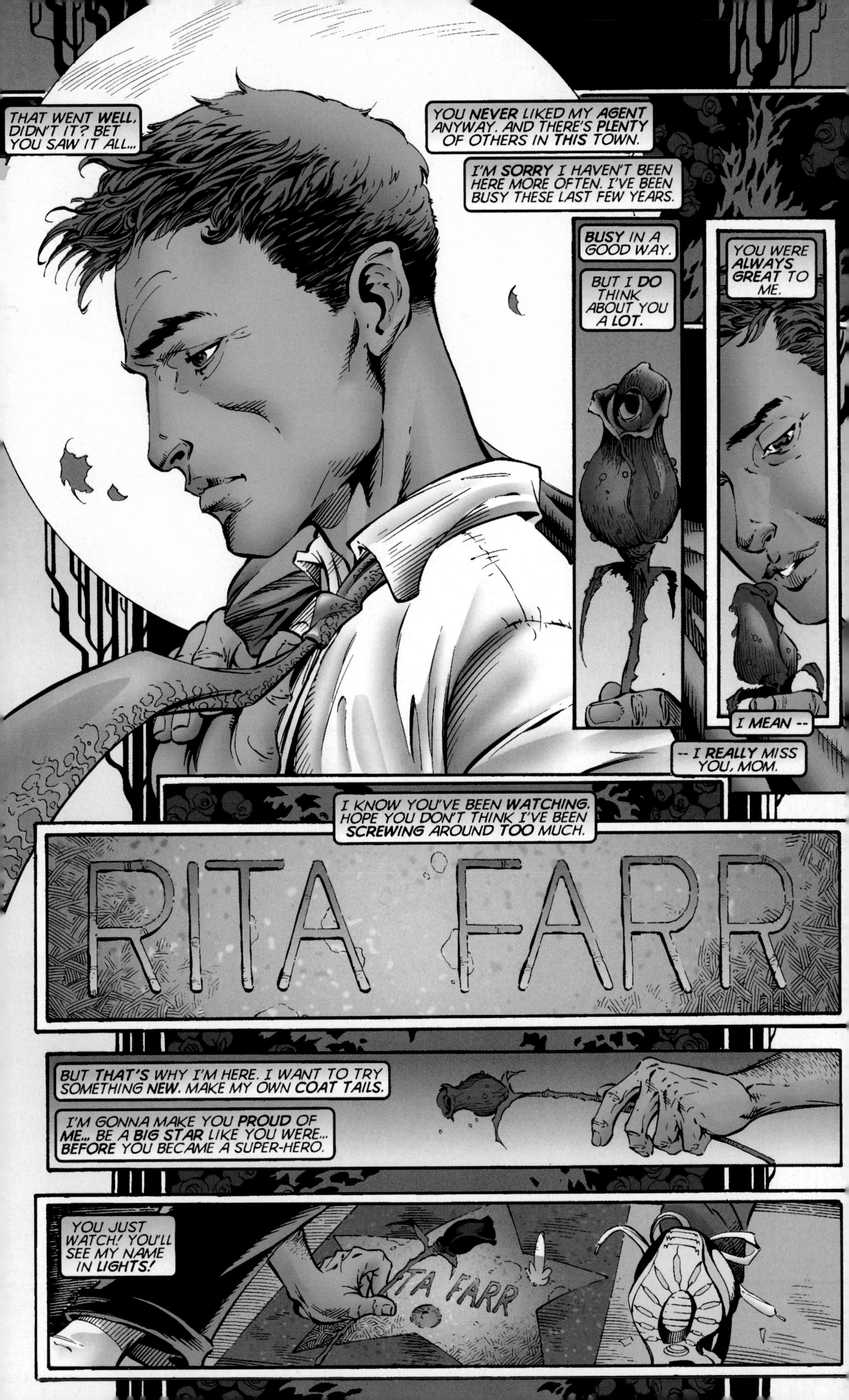
THAT WENT WELL, DIDN'T IT? BET YOU SAW IT ALL...
YOU NEVER LIKED MY AGENT ANYWAY. AND THERE'S PLENTY OF OTHERS IN THIS TOWN.
I'M SORRY I HAVEN'T BEEN HERE MORE OFTEN. I'VE BEEN BUSY THESE LAST FEW YEARS.
BUSY IN A GOOD WAY.
BUT I DO THINK ABOUT YOU A LOT.
YOU WERE ALWAYS GREAT TO ME.
I MEAN --
-- I REALLY MISS YOU, MOM.
I KNOW YOU'VE BEEN WATCHING. HOPE YOU DON'T THINK I'VE BEEN SCREWING AROUND TOO MUCH.
RITA FARR
BUT THAT'S WHY I'M HERE. I WANT TO TRY SOMETHING NEW. MAKE MY OWN COAT TAILS.
I'M GONNA MAKE YOU PROUD OF ME... BE A BIG STAR LIKE YOU WERE... BEFORE YOU BECAME A SUPER-HERO.
YOU JUST WATCH! YOU'LL SEE MY NAME IN LIGHTS!
TA FARR

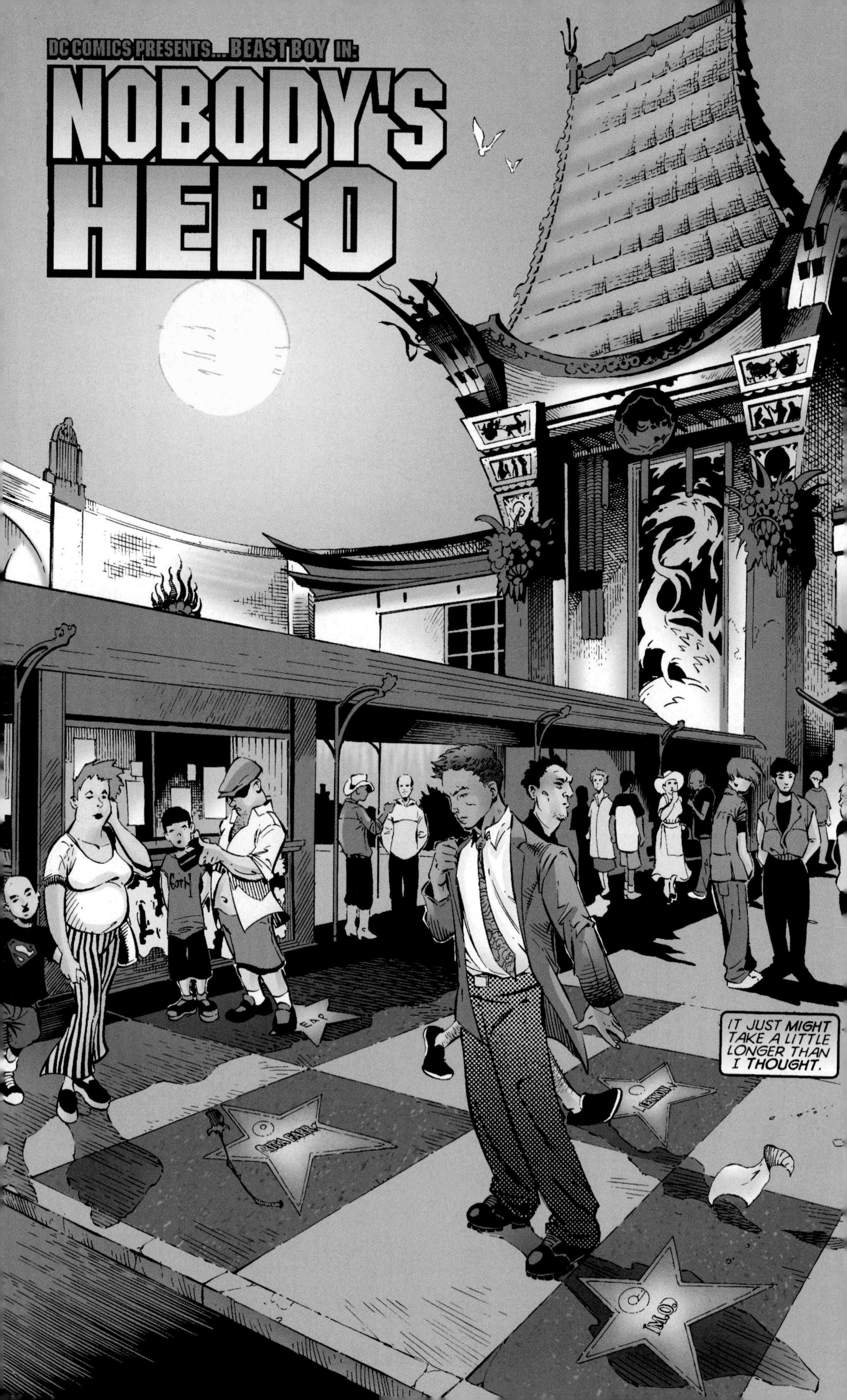
DC COMICS PRESENTS... BEAST BOY IN:
NOBODY'S HERO
IT JUST MIGHT TAKE A LITTLE LONGER THAN I THOUGHT.

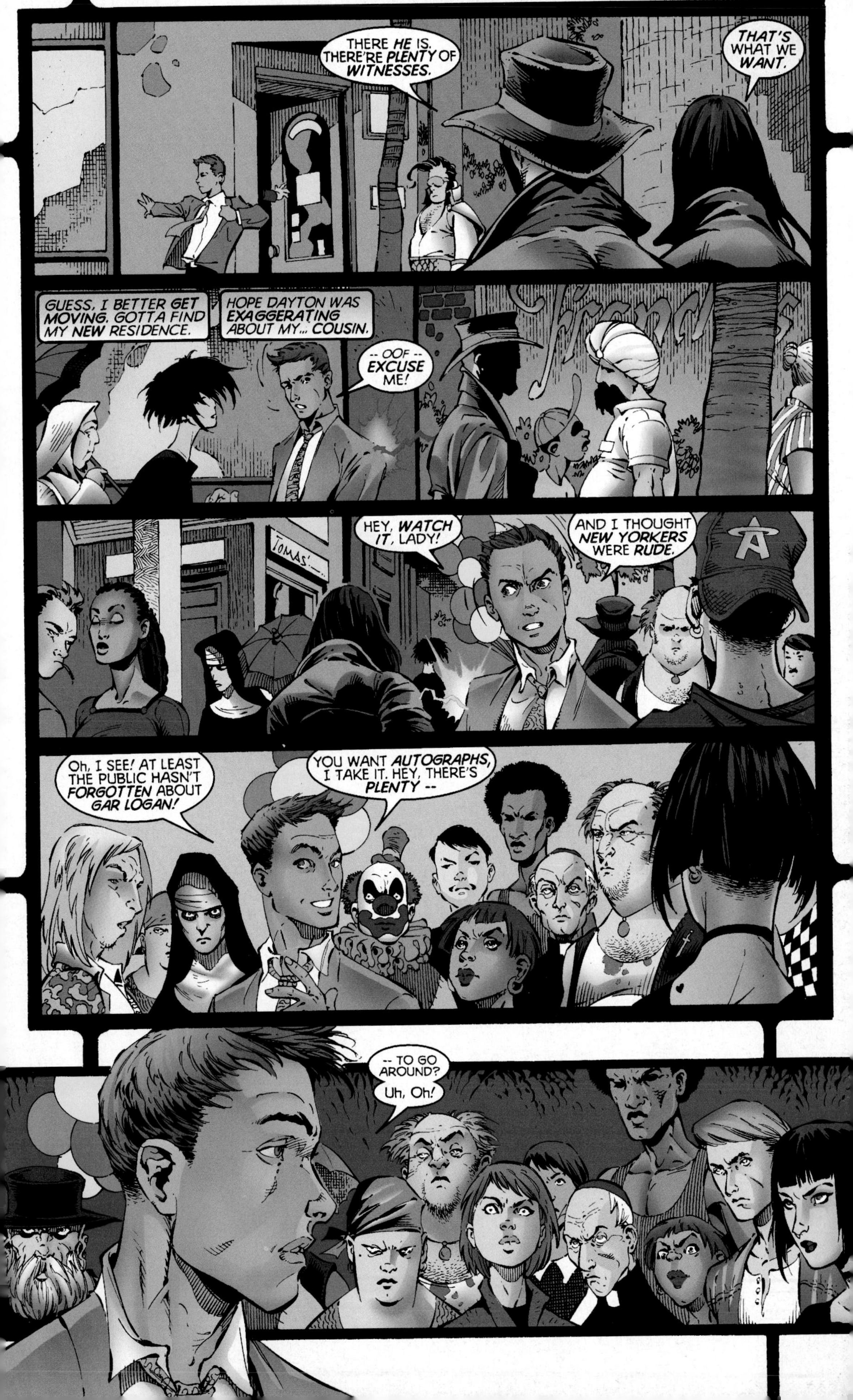
THERE HE IS. THERE'RE PLENTY OF WITNESSES.
THAT'S WHAT WE WANT.
GUESS, I BETTER GET MOVING. GOTTA FIND MY NEW RESIDENCE.
HOPE DAYTON WAS EXAGGERATING ABOUT MY... COUSIN.
-- OOF -- EXCUSE ME!
HEY, WATCH IT, LADY!
AND I THOUGHT NEW YORKERS WERE RUDE.
Oh, I SEE! AT LEAST THE PUBLIC HASN'T FORGOTTEN ABOUT GAR LOGAN!
YOU WANT AUTOGRAPHS, I TAKE IT. HEY, THERE'S PLENTY --
-- TO GO AROUND?
Uh, Oh!

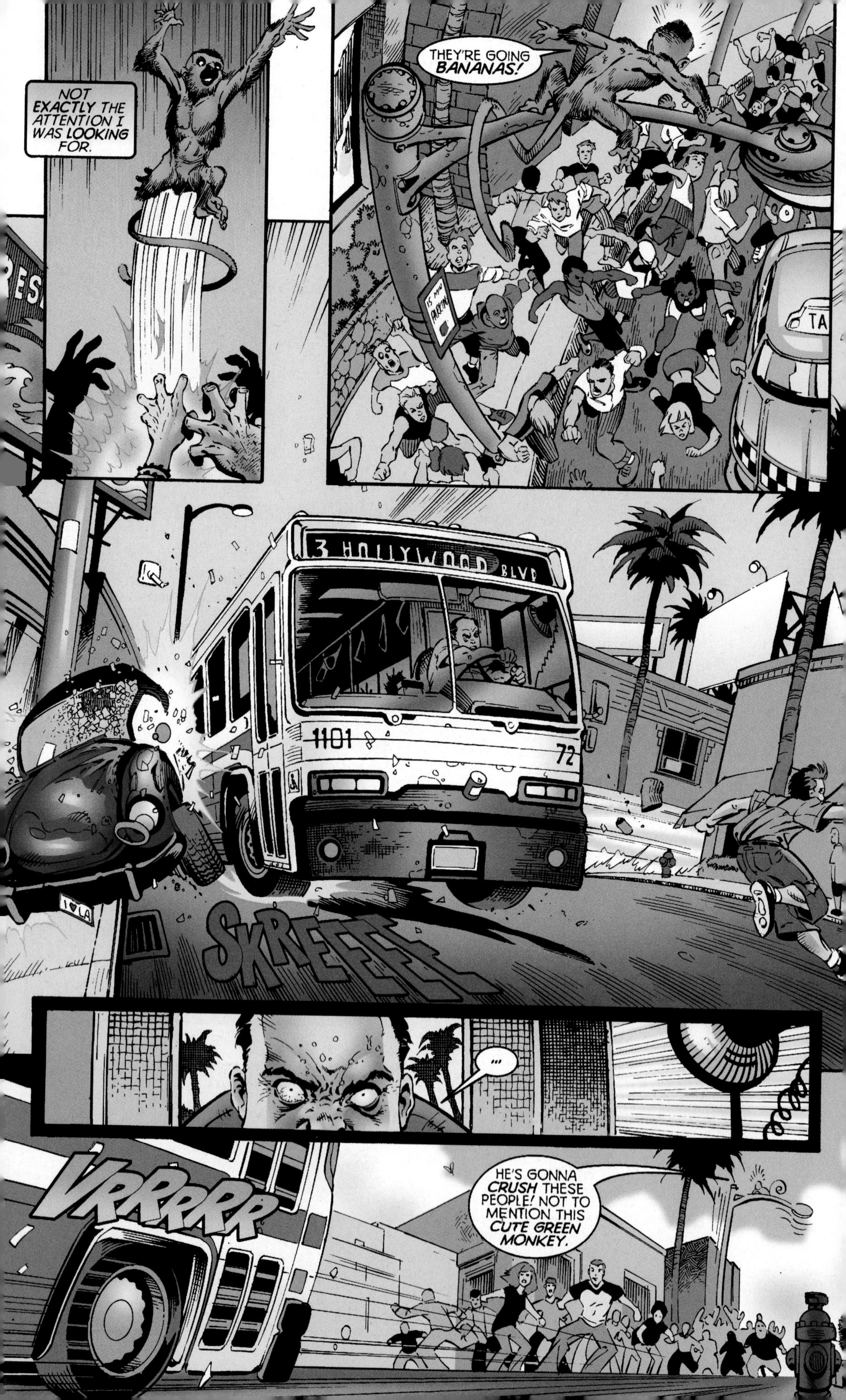
NOT EXACTLY THE ATTENTION I WAS LOOKING FOR.
THEY'RE GOING BANANAS!
15 MIN PARKING
3 HOLLYWOOD BLVD
1101
72
I ♥ LA
SKREEEE
...
VRRRRR
HE'S GONNA CRUSH THESE PEOPLE! NOT TO MENTION THIS CUTE GREEN MONKEY.

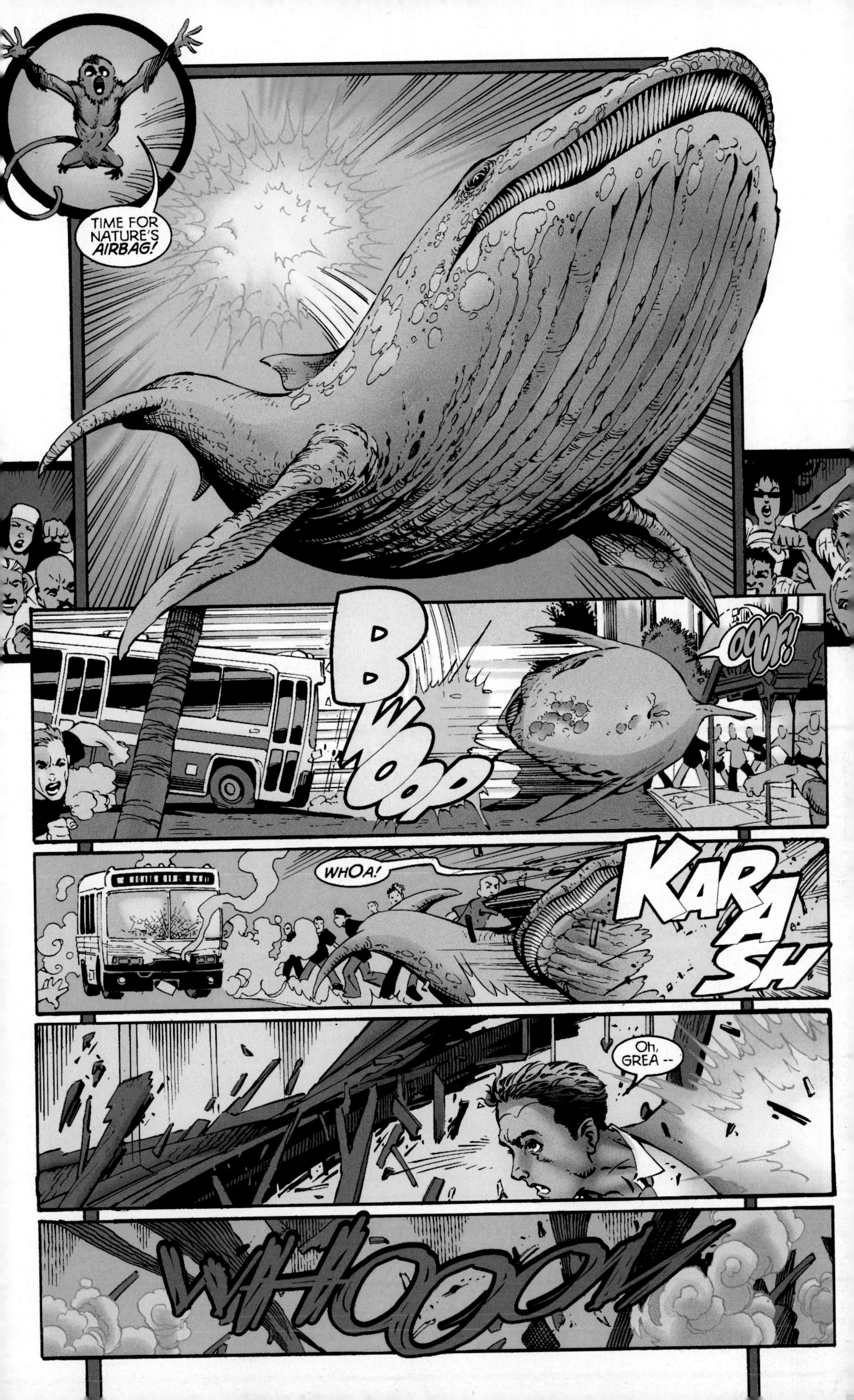
TIME FOR NATURE'S AIRBAG!
BWOOP
OOOF!
WHOA!
KARASH
Oh, GREA --
WHOOOM

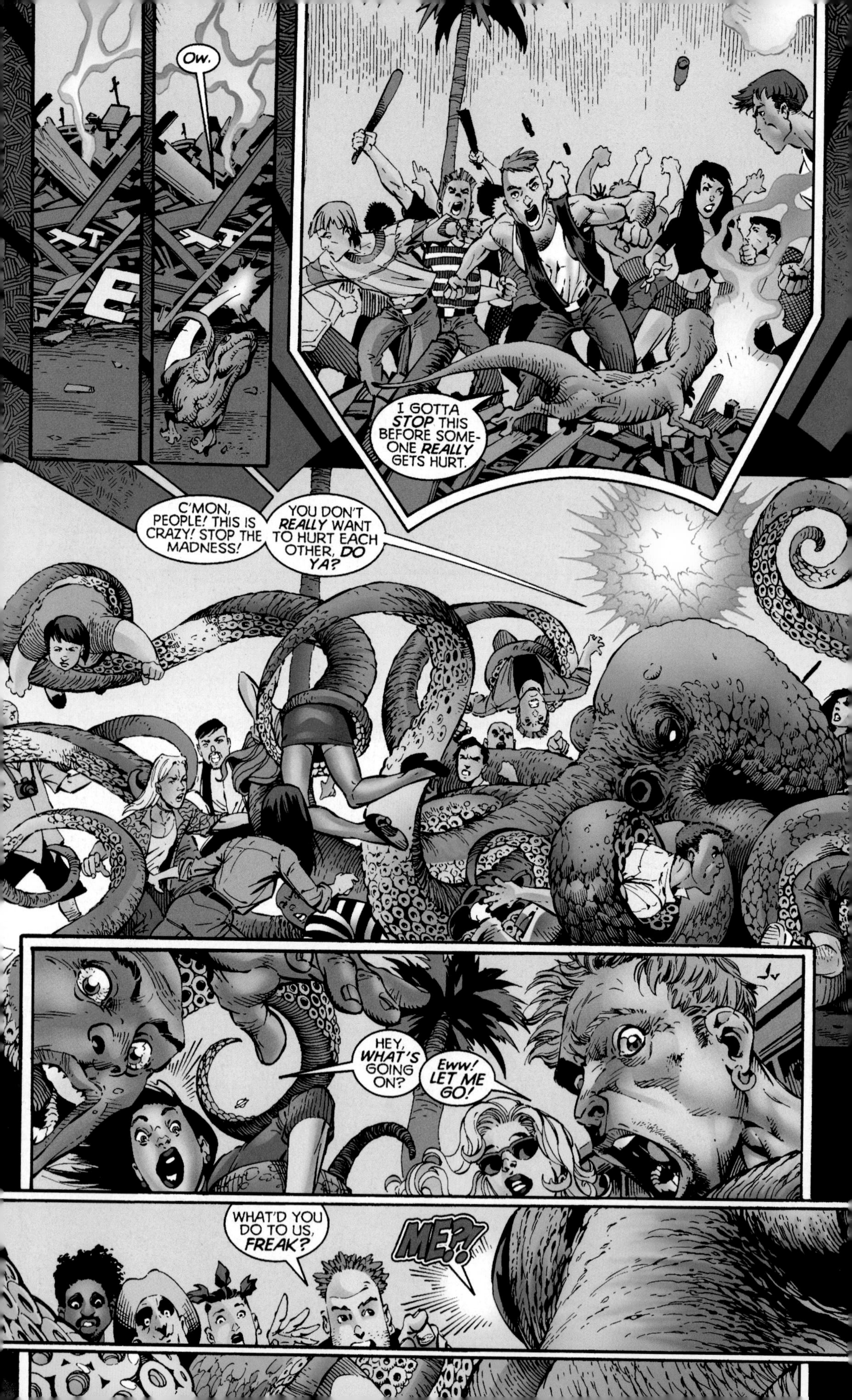
Ow.
I GOTTA STOP THIS BEFORE SOME-ONE REALLY GETS HURT.
C'MON, PEOPLE! THIS IS CRAZY! STOP THE MADNESS!
YOU DON'T REALLY WANT TO HURT EACH OTHER, DO YA?
HEY, WHAT'S GOING ON?
Eww! LET ME GO!
WHAT'D YOU DO TO US, FREAK?
ME?!

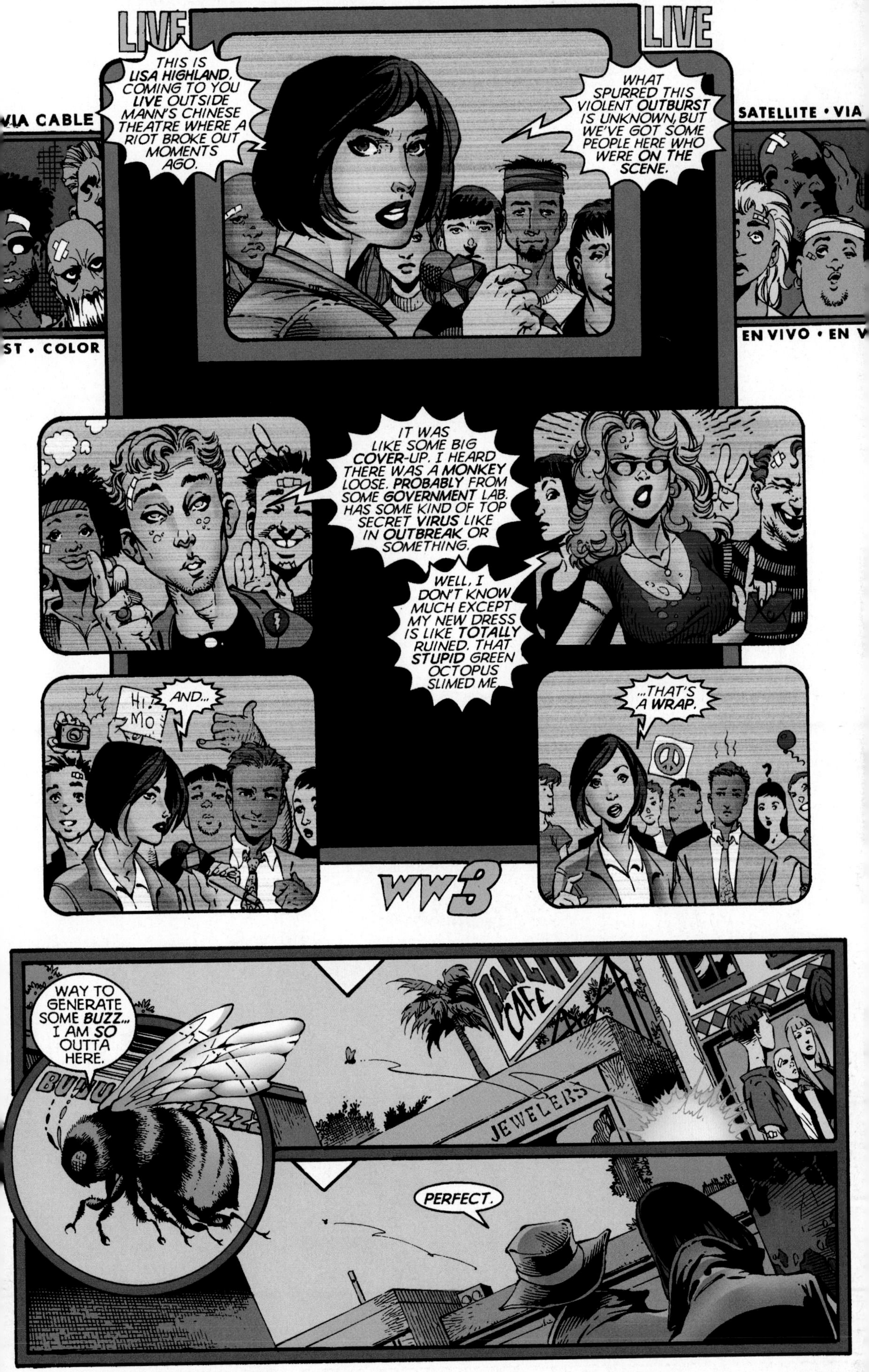
LIVE
LIVE
VIA CABLE
SATELLITE • VIA
ST • COLOR
EN VIVO • EN V
THIS IS LISA HIGHLAND, COMING TO YOU LIVE OUTSIDE MANN'S CHINESE THEATRE WHERE A RIOT BROKE OUT MOMENTS AGO.
WHAT SPURRED THIS VIOLENT OUTBURST IS UNKNOWN, BUT WE'VE GOT SOME PEOPLE HERE WHO WERE ON THE SCENE.
IT WAS LIKE SOME BIG COVER-UP. I HEARD THERE WAS A MONKEY LOOSE. PROBABLY FROM SOME GOVERNMENT LAB. HAS SOME KIND OF TOP SECRET VIRUS LIKE IN OUTBREAK OR SOMETHING.
WELL, I DON'T KNOW MUCH EXCEPT MY NEW DRESS IS LIKE TOTALLY RUINED. THAT STUPID GREEN OCTOPUS SLIMED ME.
HI! MO
AND...
...THAT'S A WRAP.
WW3
WAY TO GENERATE SOME BUZZ... I AM SO OUTTA HERE.
BUZZZZZ
CAFE
JEWELERS
PERFECT.

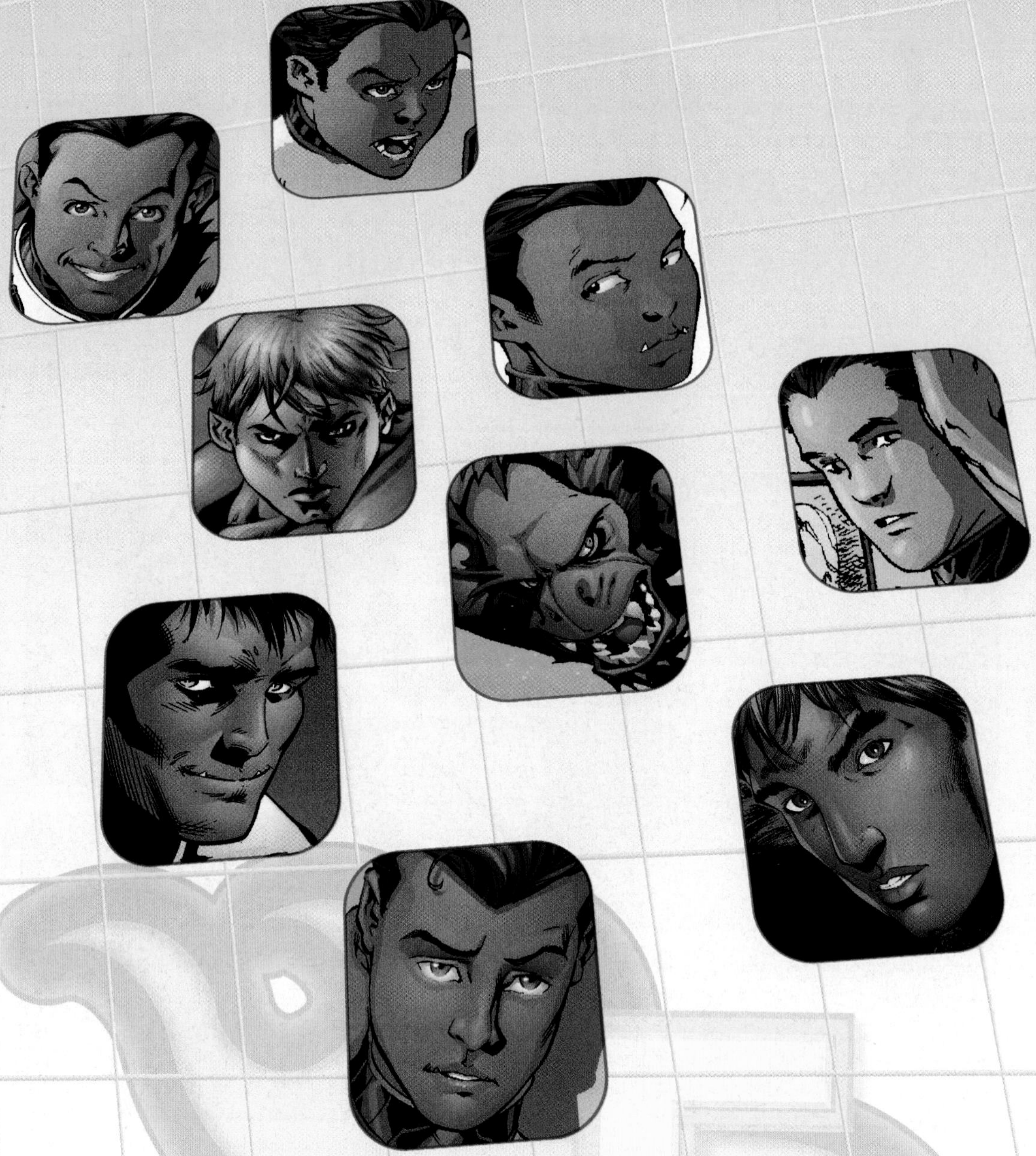

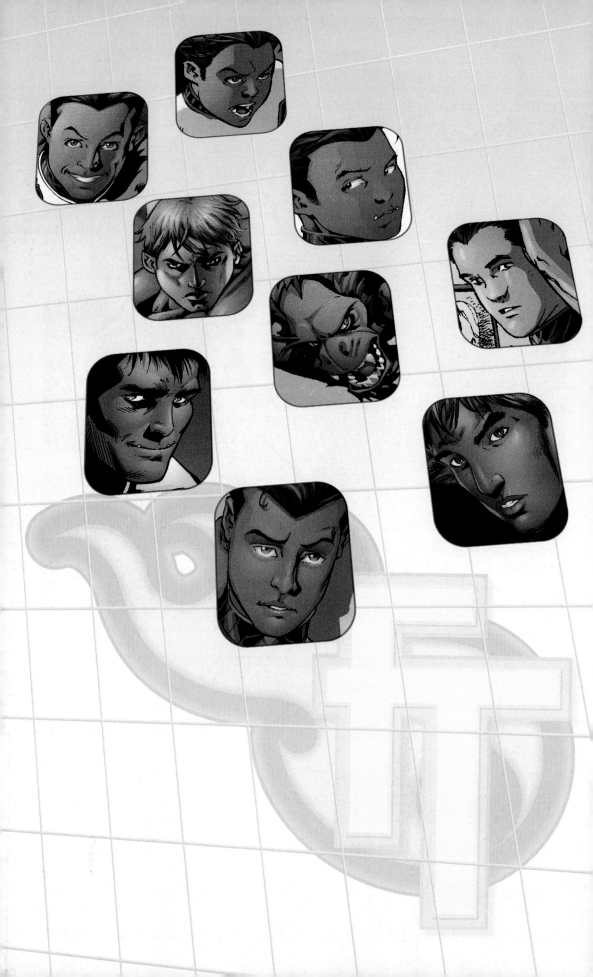

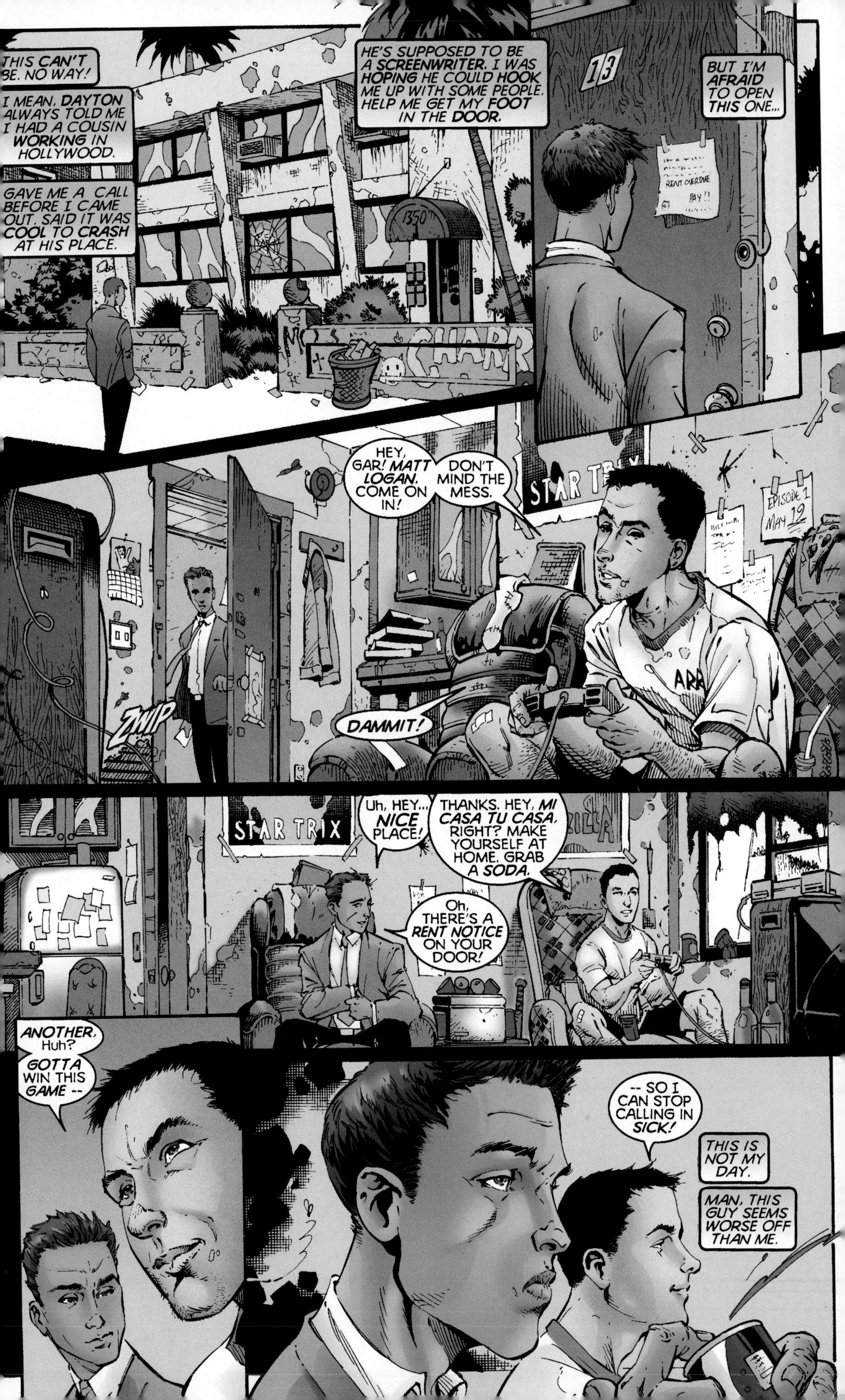
THIS CAN'T BE. NO WAY!
I MEAN, DAYTON ALWAYS TOLD ME I HAD A COUSIN WORKING IN HOLLYWOOD.
GAVE ME A CALL BEFORE I CAME OUT. SAID IT WAS COOL TO CRASH AT HIS PLACE.
1350
CHARR
HE'S SUPPOSED TO BE A SCREENWRITER. I WAS HOPING HE COULD HOOK ME UP WITH SOME PEOPLE. HELP ME GET MY FOOT IN THE DOOR.
13
RENT OVERDUE PAY!!
BUT I'M AFRAID TO OPEN THIS ONE...
HEY, GAR! MATT LOGAN. COME ON IN!
DON'T MIND THE MESS.
STAR TRIX
EPISODE 1 MAY 19
ZWIP
DAMMIT!
STAR TRIX
Uh, HEY... NICE PLACE!
THANKS. HEY, MI CASA TU CASA, RIGHT? MAKE YOURSELF AT HOME. GRAB A SODA.
Oh, THERE'S A RENT NOTICE ON YOUR DOOR!
ANOTHER, Huh? GOTTA WIN THIS GAME --
-- SO I CAN STOP CALLING IN SICK!
THIS IS NOT MY DAY.
MAN, THIS GUY SEEMS WORSE OFF THAN ME.

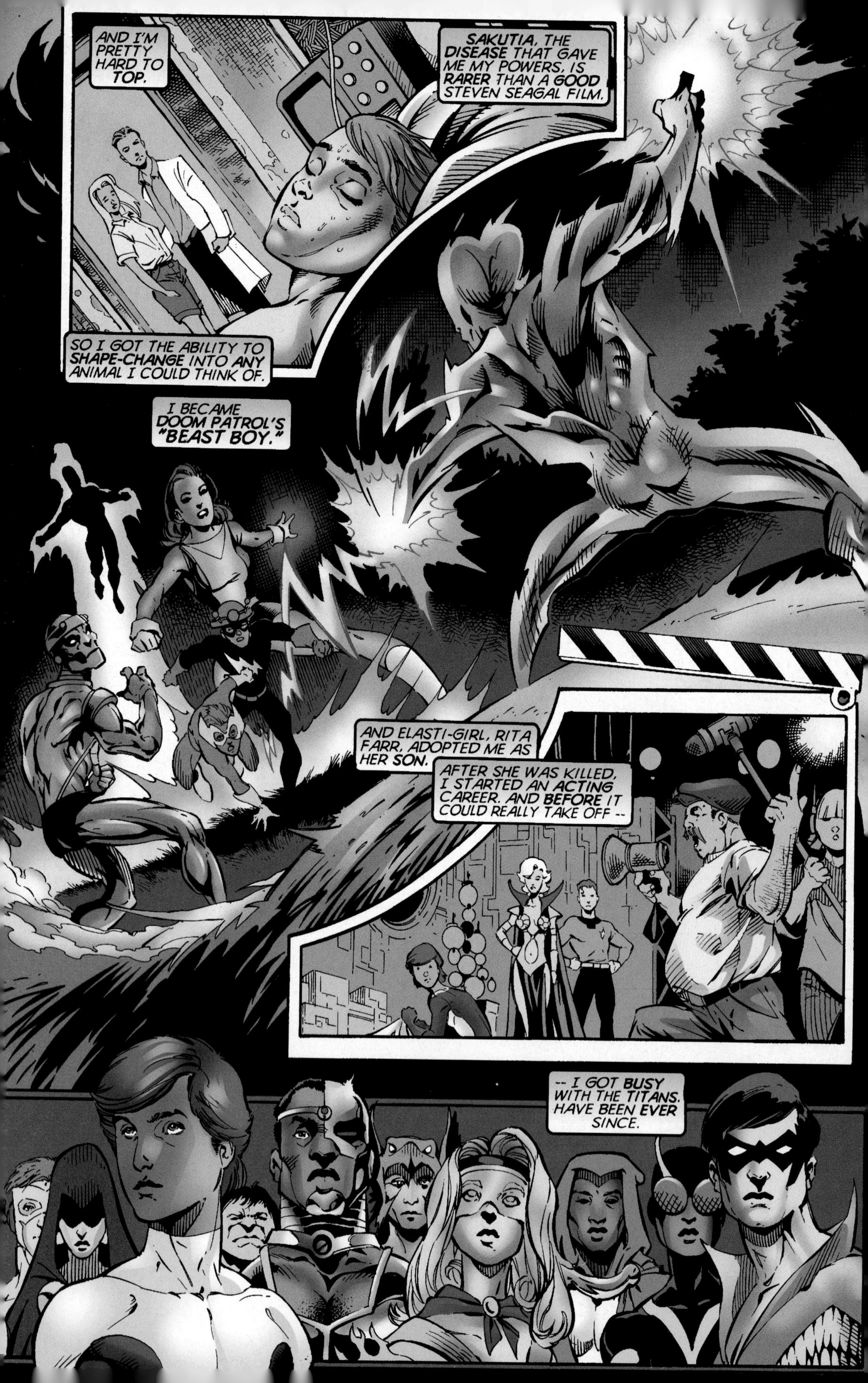
AND I'M PRETTY HARD TO TOP.
SAKUTIA, THE DISEASE THAT GAVE ME MY POWERS, IS RARER THAN A GOOD STEVEN SEAGAL FILM.
SO I GOT THE ABILITY TO SHAPE-CHANGE INTO ANY ANIMAL I COULD THINK OF.
I BECAME DOOM PATROL'S "BEAST BOY."
AND ELASTI-GIRL, RITA FARR, ADOPTED ME AS HER SON.
AFTER SHE WAS KILLED, I STARTED AN ACTING CAREER. AND BEFORE IT COULD REALLY TAKE OFF --
-- I GOT BUSY WITH THE TITANS. HAVE BEEN EVER SINCE.

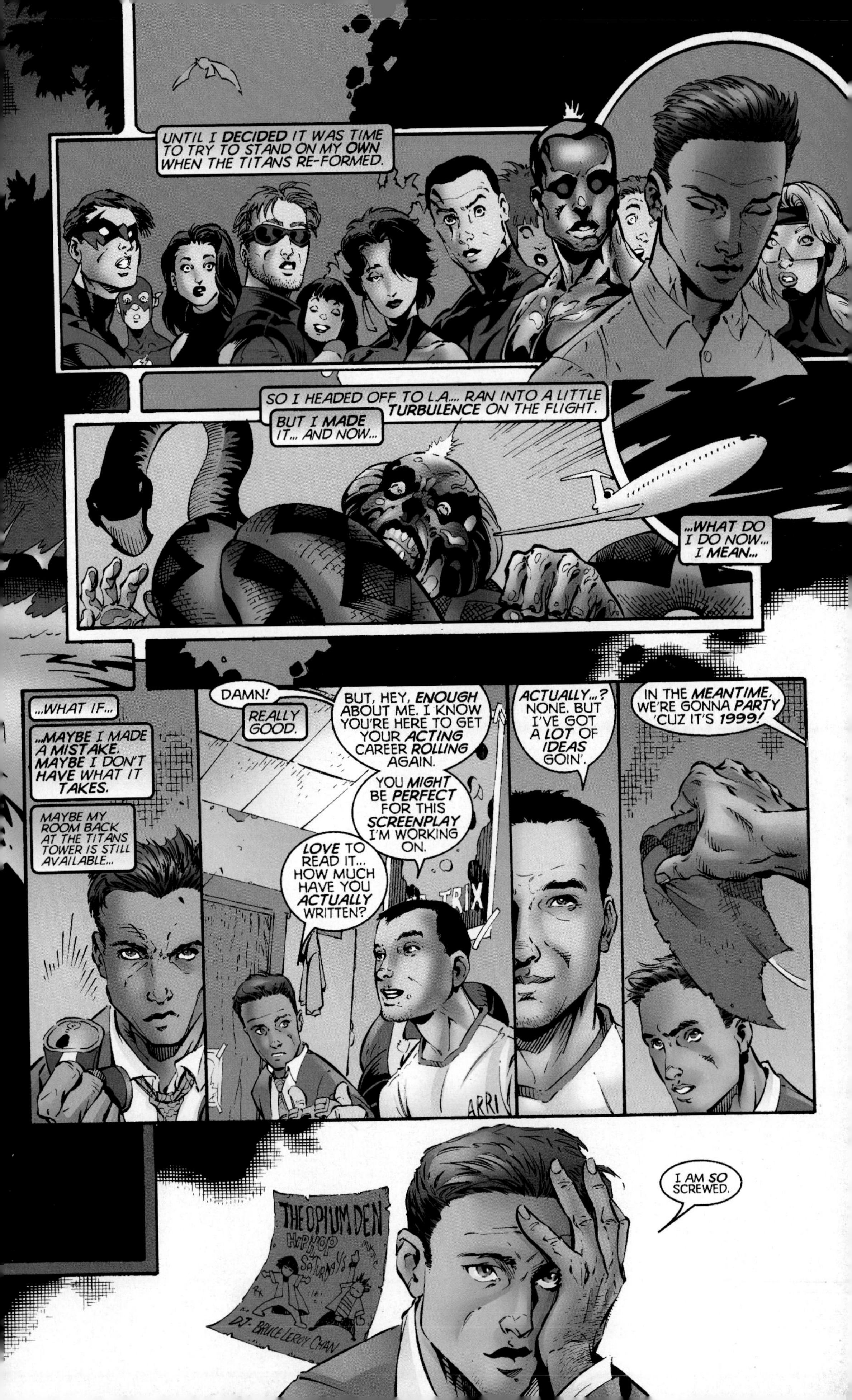
UNTIL I DECIDED IT WAS TIME TO TRY TO STAND ON MY OWN WHEN THE TITANS RE-FORMED.
SO I HEADED OFF TO L.A.... RAN INTO A LITTLE TURBULENCE ON THE FLIGHT.
BUT I MADE IT... AND NOW...
...WHAT DO I DO NOW... I MEAN...
...WHAT IF...
...MAYBE I MADE A MISTAKE. MAYBE I DON'T HAVE WHAT IT TAKES.
MAYBE MY ROOM BACK AT THE TITANS TOWER IS STILL AVAILABLE...
DAMN!
REALLY GOOD.
BUT, HEY, ENOUGH ABOUT ME. I KNOW YOU'RE HERE TO GET YOUR ACTING CAREER ROLLING AGAIN.
YOU MIGHT BE PERFECT FOR THIS SCREENPLAY I'M WORKING ON.
LOVE TO READ IT... HOW MUCH HAVE YOU ACTUALLY WRITTEN?
ACTUALLY...? NONE. BUT I'VE GOT A LOT OF IDEAS GOIN'.
IN THE MEANTIME, WE'RE GONNA PARTY 'CUZ IT'S 1999!
THE OPIUM DEN
HIP HOP SATURDAYS
DJ- BRUCE LEROY CHAN
I AM SO SCREWED.

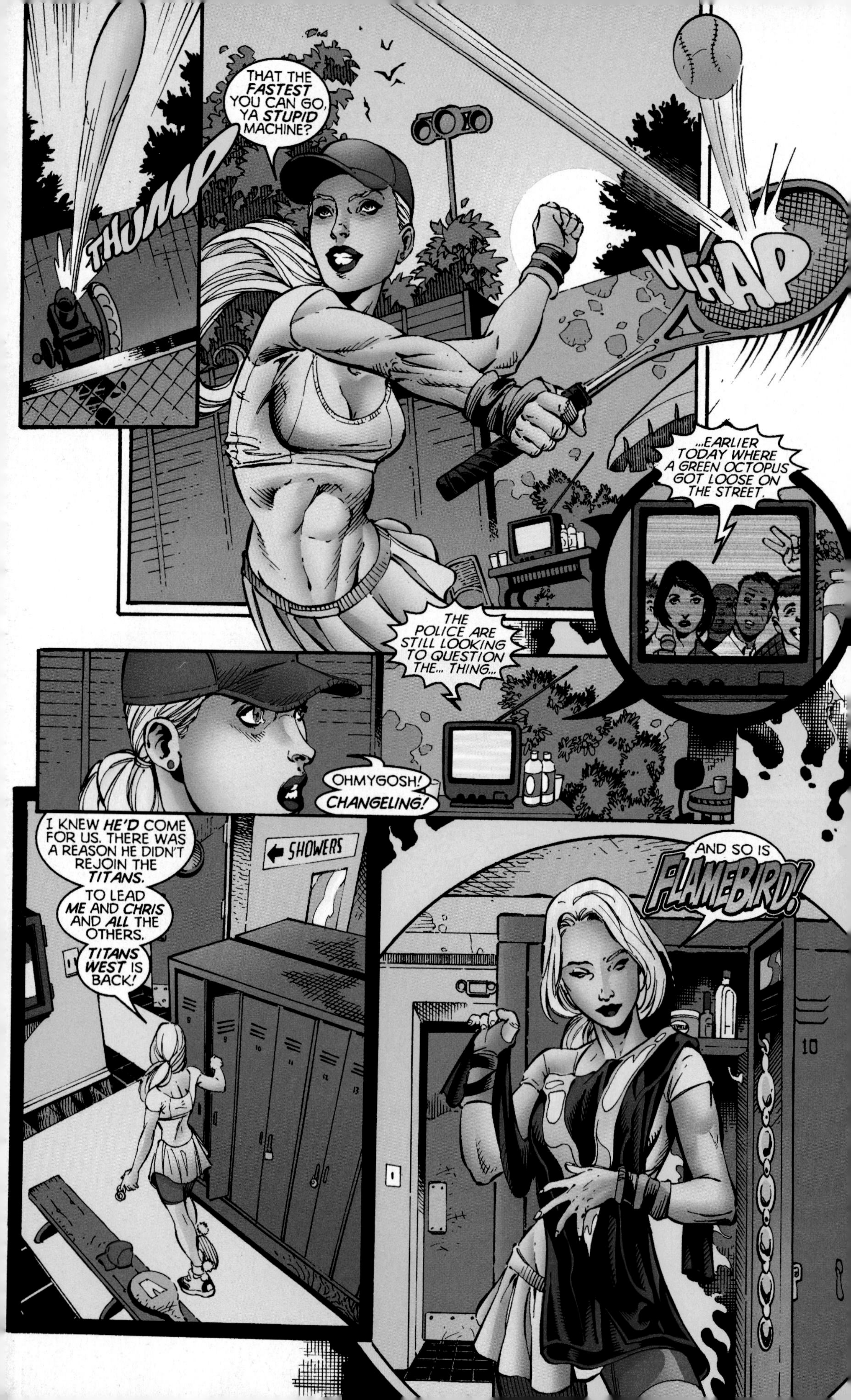
THAT THE FASTEST YOU CAN GO, YA STUPID MACHINE?
THUMP
WHAP
...EARLIER TODAY WHERE A GREEN OCTOPUS GOT LOOSE ON THE STREET.
THE POLICE ARE STILL LOOKING TO QUESTION THE... THING...
OHMYGOSH!
CHANGELING!
I KNEW HE'D COME FOR US. THERE WAS A REASON HE DIDN'T REJOIN THE TITANS.
TO LEAD ME AND CHRIS AND ALL THE OTHERS.
TITANS WEST IS BACK!
SHOWERS
AND SO IS FLAMEBIRD!
10

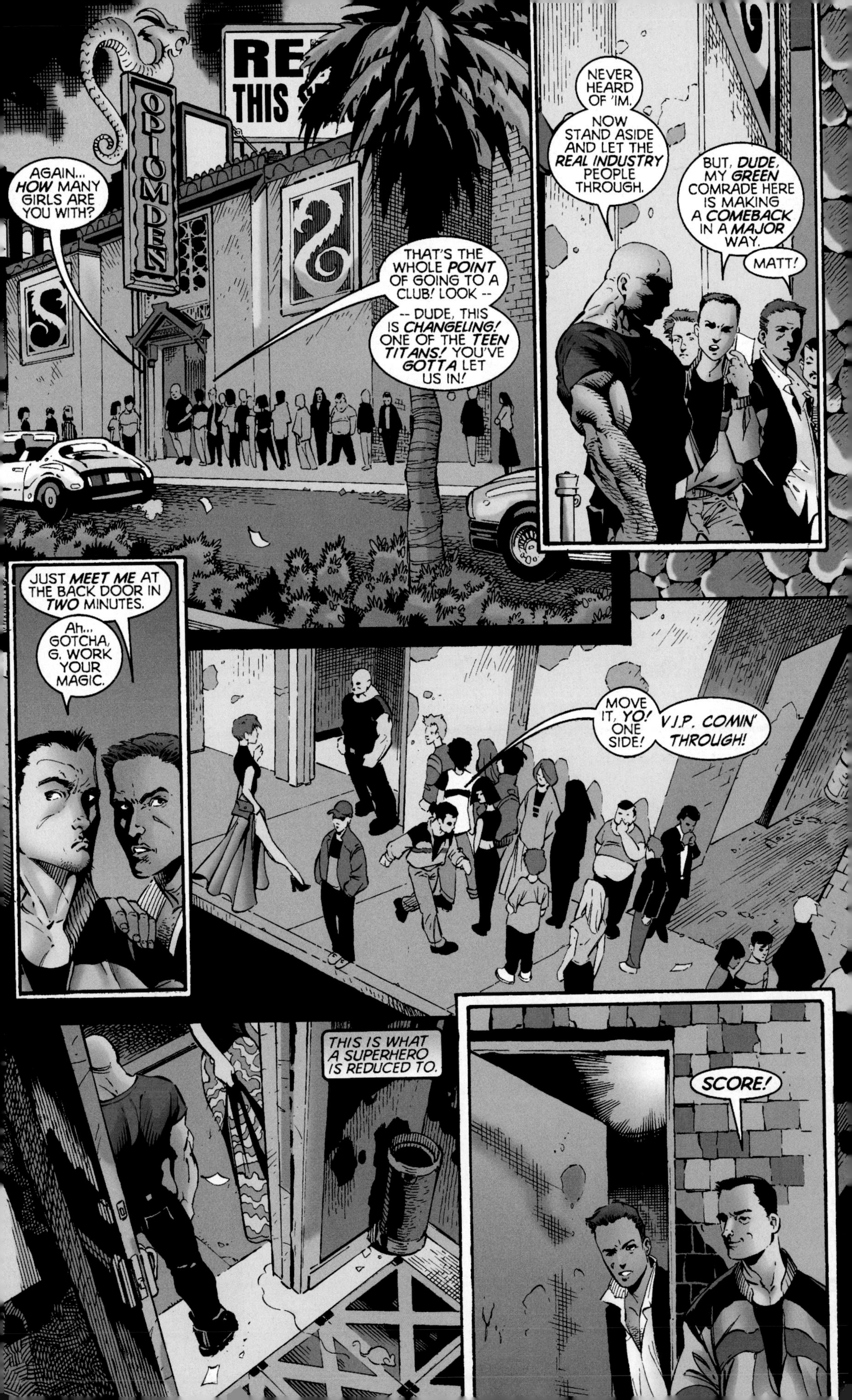
RE
THIS
OPIUM DEN
AGAIN... HOW MANY GIRLS ARE YOU WITH?
THAT'S THE WHOLE POINT OF GOING TO A CLUB! LOOK --
-- DUDE, THIS IS CHANGELING! ONE OF THE TEEN TITANS! YOU'VE GOTTA LET US IN!
NEVER HEARD OF 'IM.
NOW STAND ASIDE AND LET THE REAL INDUSTRY PEOPLE THROUGH.
BUT, DUDE, MY GREEN COMRADE HERE IS MAKING A COMEBACK IN A MAJOR WAY.
MATT!
JUST MEET ME AT THE BACK DOOR IN TWO MINUTES.
Ah... GOTCHA, G. WORK YOUR MAGIC.
MOVE IT, YO! ONE SIDE!
V.I.P. COMIN' THROUGH!
THIS IS WHAT A SUPERHERO IS REDUCED TO.
SCORE!

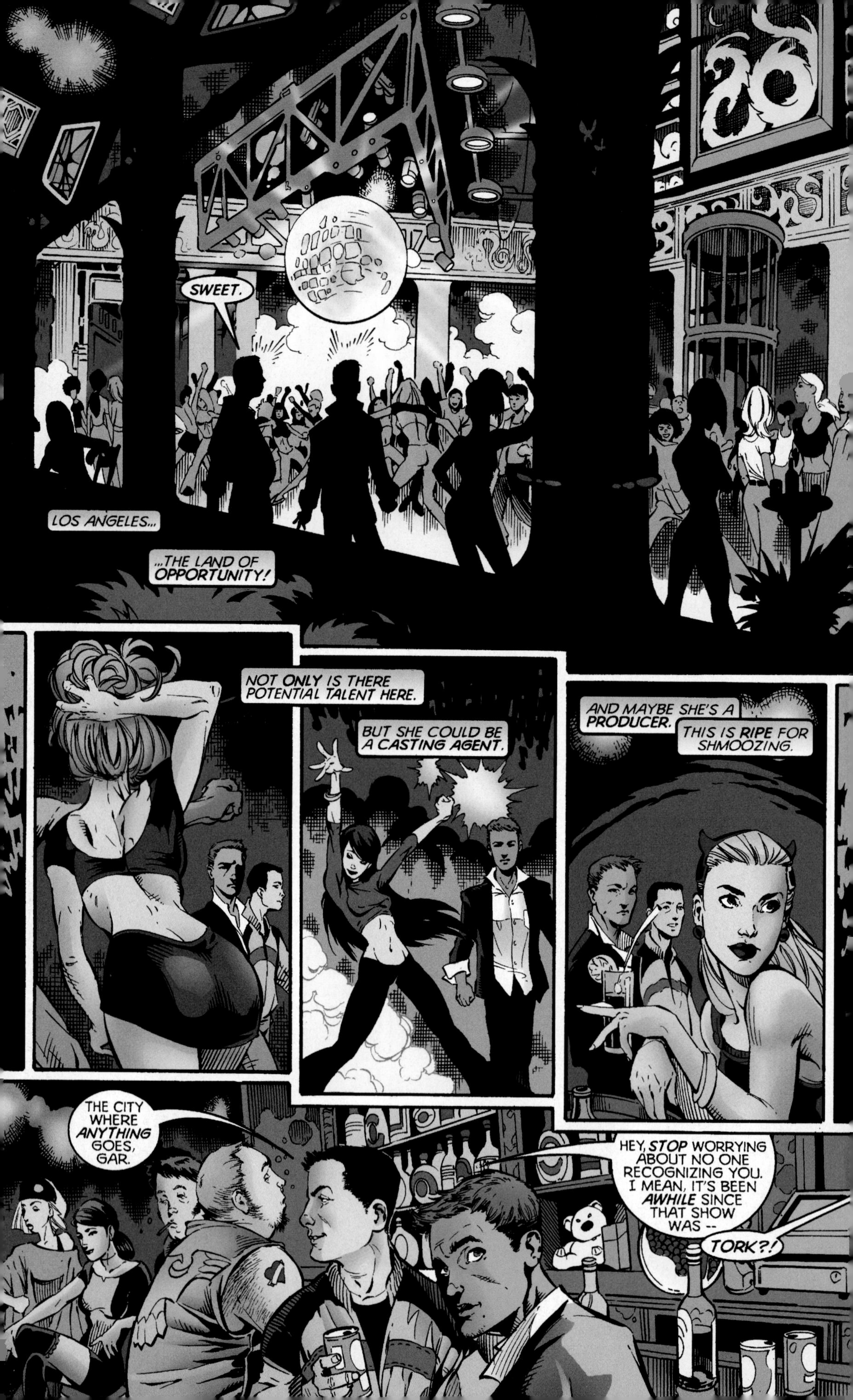
SWEET.
LOS ANGELES...
...THE LAND OF OPPORTUNITY!
NOT ONLY IS THERE POTENTIAL TALENT HERE.
BUT SHE COULD BE A CASTING AGENT.
AND MAYBE SHE'S A PRODUCER.
THIS IS RIPE FOR SHMOOZING.
THE CITY WHERE ANYTHING GOES, GAR.
HEY, STOP WORRYING ABOUT NO ONE RECOGNIZING YOU. I MEAN, IT'S BEEN AWHILE SINCE THAT SHOW WAS --
TORK?!

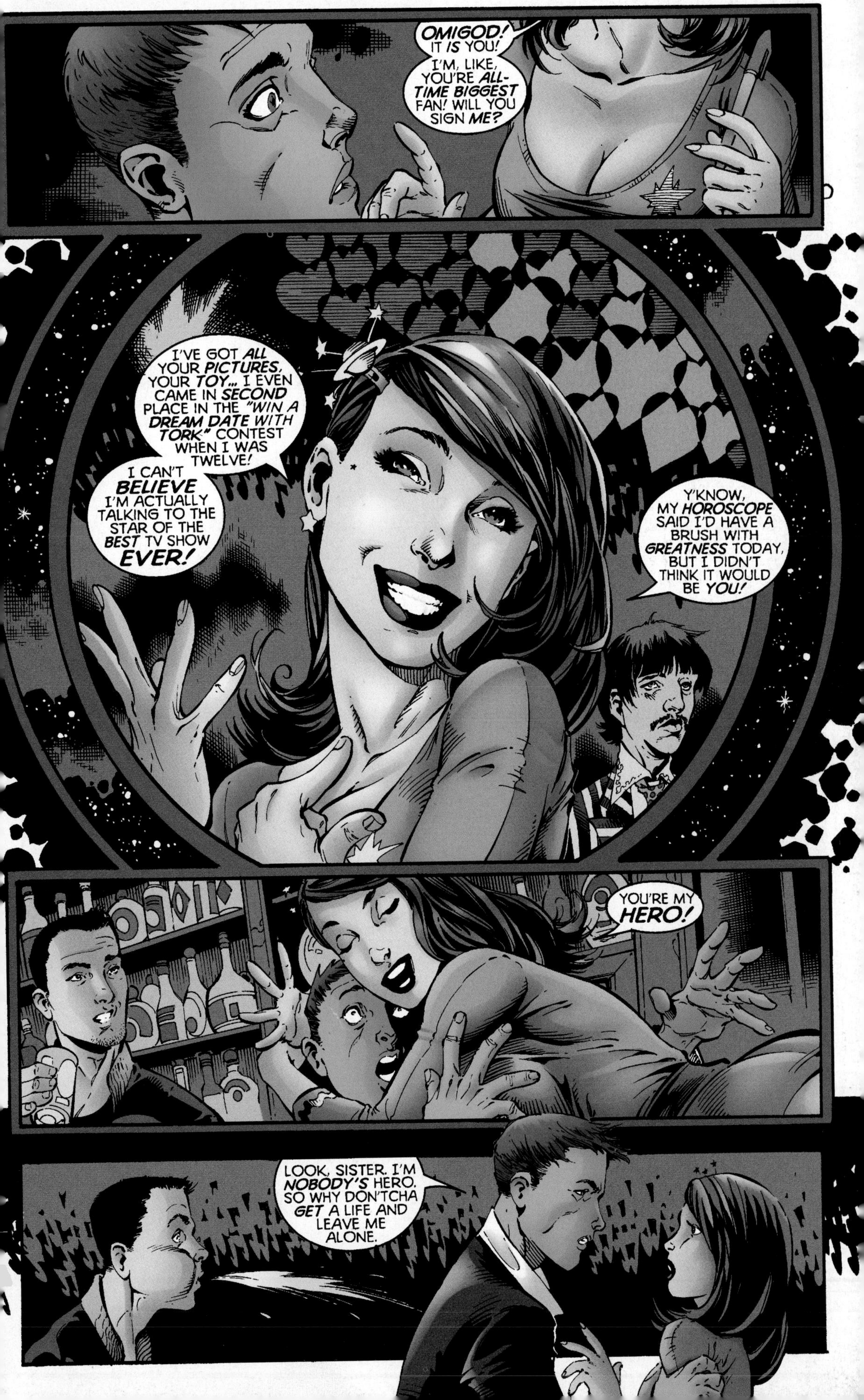

OMIGOD! IT IS YOU! I'M, LIKE, YOU'RE ALL-TIME BIGGEST FAN! WILL YOU SIGN ME?
I'VE GOT ALL YOUR PICTURES, YOUR TOY... I EVEN CAME IN SECOND PLACE IN THE "WIN A DREAM DATE WITH TORK" CONTEST WHEN I WAS TWELVE!
I CAN'T BELIEVE I'M ACTUALLY TALKING TO THE STAR OF THE BEST TV SHOW EVER!
Y'KNOW, MY HOROSCOPE SAID I'D HAVE A BRUSH WITH GREATNESS TODAY, BUT I DIDN'T THINK IT WOULD BE YOU!
YOU'RE MY HERO!
LOOK, SISTER. I'M NOBODY'S HERO. SO WHY DON'TCHA GET A LIFE AND LEAVE ME ALONE.

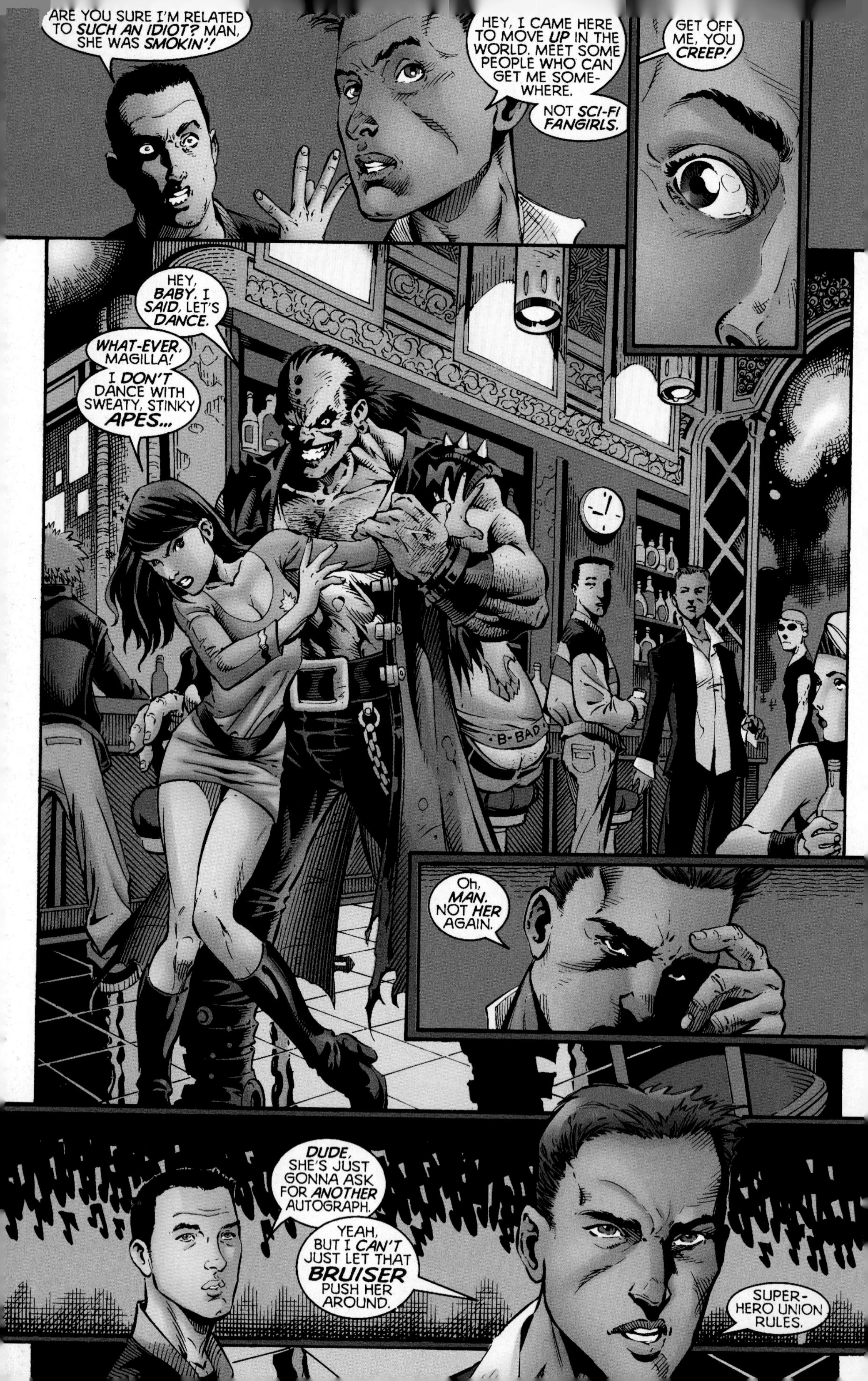

ARE YOU SURE I'M RELATED TO SUCH AN IDIOT? MAN, SHE WAS SMOKIN'!
HEY, I CAME HERE TO MOVE UP IN THE WORLD. MEET SOME PEOPLE WHO CAN GET ME SOME-WHERE.
NOT SCI-FI FANGIRLS.
GET OFF ME, YOU CREEP!
HEY, BABY. I SAID, LET'S DANCE.
WHAT-EVER, MAGILLA!
I DON'T DANCE WITH SWEATY, STINKY APES...
B-BAD
Oh, MAN. NOT HER AGAIN.
DUDE, SHE'S JUST GONNA ASK FOR ANOTHER AUTOGRAPH.
YEAH, BUT I CAN'T JUST LET THAT BRUISER PUSH HER AROUND.
SUPER-HERO UNION RULES.

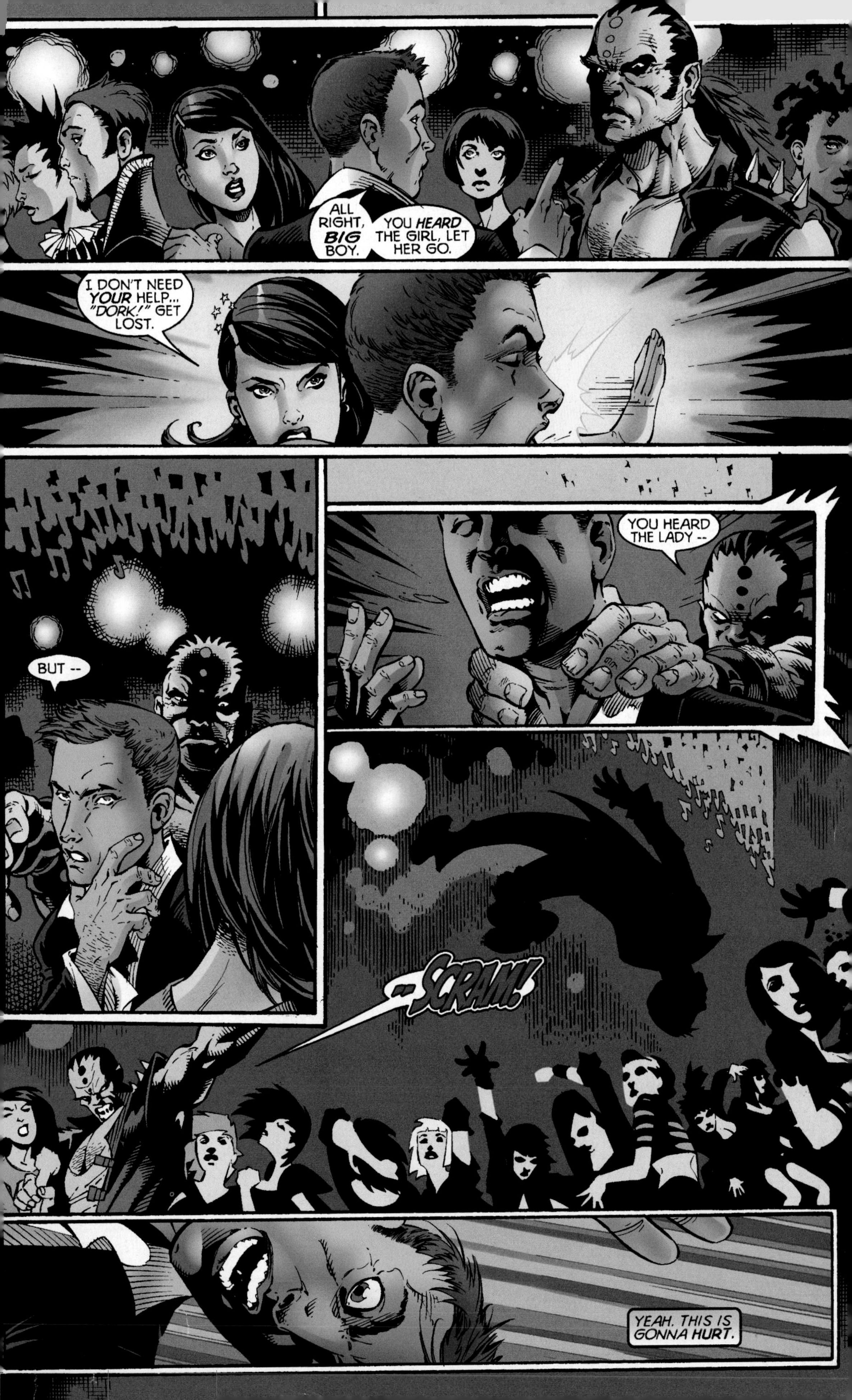
ALL RIGHT, BIG BOY.
YOU HEARD THE GIRL, LET HER GO.
I DON'T NEED YOUR HELP... "DORK!" GET LOST.
BUT --
YOU HEARD THE LADY --
-- SCRAM!
YEAH. THIS IS GONNA HURT.

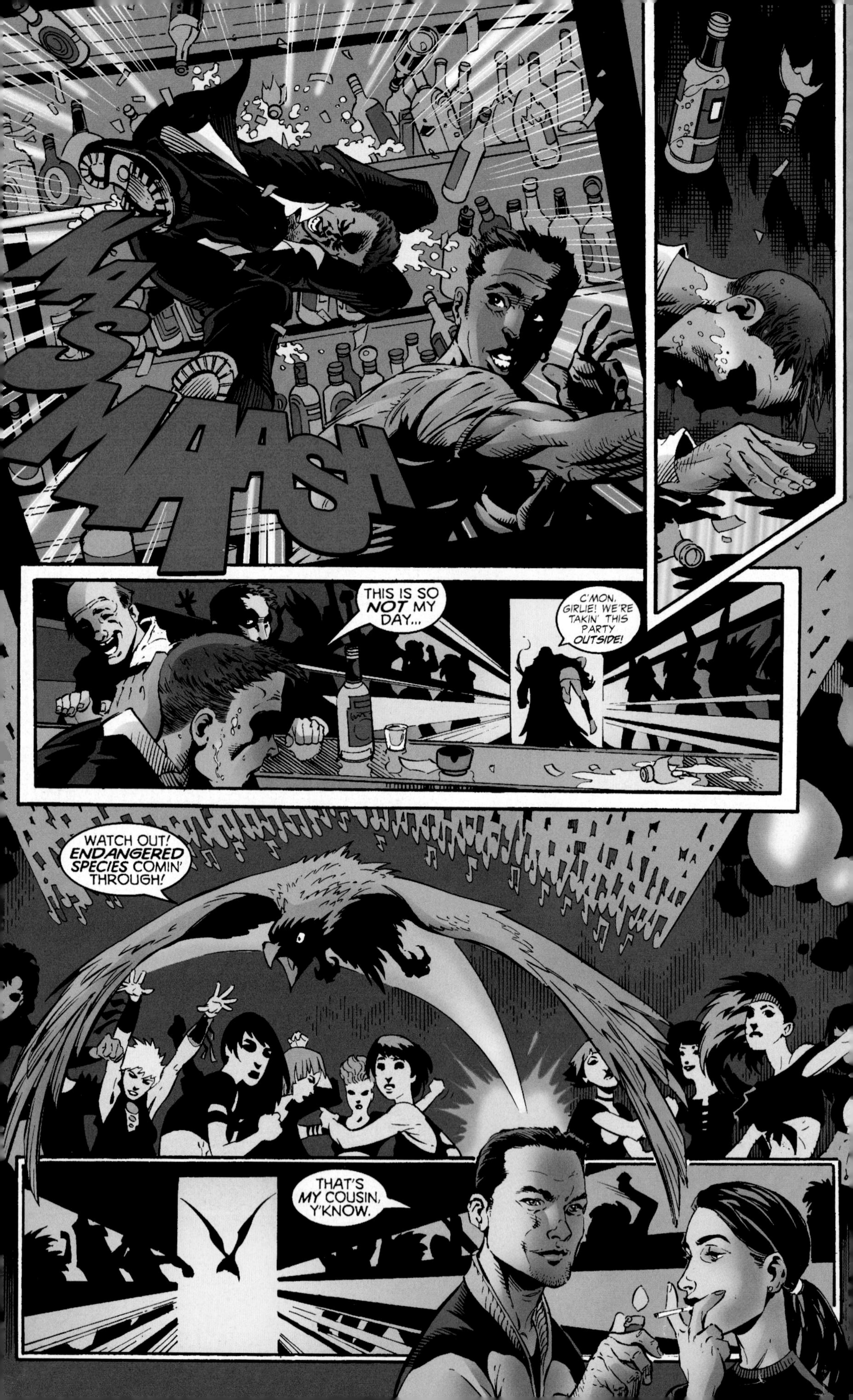
SMASH
THIS IS SO NOT MY DAY...
C'MON, GIRLIE! WE'RE TAKIN' THIS PARTY OUTSIDE!
WATCH OUT! ENDANGERED SPECIES COMIN' THROUGH!
THAT'S MY COUSIN, Y'KNOW.

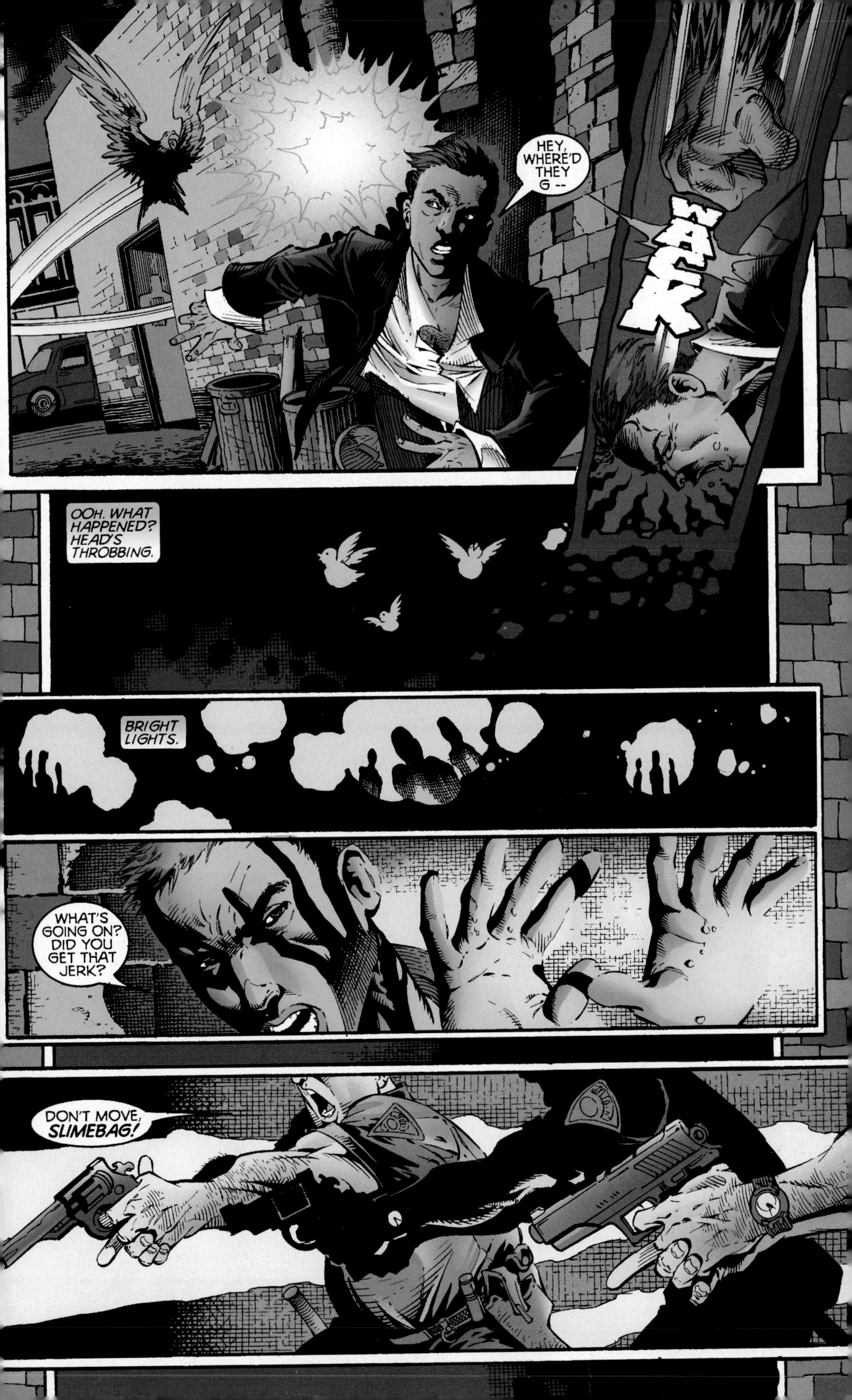
HEY, WHERE'D THEY G --
WACK
OOH. WHAT HAPPENED? HEAD'S THROBBING.
BRIGHT LIGHTS.
WHAT'S GOING ON? DID YOU GET THAT JERK?
DON'T MOVE, SLIMEBAG!

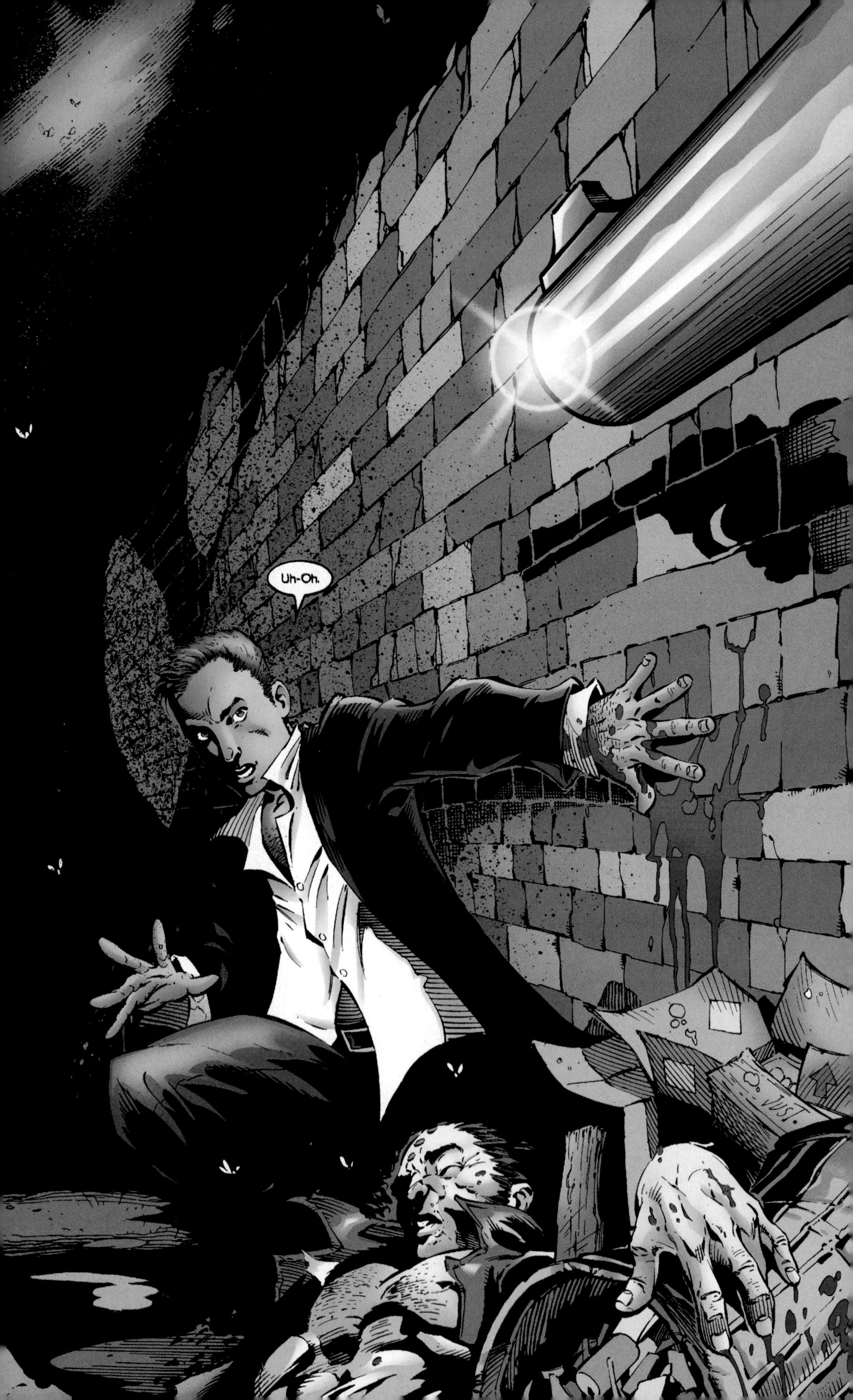
Uh-Oh.

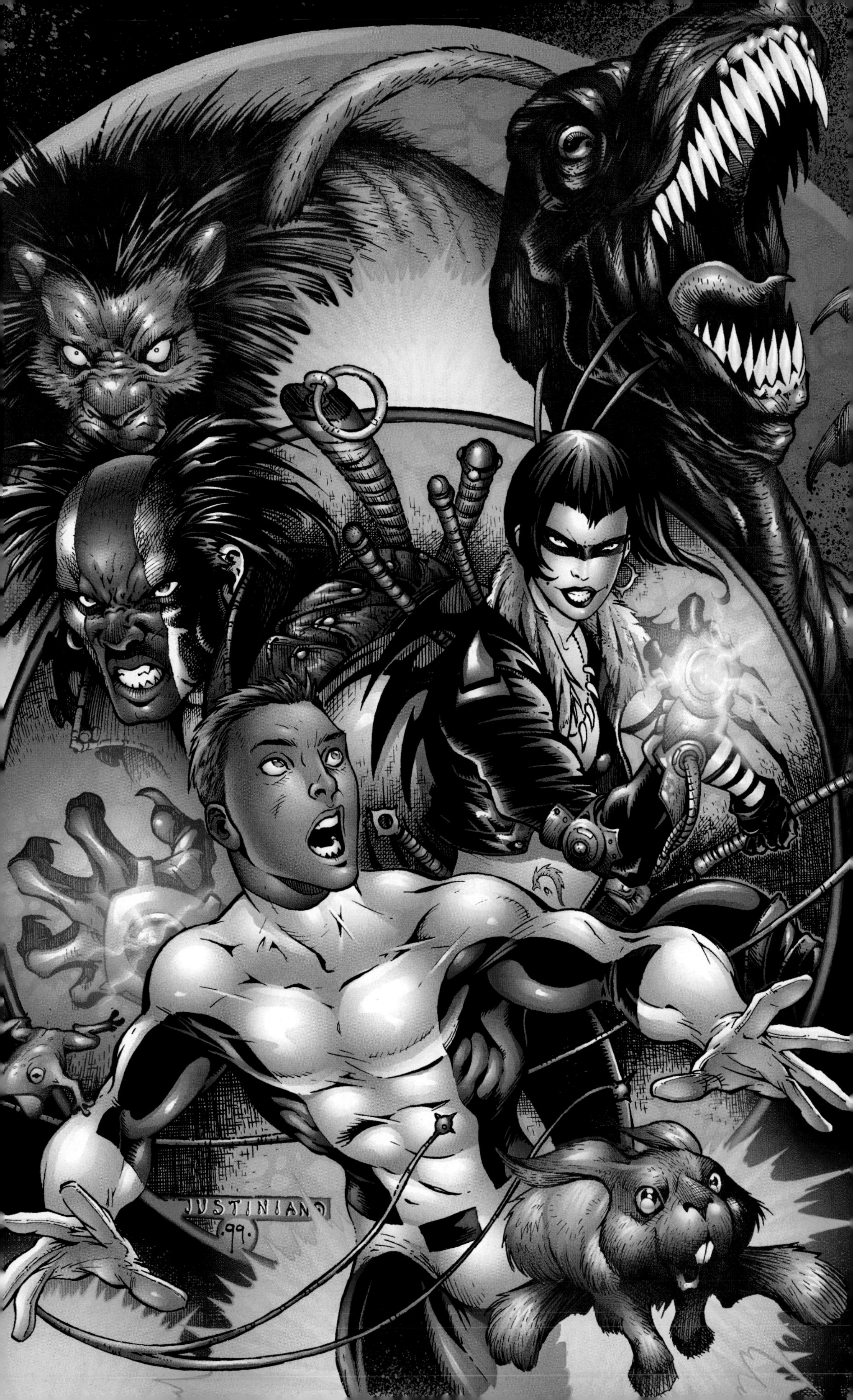
JUSTINIANO
·99·

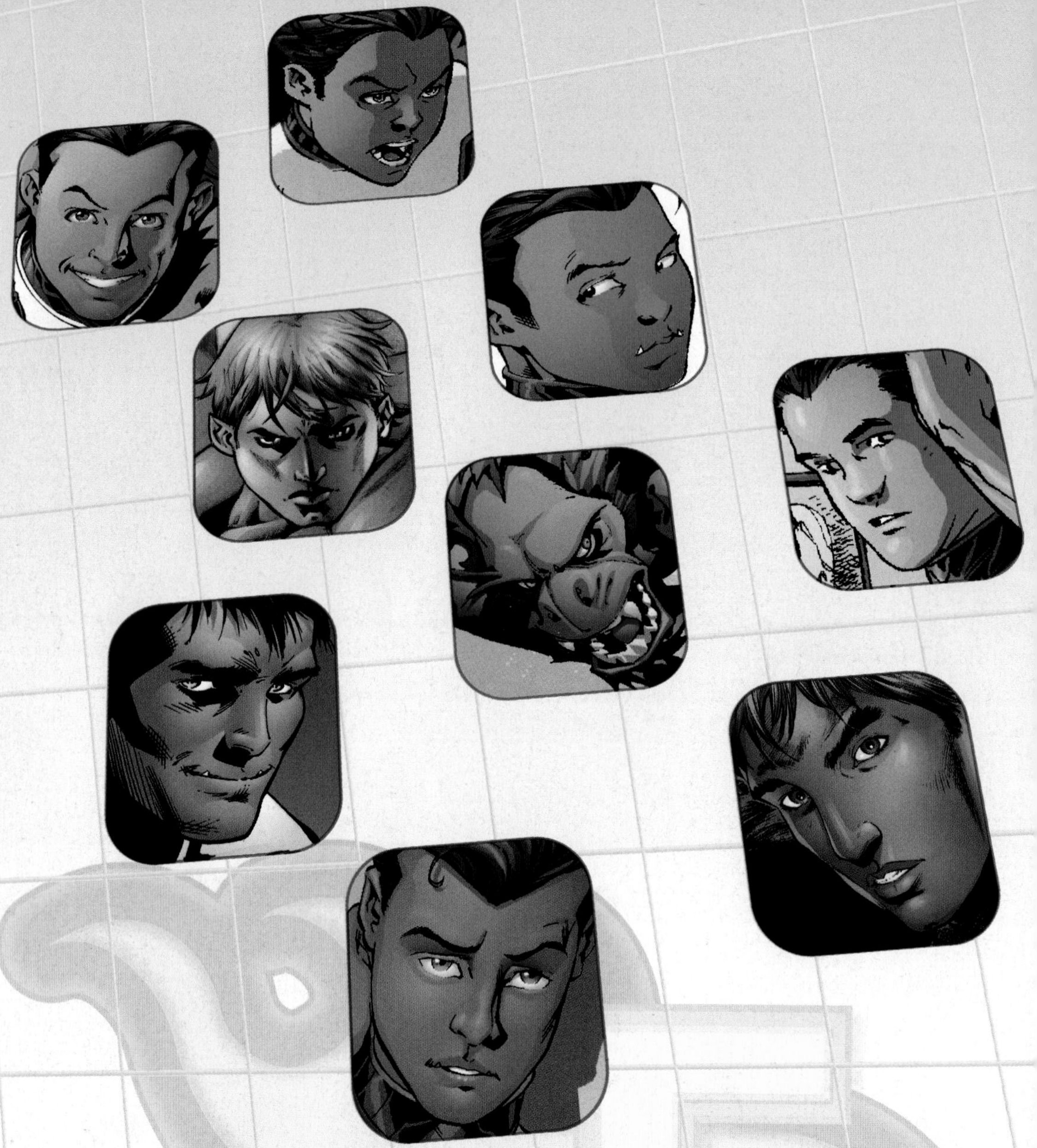

BEAST BOY #2

GEOFF JOHNS
BEN RAAB
Writers

JUSTINIANO
Penciller

CHRIS IVY
Inker

JASON WRIGHT
Colorist

COMICRAFT
Letterer

JUSTINIANO
Cover Artist

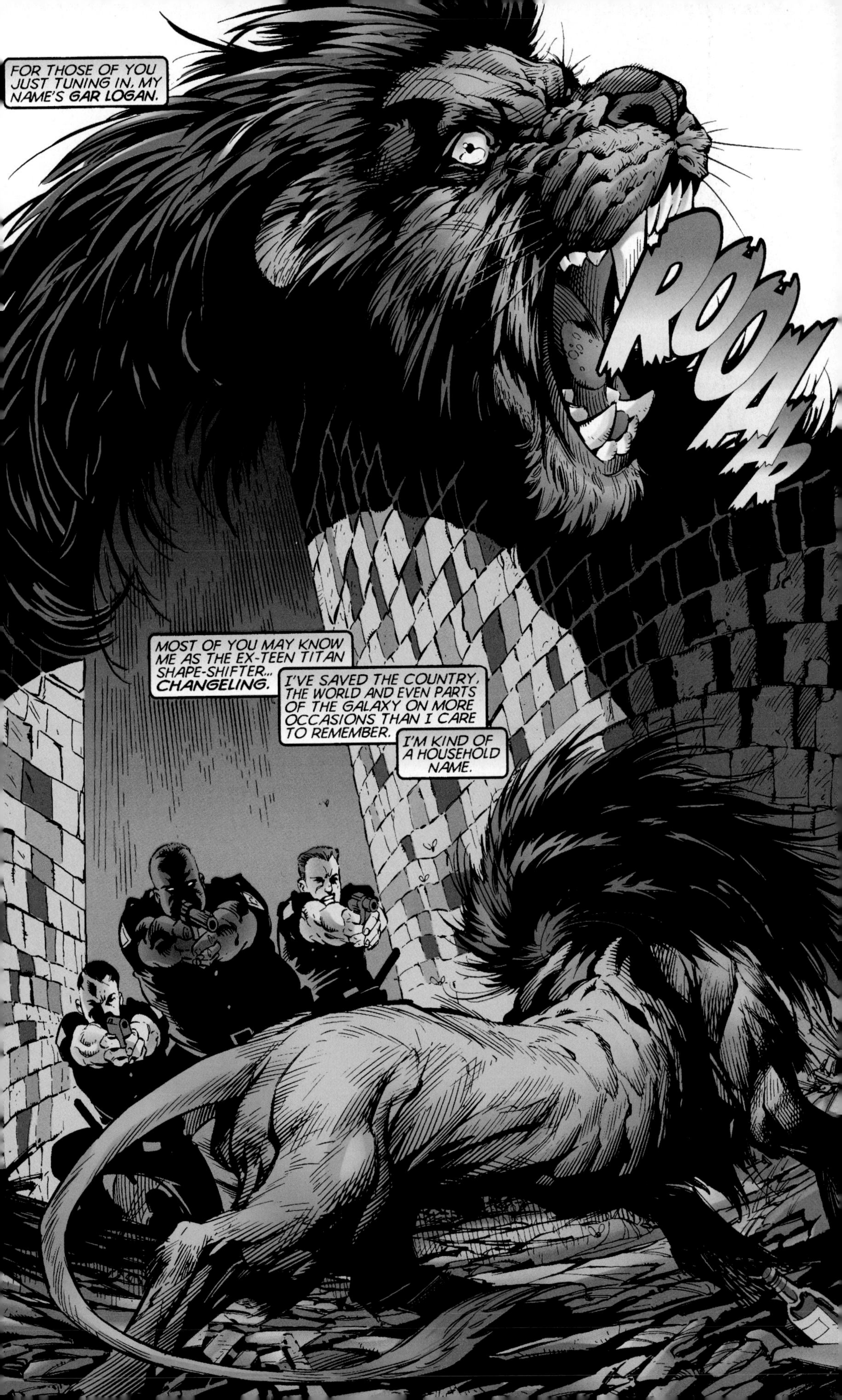

FOR THOSE OF YOU JUST TUNING IN, MY NAME'S GAR LOGAN.
ROOOAAR
MOST OF YOU MAY KNOW ME AS THE EX-TEEN TITAN SHAPE-SHIFTER... CHANGELING.
I'VE SAVED THE COUNTRY, THE WORLD AND EVEN PARTS OF THE GALAXY ON MORE OCCASIONS THAN I CARE TO REMEMBER.
I'M KIND OF A HOUSEHOLD NAME.

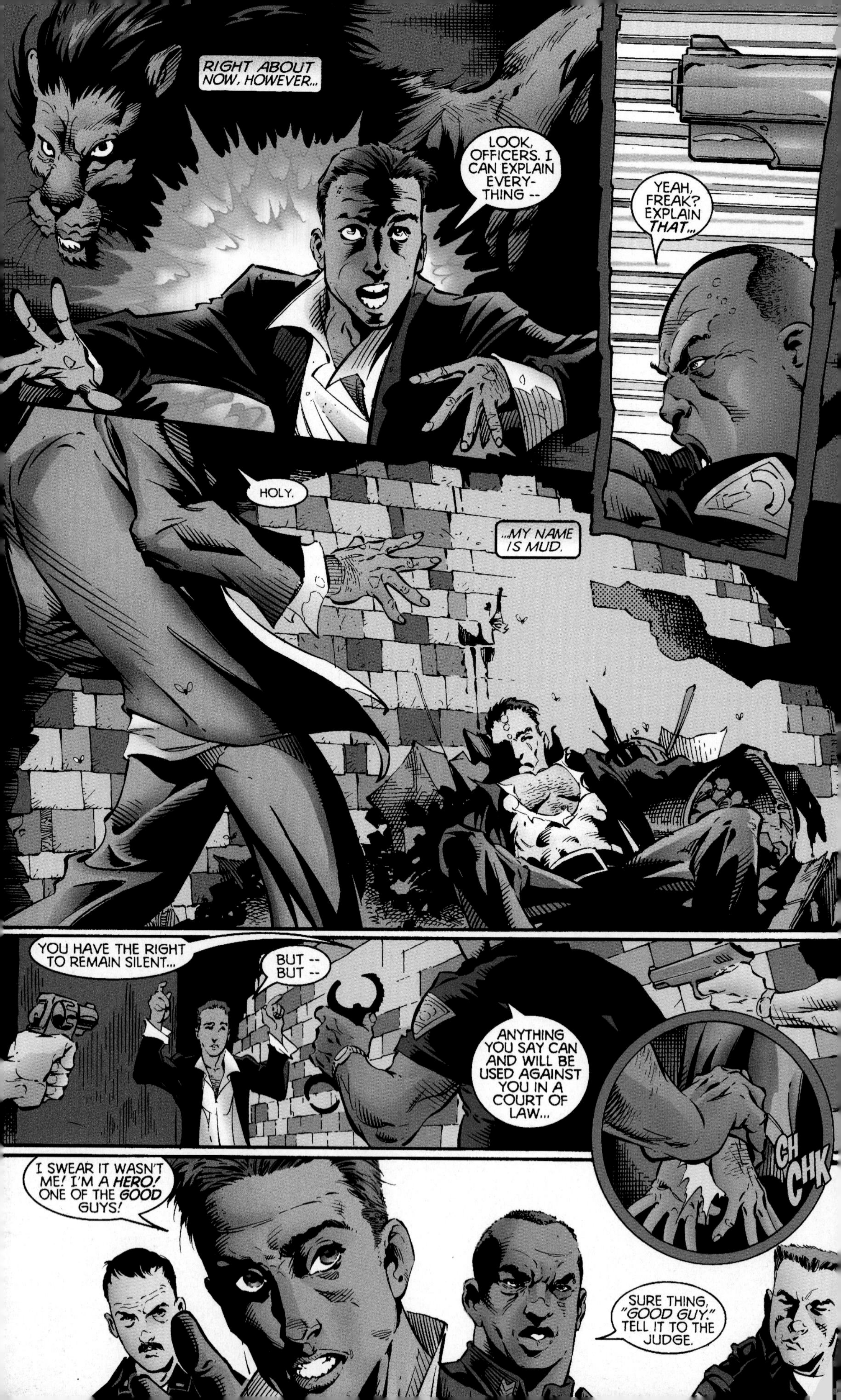

RIGHT ABOUT NOW, HOWEVER...
LOOK, OFFICERS. I CAN EXPLAIN EVERY-THING --
YEAH, FREAK? EXPLAIN THAT...
HOLY.
...MY NAME IS MUD.
YOU HAVE THE RIGHT TO REMAIN SILENT...
BUT -- BUT --
ANYTHING YOU SAY CAN AND WILL BE USED AGAINST YOU IN A COURT OF LAW...
CH CHK
I SWEAR IT WASN'T ME! I'M A HERO! ONE OF THE GOOD GUYS!
SURE THING, "GOOD GUY." TELL IT TO THE JUDGE.

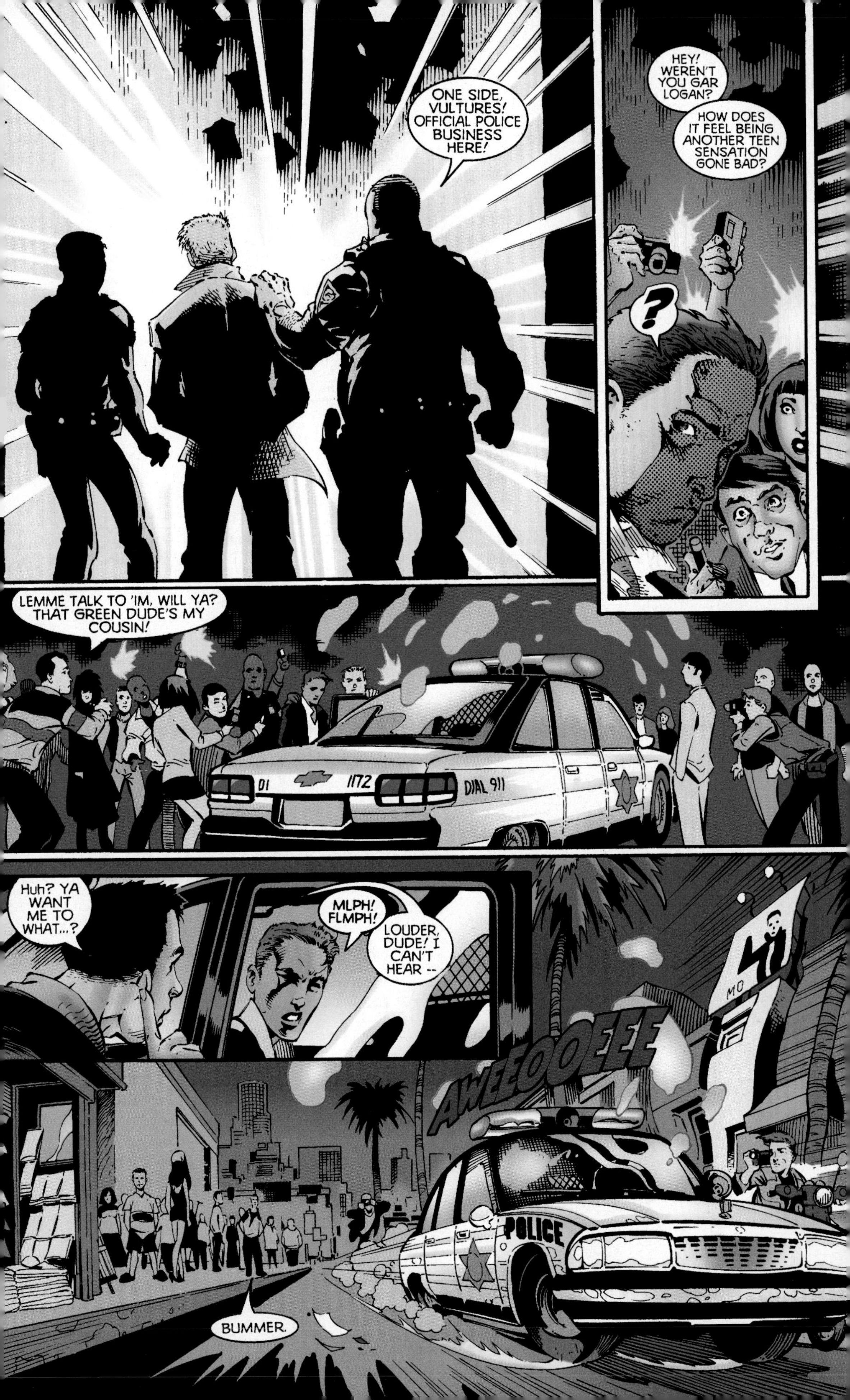
ONE SIDE, VULTURES! OFFICIAL POLICE BUSINESS HERE!
HEY! WEREN'T YOU GAR LOGAN?
HOW DOES IT FEEL BEING ANOTHER TEEN SENSATION GONE BAD?
?
LEMME TALK TO 'IM, WILL YA? THAT GREEN DUDE'S MY COUSIN!
D1
1172
DIAL 911
Huh? YA WANT ME TO WHAT...?
MLPH! FLMPH!
LOUDER, DUDE! I CAN'T HEAR --
AWEEOOEEE
POLICE
BUMMER.

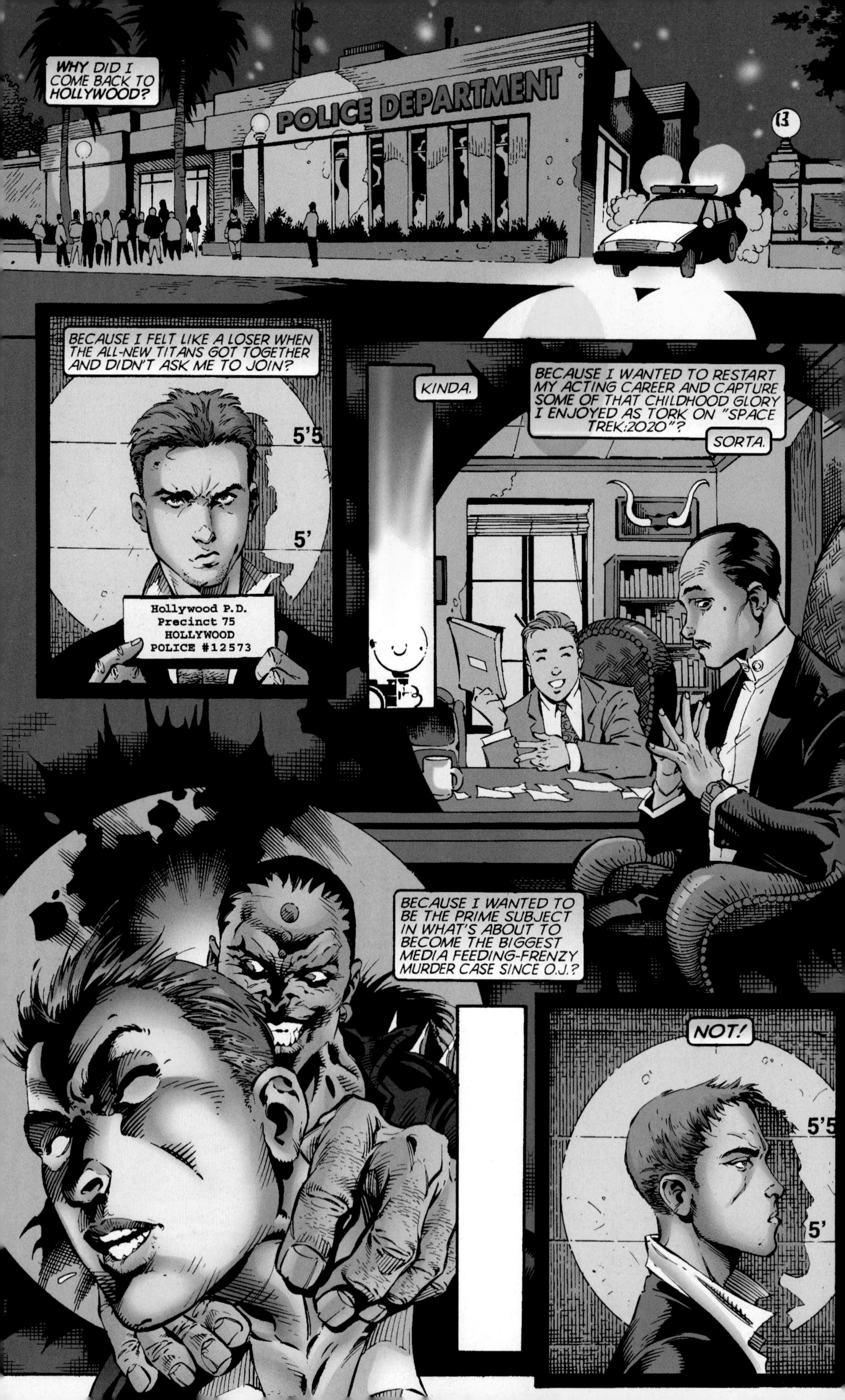
WHY DID I COME BACK TO HOLLYWOOD?
POLICE DEPARTMENT
13
BECAUSE I FELT LIKE A LOSER WHEN THE ALL-NEW TITANS GOT TOGETHER AND DIDN'T ASK ME TO JOIN?
5'5
5'
Hollywood P.D.
Precinct 75
HOLLYWOOD
POLICE #12573
KINDA.
BECAUSE I WANTED TO RESTART MY ACTING CAREER AND CAPTURE SOME OF THAT CHILDHOOD GLORY I ENJOYED AS TORK ON "SPACE TREK:2020"?
SORTA.
BECAUSE I WANTED TO BE THE PRIME SUBJECT IN WHAT'S ABOUT TO BECOME THE BIGGEST MEDIA FEEDING-FRENZY MURDER CASE SINCE O.J.?
NOT!
5'5
5'

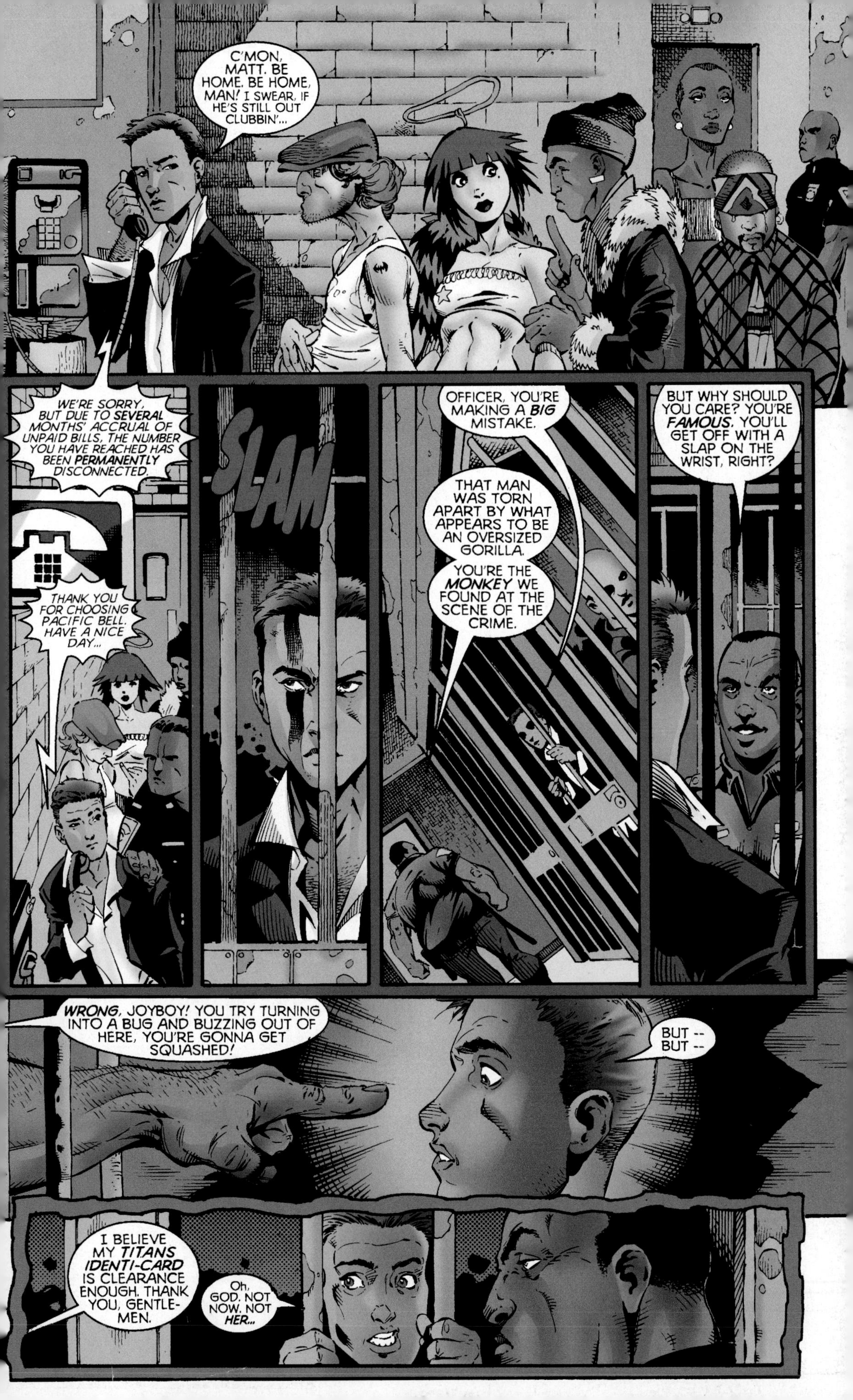
C'MON, MATT. BE HOME. BE HOME, MAN! I SWEAR, IF HE'S STILL OUT CLUBBIN'...
WE'RE SORRY, BUT DUE TO SEVERAL MONTHS' ACCRUAL OF UNPAID BILLS, THE NUMBER YOU HAVE REACHED HAS BEEN PERMANENTLY DISCONNECTED.
THANK YOU FOR CHOOSING PACIFIC BELL. HAVE A NICE DAY...
SLAM
OFFICER, YOU'RE MAKING A BIG MISTAKE.
THAT MAN WAS TORN APART BY WHAT APPEARS TO BE AN OVERSIZED GORILLA.
YOU'RE THE MONKEY WE FOUND AT THE SCENE OF THE CRIME.
BUT WHY SHOULD YOU CARE? YOU'RE FAMOUS. YOU'LL GET OFF WITH A SLAP ON THE WRIST, RIGHT?
WRONG, JOYBOY! YOU TRY TURNING INTO A BUG AND BUZZING OUT OF HERE, YOU'RE GONNA GET SQUASHED!
BUT -- BUT --
I BELIEVE MY TITANS IDENTI-CARD IS CLEARANCE ENOUGH. THANK YOU, GENTLE-MEN.
Oh, GOD. NOT NOW. NOT HER...

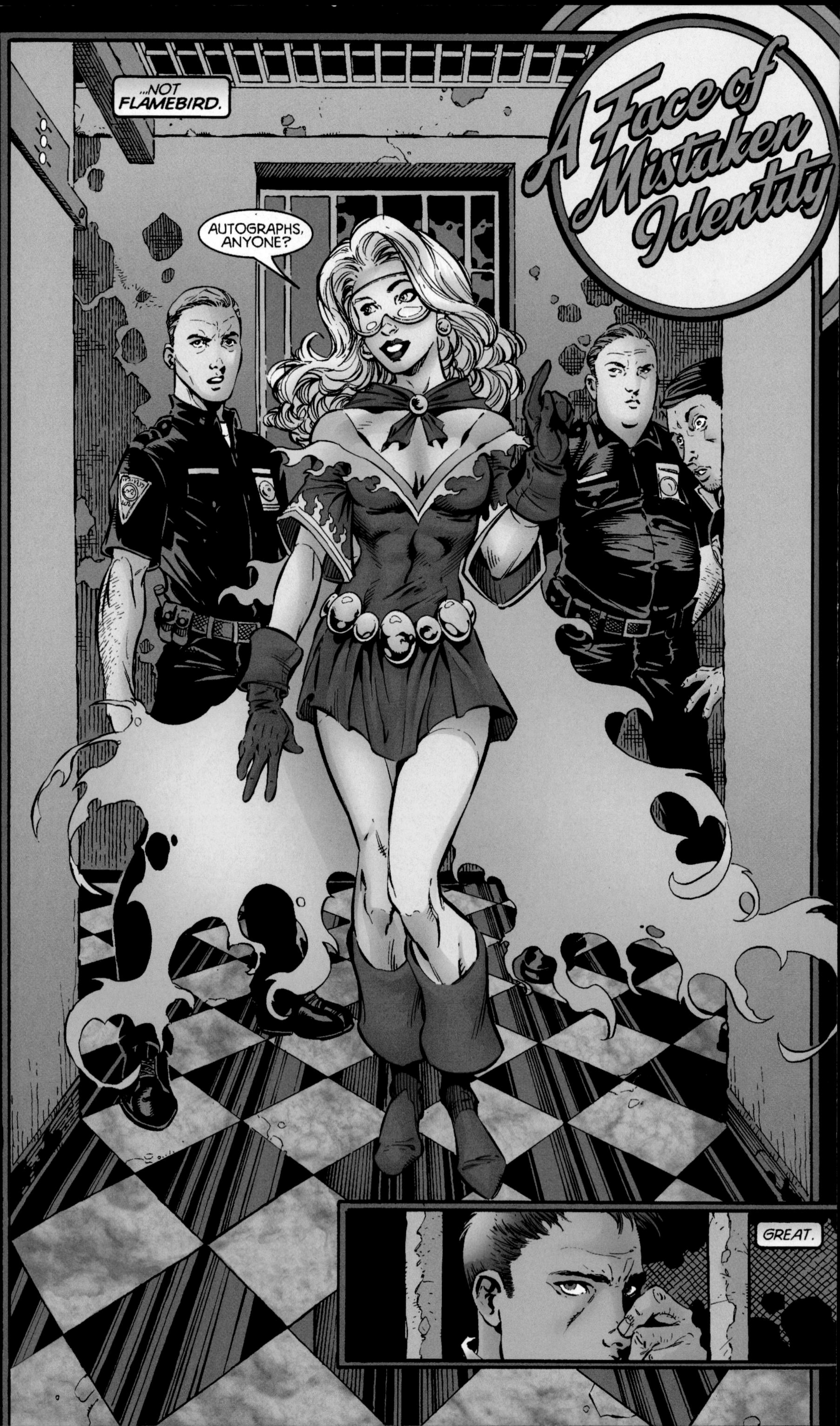
...NOT FLAMEBIRD.
A Face of Mistaken Identity
AUTOGRAPHS, ANYONE?
GREAT.

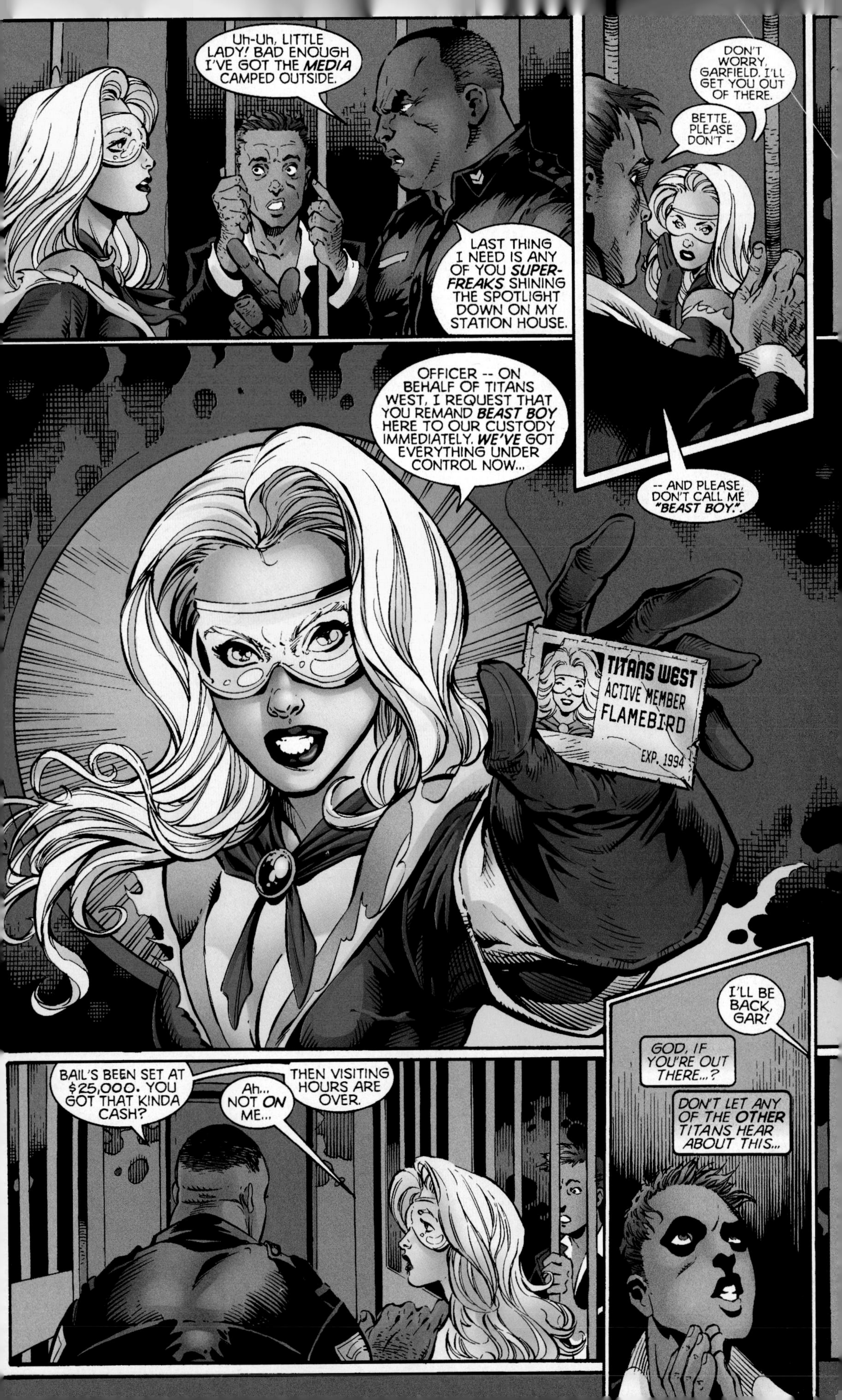
Uh-Uh, LITTLE LADY! BAD ENOUGH I'VE GOT THE *MEDIA* CAMPED OUTSIDE.
LAST THING I NEED IS ANY OF YOU *SUPER-FREAKS* SHINING THE SPOTLIGHT DOWN ON MY STATION HOUSE.
DON'T WORRY, GARFIELD. I'LL GET YOU OUT OF THERE.
BETTE, PLEASE DON'T --
OFFICER -- ON BEHALF OF TITANS WEST, I REQUEST THAT YOU REMAND *BEAST BOY* HERE TO OUR CUSTODY IMMEDIATELY. *WE'VE* GOT EVERYTHING UNDER CONTROL NOW...
-- AND PLEASE, DON'T CALL ME *"BEAST BOY."*
TITANS WEST
ACTIVE MEMBER
FLAMEBIRD
EXP. 1994
BAIL'S BEEN SET AT $25,000. YOU GOT THAT KINDA CASH?
Ah... NOT *ON* ME...
THEN VISITING HOURS ARE OVER.
I'LL BE BACK, GAR!
GOD, IF YOU'RE OUT THERE...?
DON'T LET ANY OF THE *OTHER* TITANS HEAR ABOUT THIS...

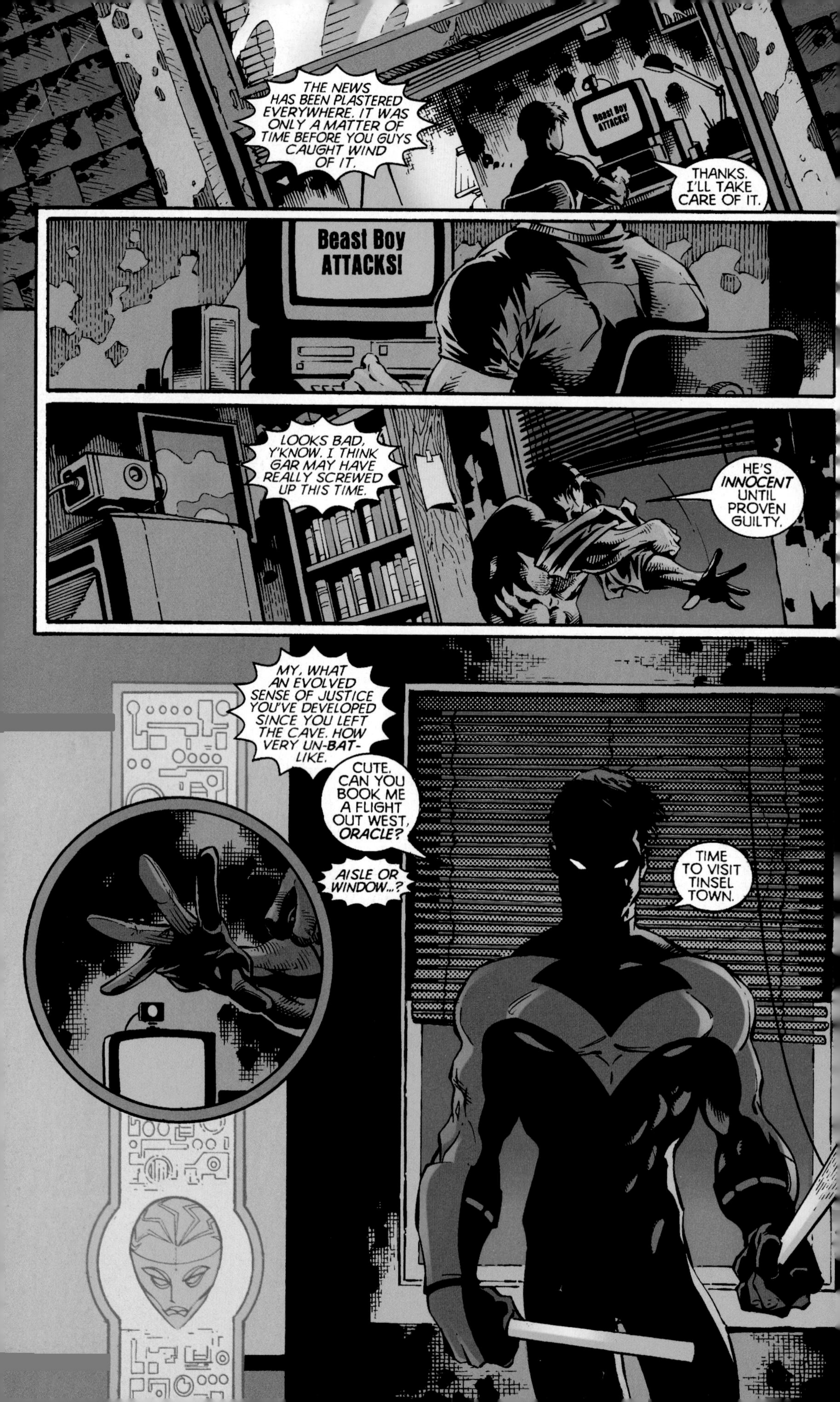

THE NEWS HAS BEEN PLASTERED EVERYWHERE. IT WAS ONLY A MATTER OF TIME BEFORE YOU GUYS CAUGHT WIND OF IT.
Beast Boy ATTACKS!
THANKS. I'LL TAKE CARE OF IT.
Beast Boy ATTACKS!
LOOKS BAD, Y'KNOW. I THINK GAR MAY HAVE REALLY SCREWED UP THIS TIME.
HE'S INNOCENT UNTIL PROVEN GUILTY.
MY, WHAT AN EVOLVED SENSE OF JUSTICE YOU'VE DEVELOPED SINCE YOU LEFT THE CAVE. HOW VERY UN-BAT-LIKE.
CUTE. CAN YOU BOOK ME A FLIGHT OUT WEST, ORACLE?
AISLE OR WINDOW...?
TIME TO VISIT TINSEL TOWN.

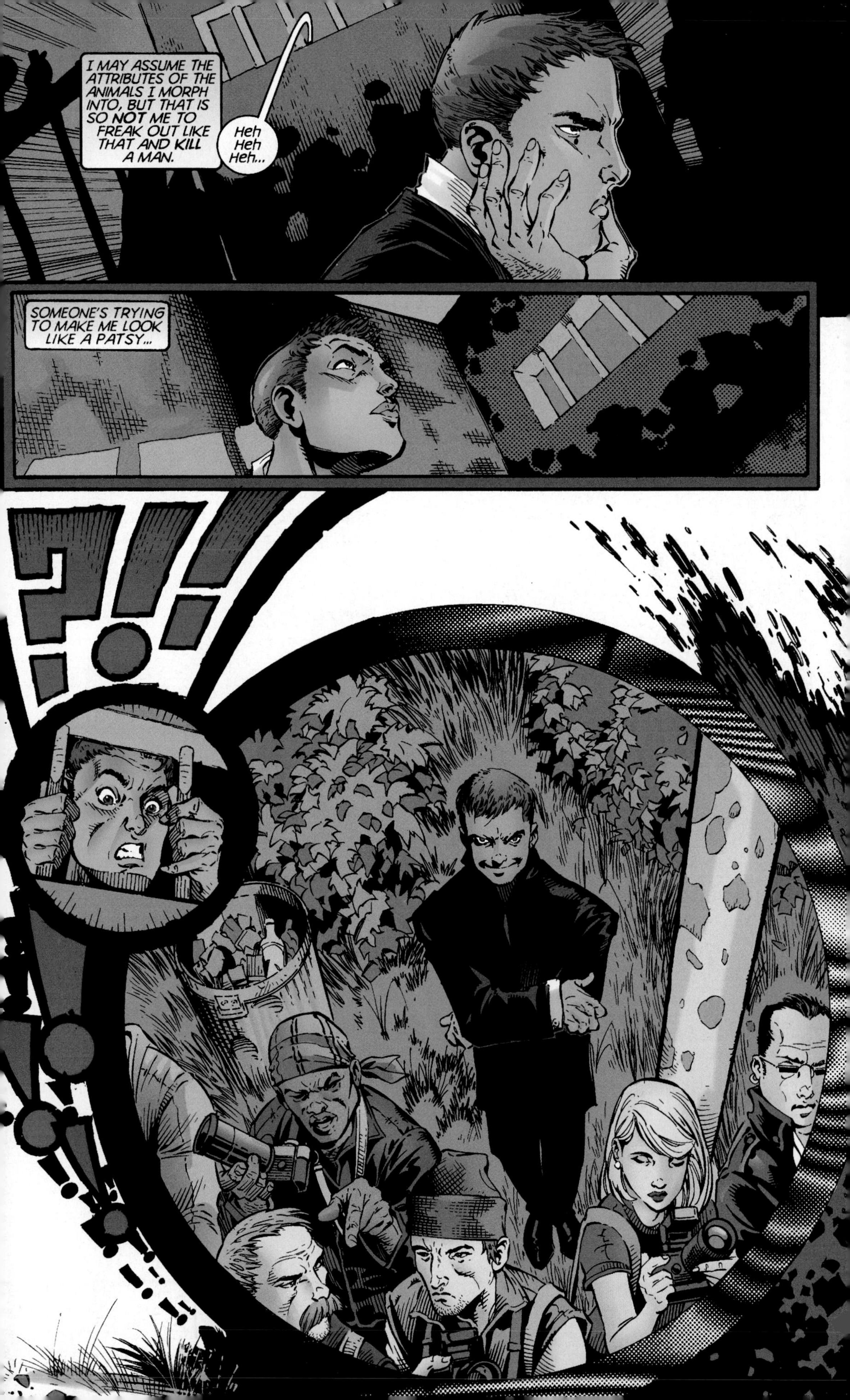
I MAY ASSUME THE ATTRIBUTES OF THE ANIMALS I MORPH INTO, BUT THAT IS SO NOT ME TO FREAK OUT LIKE THAT AND KILL A MAN.
Heh Heh Heh...
SOMEONE'S TRYING TO MAKE ME LOOK LIKE A PATSY...
?!!

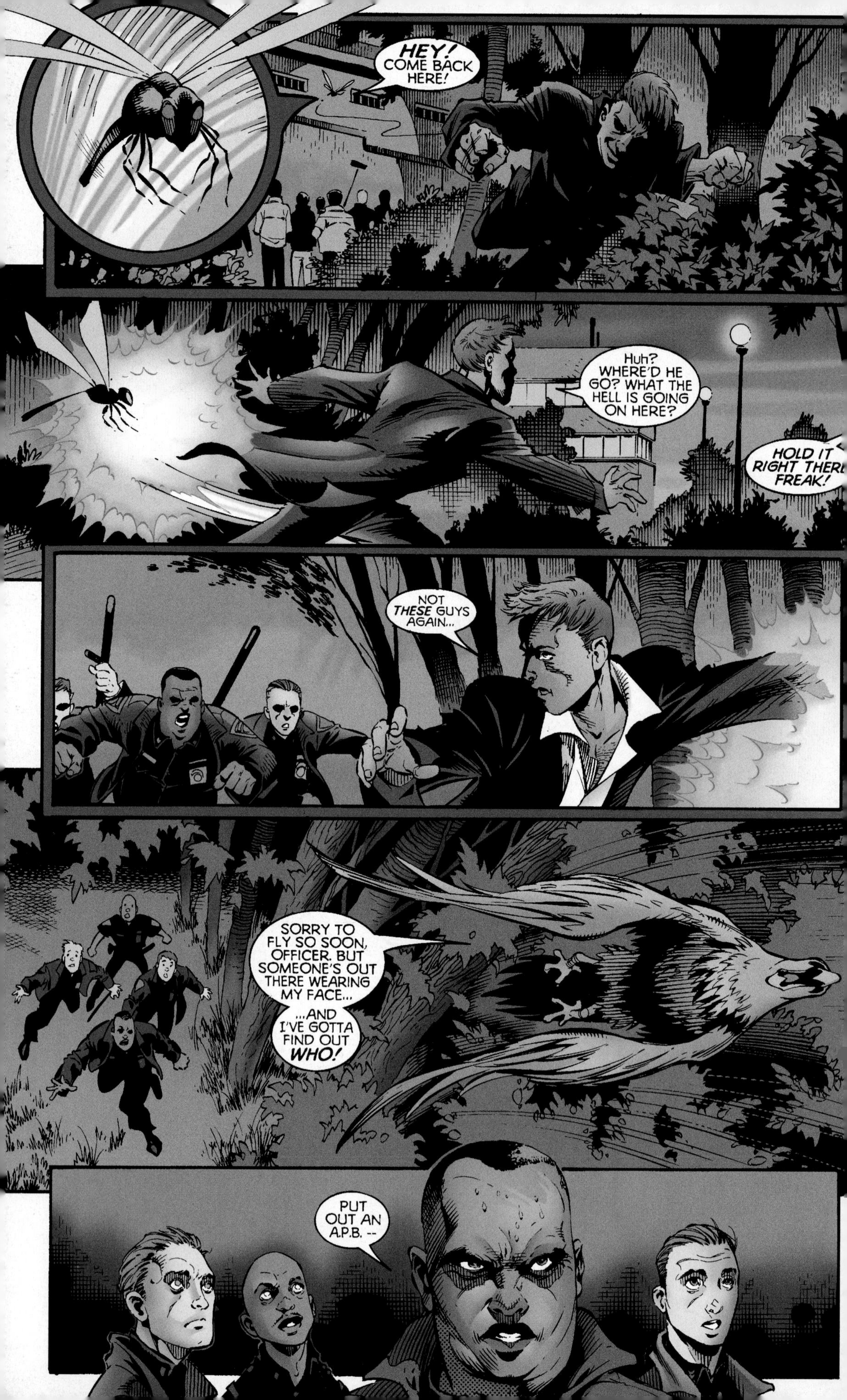
HEY! COME BACK HERE!
Huh? WHERE'D HE GO? WHAT THE HELL IS GOING ON HERE?
HOLD IT RIGHT THERE FREAK!
NOT THESE GUYS AGAIN...
SORRY TO FLY SO SOON, OFFICER. BUT SOMEONE'S OUT THERE WEARING MY FACE...
...AND I'VE GOTTA FIND OUT WHO!
PUT OUT AN A.P.B. --

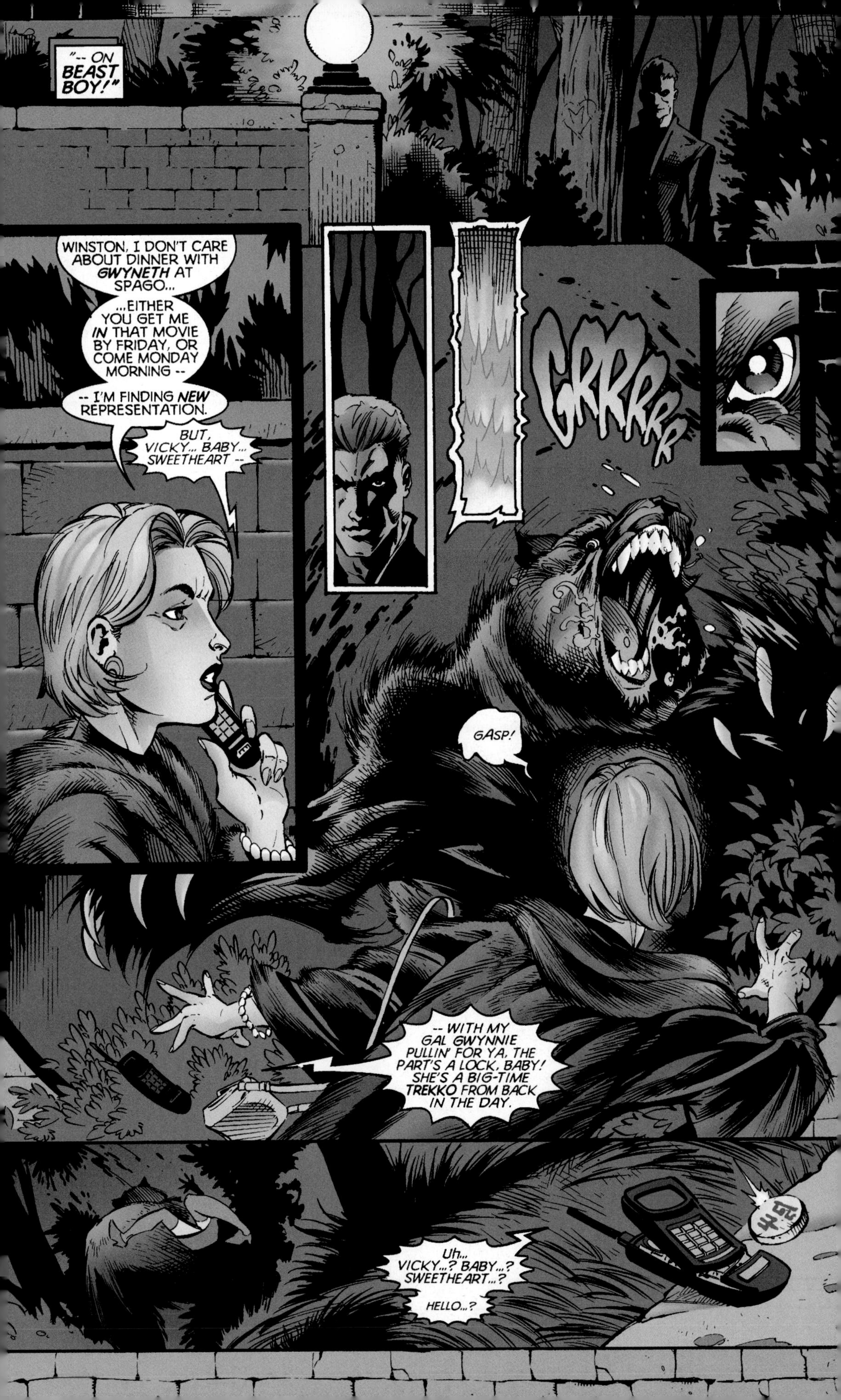
"-- ON BEAST BOY!"
WINSTON, I DON'T CARE ABOUT DINNER WITH GWYNETH AT SPAGO...
...EITHER YOU GET ME IN THAT MOVIE BY FRIDAY, OR COME MONDAY MORNING --
-- I'M FINDING NEW REPRESENTATION.
BUT, VICKY... BABY... SWEETHEART --
GRRRRR
GASP!
-- WITH MY GAL GWYNNIE PULLIN' FOR YA, THE PART'S A LOCK, BABY! SHE'S A BIG-TIME TREKKO FROM BACK IN THE DAY.
Uh... VICKY...? BABY...? SWEETHEART...?
HELLO...?

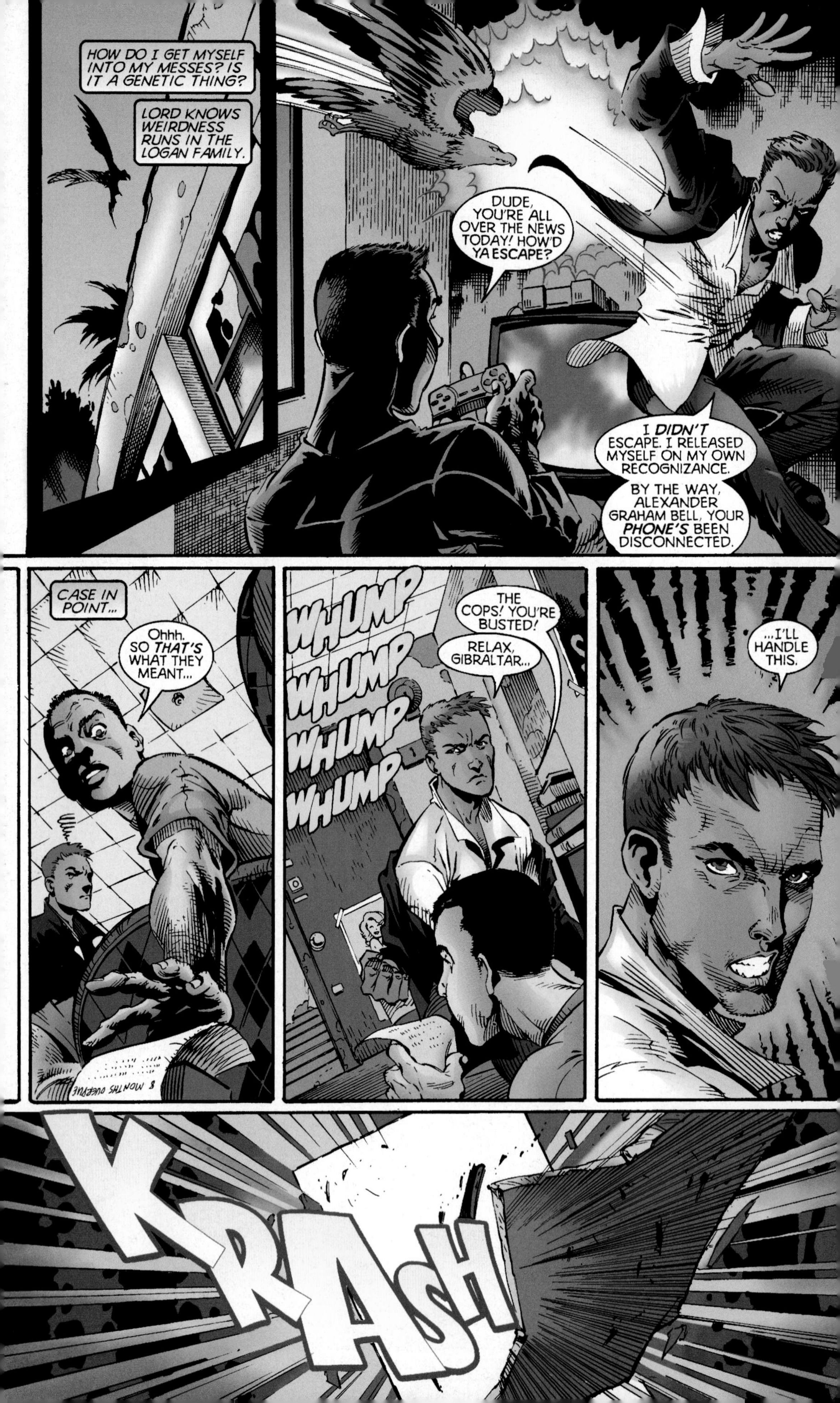
HOW DO I GET MYSELF INTO MY MESSES? IS IT A GENETIC THING?
LORD KNOWS WEIRDNESS RUNS IN THE LOGAN FAMILY.
DUDE, YOU'RE ALL OVER THE NEWS TODAY! HOW'D YA ESCAPE?
I *DIDN'T* ESCAPE. I RELEASED MYSELF ON MY OWN RECOGNIZANCE.
BY THE WAY, ALEXANDER GRAHAM BELL, YOUR *PHONE'S* BEEN DISCONNECTED.
CASE IN POINT...
Ohhh. SO *THAT'S* WHAT THEY MEANT...
3 MONTHS OVERDUE
WHUMP WHUMP WHUMP WHUMP
THE COPS! YOU'RE BUSTED!
RELAX, GIBRALTAR...
...I'LL HANDLE THIS.
KRASH

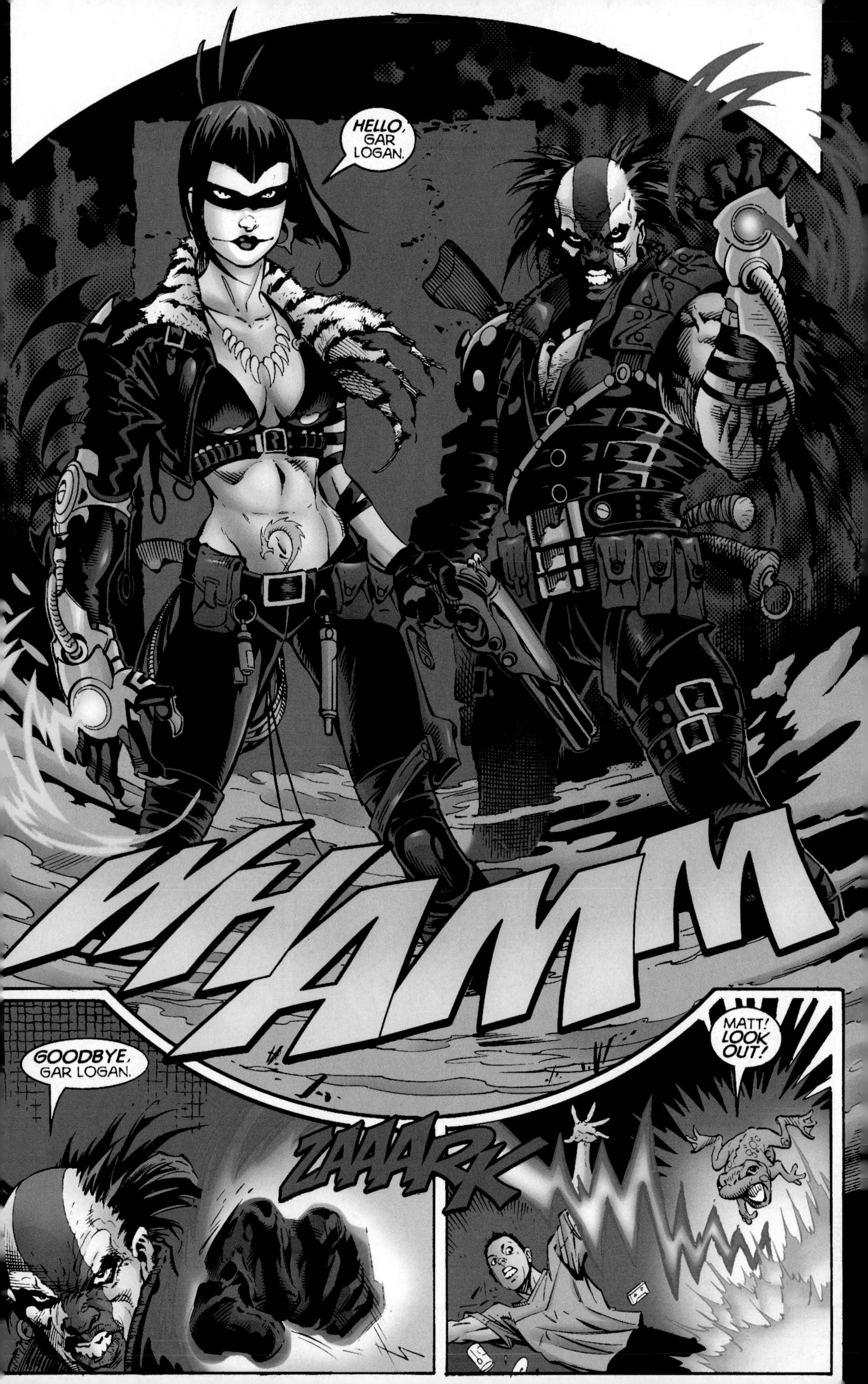
HELLO, GAR LOGAN.
WHAMM
GOODBYE, GAR LOGAN.
ZAAARK
MATT! LOOK OUT!

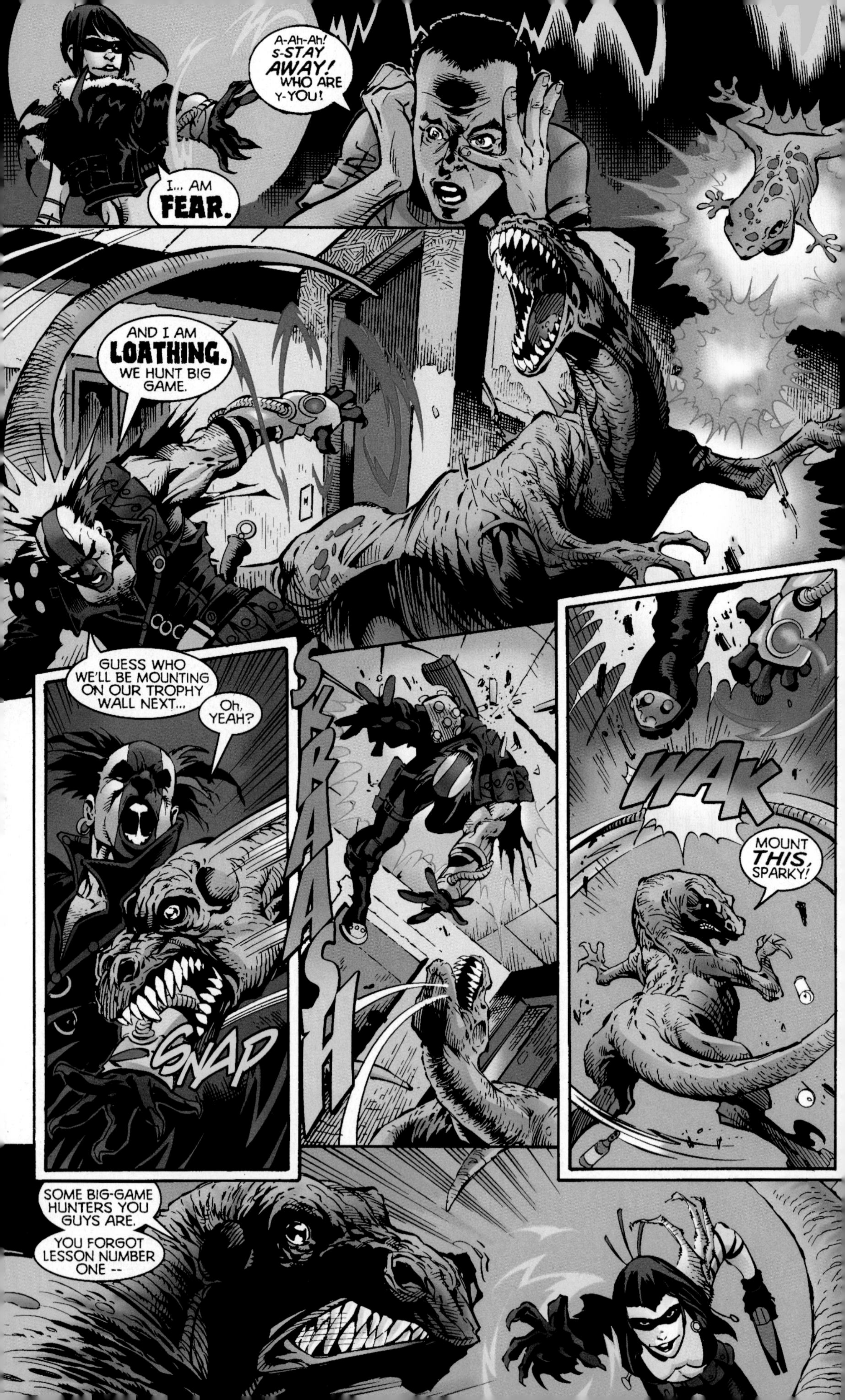
A-Ah-Ah! S-STAY AWAY! WHO ARE Y-YOU!
I... AM FEAR.
AND I AM LOATHING. WE HUNT BIG GAME.
GUESS WHO WE'LL BE MOUNTING ON OUR TROPHY WALL NEXT...
Oh, YEAH?
SNAP
SKRAAAH
WAK
MOUNT THIS, SPARKY!
SOME BIG-GAME HUNTERS YOU GUYS ARE.
YOU FORGOT LESSON NUMBER ONE --

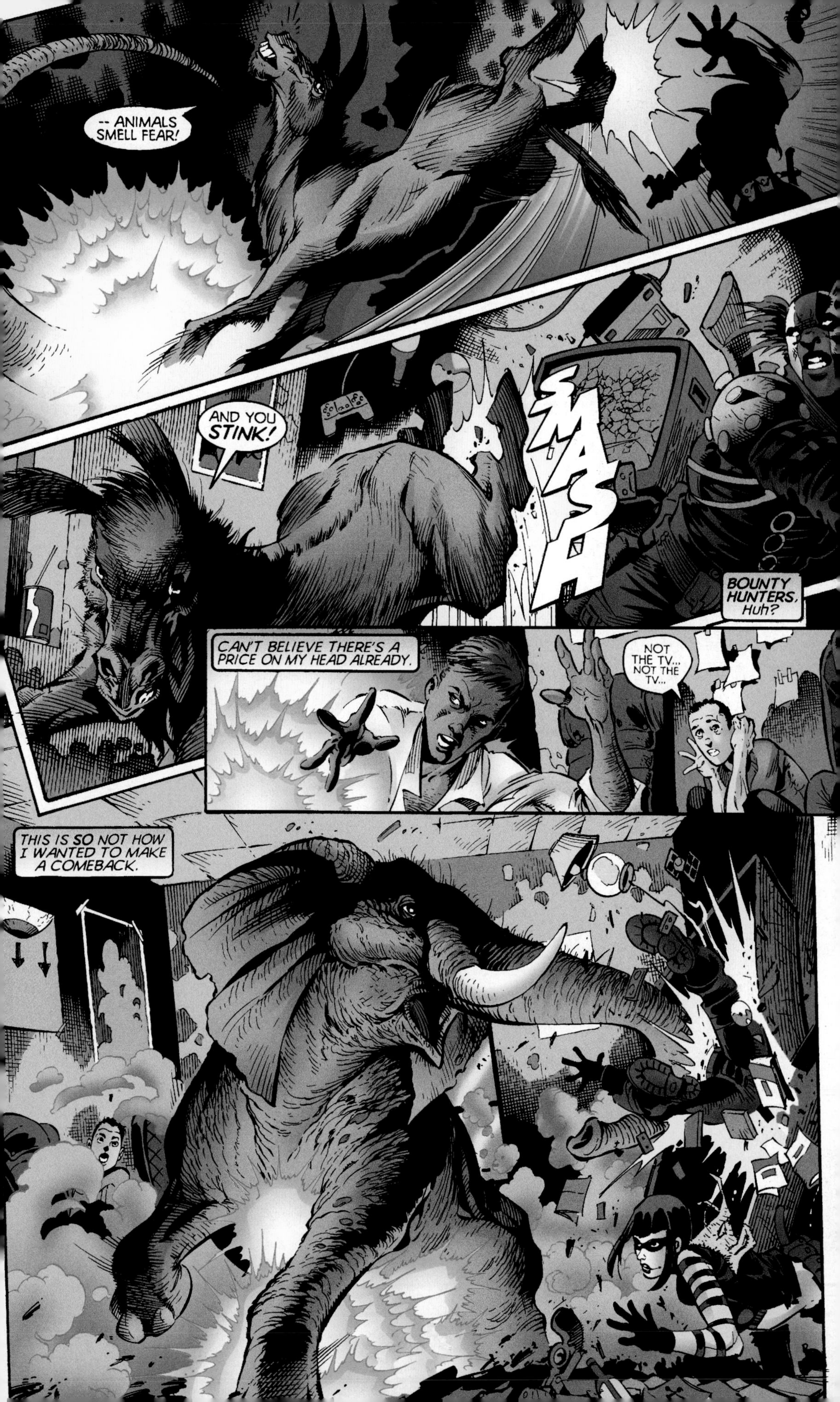
-- ANIMALS SMELL FEAR!
AND YOU STINK!
SMASH
BOUNTY HUNTERS, Huh?
CAN'T BELIEVE THERE'S A PRICE ON MY HEAD ALREADY.
NOT THE TV... NOT THE TV...
THIS IS SO NOT HOW I WANTED TO MAKE A COMEBACK.

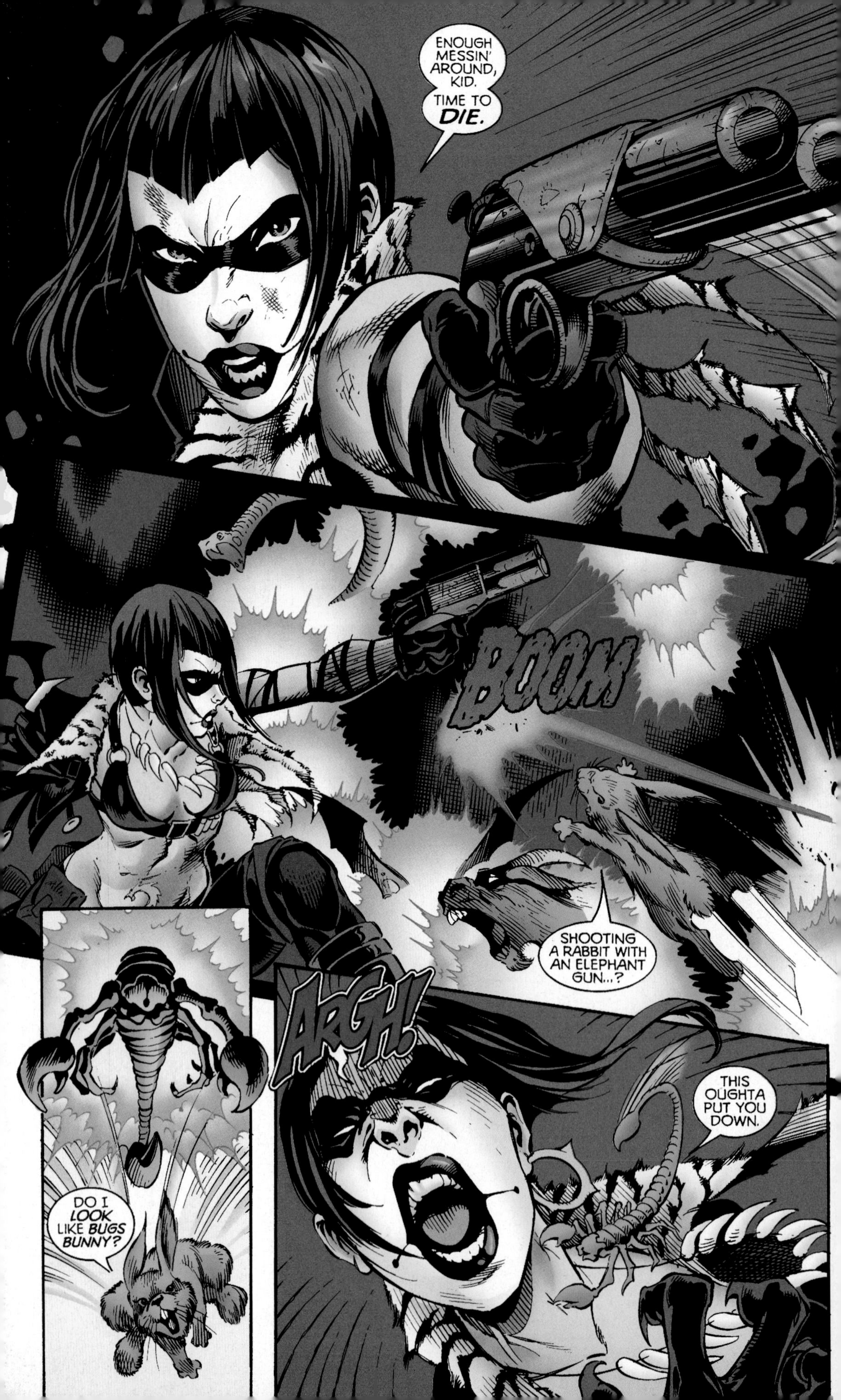
ENOUGH MESSIN' AROUND, KID. TIME TO *DIE.*
BOOM
SHOOTING A RABBIT WITH AN ELEPHANT GUN...?
DO I *LOOK* LIKE *BUGS BUNNY?*
ARGH!
THIS OUGHTA PUT YOU DOWN.

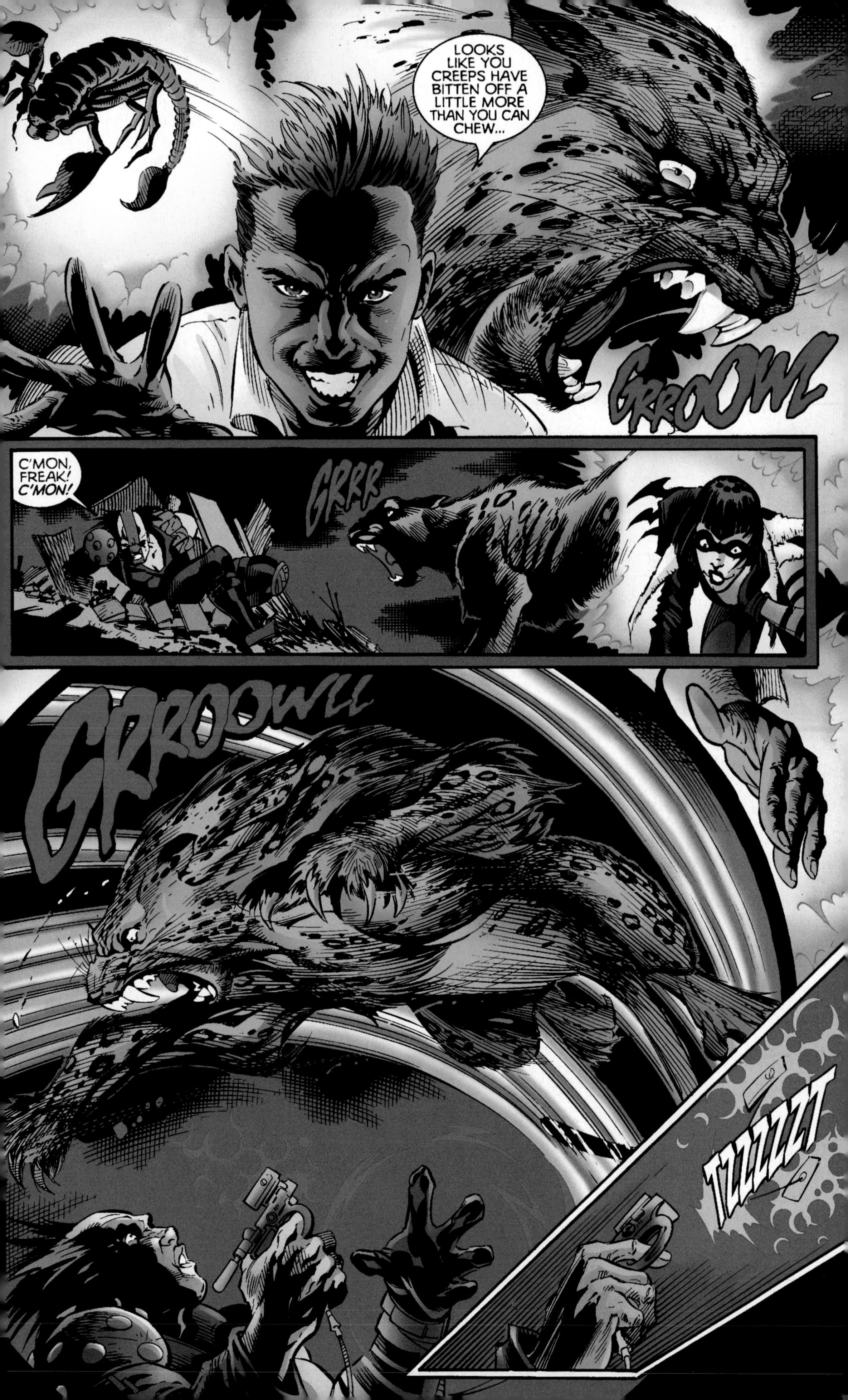

LOOKS LIKE YOU CREEPS HAVE BITTEN OFF A LITTLE MORE THAN YOU CAN CHEW...
GRROOWL
C'MON, FREAK! C'MON!
GRRR
GRROOWLL
TZZZZZZT

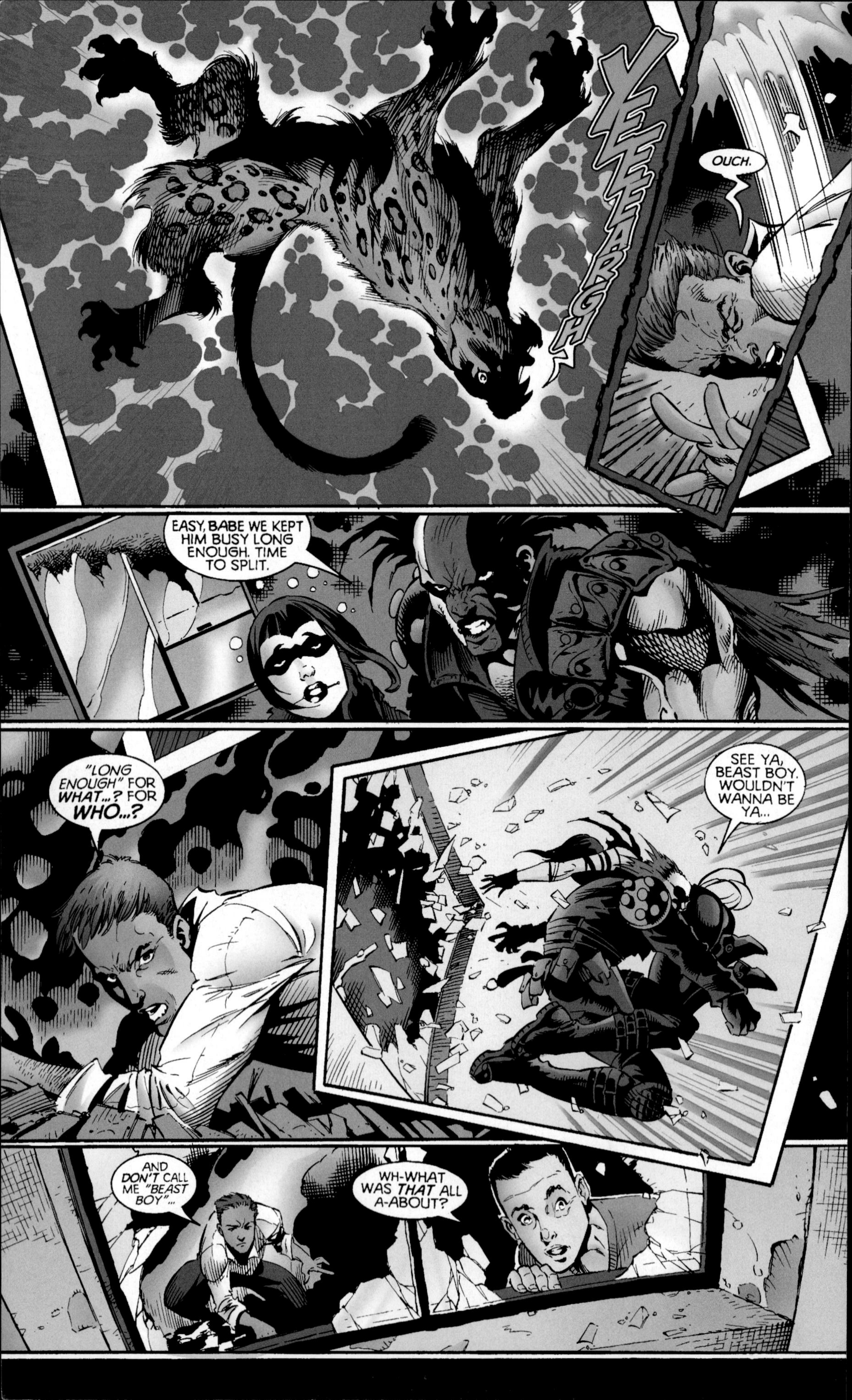
YEEEARGH
OUCH.
EASY, BABE WE KEPT HIM BUSY LONG ENOUGH. TIME TO SPLIT.
"LONG ENOUGH" FOR WHAT...? FOR WHO...?
SEE YA, BEAST BOY. WOULDN'T WANNA BE YA...
AND DON'T CALL ME "BEAST BOY"...
WH-WHAT WAS THAT ALL A-ABOUT?

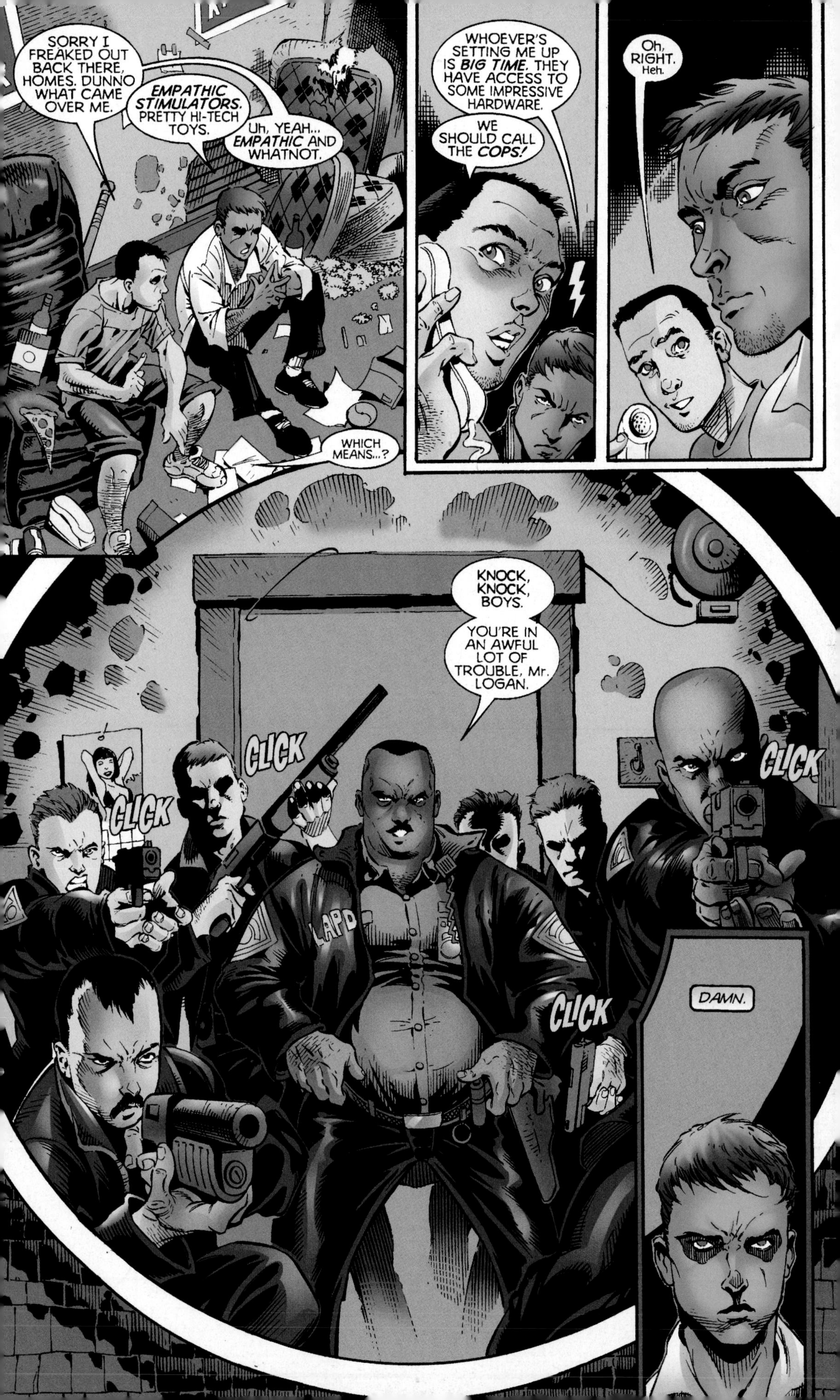

SORRY I FREAKED OUT BACK THERE, HOMES. DUNNO WHAT CAME OVER ME.
EMPATHIC STIMULATORS. PRETTY HI-TECH TOYS.
Uh, YEAH... EMPATHIC AND WHATNOT.
WHICH MEANS...?
WHOEVER'S SETTING ME UP IS BIG TIME. THEY HAVE ACCESS TO SOME IMPRESSIVE HARDWARE.
WE SHOULD CALL THE COPS!
Oh, RIGHT. Heh.
KNOCK, KNOCK, BOYS.
YOU'RE IN AN AWFUL LOT OF TROUBLE, Mr. LOGAN.
CLICK
CLICK
CLICK
CLICK
LAPD
DAMN.

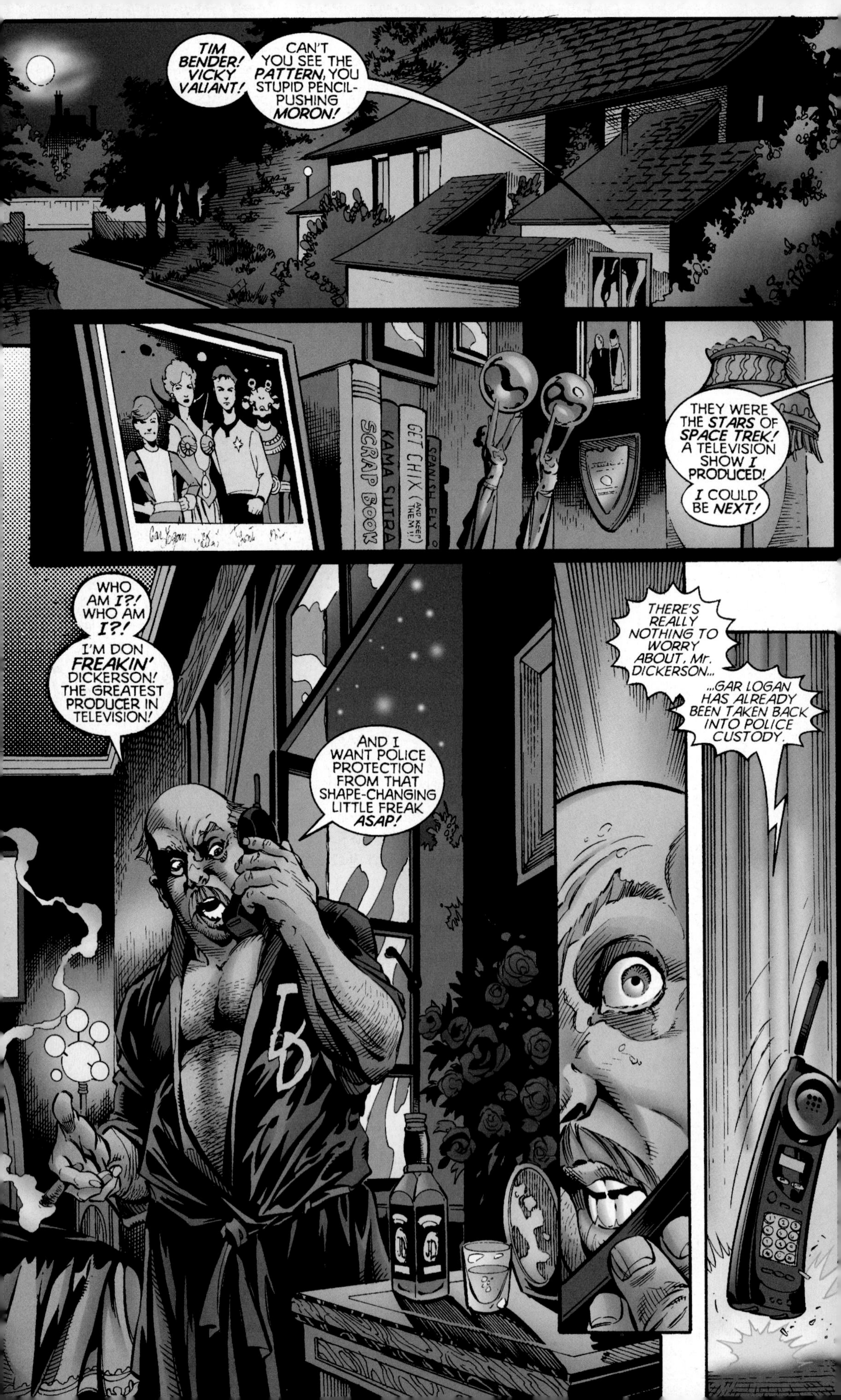

TIM BENDER! VICKY VALIANT!
CAN'T YOU SEE THE PATTERN, YOU STUPID PENCIL-PUSHING MORON!
SCRAP BOOK
KAMA SUTRA
GET CHIX (AND KEEP THEM!!)
SPANISH FLY
THEY WERE THE STARS OF SPACE TREK! A TELEVISION SHOW I PRODUCED!
I COULD BE NEXT!
WHO AM I?! WHO AM I?!
I'M DON FREAKIN' DICKERSON! THE GREATEST PRODUCER IN TELEVISION!
AND I WANT POLICE PROTECTION FROM THAT SHAPE-CHANGING LITTLE FREAK ASAP!
THERE'S REALLY NOTHING TO WORRY ABOUT, Mr. DICKERSON...
...GAR LOGAN HAS ALREADY BEEN TAKEN BACK INTO POLICE CUSTODY.

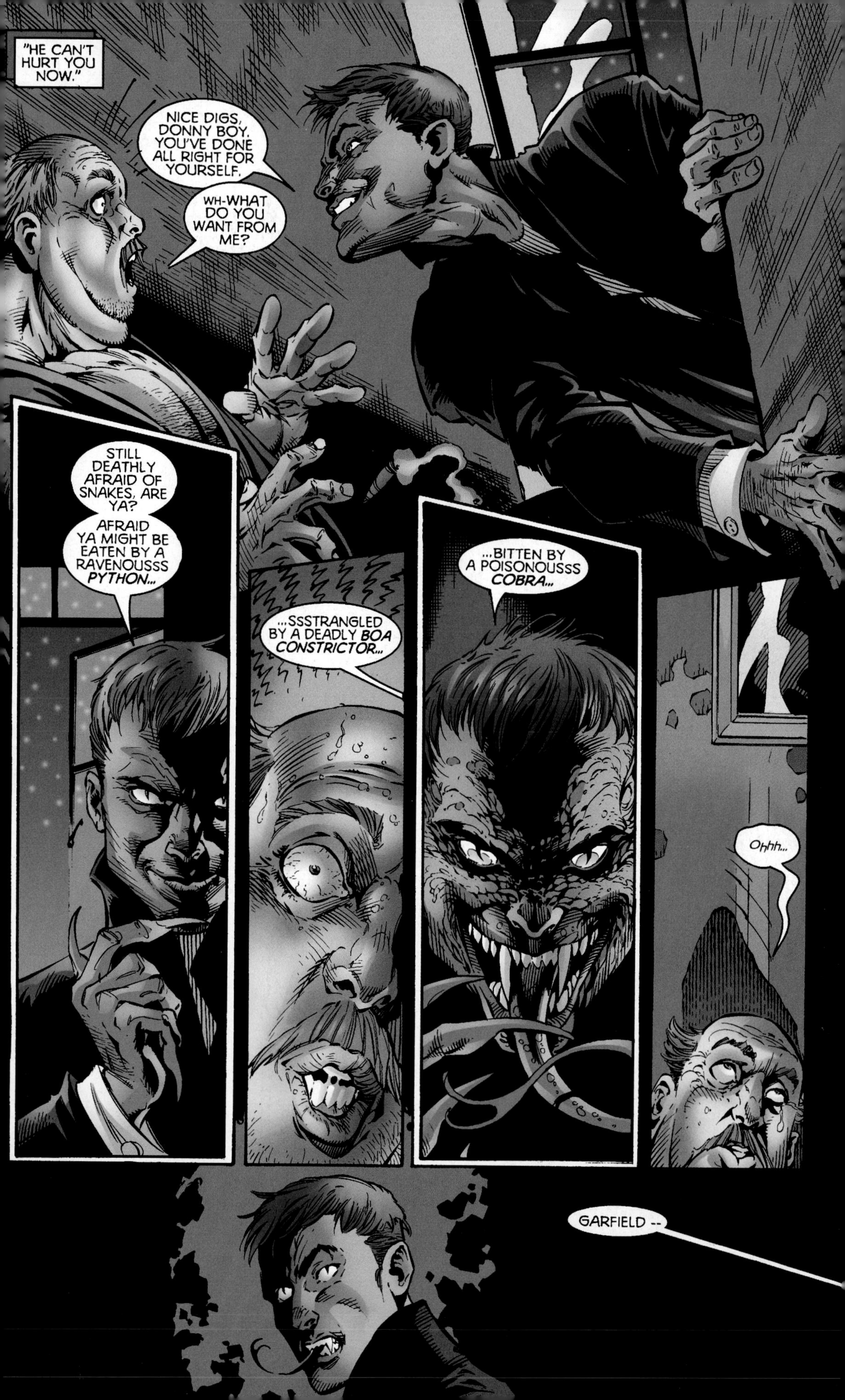

"HE CAN'T HURT YOU NOW."
NICE DIGS, DONNY BOY. YOU'VE DONE ALL RIGHT FOR YOURSELF.
WH-WHAT DO YOU WANT FROM ME?
STILL DEATHLY AFRAID OF SNAKES, ARE YA?
AFRAID YA MIGHT BE EATEN BY A RAVENOUSSS *PYTHON*...
...SSSTRANGLED BY A DEADLY *BOA CONSTRICTOR*...
...BITTEN BY A POISONOUSSS *COBRA*...
Ohhh...
GARFIELD --

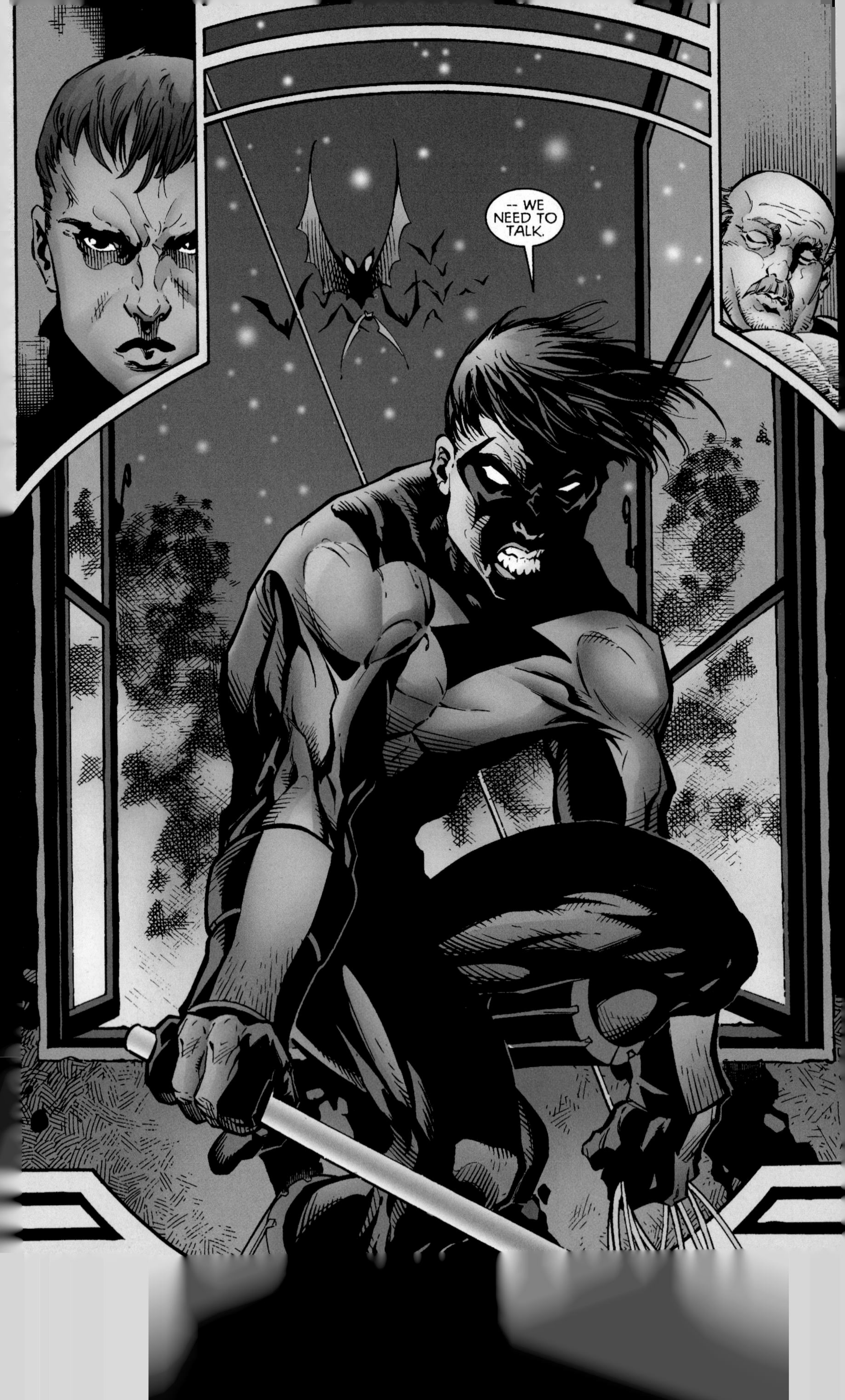
-- WE NEED TO TALK.

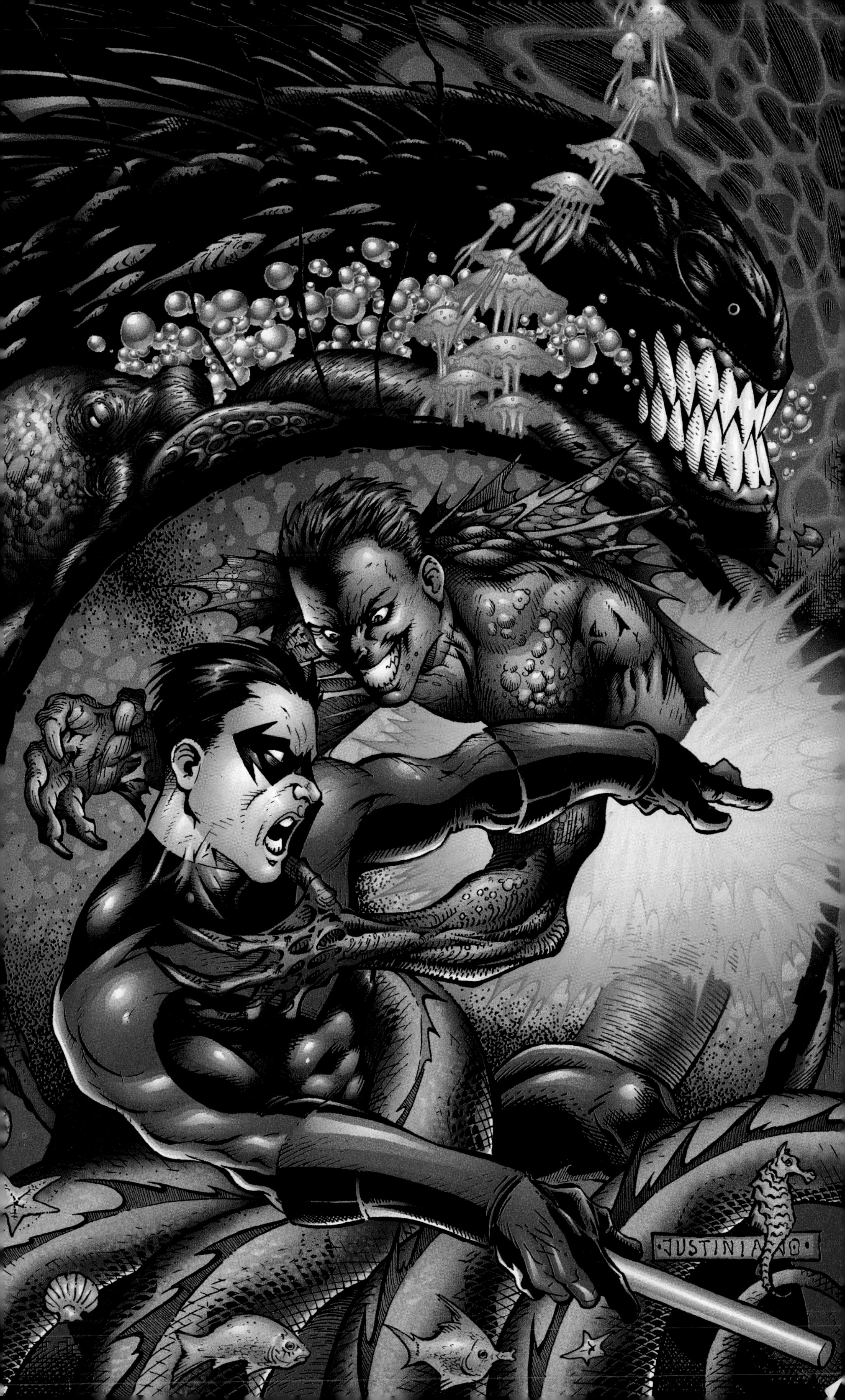

JUSTINIANO

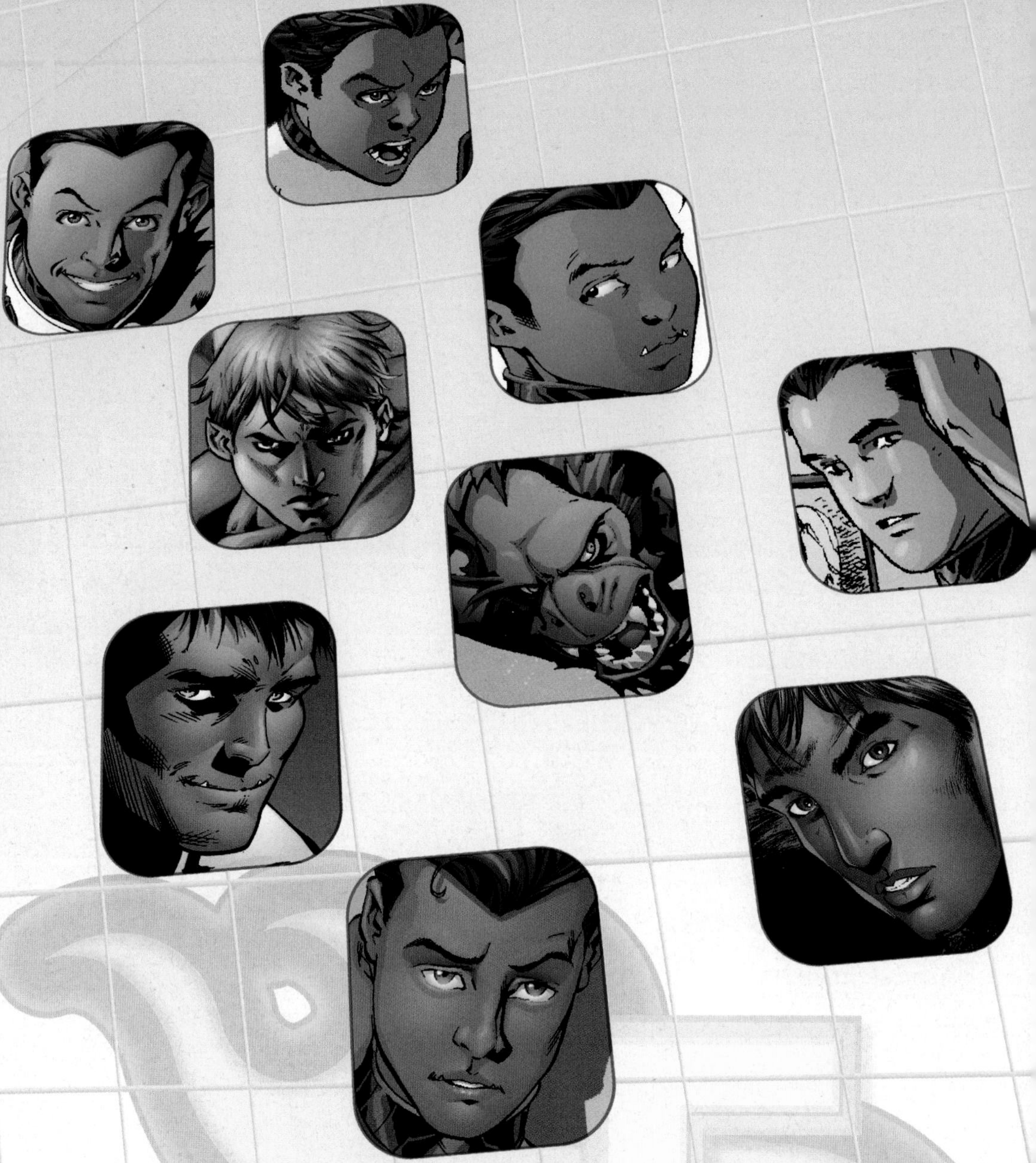

BEAST BOY #3

GEOFF JOHNS
BEN RAAB
Writers

JUSTINIANO
Penciller

CHRIS IVY
Inker

JASON WRIGHT
Colorist

COMICRAFT
Letterer

JUSTINIANO
Cover Artist

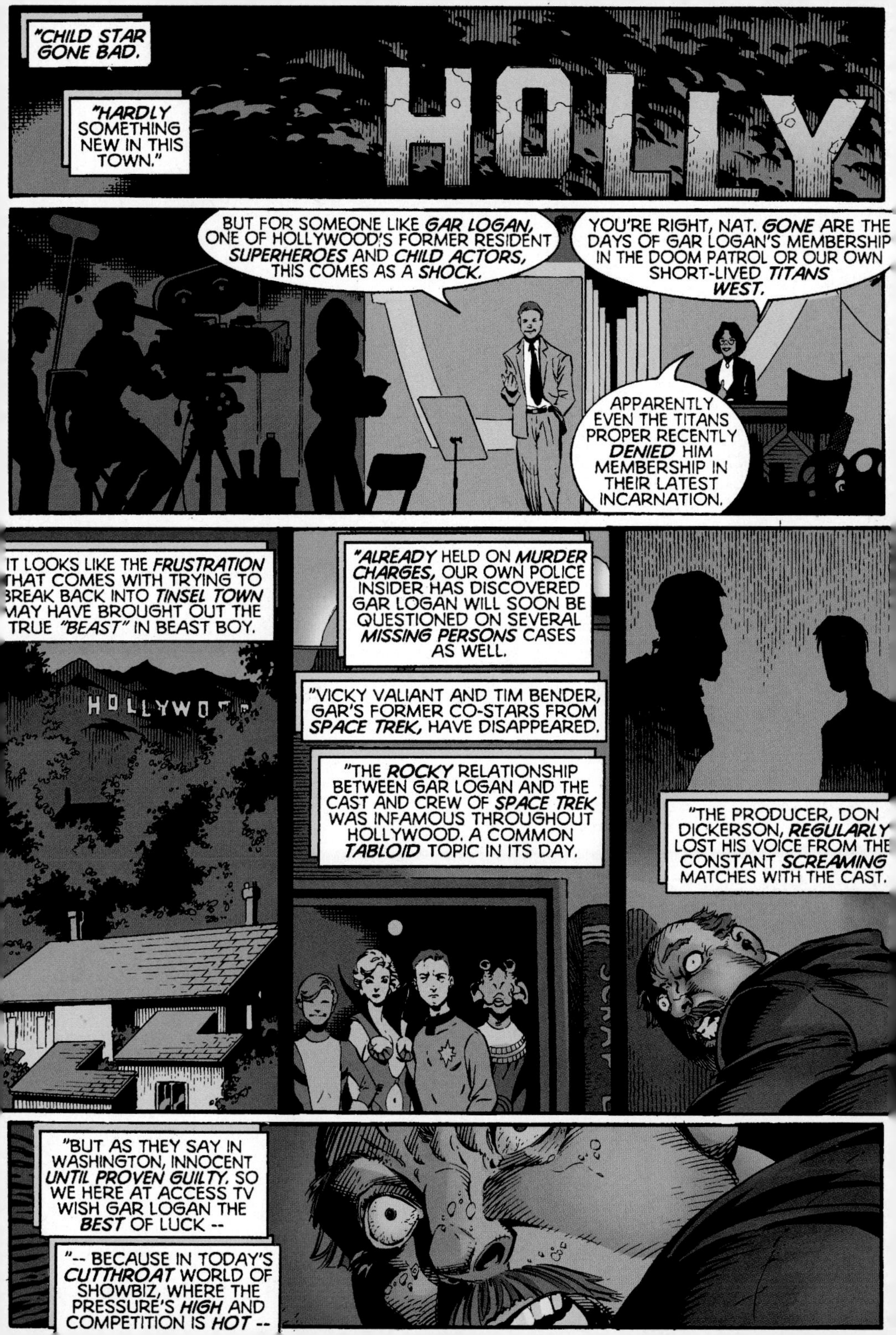
"CHILD STAR GONE BAD.
"HARDLY SOMETHING NEW IN THIS TOWN."
HOLLY
BUT FOR SOMEONE LIKE GAR LOGAN, ONE OF HOLLYWOOD'S FORMER RESIDENT SUPERHEROES AND CHILD ACTORS, THIS COMES AS A SHOCK.
YOU'RE RIGHT, NAT. GONE ARE THE DAYS OF GAR LOGAN'S MEMBERSHIP IN THE DOOM PATROL OR OUR OWN SHORT-LIVED TITANS WEST.
APPARENTLY EVEN THE TITANS PROPER RECENTLY DENIED HIM MEMBERSHIP IN THEIR LATEST INCARNATION.
IT LOOKS LIKE THE FRUSTRATION THAT COMES WITH TRYING TO BREAK BACK INTO TINSEL TOWN MAY HAVE BROUGHT OUT THE TRUE "BEAST" IN BEAST BOY.
HOLLYWO
"ALREADY HELD ON MURDER CHARGES, OUR OWN POLICE INSIDER HAS DISCOVERED GAR LOGAN WILL SOON BE QUESTIONED ON SEVERAL MISSING PERSONS CASES AS WELL.
"VICKY VALIANT AND TIM BENDER, GAR'S FORMER CO-STARS FROM SPACE TREK, HAVE DISAPPEARED.
"THE ROCKY RELATIONSHIP BETWEEN GAR LOGAN AND THE CAST AND CREW OF SPACE TREK WAS INFAMOUS THROUGHOUT HOLLYWOOD. A COMMON TABLOID TOPIC IN ITS DAY.
"THE PRODUCER, DON DICKERSON, REGULARLY LOST HIS VOICE FROM THE CONSTANT SCREAMING MATCHES WITH THE CAST.
"BUT AS THEY SAY IN WASHINGTON, INNOCENT UNTIL PROVEN GUILTY. SO WE HERE AT ACCESS TV WISH GAR LOGAN THE BEST OF LUCK --
"-- BECAUSE IN TODAY'S CUTTHROAT WORLD OF SHOWBIZ, WHERE THE PRESSURE'S HIGH AND COMPETITION IS HOT --

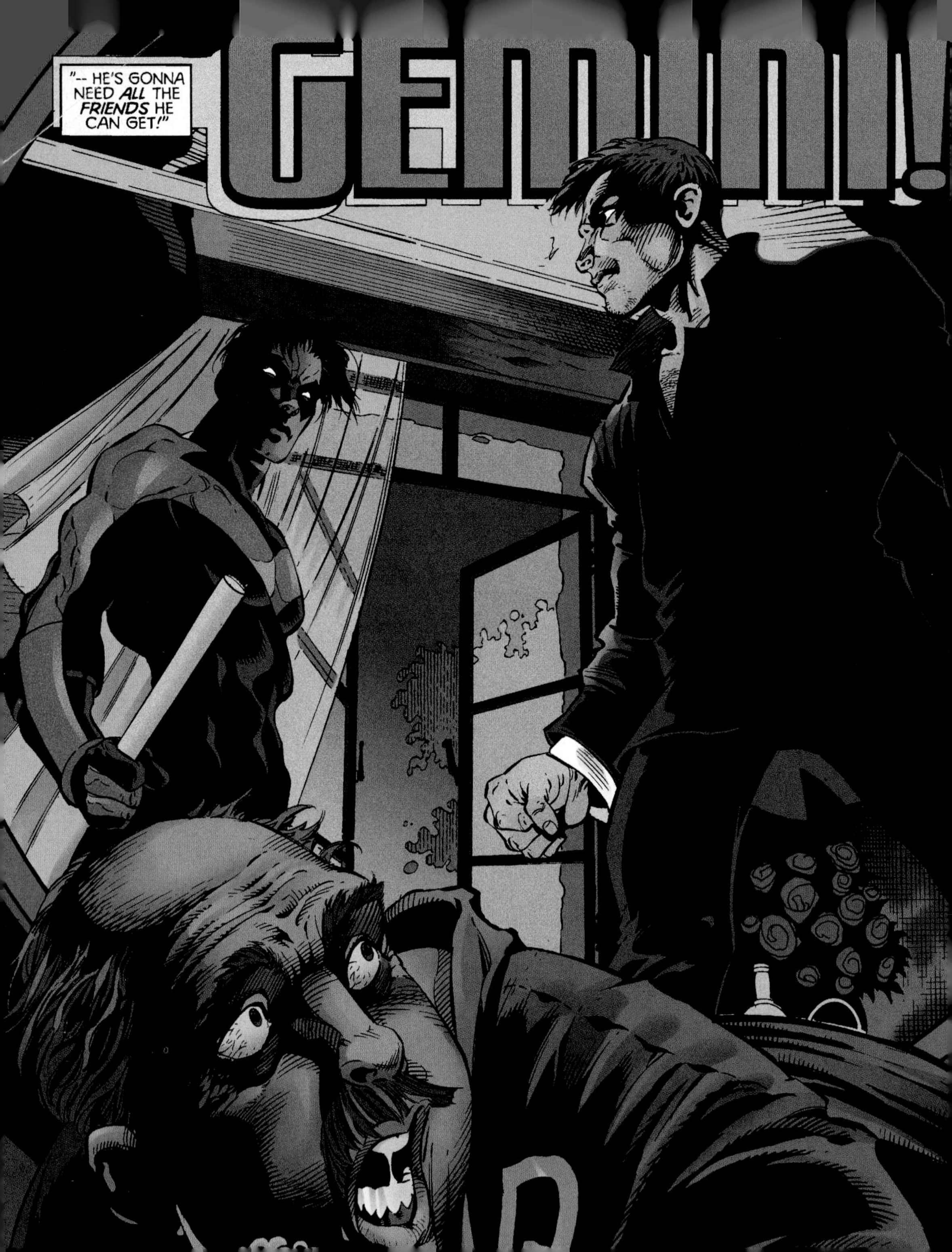
"-- HE'S GONNA NEED ALL THE FRIENDS HE CAN GET!"
GEMINI!

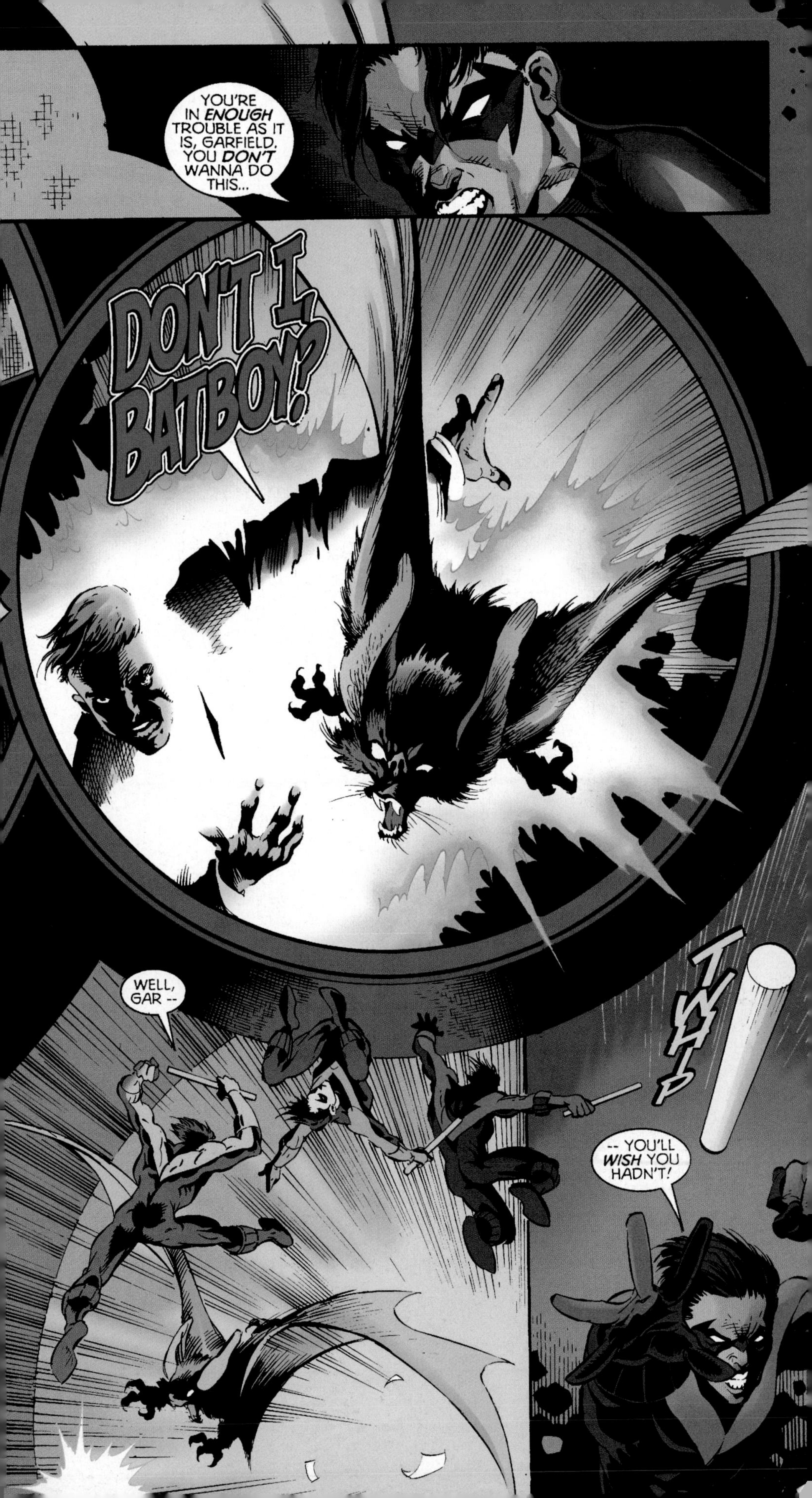

YOU'RE IN *ENOUGH* TROUBLE AS IT IS, GARFIELD. YOU *DON'T* WANNA DO THIS...
DON'T I, BATBOY?
WELL, GAR --
TWHIP
-- YOU'LL *WISH* YOU HADN'T!

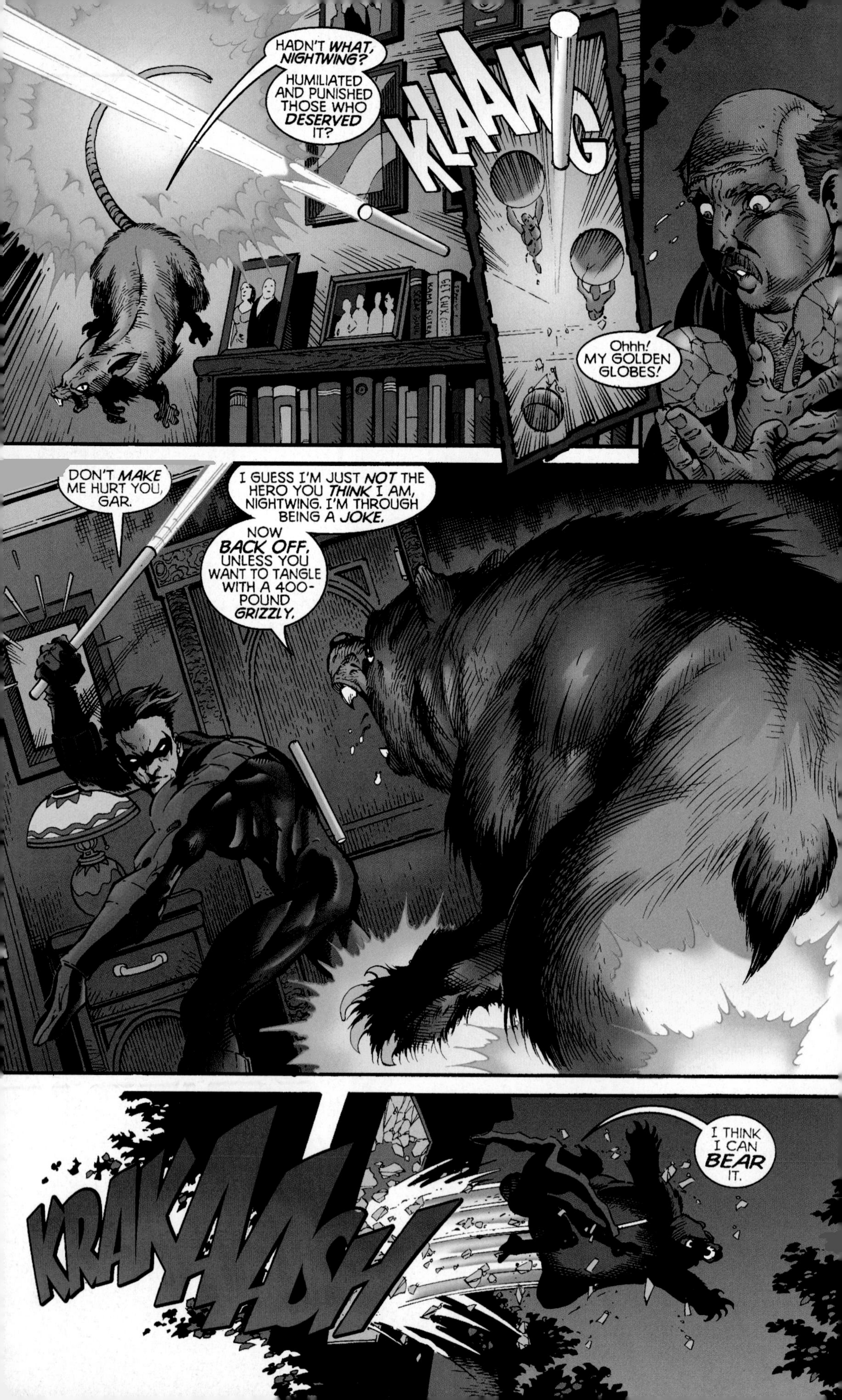
HADN'T WHAT, NIGHTWING? HUMILIATED AND PUNISHED THOSE WHO DESERVED IT?
KLAANG
Ohhh! MY GOLDEN GLOBES!
DON'T MAKE ME HURT YOU, GAR.
I GUESS I'M JUST NOT THE HERO YOU THINK I AM, NIGHTWING. I'M THROUGH BEING A JOKE.
NOW BACK OFF, UNLESS YOU WANT TO TANGLE WITH A 400-POUND GRIZZLY.
KRAKADOSH!
I THINK I CAN BEAR IT.

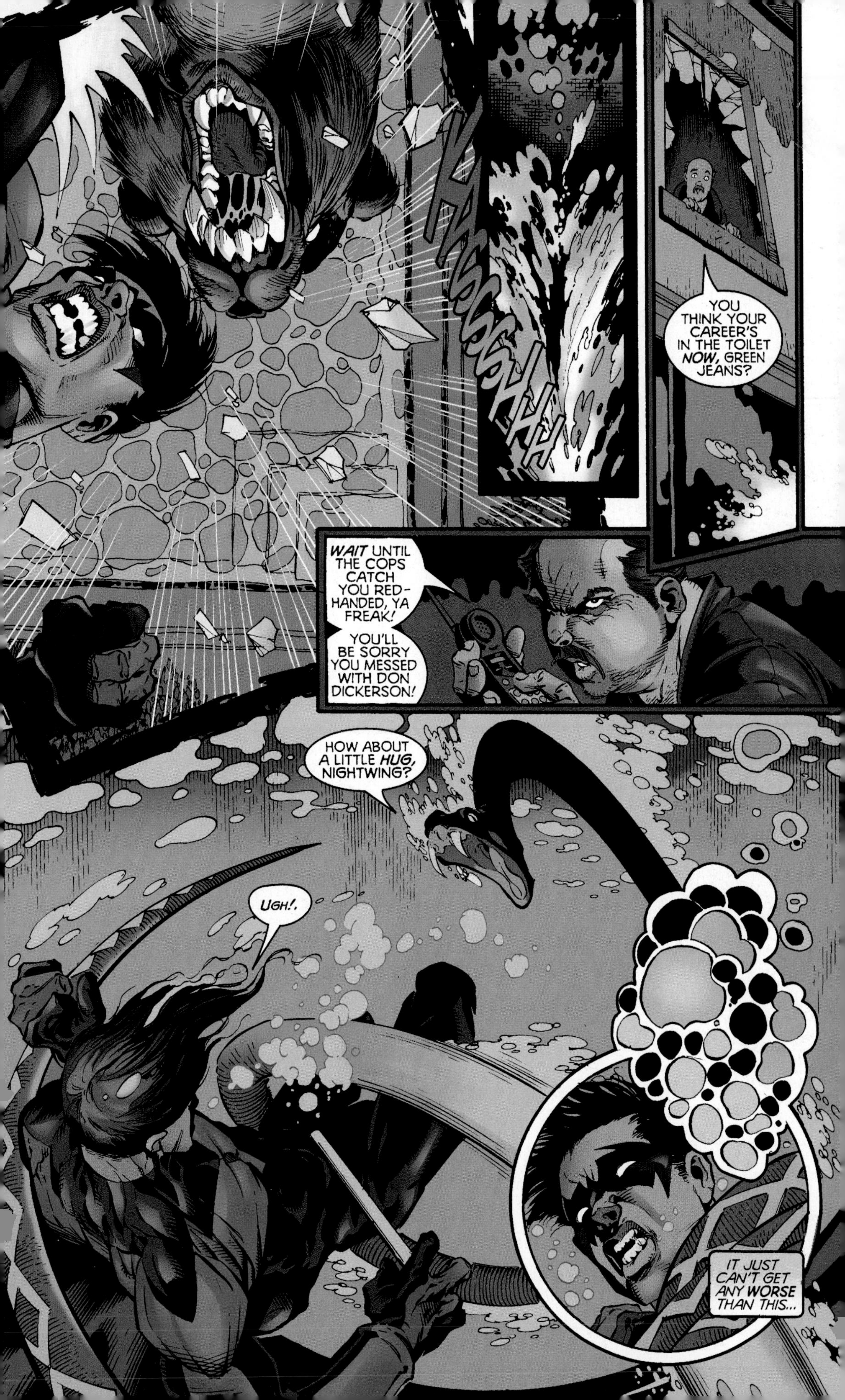
KRAAASHHH
YOU THINK YOUR CAREER'S IN THE TOILET *NOW*, GREEN JEANS?
WAIT UNTIL THE COPS CATCH YOU RED-HANDED, YA FREAK!
YOU'LL BE SORRY YOU MESSED WITH DON DICKERSON!
HOW ABOUT A LITTLE *HUG*, NIGHTWING?
UGH!.
IT JUST CAN'T GET ANY *WORSE* THAN THIS...

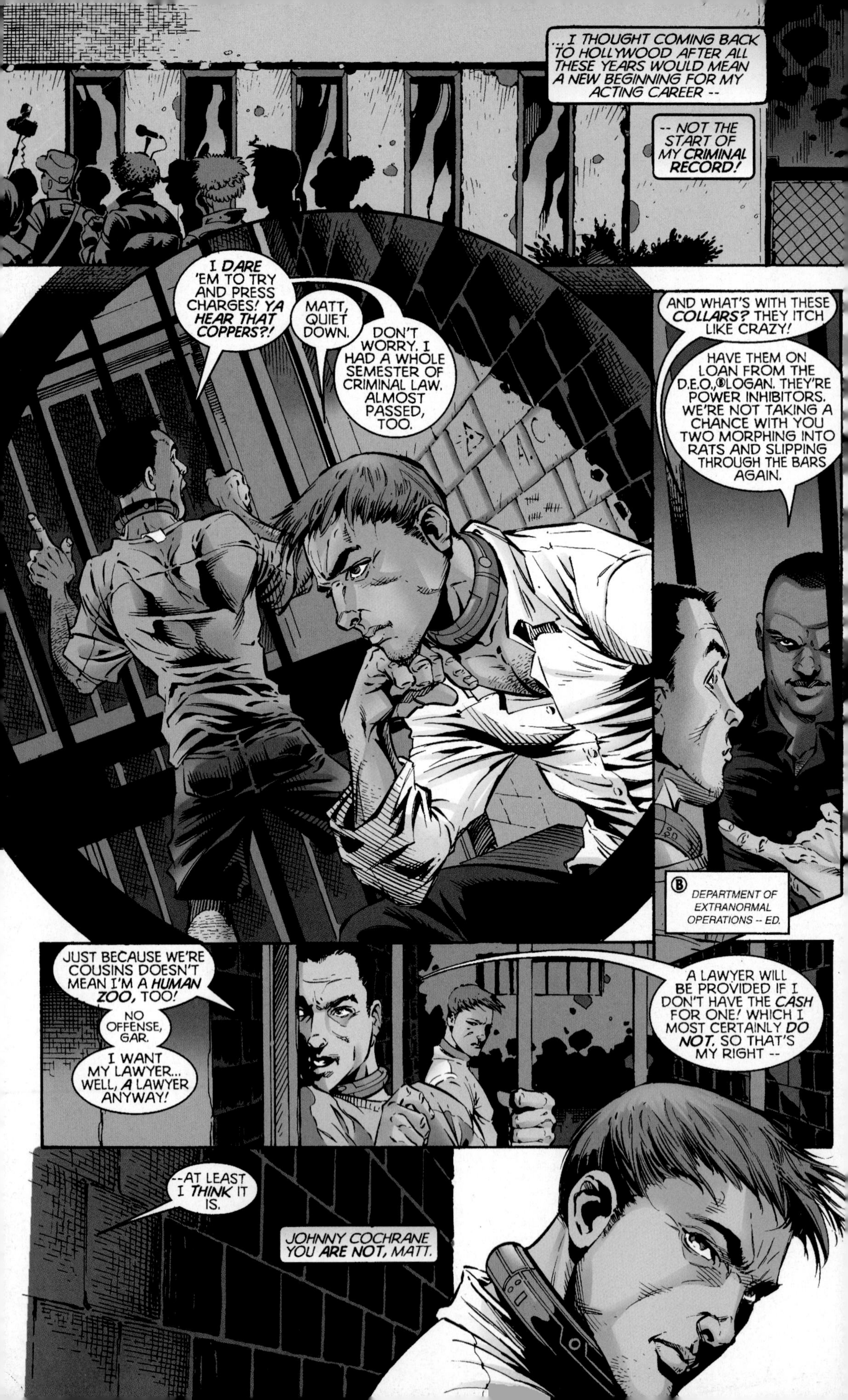
...I THOUGHT COMING BACK TO HOLLYWOOD AFTER ALL THESE YEARS WOULD MEAN A NEW BEGINNING FOR MY ACTING CAREER --
-- NOT THE START OF MY CRIMINAL RECORD!
I DARE 'EM TO TRY AND PRESS CHARGES! YA HEAR THAT COPPERS?!
MATT, QUIET DOWN.
DON'T WORRY. I HAD A WHOLE SEMESTER OF CRIMINAL LAW. ALMOST PASSED, TOO.
AND WHAT'S WITH THESE COLLARS? THEY ITCH LIKE CRAZY!
HAVE THEM ON LOAN FROM THE D.E.O.,(B) LOGAN. THEY'RE POWER INHIBITORS. WE'RE NOT TAKING A CHANCE WITH YOU TWO MORPHING INTO RATS AND SLIPPING THROUGH THE BARS AGAIN.
(B) DEPARTMENT OF EXTRANORMAL OPERATIONS -- ED.
JUST BECAUSE WE'RE COUSINS DOESN'T MEAN I'M A HUMAN ZOO, TOO!
NO OFFENSE, GAR.
I WANT MY LAWYER... WELL, A LAWYER ANYWAY!
A LAWYER WILL BE PROVIDED IF I DON'T HAVE THE CASH FOR ONE! WHICH I MOST CERTAINLY DO NOT, SO THAT'S MY RIGHT --
--AT LEAST I THINK IT IS.
JOHNNY COCHRANE YOU ARE NOT, MATT.

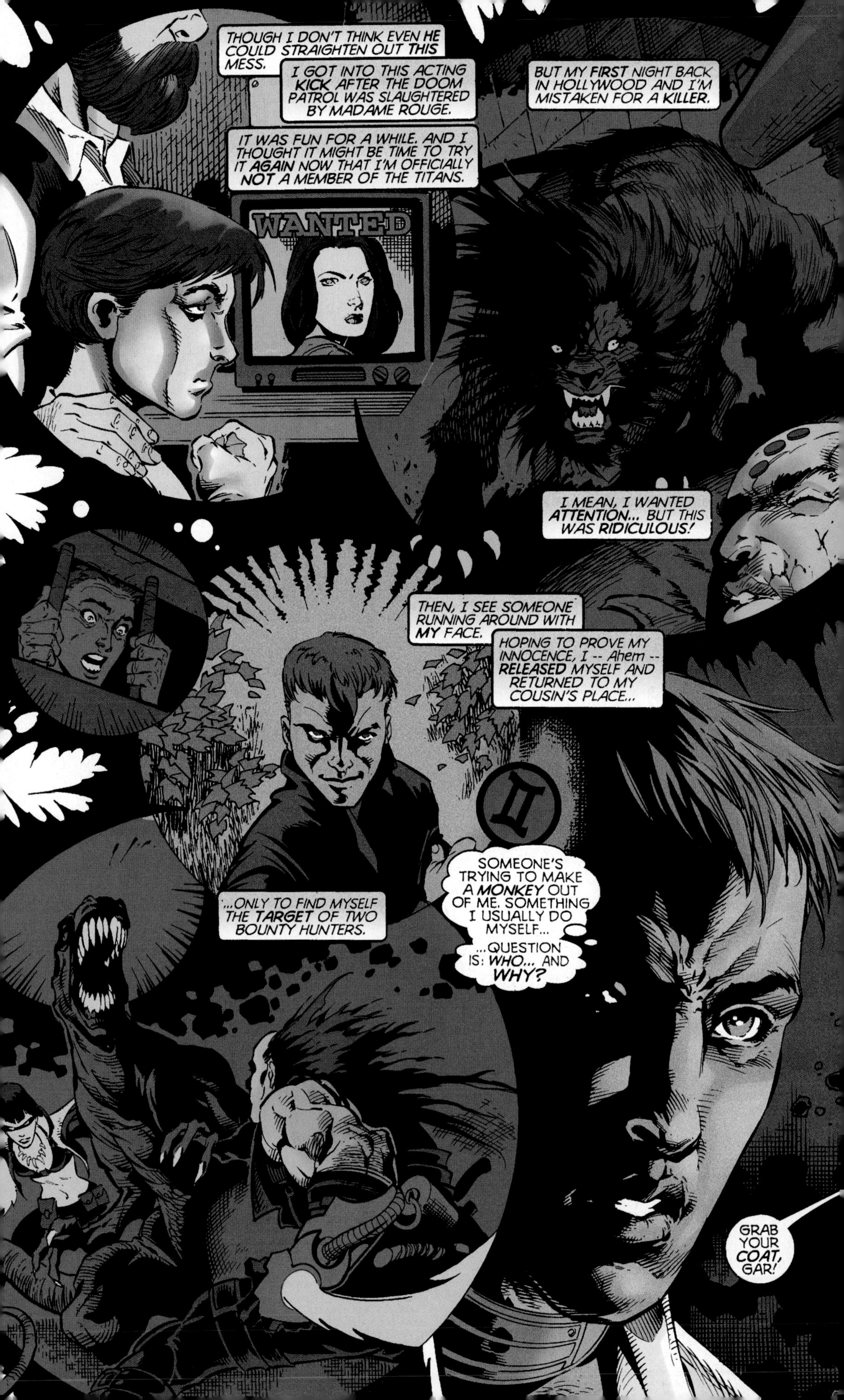
THOUGH I DON'T THINK EVEN HE COULD STRAIGHTEN OUT THIS MESS.
I GOT INTO THIS ACTING KICK AFTER THE DOOM PATROL WAS SLAUGHTERED BY MADAME ROUGE.
IT WAS FUN FOR A WHILE. AND I THOUGHT IT MIGHT BE TIME TO TRY IT AGAIN NOW THAT I'M OFFICIALLY NOT A MEMBER OF THE TITANS.
WANTED
BUT MY FIRST NIGHT BACK IN HOLLYWOOD AND I'M MISTAKEN FOR A KILLER.
I MEAN, I WANTED ATTENTION... BUT THIS WAS RIDICULOUS!
THEN, I SEE SOMEONE RUNNING AROUND WITH MY FACE.
HOPING TO PROVE MY INNOCENCE, I -- Ahem -- RELEASED MYSELF AND RETURNED TO MY COUSIN'S PLACE...
...ONLY TO FIND MYSELF THE TARGET OF TWO BOUNTY HUNTERS.
SOMEONE'S TRYING TO MAKE A MONKEY OUT OF ME. SOMETHING I USUALLY DO MYSELF...
...QUESTION IS: WHO... AND WHY?
GRAB YOUR COAT, GAR!

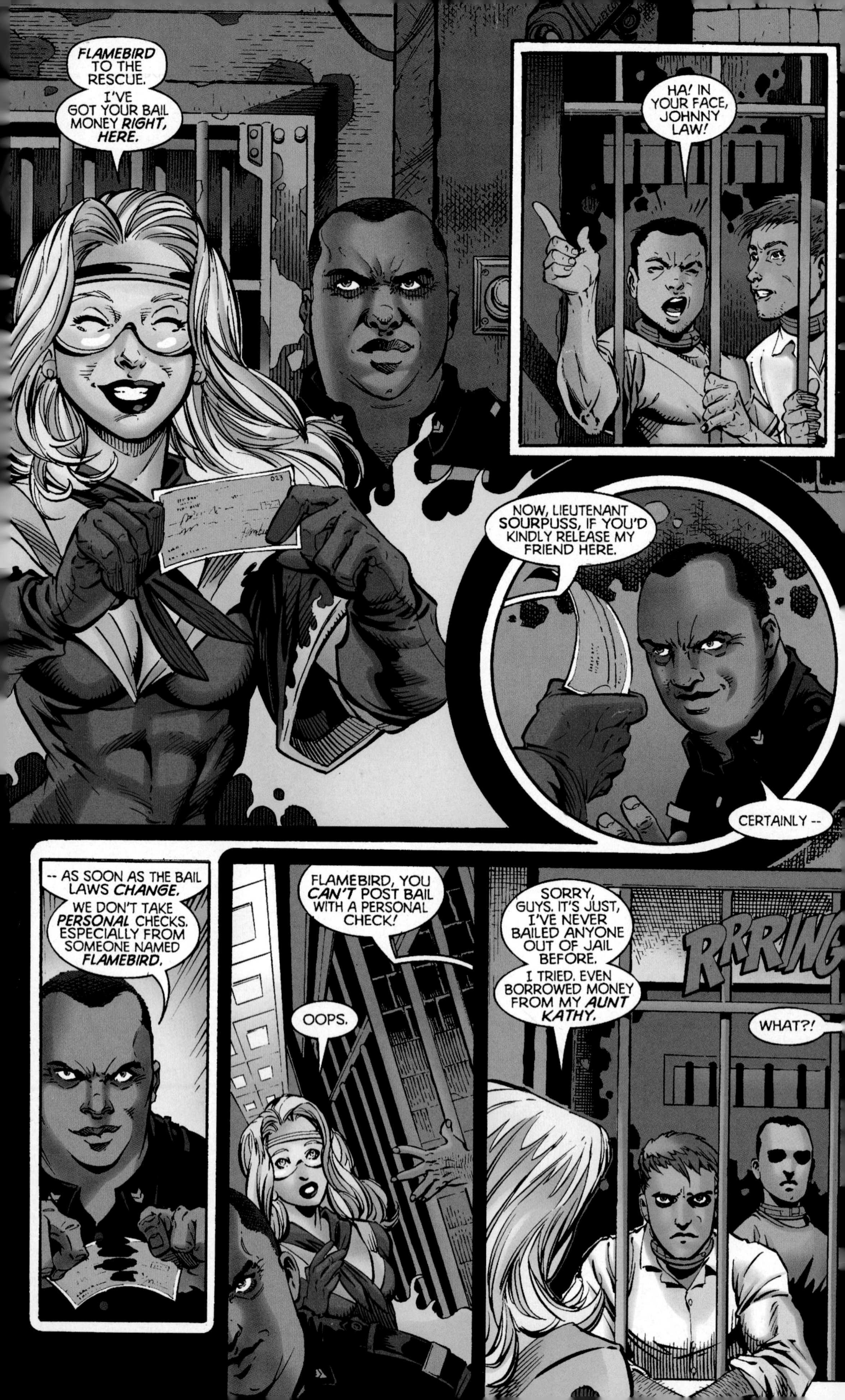
FLAMEBIRD TO THE RESCUE.
I'VE GOT YOUR BAIL MONEY RIGHT, HERE.
HA! IN YOUR FACE, JOHNNY LAW!
NOW, LIEUTENANT SOURPUSS, IF YOU'D KINDLY RELEASE MY FRIEND HERE.
CERTAINLY --
-- AS SOON AS THE BAIL LAWS CHANGE.
WE DON'T TAKE PERSONAL CHECKS. ESPECIALLY FROM SOMEONE NAMED FLAMEBIRD.
FLAMEBIRD, YOU CAN'T POST BAIL WITH A PERSONAL CHECK!
OOPS.
SORRY, GUYS. IT'S JUST, I'VE NEVER BAILED ANYONE OUT OF JAIL BEFORE.
I TRIED. EVEN BORROWED MONEY FROM MY AUNT KATHY.
RRRING
WHAT?!

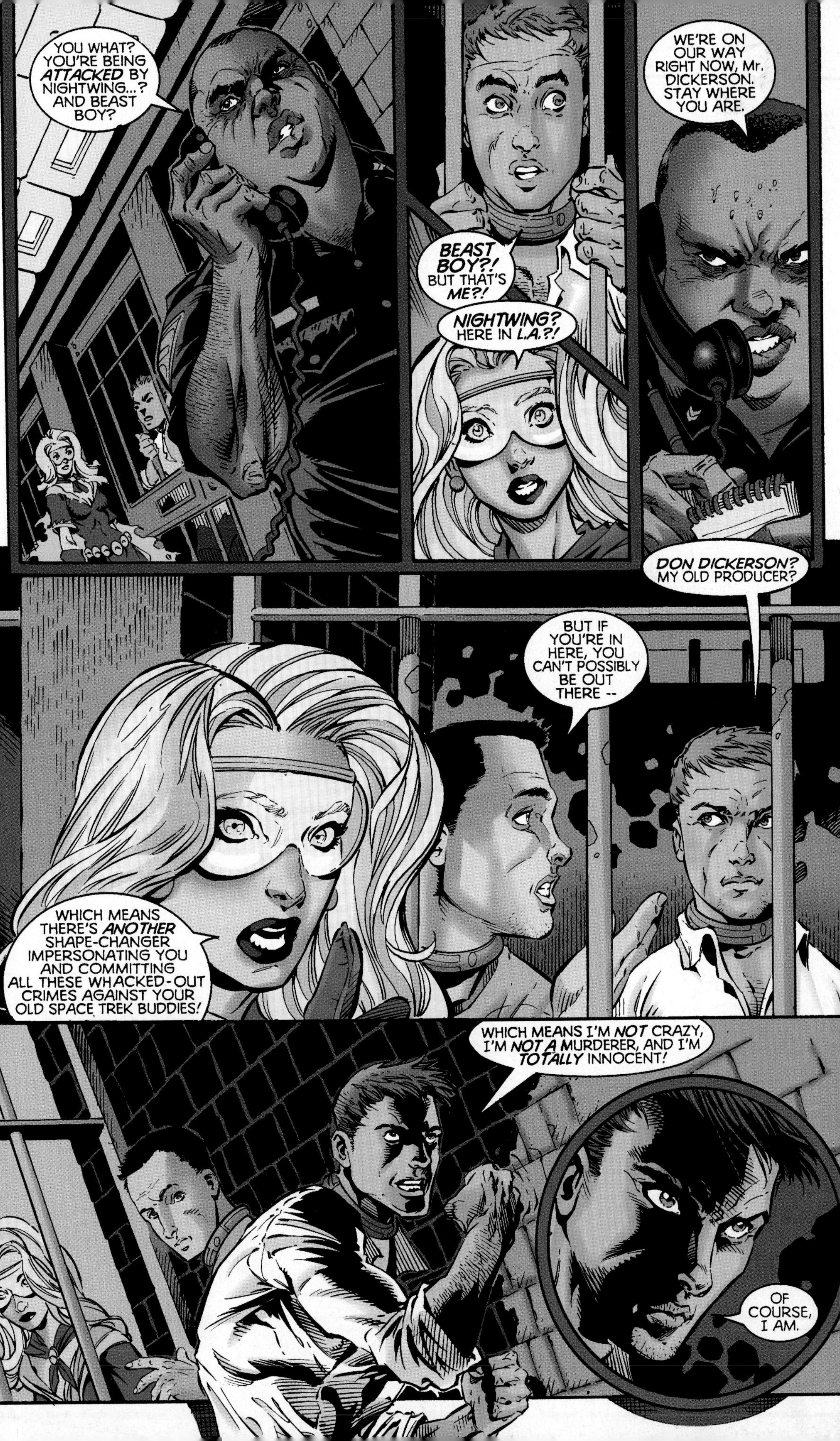
YOU WHAT? YOU'RE BEING ATTACKED BY NIGHTWING...? AND BEAST BOY?
BEAST BOY?! BUT THAT'S ME?!
NIGHTWING? HERE IN L.A.?!
WE'RE ON OUR WAY RIGHT NOW, Mr. DICKERSON. STAY WHERE YOU ARE.
DON DICKERSON? MY OLD PRODUCER?
BUT IF YOU'RE IN HERE, YOU CAN'T POSSIBLY BE OUT THERE --
WHICH MEANS THERE'S ANOTHER SHAPE-CHANGER IMPERSONATING YOU AND COMMITTING ALL THESE WHACKED-OUT CRIMES AGAINST YOUR OLD SPACE TREK BUDDIES!
WHICH MEANS I'M NOT CRAZY, I'M NOT A MURDERER, AND I'M TOTALLY INNOCENT!
OF COURSE, I AM.

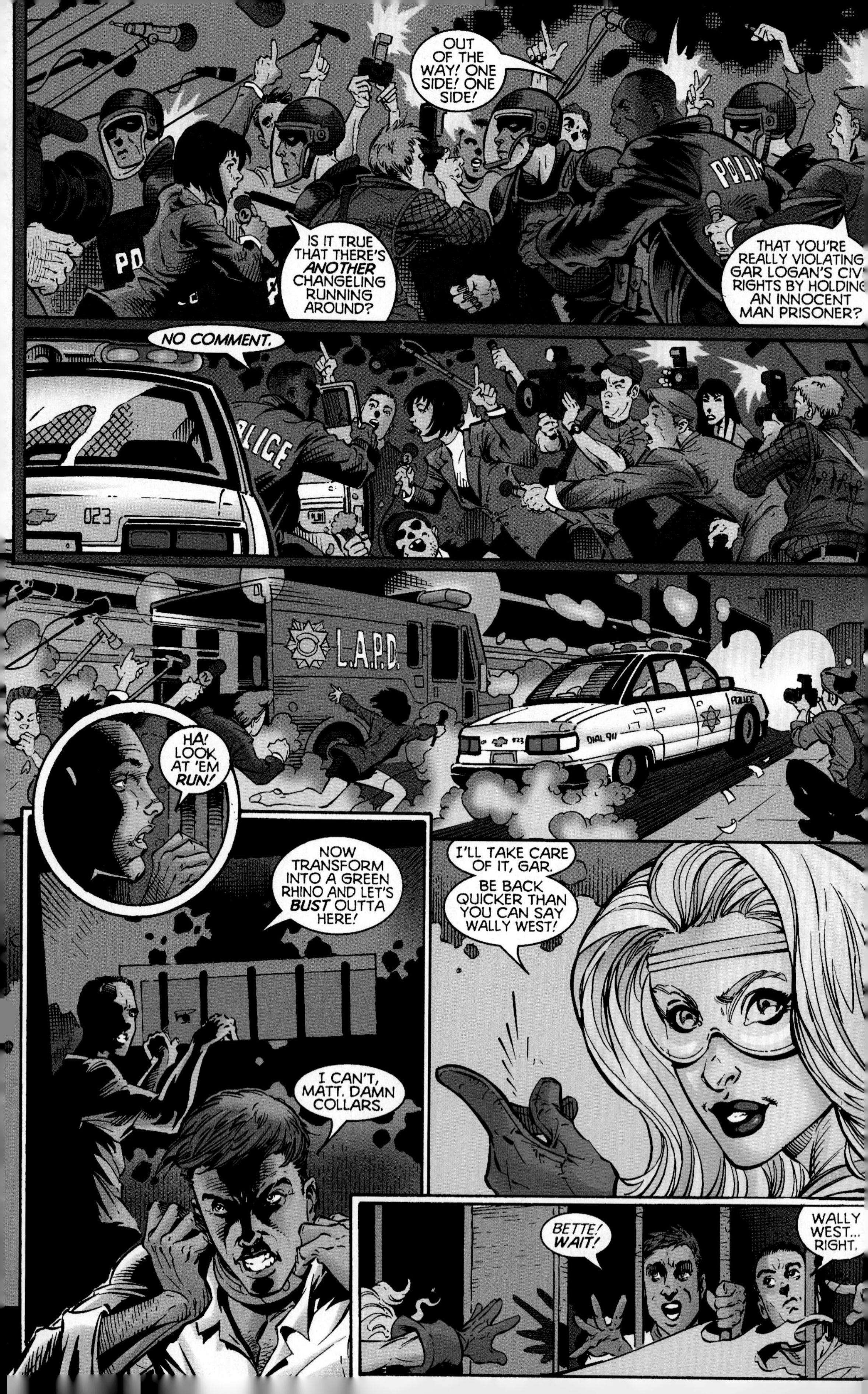

OUT OF THE WAY! ONE SIDE! ONE SIDE!
IS IT TRUE THAT THERE'S **ANOTHER** CHANGELING RUNNING AROUND?
THAT YOU'RE REALLY VIOLATING GAR LOGAN'S CIV RIGHTS BY HOLDING AN INNOCENT MAN PRISONER?
POLI
PO
NO COMMENT.
POLICE
023
L.A.P.D.
POLICE
DIAL 911
HA! LOOK AT 'EM **RUN!**
NOW TRANSFORM INTO A GREEN RHINO AND LET'S **BUST** OUTTA HERE!
I CAN'T, MATT. DAMN COLLARS.
I'LL TAKE CARE OF IT, GAR.
BE BACK QUICKER THAN YOU CAN SAY WALLY WEST!
BETTE! **WAIT!**
WALLY WEST... RIGHT.

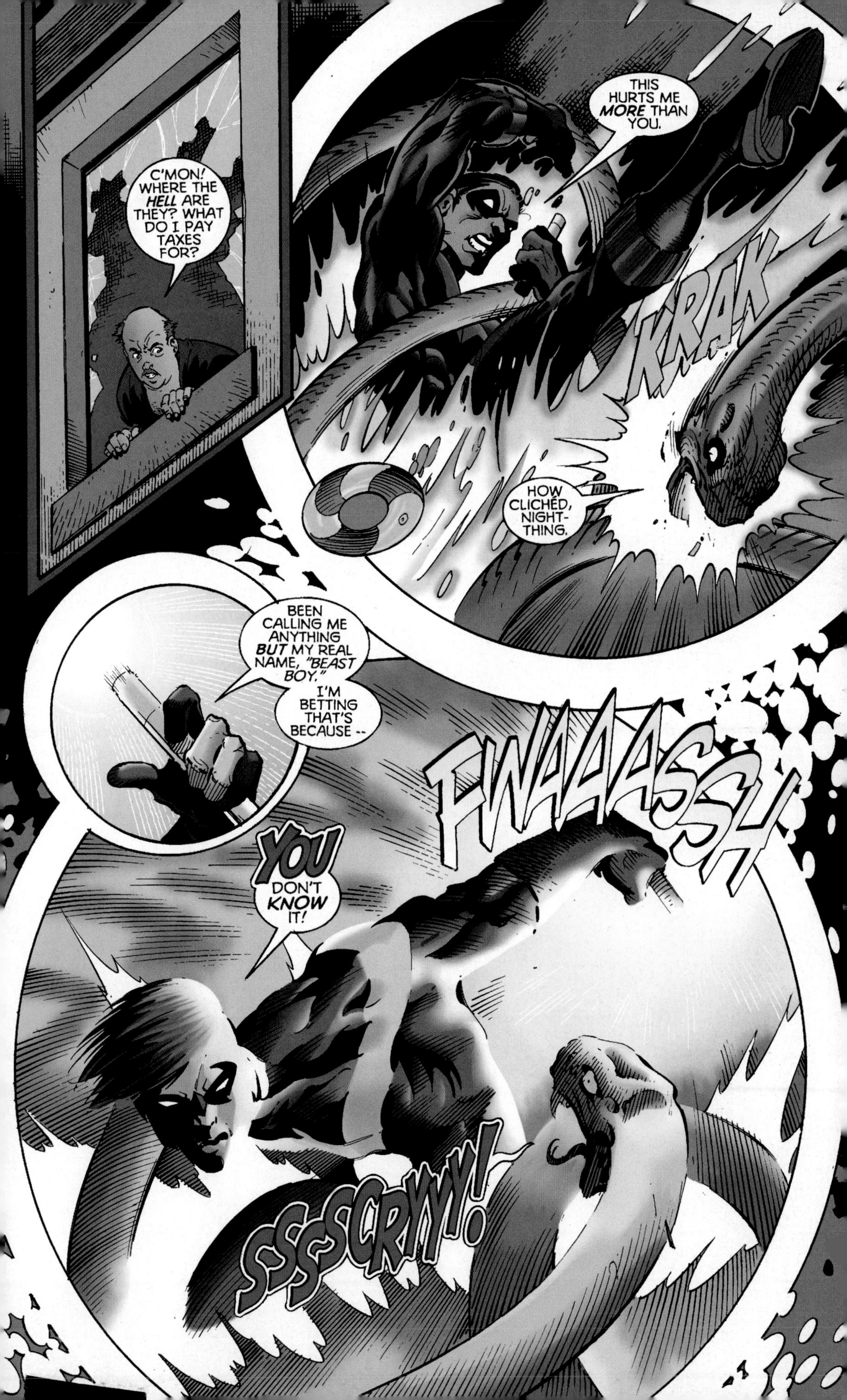
C'MON! WHERE THE HELL ARE THEY? WHAT DO I PAY TAXES FOR?
THIS HURTS ME MORE THAN YOU.
KRAK
HOW CLICHÉD, NIGHT-THING.
BEEN CALLING ME ANYTHING BUT MY REAL NAME, "BEAST BOY."
I'M BETTING THAT'S BECAUSE --
FWAAAASSH
YOU DON'T KNOW IT!
SSSSCRYYY!

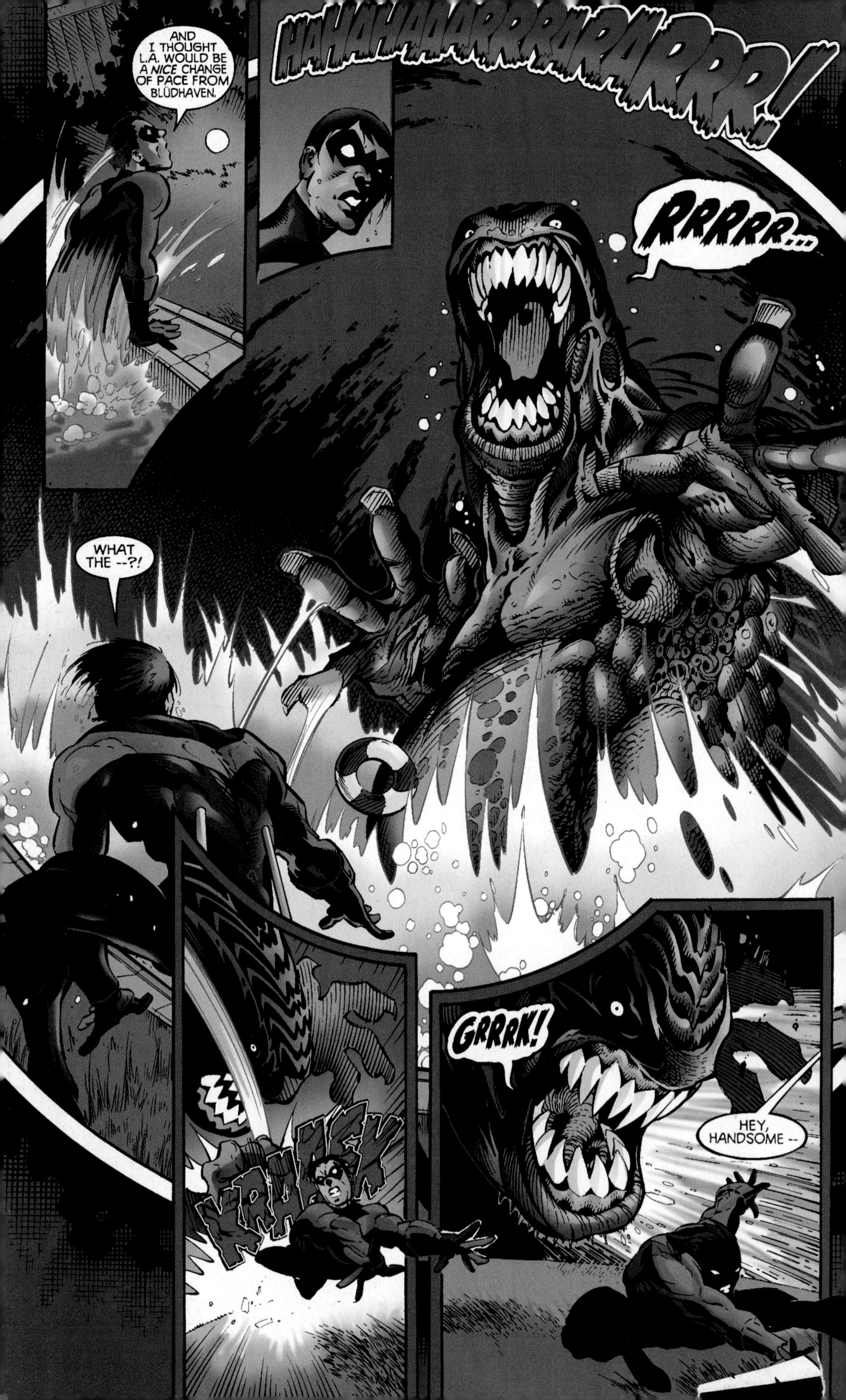
AND I THOUGHT L.A. WOULD BE A NICE CHANGE OF PACE FROM BLÜDHAVEN.
HAHAHAHAARRRRARARRRR!
RRRRR...
WHAT THE --?!
KRAKK
GRRRK!
HEY, HANDSOME --

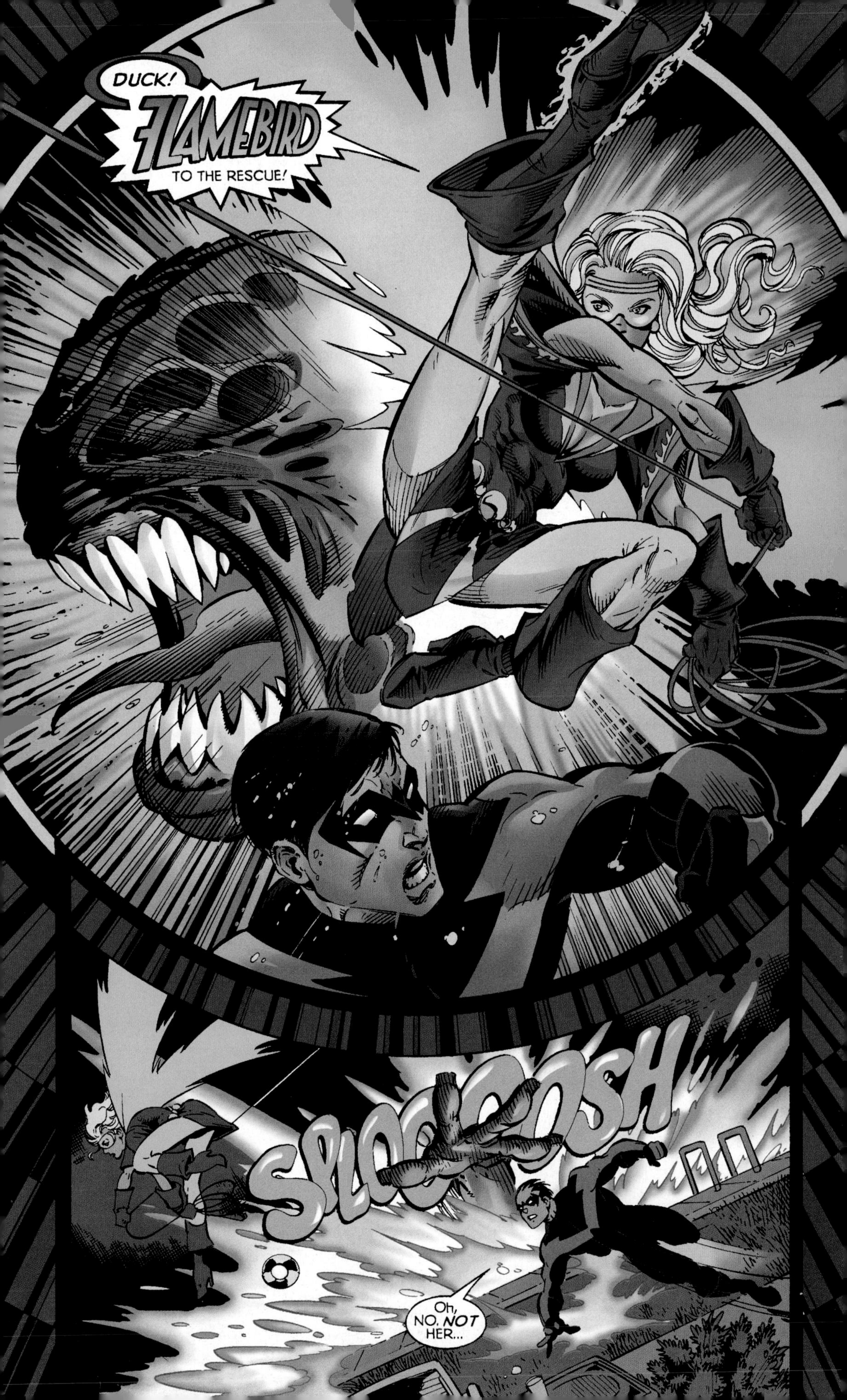
DUCK!
FLAMEBIRD
TO THE RESCUE!
SPLOOOOOSH
Oh, NO. NOT HER...

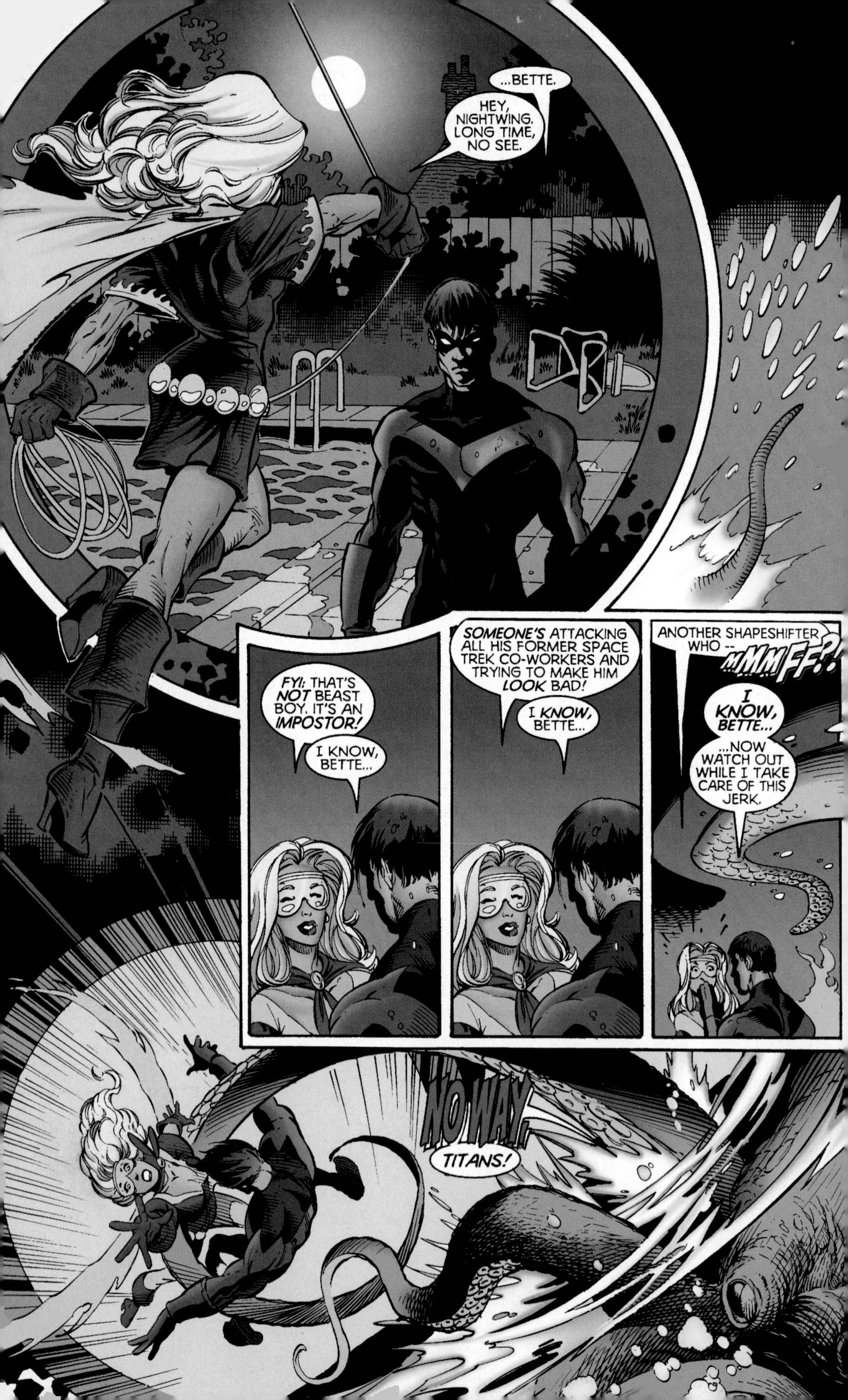
HEY, NIGHTWING. LONG TIME, NO SEE.
...BETTE.
FYI: THAT'S NOT BEAST BOY. IT'S AN IMPOSTOR!
I KNOW, BETTE...
SOMEONE'S ATTACKING ALL HIS FORMER SPACE TREK CO-WORKERS AND TRYING TO MAKE HIM LOOK BAD!
I KNOW, BETTE...
ANOTHER SHAPESHIFTER WHO --
MMMFF?!
I KNOW, BETTE...
...NOW WATCH OUT WHILE I TAKE CARE OF THIS JERK.
NO WAY,
TITANS!

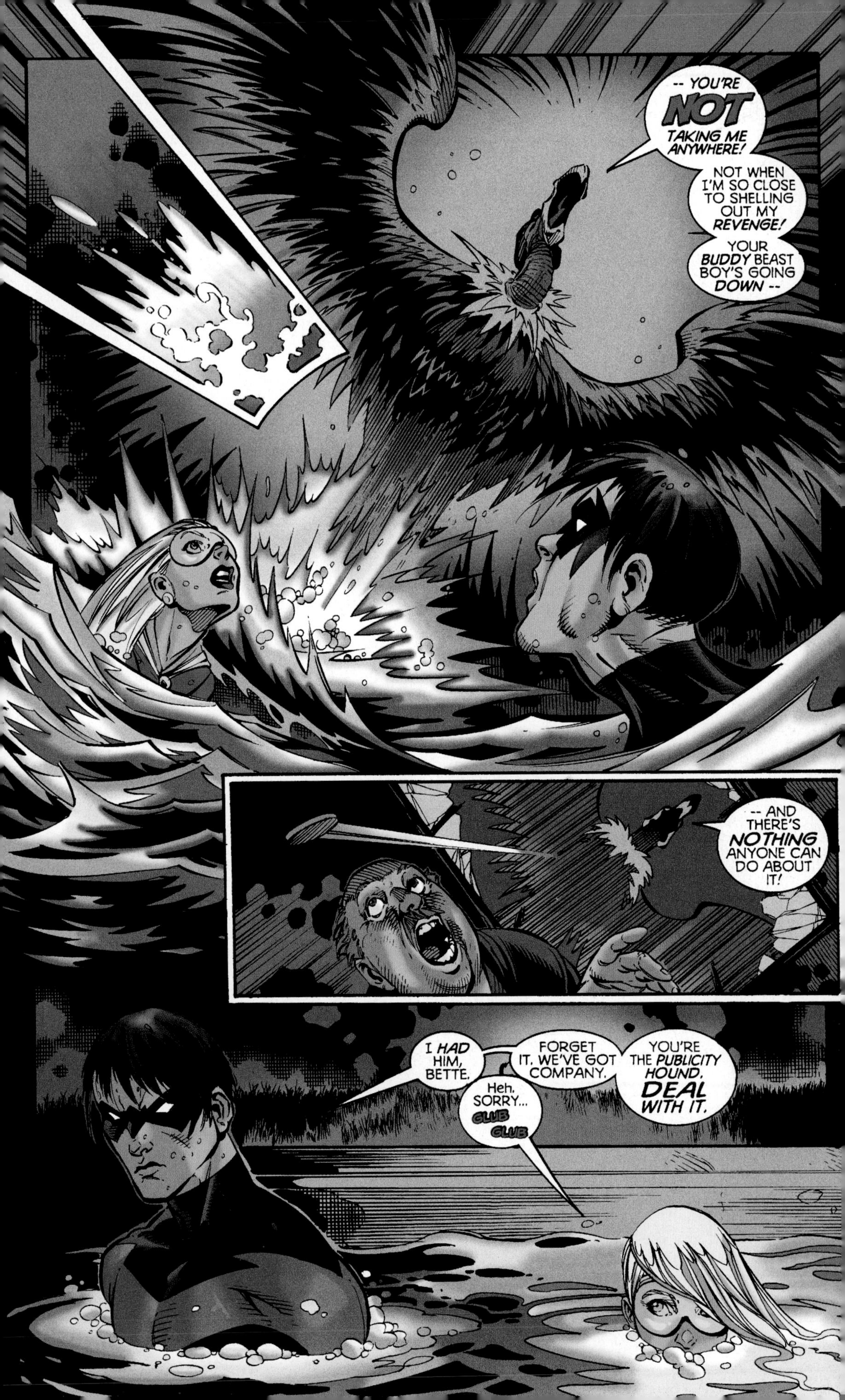
-- YOU'RE NOT TAKING ME ANYWHERE!
NOT WHEN I'M SO CLOSE TO SHELLING OUT MY REVENGE!
YOUR BUDDY BEAST BOY'S GOING DOWN --
-- AND THERE'S NOTHING ANYONE CAN DO ABOUT IT!
I HAD HIM, BETTE.
FORGET IT. WE'VE GOT COMPANY.
YOU'RE THE PUBLICITY HOUND. DEAL WITH IT.
Heh. SORRY... GLUB GLUB

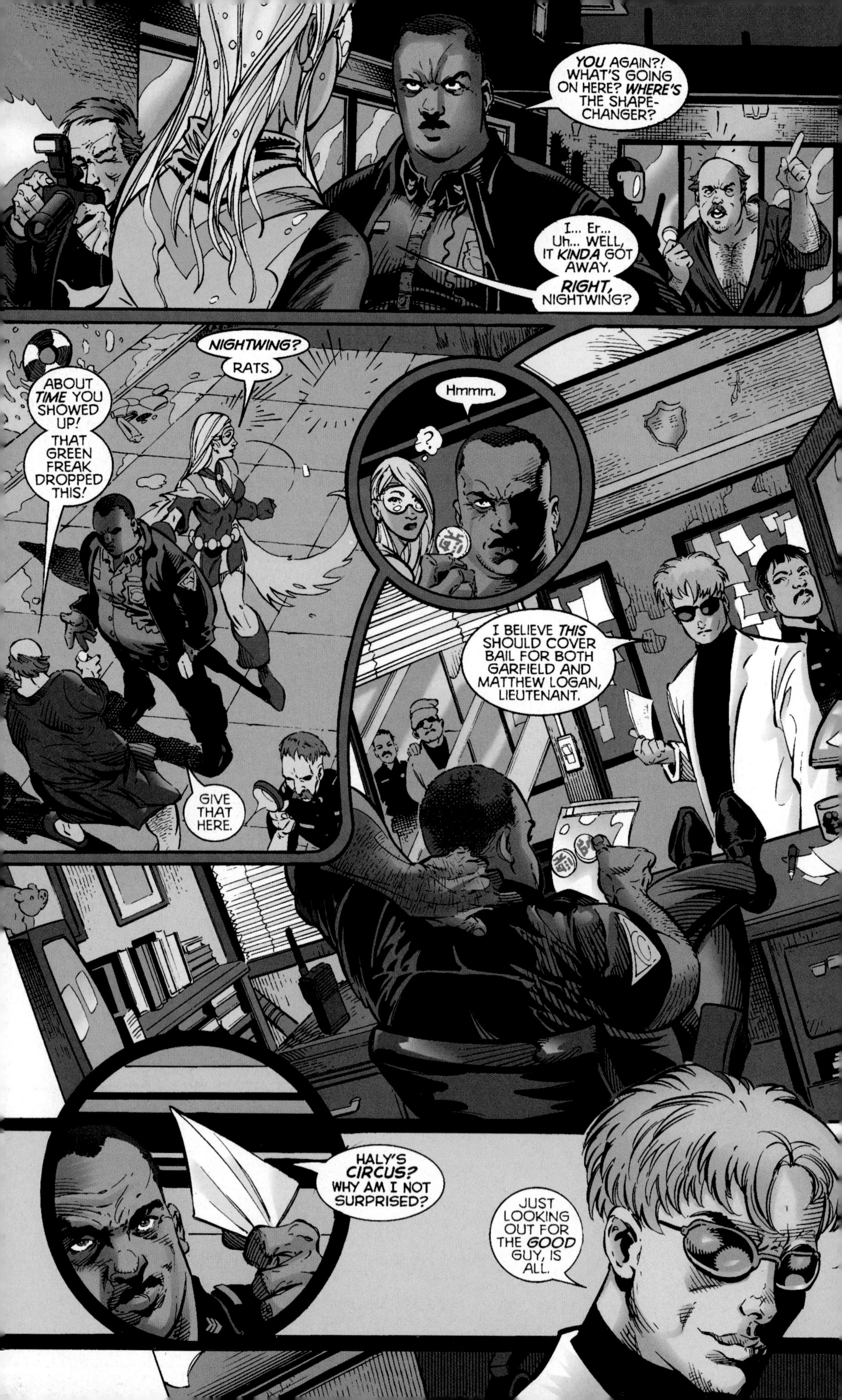

YOU AGAIN?! WHAT'S GOING ON HERE? WHERE'S THE SHAPE-CHANGER?
I... Er... Uh... WELL, IT KINDA GOT AWAY.
RIGHT, NIGHTWING?
NIGHTWING? RATS.
ABOUT TIME YOU SHOWED UP!
THAT GREEN FREAK DROPPED THIS!
GIVE THAT HERE.
Hmmm.
?
I BELIEVE THIS SHOULD COVER BAIL FOR BOTH GARFIELD AND MATTHEW LOGAN, LIEUTENANT.
HALY'S CIRCUS? WHY AM I NOT SURPRISED?
JUST LOOKING OUT FOR THE GOOD GUY, IS ALL.

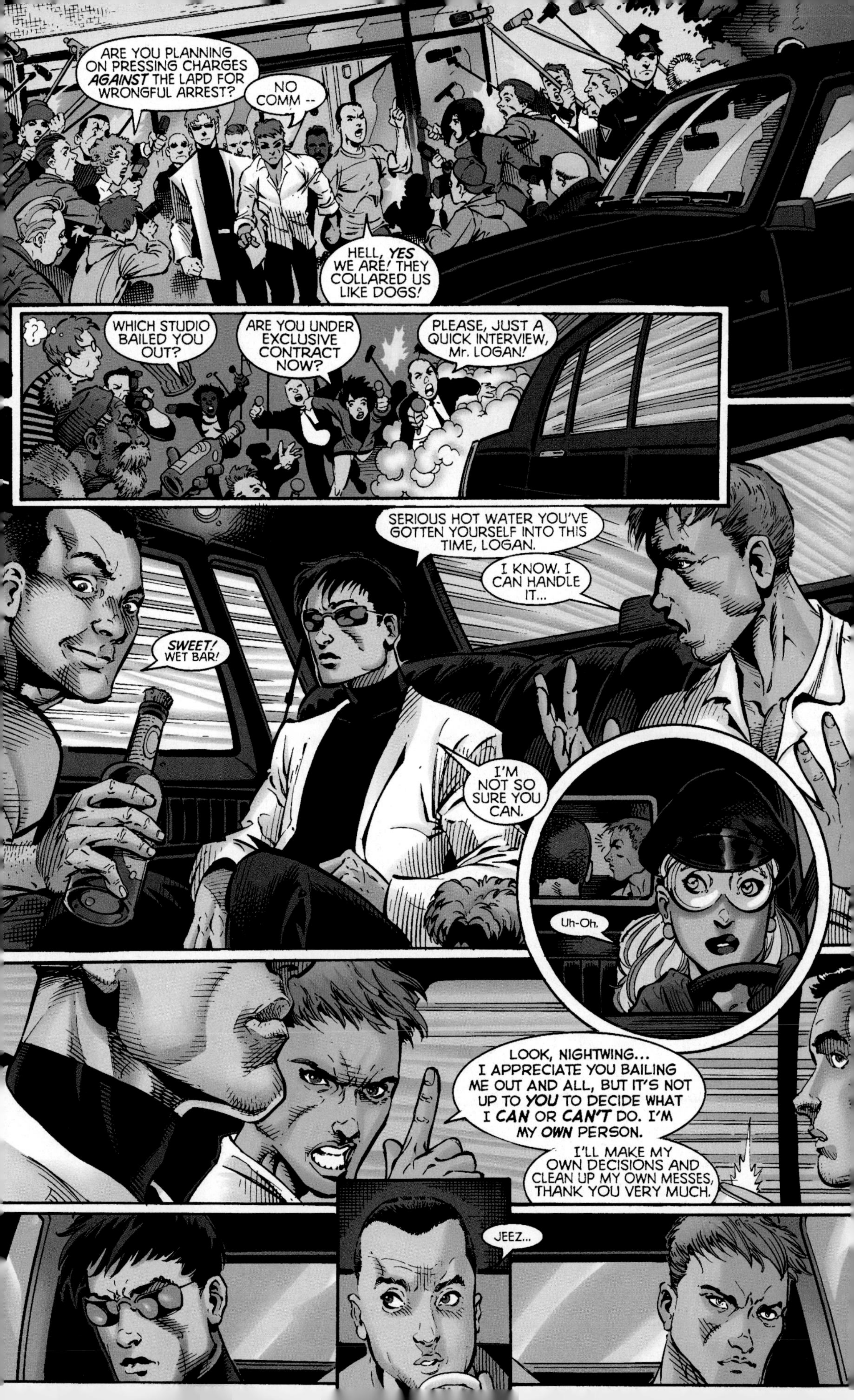
ARE YOU PLANNING ON PRESSING CHARGES AGAINST THE LAPD FOR WRONGFUL ARREST?
NO COMM --
HELL, YES WE ARE! THEY COLLARED US LIKE DOGS!
WHICH STUDIO BAILED YOU OUT?
ARE YOU UNDER EXCLUSIVE CONTRACT NOW?
PLEASE, JUST A QUICK INTERVIEW, Mr. LOGAN!
SERIOUS HOT WATER YOU'VE GOTTEN YOURSELF INTO THIS TIME, LOGAN.
I KNOW. I CAN HANDLE IT...
SWEET! WET BAR!
I'M NOT SO SURE YOU CAN.
Uh-Oh.
LOOK, NIGHTWING... I APPRECIATE YOU BAILING ME OUT AND ALL, BUT IT'S NOT UP TO YOU TO DECIDE WHAT I CAN OR CAN'T DO. I'M MY OWN PERSON.
I'LL MAKE MY OWN DECISIONS AND CLEAN UP MY OWN MESSES, THANK YOU VERY MUCH.
JEEZ...

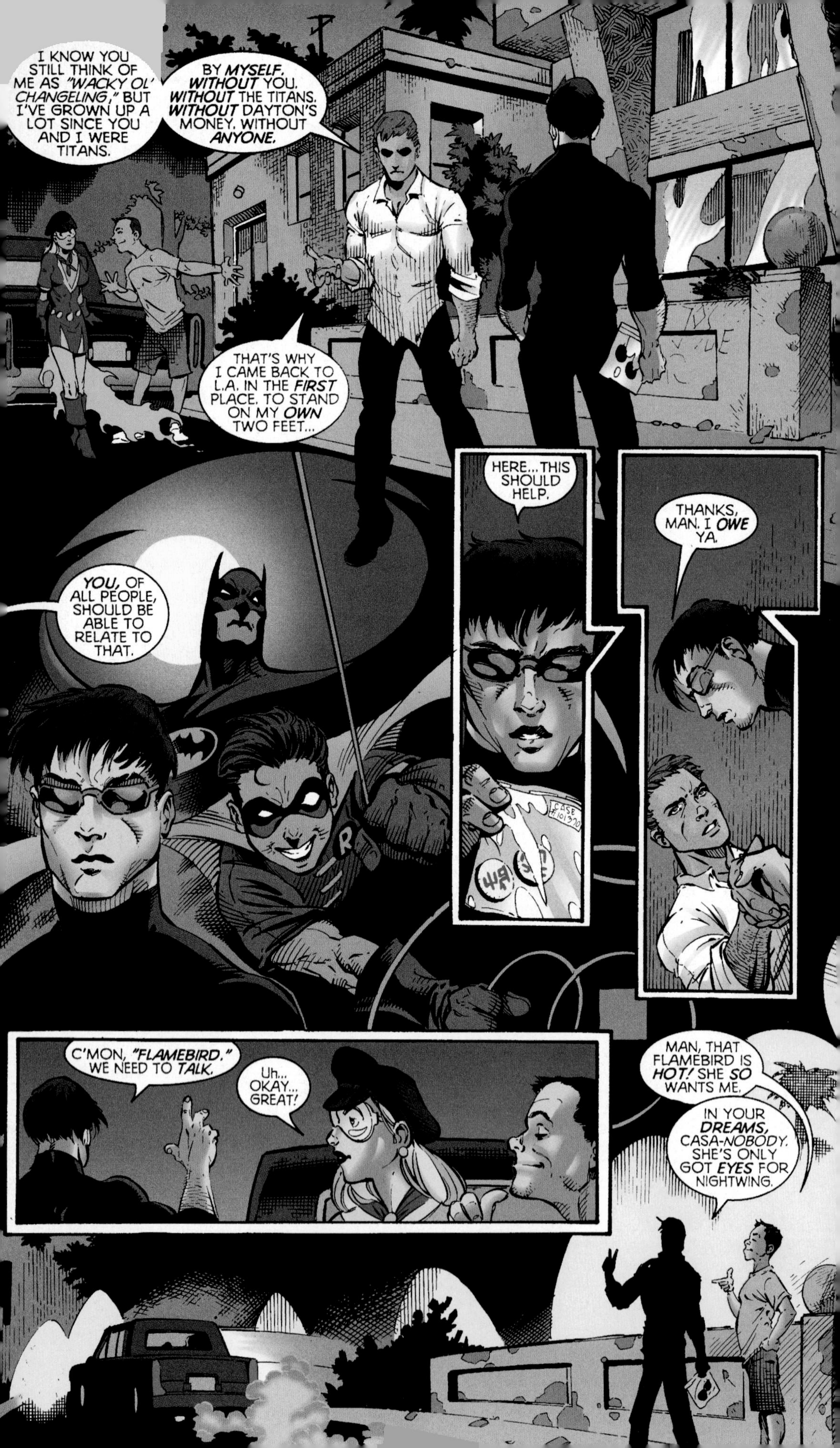

I KNOW YOU STILL THINK OF ME AS "WACKY OL' CHANGELING," BUT I'VE GROWN UP A LOT SINCE YOU AND I WERE TITANS.
BY MYSELF. WITHOUT YOU. WITHOUT THE TITANS. WITHOUT DAYTON'S MONEY. WITHOUT ANYONE.
THAT'S WHY I CAME BACK TO L.A. IN THE FIRST PLACE. TO STAND ON MY OWN TWO FEET...
YOU, OF ALL PEOPLE, SHOULD BE ABLE TO RELATE TO THAT.
HERE...THIS SHOULD HELP.
CASE #101370
THANKS, MAN. I OWE YA.
C'MON, "FLAMEBIRD." WE NEED TO TALK.
Uh... OKAY... GREAT!
MAN, THAT FLAMEBIRD IS HOT! SHE SO WANTS ME.
IN YOUR DREAMS, CASA-NOBODY. SHE'S ONLY GOT EYES FOR NIGHTWING.

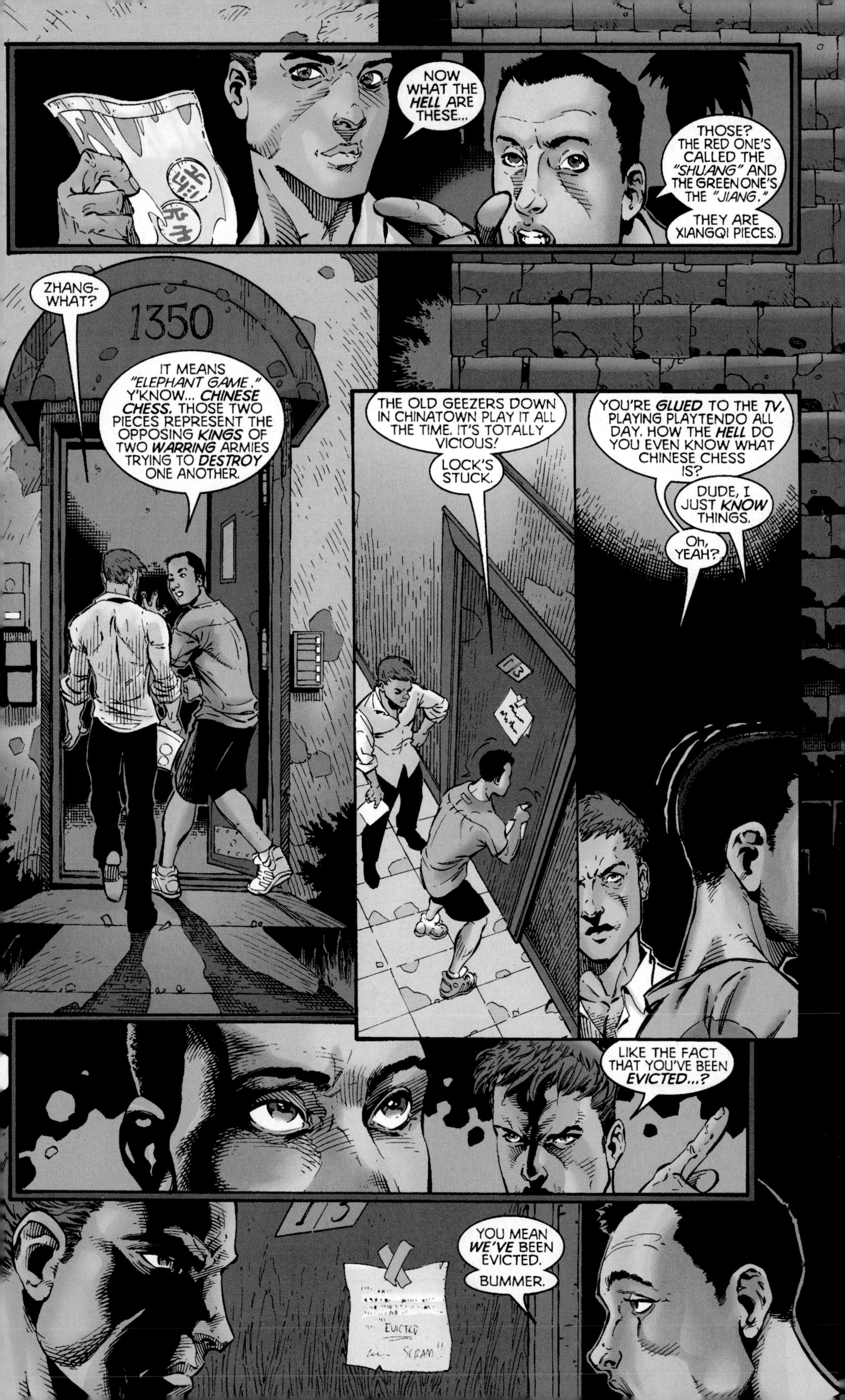

NOW WHAT THE HELL ARE THESE...
THOSE? THE RED ONE'S CALLED THE "SHUANG" AND THE GREEN ONE'S THE "JIANG."
THEY ARE XIANGQI PIECES.
ZHANG-WHAT?
1350
IT MEANS "ELEPHANT GAME." Y'KNOW... CHINESE CHESS. THOSE TWO PIECES REPRESENT THE OPPOSING KINGS OF TWO WARRING ARMIES TRYING TO DESTROY ONE ANOTHER.
THE OLD GEEZERS DOWN IN CHINATOWN PLAY IT ALL THE TIME. IT'S TOTALLY VICIOUS!
LOCK'S STUCK.
YOU'RE GLUED TO THE TV, PLAYING PLAYTENDO ALL DAY. HOW THE HELL DO YOU EVEN KNOW WHAT CHINESE CHESS IS?
DUDE, I JUST KNOW THINGS.
Oh, YEAH?
LIKE THE FACT THAT YOU'VE BEEN EVICTED...?
EVICTED
SCRAM!!
YOU MEAN WE'VE BEEN EVICTED.
BUMMER.

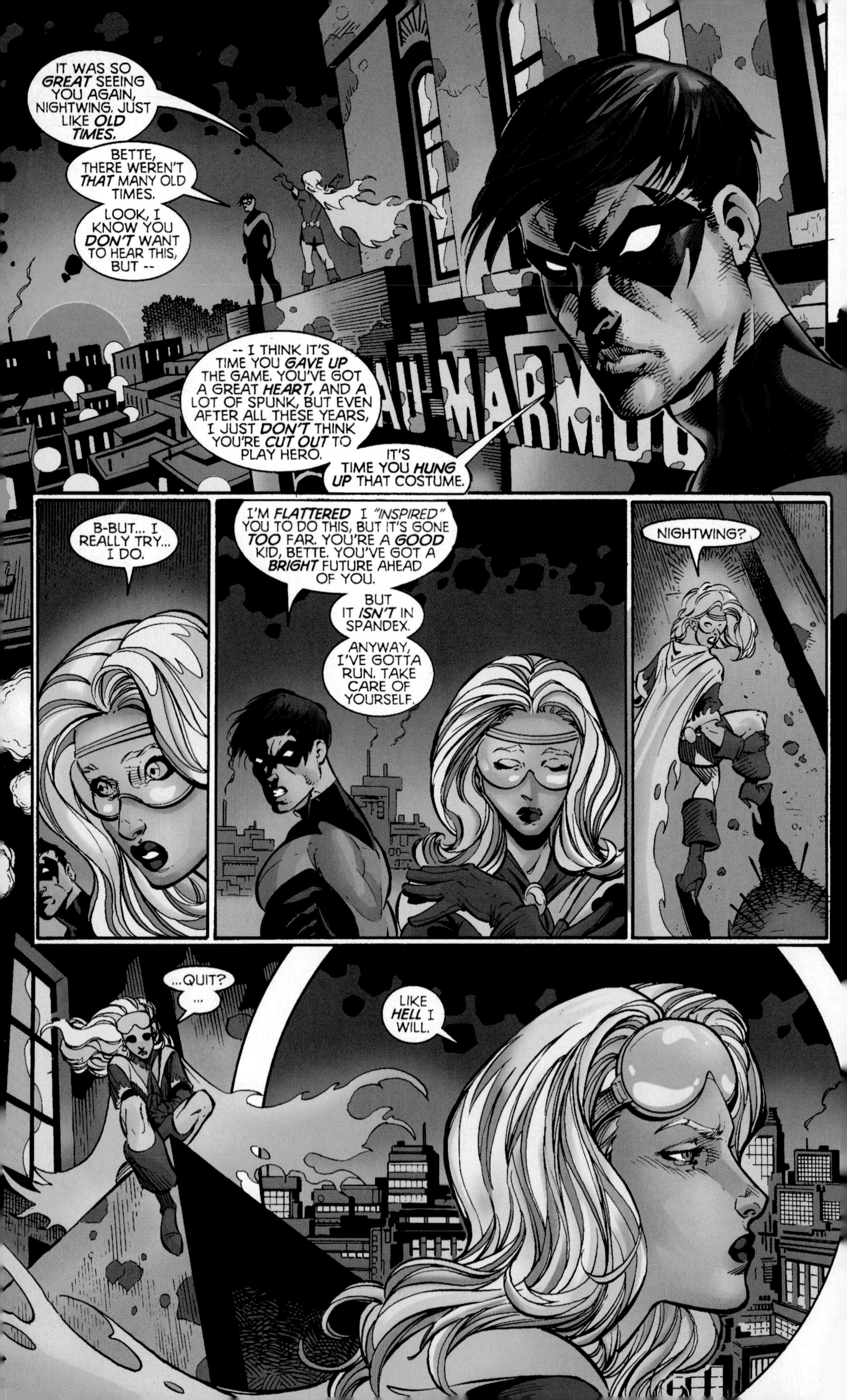
IT WAS SO GREAT SEEING YOU AGAIN, NIGHTWING. JUST LIKE OLD TIMES.
BETTE, THERE WEREN'T THAT MANY OLD TIMES.
LOOK, I KNOW YOU DON'T WANT TO HEAR THIS, BUT --
-- I THINK IT'S TIME YOU GAVE UP THE GAME. YOU'VE GOT A GREAT HEART, AND A LOT OF SPUNK, BUT EVEN AFTER ALL THESE YEARS, I JUST DON'T THINK YOU'RE CUT OUT TO PLAY HERO.
IT'S TIME YOU HUNG UP THAT COSTUME.
B-BUT... I REALLY TRY... I DO.
I'M FLATTERED I "INSPIRED" YOU TO DO THIS, BUT IT'S GONE TOO FAR. YOU'RE A GOOD KID, BETTE. YOU'VE GOT A BRIGHT FUTURE AHEAD OF YOU.
BUT IT ISN'T IN SPANDEX.
ANYWAY, I'VE GOTTA RUN. TAKE CARE OF YOURSELF.
NIGHTWING?
...QUIT? ...
LIKE HELL I WILL.

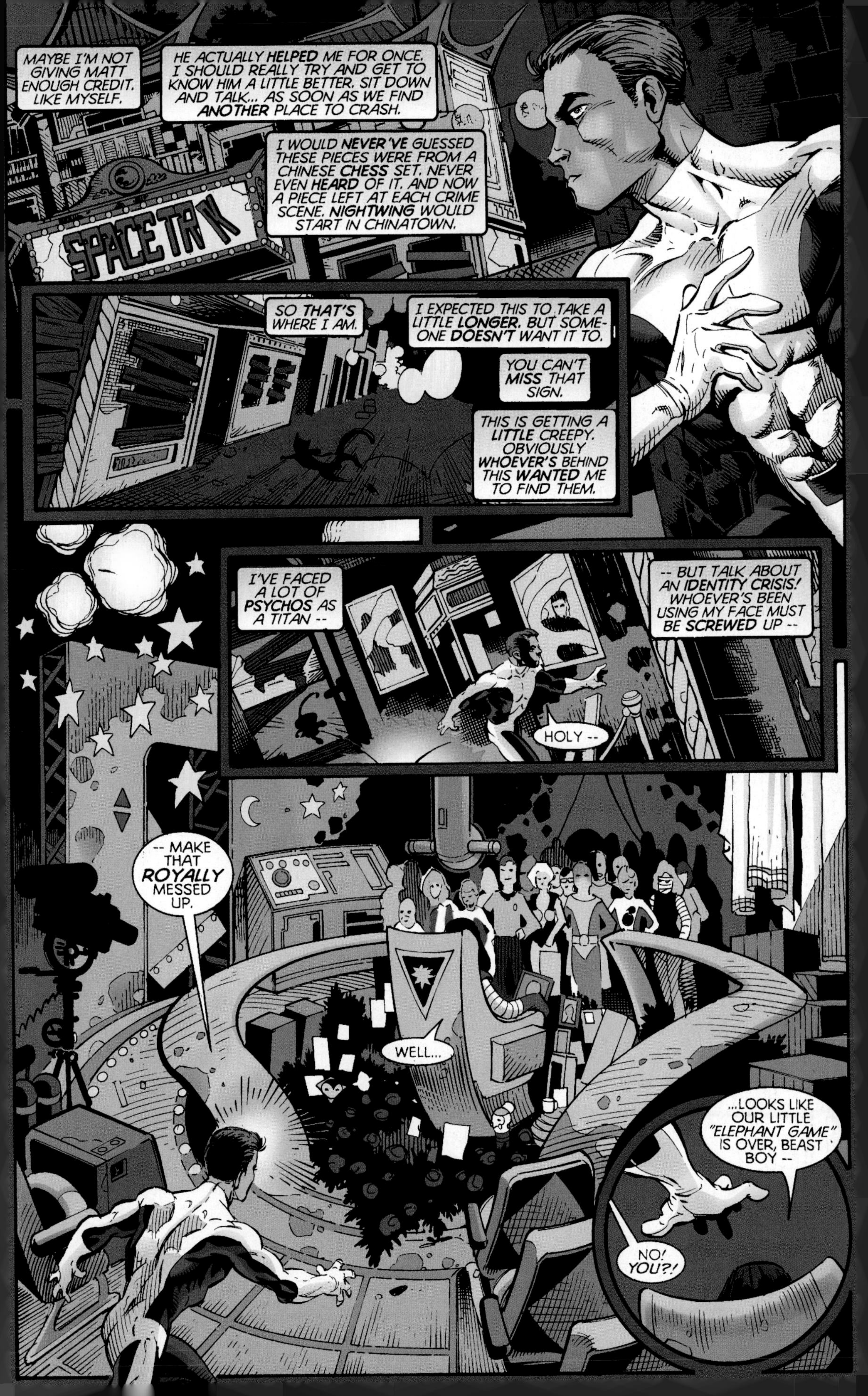
MAYBE I'M NOT GIVING MATT ENOUGH CREDIT. LIKE MYSELF.
HE ACTUALLY HELPED ME FOR ONCE. I SHOULD REALLY TRY AND GET TO KNOW HIM A LITTLE BETTER. SIT DOWN AND TALK... AS SOON AS WE FIND ANOTHER PLACE TO CRASH.
I WOULD NEVER'VE GUESSED THESE PIECES WERE FROM A CHINESE CHESS SET. NEVER EVEN HEARD OF IT. AND NOW A PIECE LEFT AT EACH CRIME SCENE. NIGHTWING WOULD START IN CHINATOWN.
SPACE TR K
SO THAT'S WHERE I AM.
I EXPECTED THIS TO TAKE A LITTLE LONGER. BUT SOMEONE DOESN'T WANT IT TO.
YOU CAN'T MISS THAT SIGN.
THIS IS GETTING A LITTLE CREEPY. OBVIOUSLY WHOEVER'S BEHIND THIS WANTED ME TO FIND THEM.
I'VE FACED A LOT OF PSYCHOS AS A TITAN --
-- BUT TALK ABOUT AN IDENTITY CRISIS! WHOEVER'S BEEN USING MY FACE MUST BE SCREWED UP --
HOLY --
-- MAKE THAT ROYALLY MESSED UP.
WELL...
...LOOKS LIKE OUR LITTLE "ELEPHANT GAME" IS OVER, BEAST BOY --
NO! YOU?!

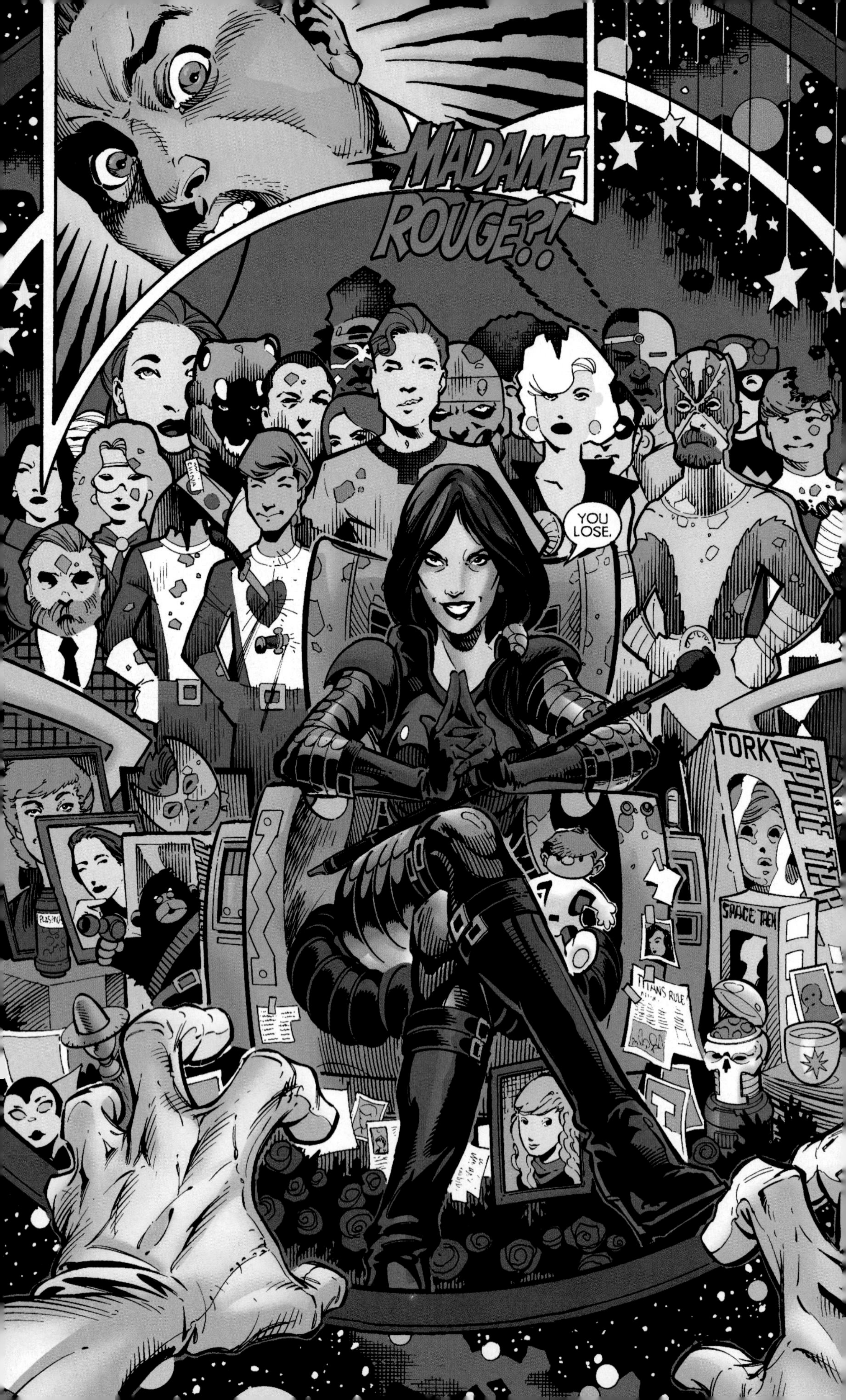
MADAME ROUGE?!
YOU LOSE.
TORK
SPACE TREK
TITANS RULE

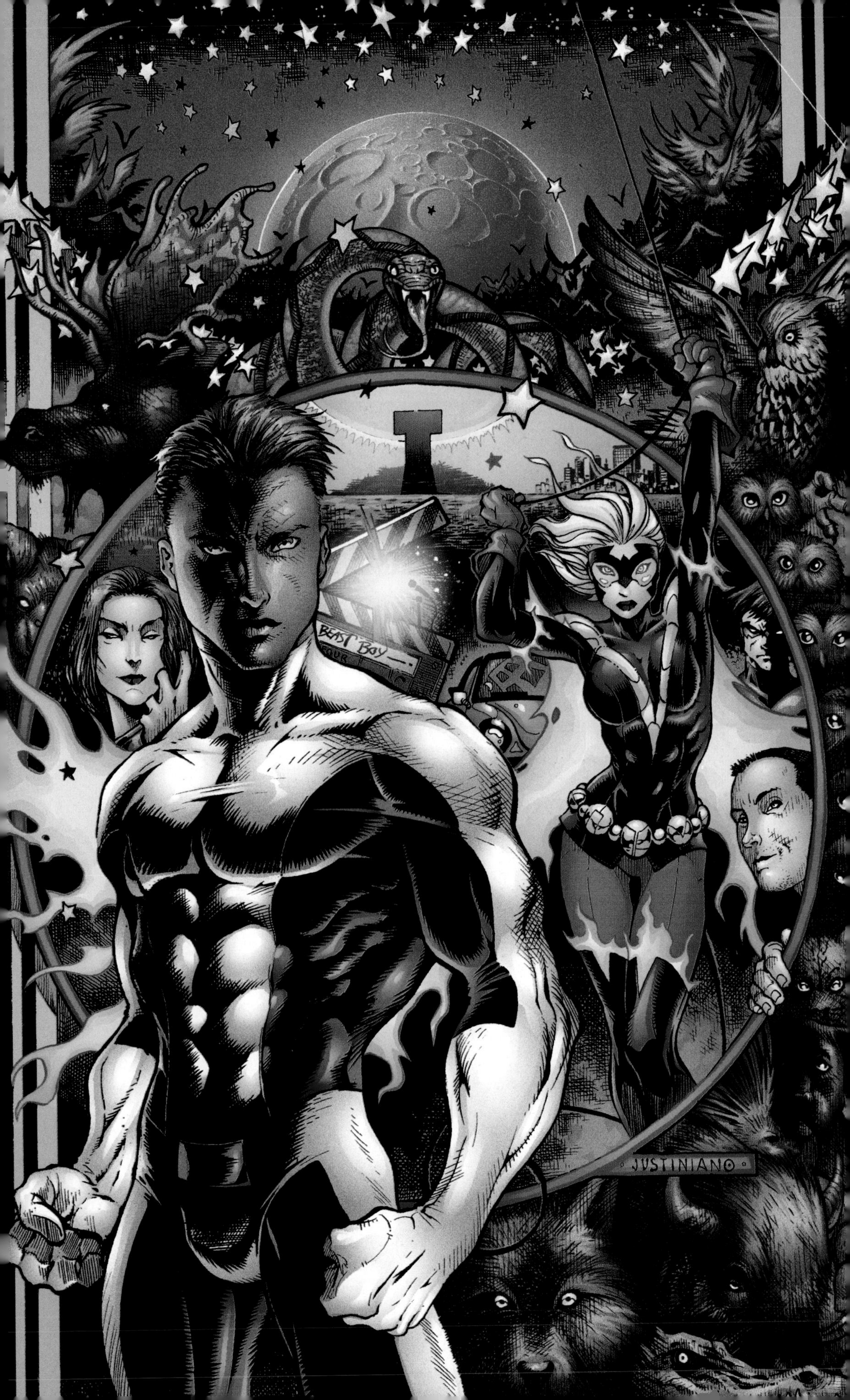
BEAST BOY
JUSTINIANO

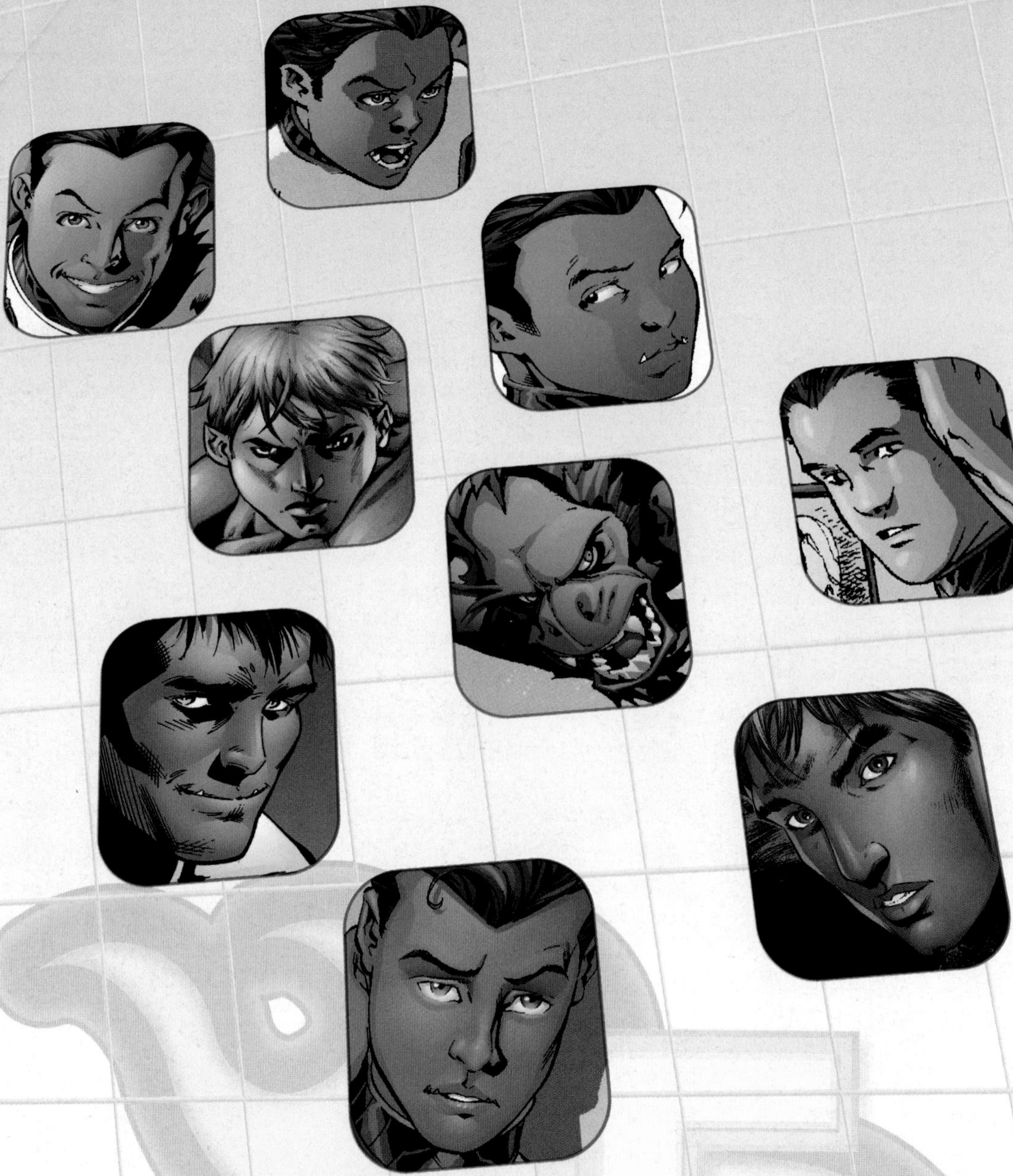

BEAST BOY #4

GEOFF JOHNS
BEN RAAB
Writers

JUSTINIANO
Penciller

CHRIS IVY
Inker

JASON WRIGHT
Colorist

COMICRAFT
Letterer

JUSTINIANO
Cover Artist

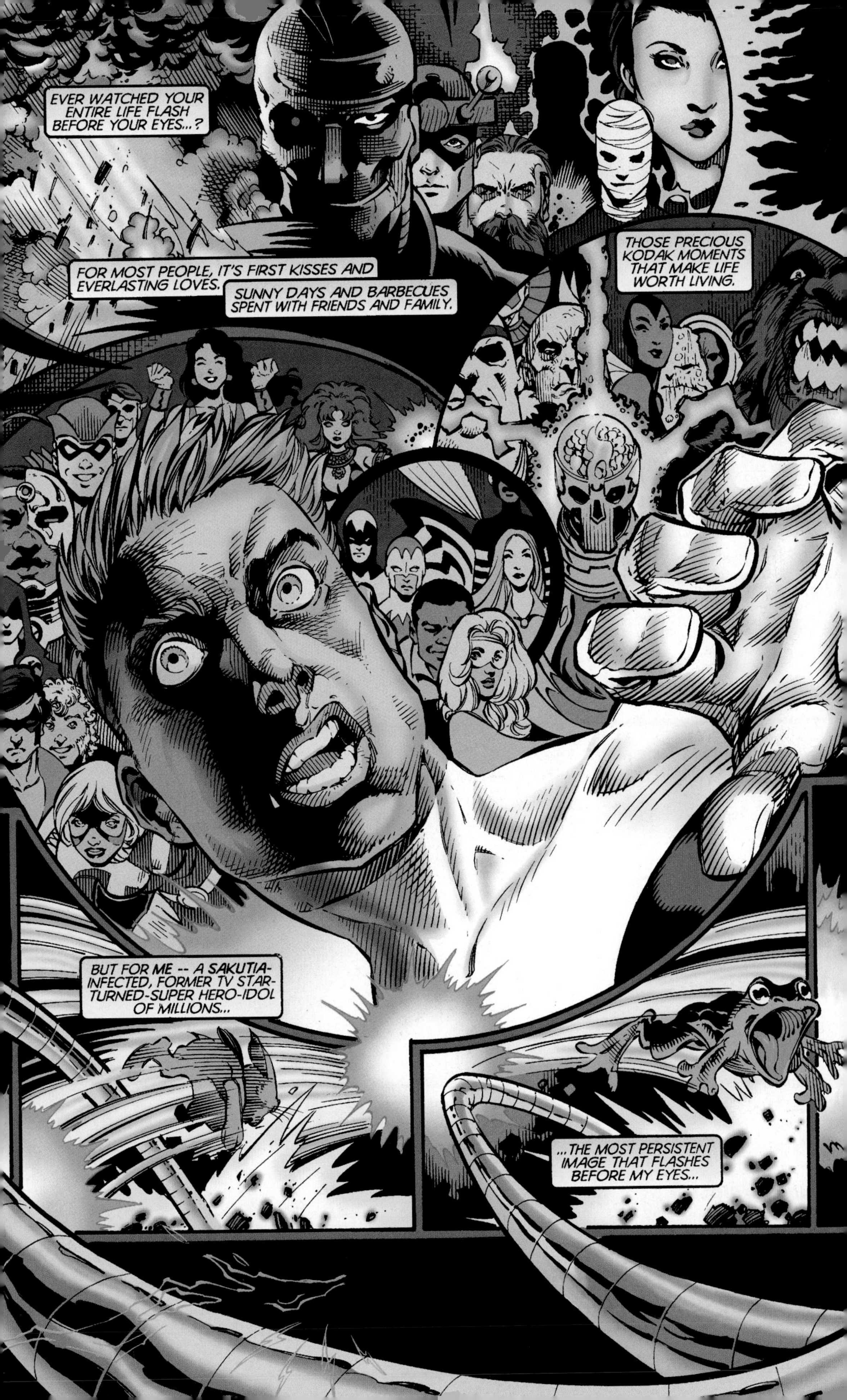
EVER WATCHED YOUR ENTIRE LIFE FLASH BEFORE YOUR EYES...?
FOR MOST PEOPLE, IT'S FIRST KISSES AND EVERLASTING LOVES.
SUNNY DAYS AND BARBECUES SPENT WITH FRIENDS AND FAMILY.
THOSE PRECIOUS KODAK MOMENTS THAT MAKE LIFE WORTH LIVING.
BUT FOR ME -- A SAKUTIA-INFECTED, FORMER TV STAR-TURNED-SUPER HERO-IDOL OF MILLIONS...
...THE MOST PERSISTENT IMAGE THAT FLASHES BEFORE MY EYES...

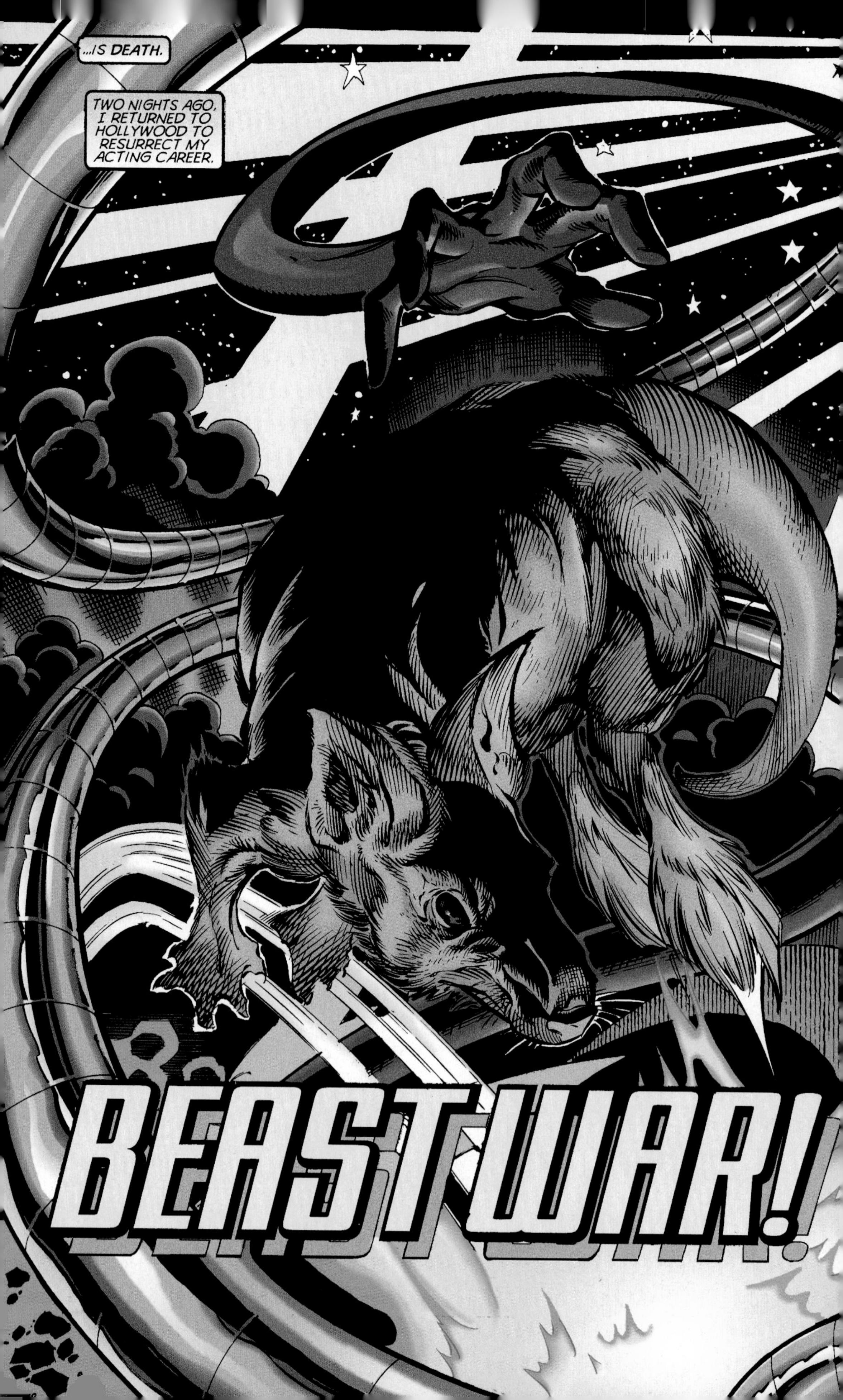
...IS DEATH.
TWO NIGHTS AGO, I RETURNED TO HOLLYWOOD TO RESURRECT MY ACTING CAREER.
BEAST WAR!

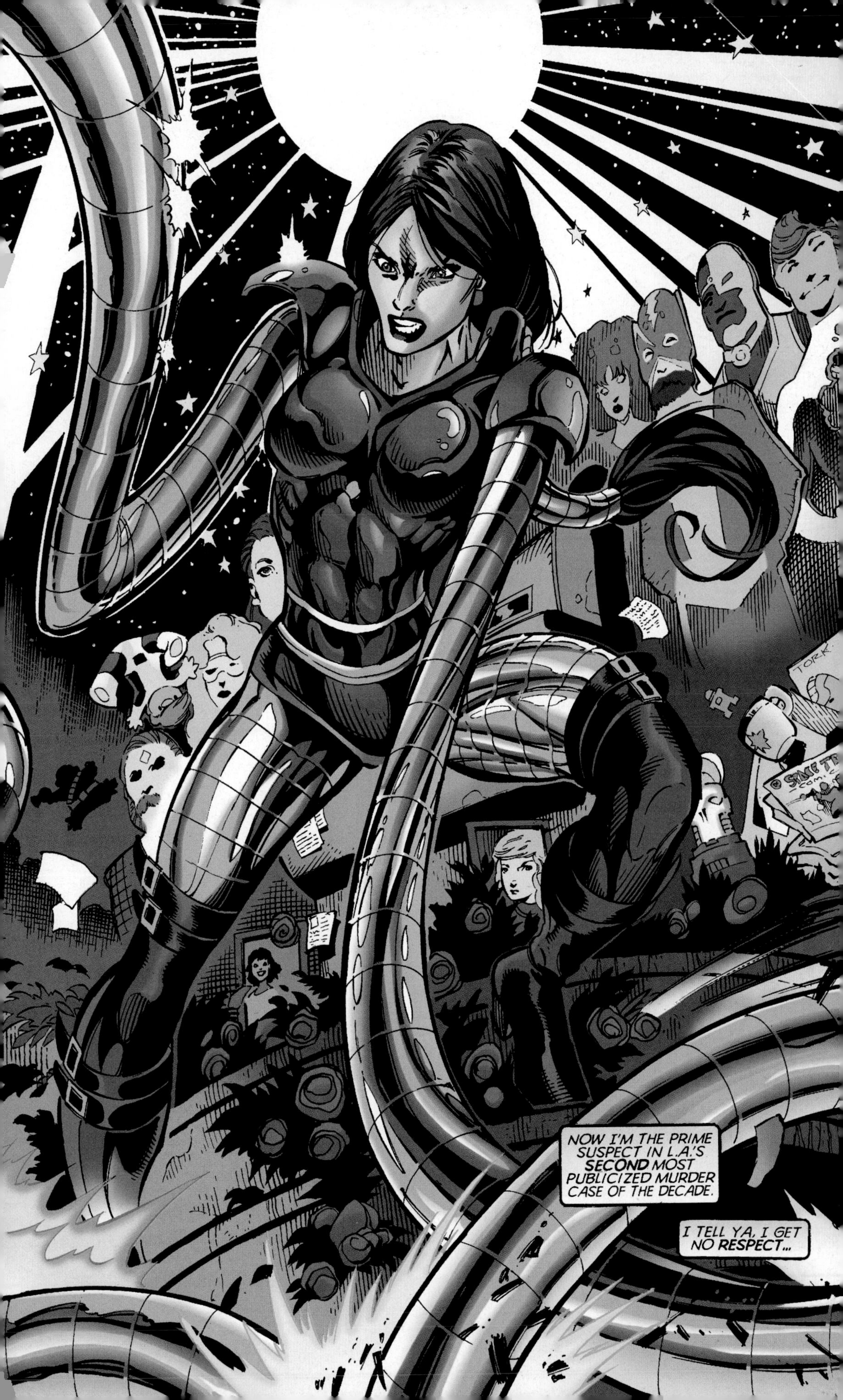
NOW I'M THE PRIME SUSPECT IN L.A.'S **SECOND** MOST PUBLICIZED MURDER CASE OF THE DECADE.
I TELL YA, I GET NO **RESPECT**...

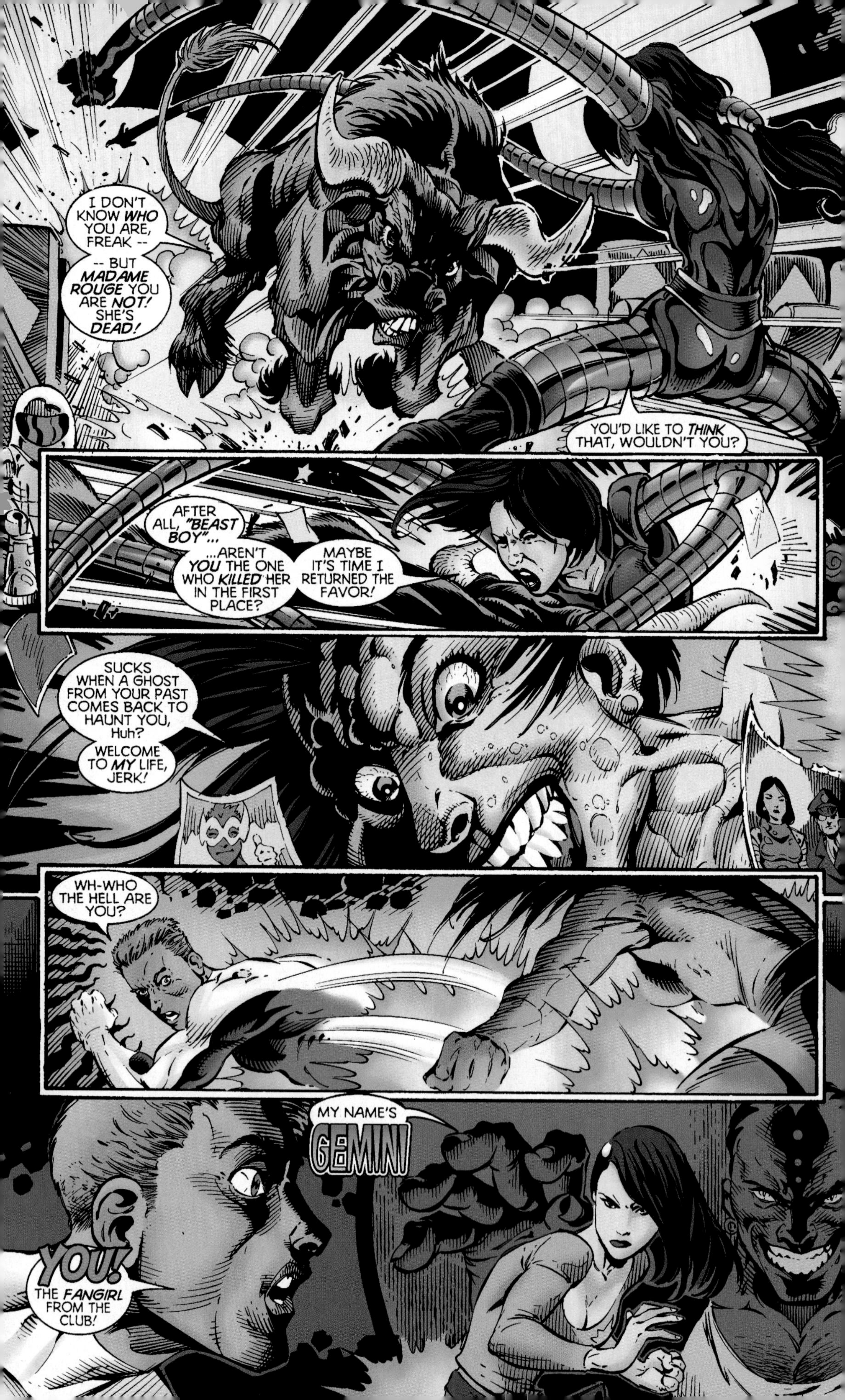
I DON'T KNOW WHO YOU ARE, FREAK --
-- BUT MADAME ROUGE YOU ARE NOT! SHE'S DEAD!
YOU'D LIKE TO THINK THAT, WOULDN'T YOU?
AFTER ALL, "BEAST BOY"...
...AREN'T YOU THE ONE WHO KILLED HER IN THE FIRST PLACE?
MAYBE IT'S TIME I RETURNED THE FAVOR!
SUCKS WHEN A GHOST FROM YOUR PAST COMES BACK TO HAUNT YOU, Huh?
WELCOME TO MY LIFE, JERK!
WH-WHO THE HELL ARE YOU?
MY NAME'S
GEMINI
YOU! THE FANGIRL FROM THE CLUB!

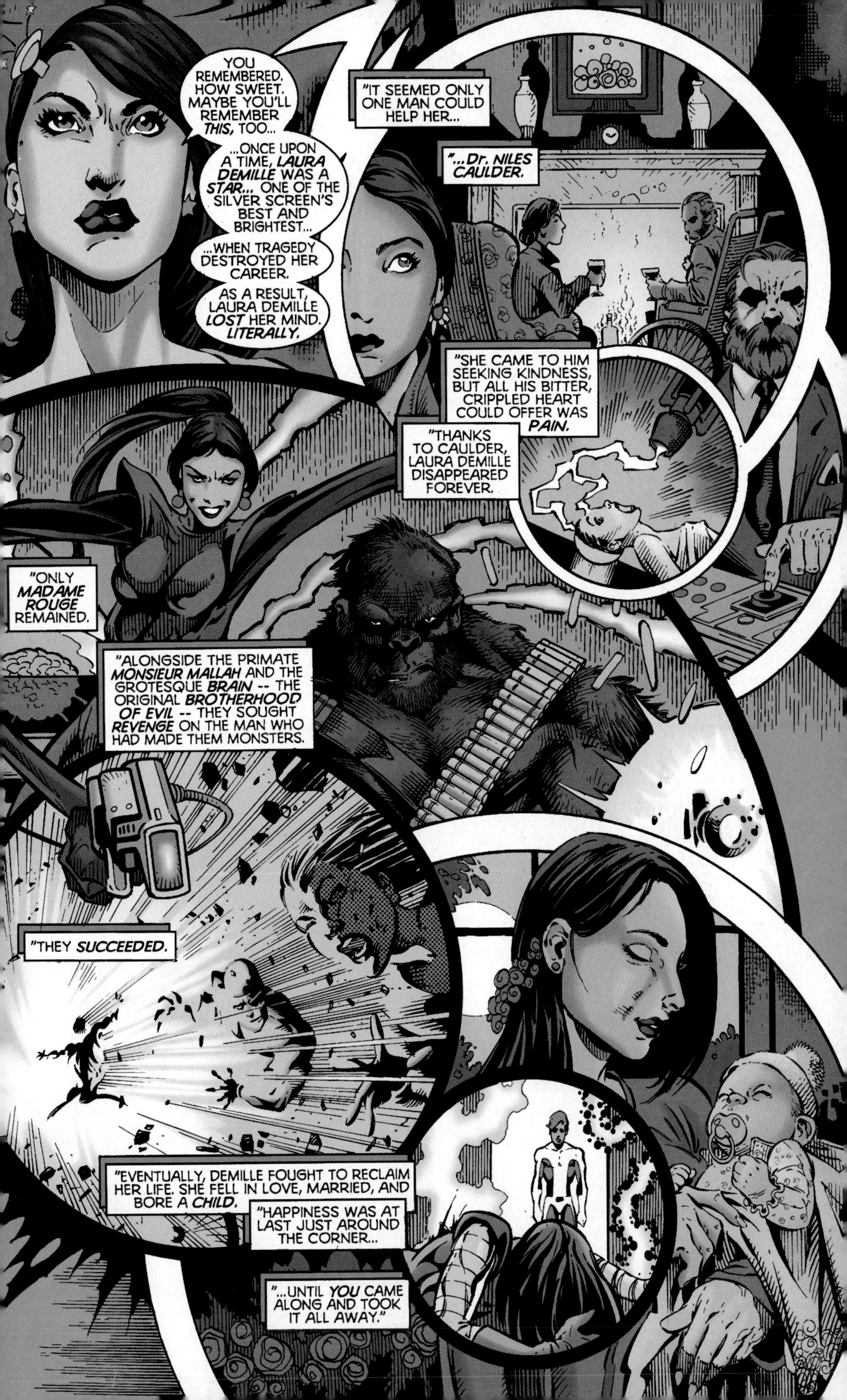

YOU REMEMBERED. HOW SWEET. MAYBE YOU'LL REMEMBER *THIS,* TOO...
...ONCE UPON A TIME, *LAURA DEMILLE* WAS A *STAR...* ONE OF THE SILVER SCREEN'S BEST AND BRIGHTEST...
...WHEN TRAGEDY DESTROYED HER CAREER.
AS A RESULT, LAURA DEMILLE *LOST* HER MIND. *LITERALLY.*
"IT SEEMED ONLY ONE MAN COULD HELP HER...
"...*Dr. NILES CAULDER.*
"SHE CAME TO HIM SEEKING KINDNESS, BUT ALL HIS BITTER, CRIPPLED HEART COULD OFFER WAS *PAIN.*
"THANKS TO CAULDER, LAURA DEMILLE DISAPPEARED FOREVER.
"ONLY *MADAME ROUGE* REMAINED.
"ALONGSIDE THE PRIMATE *MONSIEUR MALLAH* AND THE GROTESQUE *BRAIN* -- THE ORIGINAL *BROTHERHOOD OF EVIL* -- THEY SOUGHT *REVENGE* ON THE MAN WHO HAD MADE THEM MONSTERS.
"THEY *SUCCEEDED.*
"EVENTUALLY, DEMILLE FOUGHT TO RECLAIM HER LIFE. SHE FELL IN LOVE, MARRIED, AND BORE A *CHILD.*
"HAPPINESS WAS AT LAST JUST AROUND THE CORNER...
"...UNTIL *YOU* CAME ALONG AND TOOK IT ALL AWAY."

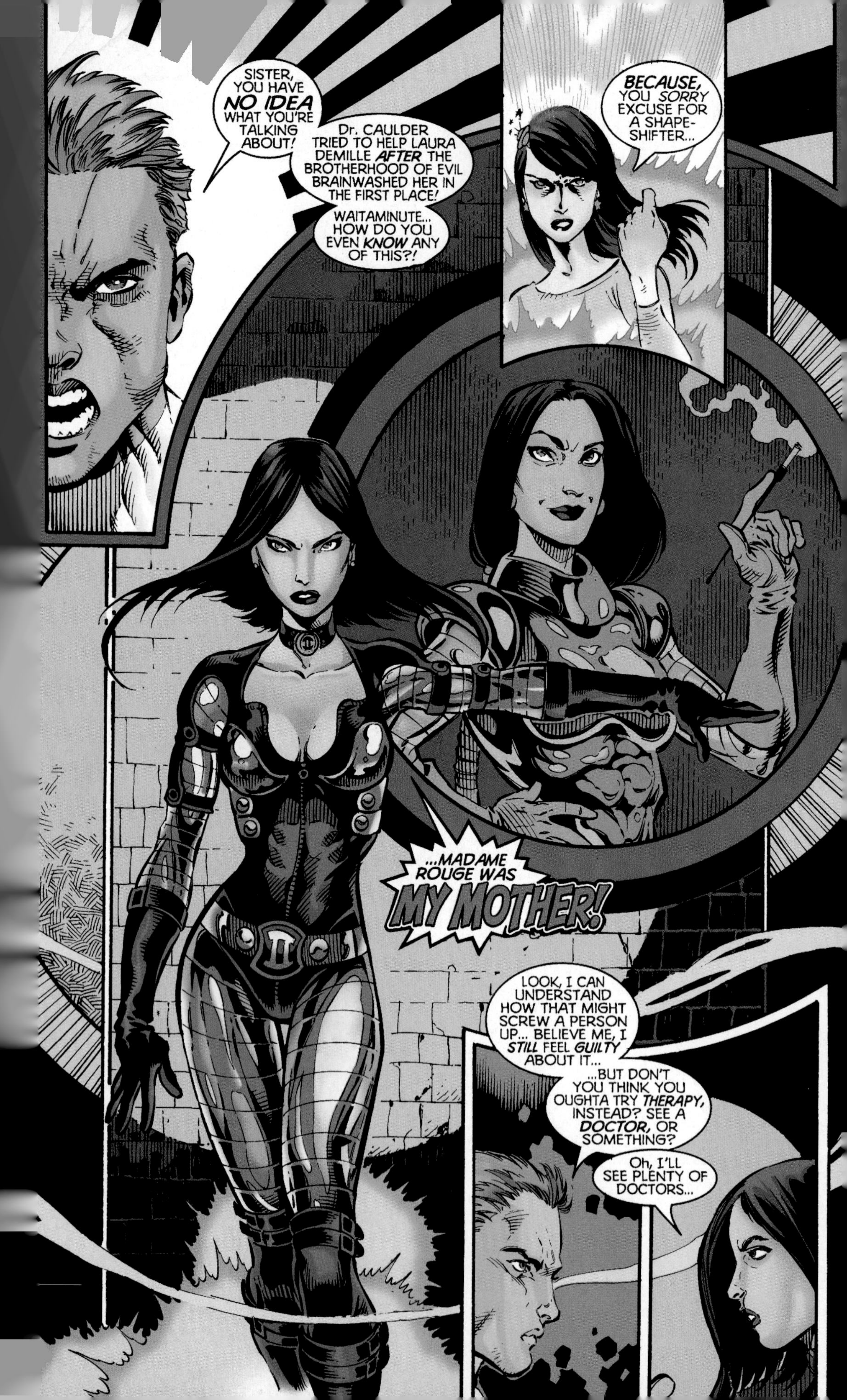
SISTER, YOU HAVE NO IDEA WHAT YOU'RE TALKING ABOUT!
Dr. CAULDER TRIED TO HELP LAURA DEMILLE AFTER THE BROTHERHOOD OF EVIL BRAINWASHED HER IN THE FIRST PLACE!
WAITAMINUTE... HOW DO YOU EVEN KNOW ANY OF THIS?!
BECAUSE, YOU SORRY EXCUSE FOR A SHAPE-SHIFTER...
...MADAME ROUGE WAS MY MOTHER!
LOOK, I CAN UNDERSTAND HOW THAT MIGHT SCREW A PERSON UP... BELIEVE ME, I STILL FEEL GUILTY ABOUT IT...
...BUT DON'T YOU THINK YOU OUGHTA TRY THERAPY, INSTEAD? SEE A DOCTOR, OR SOMETHING?
Oh, I'LL SEE PLENTY OF DOCTORS...

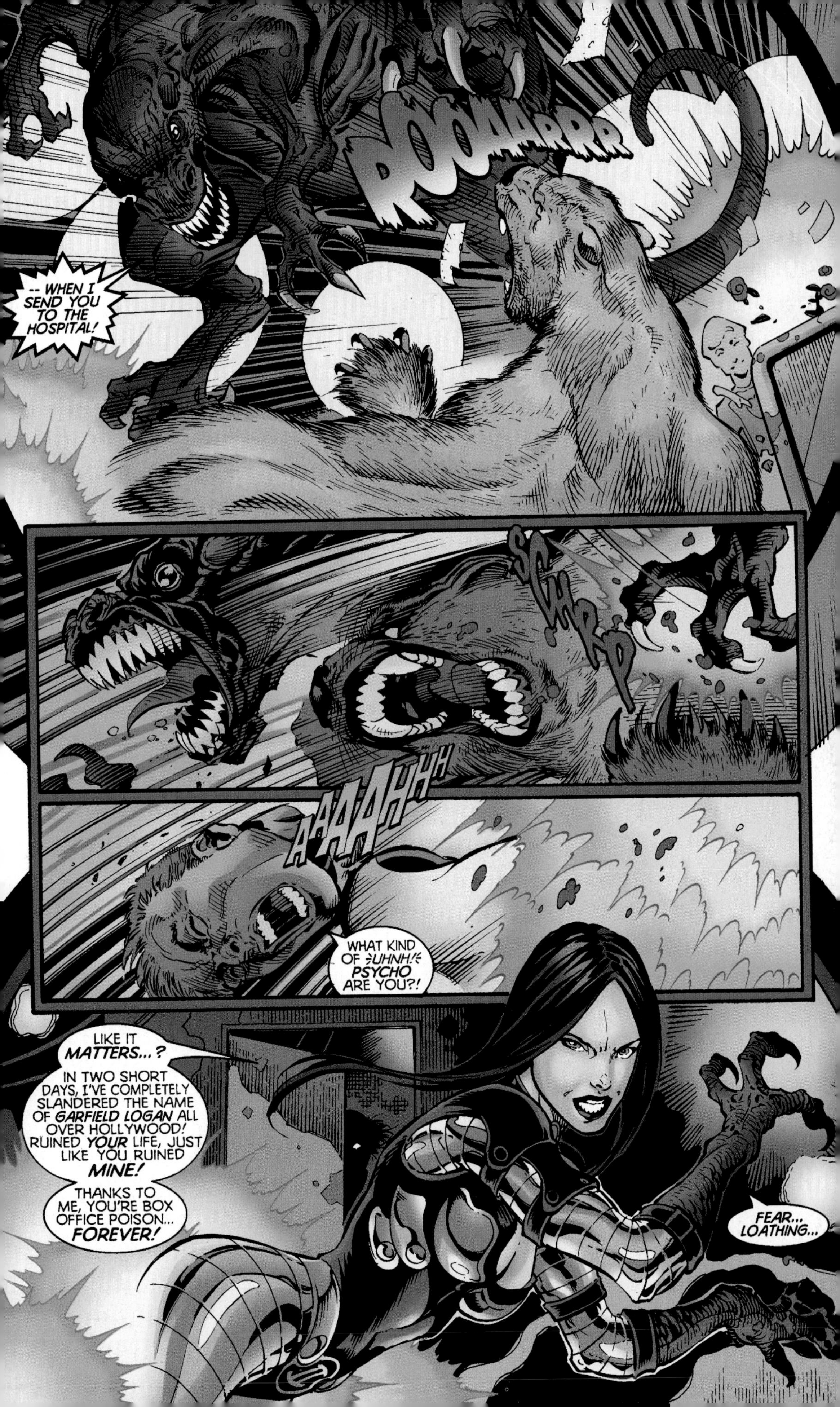
ROOOAARRR
-- WHEN I SEND YOU TO THE HOSPITAL!
SCHRRP
AAAAHHH
WHAT KIND OF ⚡UHNH!⚡ PSYCHO ARE YOU?!
LIKE IT MATTERS...?
IN TWO SHORT DAYS, I'VE COMPLETELY SLANDERED THE NAME OF GARFIELD LOGAN ALL OVER HOLLYWOOD! RUINED YOUR LIFE, JUST LIKE YOU RUINED MINE!
THANKS TO ME, YOU'RE BOX OFFICE POISON... FOREVER!
FEAR... LOATHING...

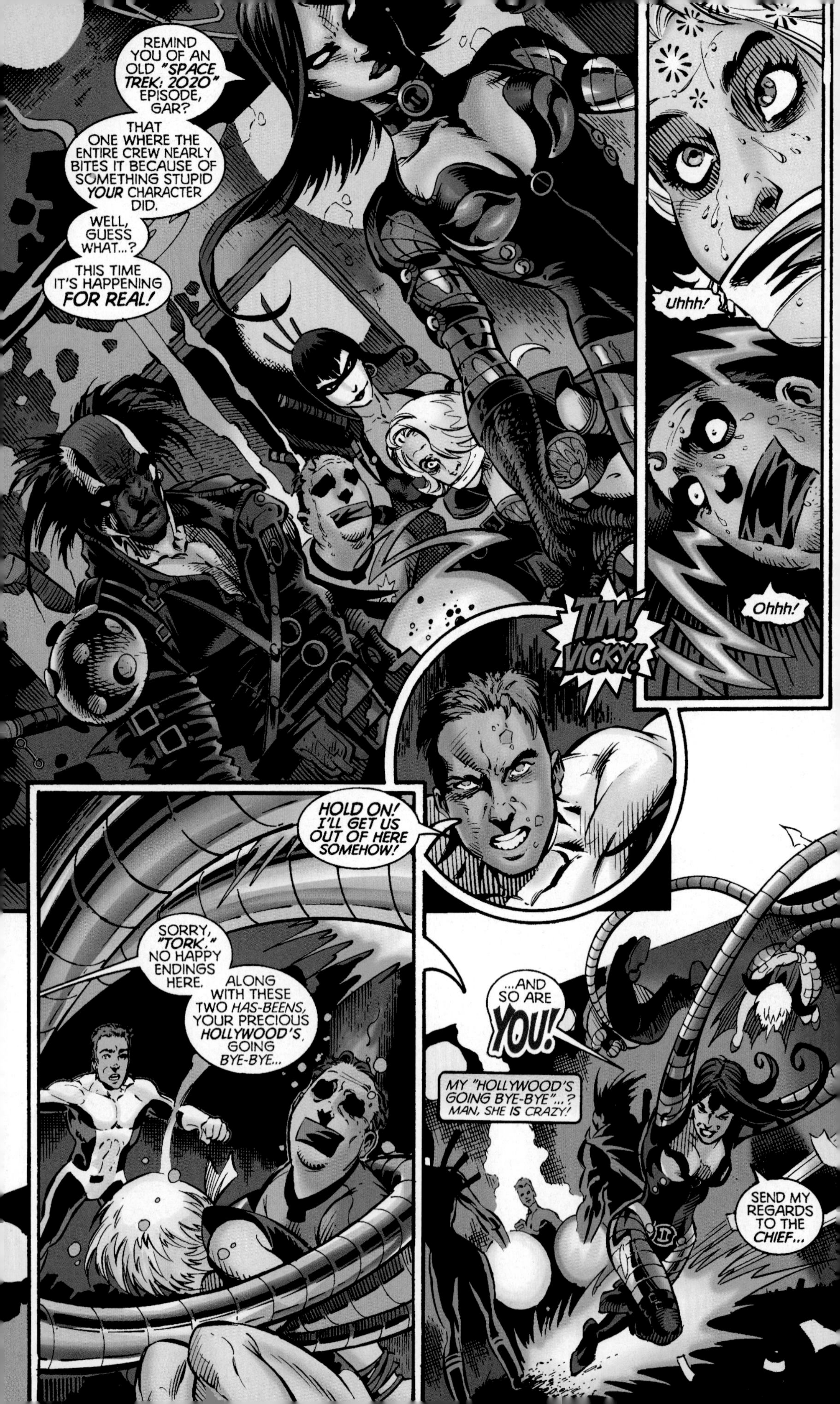

REMIND YOU OF AN OLD "SPACE TREK: 2020" EPISODE, GAR?
THAT ONE WHERE THE ENTIRE CREW NEARLY BITES IT BECAUSE OF SOMETHING STUPID YOUR CHARACTER DID.
WELL, GUESS WHAT...?
THIS TIME IT'S HAPPENING FOR REAL!
Uhhh!
Ohhh!
TIM! VICKY!
HOLD ON! I'LL GET US OUT OF HERE SOMEHOW!
SORRY, "TORK." NO HAPPY ENDINGS HERE.
ALONG WITH THESE TWO HAS-BEENS, YOUR PRECIOUS HOLLYWOOD'S GOING BYE-BYE...
...AND SO ARE YOU!
MY "HOLLYWOOD'S GOING BYE-BYE"...? MAN, SHE IS CRAZY!
SEND MY REGARDS TO THE CHIEF...

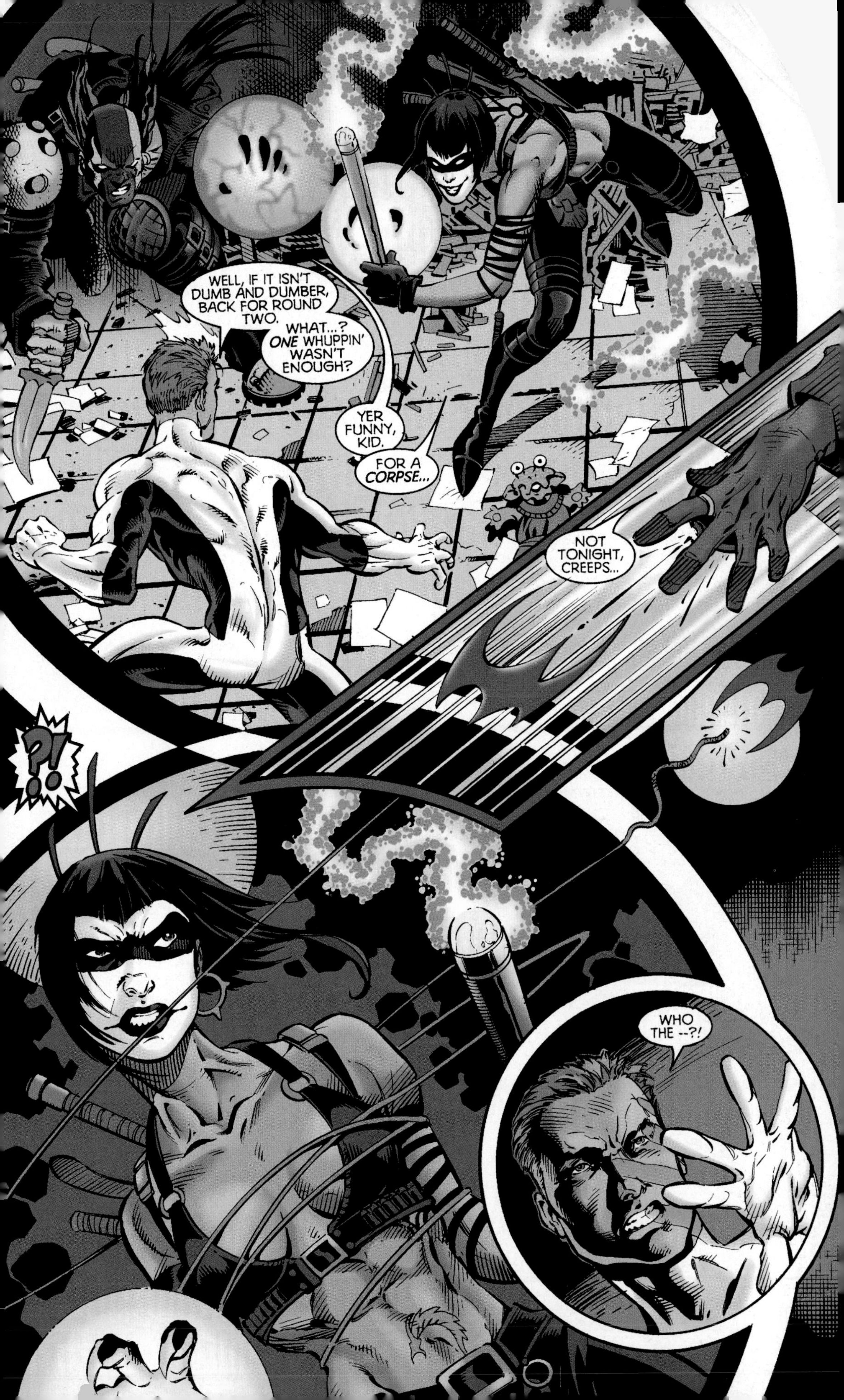
WELL, IF IT ISN'T DUMB AND DUMBER, BACK FOR ROUND TWO.
WHAT...? ONE WHUPPIN' WASN'T ENOUGH?
YER FUNNY, KID.
FOR A CORPSE...
NOT TONIGHT, CREEPS...
?!
WHO THE --?!

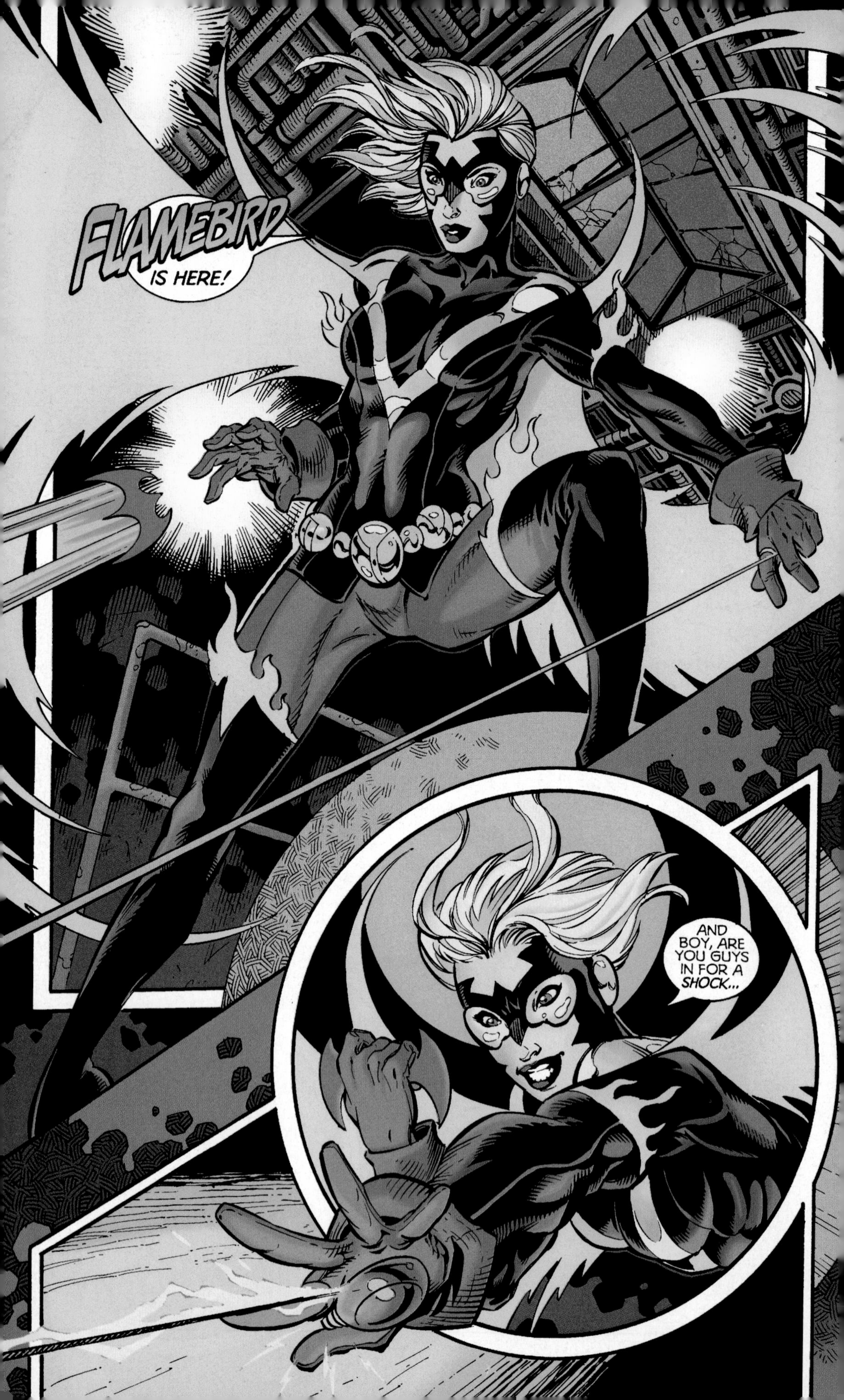
FLAMEBIRD
IS HERE!
AND BOY, ARE YOU GUYS IN FOR A SHOCK...

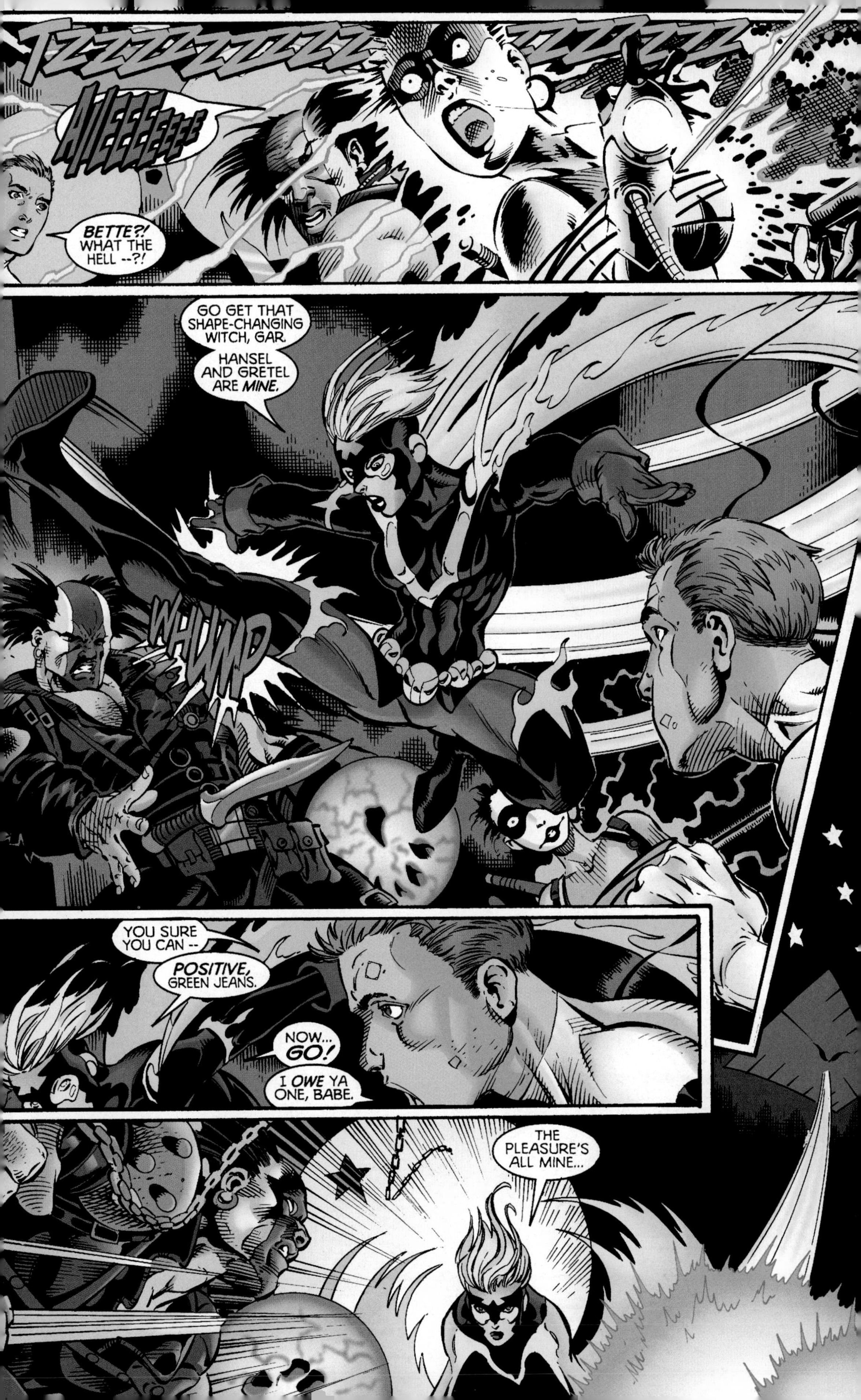
TZZZZZZZZZZZZZZZZZZZZZ
AIEEEEEeee
BETTE?! WHAT THE HELL --?!
GO GET THAT SHAPE-CHANGING WITCH, GAR.
HANSEL AND GRETEL ARE MINE.
WHUMP
YOU SURE YOU CAN --
POSITIVE, GREEN JEANS.
NOW... GO!
I OWE YA ONE, BABE.
THE PLEASURE'S ALL MINE...

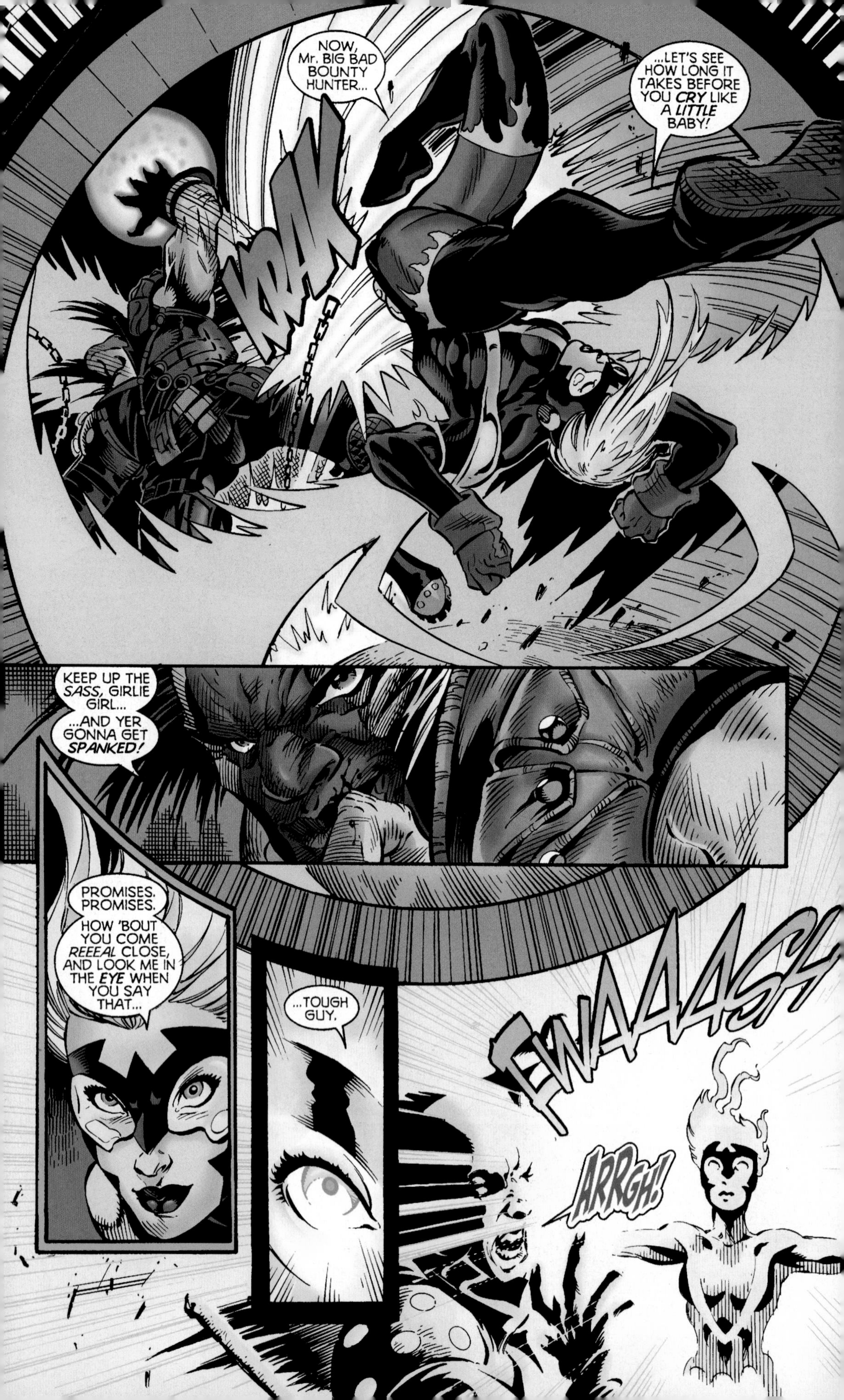
NOW, Mr. BIG BAD BOUNTY HUNTER...
...LET'S SEE HOW LONG IT TAKES BEFORE YOU *CRY* LIKE A *LITTLE* BABY!
KRAK
KEEP UP THE *SASS,* GIRLIE GIRL...
...AND YER GONNA GET *SPANKED!*
PROMISES. PROMISES.
HOW 'BOUT YOU COME *REEEAL* CLOSE, AND LOOK ME IN THE *EYE* WHEN YOU SAY THAT...
...TOUGH GUY.
FWAAASH
ARRGH!

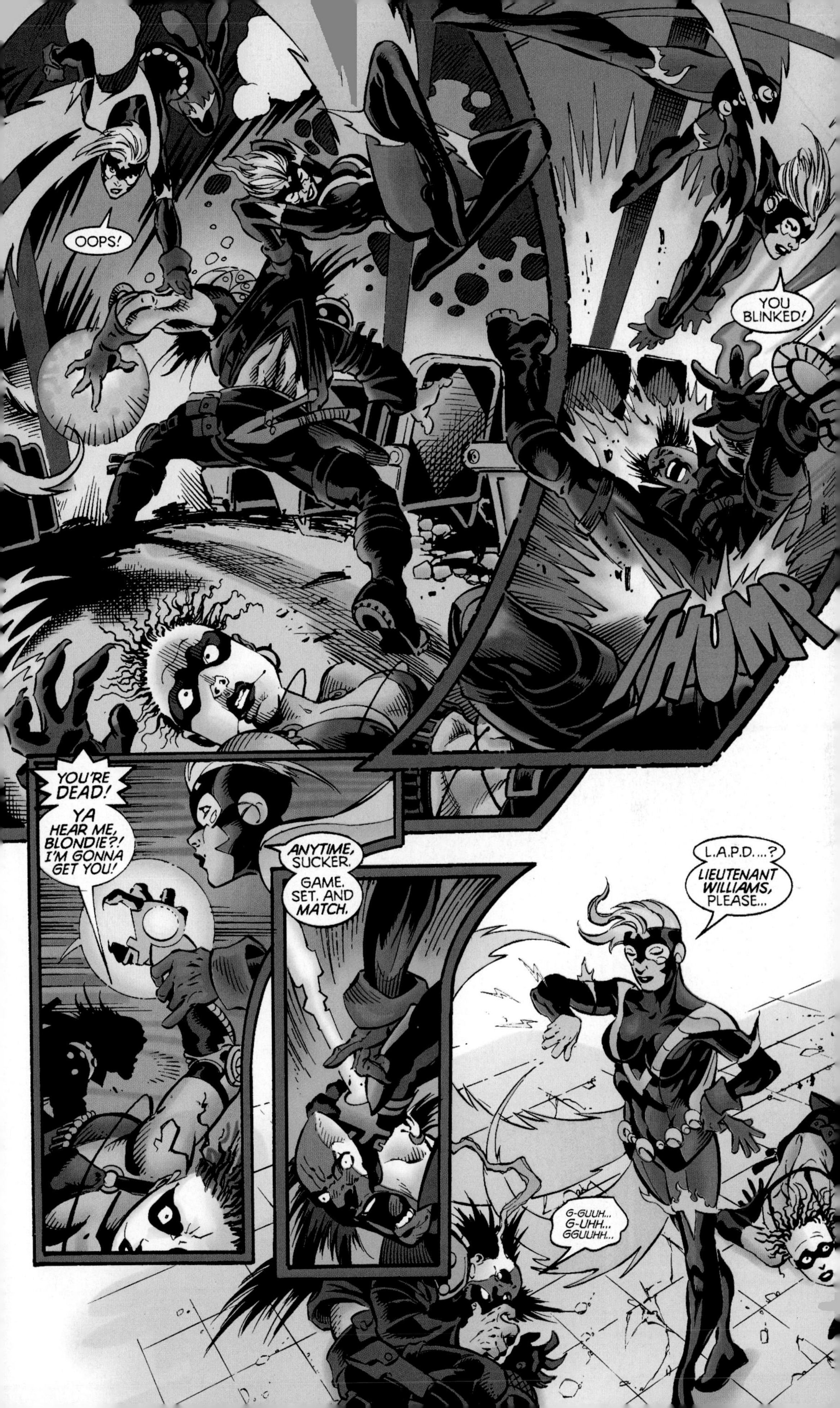
OOPS!
YOU BLINKED!
THUMP
YOU'RE DEAD!
YA HEAR ME, BLONDIE?! I'M GONNA GET YOU!
ANYTIME, SUCKER.
GAME. SET. AND MATCH.
L.A.P.D....?
LIEUTENANT WILLIAMS, PLEASE...
G-GUUH... G-UHH... GGUUHH...

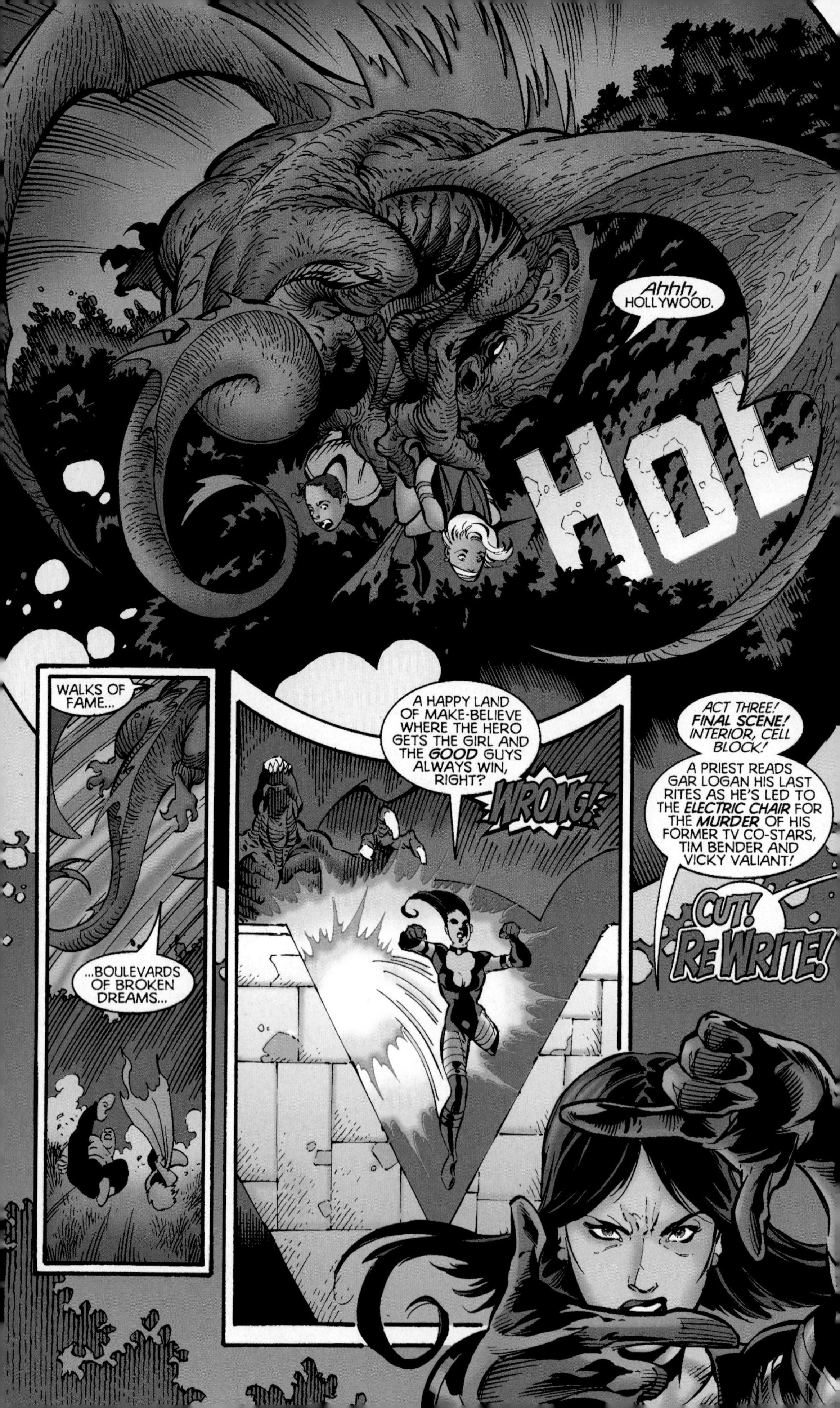

Ahhh, HOLLYWOOD.
HOL
WALKS OF FAME...
...BOULEVARDS OF BROKEN DREAMS...
A HAPPY LAND OF MAKE-BELIEVE WHERE THE HERO GETS THE GIRL AND THE GOOD GUYS ALWAYS WIN, RIGHT?
WRONG!
ACT THREE! FINAL SCENE! INTERIOR, CELL BLOCK!
A PRIEST READS GAR LOGAN HIS LAST RITES AS HE'S LED TO THE ELECTRIC CHAIR FOR THE MURDER OF HIS FORMER TV CO-STARS, TIM BENDER AND VICKY VALIANT!
CUT! RE-WRITE!

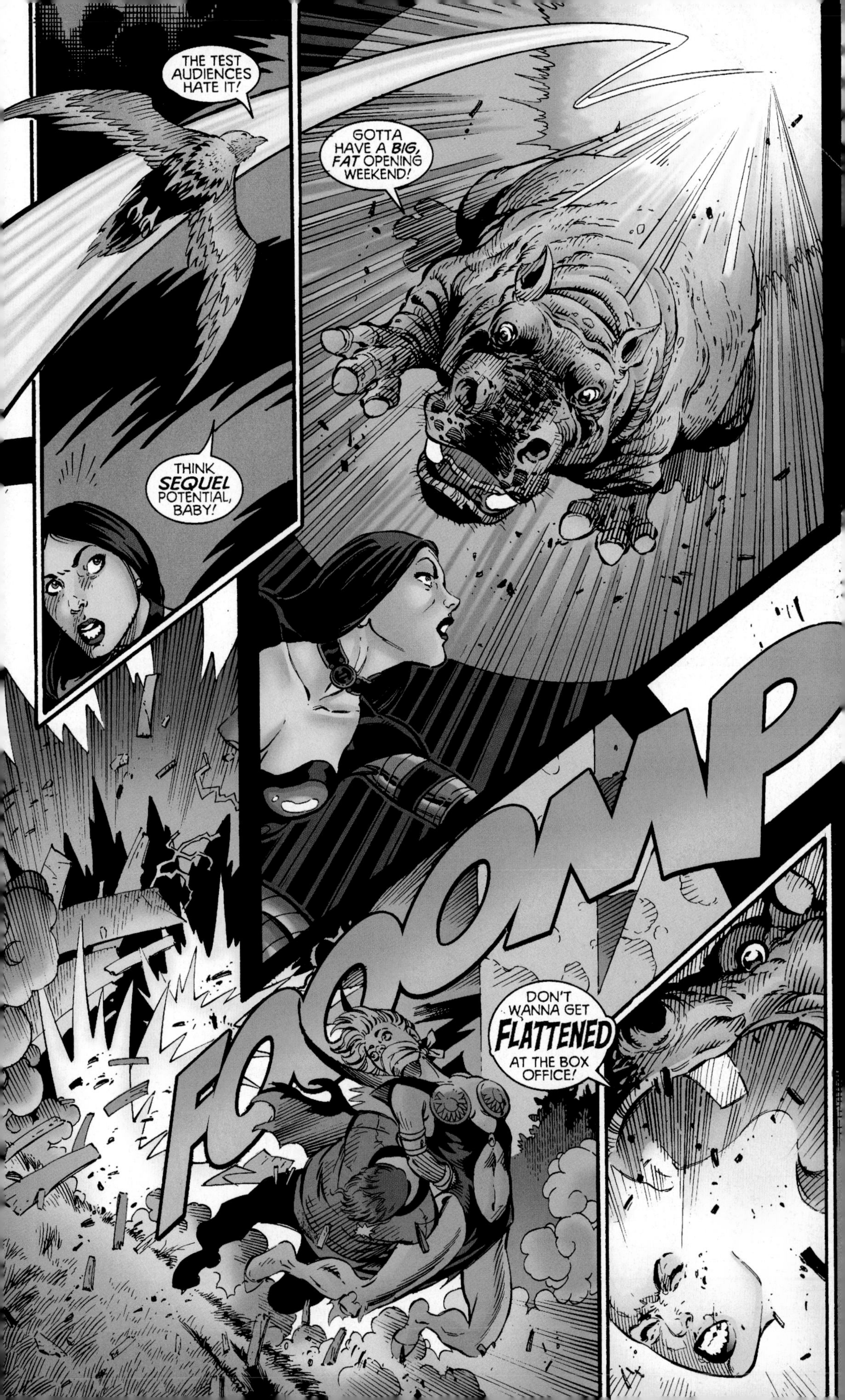

THE TEST AUDIENCES HATE IT!
GOTTA HAVE A BIG, FAT OPENING WEEKEND!
THINK SEQUEL POTENTIAL, BABY!
FOOOMP
DON'T WANNA GET FLATTENED AT THE BOX OFFICE!

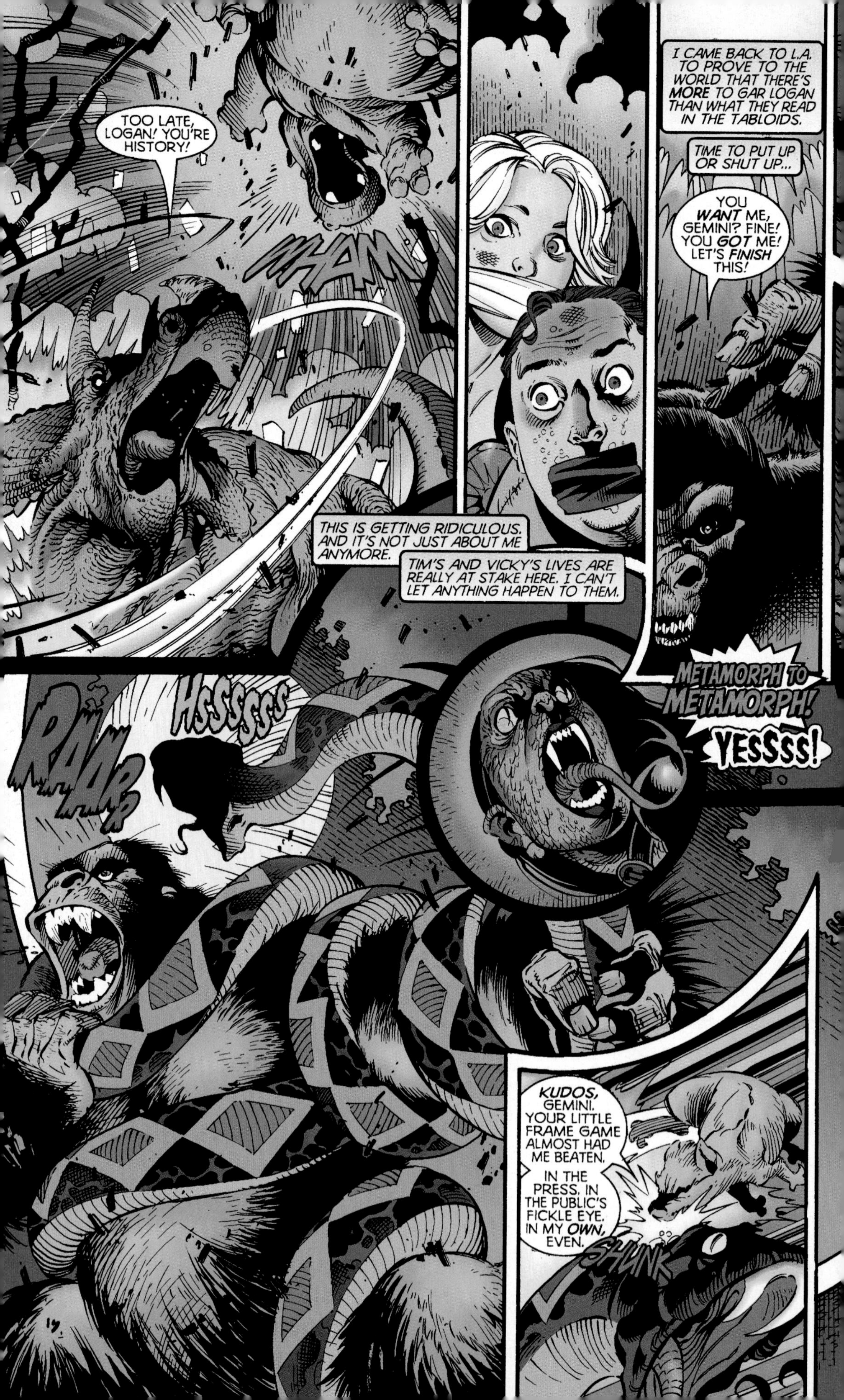
TOO LATE, LOGAN! YOU'RE HISTORY!
WHAM
I CAME BACK TO L.A. TO PROVE TO THE WORLD THAT THERE'S MORE TO GAR LOGAN THAN WHAT THEY READ IN THE TABLOIDS.
TIME TO PUT UP OR SHUT UP...
YOU WANT ME, GEMINI!? FINE! YOU GOT ME! LET'S FINISH THIS!
THIS IS GETTING RIDICULOUS. AND IT'S NOT JUST ABOUT ME ANYMORE.
TIM'S AND VICKY'S LIVES ARE REALLY AT STAKE HERE. I CAN'T LET ANYTHING HAPPEN TO THEM.
RAARR
HSSSSSS
METAMORPH TO METAMORPH!
YESSSS!
KUDOS, GEMINI. YOUR LITTLE FRAME GAME ALMOST HAD ME BEATEN.
IN THE PRESS. IN THE PUBLIC'S FICKLE EYE. IN MY OWN, EVEN.
SHUNK

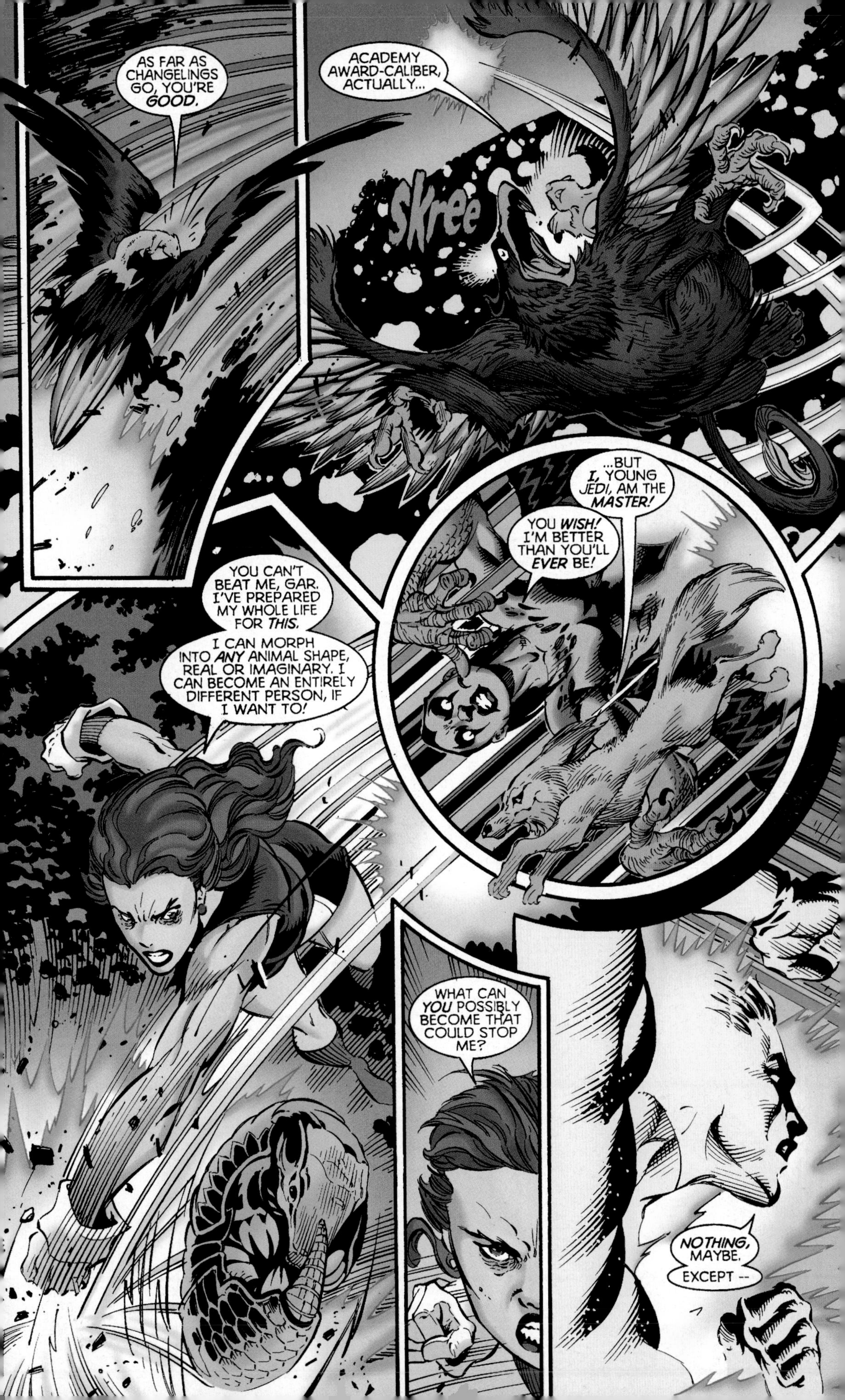
AS FAR AS CHANGELINGS GO, YOU'RE GOOD.
ACADEMY AWARD-CALIBER, ACTUALLY...
SKREE
...BUT I, YOUNG JEDI, AM THE MASTER!
YOU WISH! I'M BETTER THAN YOU'LL EVER BE!
YOU CAN'T BEAT ME, GAR. I'VE PREPARED MY WHOLE LIFE FOR THIS.
I CAN MORPH INTO ANY ANIMAL SHAPE, REAL OR IMAGINARY. I CAN BECOME AN ENTIRELY DIFFERENT PERSON, IF I WANT TO!
WHAT CAN YOU POSSIBLY BECOME THAT COULD STOP ME?
NOTHING, MAYBE.
EXCEPT --

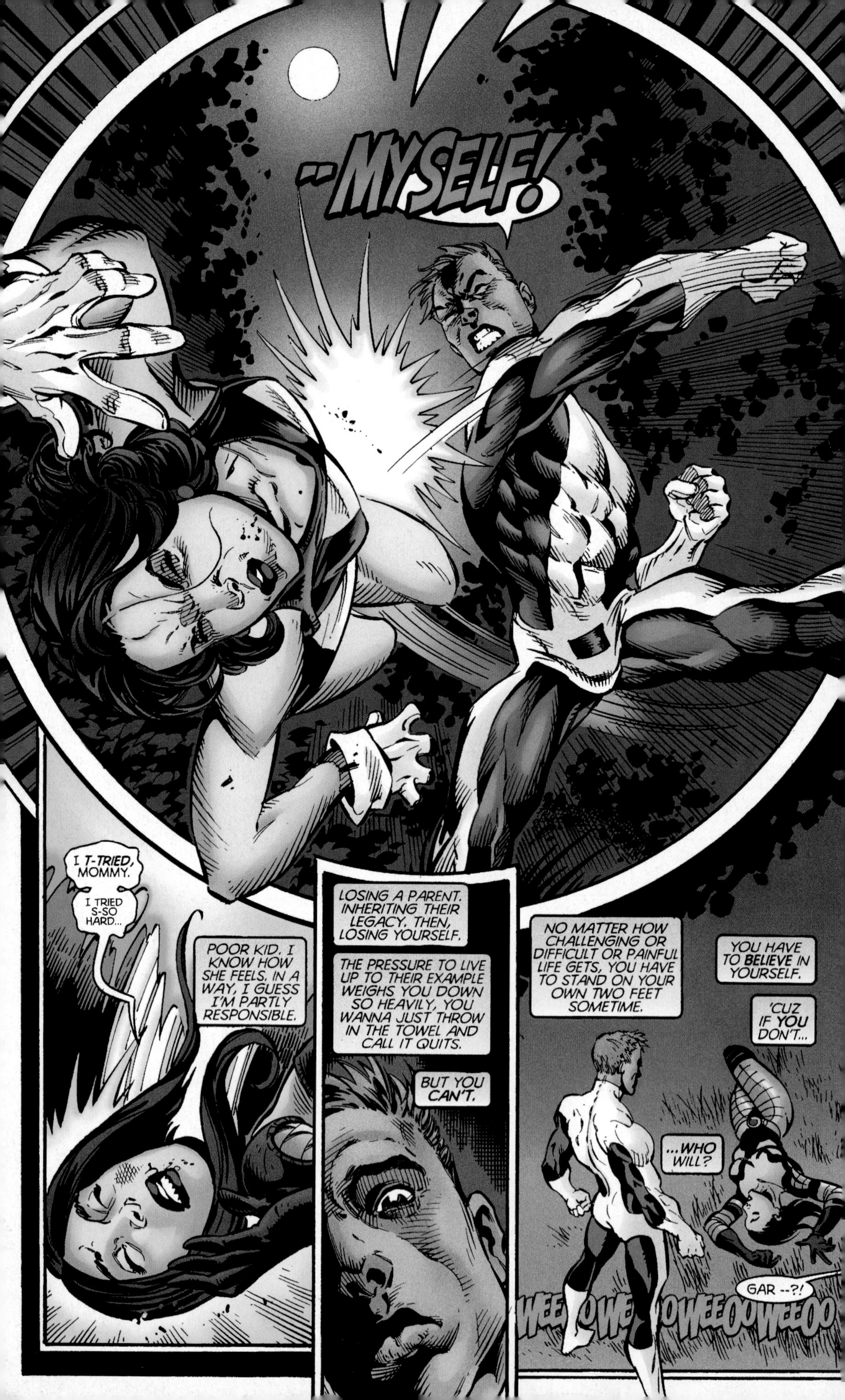
--MYSELF!
I T-TRIED, MOMMY.
I TRIED S-SO HARD...
POOR KID. I KNOW HOW SHE FEELS. IN A WAY, I GUESS I'M PARTLY RESPONSIBLE.
LOSING A PARENT. INHERITING THEIR LEGACY. THEN, LOSING YOURSELF.
THE PRESSURE TO LIVE UP TO THEIR EXAMPLE WEIGHS YOU DOWN SO HEAVILY, YOU WANNA JUST THROW IN THE TOWEL AND CALL IT QUITS.
BUT YOU CAN'T.
NO MATTER HOW CHALLENGING OR DIFFICULT OR PAINFUL LIFE GETS, YOU HAVE TO STAND ON YOUR OWN TWO FEET SOMETIME.
YOU HAVE TO BELIEVE IN YOURSELF.
'CUZ IF YOU DON'T...
...WHO WILL?
GAR --?!

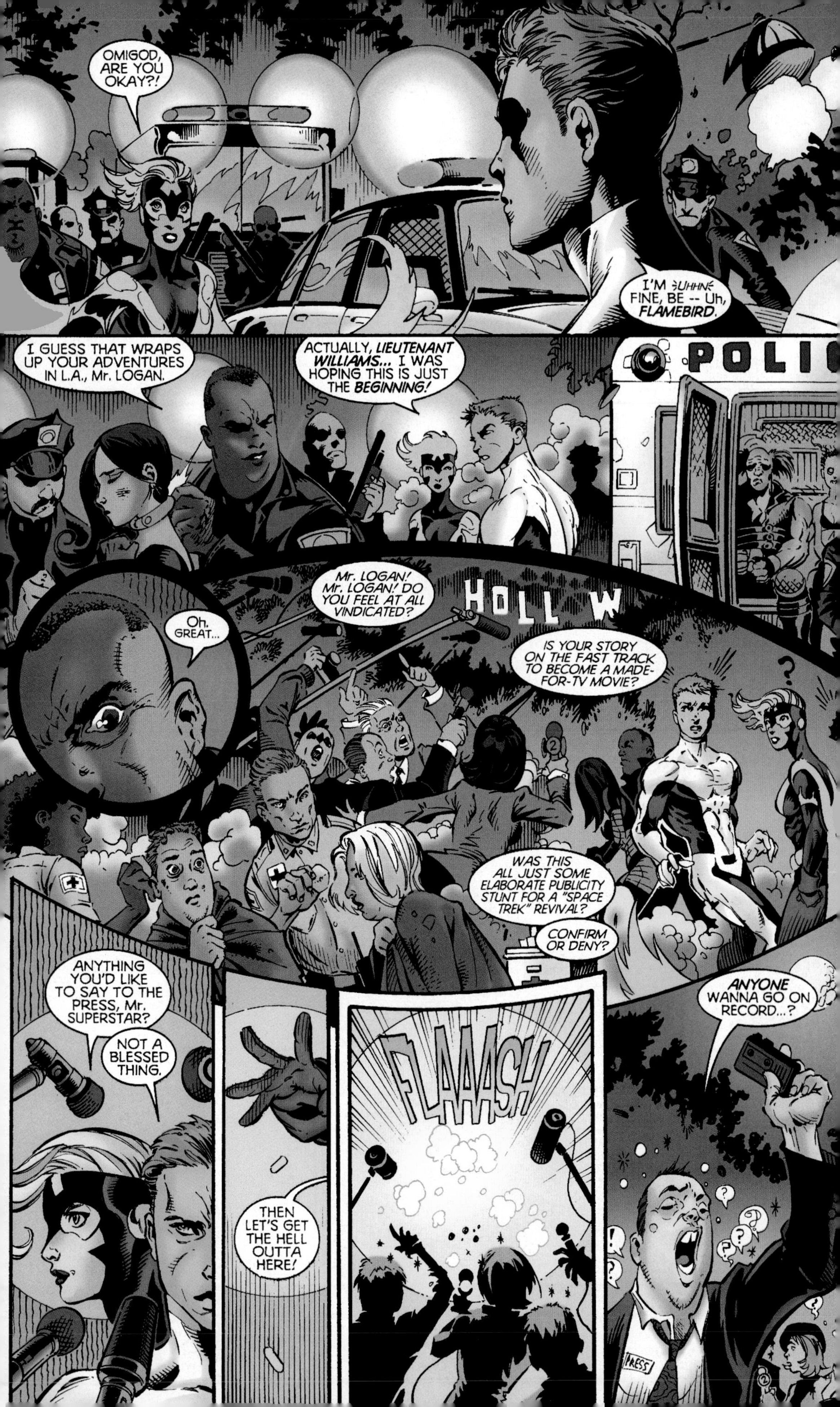
OMIGOD, ARE YOU OKAY?!
I'M UHHN FINE, BE -- Uh, FLAMEBIRD.
I GUESS THAT WRAPS UP YOUR ADVENTURES IN L.A., Mr. LOGAN.
ACTUALLY, LIEUTENANT WILLIAMS... I WAS HOPING THIS IS JUST THE BEGINNING!
POLI
Oh. GREAT...
Mr. LOGAN! Mr. LOGAN! DO YOU FEEL AT ALL VINDICATED?
HOLL W
IS YOUR STORY ON THE FAST TRACK TO BECOME A MADE-FOR-TV MOVIE?
WAS THIS ALL JUST SOME ELABORATE PUBLICITY STUNT FOR A "SPACE TREK" REVIVAL?
CONFIRM OR DENY?
ANYTHING YOU'D LIKE TO SAY TO THE PRESS, Mr. SUPERSTAR?
NOT A BLESSED THING.
THEN LET'S GET THE HELL OUTTA HERE!
FLAAASH
ANYONE WANNA GO ON RECORD...?
PRESS

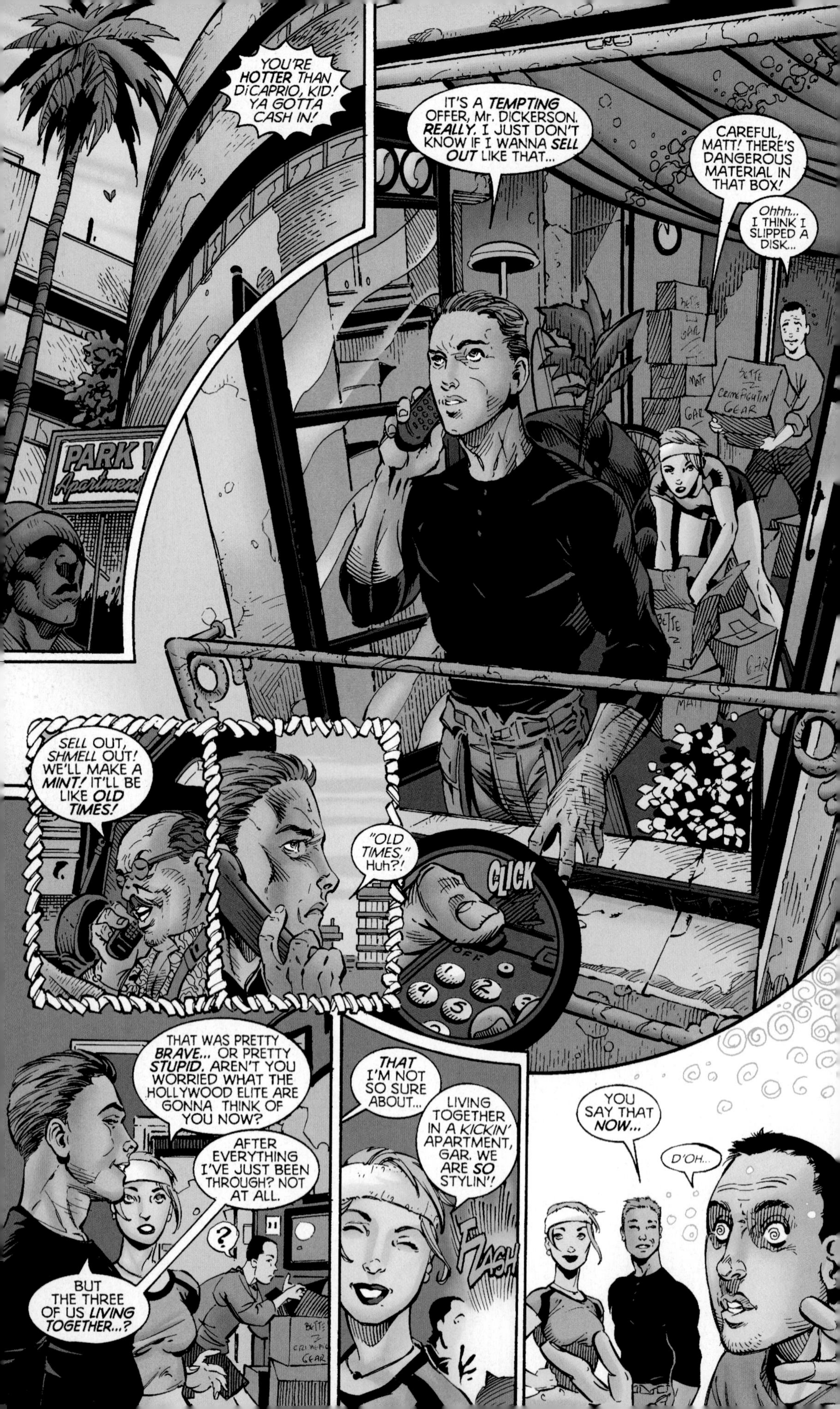

YOU'RE HOTTER THAN DiCAPRIO, KID! YA GOTTA CASH IN!
IT'S A TEMPTING OFFER, Mr. DICKERSON. REALLY. I JUST DON'T KNOW IF I WANNA SELL OUT LIKE THAT...
CAREFUL, MATT! THERE'S DANGEROUS MATERIAL IN THAT BOX!
Ohhh... I THINK I SLIPPED A DISK...
PARK
Apartment
BETTE
GAR
MATT
BETTE 2 CRIMEFIGHTIN' GEAR
SELL OUT, SHMELL OUT! WE'LL MAKE A MINT! IT'LL BE LIKE OLD TIMES!
"OLD TIMES," Huh?!
CLICK
OFF
THAT WAS PRETTY BRAVE... OR PRETTY STUPID. AREN'T YOU WORRIED WHAT THE HOLLYWOOD ELITE ARE GONNA THINK OF YOU NOW?
AFTER EVERYTHING I'VE JUST BEEN THROUGH? NOT AT ALL.
BUT THE THREE OF US LIVING TOGETHER...?
?
THAT I'M NOT SO SURE ABOUT...
LIVING TOGETHER IN A KICKIN' APARTMENT, GAR, WE ARE SO STYLIN'!
FLASH
YOU SAY THAT NOW...
D'OH...

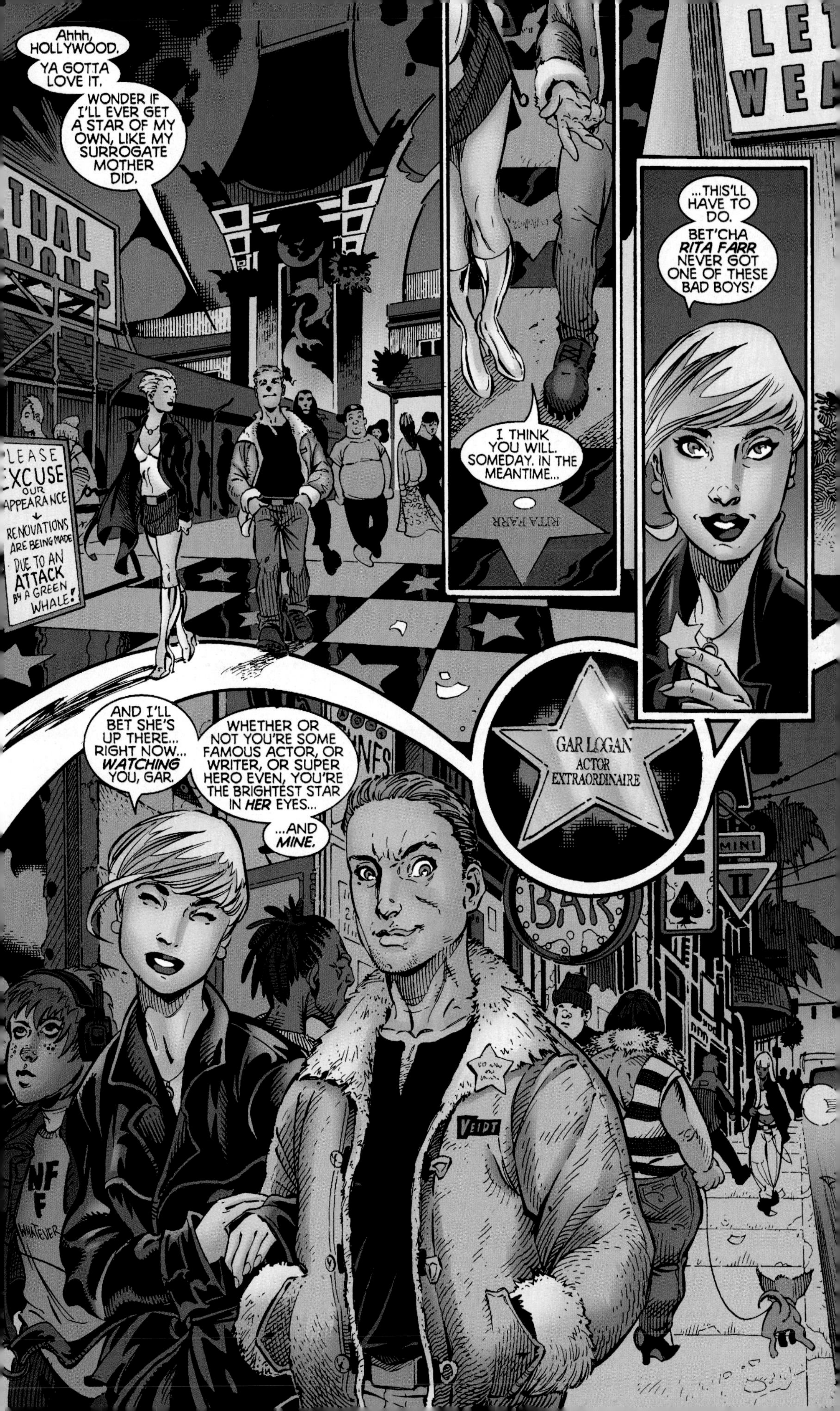

Ahhh, HOLLYWOOD.
YA GOTTA LOVE IT.
WONDER IF I'LL EVER GET A STAR OF MY OWN, LIKE MY SURROGATE MOTHER DID.
LEASE EXCUSE OUR APPEARANCE RENOVATIONS ARE BEING MADE DUE TO AN ATTACK BY A GREEN WHALE!
I THINK YOU WILL. SOMEDAY. IN THE MEANTIME...
RITA FARR
...THIS'LL HAVE TO DO. BET'CHA RITA FARR NEVER GOT ONE OF THESE BAD BOYS!
GAR LOGAN ACTOR EXTRAORDINAIRE
AND I'LL BET SHE'S UP THERE... RIGHT NOW... WATCHING YOU, GAR.
WHETHER OR NOT YOU'RE SOME FAMOUS ACTOR, OR WRITER, OR SUPER HERO EVEN, YOU'RE THE BRIGHTEST STAR IN HER EYES...
...AND MINE.
BAR
VEIDT
NF F WHATEVER

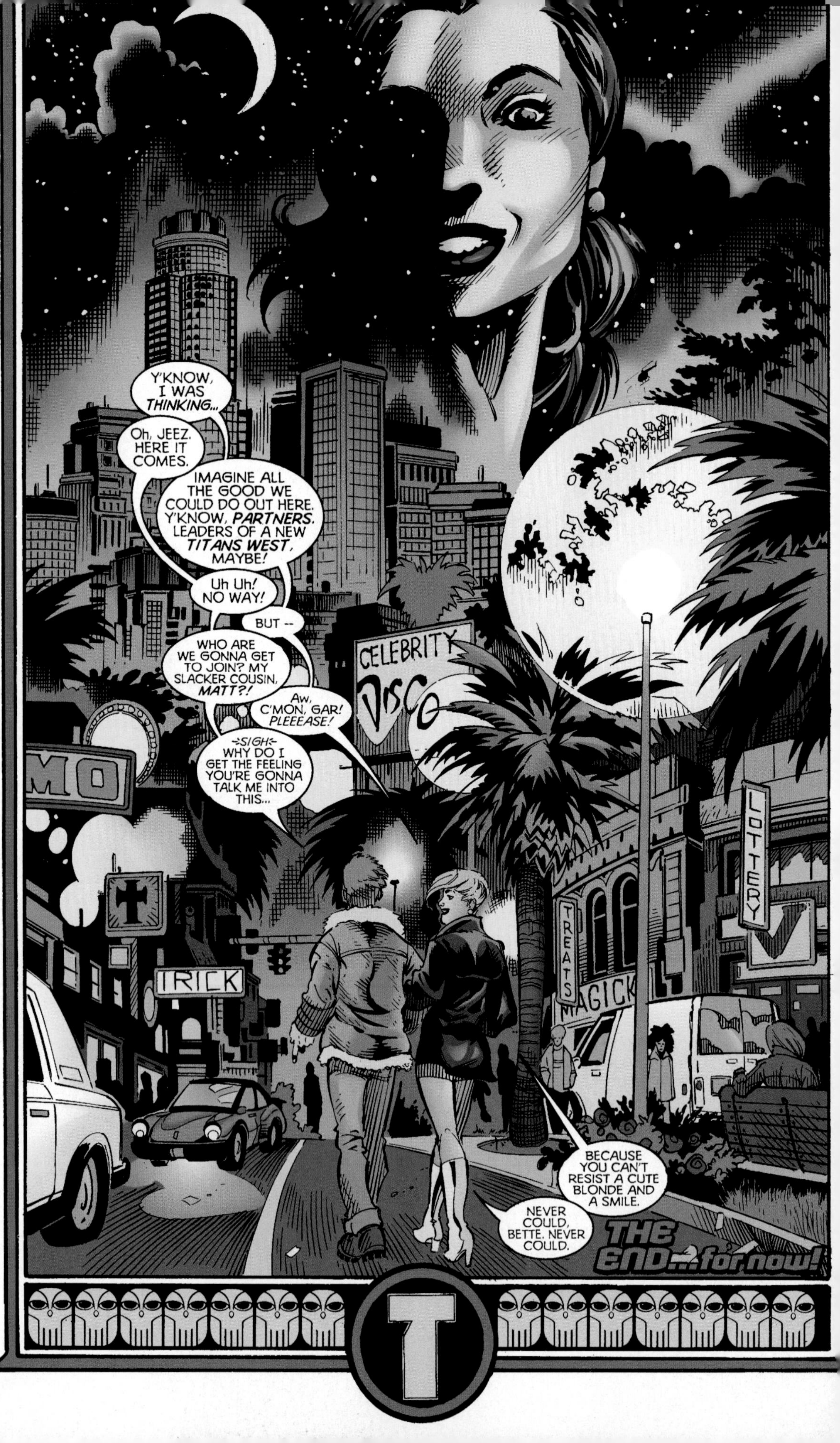
Y'KNOW, I WAS THINKING...
Oh, JEEZ. HERE IT COMES.
IMAGINE ALL THE GOOD WE COULD DO OUT HERE. Y'KNOW, PARTNERS. LEADERS OF A NEW TITANS WEST, MAYBE!
Uh Uh! NO WAY!
BUT --
WHO ARE WE GONNA GET TO JOIN? MY SLACKER COUSIN, MATT?!
AW, C'MON, GAR! PLEEEASE!
-SIGH- WHY DO I GET THE FEELING YOU'RE GONNA TALK ME INTO THIS...
BECAUSE YOU CAN'T RESIST A CUTE BLONDE AND A SMILE.
NEVER COULD, BETTE. NEVER COULD.
CELEBRITY DISCO
MO
IRICK
TREATS
MAGICK
LOTTERY
THE END... for now!

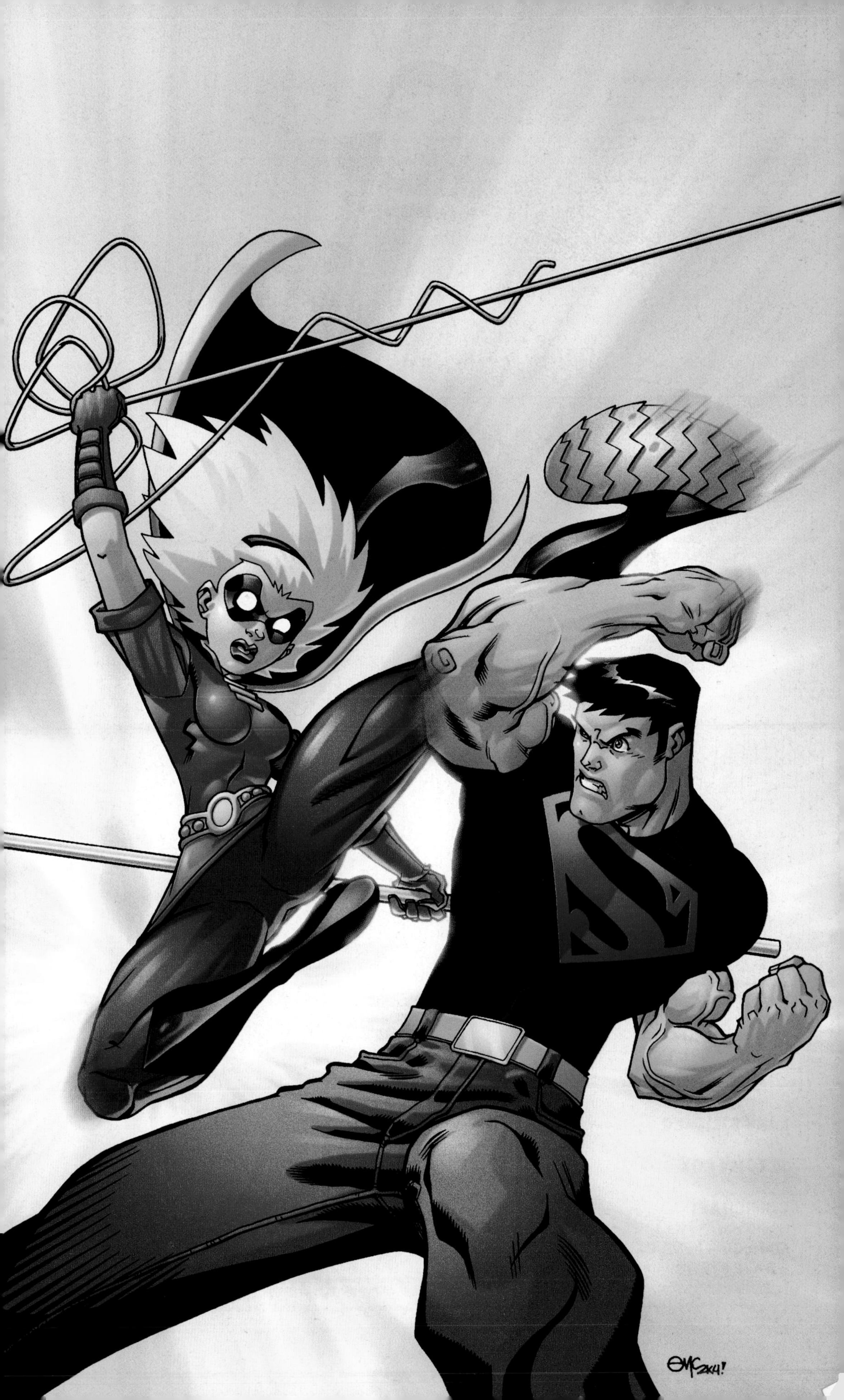

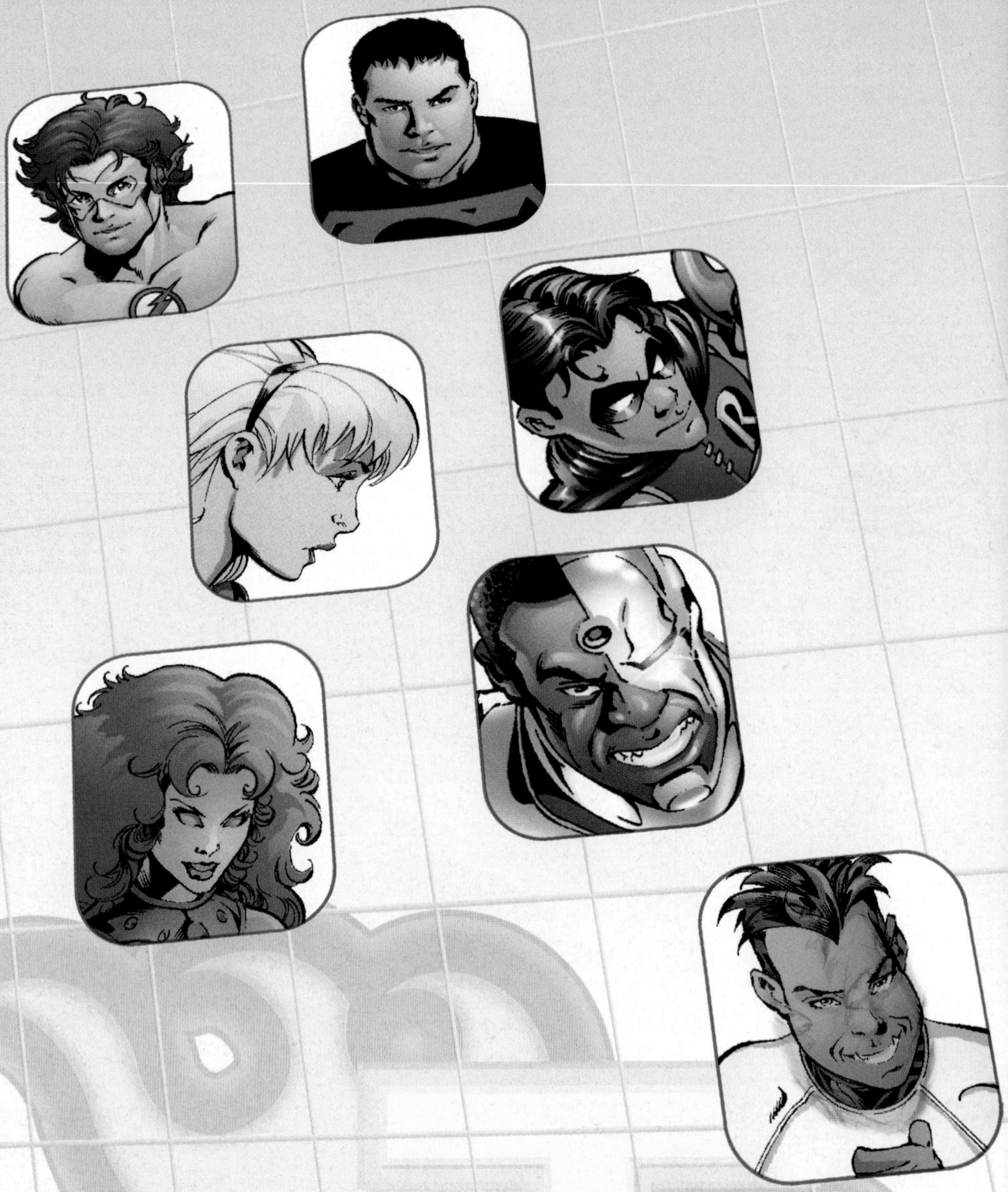

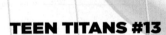

TEEN TITANS #13

GEOFF JOHNS
Writer

TOM GRUMMETT
Penciller

LARY STUCKER
Inker

JEROMY COX
Colorist

COMICRAFT
Letterer

ED McGUINNESS, DEXTER VINES & DAVE STEWART
Cover Artists

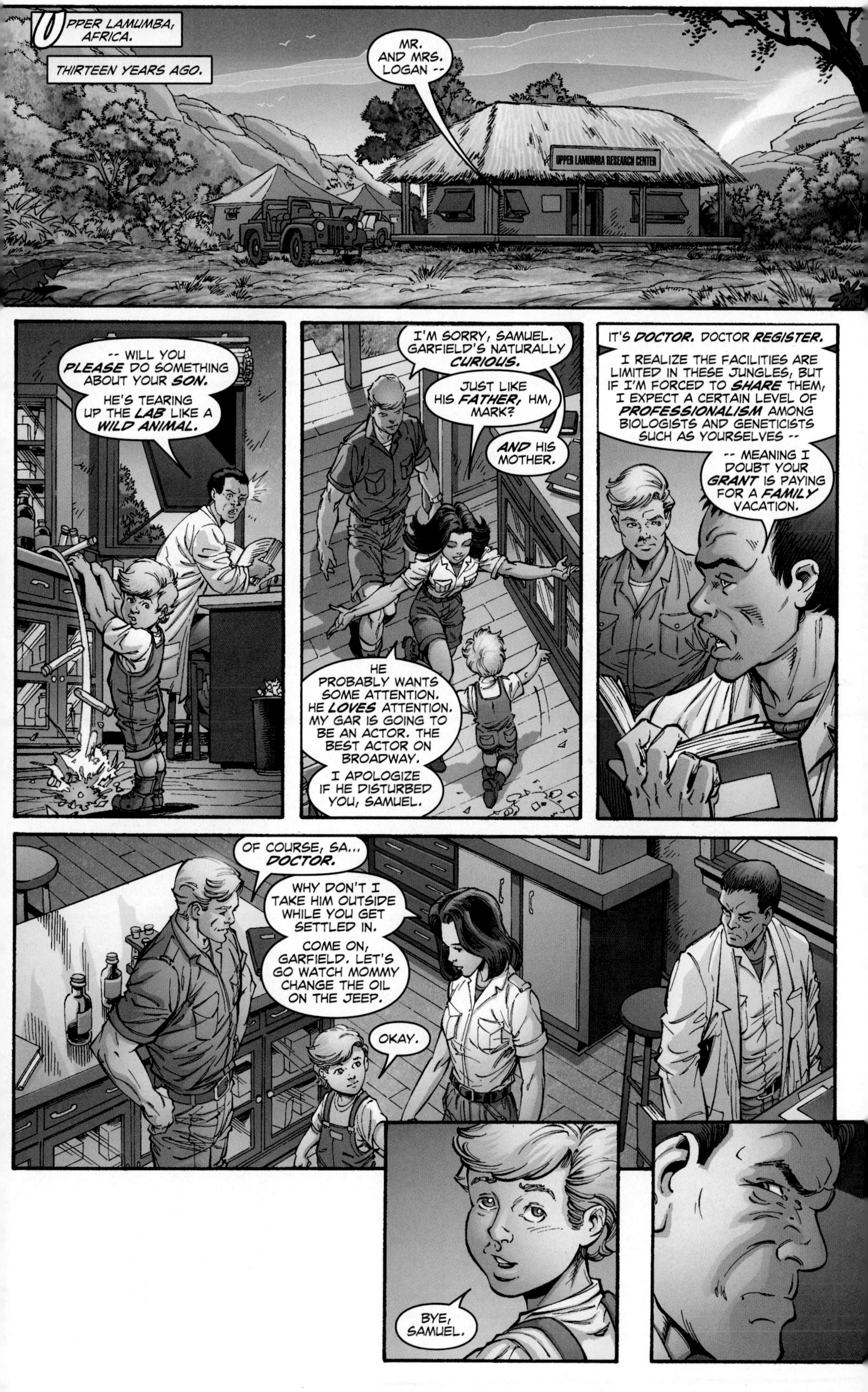
UPPER LAMUMBA, AFRICA.
THIRTEEN YEARS AGO.
MR. AND MRS. LOGAN --
UPPER LAMUMBA RESEARCH CENTER
-- WILL YOU PLEASE DO SOMETHING ABOUT YOUR SON.
HE'S TEARING UP THE LAB LIKE A WILD ANIMAL.
I'M SORRY, SAMUEL. GARFIELD'S NATURALLY CURIOUS.
JUST LIKE HIS FATHER, HM, MARK?
AND HIS MOTHER.
HE PROBABLY WANTS SOME ATTENTION. HE LOVES ATTENTION. MY GAR IS GOING TO BE AN ACTOR. THE BEST ACTOR ON BROADWAY.
I APOLOGIZE IF HE DISTURBED YOU, SAMUEL.
IT'S DOCTOR. DOCTOR REGISTER.
I REALIZE THE FACILITIES ARE LIMITED IN THESE JUNGLES, BUT IF I'M FORCED TO SHARE THEM, I EXPECT A CERTAIN LEVEL OF PROFESSIONALISM AMONG BIOLOGISTS AND GENETICISTS SUCH AS YOURSELVES --
-- MEANING I DOUBT YOUR GRANT IS PAYING FOR A FAMILY VACATION.
OF COURSE, SA... DOCTOR.
WHY DON'T I TAKE HIM OUTSIDE WHILE YOU GET SETTLED IN.
COME ON, GARFIELD. LET'S GO WATCH MOMMY CHANGE THE OIL ON THE JEEP.
OKAY.
BYE, SAMUEL.

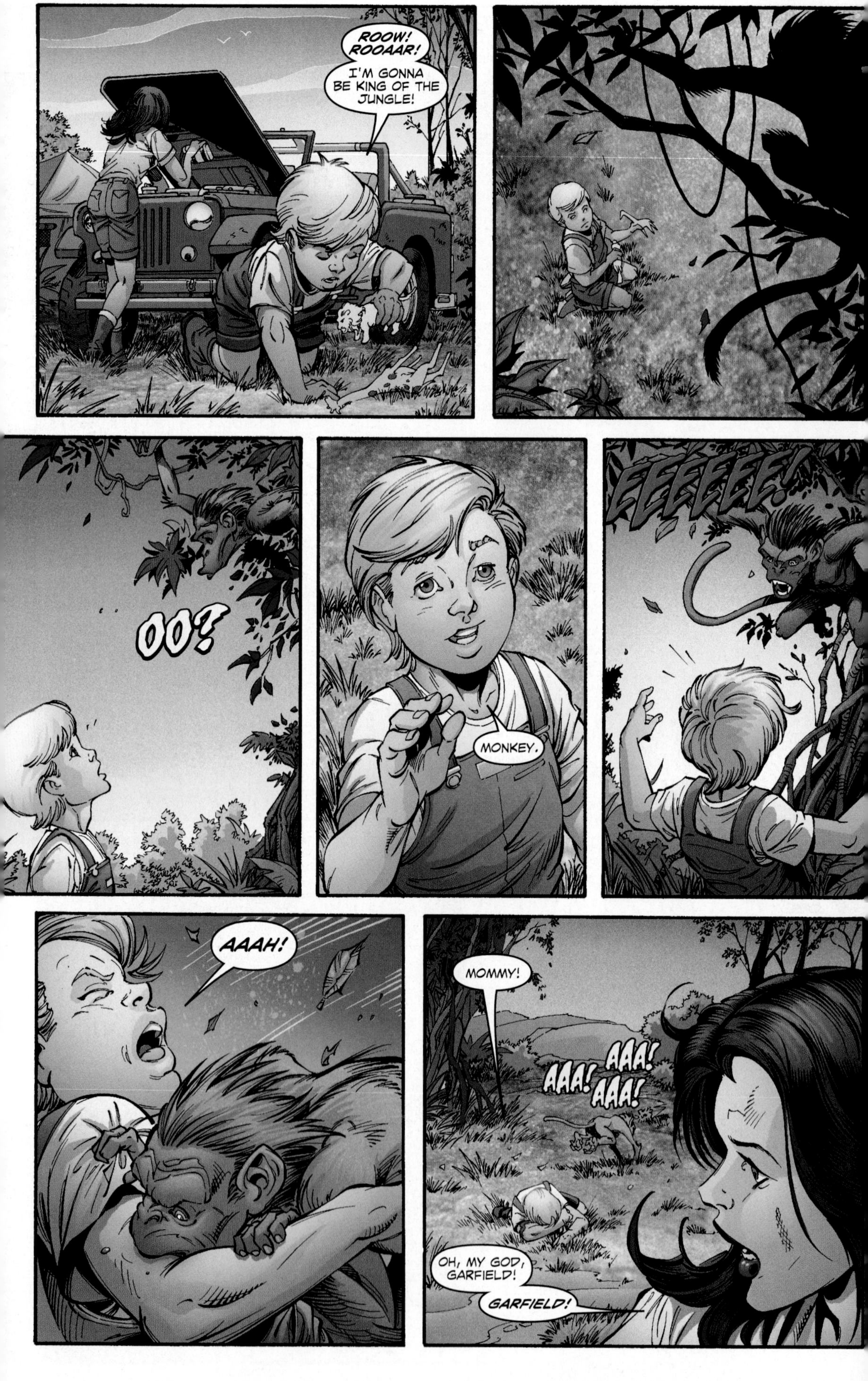
ROOW! ROOAAR!
I'M GONNA BE KING OF THE JUNGLE!
OO?
MONKEY.
EEEEEE!
AAAH!
MOMMY!
AAA! AAA! AAA!
OH, MY GOD, GARFIELD!
GARFIELD!

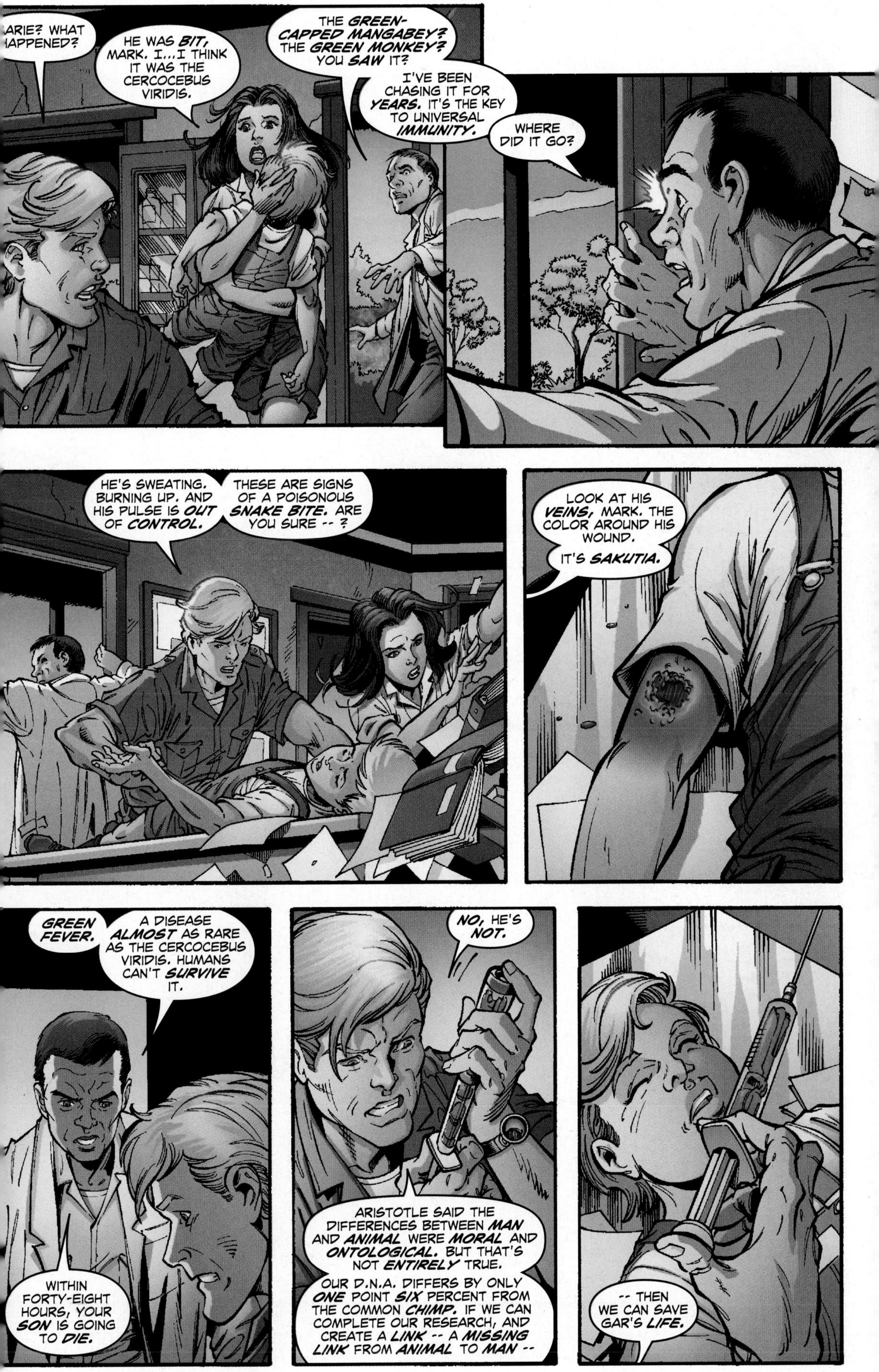

ARIE? WHAT
HAPPENED?
HE WAS BIT, MARK. I...I THINK IT WAS THE CERCOCEBUS VIRIDIS.
THE GREEN-CAPPED MANGABEY? THE GREEN MONKEY? YOU SAW IT?
I'VE BEEN CHASING IT FOR YEARS. IT'S THE KEY TO UNIVERSAL IMMUNITY.
WHERE DID IT GO?
HE'S SWEATING. BURNING UP. AND HIS PULSE IS OUT OF CONTROL.
THESE ARE SIGNS OF A POISONOUS SNAKE BITE. ARE YOU SURE -- ?
LOOK AT HIS VEINS, MARK. THE COLOR AROUND HIS WOUND.
IT'S SAKUTIA.
GREEN FEVER.
A DISEASE ALMOST AS RARE AS THE CERCOCEBUS VIRIDIS. HUMANS CAN'T SURVIVE IT.
WITHIN FORTY-EIGHT HOURS, YOUR SON IS GOING TO DIE.
NO, HE'S NOT.
ARISTOTLE SAID THE DIFFERENCES BETWEEN MAN AND ANIMAL WERE MORAL AND ONTOLOGICAL. BUT THAT'S NOT ENTIRELY TRUE.
OUR D.N.A. DIFFERS BY ONLY ONE POINT SIX PERCENT FROM THE COMMON CHIMP. IF WE CAN COMPLETE OUR RESEARCH, AND CREATE A LINK -- A MISSING LINK FROM ANIMAL TO MAN --
-- THEN WE CAN SAVE GAR'S LIFE.

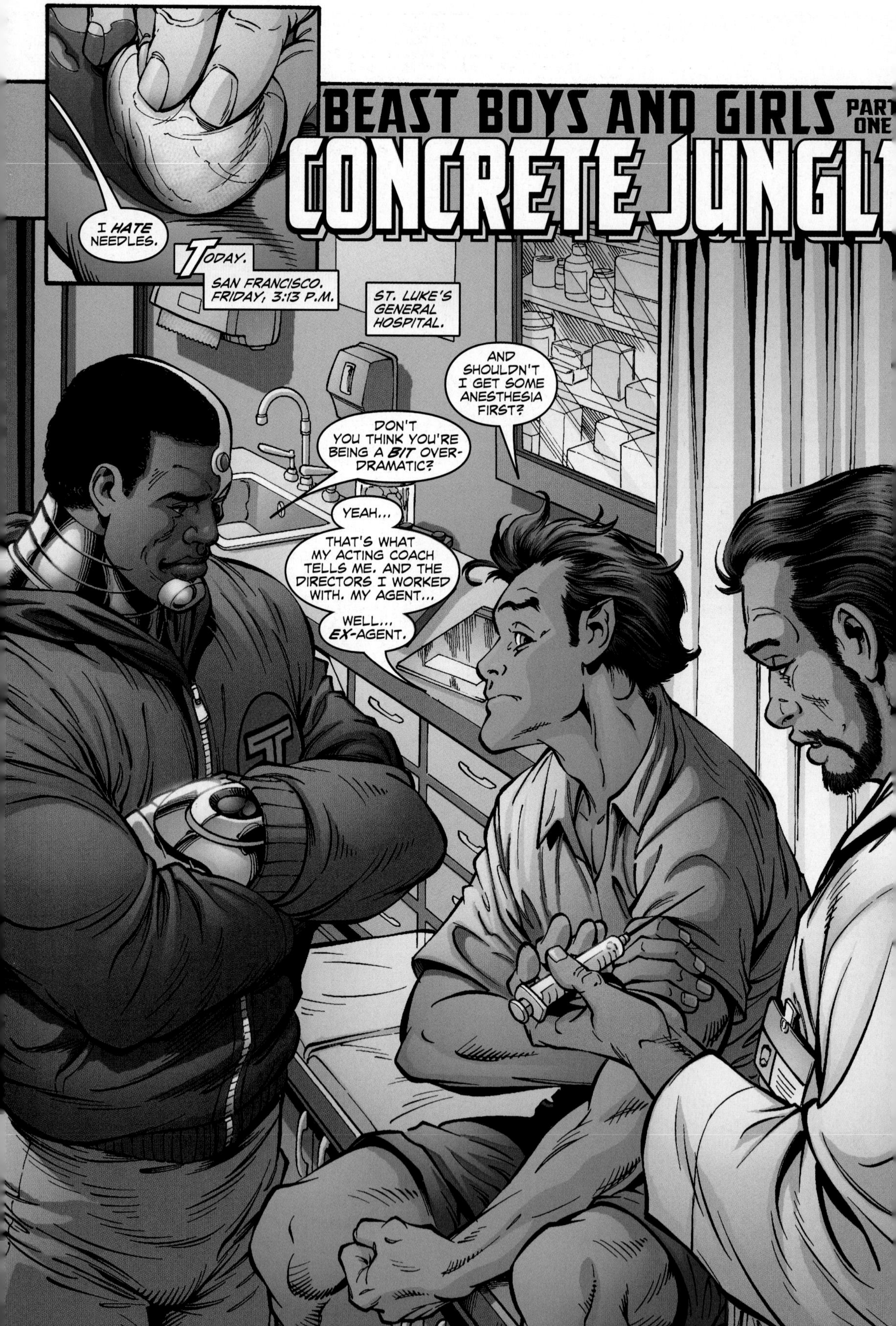
I HATE NEEDLES.
BEAST BOYS AND GIRLS PART ONE
CONCRETE JUNGLE
TODAY.
SAN FRANCISCO. FRIDAY, 3:13 P.M.
ST. LUKE'S GENERAL HOSPITAL.
AND SHOULDN'T I GET SOME ANESTHESIA FIRST?
DON'T YOU THINK YOU'RE BEING A BIT OVER-DRAMATIC?
YEAH...
THAT'S WHAT MY ACTING COACH TELLS ME. AND THE DIRECTORS I WORKED WITH. MY AGENT...
WELL... EX-AGENT.

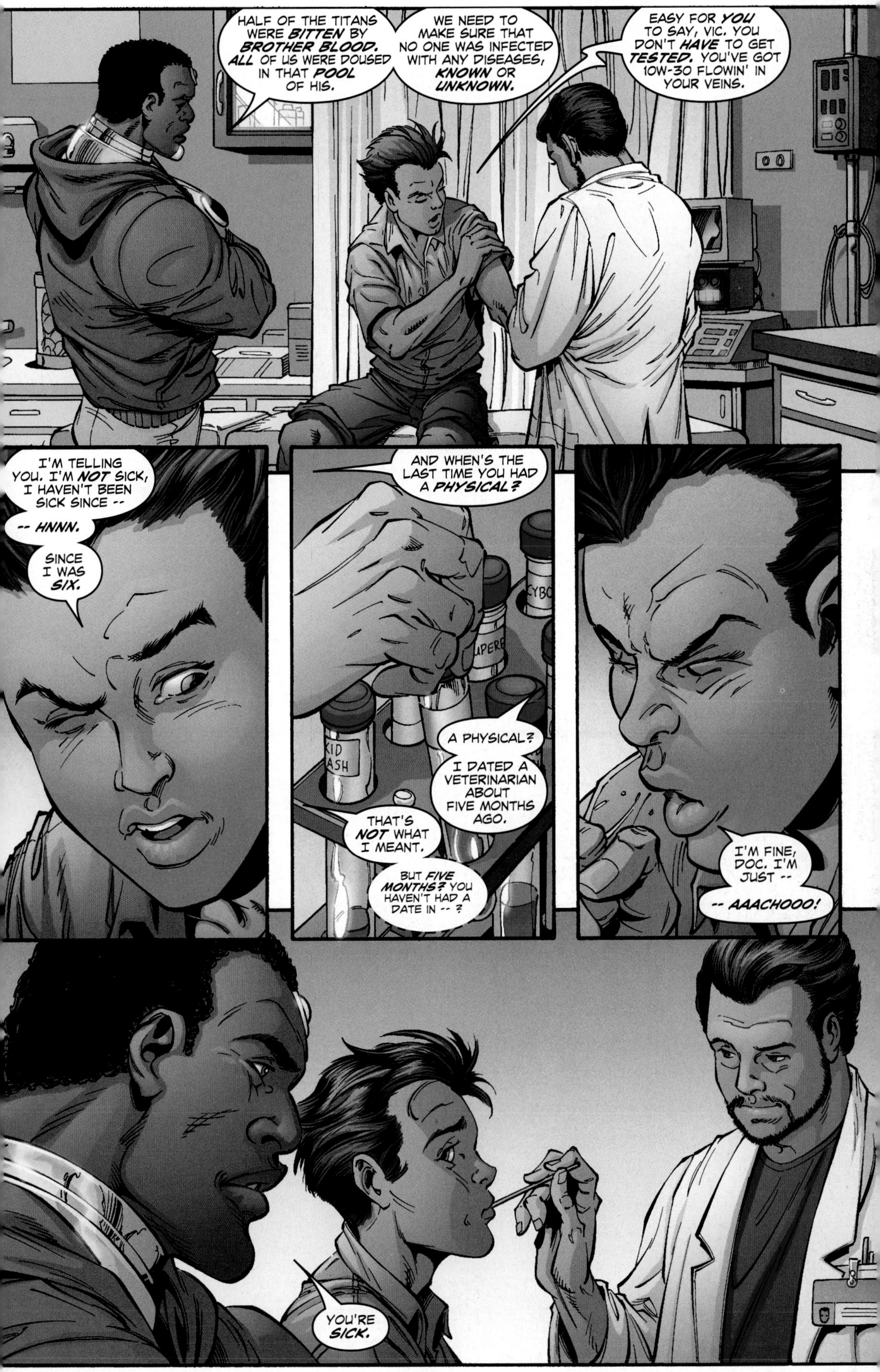

HALF OF THE TITANS WERE **BITTEN** BY **BROTHER BLOOD. ALL** OF US WERE DOUSED IN THAT **POOL** OF HIS.
WE NEED TO MAKE SURE THAT NO ONE WAS INFECTED WITH ANY DISEASES, **KNOWN** OR **UNKNOWN.**
EASY FOR **YOU** TO SAY, VIC. YOU DON'T **HAVE** TO GET **TESTED.** YOU'VE GOT 10W-30 FLOWIN' IN YOUR VEINS.
I'M TELLING YOU. I'M **NOT** SICK, I HAVEN'T BEEN SICK SINCE --
-- **HNNN.**
SINCE I WAS **SIX.**
AND WHEN'S THE LAST TIME YOU HAD A **PHYSICAL?**
A PHYSICAL?
I DATED A VETERINARIAN ABOUT FIVE MONTHS AGO.
THAT'S **NOT** WHAT I MEANT.
BUT **FIVE MONTHS?** YOU HAVEN'T HAD A DATE IN -- ?
I'M FINE, DOC. I'M JUST --
-- **AAACHOOO!**
YOU'RE **SICK.**

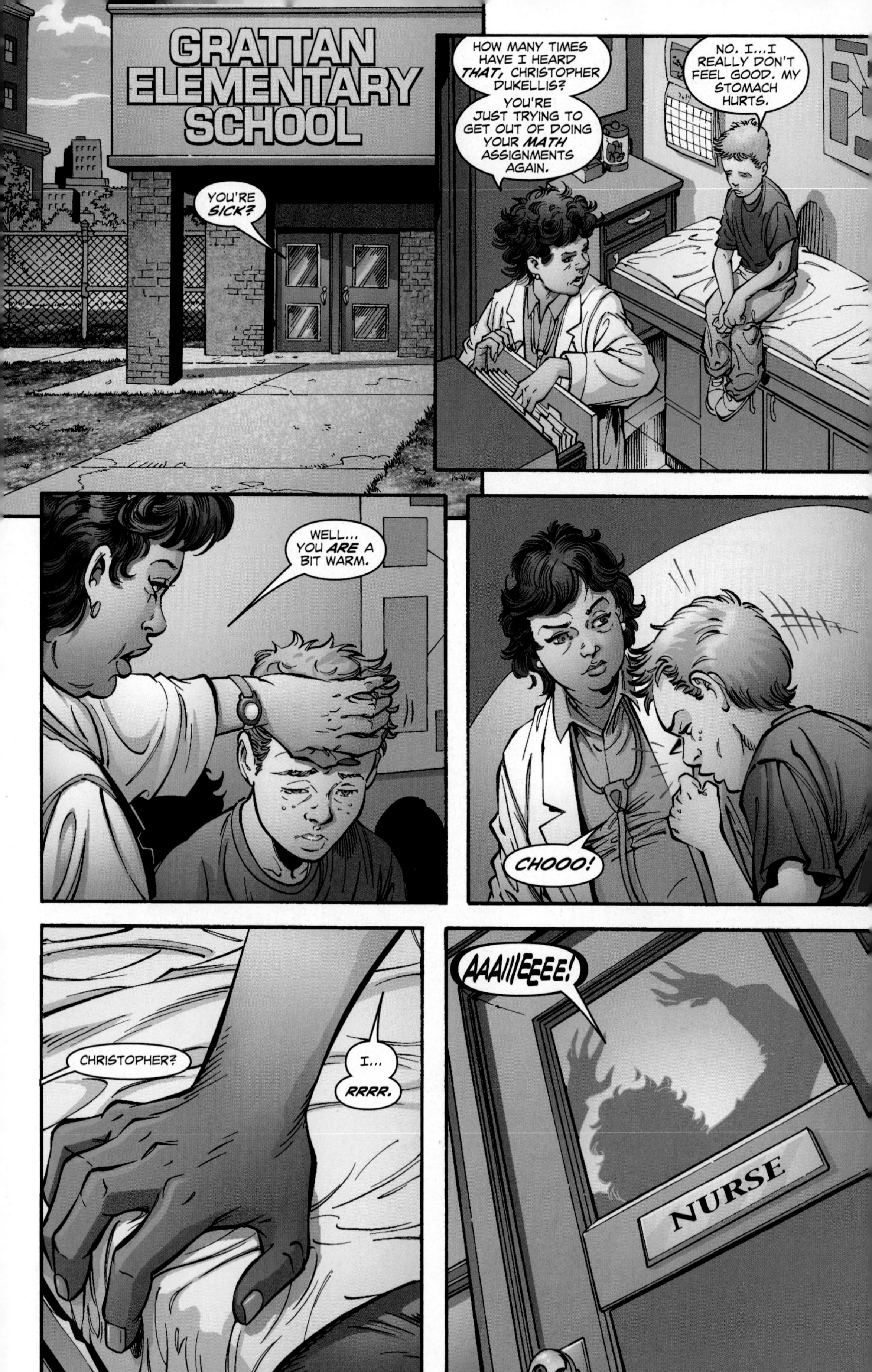

GRATTAN ELEMENTARY SCHOOL
YOU'RE SICK?
HOW MANY TIMES HAVE I HEARD THAT, CHRISTOPHER DUKELLIS?
YOU'RE JUST TRYING TO GET OUT OF DOING YOUR MATH ASSIGNMENTS AGAIN.
NO. I...I REALLY DON'T FEEL GOOD. MY STOMACH HURTS.
WELL... YOU ARE A BIT WARM.
CHOOO!
CHRISTOPHER?
I... RRRR.
AAAIIIEEEE!
NURSE

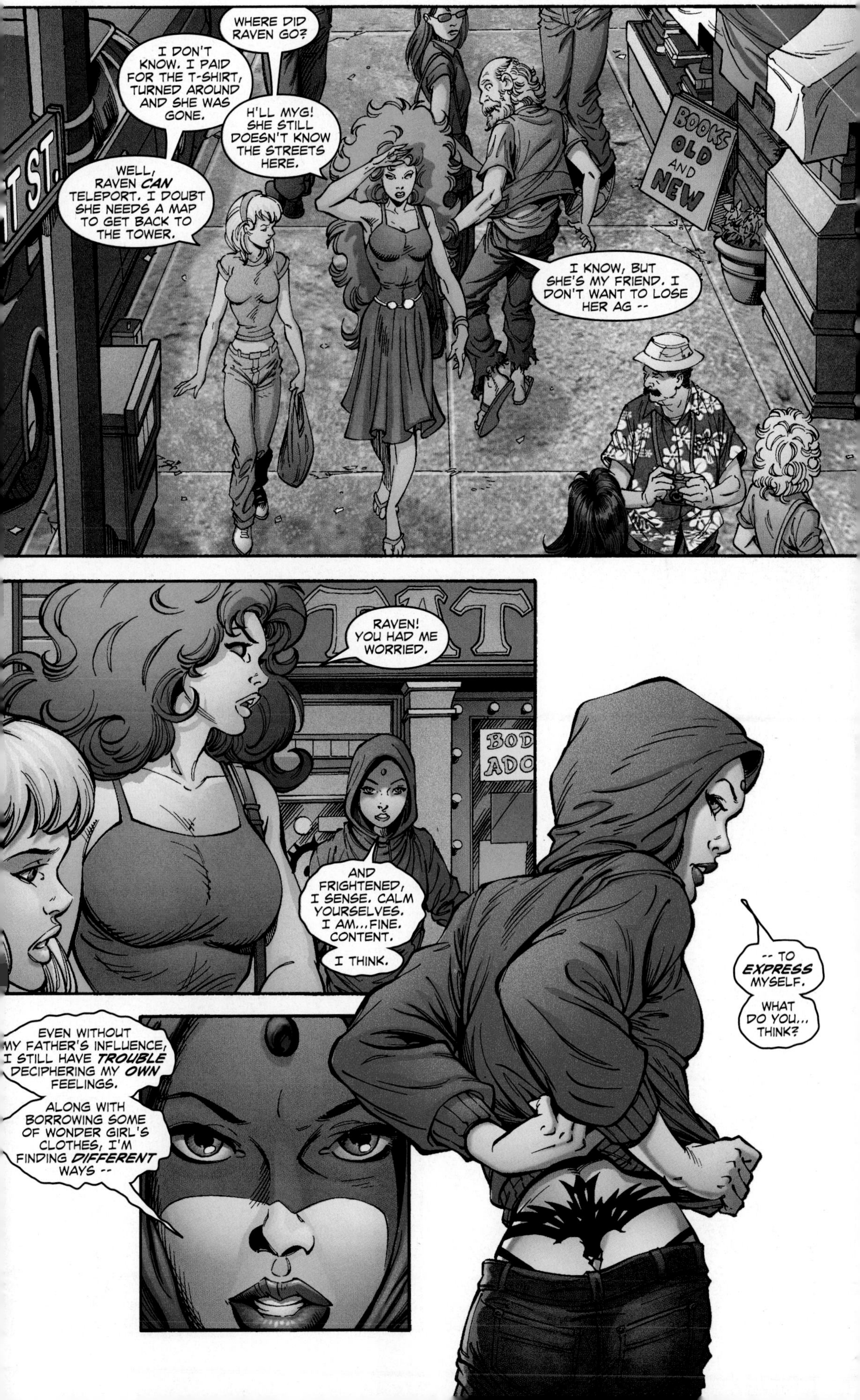
WHERE DID RAVEN GO?
I DON'T KNOW. I PAID FOR THE T-SHIRT, TURNED AROUND AND SHE WAS GONE.
H'LL MYG! SHE STILL DOESN'T KNOW THE STREETS HERE.
WELL, RAVEN CAN TELEPORT. I DOUBT SHE NEEDS A MAP TO GET BACK TO THE TOWER.
I KNOW, BUT SHE'S MY FRIEND. I DON'T WANT TO LOSE HER AG --
BOOKS OLD AND NEW
RAVEN! YOU HAD ME WORRIED.
AND FRIGHTENED, I SENSE. CALM YOURSELVES. I AM...FINE. CONTENT.
I THINK.
EVEN WITHOUT MY FATHER'S INFLUENCE, I STILL HAVE TROUBLE DECIPHERING MY OWN FEELINGS.
ALONG WITH BORROWING SOME OF WONDER GIRL'S CLOTHES, I'M FINDING DIFFERENT WAYS --
-- TO EXPRESS MYSELF.
WHAT DO YOU... THINK?

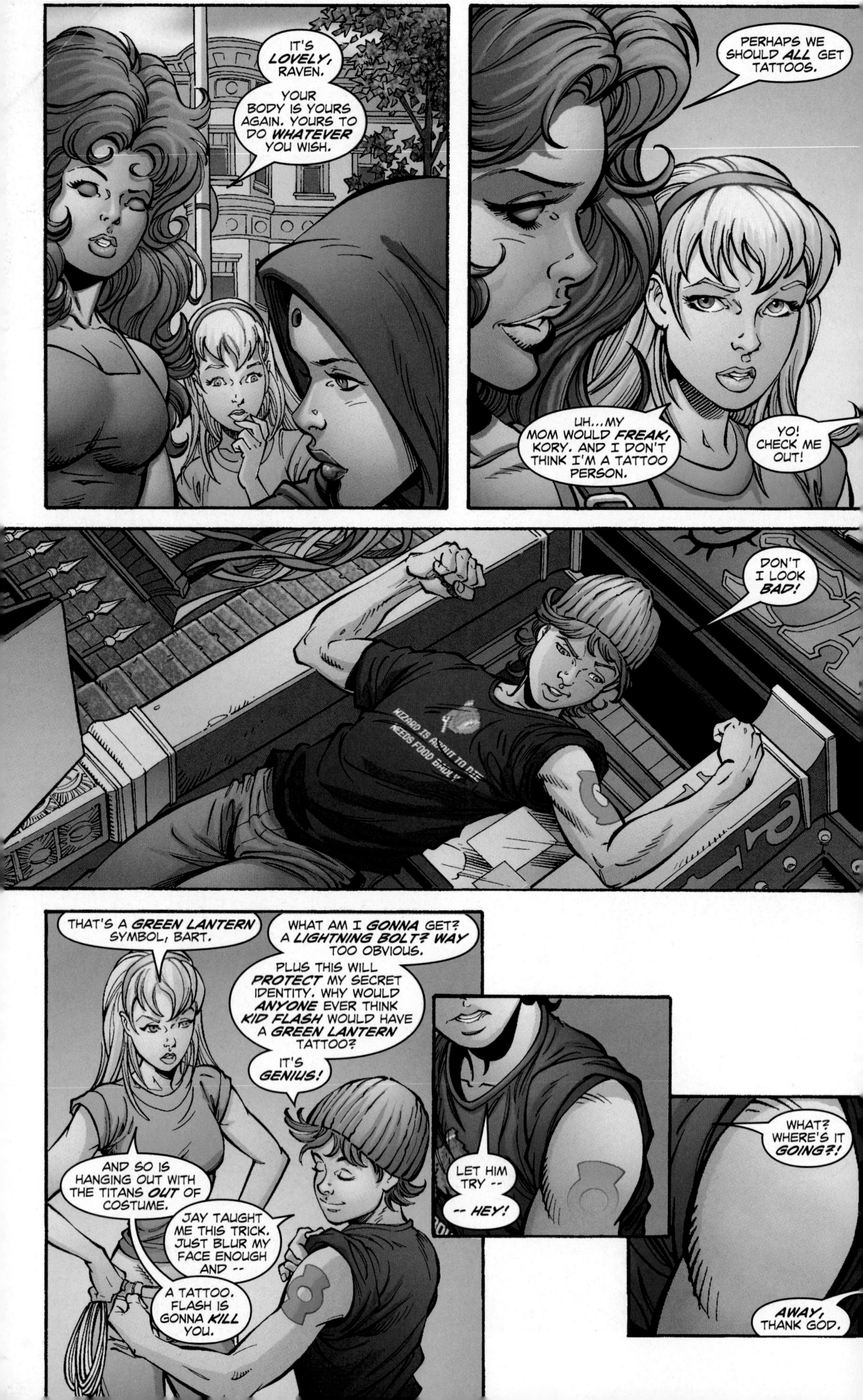

IT'S *LOVELY,* RAVEN.
YOUR BODY IS YOURS AGAIN. YOURS TO DO *WHATEVER* YOU WISH.
PERHAPS WE SHOULD *ALL* GET TATTOOS.
UH...MY MOM WOULD *FREAK,* KORY. AND I DON'T THINK I'M A TATTOO PERSON.
YO! CHECK ME OUT!
DON'T I LOOK *BAD!*
THAT'S A *GREEN LANTERN* SYMBOL, BART.
WHAT AM I *GONNA* GET? A *LIGHTNING BOLT? WAY* TOO OBVIOUS.
PLUS THIS WILL *PROTECT* MY SECRET IDENTITY. WHY WOULD *ANYONE* EVER THINK *KID FLASH* WOULD HAVE A *GREEN LANTERN* TATTOO?
IT'S *GENIUS!*
AND SO IS HANGING OUT WITH THE TITANS *OUT* OF COSTUME.
JAY TAUGHT ME THIS TRICK. JUST BLUR MY FACE ENOUGH AND --
A TATTOO. FLASH IS GONNA *KILL* YOU.
LET HIM TRY --
-- *HEY!*
WHAT? WHERE'S IT *GOING?!*
AWAY, THANK GOD.

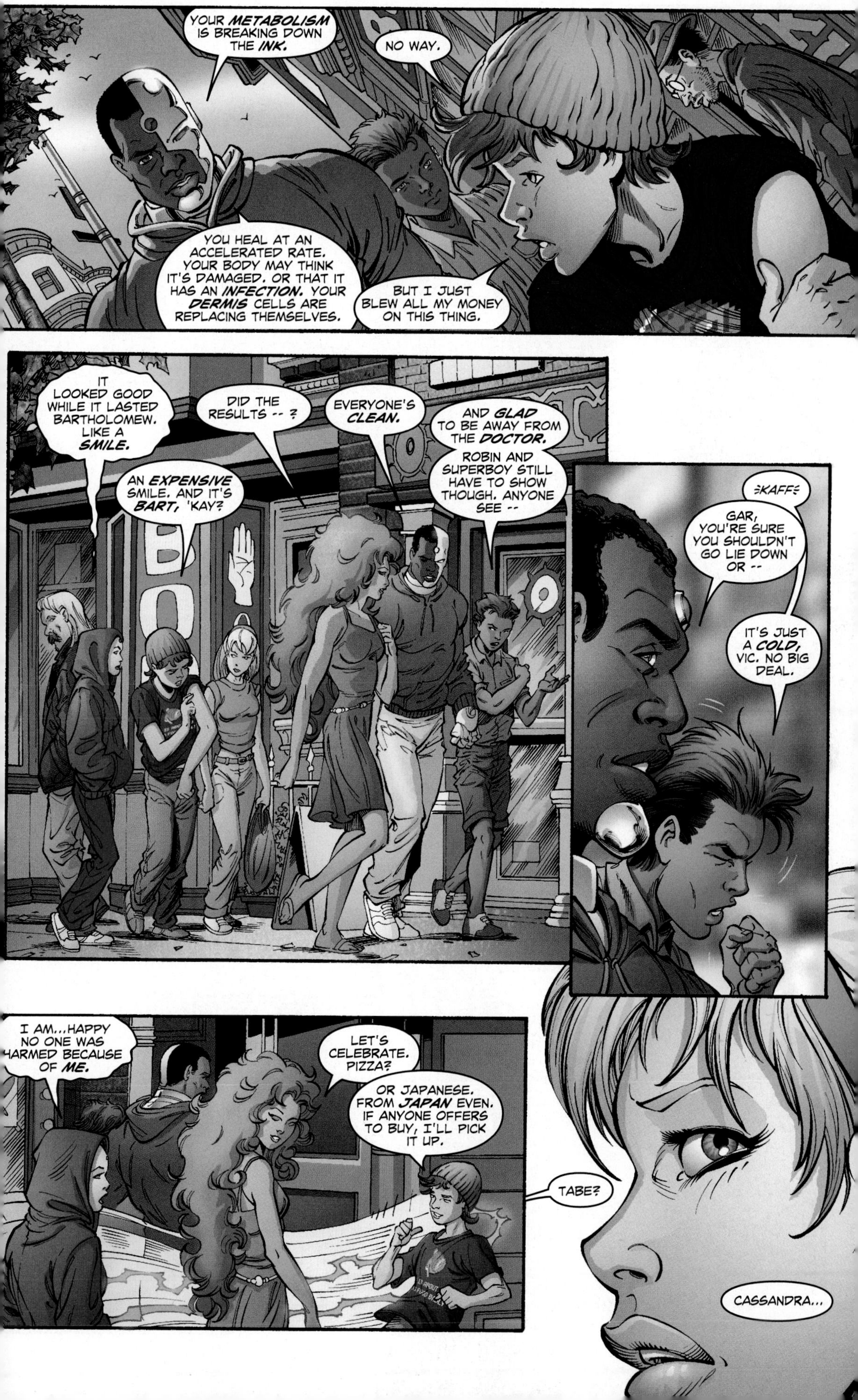
YOUR METABOLISM IS BREAKING DOWN THE INK.
NO WAY.
YOU HEAL AT AN ACCELERATED RATE. YOUR BODY MAY THINK IT'S DAMAGED. OR THAT IT HAS AN INFECTION. YOUR DERMIS CELLS ARE REPLACING THEMSELVES.
BUT I JUST BLEW ALL MY MONEY ON THIS THING.
IT LOOKED GOOD WHILE IT LASTED BARTHOLOMEW. LIKE A SMILE.
AN EXPENSIVE SMILE. AND IT'S BART, 'KAY?
DID THE RESULTS -- ?
EVERYONE'S CLEAN.
AND GLAD TO BE AWAY FROM THE DOCTOR.
ROBIN AND SUPERBOY STILL HAVE TO SHOW THOUGH. ANYONE SEE --
KAFF
GAR, YOU'RE SURE YOU SHOULDN'T GO LIE DOWN OR --
IT'S JUST A COLD, VIC. NO BIG DEAL.
I AM...HAPPY NO ONE WAS HARMED BECAUSE OF ME.
LET'S CELEBRATE. PIZZA?
OR JAPANESE. FROM JAPAN EVEN. IF ANYONE OFFERS TO BUY, I'LL PICK IT UP.
TABE?
CASSANDRA...

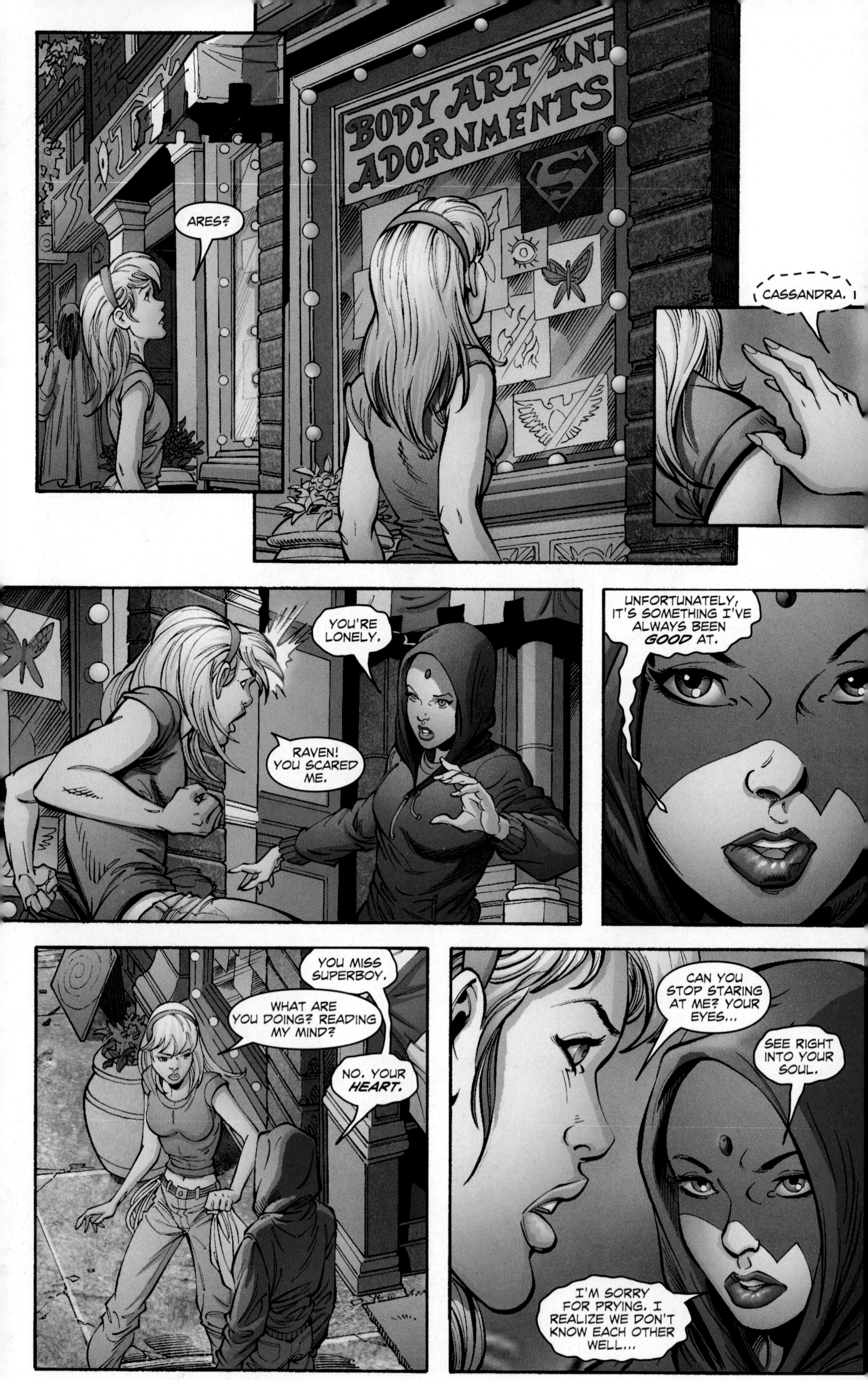
BODY ART AND ADORNMENTS
ARES?
CASSANDRA.
YOU'RE LONELY.
RAVEN! YOU SCARED ME.
UNFORTUNATELY, IT'S SOMETHING I'VE ALWAYS BEEN *GOOD* AT.
YOU MISS SUPERBOY.
WHAT ARE YOU DOING? READING MY MIND?
NO. YOUR *HEART.*
CAN YOU STOP STARING AT ME? YOUR EYES...
SEE RIGHT INTO YOUR SOUL.
I'M SORRY FOR PRYING. I REALIZE WE DON'T KNOW EACH OTHER WELL...

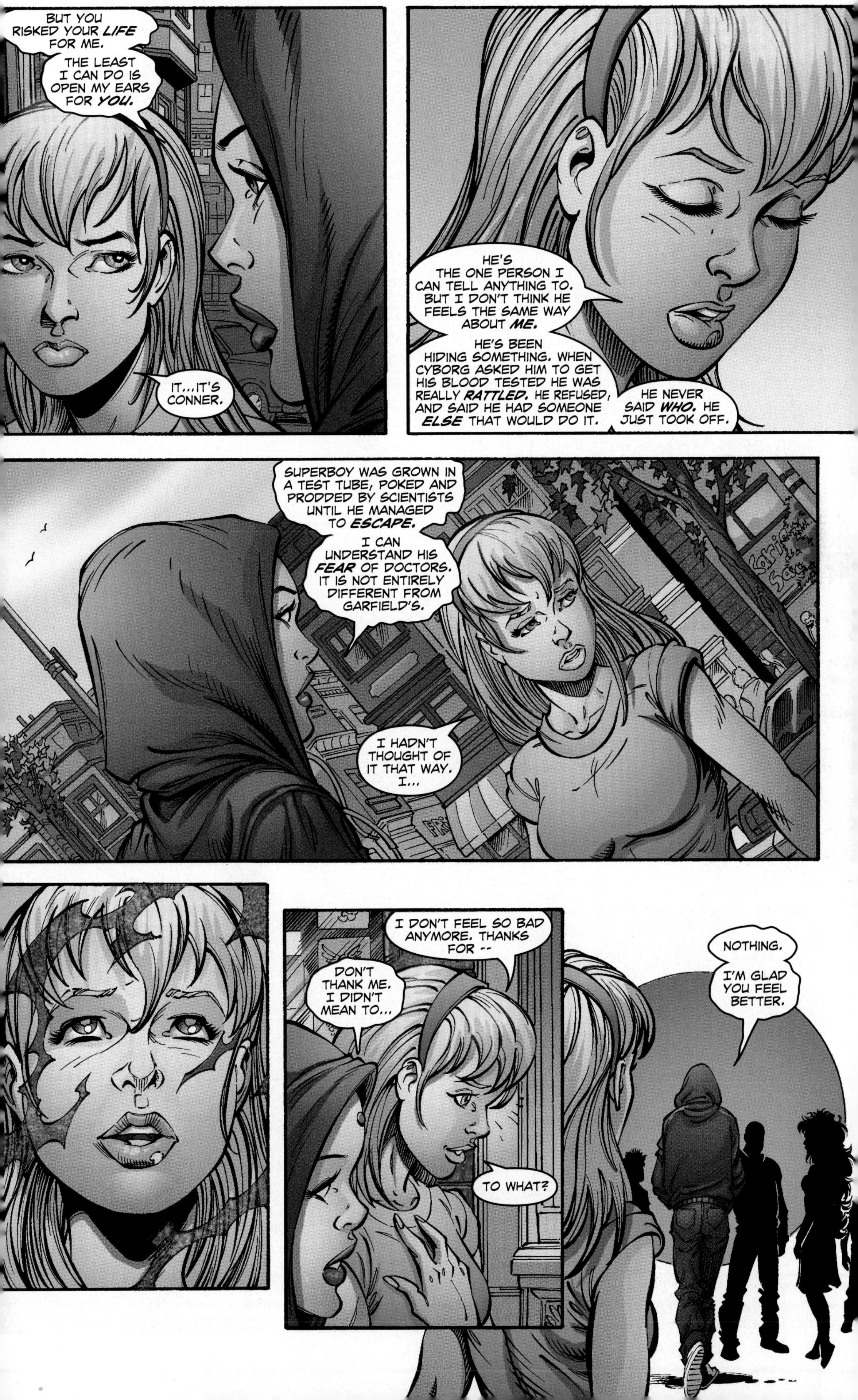
BUT YOU RISKED YOUR LIFE FOR ME.
THE LEAST I CAN DO IS OPEN MY EARS FOR YOU.
IT...IT'S CONNER.
HE'S THE ONE PERSON I CAN TELL ANYTHING TO. BUT I DON'T THINK HE FEELS THE SAME WAY ABOUT ME.
HE'S BEEN HIDING SOMETHING. WHEN CYBORG ASKED HIM TO GET HIS BLOOD TESTED HE WAS REALLY RATTLED. HE REFUSED, AND SAID HE HAD SOMEONE ELSE THAT WOULD DO IT.
HE NEVER SAID WHO. HE JUST TOOK OFF.
SUPERBOY WAS GROWN IN A TEST TUBE, POKED AND PRODDED BY SCIENTISTS UNTIL HE MANAGED TO ESCAPE.
I CAN UNDERSTAND HIS FEAR OF DOCTORS. IT IS NOT ENTIRELY DIFFERENT FROM GARFIELD'S.
I HADN'T THOUGHT OF IT THAT WAY. I...
I DON'T FEEL SO BAD ANYMORE. THANKS FOR --
DON'T THANK ME. I DIDN'T MEAN TO...
TO WHAT?
NOTHING.
I'M GLAD YOU FEEL BETTER.

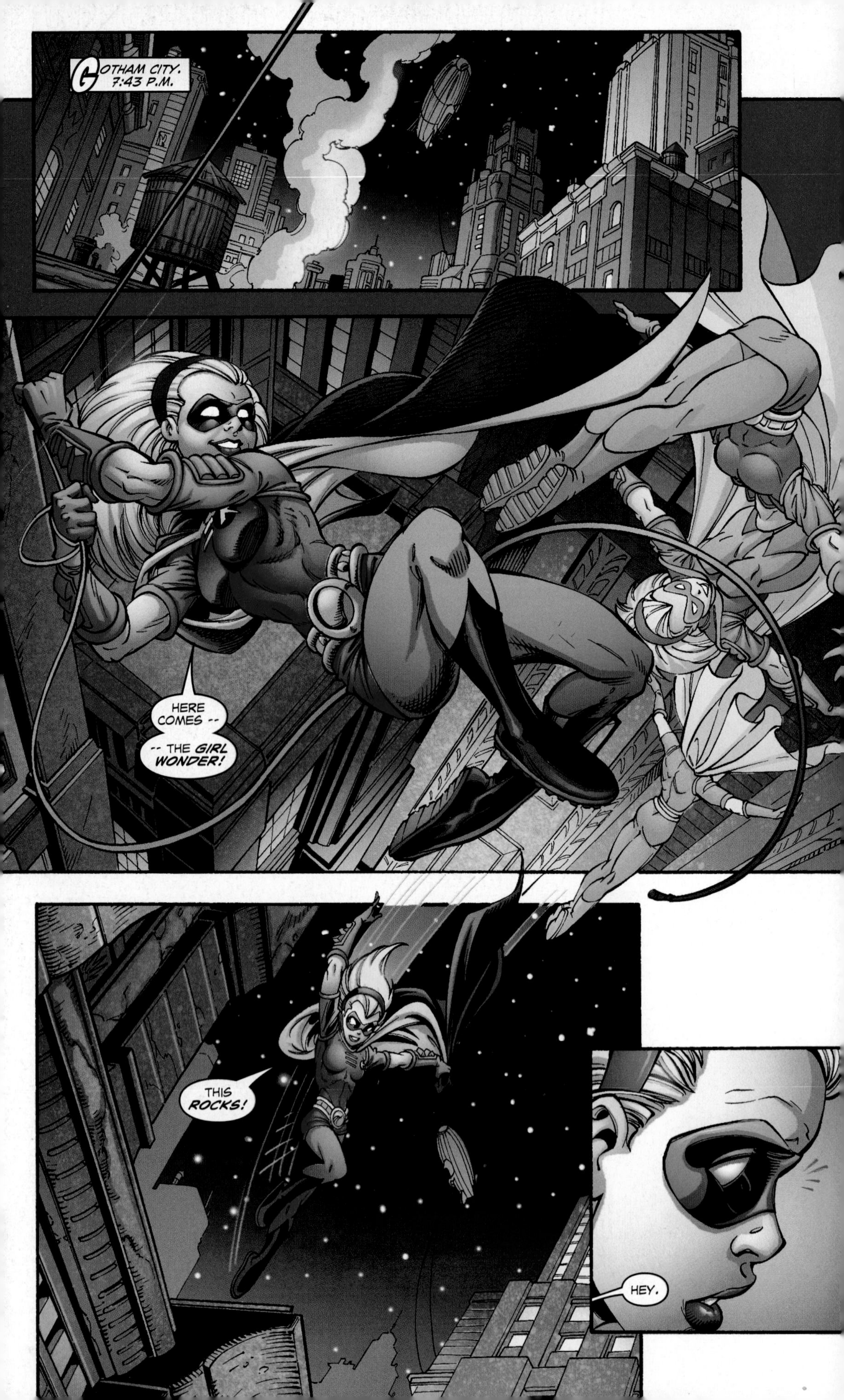
GOTHAM CITY.
7:43 P.M.
HERE COMES --
-- THE *GIRL WONDER!*
THIS *ROCKS!*
HEY.

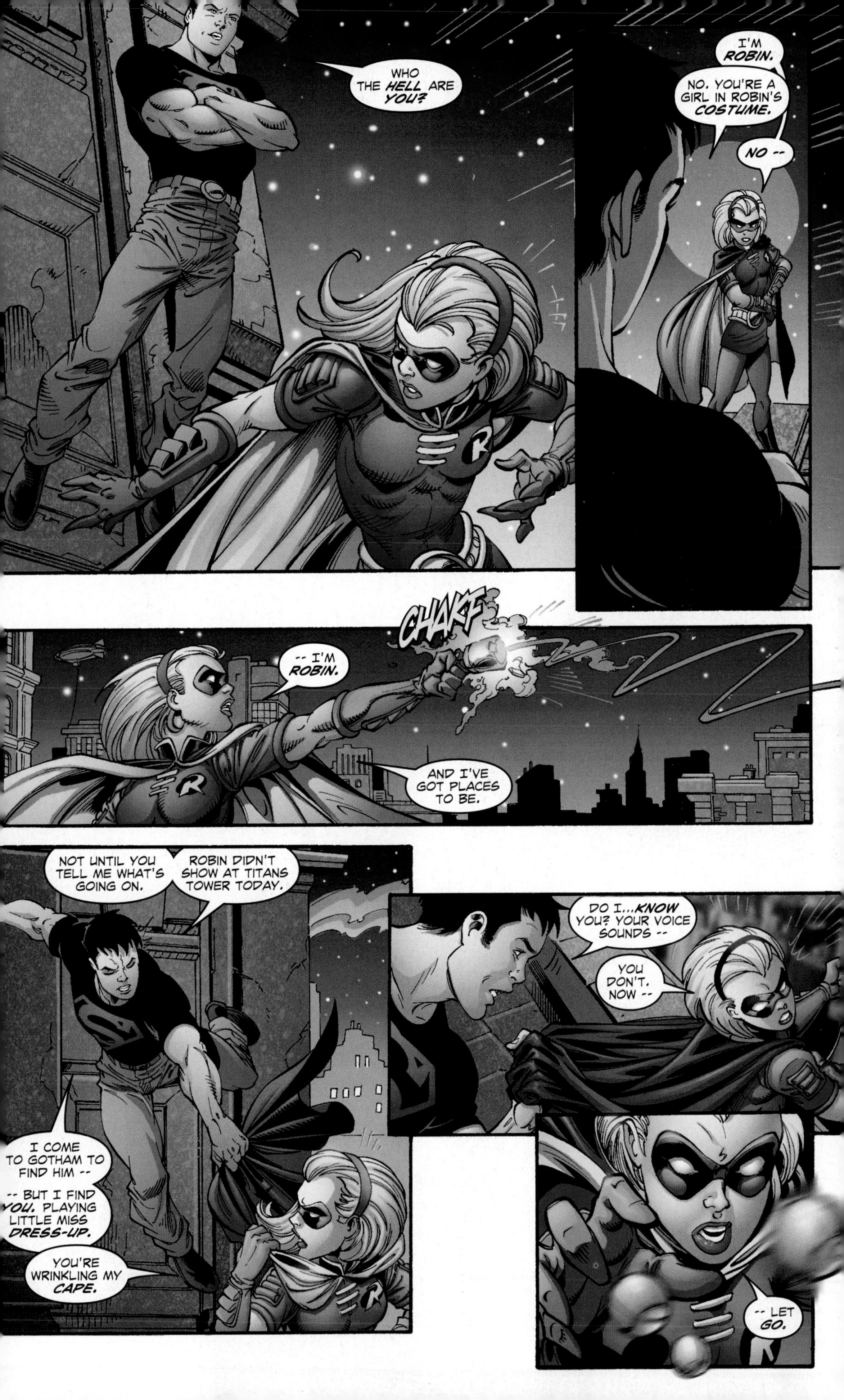
WHO THE HELL ARE YOU?
I'M ROBIN.
NO. YOU'RE A GIRL IN ROBIN'S COSTUME.
NO --
CHAKF
-- I'M ROBIN.
AND I'VE GOT PLACES TO BE.
NOT UNTIL YOU TELL ME WHAT'S GOING ON.
ROBIN DIDN'T SHOW AT TITANS TOWER TODAY.
I COME TO GOTHAM TO FIND HIM --
-- BUT I FIND YOU. PLAYING LITTLE MISS DRESS-UP.
YOU'RE WRINKLING MY CAPE.
DO I...KNOW YOU? YOUR VOICE SOUNDS --
YOU DON'T. NOW --
-- LET GO.

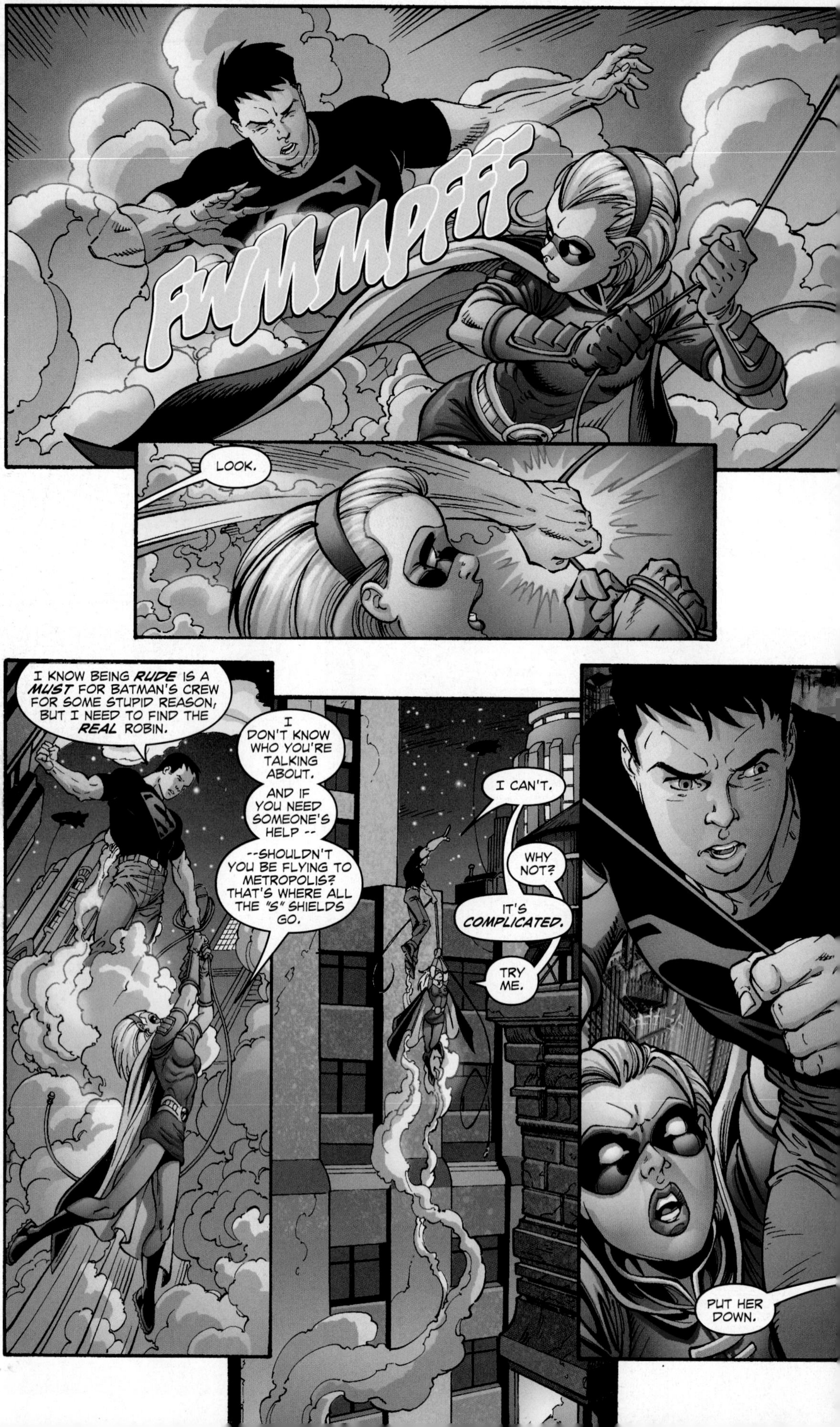
FWMMPFFF
LOOK.
I KNOW BEING RUDE IS A MUST FOR BATMAN'S CREW FOR SOME STUPID REASON, BUT I NEED TO FIND THE REAL ROBIN.
I DON'T KNOW WHO YOU'RE TALKING ABOUT.
AND IF YOU NEED SOMEONE'S HELP --
--SHOULDN'T YOU BE FLYING TO METROPOLIS? THAT'S WHERE ALL THE "S" SHIELDS GO.
I CAN'T.
WHY NOT?
IT'S COMPLICATED.
TRY ME.
PUT HER DOWN.

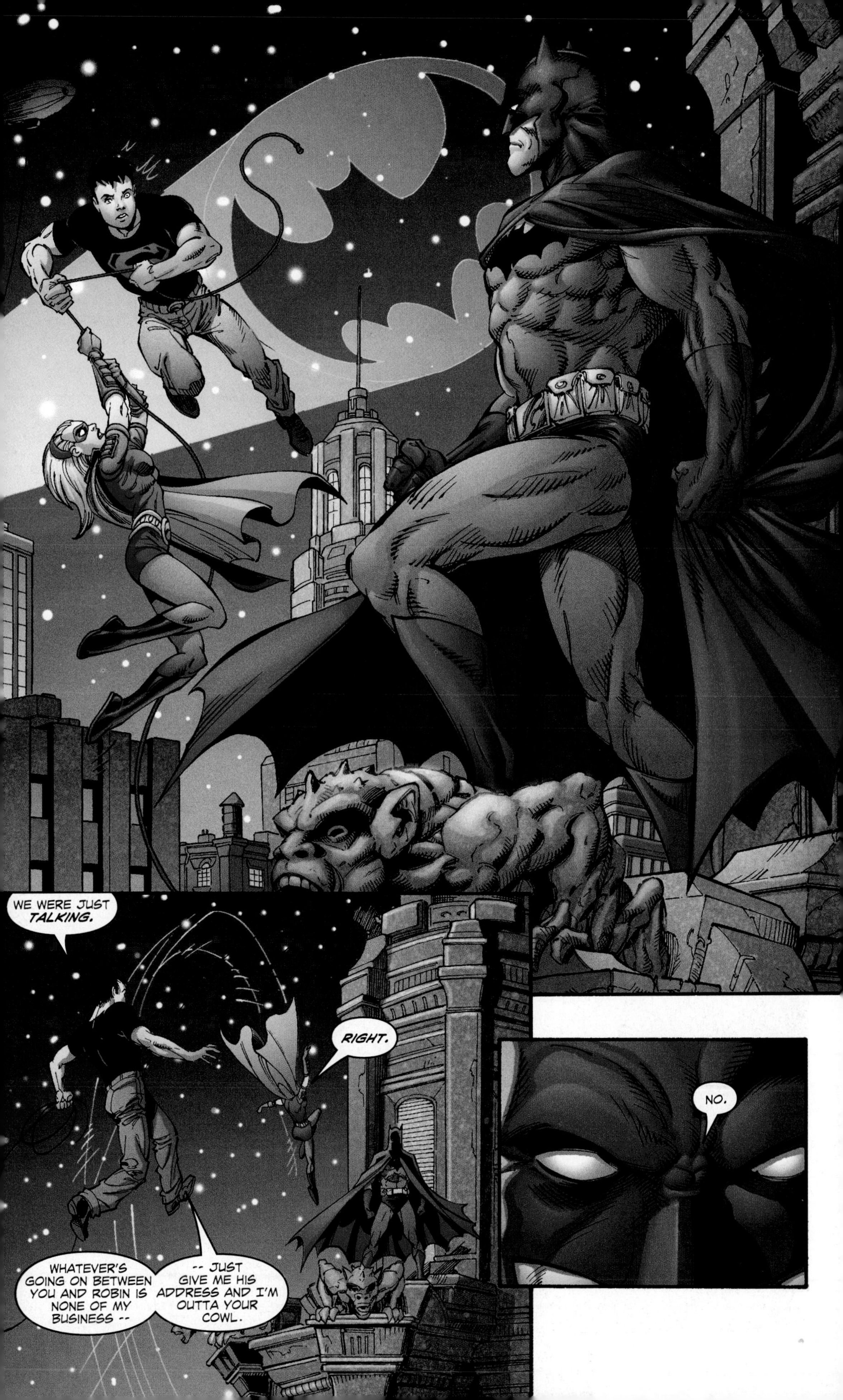
WE WERE JUST *TALKING.*
RIGHT.
WHATEVER'S GOING ON BETWEEN YOU AND ROBIN IS NONE OF MY BUSINESS --
-- JUST GIVE ME HIS ADDRESS AND I'M OUTTA YOUR COWL.
NO.

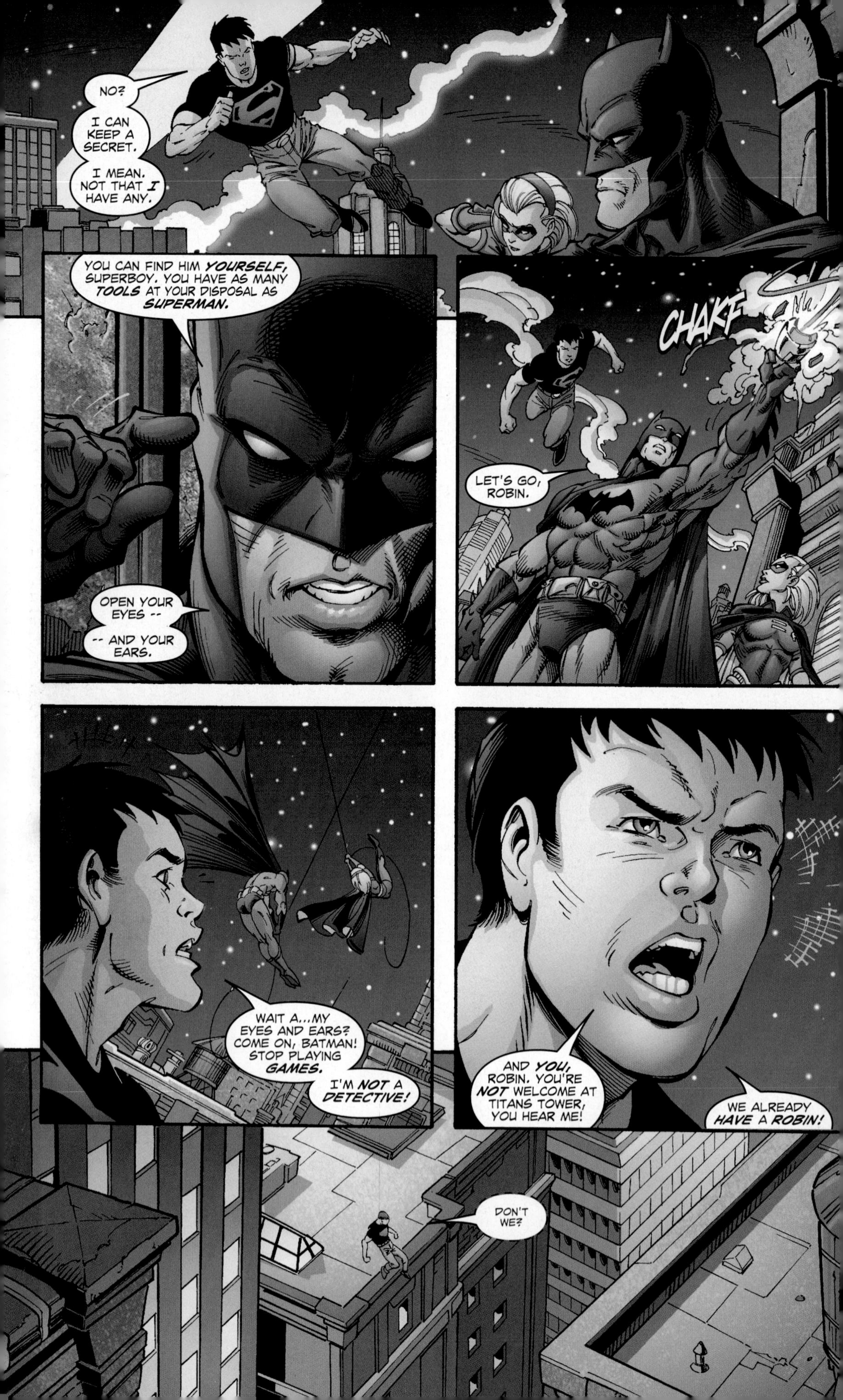
NO?
I CAN KEEP A SECRET.
I MEAN. NOT THAT I HAVE ANY.
YOU CAN FIND HIM YOURSELF, SUPERBOY. YOU HAVE AS MANY TOOLS AT YOUR DISPOSAL AS SUPERMAN.
OPEN YOUR EYES --
-- AND YOUR EARS.
CHAKF
LET'S GO, ROBIN.
WAIT A...MY EYES AND EARS? COME ON, BATMAN! STOP PLAYING GAMES.
I'M NOT A DETECTIVE!
AND YOU, ROBIN. YOU'RE NOT WELCOME AT TITANS TOWER, YOU HEAR ME!
WE ALREADY HAVE A ROBIN!
DON'T WE?

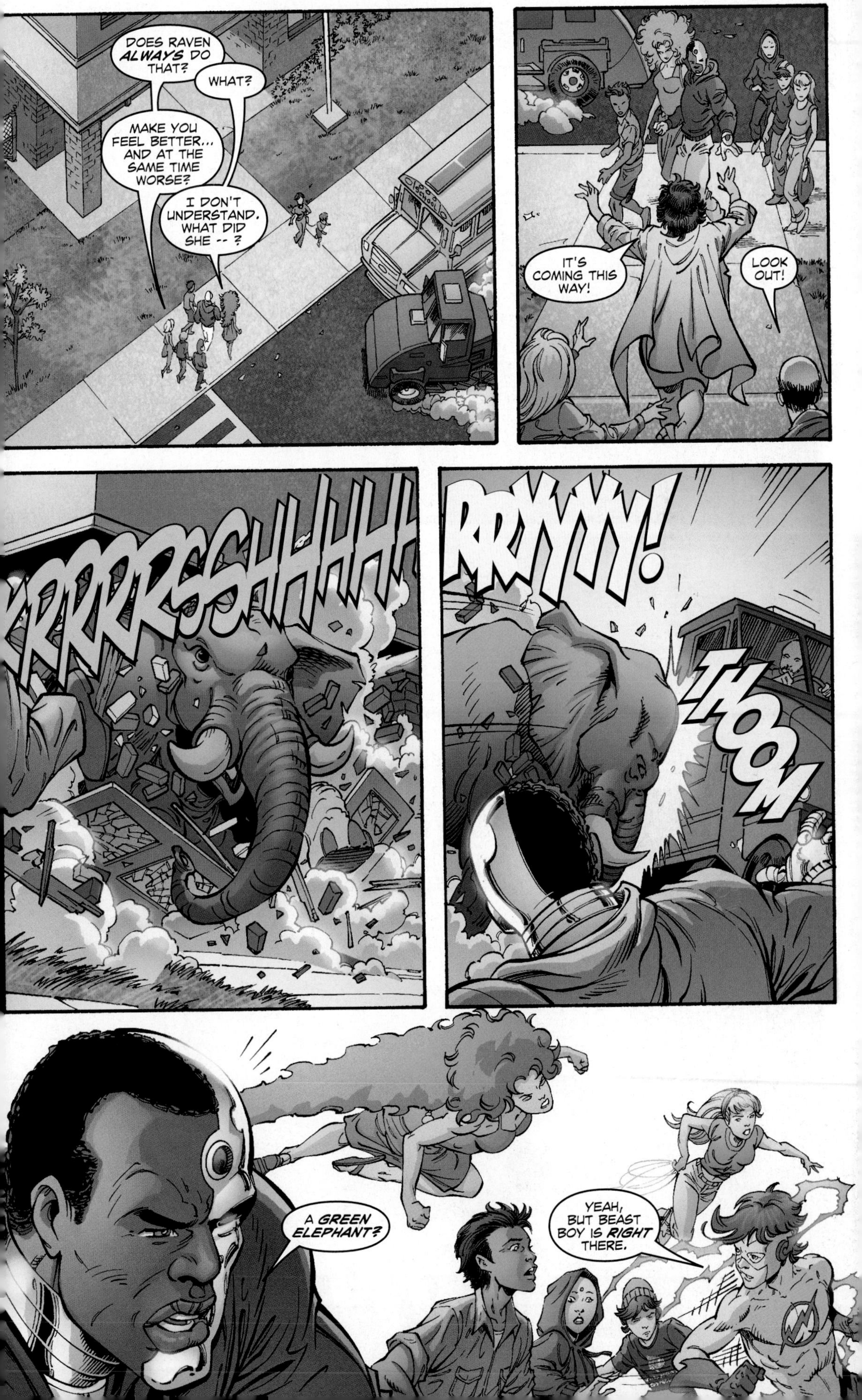
DOES RAVEN *ALWAYS* DO THAT?
WHAT?
MAKE YOU FEEL BETTER... AND AT THE SAME TIME WORSE?
I DON'T UNDERSTAND. WHAT DID SHE -- ?
IT'S COMING THIS WAY!
LOOK OUT!
KRRRRSHHHHH
RRYYYY!
THOOM
A *GREEN ELEPHANT?*
YEAH, BUT BEAST BOY IS *RIGHT* THERE.

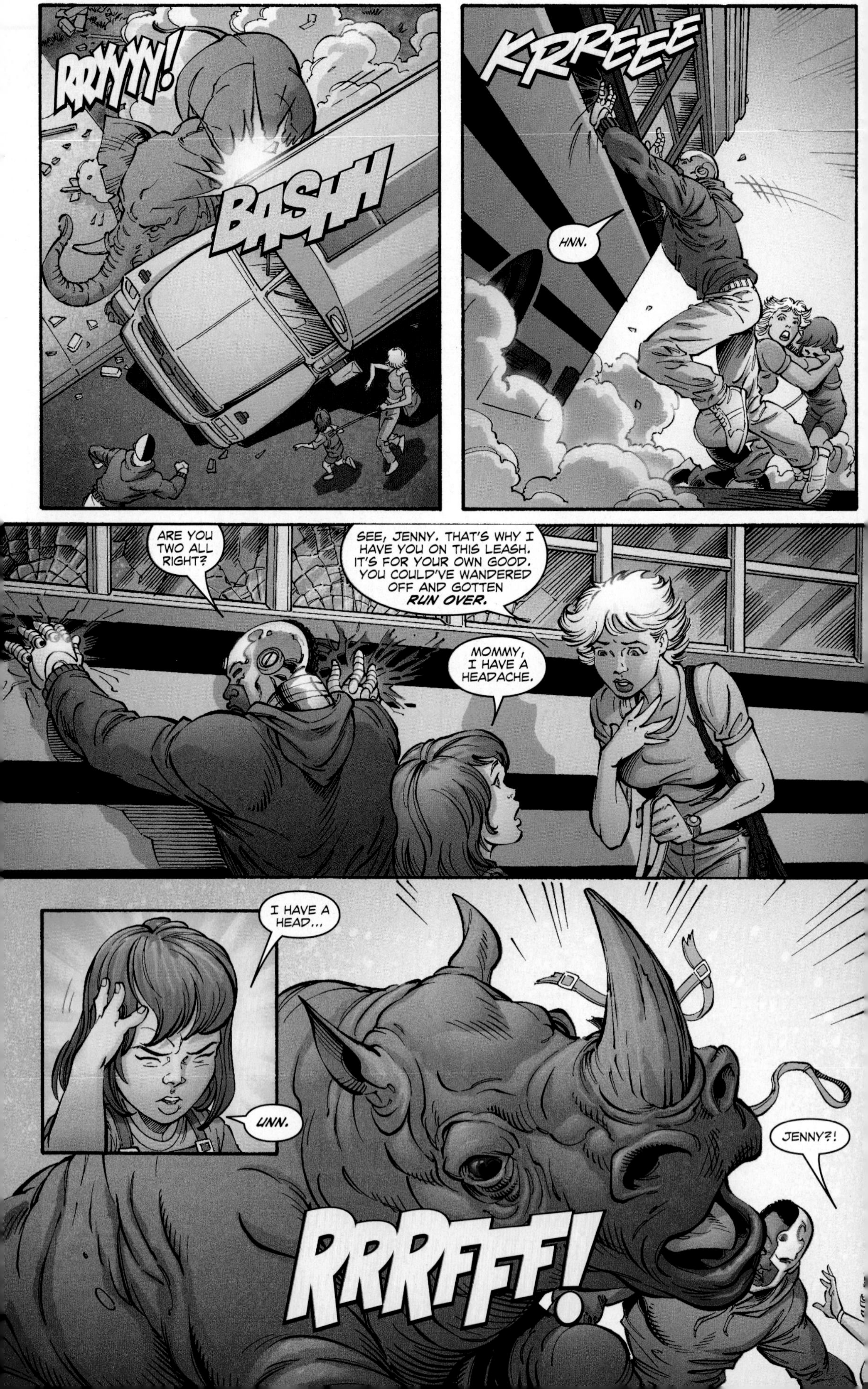
RRYYYY!
BASHH
KRREEE
HNN.
ARE YOU TWO ALL RIGHT?
SEE, JENNY. THAT'S WHY I HAVE YOU ON THIS LEASH. IT'S FOR YOUR OWN GOOD. YOU COULD'VE WANDERED OFF AND GOTTEN *RUN OVER.*
MOMMY, I HAVE A HEADACHE.
I HAVE A HEAD...
UNN.
JENNY?!
RRRFFF!

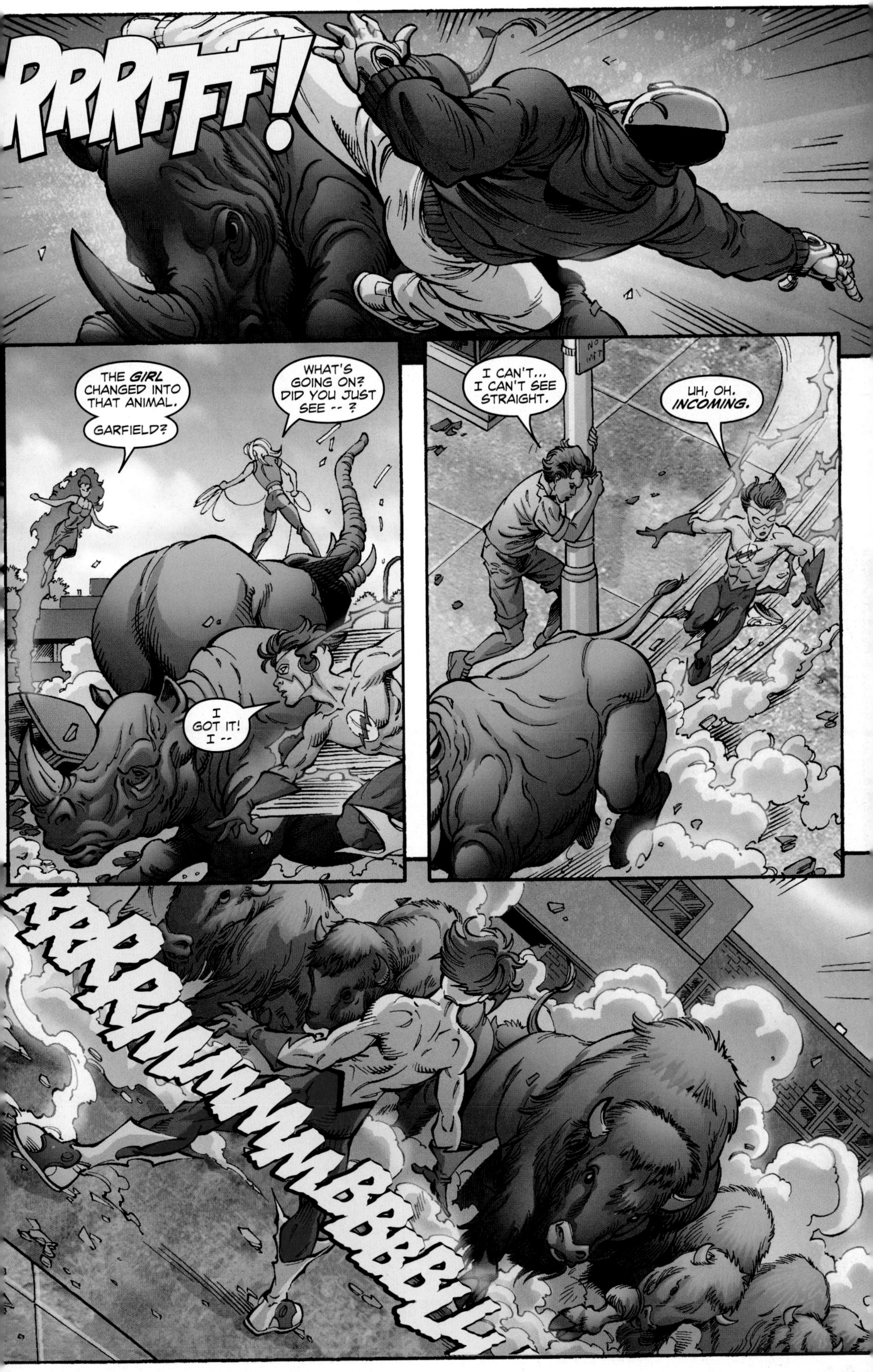
RRRFFF!
THE GIRL CHANGED INTO THAT ANIMAL.
GARFIELD?
WHAT'S GOING ON? DID YOU JUST SEE -- ?
I GOT IT! I --
I CAN'T... I CAN'T SEE STRAIGHT.
UH, OH. INCOMING.
RRRRMMMMBBBBLL

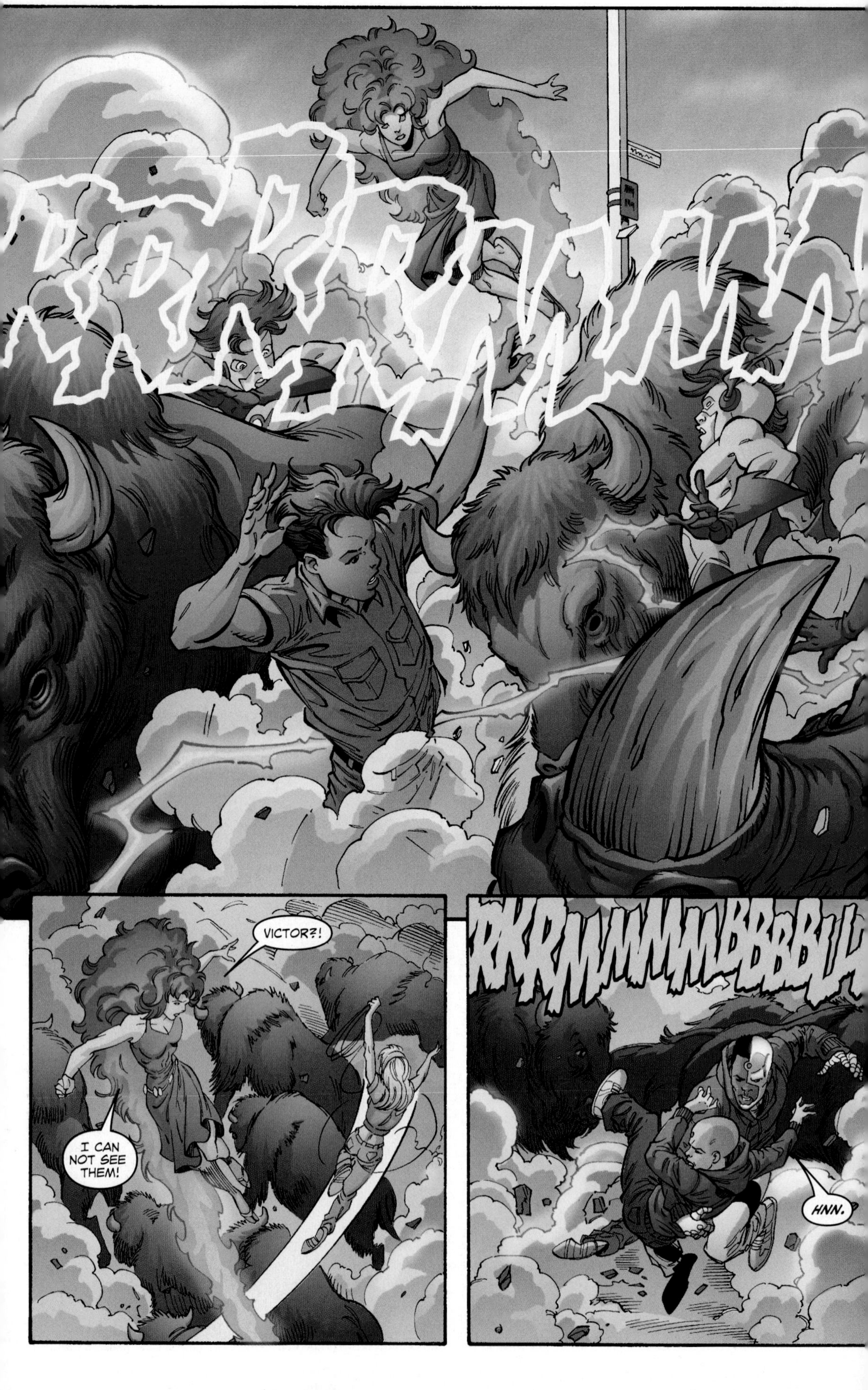
VICTOR?!
I CAN NOT SEE THEM!
RKRMMMMMBBBBL
HNN.

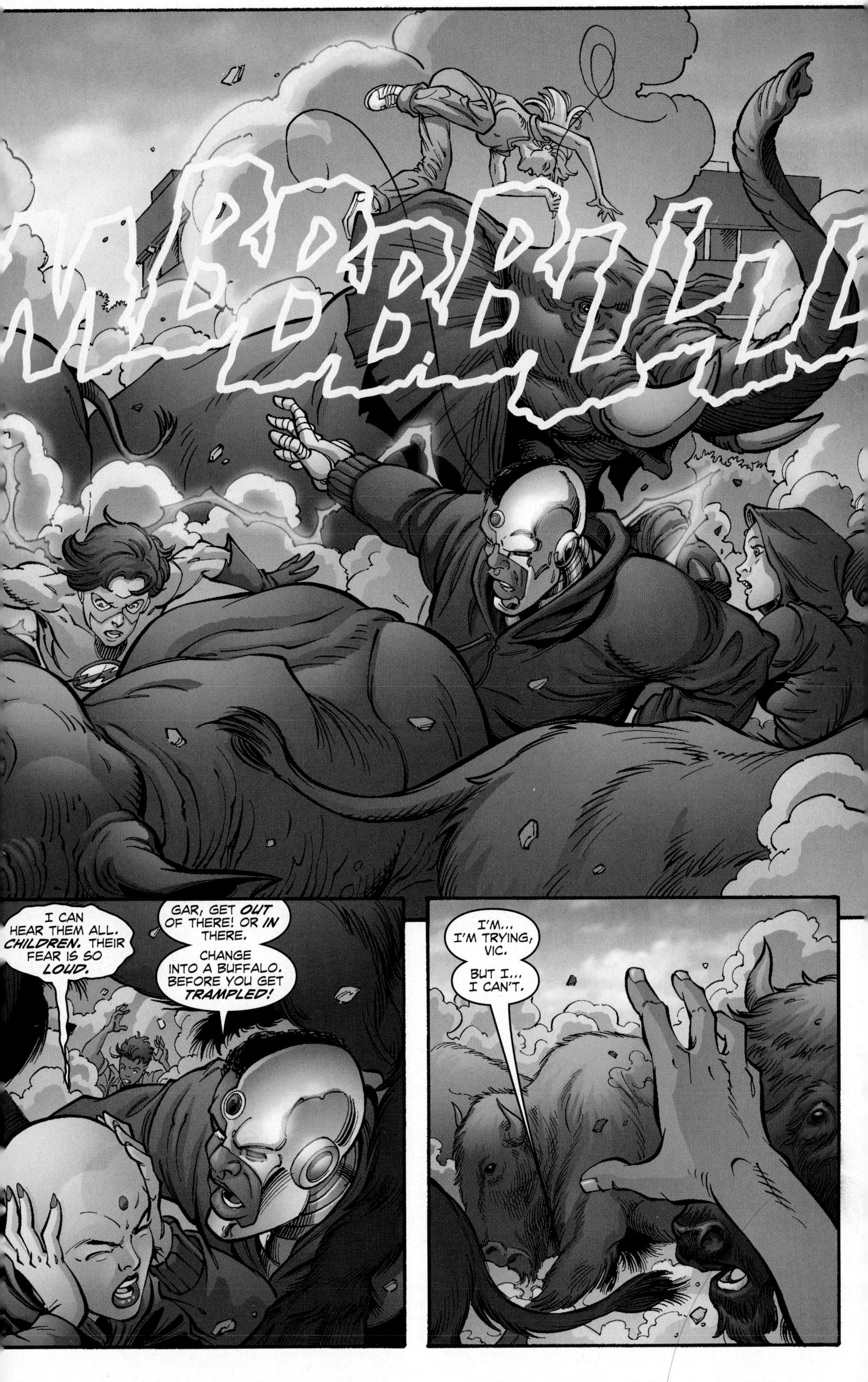
I CAN HEAR THEM ALL. CHILDREN. THEIR FEAR IS SO LOUD.
GAR, GET OUT OF THERE! OR IN THERE.
CHANGE INTO A BUFFALO. BEFORE YOU GET TRAMPLED!
I'M... I'M TRYING, VIC.
BUT I... I CAN'T.

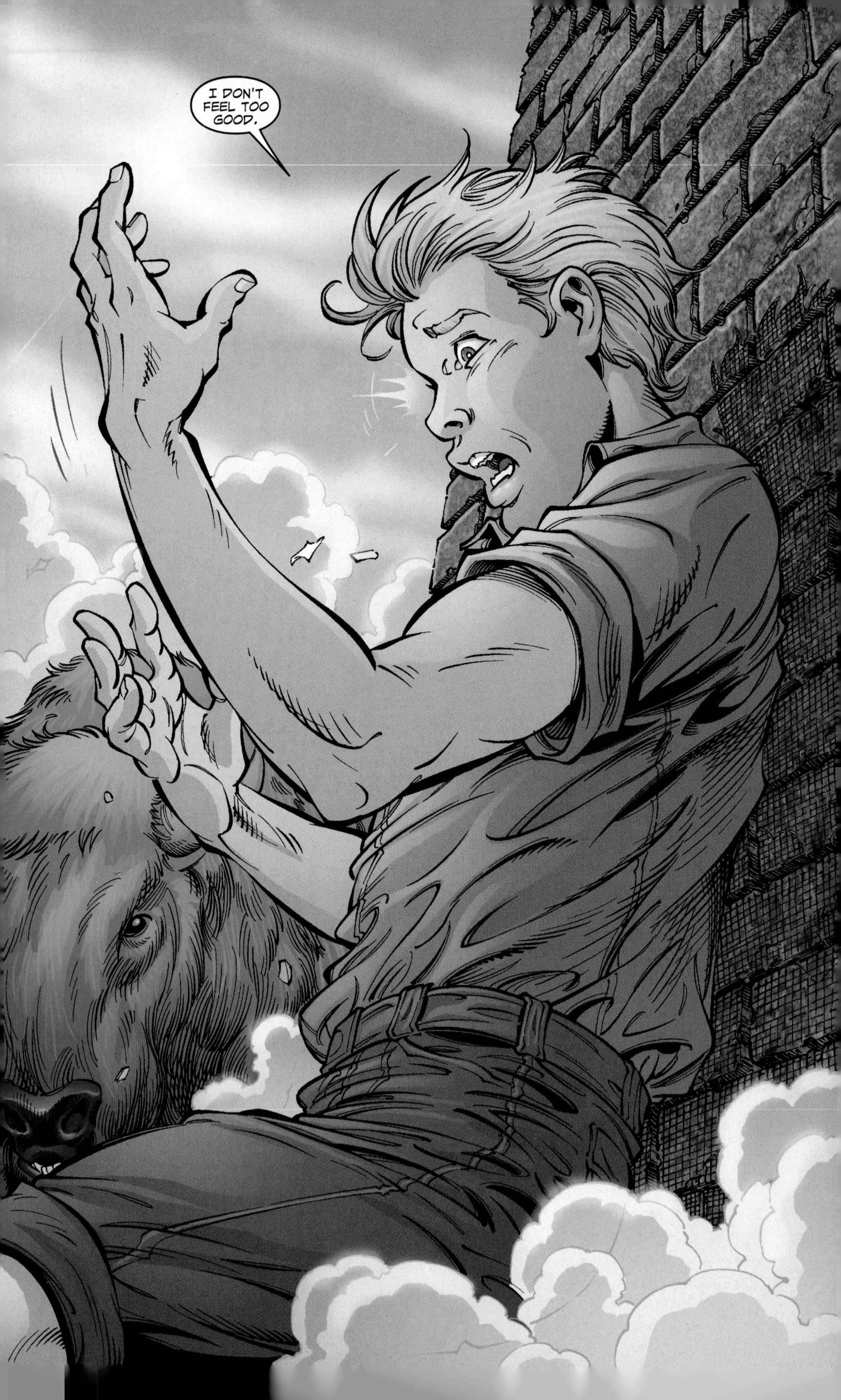
I DON'T FEEL TOO GOOD.

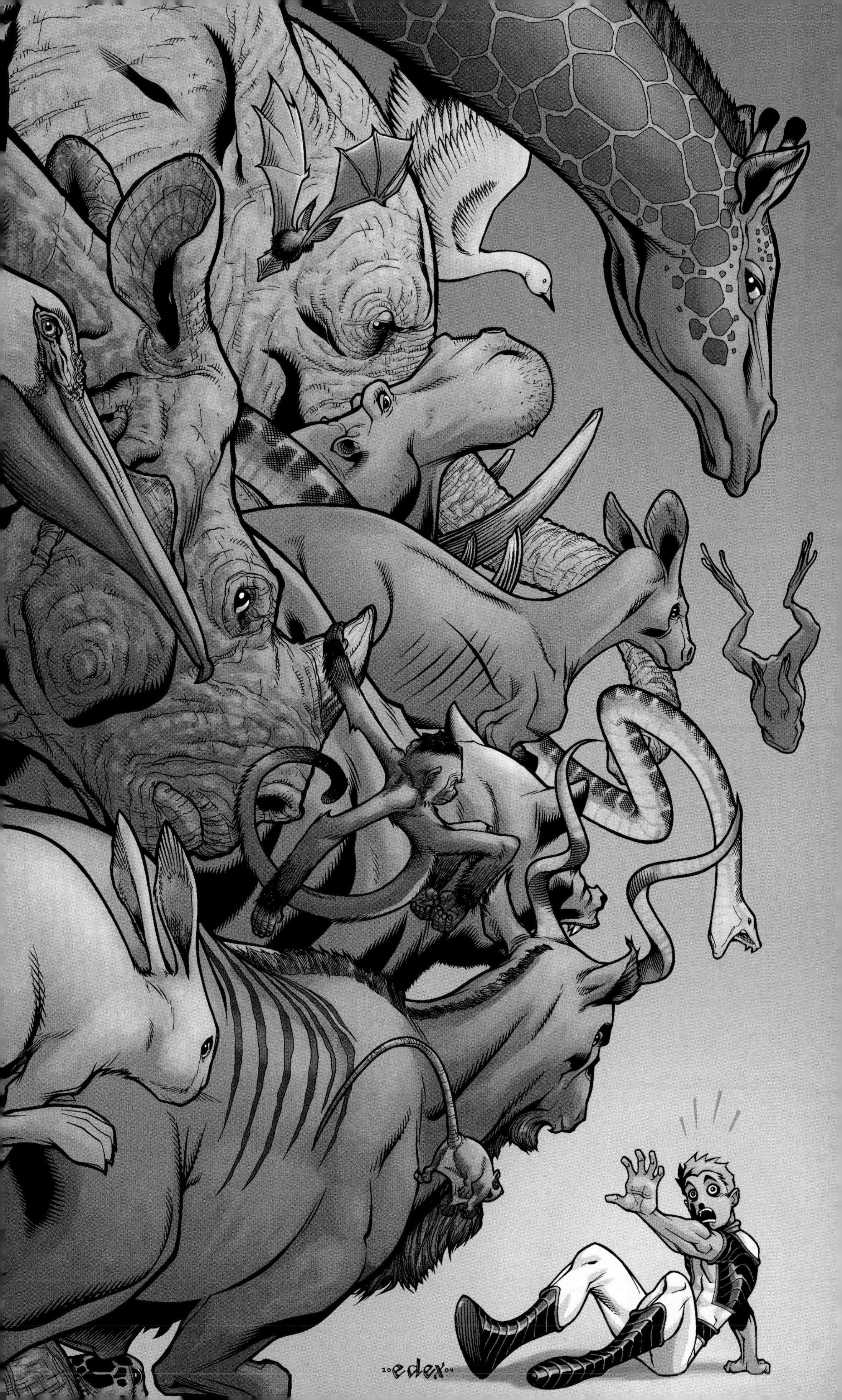
20 edex 04

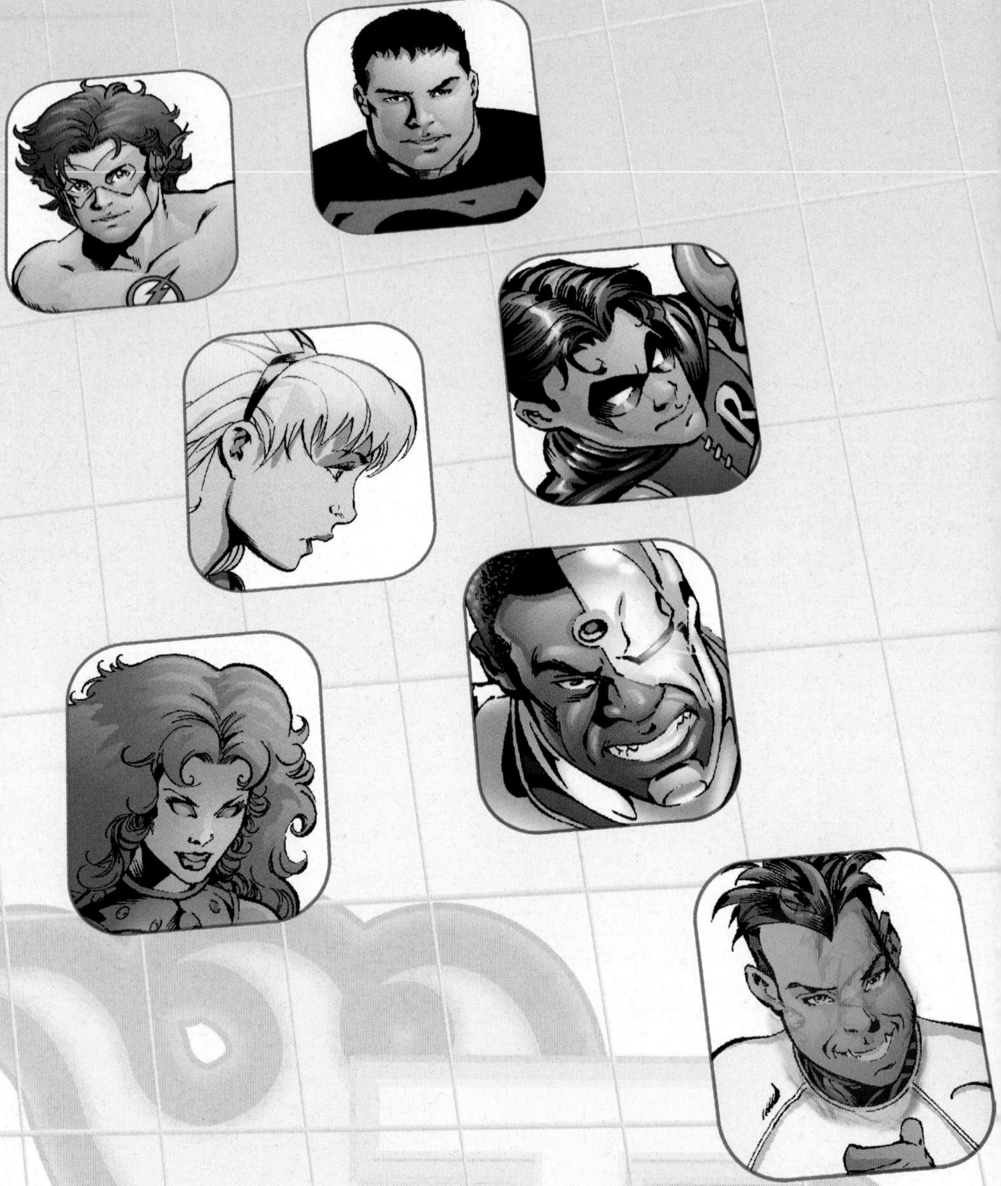

TEEN TITANS #14

GEOFF JOHNS
Writer

TOM GRUMMETT
Penciller

LARY STUCKER
Inker

JEROMY COX
Colorist

COMICRAFT
Letterer

ED McGUINNESS, DEXTER VINES & DAVE STEWART
Cover Artists

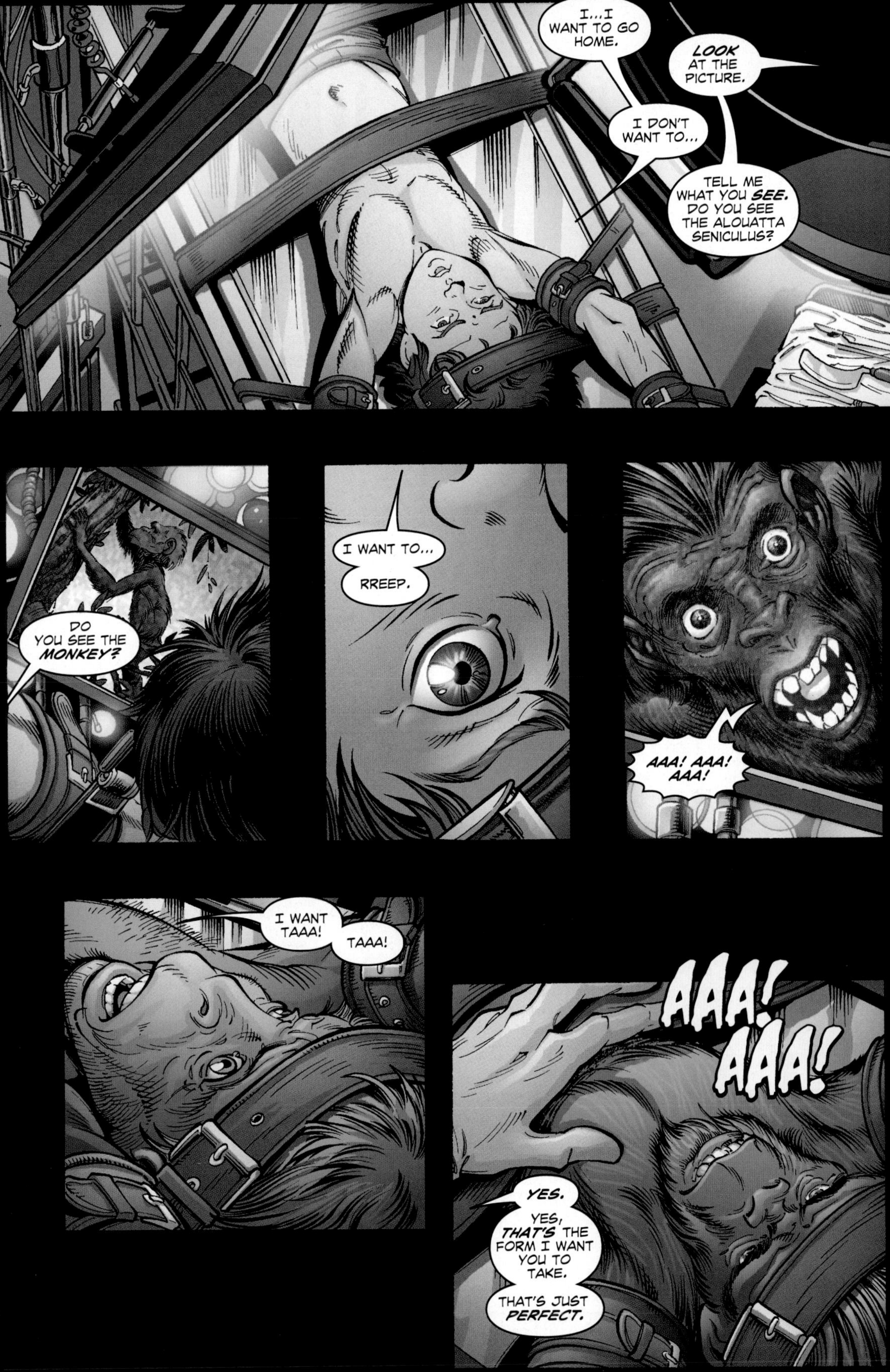
I...I WANT TO GO HOME.
LOOK AT THE PICTURE.
I DON'T WANT TO...
TELL ME WHAT YOU SEE. DO YOU SEE THE ALOUATTA SENICULUS?
DO YOU SEE THE MONKEY?
I WANT TO...
RREEP.
AAA! AAA! AAA!
I WANT TAAA!
TAAA!
AAA! AAA!
YES.
YES, THAT'S THE FORM I WANT YOU TO TAKE.
THAT'S JUST PERFECT.

BEAST BOYS AND GIRLS PART TWO

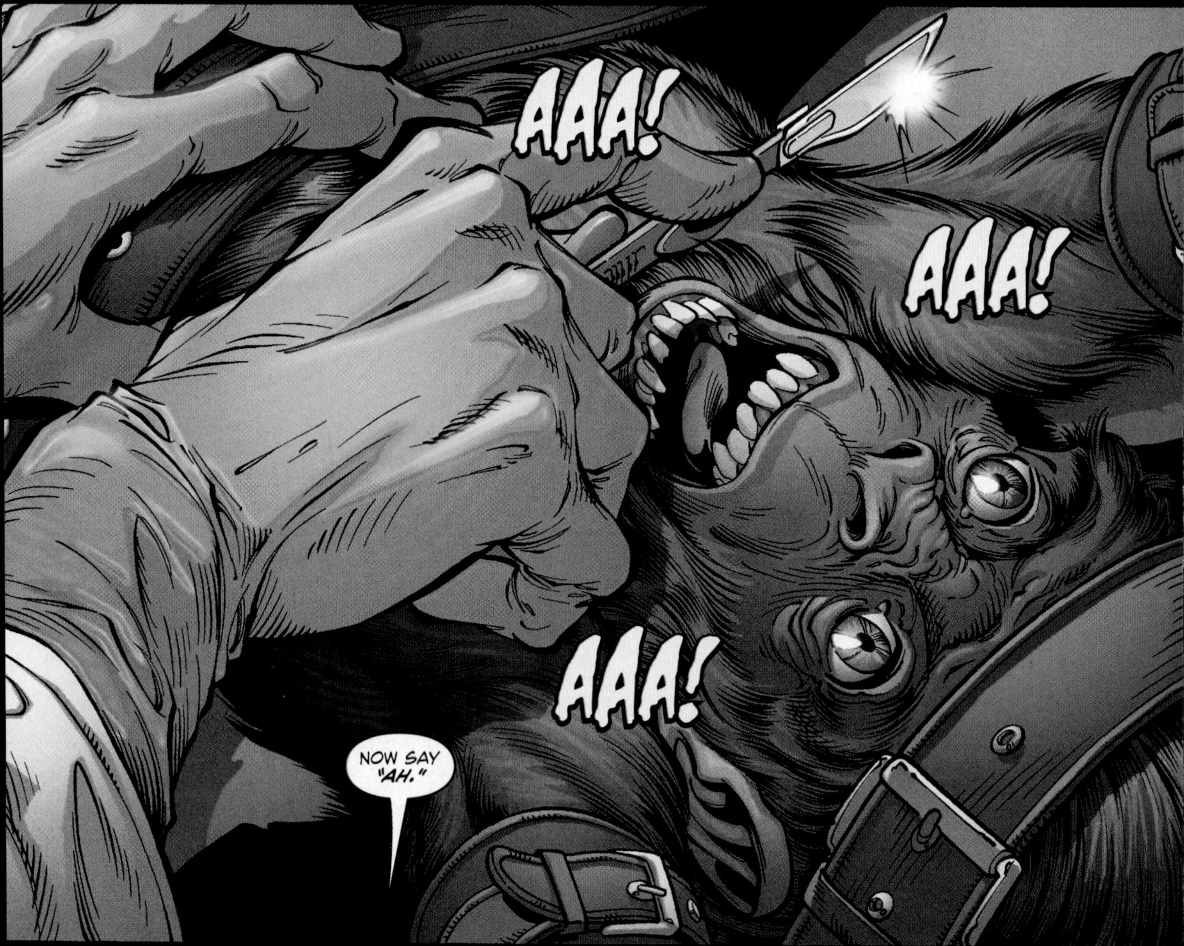

AAA!
AAA!
AAA!
NOW SAY "AH."

WILD LIFE

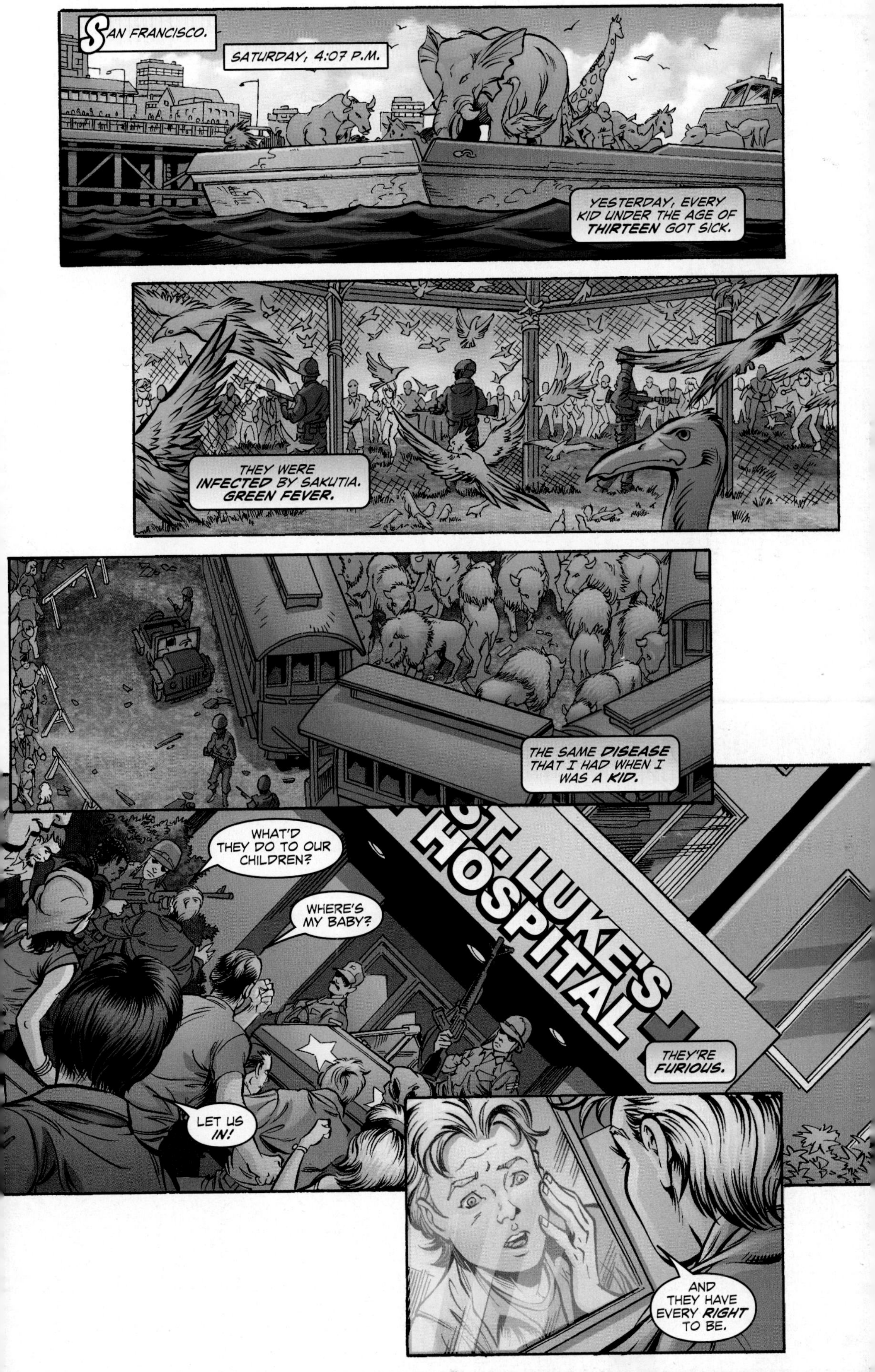
SAN FRANCISCO.
SATURDAY, 4:07 P.M.
YESTERDAY, EVERY KID UNDER THE AGE OF THIRTEEN GOT SICK.
THEY WERE INFECTED BY SAKUTIA. GREEN FEVER.
THE SAME DISEASE THAT I HAD WHEN I WAS A KID.
WHAT'D THEY DO TO OUR CHILDREN?
WHERE'S MY BABY?
ST. LUKE'S HOSPITAL
THEY'RE FURIOUS.
LET US IN!
AND THEY HAVE EVERY RIGHT TO BE.

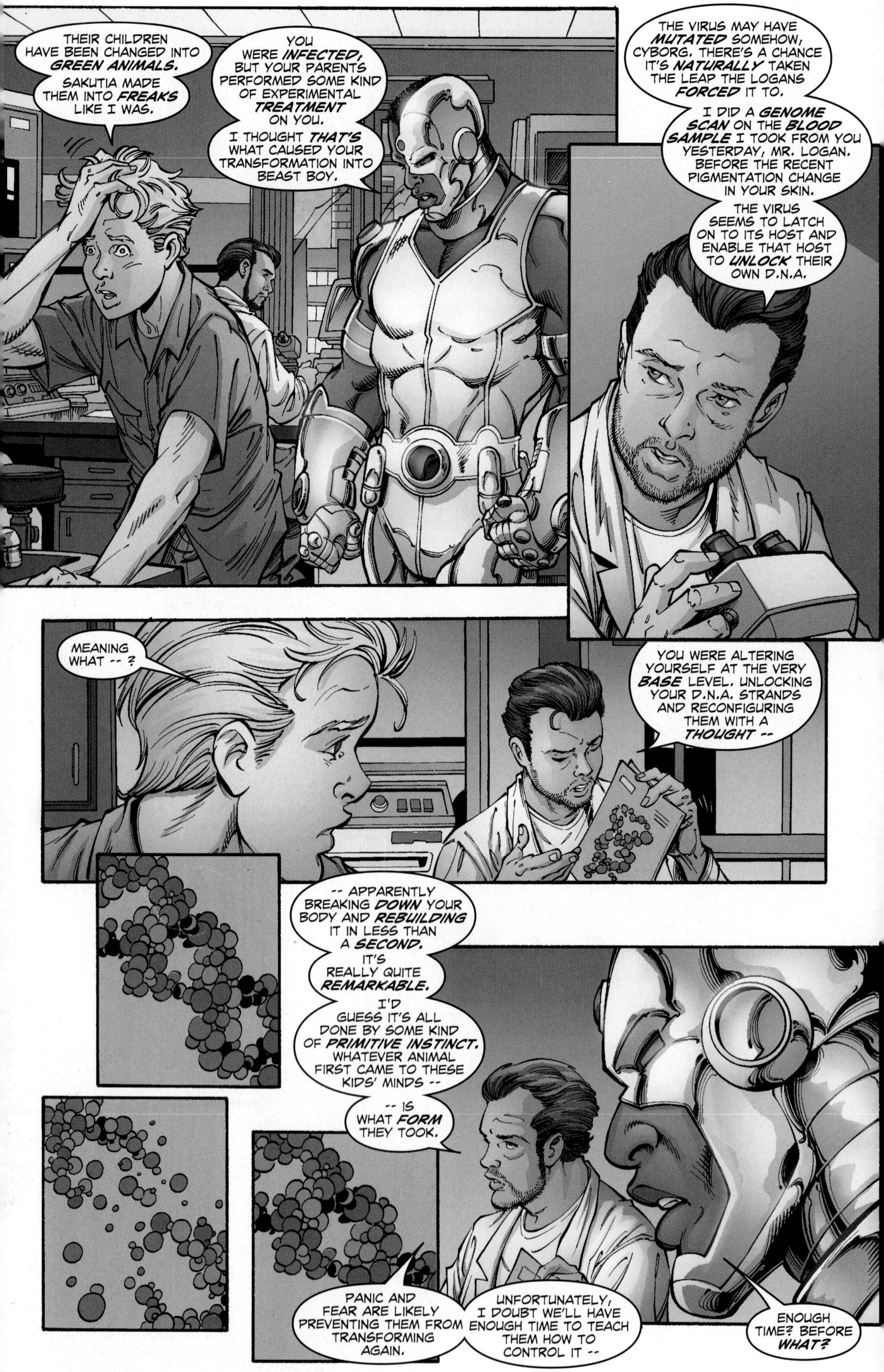
THEIR CHILDREN HAVE BEEN CHANGED INTO GREEN ANIMALS.
SAKUTIA MADE THEM INTO FREAKS LIKE I WAS.
YOU WERE INFECTED, BUT YOUR PARENTS PERFORMED SOME KIND OF EXPERIMENTAL TREATMENT ON YOU.
I THOUGHT THAT'S WHAT CAUSED YOUR TRANSFORMATION INTO BEAST BOY.
THE VIRUS MAY HAVE MUTATED SOMEHOW, CYBORG. THERE'S A CHANCE IT'S NATURALLY TAKEN THE LEAP THE LOGANS FORCED IT TO.
I DID A GENOME SCAN ON THE BLOOD SAMPLE I TOOK FROM YOU YESTERDAY, MR. LOGAN. BEFORE THE RECENT PIGMENTATION CHANGE IN YOUR SKIN.
THE VIRUS SEEMS TO LATCH ON TO ITS HOST AND ENABLE THAT HOST TO UNLOCK THEIR OWN D.N.A.
MEANING WHAT -- ?
YOU WERE ALTERING YOURSELF AT THE VERY BASE LEVEL. UNLOCKING YOUR D.N.A. STRANDS AND RECONFIGURING THEM WITH A THOUGHT --
-- APPARENTLY BREAKING DOWN YOUR BODY AND REBUILDING IT IN LESS THAN A SECOND.
IT'S REALLY QUITE REMARKABLE.
I'D GUESS IT'S ALL DONE BY SOME KIND OF PRIMITIVE INSTINCT. WHATEVER ANIMAL FIRST CAME TO THESE KIDS' MINDS --
-- IS WHAT FORM THEY TOOK.
PANIC AND FEAR ARE LIKELY PREVENTING THEM FROM TRANSFORMING AGAIN.
UNFORTUNATELY, I DOUBT WE'LL HAVE ENOUGH TIME TO TEACH THEM HOW TO CONTROL IT --
ENOUGH TIME? BEFORE WHAT?

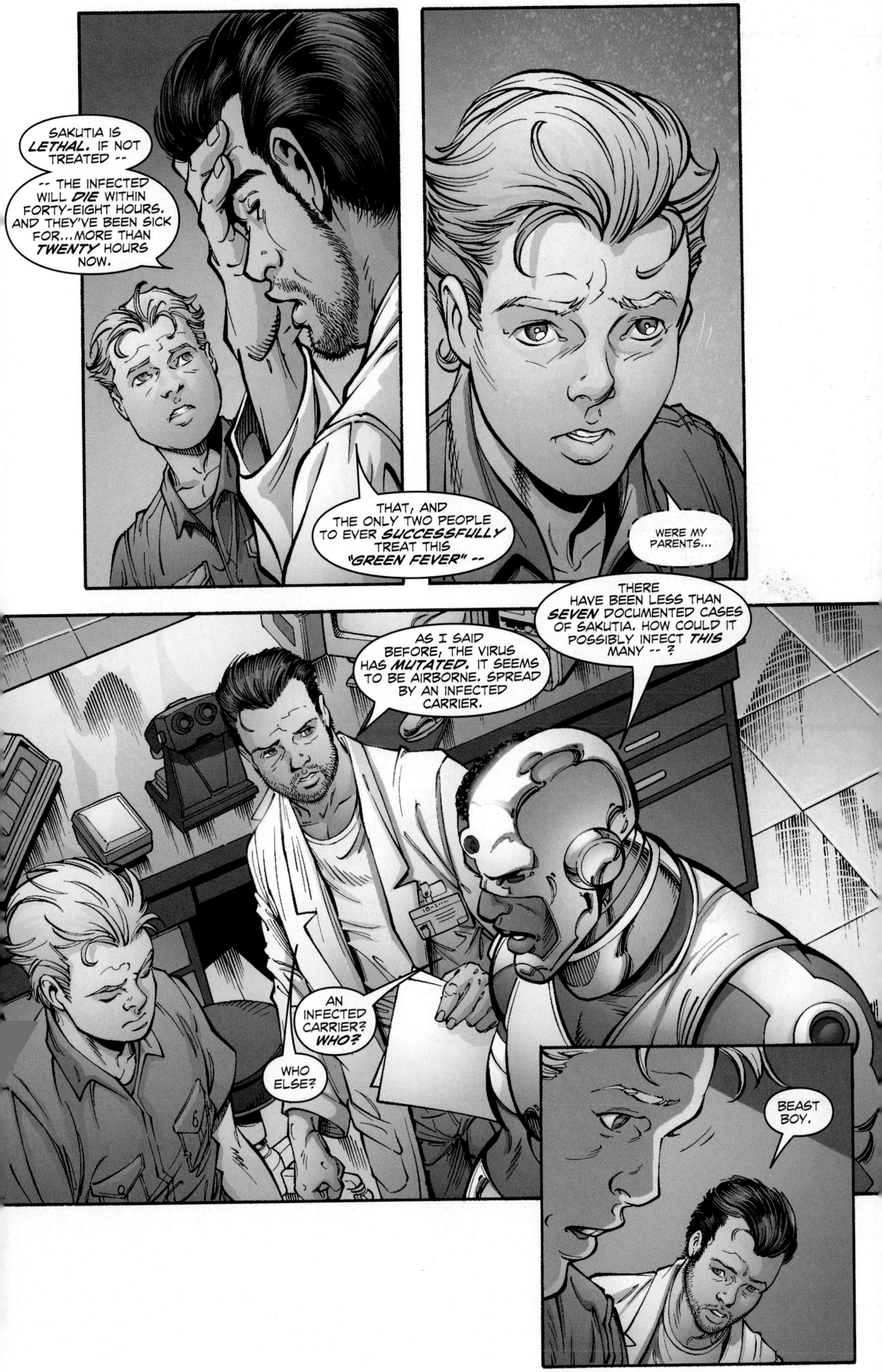
SAKUTIA IS LETHAL. IF NOT TREATED --
-- THE INFECTED WILL DIE WITHIN FORTY-EIGHT HOURS. AND THEY'VE BEEN SICK FOR...MORE THAN TWENTY HOURS NOW.
THAT, AND THE ONLY TWO PEOPLE TO EVER SUCCESSFULLY TREAT THIS "GREEN FEVER" --
WERE MY PARENTS...
THERE HAVE BEEN LESS THAN SEVEN DOCUMENTED CASES OF SAKUTIA. HOW COULD IT POSSIBLY INFECT THIS MANY -- ?
AS I SAID BEFORE, THE VIRUS HAS MUTATED. IT SEEMS TO BE AIRBORNE. SPREAD BY AN INFECTED CARRIER.
AN INFECTED CARRIER? WHO?
WHO ELSE?
BEAST BOY.

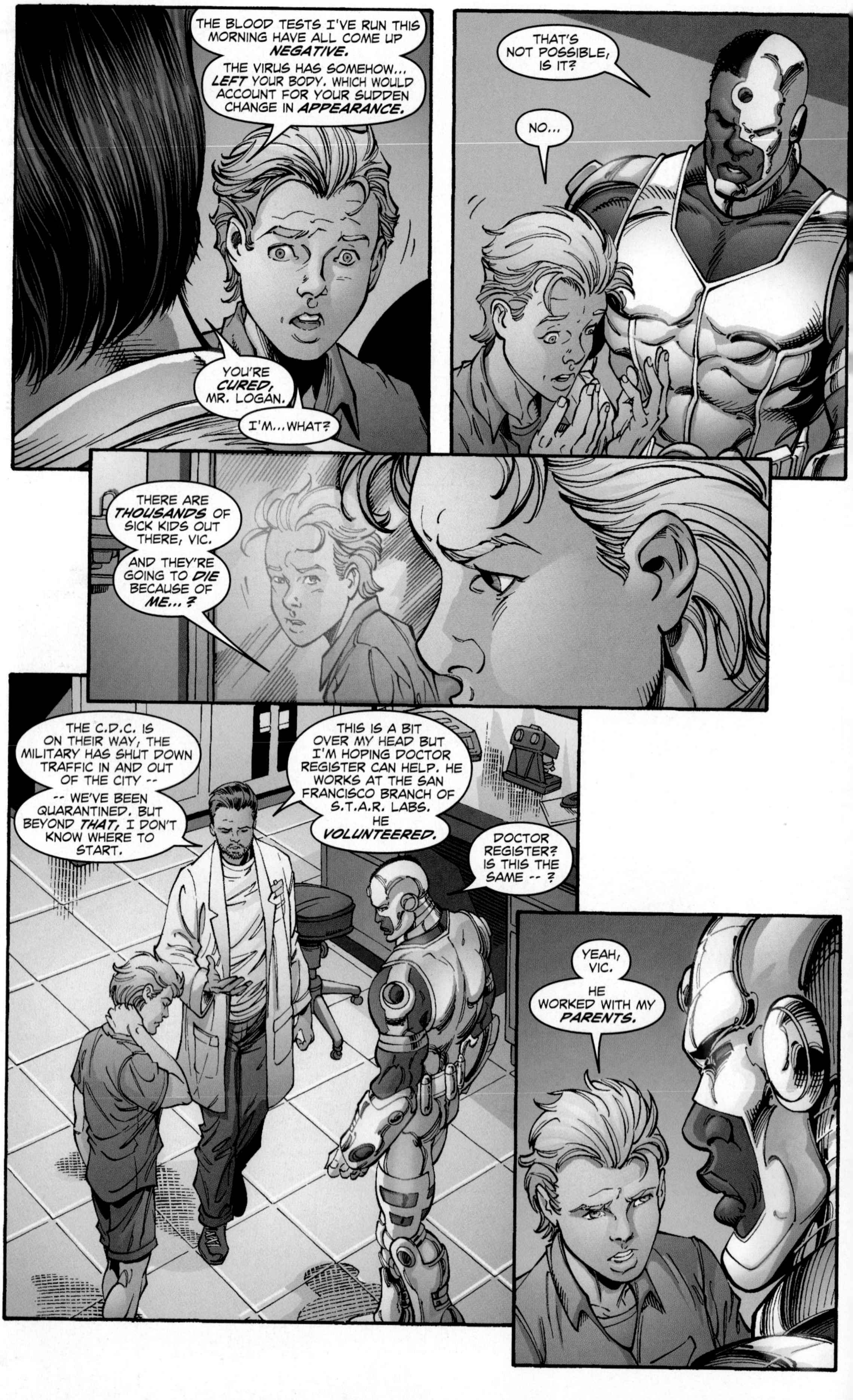
THE BLOOD TESTS I'VE RUN THIS MORNING HAVE ALL COME UP *NEGATIVE.*
THE VIRUS HAS SOMEHOW... *LEFT* YOUR BODY. WHICH WOULD ACCOUNT FOR YOUR SUDDEN CHANGE IN *APPEARANCE.*
YOU'RE *CURED,* MR. LOGAN.
I'M...WHAT?
THAT'S NOT POSSIBLE, IS IT?
NO...
THERE ARE *THOUSANDS* OF SICK KIDS OUT THERE, VIC.
AND THEY'RE GOING TO *DIE* BECAUSE OF *ME...?*
THE C.D.C. IS ON THEIR WAY, THE MILITARY HAS SHUT DOWN TRAFFIC IN AND OUT OF THE CITY --
-- WE'VE BEEN QUARANTINED. BUT BEYOND *THAT,* I DON'T KNOW WHERE TO START.
THIS IS A BIT OVER MY HEAD BUT I'M HOPING DOCTOR REGISTER CAN HELP. HE WORKS AT THE SAN FRANCISCO BRANCH OF S.T.A.R. LABS.
HE *VOLUNTEERED.*
DOCTOR REGISTER? IS THIS THE SAME -- ?
YEAH, VIC.
HE WORKED WITH MY *PARENTS.*

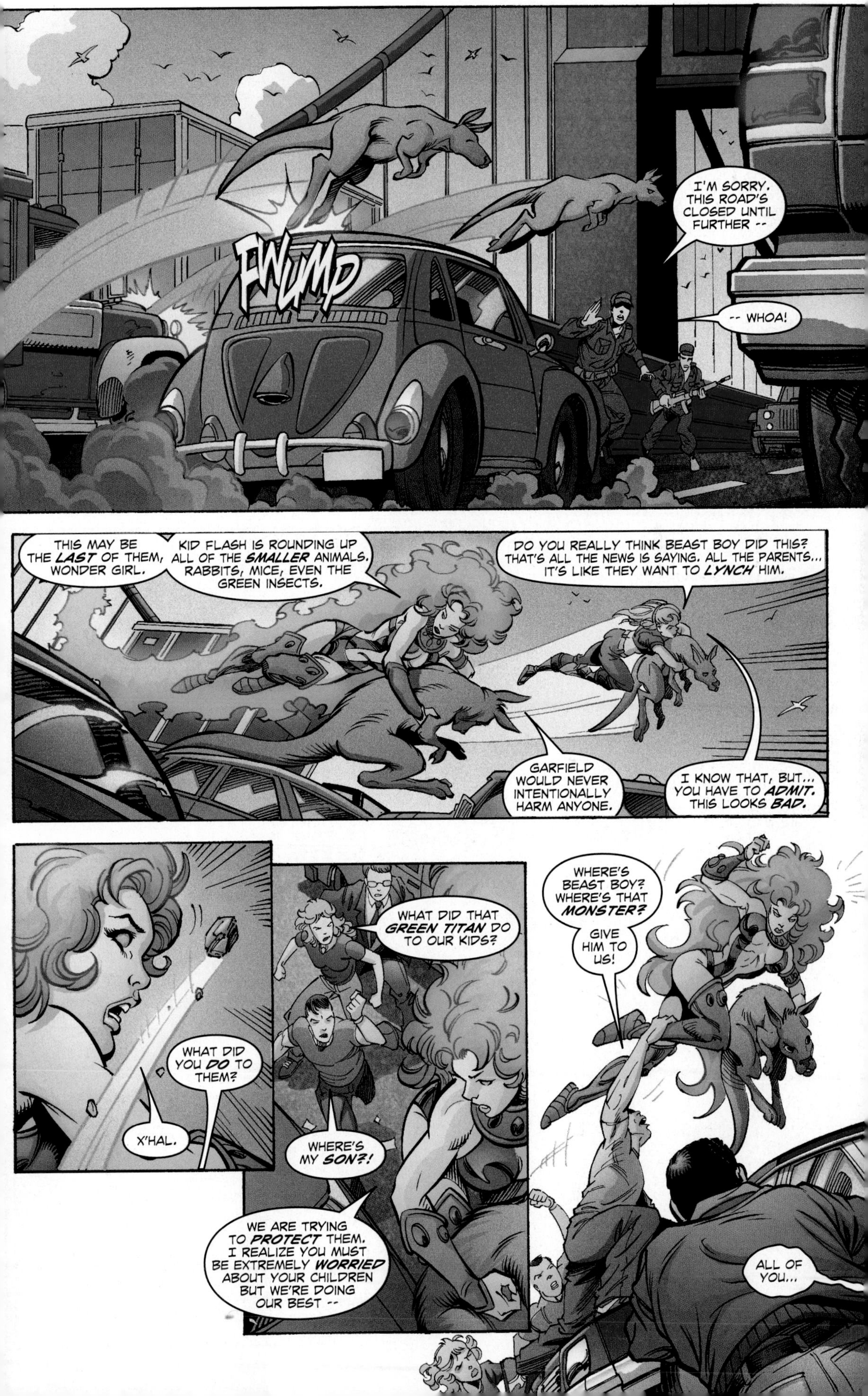
FWUMP
I'M SORRY. THIS ROAD'S CLOSED UNTIL FURTHER --
-- WHOA!
THIS MAY BE THE LAST OF THEM, WONDER GIRL.
KID FLASH IS ROUNDING UP ALL OF THE SMALLER ANIMALS. RABBITS, MICE, EVEN THE GREEN INSECTS.
DO YOU REALLY THINK BEAST BOY DID THIS? THAT'S ALL THE NEWS IS SAYING. ALL THE PARENTS... IT'S LIKE THEY WANT TO LYNCH HIM.
GARFIELD WOULD NEVER INTENTIONALLY HARM ANYONE.
I KNOW THAT, BUT... YOU HAVE TO ADMIT. THIS LOOKS BAD.
WHAT DID YOU DO TO THEM?
X'HAL.
WHAT DID THAT GREEN TITAN DO TO OUR KIDS?
WHERE'S MY SON?!
WE ARE TRYING TO PROTECT THEM. I REALIZE YOU MUST BE EXTREMELY WORRIED ABOUT YOUR CHILDREN BUT WE'RE DOING OUR BEST --
WHERE'S BEAST BOY? WHERE'S THAT MONSTER?
GIVE HIM TO US!
ALL OF YOU...

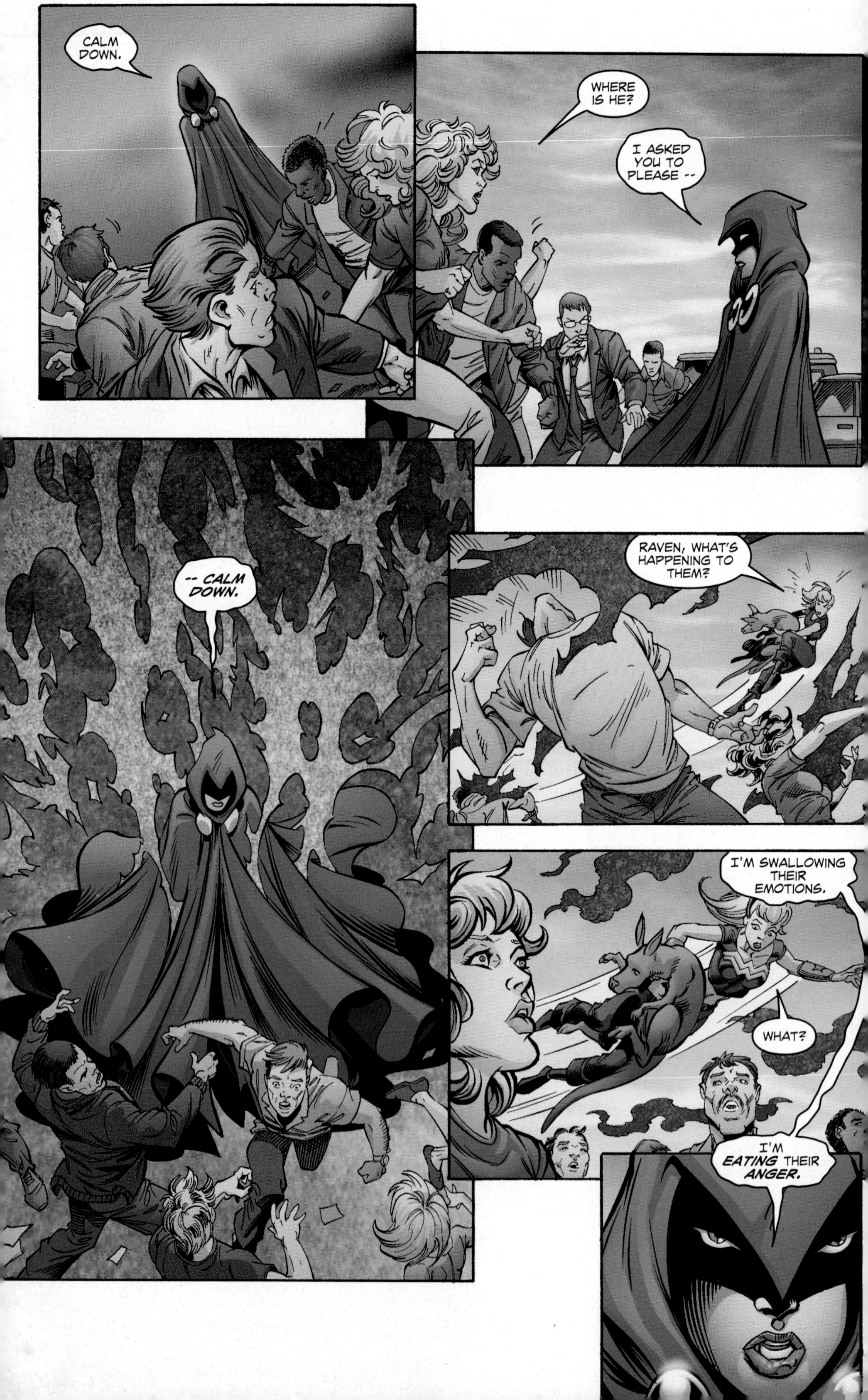
CALM DOWN.
WHERE IS HE?
I ASKED YOU TO PLEASE --
-- CALM DOWN.
RAVEN, WHAT'S HAPPENING TO THEM?
I'M SWALLOWING THEIR EMOTIONS.
WHAT?
I'M EATING THEIR ANGER.

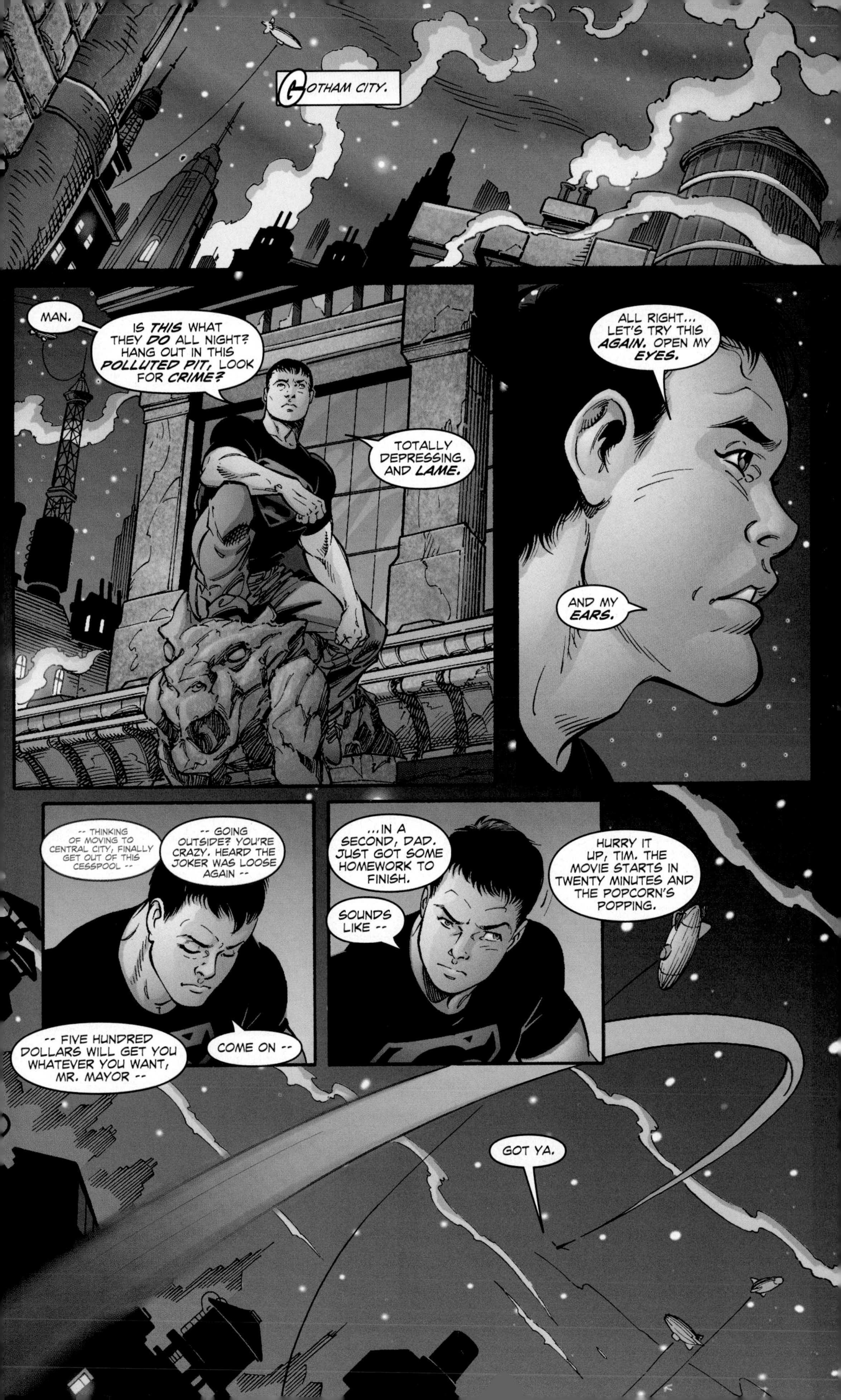
GOTHAM CITY.
MAN.
IS THIS WHAT THEY DO ALL NIGHT? HANG OUT IN THIS POLLUTED PIT, LOOK FOR CRIME?
TOTALLY DEPRESSING. AND LAME.
ALL RIGHT... LET'S TRY THIS AGAIN. OPEN MY EYES.
AND MY EARS.
-- THINKING OF MOVING TO CENTRAL CITY, FINALLY GET OUT OF THIS CESSPOOL --
-- GOING OUTSIDE? YOU'RE CRAZY. HEARD THE JOKER WAS LOOSE AGAIN --
-- FIVE HUNDRED DOLLARS WILL GET YOU WHATEVER YOU WANT, MR. MAYOR --
COME ON --
...IN A SECOND, DAD. JUST GOT SOME HOMEWORK TO FINISH.
SOUNDS LIKE --
HURRY IT UP, TIM. THE MOVIE STARTS IN TWENTY MINUTES AND THE POPCORN'S POPPING.
GOT YA.

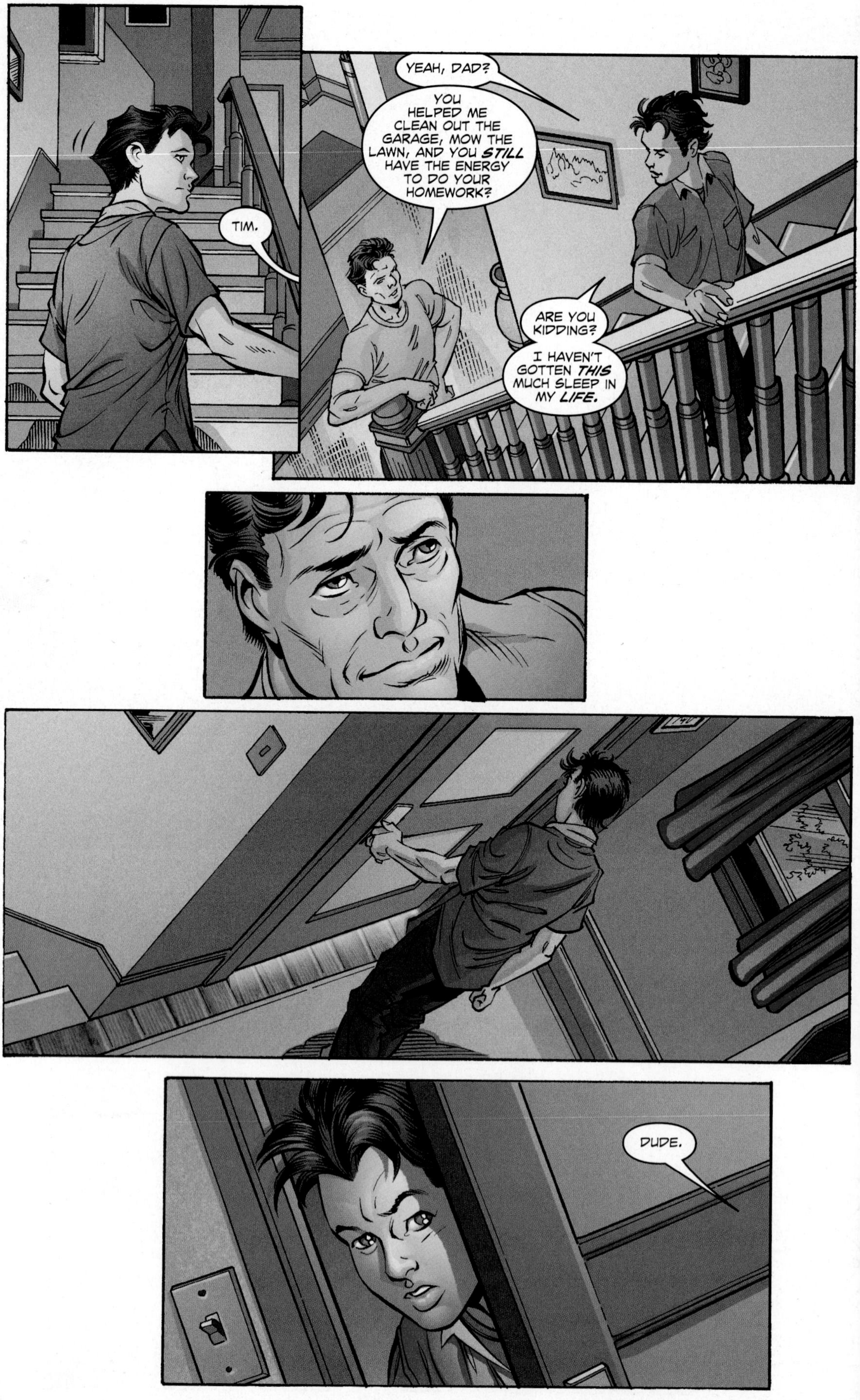
TIM.
YEAH, DAD?
YOU HELPED ME CLEAN OUT THE GARAGE, MOW THE LAWN, AND YOU STILL HAVE THE ENERGY TO DO YOUR HOMEWORK?
ARE YOU KIDDING?
I HAVEN'T GOTTEN THIS MUCH SLEEP IN MY LIFE.
DUDE.

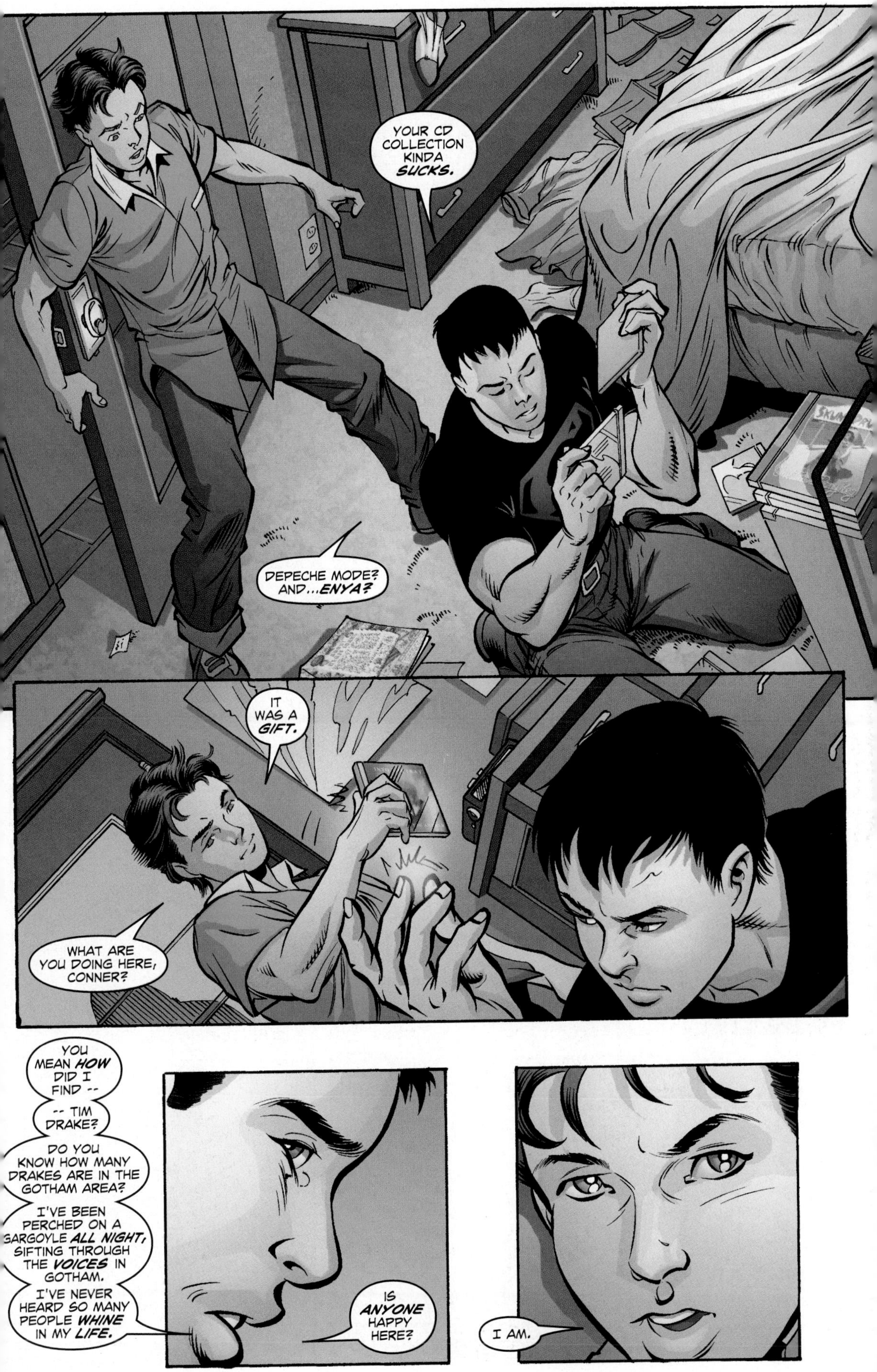
YOUR CD COLLECTION KINDA SUCKS.
DEPECHE MODE? AND...ENYA?
IT WAS A GIFT.
WHAT ARE YOU DOING HERE, CONNER?
YOU MEAN HOW DID I FIND --
-- TIM DRAKE?
DO YOU KNOW HOW MANY DRAKES ARE IN THE GOTHAM AREA?
I'VE BEEN PERCHED ON A GARGOYLE ALL NIGHT, SIFTING THROUGH THE VOICES IN GOTHAM.
I'VE NEVER HEARD SO MANY PEOPLE WHINE IN MY LIFE.
IS ANYONE HAPPY HERE?
I AM.

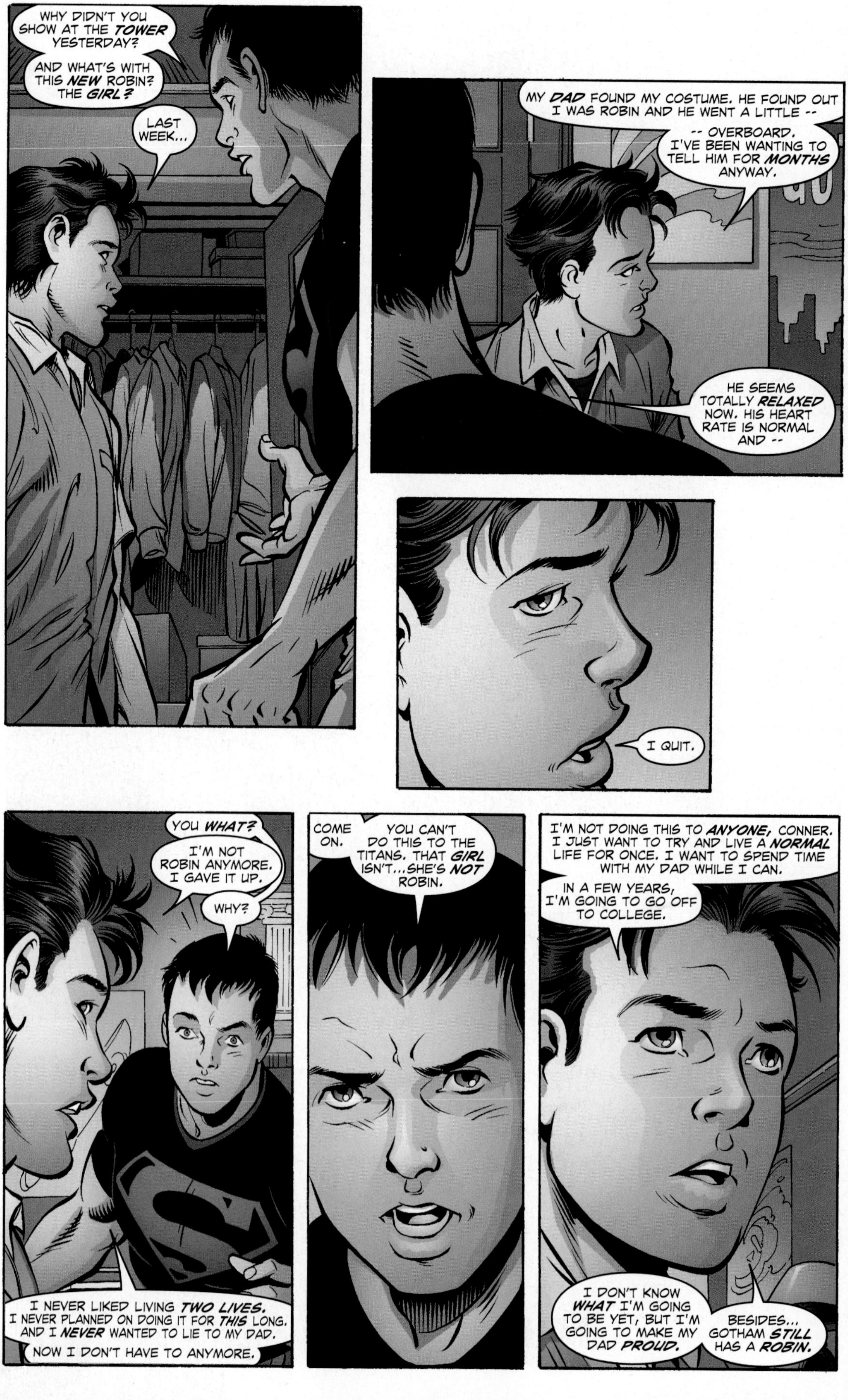

WHY DIDN'T YOU SHOW AT THE TOWER YESTERDAY?
AND WHAT'S WITH THIS NEW ROBIN? THE GIRL?
LAST WEEK...
MY DAD FOUND MY COSTUME. HE FOUND OUT I WAS ROBIN AND HE WENT A LITTLE --
-- OVERBOARD. I'VE BEEN WANTING TO TELL HIM FOR MONTHS ANYWAY.
HE SEEMS TOTALLY RELAXED NOW. HIS HEART RATE IS NORMAL AND --
I QUIT.
YOU WHAT?
I'M NOT ROBIN ANYMORE. I GAVE IT UP.
WHY?
I NEVER LIKED LIVING TWO LIVES. I NEVER PLANNED ON DOING IT FOR THIS LONG. AND I NEVER WANTED TO LIE TO MY DAD.
NOW I DON'T HAVE TO ANYMORE.
COME ON.
YOU CAN'T DO THIS TO THE TITANS. THAT GIRL ISN'T...SHE'S NOT ROBIN.
I'M NOT DOING THIS TO ANYONE, CONNER. I JUST WANT TO TRY AND LIVE A NORMAL LIFE FOR ONCE. I WANT TO SPEND TIME WITH MY DAD WHILE I CAN.
IN A FEW YEARS, I'M GOING TO GO OFF TO COLLEGE.
I DON'T KNOW WHAT I'M GOING TO BE YET, BUT I'M GOING TO MAKE MY DAD PROUD.
BESIDES... GOTHAM STILL HAS A ROBIN.

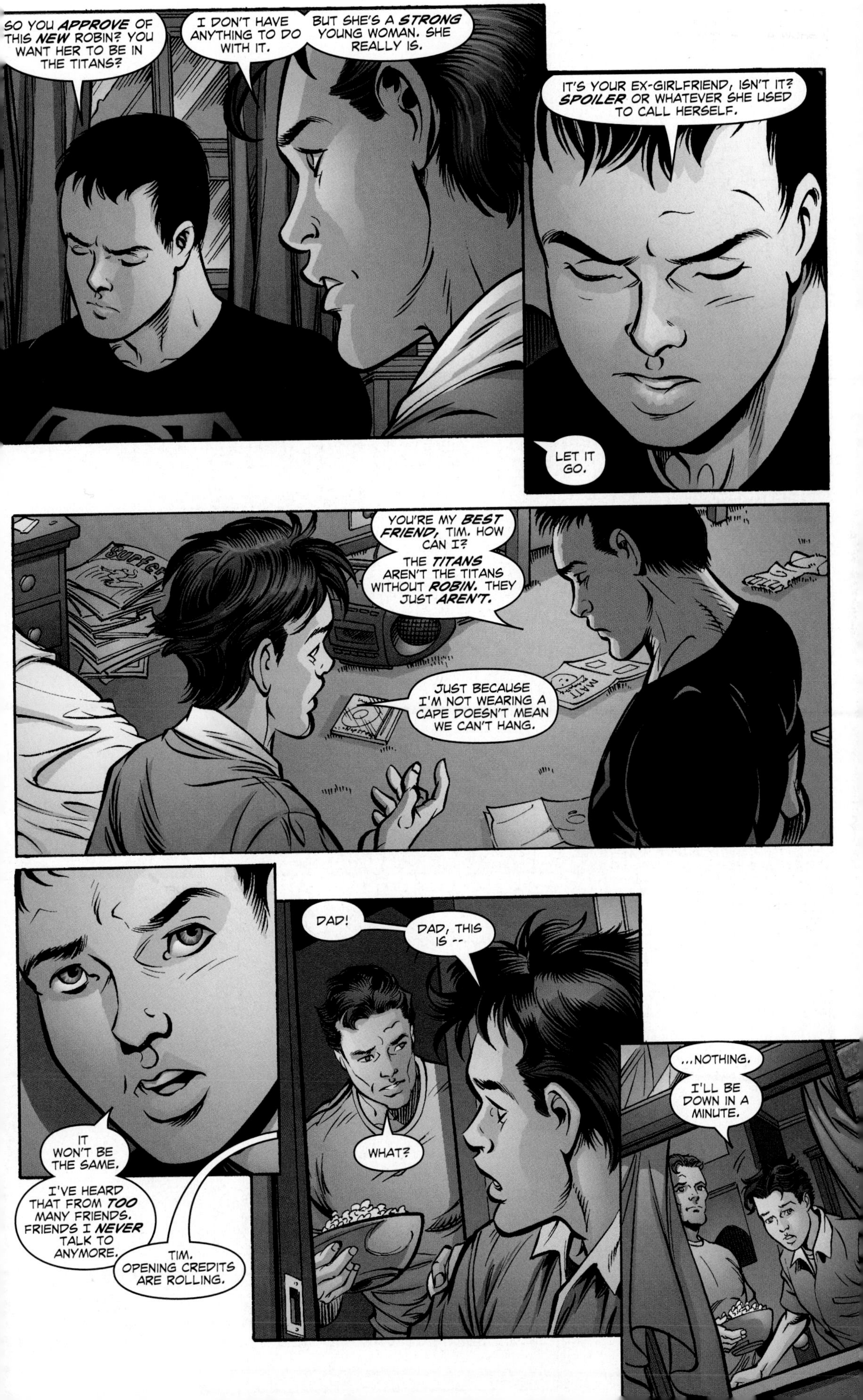

SO YOU APPROVE OF THIS NEW ROBIN? YOU WANT HER TO BE IN THE TITANS?
I DON'T HAVE ANYTHING TO DO WITH IT.
BUT SHE'S A STRONG YOUNG WOMAN. SHE REALLY IS.
IT'S YOUR EX-GIRLFRIEND, ISN'T IT? SPOILER OR WHATEVER SHE USED TO CALL HERSELF.
LET IT GO.
YOU'RE MY BEST FRIEND, TIM. HOW CAN I?
THE TITANS AREN'T THE TITANS WITHOUT ROBIN. THEY JUST AREN'T.
JUST BECAUSE I'M NOT WEARING A CAPE DOESN'T MEAN WE CAN'T HANG.
IT WON'T BE THE SAME.
I'VE HEARD THAT FROM TOO MANY FRIENDS. FRIENDS I NEVER TALK TO ANYMORE.
TIM. OPENING CREDITS ARE ROLLING.
DAD!
DAD, THIS IS --
WHAT?
...NOTHING.
I'LL BE DOWN IN A MINUTE.

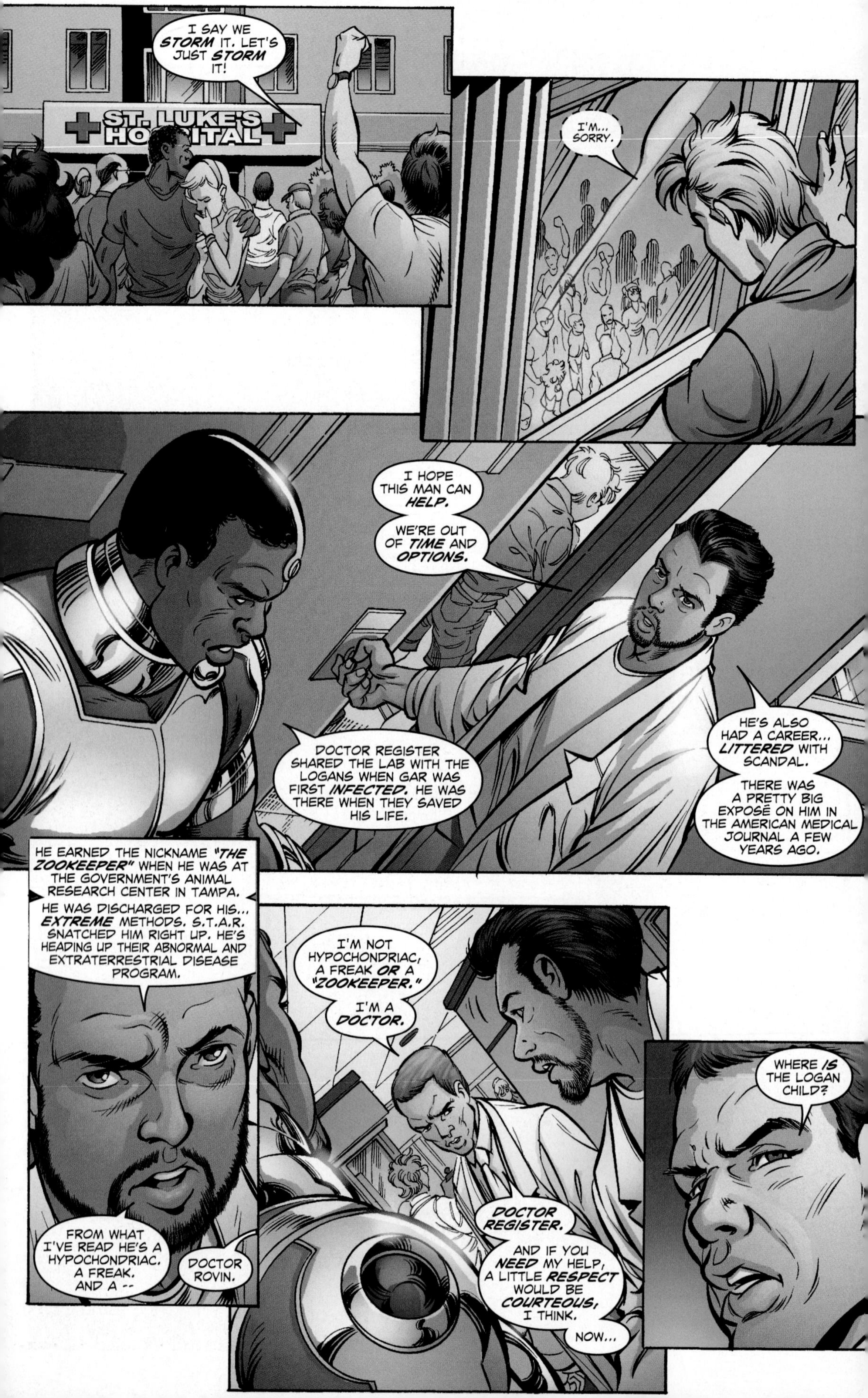

I SAY WE STORM IT. LET'S JUST STORM IT!
ST. LUKE'S HO ITAL
I'M... SORRY.
I HOPE THIS MAN CAN HELP.
WE'RE OUT OF TIME AND OPTIONS.
DOCTOR REGISTER SHARED THE LAB WITH THE LOGANS WHEN GAR WAS FIRST INFECTED. HE WAS THERE WHEN THEY SAVED HIS LIFE.
HE'S ALSO HAD A CAREER... LITTERED WITH SCANDAL.
THERE WAS A PRETTY BIG EXPOSÉ ON HIM IN THE AMERICAN MEDICAL JOURNAL A FEW YEARS AGO.
HE EARNED THE NICKNAME "THE ZOOKEEPER" WHEN HE WAS AT THE GOVERNMENT'S ANIMAL RESEARCH CENTER IN TAMPA.
HE WAS DISCHARGED FOR HIS... EXTREME METHODS. S.T.A.R. SNATCHED HIM RIGHT UP. HE'S HEADING UP THEIR ABNORMAL AND EXTRATERRESTRIAL DISEASE PROGRAM.
FROM WHAT I'VE READ HE'S A HYPOCHONDRIAC. A FREAK. AND A --
DOCTOR ROVIN.
I'M NOT HYPOCHONDRIAC, A FREAK OR A "ZOOKEEPER."
I'M A DOCTOR.
DOCTOR REGISTER.
AND IF YOU NEED MY HELP, A LITTLE RESPECT WOULD BE COURTEOUS, I THINK.
NOW...
WHERE IS THE LOGAN CHILD?

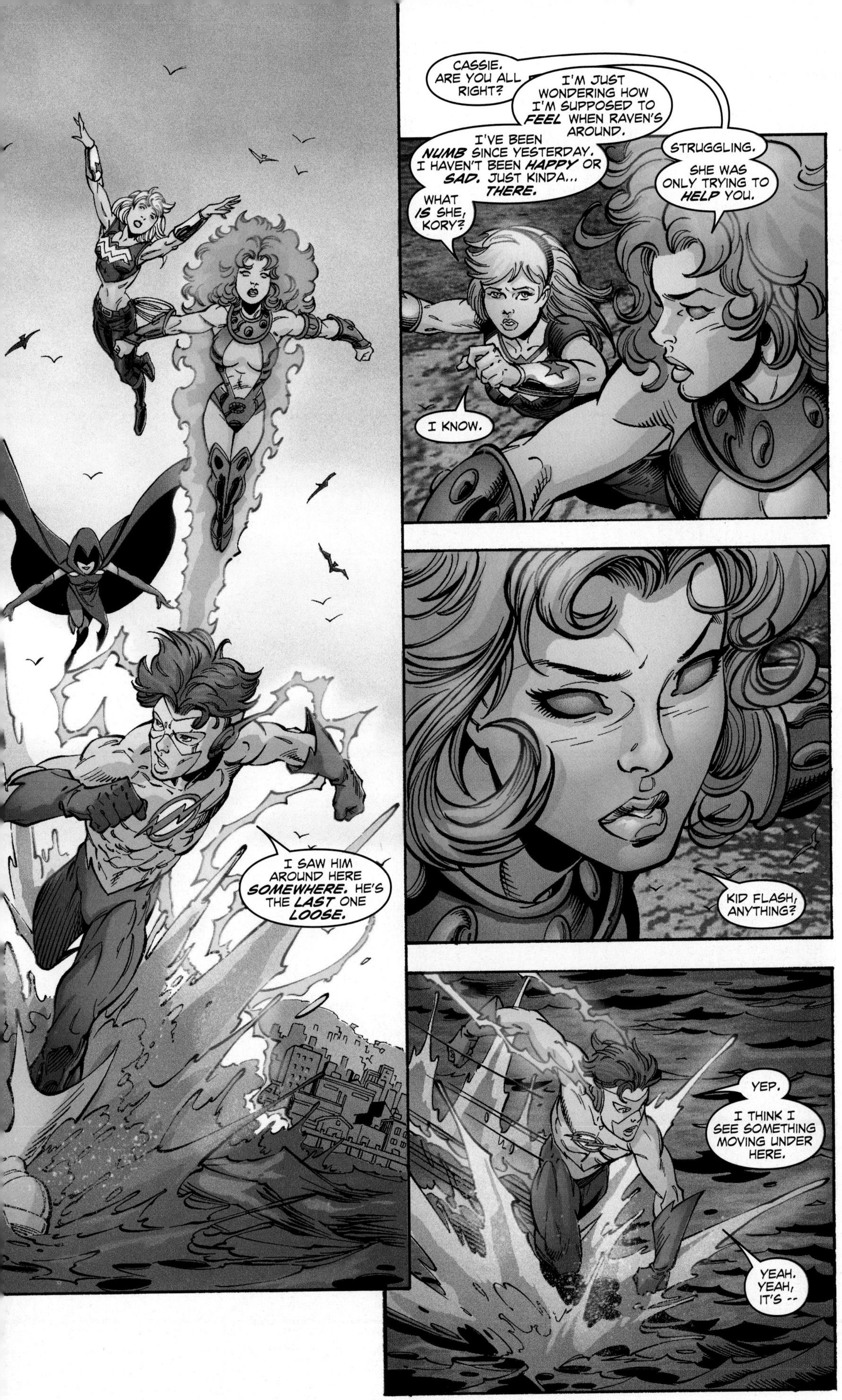
I SAW HIM AROUND HERE SOMEWHERE. HE'S THE LAST ONE LOOSE.
CASSIE. ARE YOU ALL RIGHT?
I'M JUST WONDERING HOW I'M SUPPOSED TO FEEL WHEN RAVEN'S AROUND.
STRUGGLING.
SHE WAS ONLY TRYING TO HELP YOU.
I'VE BEEN NUMB SINCE YESTERDAY. I HAVEN'T BEEN HAPPY OR SAD. JUST KINDA... THERE.
WHAT IS SHE, KORY?
I KNOW.
KID FLASH, ANYTHING?
YEP.
I THINK I SEE SOMETHING MOVING UNDER HERE.
YEAH. YEAH, IT'S --

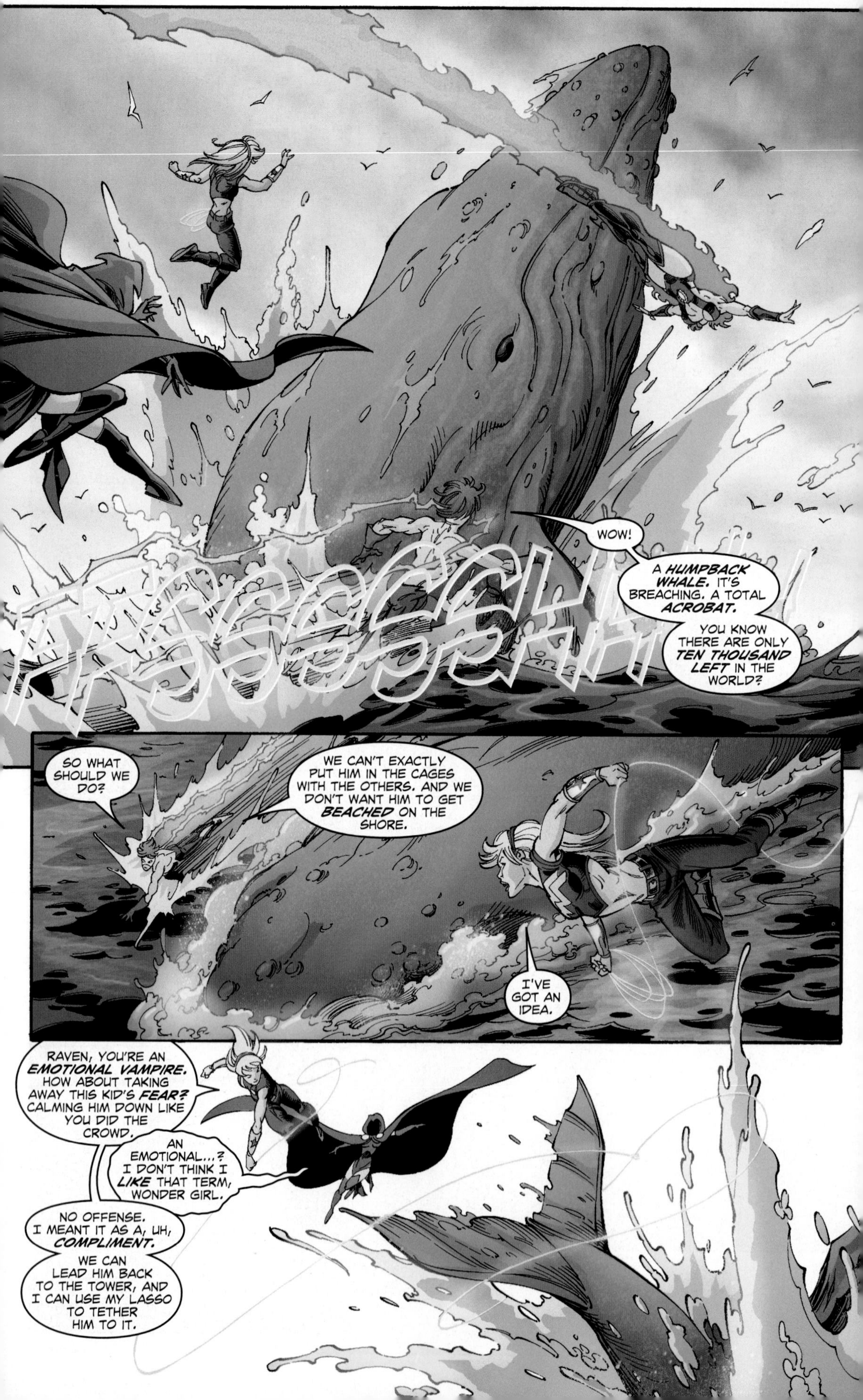

FFSSSCHHH!
WOW!
A HUMPBACK WHALE. IT'S BREACHING. A TOTAL ACROBAT.
YOU KNOW THERE ARE ONLY TEN THOUSAND LEFT IN THE WORLD?
SO WHAT SHOULD WE DO?
WE CAN'T EXACTLY PUT HIM IN THE CAGES WITH THE OTHERS. AND WE DON'T WANT HIM TO GET BEACHED ON THE SHORE.
I'VE GOT AN IDEA.
RAVEN, YOU'RE AN EMOTIONAL VAMPIRE. HOW ABOUT TAKING AWAY THIS KID'S FEAR? CALMING HIM DOWN LIKE YOU DID THE CROWD.
AN EMOTIONAL...? I DON'T THINK I LIKE THAT TERM, WONDER GIRL.
NO OFFENSE. I MEANT IT AS A, UH, COMPLIMENT.
WE CAN LEAD HIM BACK TO THE TOWER, AND I CAN USE MY LASSO TO TETHER HIM TO IT.

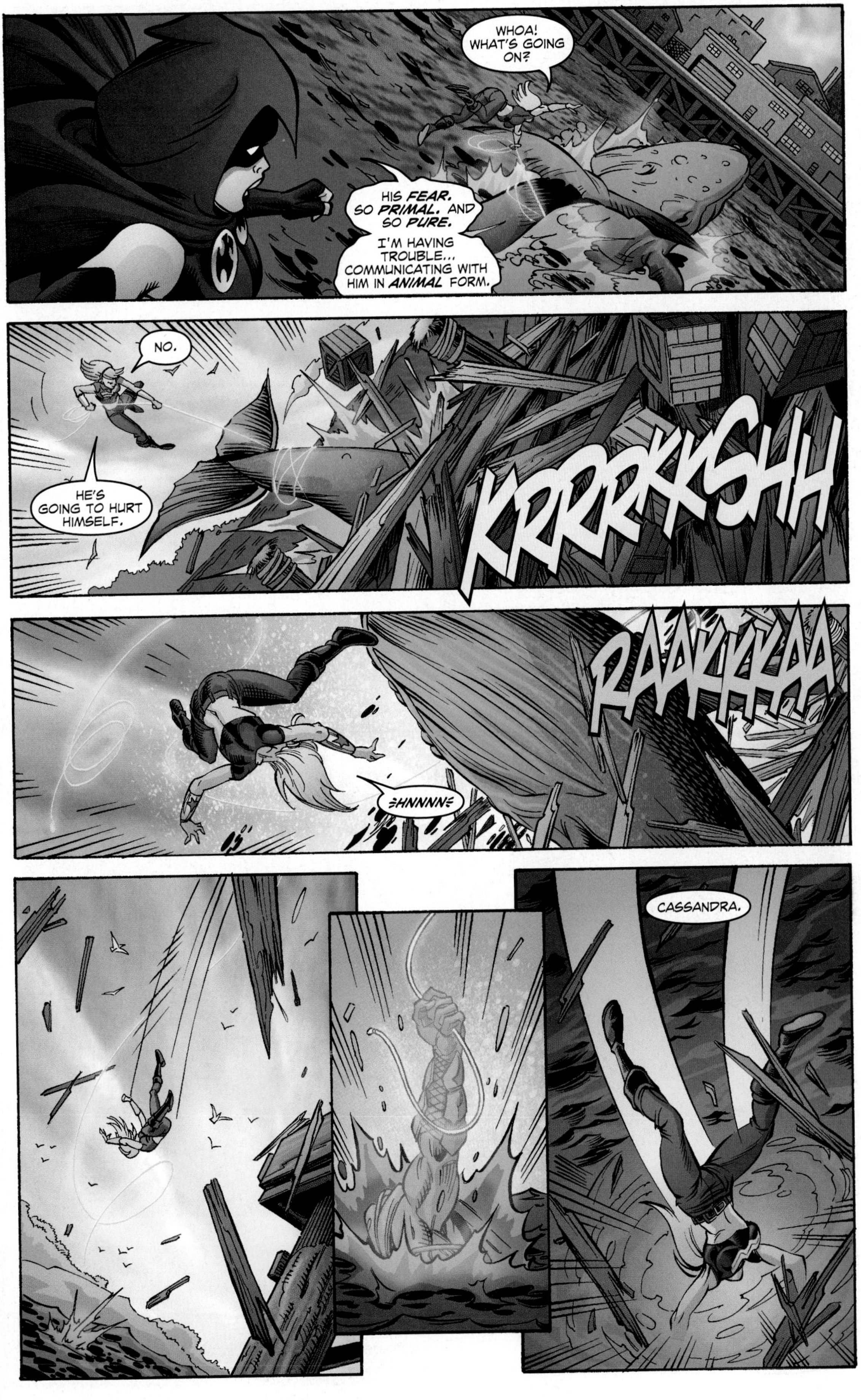

WHOA! WHAT'S GOING ON?
HIS FEAR. SO PRIMAL. AND SO PURE.
I'M HAVING TROUBLE... COMMUNICATING WITH HIM IN ANIMAL FORM.
NO.
HE'S GOING TO HURT HIMSELF.
KRRRKSHH
RAAKKKAA
HNNNN
CASSANDRA.

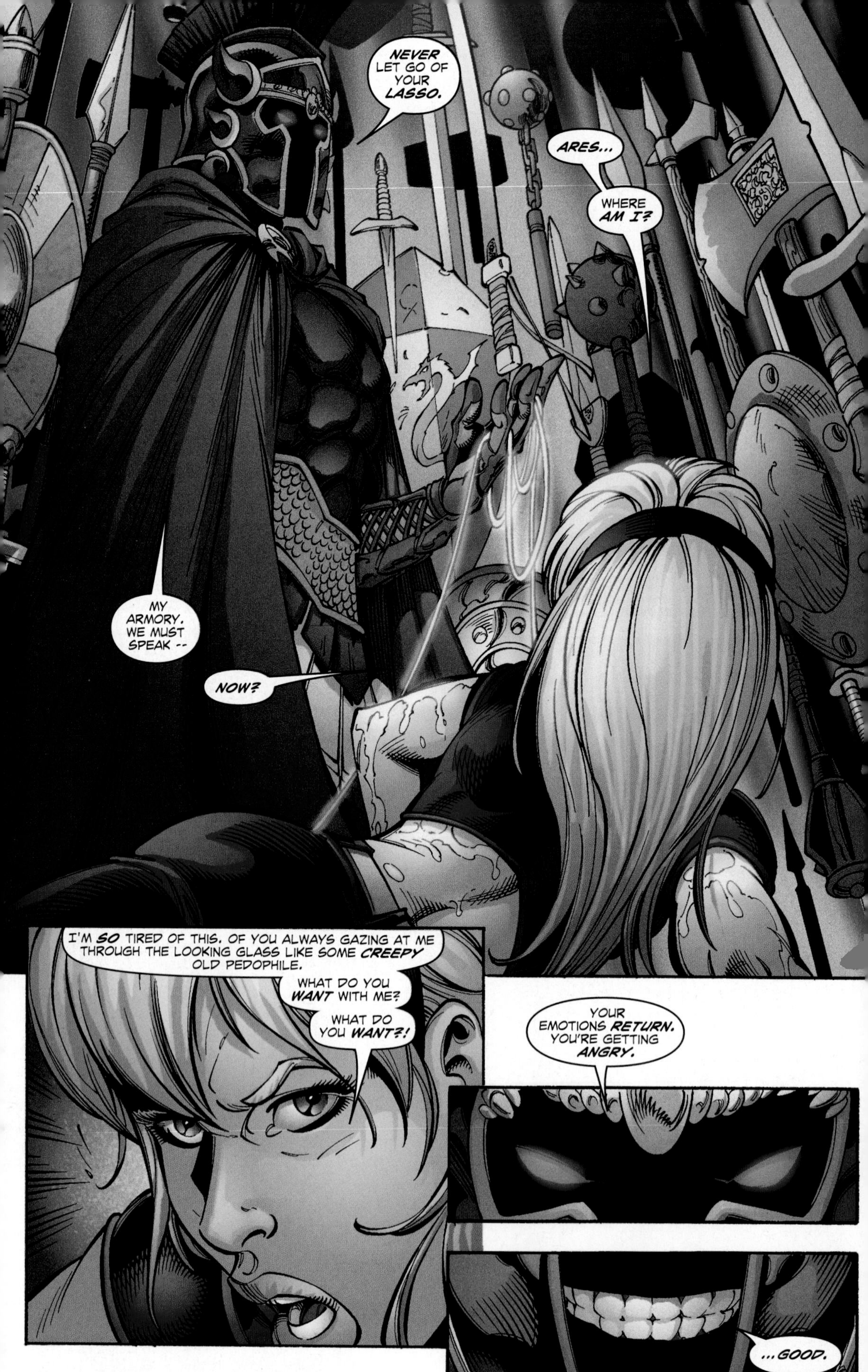
NEVER LET GO OF YOUR LASSO.
ARES...
WHERE AM I?
MY ARMORY. WE MUST SPEAK --
NOW?
I'M SO TIRED OF THIS. OF YOU ALWAYS GAZING AT ME THROUGH THE LOOKING GLASS LIKE SOME CREEPY OLD PEDOPHILE.
WHAT DO YOU WANT WITH ME?
WHAT DO YOU WANT?!
YOUR EMOTIONS RETURN. YOU'RE GETTING ANGRY.
...GOOD.

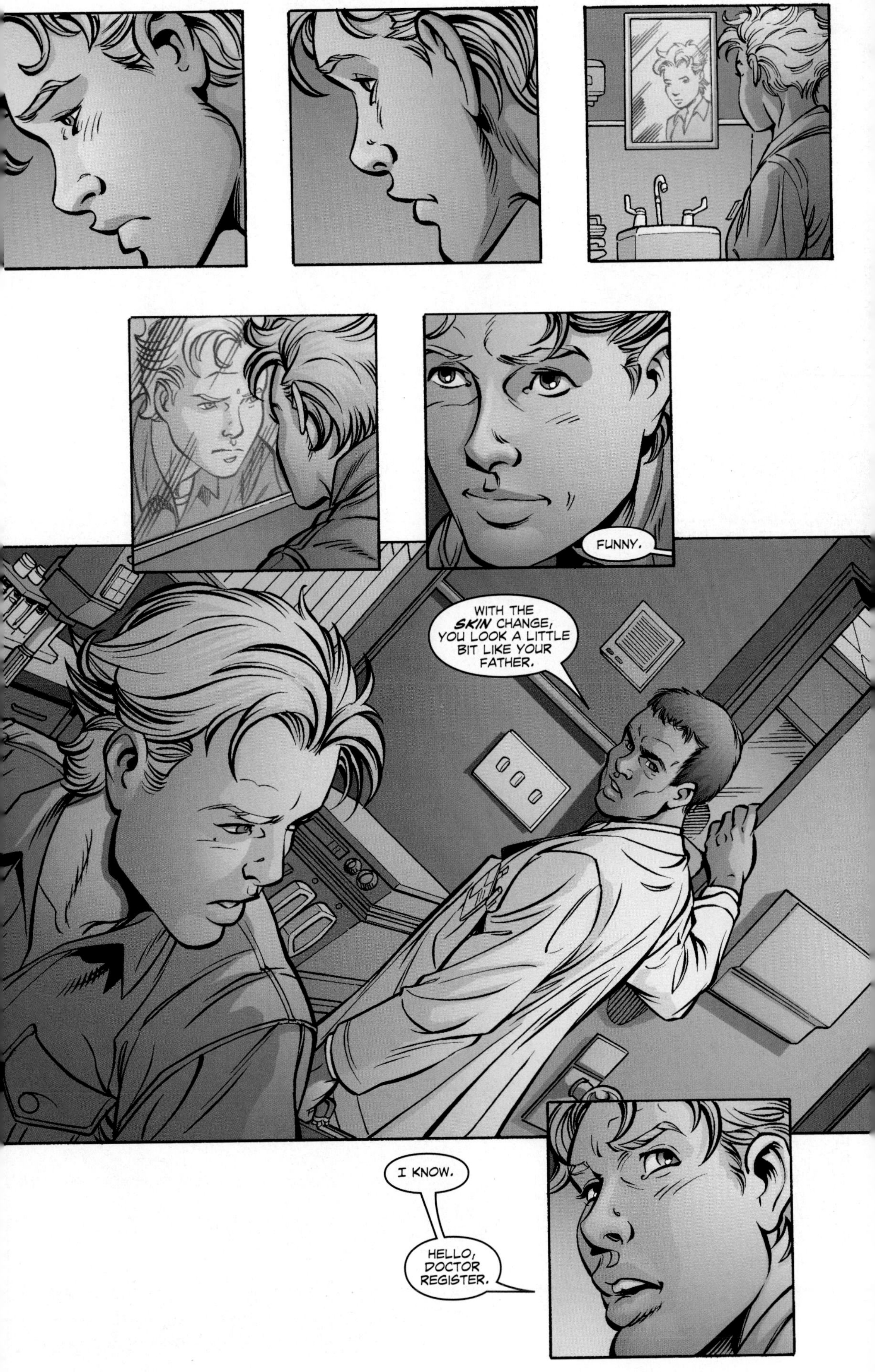
FUNNY.
WITH THE SKIN CHANGE, YOU LOOK A LITTLE BIT LIKE YOUR FATHER.
I KNOW.
HELLO, DOCTOR REGISTER.

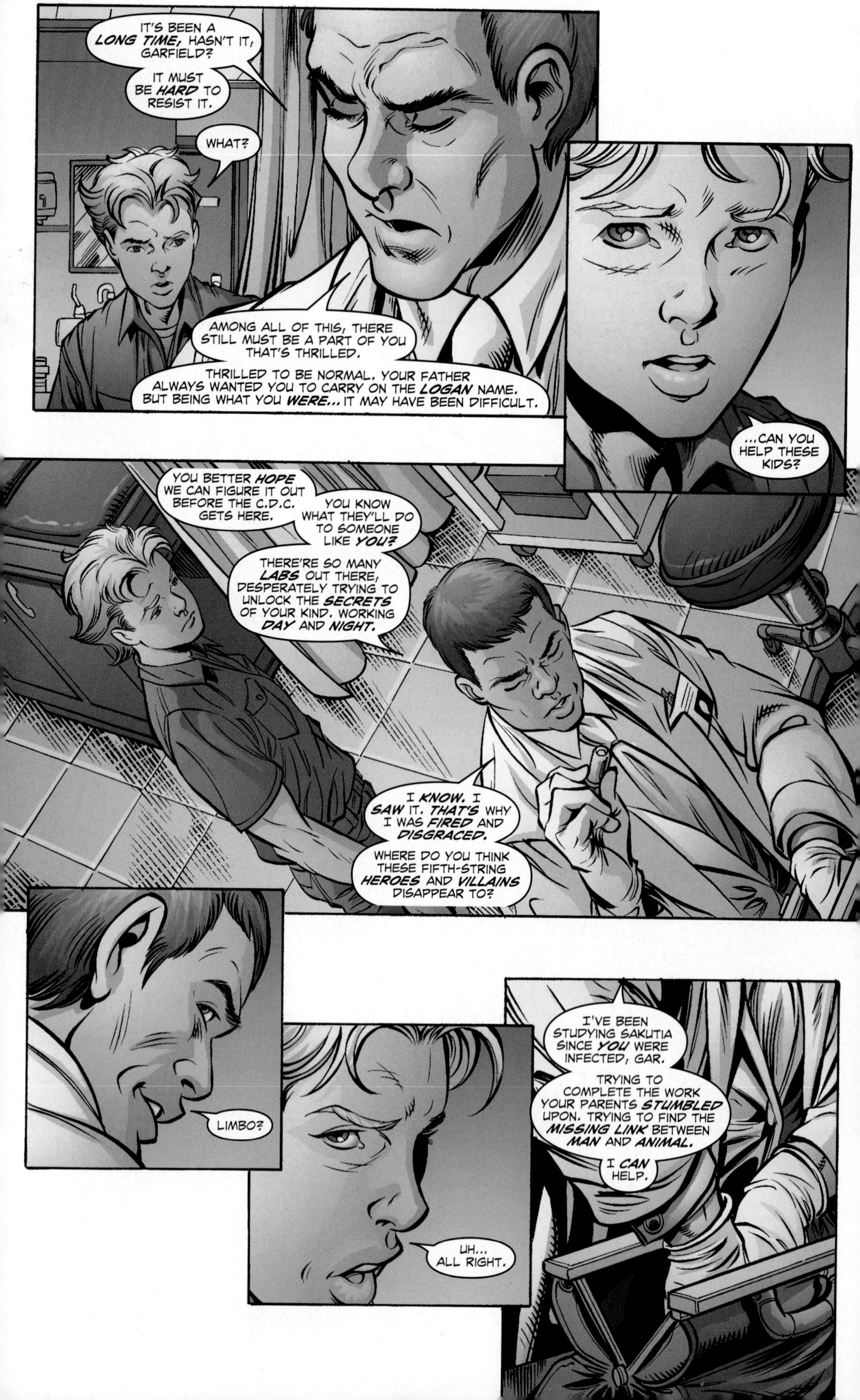
IT'S BEEN A LONG TIME, HASN'T IT, GARFIELD?
IT MUST BE HARD TO RESIST IT.
WHAT?
AMONG ALL OF THIS, THERE STILL MUST BE A PART OF YOU THAT'S THRILLED.
THRILLED TO BE NORMAL. YOUR FATHER ALWAYS WANTED YOU TO CARRY ON THE LOGAN NAME. BUT BEING WHAT YOU WERE... IT MAY HAVE BEEN DIFFICULT.
...CAN YOU HELP THESE KIDS?
YOU BETTER HOPE WE CAN FIGURE IT OUT BEFORE THE C.D.C. GETS HERE.
YOU KNOW WHAT THEY'LL DO TO SOMEONE LIKE YOU?
THERE'RE SO MANY LABS OUT THERE, DESPERATELY TRYING TO UNLOCK THE SECRETS OF YOUR KIND. WORKING DAY AND NIGHT.
I KNOW. I SAW IT. THAT'S WHY I WAS FIRED AND DISGRACED.
WHERE DO YOU THINK THESE FIFTH-STRING HEROES AND VILLAINS DISAPPEAR TO?
LIMBO?
UH... ALL RIGHT.
I'VE BEEN STUDYING SAKUTIA SINCE YOU WERE INFECTED, GAR.
TRYING TO COMPLETE THE WORK YOUR PARENTS STUMBLED UPON. TRYING TO FIND THE MISSING LINK BETWEEN MAN AND ANIMAL.
I CAN HELP.

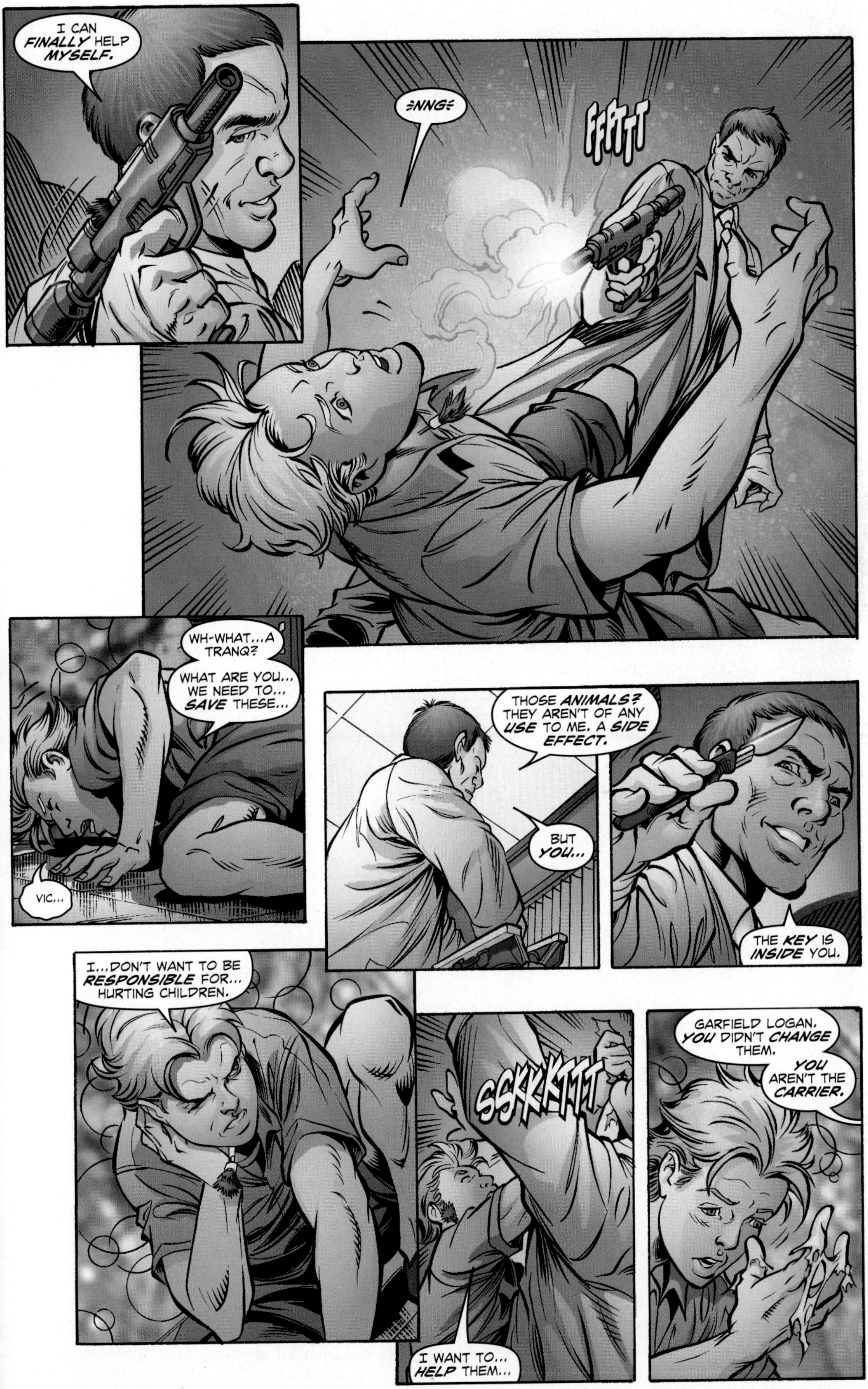
I CAN FINALLY HELP MYSELF.
NNG
FFFTTT
WH-WHAT...A TRANQ?
WHAT ARE YOU... WE NEED TO... SAVE THESE...
VIC...
THOSE ANIMALS? THEY AREN'T OF ANY USE TO ME. A SIDE EFFECT.
BUT YOU...
THE KEY IS INSIDE YOU.
I...DON'T WANT TO BE RESPONSIBLE FOR... HURTING CHILDREN.
SSKKKTTT
I WANT TO... HELP THEM...
GARFIELD LOGAN. YOU DIDN'T CHANGE THEM.
YOU AREN'T THE CARRIER.

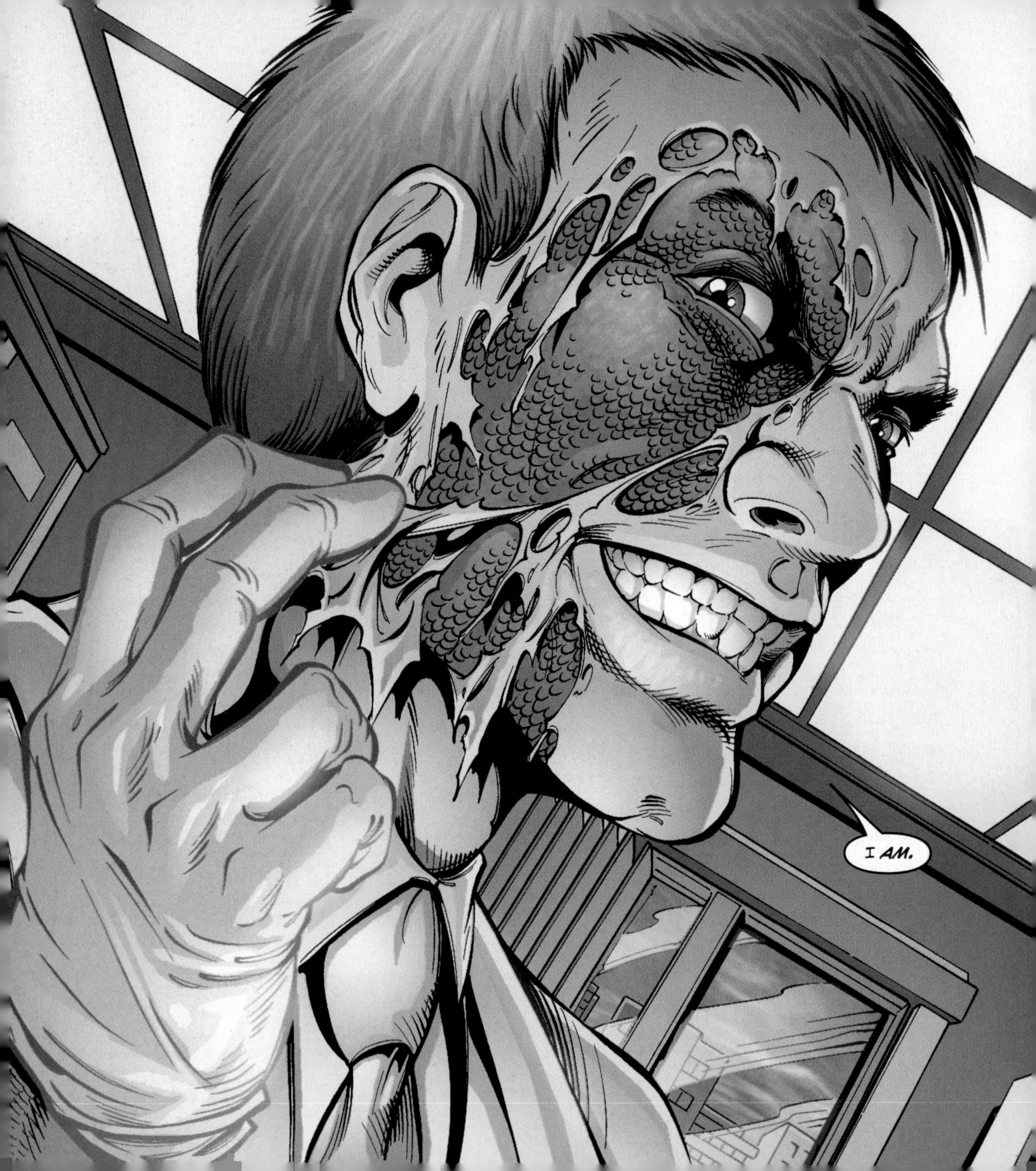
I AM.

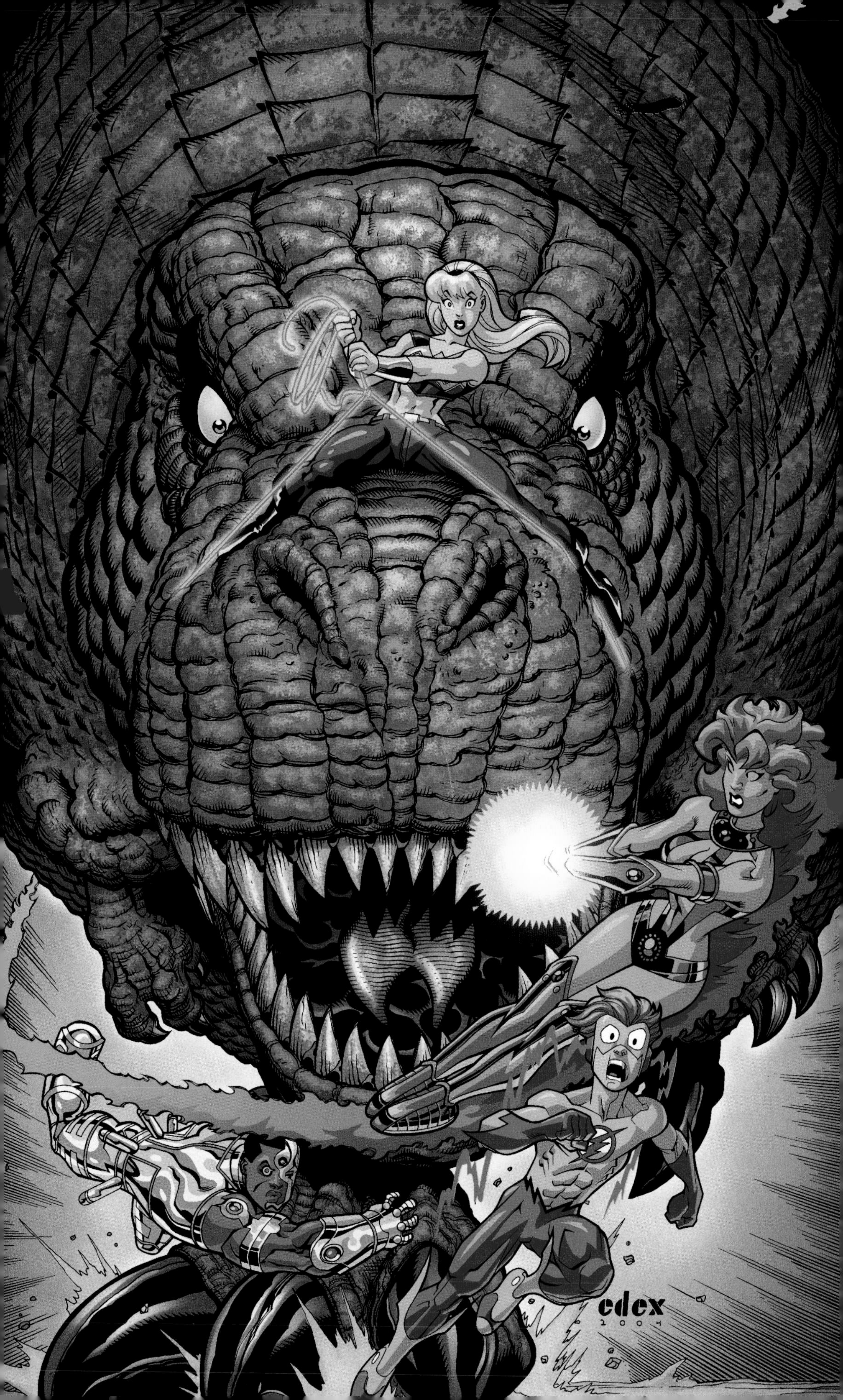
2004

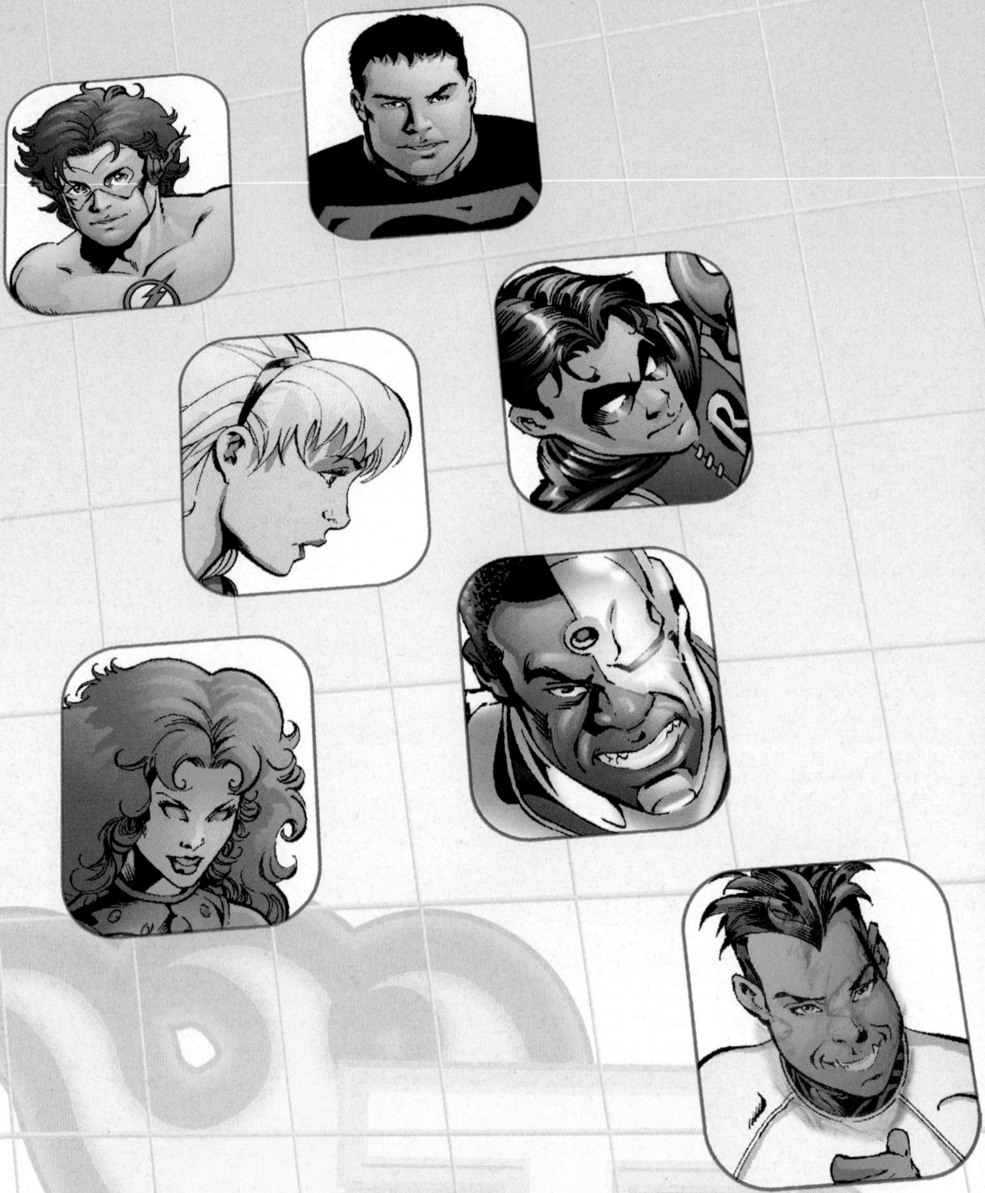

TEEN TITANS #15

GEOFF JOHNS
Writer

TOM GRUMMETT
Penciller

LARY STUCKER
Inker

JEROMY COX
Colorist

COMICRAFT
Letterer

ED McGUINNESS, DEXTER VINES & DAVE STEWART
Cover Artists

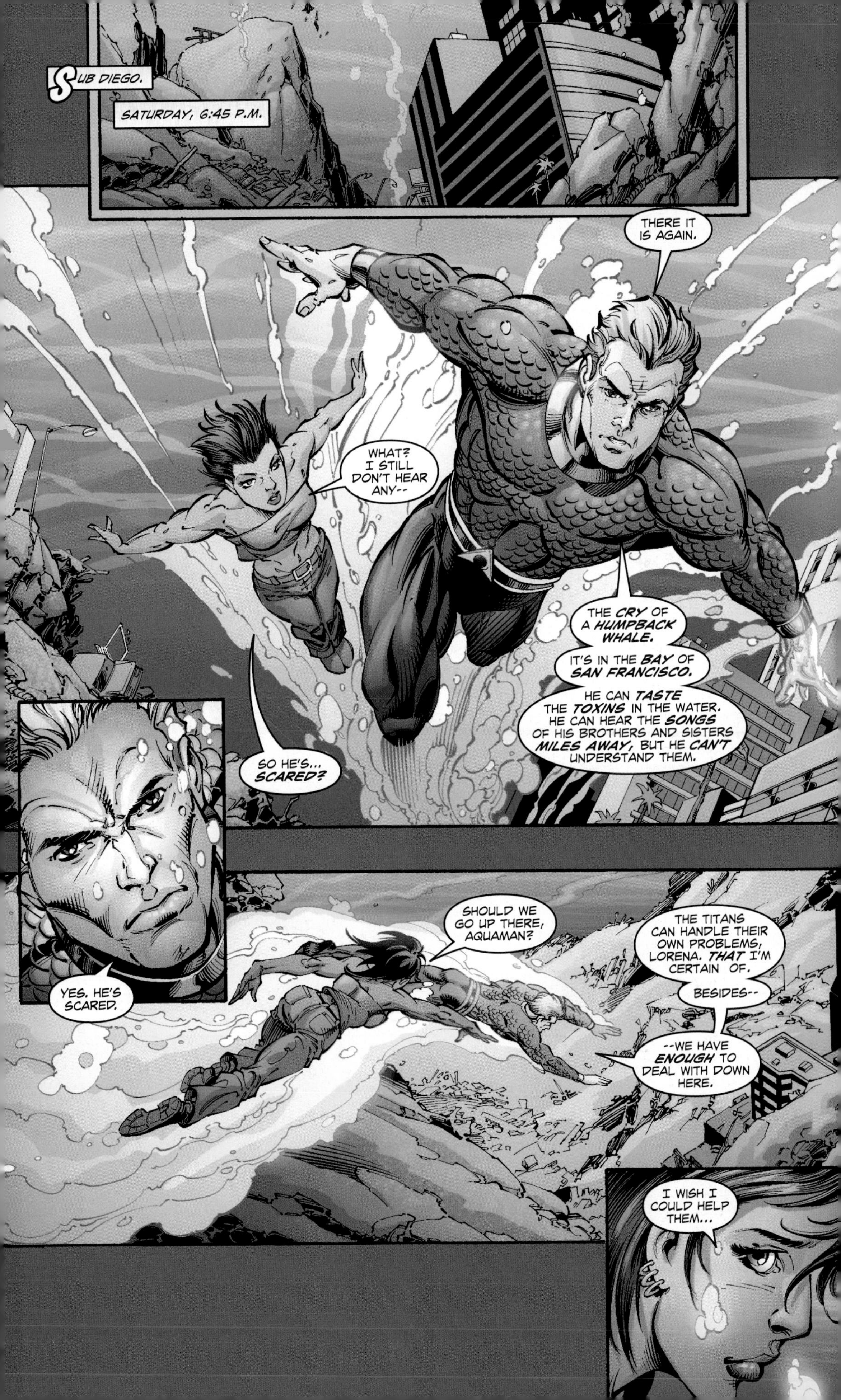

SUB DIEGO.
SATURDAY, 6:45 P.M.
THERE IT IS AGAIN.
WHAT? I STILL DON'T HEAR ANY--
THE CRY OF A HUMPBACK WHALE.
IT'S IN THE BAY OF SAN FRANCISCO.
HE CAN TASTE THE TOXINS IN THE WATER. HE CAN HEAR THE SONGS OF HIS BROTHERS AND SISTERS MILES AWAY, BUT HE CAN'T UNDERSTAND THEM.
SO HE'S... SCARED?
YES. HE'S SCARED.
SHOULD WE GO UP THERE, AQUAMAN?
THE TITANS CAN HANDLE THEIR OWN PROBLEMS, LORENA. THAT I'M CERTAIN OF.
BESIDES--
--WE HAVE ENOUGH TO DEAL WITH DOWN HERE.
I WISH I COULD HELP THEM...

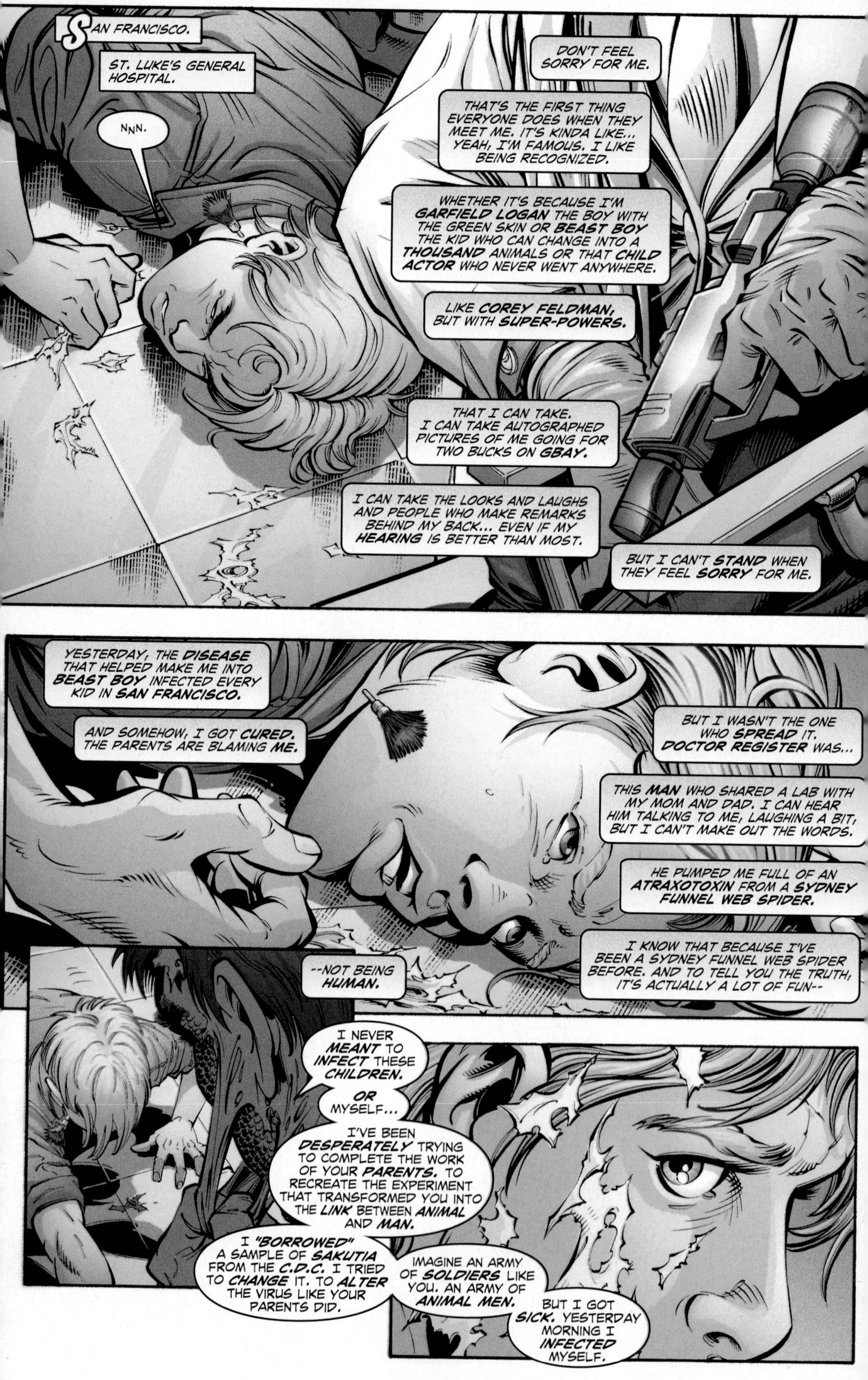
SAN FRANCISCO.
ST. LUKE'S GENERAL HOSPITAL.
NNN.
DON'T FEEL SORRY FOR ME.
THAT'S THE FIRST THING EVERYONE DOES WHEN THEY MEET ME. IT'S KINDA LIKE... YEAH, I'M FAMOUS. I LIKE BEING RECOGNIZED.
WHETHER IT'S BECAUSE I'M GARFIELD LOGAN THE BOY WITH THE GREEN SKIN OR BEAST BOY THE KID WHO CAN CHANGE INTO A THOUSAND ANIMALS OR THAT CHILD ACTOR WHO NEVER WENT ANYWHERE.
LIKE COREY FELDMAN, BUT WITH SUPER-POWERS.
THAT I CAN TAKE. I CAN TAKE AUTOGRAPHED PICTURES OF ME GOING FOR TWO BUCKS ON GBAY.
I CAN TAKE THE LOOKS AND LAUGHS AND PEOPLE WHO MAKE REMARKS BEHIND MY BACK... EVEN IF MY HEARING IS BETTER THAN MOST.
BUT I CAN'T STAND WHEN THEY FEEL SORRY FOR ME.
YESTERDAY, THE DISEASE THAT HELPED MAKE ME INTO BEAST BOY INFECTED EVERY KID IN SAN FRANCISCO.
AND SOMEHOW, I GOT CURED. THE PARENTS ARE BLAMING ME.
BUT I WASN'T THE ONE WHO SPREAD IT. DOCTOR REGISTER WAS...
THIS MAN WHO SHARED A LAB WITH MY MOM AND DAD. I CAN HEAR HIM TALKING TO ME, LAUGHING A BIT, BUT I CAN'T MAKE OUT THE WORDS.
HE PUMPED ME FULL OF AN ATRAXOTOXIN FROM A SYDNEY FUNNEL WEB SPIDER.
I KNOW THAT BECAUSE I'VE BEEN A SYDNEY FUNNEL WEB SPIDER BEFORE. AND TO TELL YOU THE TRUTH, IT'S ACTUALLY A LOT OF FUN--
--NOT BEING HUMAN.
I NEVER MEANT TO INFECT THESE CHILDREN.
OR MYSELF...
I'VE BEEN DESPERATELY TRYING TO COMPLETE THE WORK OF YOUR PARENTS. TO RECREATE THE EXPERIMENT THAT TRANSFORMED YOU INTO THE LINK BETWEEN ANIMAL AND MAN.
I "BORROWED" A SAMPLE OF SAKUTIA FROM THE C.D.C. I TRIED TO CHANGE IT. TO ALTER THE VIRUS LIKE YOUR PARENTS DID.
IMAGINE AN ARMY OF SOLDIERS LIKE YOU. AN ARMY OF ANIMAL MEN.
BUT I GOT SICK. YESTERDAY MORNING I INFECTED MYSELF.

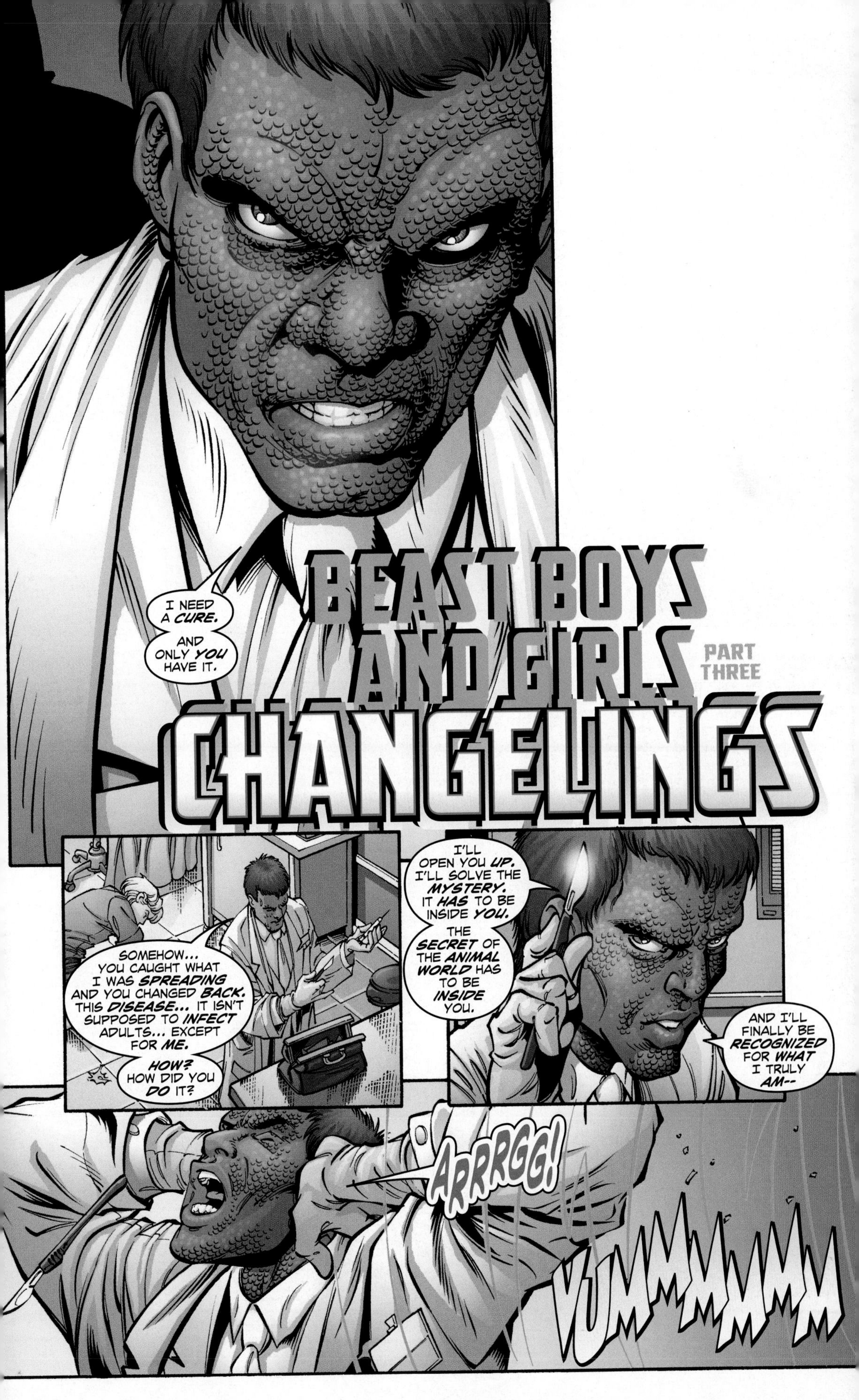
I NEED A *CURE*.
AND ONLY *YOU* HAVE IT.
BEAST BOYS AND GIRLS
PART THREE
CHANGELINGS
SOMEHOW... YOU CAUGHT WHAT I WAS *SPREADING* AND YOU CHANGED *BACK*. THIS *DISEASE*... IT ISN'T SUPPOSED TO *INFECT* ADULTS... EXCEPT FOR *ME*.
HOW? HOW DID YOU *DO* IT?
I'LL OPEN YOU *UP*. I'LL SOLVE THE *MYSTERY*. IT *HAS* TO BE INSIDE *YOU*.
THE *SECRET* OF THE *ANIMAL WORLD* HAS TO BE *INSIDE* YOU.
AND I'LL FINALLY BE *RECOGNIZED* FOR *WHAT* I TRULY *AM*--
ARRRGG!
VUMMMMMMM

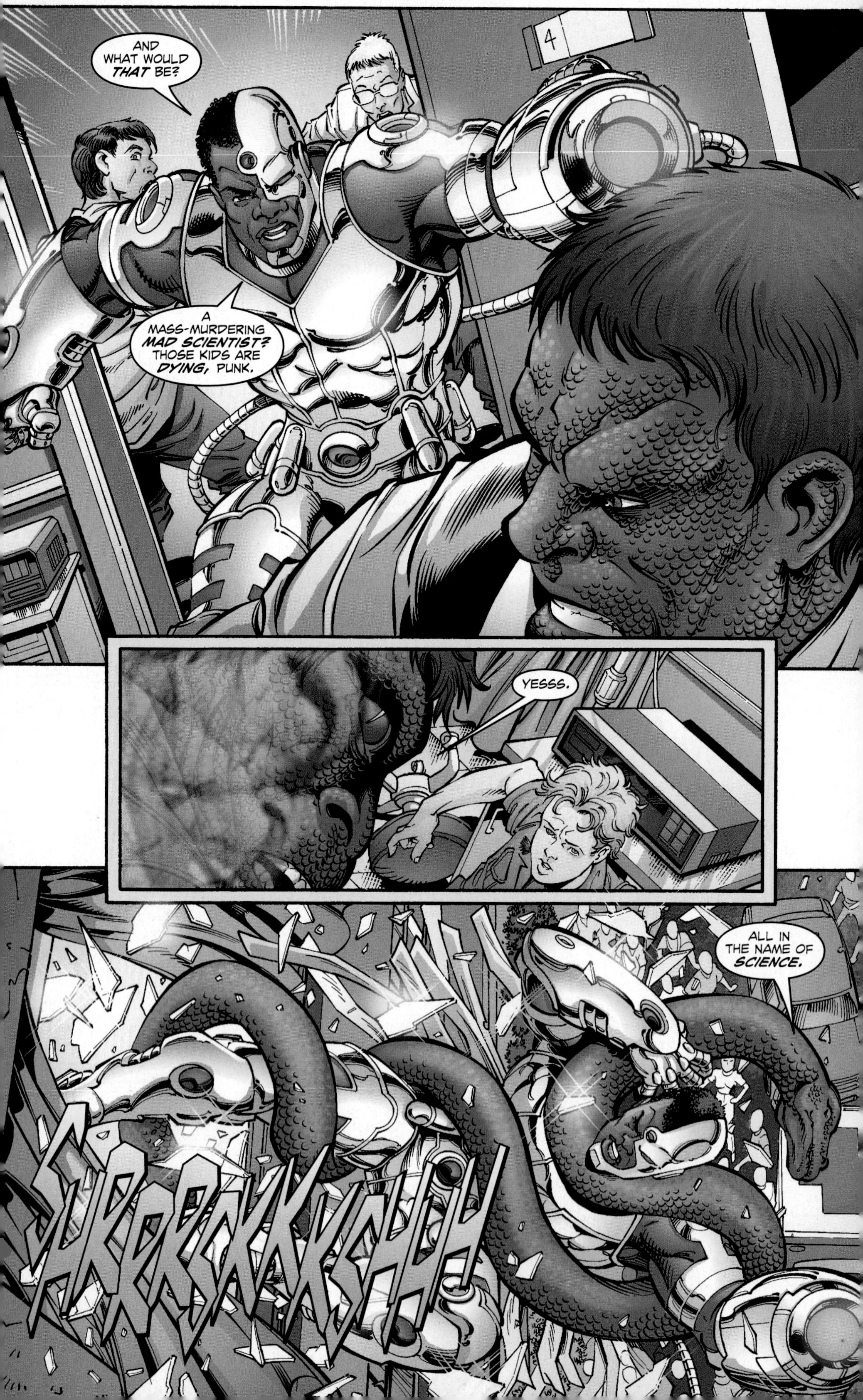

AND WHAT WOULD *THAT* BE?
A MASS-MURDERING *MAD SCIENTIST?* THOSE KIDS ARE *DYING,* PUNK.
YESSS.
ALL IN THE NAME OF *SCIENCE.*

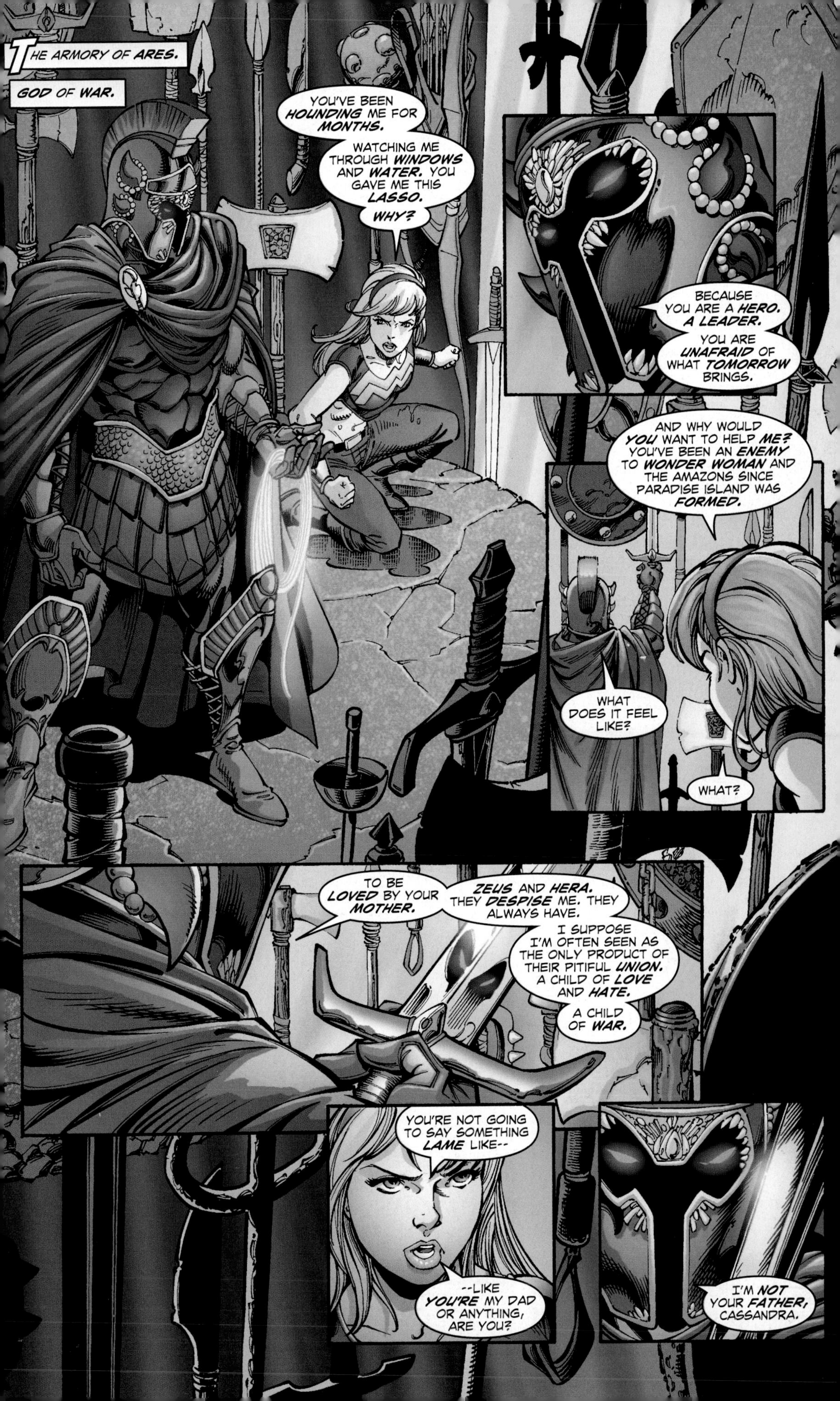
THE ARMORY OF ARES.
GOD OF WAR.
YOU'VE BEEN HOUNDING ME FOR MONTHS.
WATCHING ME THROUGH WINDOWS AND WATER. YOU GAVE ME THIS LASSO.
WHY?
BECAUSE YOU ARE A HERO. A LEADER.
YOU ARE UNAFRAID OF WHAT TOMORROW BRINGS.
AND WHY WOULD YOU WANT TO HELP ME? YOU'VE BEEN AN ENEMY TO WONDER WOMAN AND THE AMAZONS SINCE PARADISE ISLAND WAS FORMED.
WHAT DOES IT FEEL LIKE?
WHAT?
TO BE LOVED BY YOUR MOTHER.
ZEUS AND HERA. THEY DESPISE ME. THEY ALWAYS HAVE.
I SUPPOSE I'M OFTEN SEEN AS THE ONLY PRODUCT OF THEIR PITIFUL UNION. A CHILD OF LOVE AND HATE.
A CHILD OF WAR.
YOU'RE NOT GOING TO SAY SOMETHING LAME LIKE--
--LIKE YOU'RE MY DAD OR ANYTHING, ARE YOU?
I'M NOT YOUR FATHER, CASSANDRA.

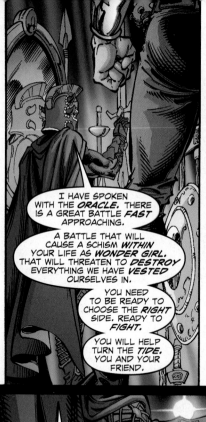

I HAVE SPOKEN WITH THE *ORACLE.* THERE IS A GREAT BATTLE *FAST* APPROACHING.

A BATTLE THAT WILL CAUSE A SCHISM *WITHIN* YOUR LIFE AS *WONDER GIRL,* THAT WILL THREATEN TO *DESTROY* EVERYTHING WE HAVE *VESTED* OURSELVES IN.

YOU NEED TO BE READY TO CHOOSE THE *RIGHT* SIDE. READY TO *FIGHT.*

YOU WILL HELP TURN THE *TIDE.* YOU AND YOUR FRIEND.

WHAT DID YOU SEE?

INNOCENCE *LOST.* A MAN *FALLS* ON THE BATTLEFIELD.

I'M *TEACHING* YOU TO FEEL ANGER, BECAUSE THAT IS WHAT WILL *FUEL* YOU WHEN YOU MOST *NEED* IT.

DO NOT LET THIS *LASSO* LEAVE YOUR *SIGHT.*

IT DOES *MORE* THAN *CHANNEL* ZEUS'S LIGHTNING.

WHAT ELSE CAN IT DO? WHAT IS IT FOR--?

GO.

FWOOSHH!

AND MAY THE *GODS* BE WITH YOU...

...BOTH.

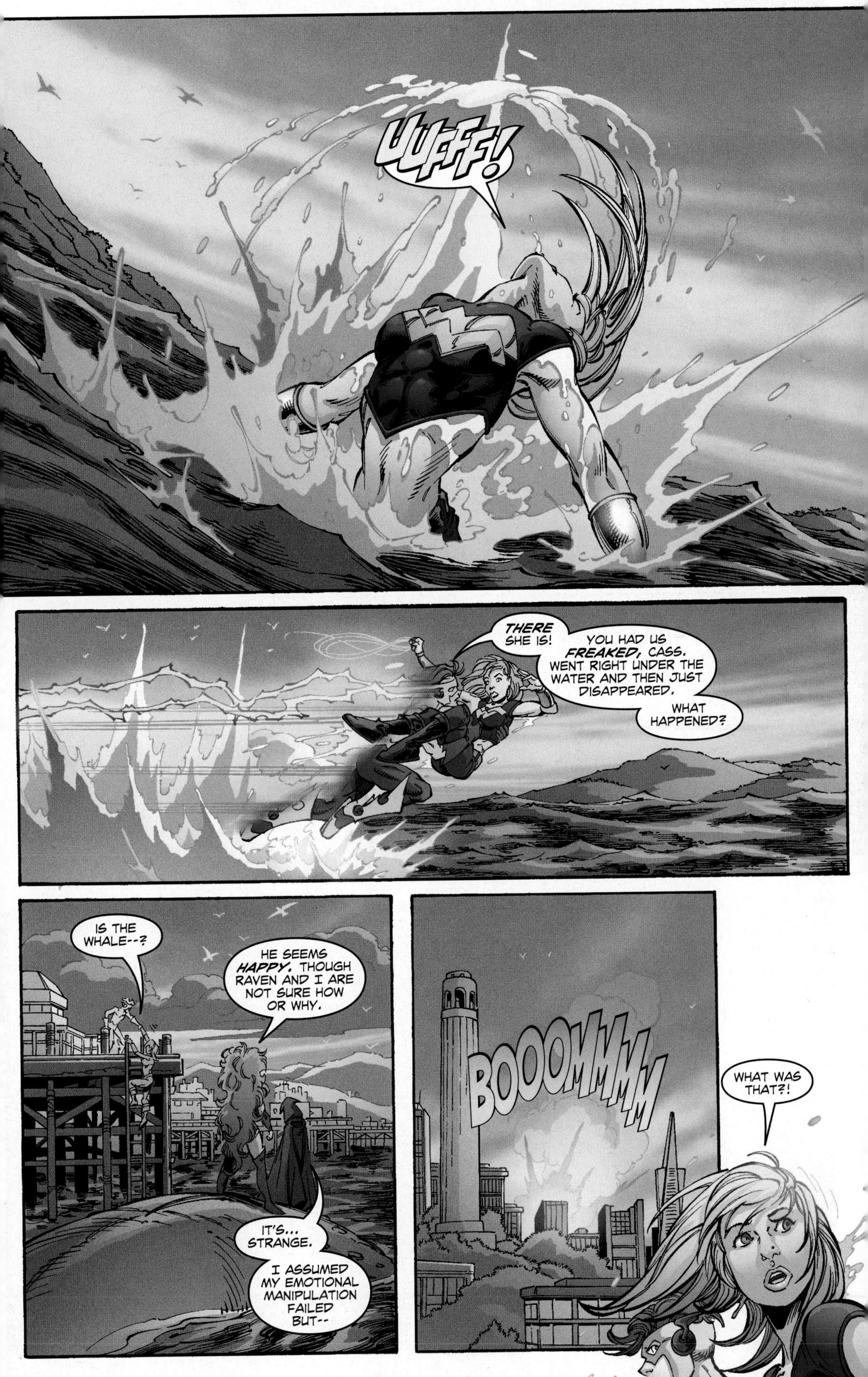

UUFFF!
THERE SHE IS!
YOU HAD US FREAKED, CASS. WENT RIGHT UNDER THE WATER AND THEN JUST DISAPPEARED.
WHAT HAPPENED?
IS THE WHALE--?
HE SEEMS HAPPY. THOUGH RAVEN AND I ARE NOT SURE HOW OR WHY.
IT'S... STRANGE.
I ASSUMED MY EMOTIONAL MANIPULATION FAILED BUT--
BOOOMMMM
WHAT WAS THAT?!

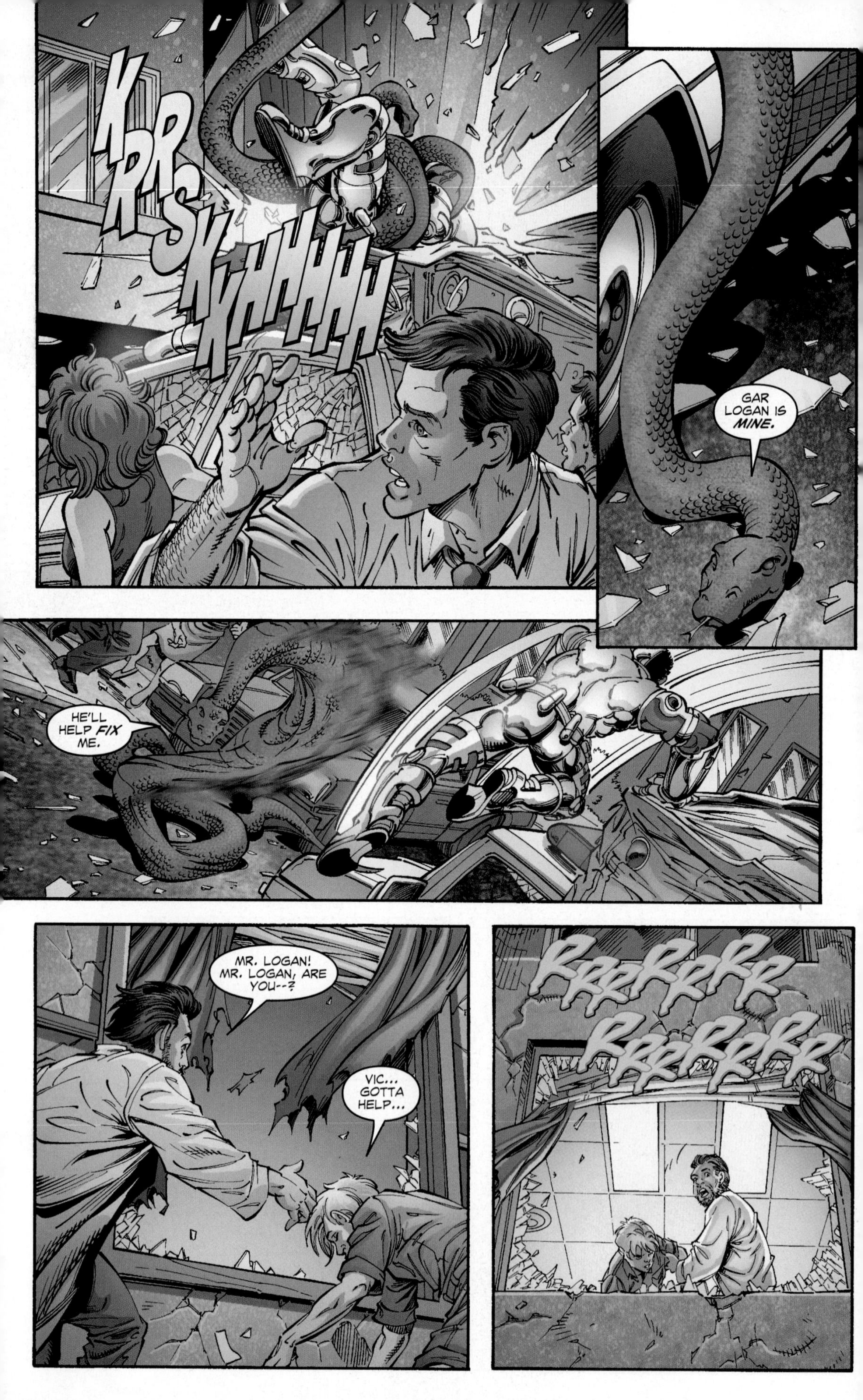
KRRSKKHHHHH
GAR LOGAN IS MINE.
HE'LL HELP FIX ME.
MR. LOGAN! MR. LOGAN, ARE YOU--?
VIC... GOTTA HELP...
RRRRRRR RRRRRRR

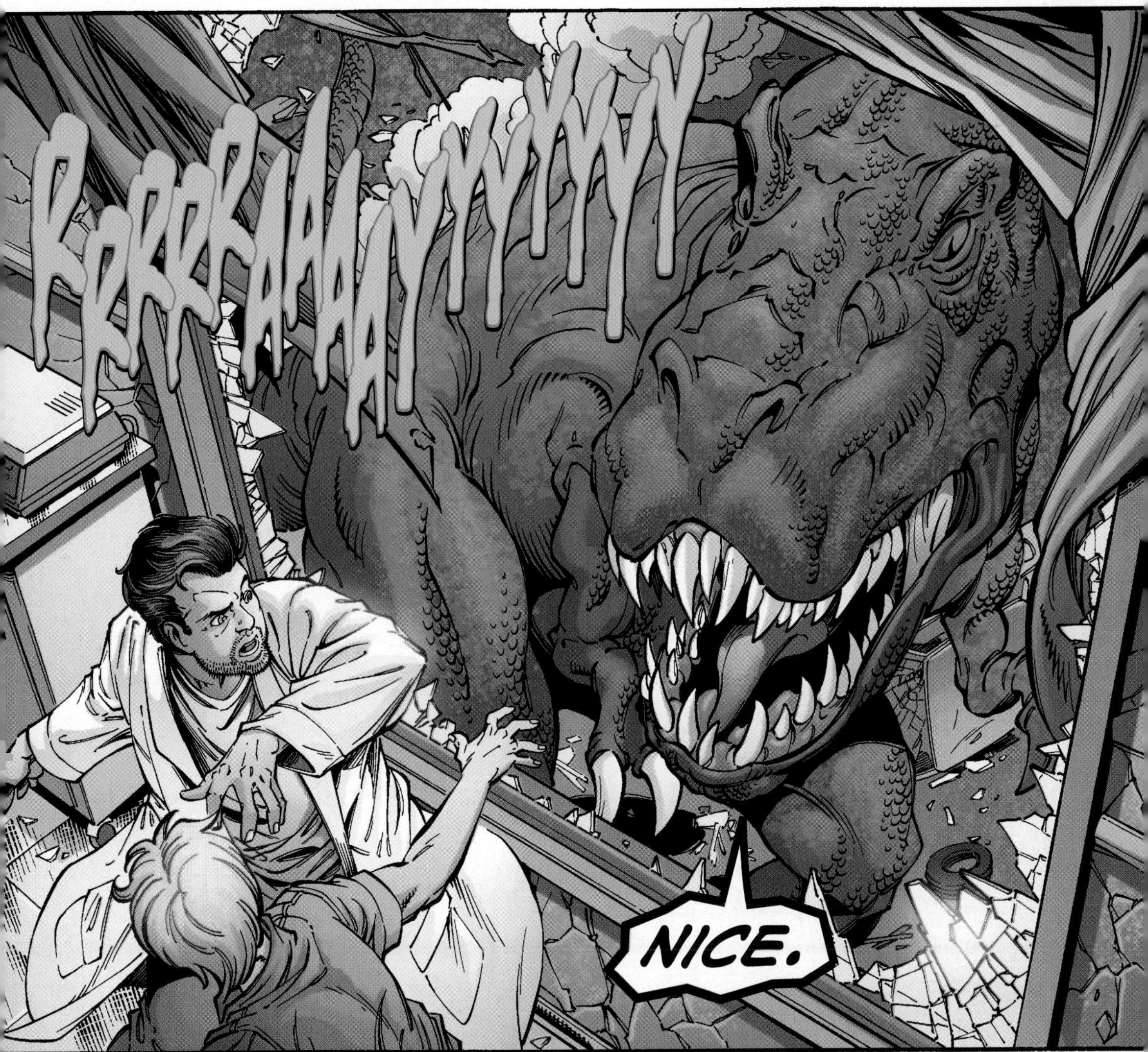
RRRRAAAAYYYYYYN
NICE.

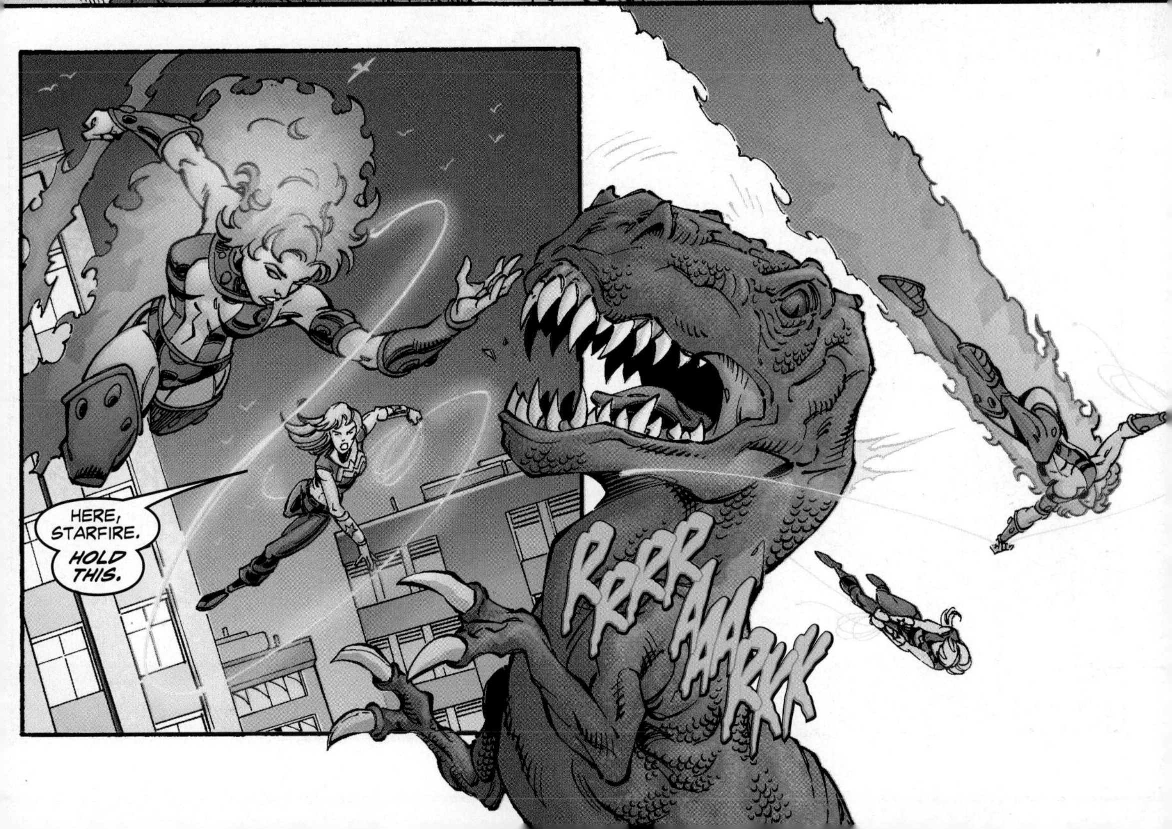
HERE, STARFIRE. HOLD THIS.
RRRRAAARKK

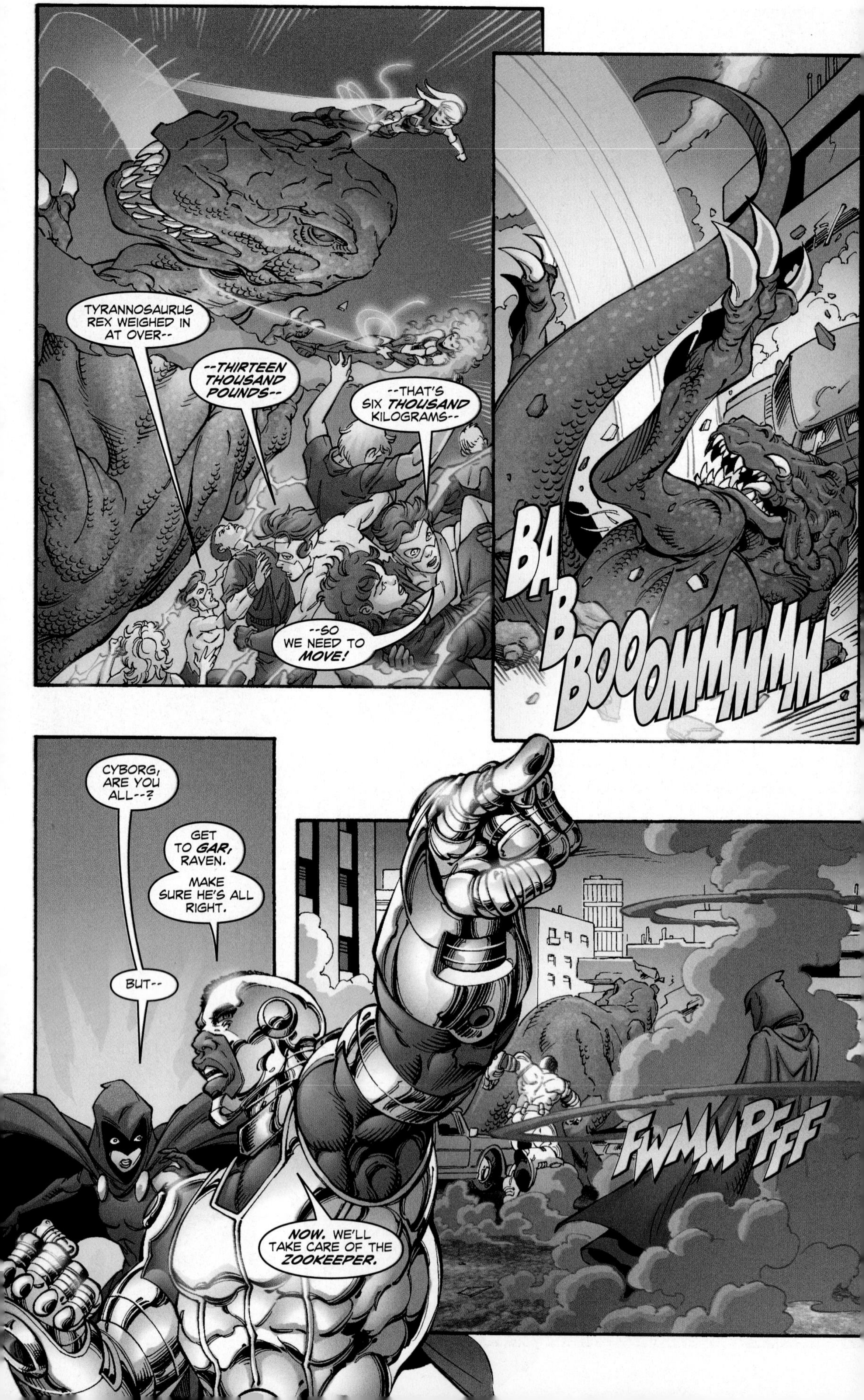
TYRANNOSAURUS REX WEIGHED IN AT OVER--
--THIRTEEN THOUSAND POUNDS--
--THAT'S SIX THOUSAND KILOGRAMS--
--SO WE NEED TO MOVE!
BA B BOOOMMMMM
CYBORG, ARE YOU ALL--?
GET TO GAR, RAVEN. MAKE SURE HE'S ALL RIGHT.
BUT--
NOW. WE'LL TAKE CARE OF THE ZOOKEEPER.
FWMMPFFF

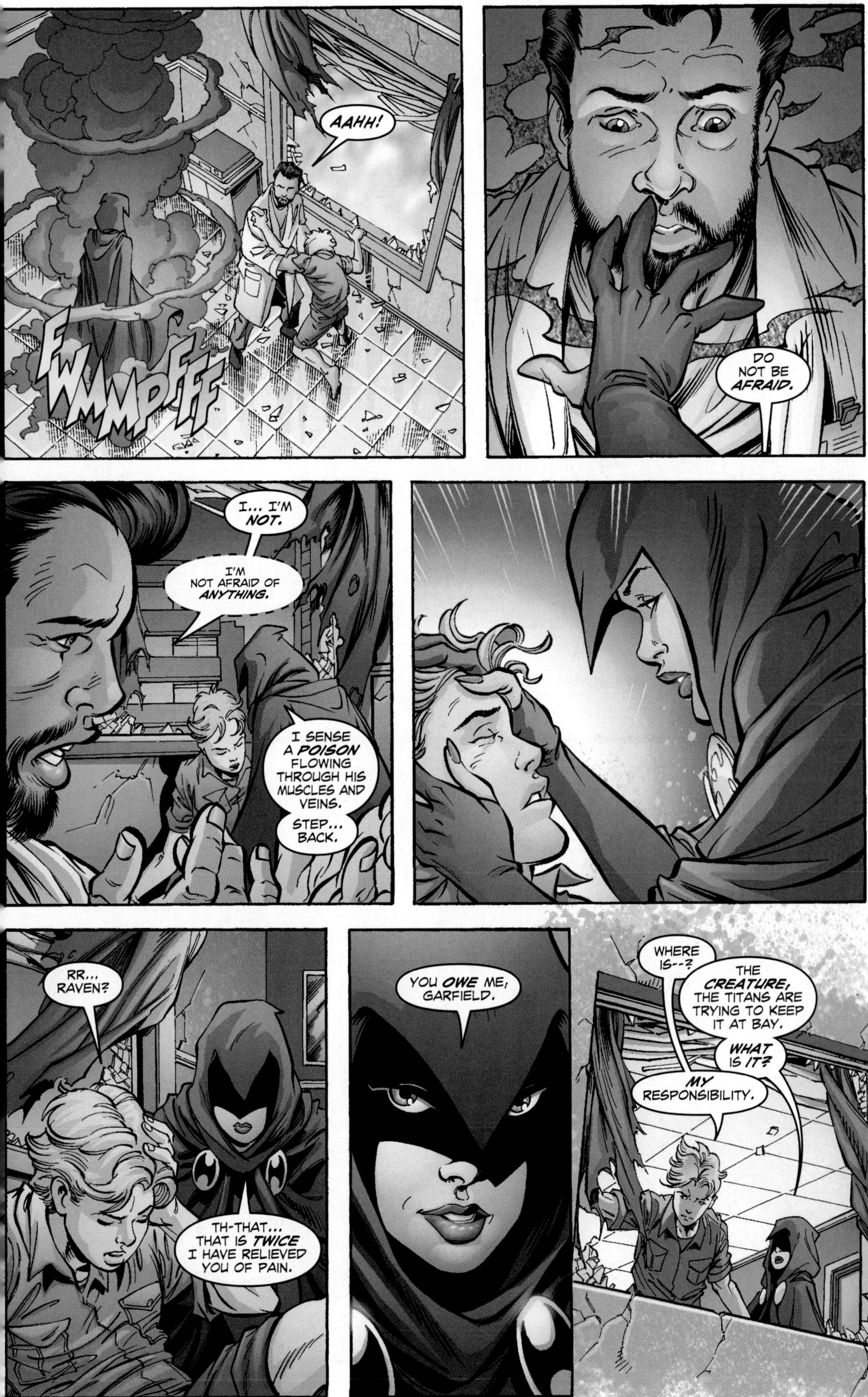
AAHH!
FWMMPFFF
DO NOT BE AFRAID.
I... I'M NOT.
I'M NOT AFRAID OF ANYTHING.
I SENSE A POISON FLOWING THROUGH HIS MUSCLES AND VEINS.
STEP... BACK.
RR... RAVEN?
TH-THAT... THAT IS TWICE I HAVE RELIEVED YOU OF PAIN.
YOU OWE ME, GARFIELD.
WHERE IS--?
THE CREATURE, THE TITANS ARE TRYING TO KEEP IT AT BAY.
WHAT IS IT?
MY RESPONSIBILITY.

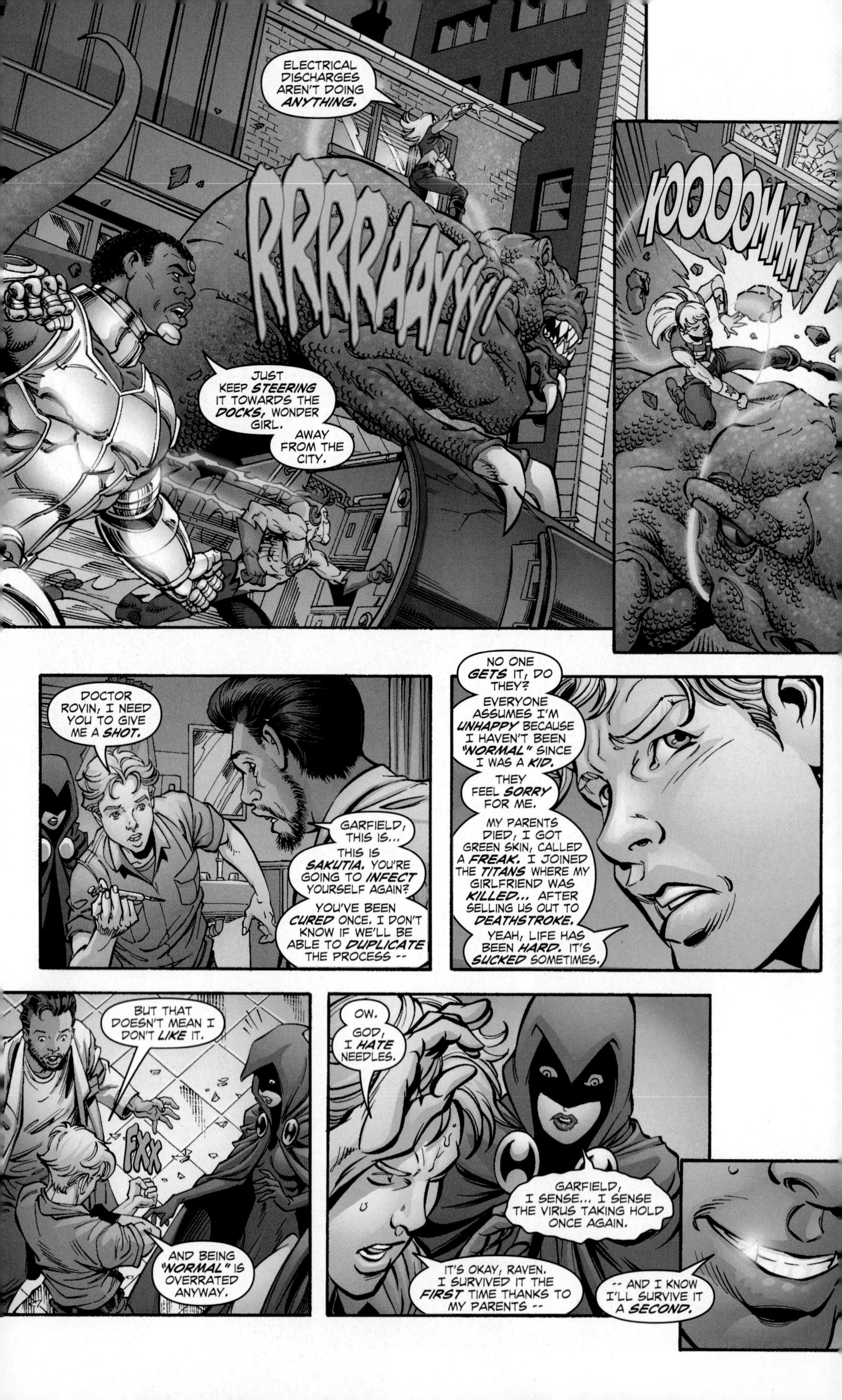

ELECTRICAL DISCHARGES AREN'T DOING ANYTHING.
RRRRAAYYY!
JUST KEEP STEERING IT TOWARDS THE DOCKS, WONDER GIRL.
AWAY FROM THE CITY.
KOOOOMMM
DOCTOR ROVIN, I NEED YOU TO GIVE ME A SHOT.
GARFIELD, THIS IS... THIS IS SAKUTIA. YOU'RE GOING TO INFECT YOURSELF AGAIN?
YOU'VE BEEN CURED ONCE. I DON'T KNOW IF WE'LL BE ABLE TO DUPLICATE THE PROCESS --
NO ONE GETS IT, DO THEY?
EVERYONE ASSUMES I'M UNHAPPY BECAUSE I HAVEN'T BEEN "NORMAL" SINCE I WAS A KID.
THEY FEEL SORRY FOR ME.
MY PARENTS DIED, I GOT GREEN SKIN, CALLED A FREAK. I JOINED THE TITANS WHERE MY GIRLFRIEND WAS KILLED... AFTER SELLING US OUT TO DEATHSTROKE.
YEAH, LIFE HAS BEEN HARD. IT'S SUCKED SOMETIMES.
BUT THAT DOESN'T MEAN I DON'T LIKE IT.
FXX
AND BEING "NORMAL" IS OVERRATED ANYWAY.
OW.
GOD, I HATE NEEDLES.
GARFIELD, I SENSE... I SENSE THE VIRUS TAKING HOLD ONCE AGAIN.
IT'S OKAY, RAVEN. I SURVIVED IT THE FIRST TIME THANKS TO MY PARENTS --
-- AND I KNOW I'LL SURVIVE IT A SECOND.

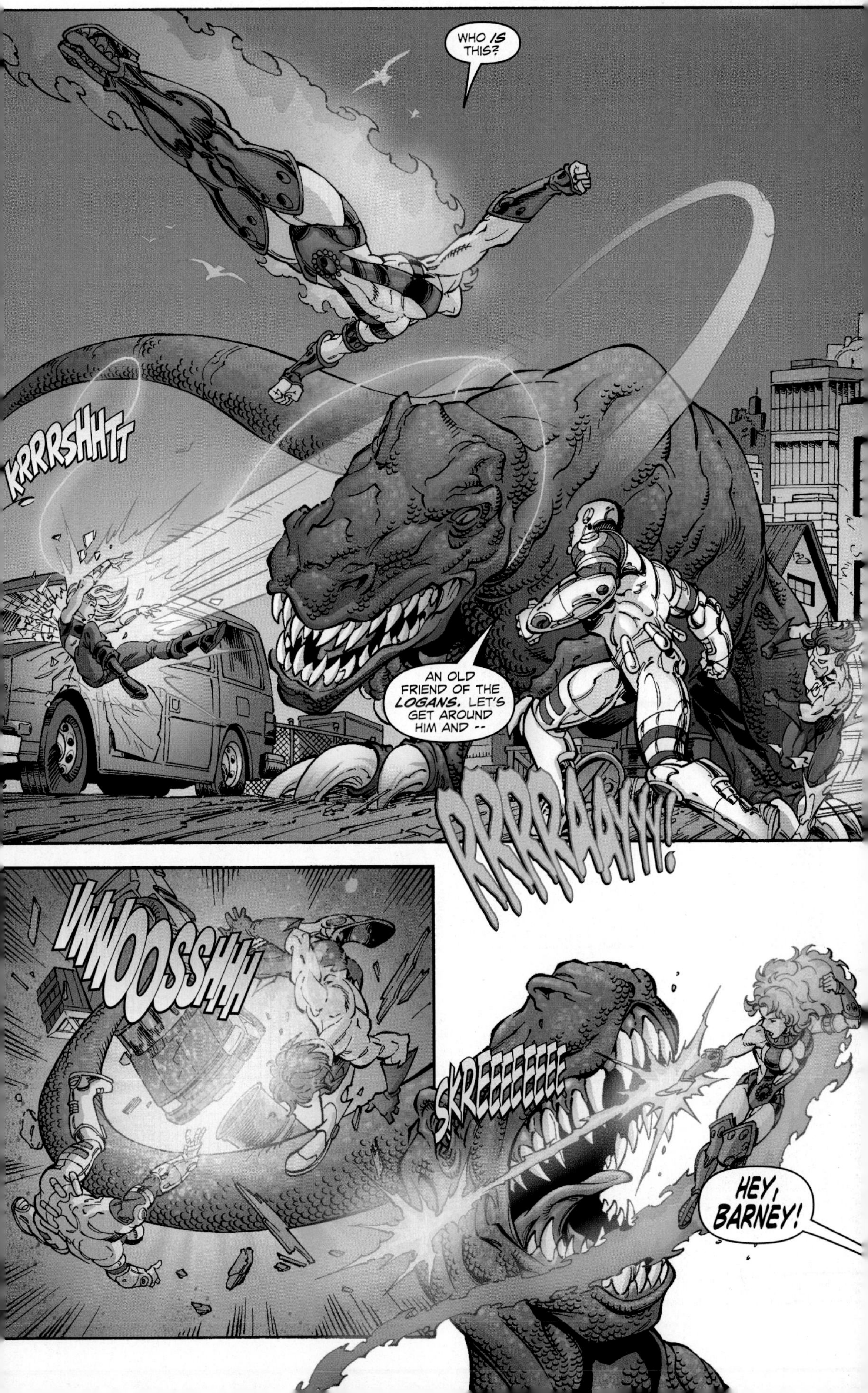
WHO IS THIS?
KRRRSHHTT
AN OLD FRIEND OF THE LOGANS. LET'S GET AROUND HIM AND --
RRRRAAYYY!
VWWOOSSHHH
SKREEEEEEEE
HEY, BARNEY!

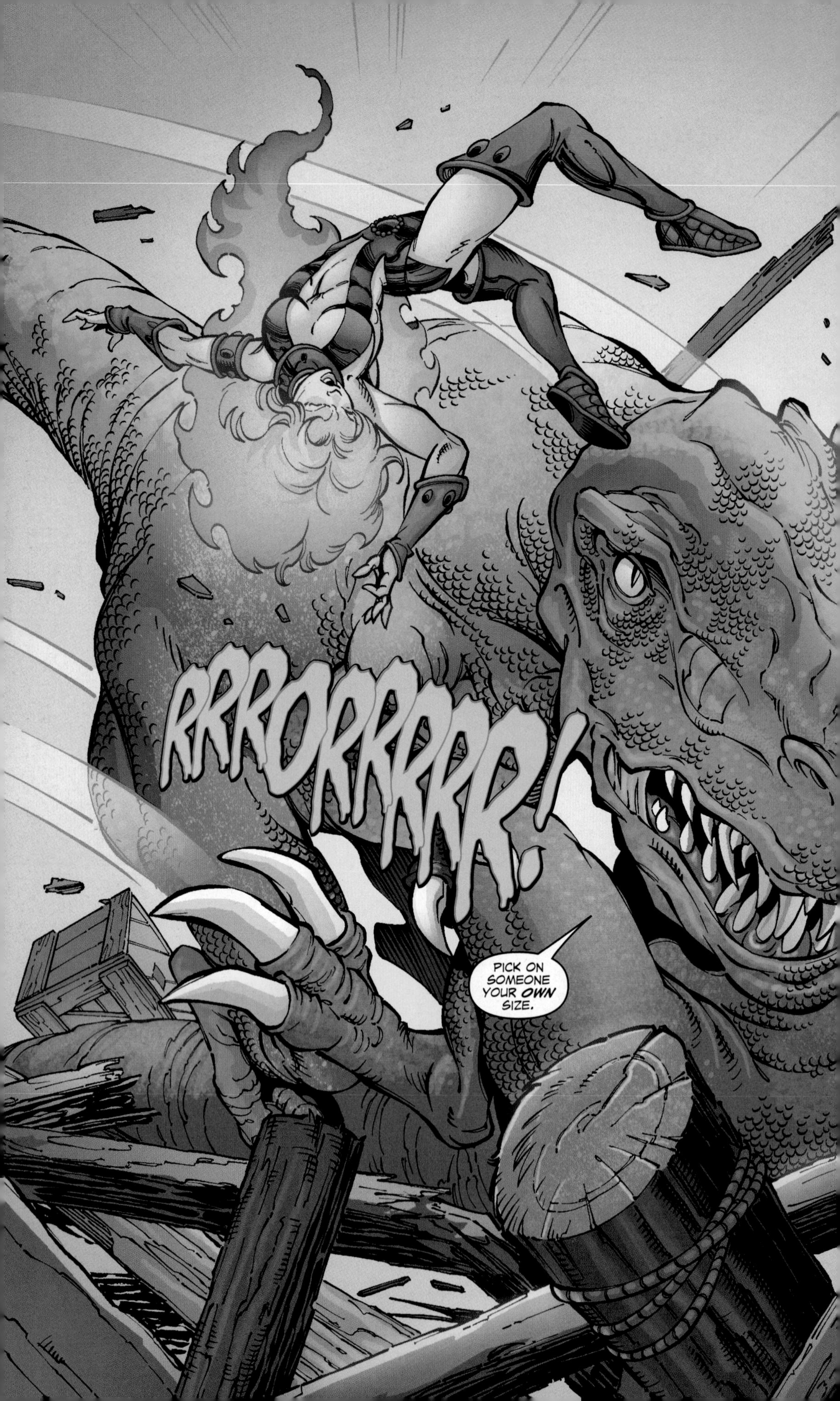
RRRORRRRR!
PICK ON SOMEONE YOUR *OWN* SIZE.

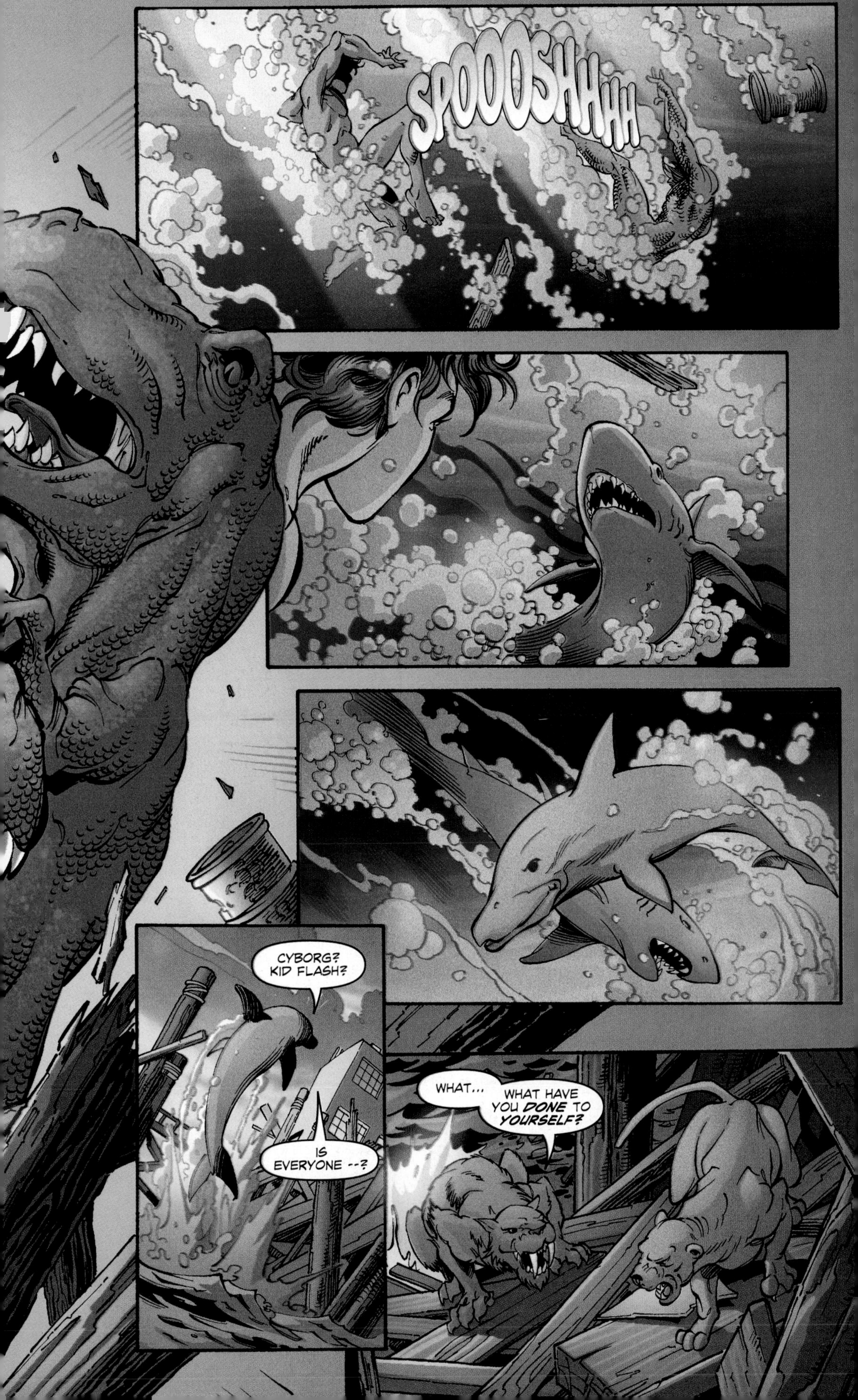
SPOOOSHHHH
CYBORG? KID FLASH?
IS EVERYONE --?
WHAT...
WHAT HAVE YOU DONE TO YOURSELF?

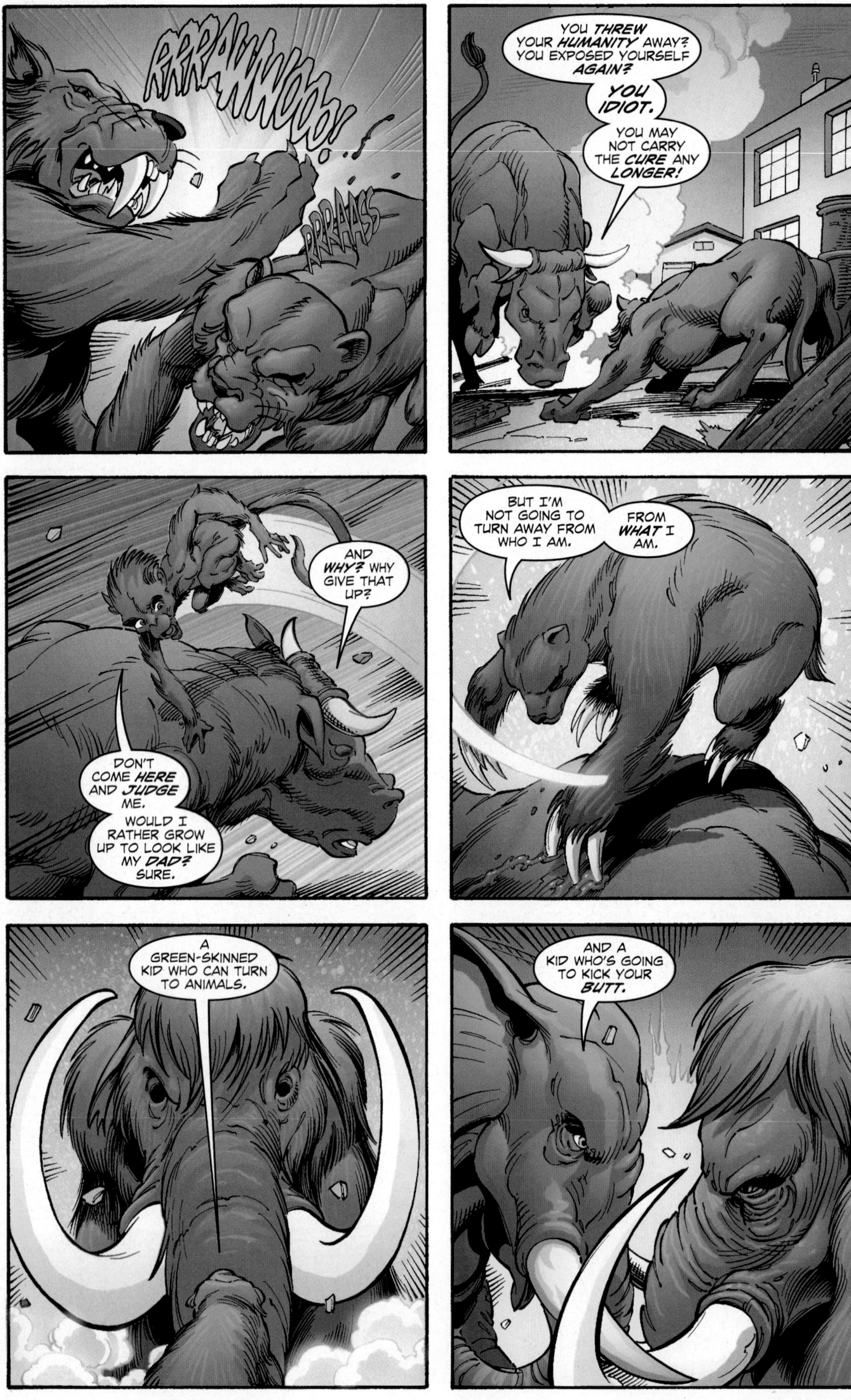
RRRAWWOOO!
RRRAASS
YOU THREW YOUR HUMANITY AWAY? YOU EXPOSED YOURSELF AGAIN?
YOU IDIOT.
YOU MAY NOT CARRY THE CURE ANY LONGER!
AND WHY? WHY GIVE THAT UP?
DON'T COME HERE AND JUDGE ME.
WOULD I RATHER GROW UP TO LOOK LIKE MY DAD? SURE.
BUT I'M NOT GOING TO TURN AWAY FROM WHO I AM.
FROM WHAT I AM.
A GREEN-SKINNED KID WHO CAN TURN TO ANIMALS.
AND A KID WHO'S GOING TO KICK YOUR BUTT.

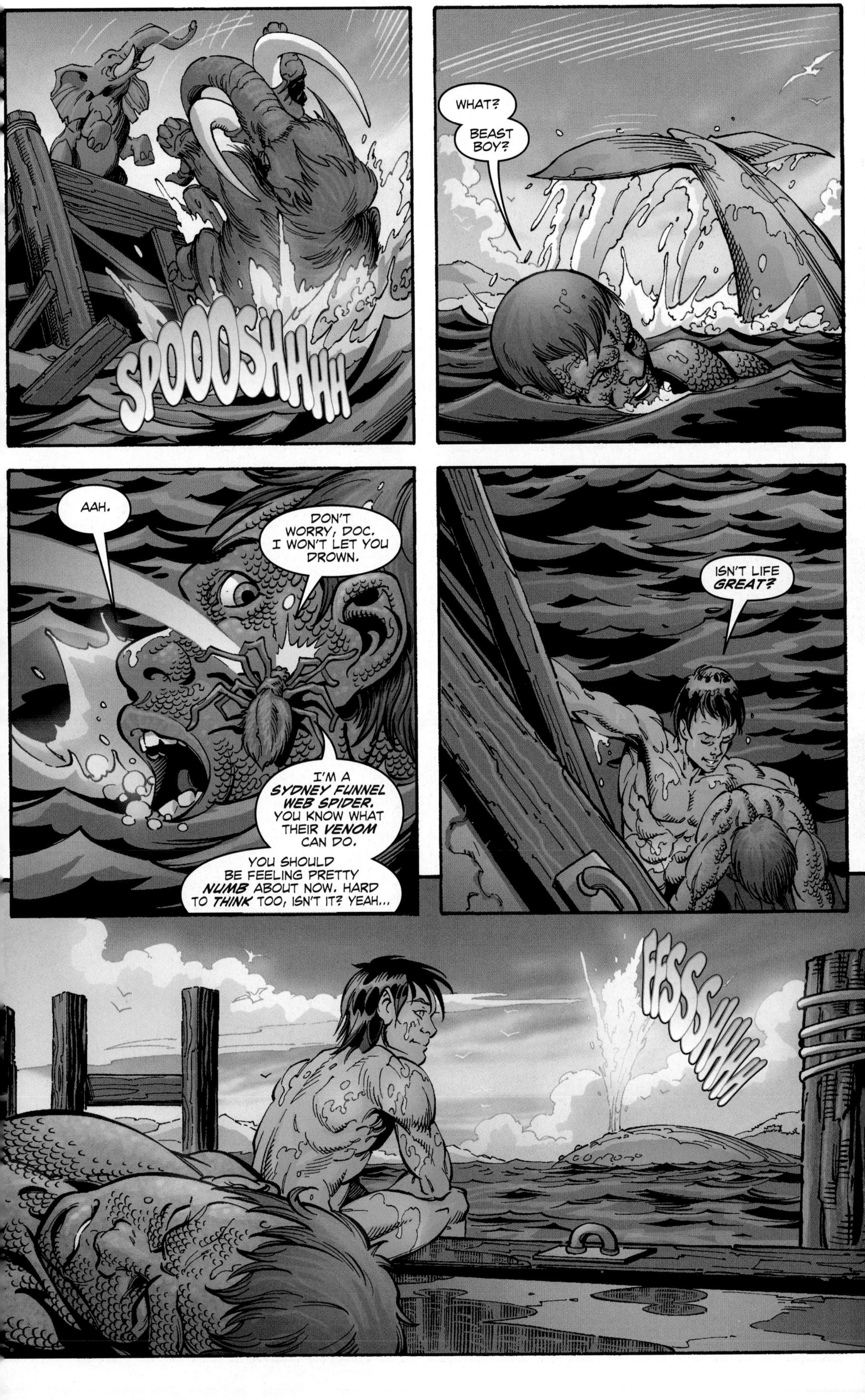

SPOOOSHHHH
WHAT?
BEAST BOY?
AAH.
DON'T WORRY, DOC. I WON'T LET YOU DROWN.
I'M A SYDNEY FUNNEL WEB SPIDER. YOU KNOW WHAT THEIR VENOM CAN DO.
YOU SHOULD BE FEELING PRETTY NUMB ABOUT NOW. HARD TO THINK TOO, ISN'T IT? YEAH...
ISN'T LIFE GREAT?
FFSSSHHHH

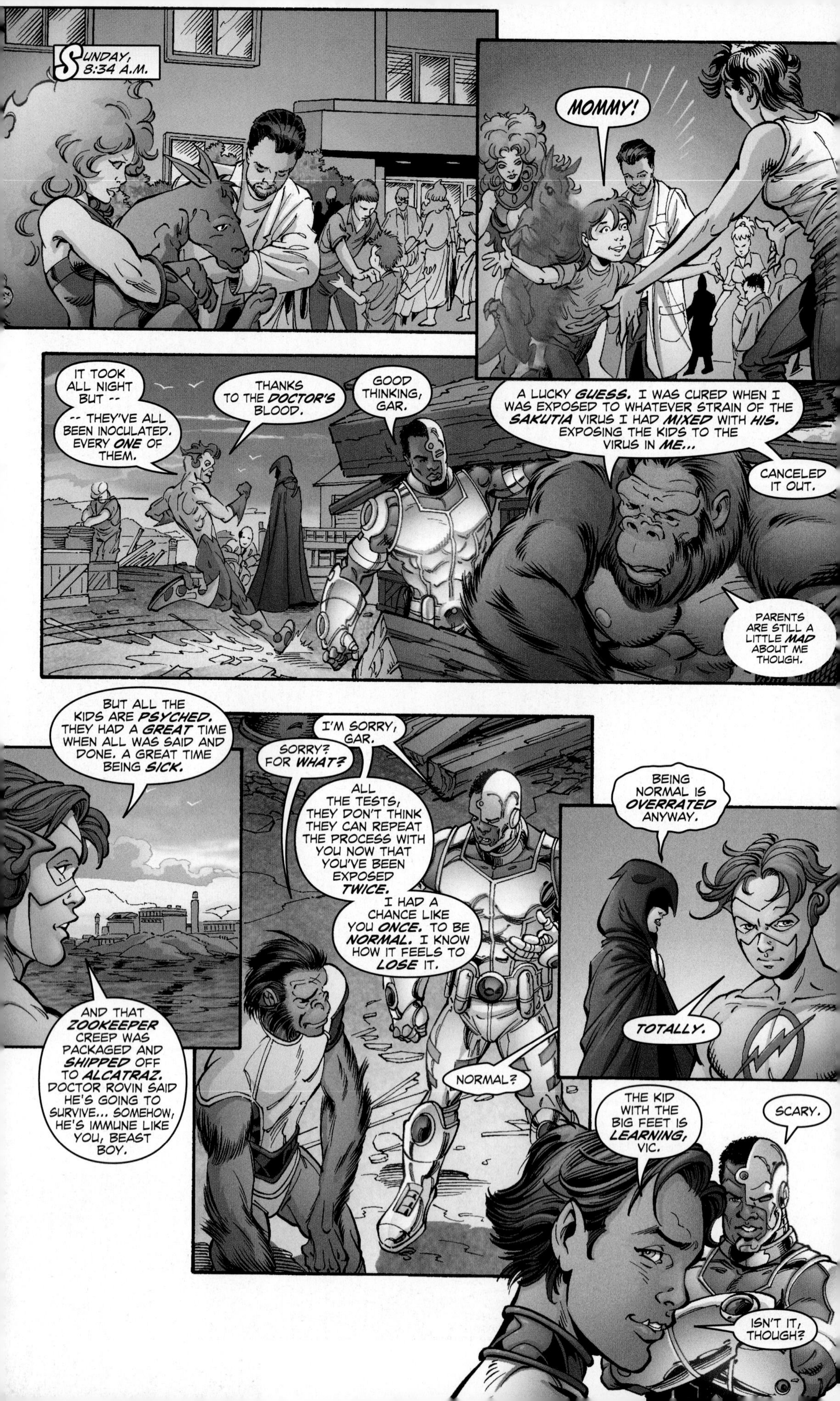
SUNDAY, 8:34 A.M.
MOMMY!
IT TOOK ALL NIGHT BUT --
-- THEY'VE ALL BEEN INOCULATED. EVERY ONE OF THEM.
THANKS TO THE DOCTOR'S BLOOD.
GOOD THINKING, GAR.
A LUCKY GUESS. I WAS CURED WHEN I WAS EXPOSED TO WHATEVER STRAIN OF THE SAKUTIA VIRUS I HAD MIXED WITH HIS. EXPOSING THE KIDS TO THE VIRUS IN ME...
CANCELED IT OUT.
PARENTS ARE STILL A LITTLE MAD ABOUT ME THOUGH.
BUT ALL THE KIDS ARE PSYCHED. THEY HAD A GREAT TIME WHEN ALL WAS SAID AND DONE. A GREAT TIME BEING SICK.
AND THAT ZOOKEEPER CREEP WAS PACKAGED AND SHIPPED OFF TO ALCATRAZ. DOCTOR ROVIN SAID HE'S GOING TO SURVIVE... SOMEHOW, HE'S IMMUNE LIKE YOU, BEAST BOY.
I'M SORRY, GAR.
SORRY? FOR WHAT?
ALL THE TESTS, THEY DON'T THINK THEY CAN REPEAT THE PROCESS WITH YOU NOW THAT YOU'VE BEEN EXPOSED TWICE.
I HAD A CHANCE LIKE YOU ONCE. TO BE NORMAL. I KNOW HOW IT FEELS TO LOSE IT.
NORMAL?
BEING NORMAL IS OVERRATED ANYWAY.
TOTALLY.
THE KID WITH THE BIG FEET IS LEARNING, VIC.
SCARY.
ISN'T IT, THOUGH?

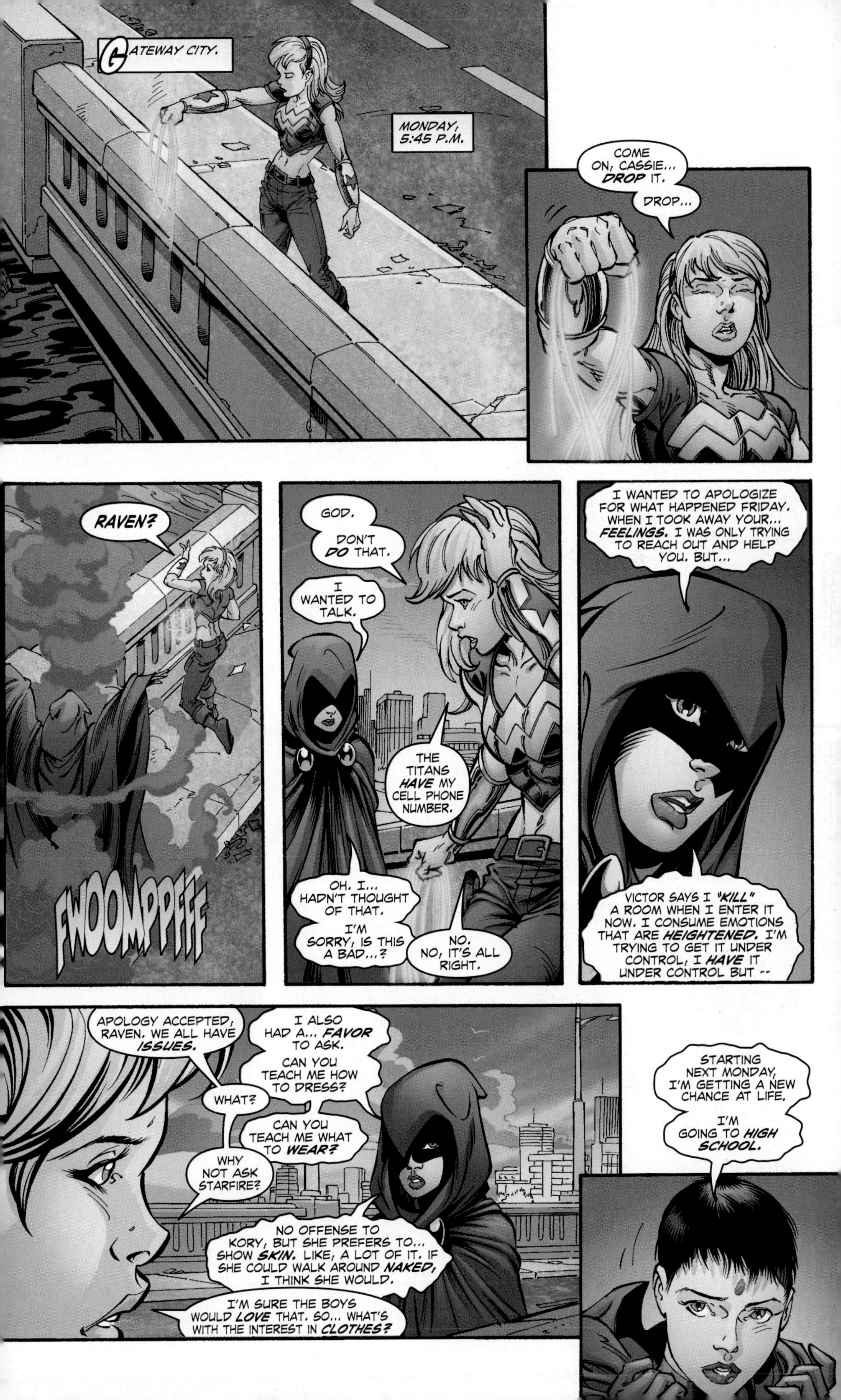
GATEWAY CITY.
MONDAY, 5:45 P.M.
COME ON, CASSIE... DROP IT.
DROP...
RAVEN?
FWOOMPFFF
GOD.
DON'T DO THAT.
I WANTED TO TALK.
THE TITANS HAVE MY CELL PHONE NUMBER.
OH. I... HADN'T THOUGHT OF THAT.
I'M SORRY, IS THIS A BAD...?
NO. NO, IT'S ALL RIGHT.
I WANTED TO APOLOGIZE FOR WHAT HAPPENED FRIDAY. WHEN I TOOK AWAY YOUR... FEELINGS. I WAS ONLY TRYING TO REACH OUT AND HELP YOU. BUT...
VICTOR SAYS I "KILL" A ROOM WHEN I ENTER IT NOW. I CONSUME EMOTIONS THAT ARE HEIGHTENED. I'M TRYING TO GET IT UNDER CONTROL, I HAVE IT UNDER CONTROL BUT --
APOLOGY ACCEPTED, RAVEN. WE ALL HAVE ISSUES.
I ALSO HAD A... FAVOR TO ASK.
CAN YOU TEACH ME HOW TO DRESS?
WHAT?
CAN YOU TEACH ME WHAT TO WEAR?
WHY NOT ASK STARFIRE?
NO OFFENSE TO KORY, BUT SHE PREFERS TO... SHOW SKIN. LIKE, A LOT OF IT. IF SHE COULD WALK AROUND NAKED, I THINK SHE WOULD.
I'M SURE THE BOYS WOULD LOVE THAT. SO... WHAT'S WITH THE INTEREST IN CLOTHES?
STARTING NEXT MONDAY, I'M GETTING A NEW CHANCE AT LIFE.
I'M GOING TO HIGH SCHOOL.

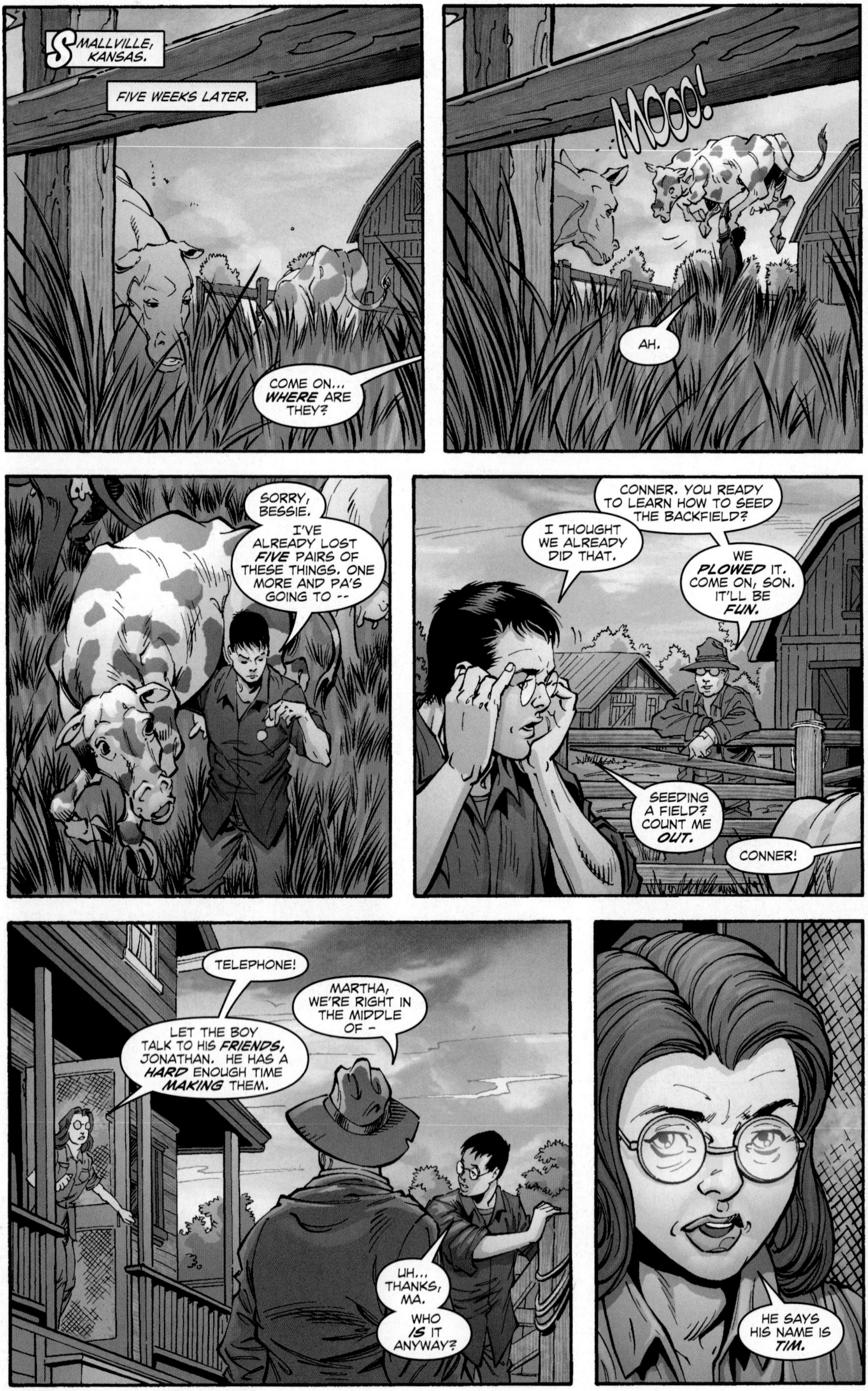
SMALLVILLE, KANSAS.
FIVE WEEKS LATER.
COME ON... WHERE ARE THEY?
MOOO!
AH.
SORRY, BESSIE.
I'VE ALREADY LOST FIVE PAIRS OF THESE THINGS. ONE MORE AND PA'S GOING TO --
CONNER. YOU READY TO LEARN HOW TO SEED THE BACKFIELD?
I THOUGHT WE ALREADY DID THAT.
WE PLOWED IT. COME ON, SON. IT'LL BE FUN.
SEEDING A FIELD? COUNT ME OUT.
CONNER!
TELEPHONE!
MARTHA, WE'RE RIGHT IN THE MIDDLE OF -
LET THE BOY TALK TO HIS FRIENDS, JONATHAN. HE HAS A HARD ENOUGH TIME MAKING THEM.
UH.. THANKS, MA.
WHO IS IT ANYWAY?
HE SAYS HIS NAME IS TIM.

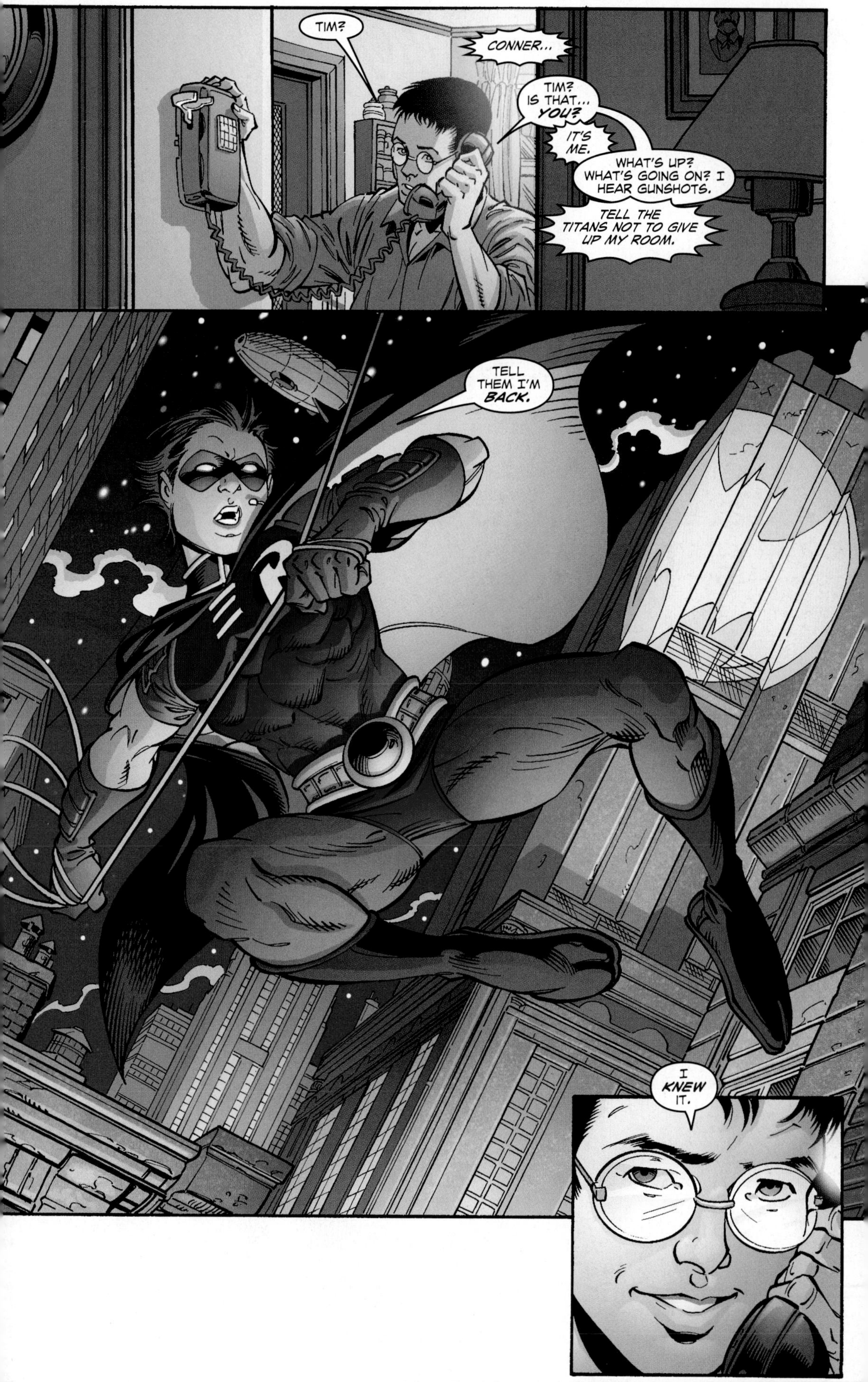
TIM?
CONNER...
TIM? IS THAT... YOU?
IT'S ME.
WHAT'S UP? WHAT'S GOING ON? I HEAR GUNSHOTS.
TELL THE TITANS NOT TO GIVE UP MY ROOM.
TELL THEM I'M BACK.
I KNEW IT.

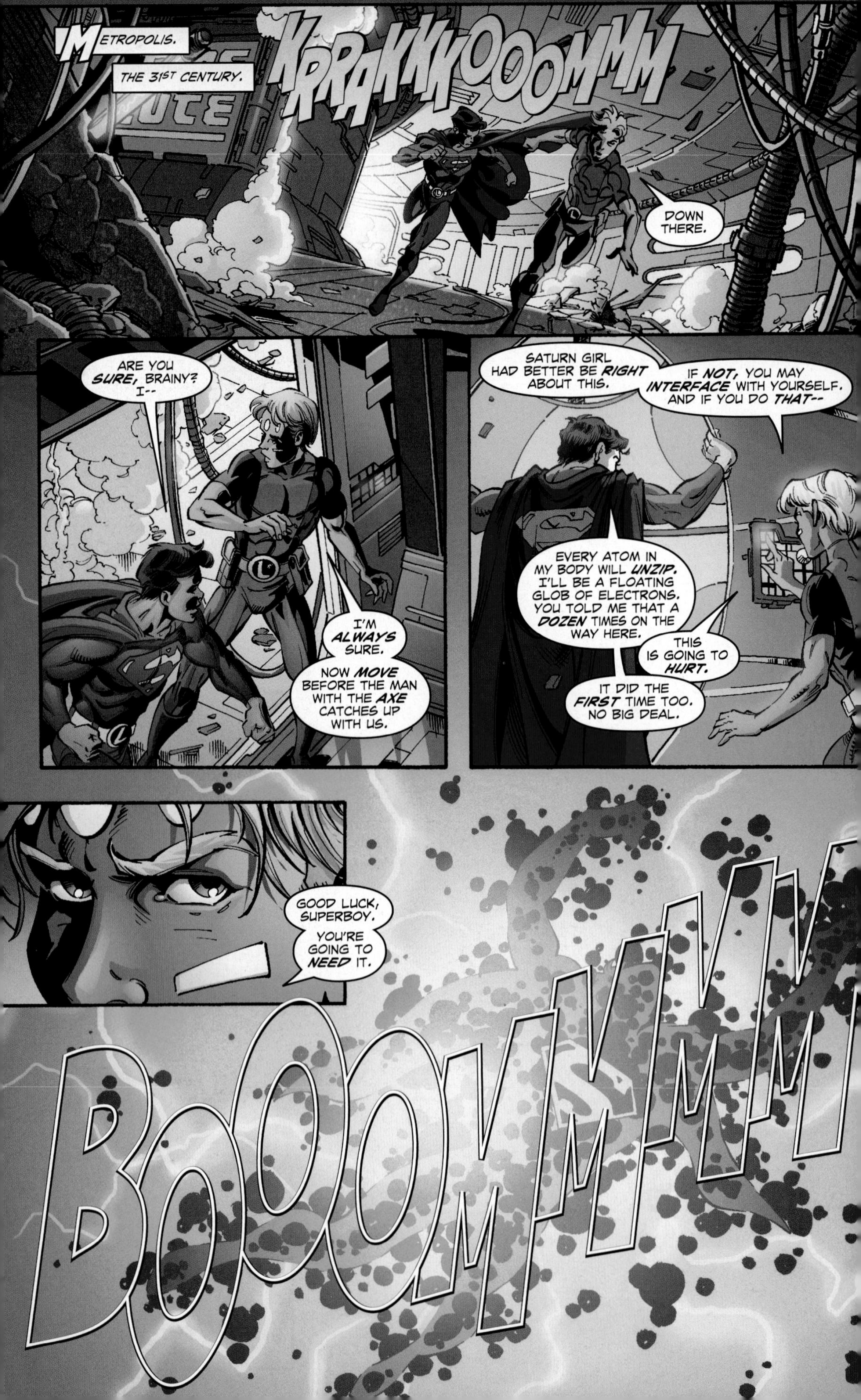
METROPOLIS.
THE 31ST CENTURY.
KRRAKKKOOOMMM
DOWN THERE.
ARE YOU SURE, BRAINY? I--
I'M ALWAYS SURE.
NOW MOVE BEFORE THE MAN WITH THE AXE CATCHES UP WITH US.
SATURN GIRL HAD BETTER BE RIGHT ABOUT THIS.
IF NOT, YOU MAY INTERFACE WITH YOURSELF. AND IF YOU DO THAT--
EVERY ATOM IN MY BODY WILL UNZIP. I'LL BE A FLOATING GLOB OF ELECTRONS. YOU TOLD ME THAT A DOZEN TIMES ON THE WAY HERE.
THIS IS GOING TO HURT.
IT DID THE FIRST TIME TOO. NO BIG DEAL.
GOOD LUCK, SUPERBOY.
YOU'RE GOING TO NEED IT.
BOOOMMMMM

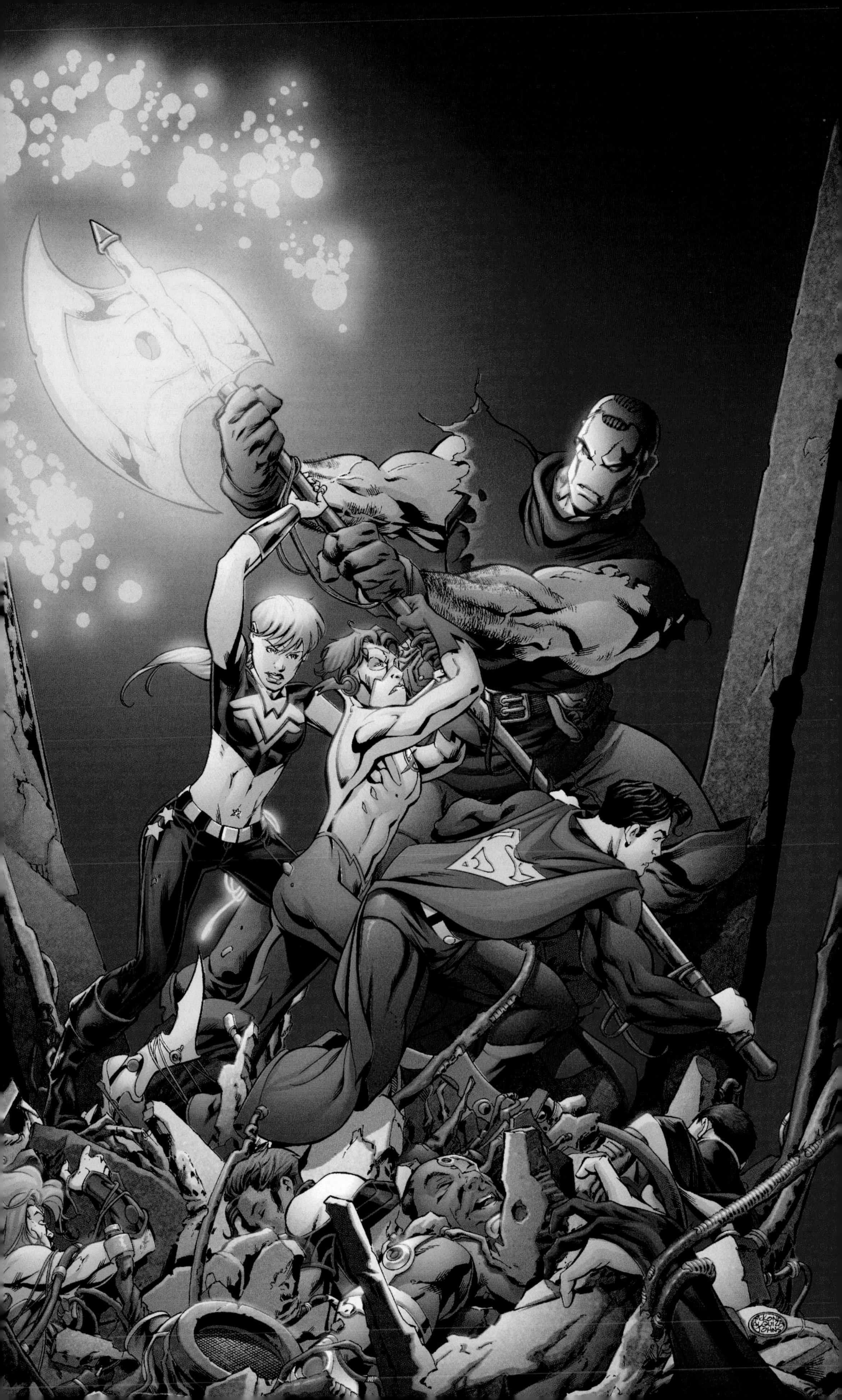

TEEN TITANS #16

GEOFF JOHNS
Writer

MIKE McKONE
Penciller

MARLO ALQUIZA
Inker

JEROMY COX
Colorist

COMICRAFT
Letterer

**MIKE McKONE, MARLO ALQUIZA
& JEROMY COX**
Cover Artists

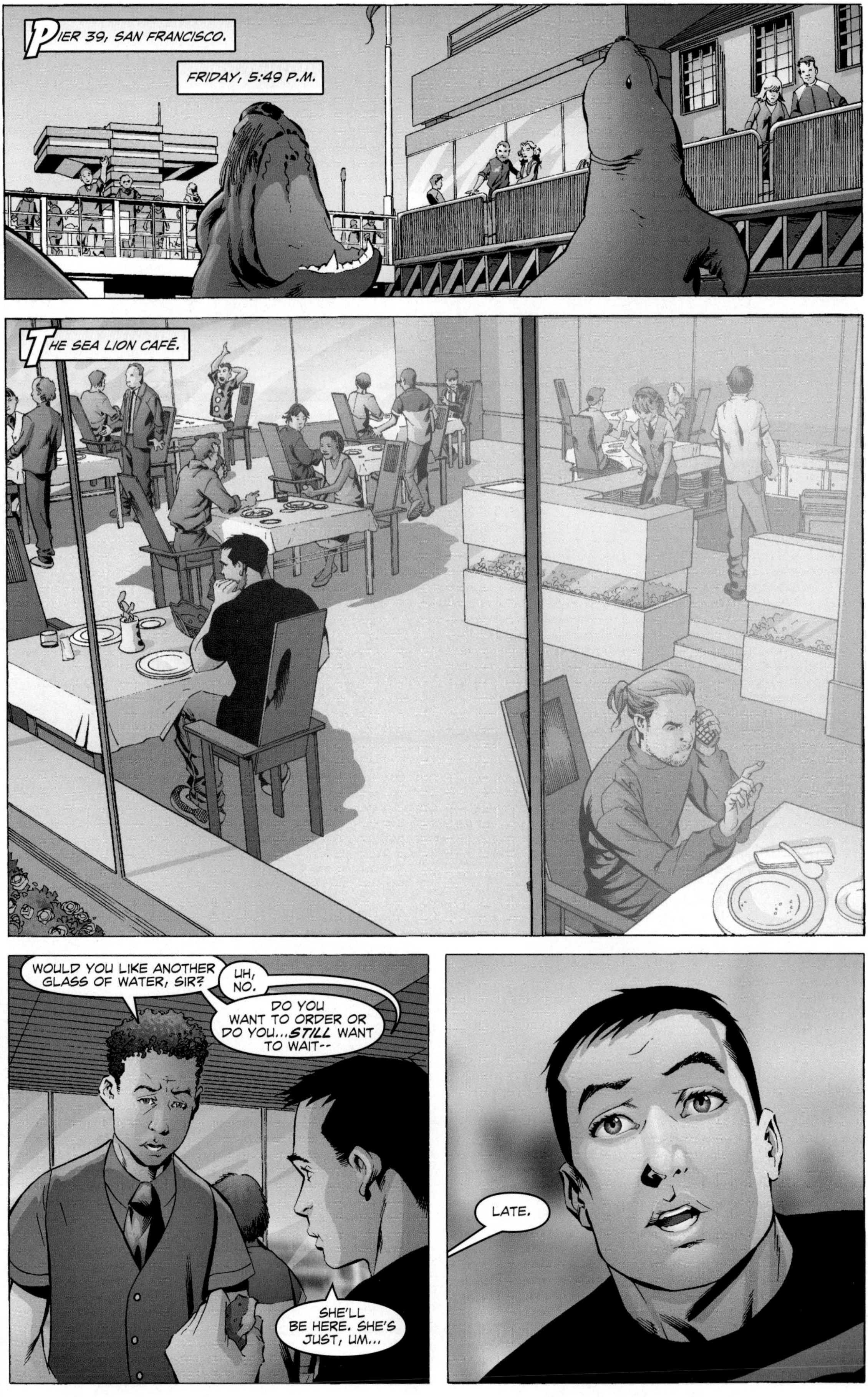
PIER 39, SAN FRANCISCO.
FRIDAY, 5:49 P.M.
THE SEA LION CAFÉ.
WOULD YOU LIKE ANOTHER GLASS OF WATER, SIR?
UH, NO.
DO YOU WANT TO ORDER OR DO YOU...STILL WANT TO WAIT--
SHE'LL BE HERE. SHE'S JUST, UM...
LATE.

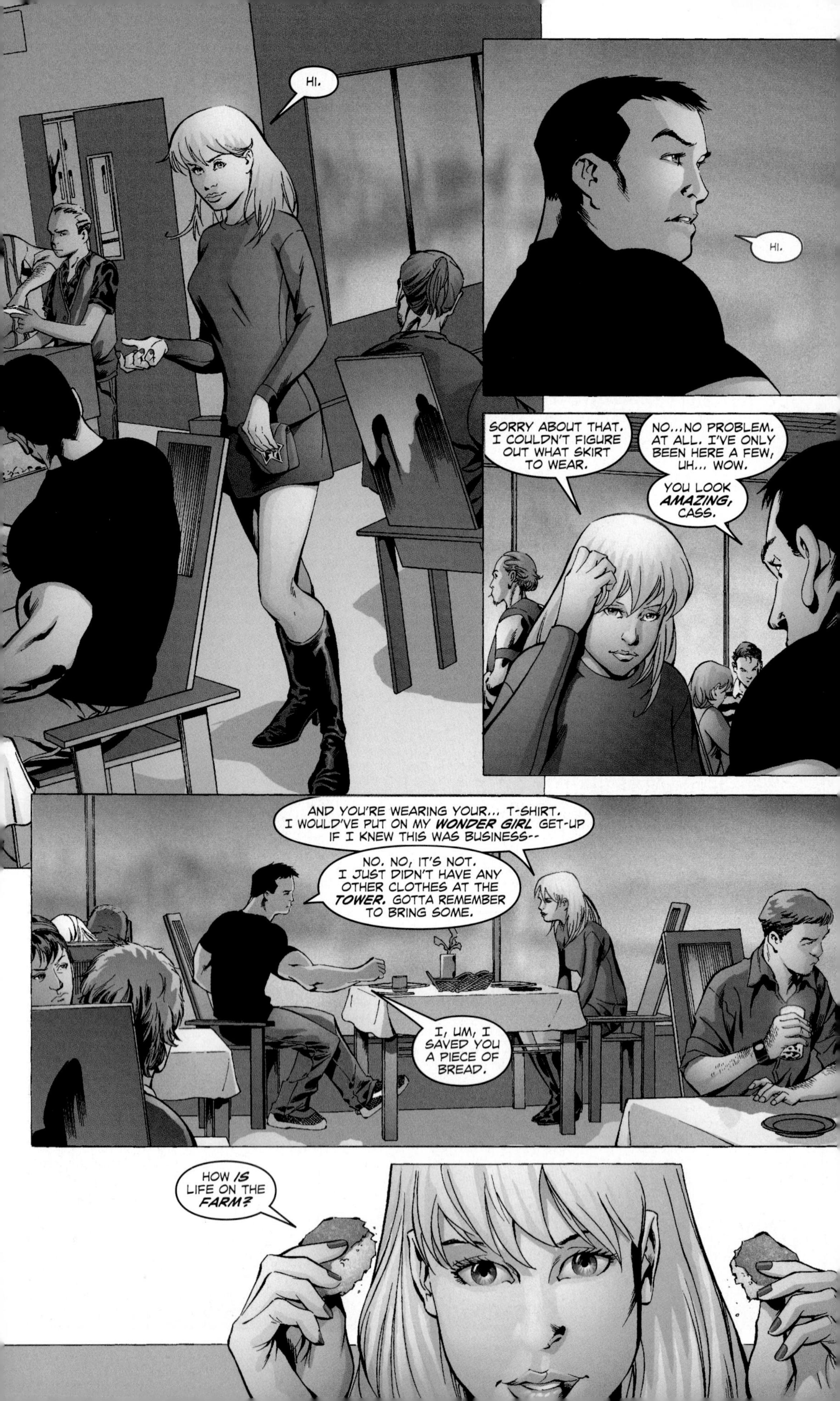
HI.
HI.
SORRY ABOUT THAT. I COULDN'T FIGURE OUT WHAT SKIRT TO WEAR.
NO...NO PROBLEM. AT ALL. I'VE ONLY BEEN HERE A FEW, UH... WOW.
YOU LOOK *AMAZING,* CASS.
AND YOU'RE WEARING YOUR... T-SHIRT. I WOULD'VE PUT ON MY *WONDER GIRL* GET-UP IF I KNEW THIS WAS BUSINESS--
NO. NO, IT'S NOT. I JUST DIDN'T HAVE ANY OTHER CLOTHES AT THE *TOWER.* GOTTA REMEMBER TO BRING SOME.
I, UM, I SAVED YOU A PIECE OF BREAD.
HOW *IS* LIFE ON THE *FARM?*

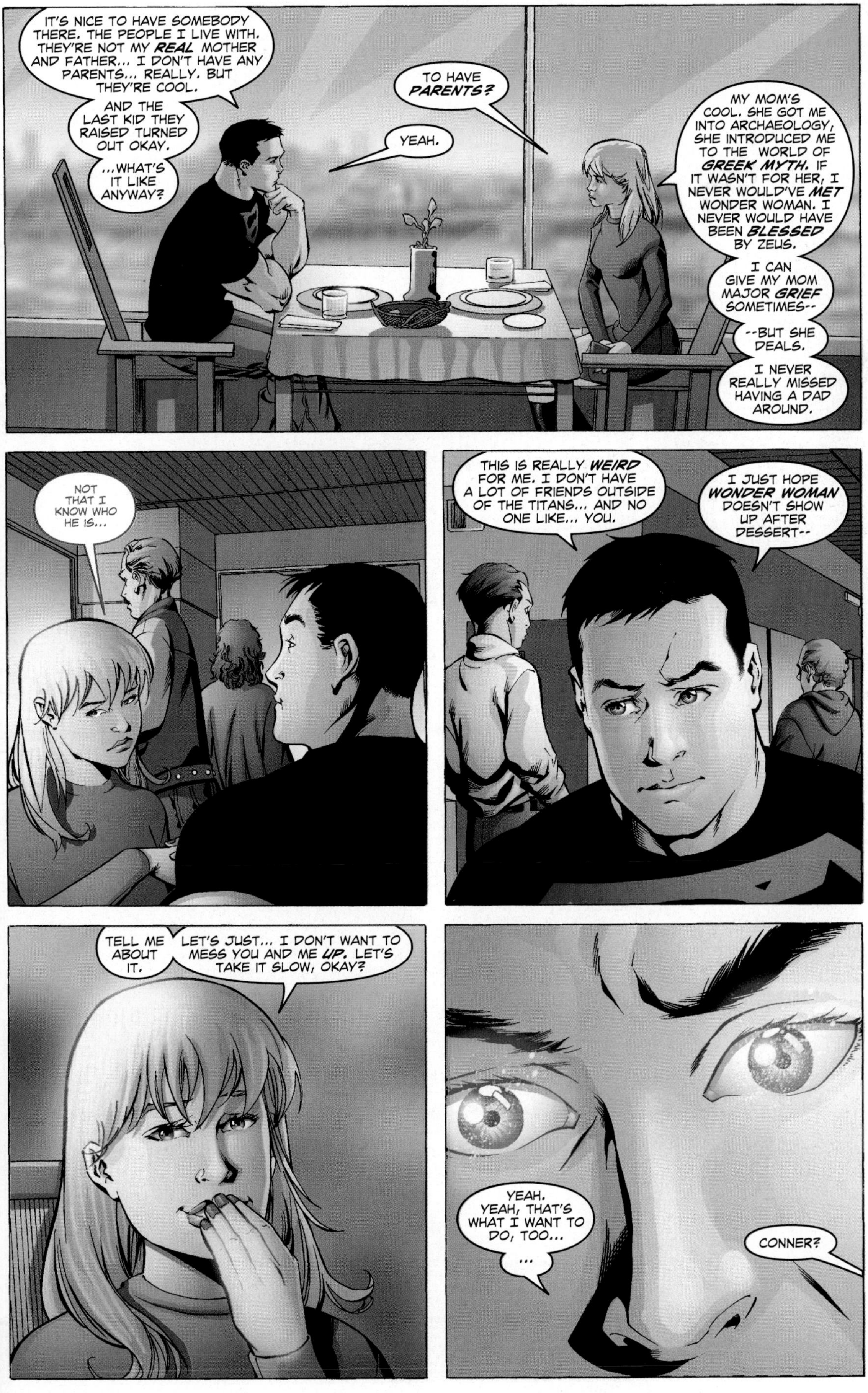
IT'S NICE TO HAVE SOMEBODY THERE. THE PEOPLE I LIVE WITH. THEY'RE NOT MY REAL MOTHER AND FATHER... I DON'T HAVE ANY PARENTS... REALLY. BUT THEY'RE COOL.
AND THE LAST KID THEY RAISED TURNED OUT OKAY.
...WHAT'S IT LIKE ANYWAY?
TO HAVE PARENTS?
YEAH.
MY MOM'S COOL. SHE GOT ME INTO ARCHAEOLOGY, SHE INTRODUCED ME TO THE WORLD OF GREEK MYTH. IF IT WASN'T FOR HER, I NEVER WOULD'VE MET WONDER WOMAN. I NEVER WOULD HAVE BEEN BLESSED BY ZEUS.
I CAN GIVE MY MOM MAJOR GRIEF SOMETIMES--
--BUT SHE DEALS.
I NEVER REALLY MISSED HAVING A DAD AROUND.
NOT THAT I KNOW WHO HE IS...
THIS IS REALLY WEIRD FOR ME. I DON'T HAVE A LOT OF FRIENDS OUTSIDE OF THE TITANS... AND NO ONE LIKE... YOU.
I JUST HOPE WONDER WOMAN DOESN'T SHOW UP AFTER DESSERT--
TELL ME ABOUT IT.
LET'S JUST... I DON'T WANT TO MESS YOU AND ME UP. LET'S TAKE IT SLOW, OKAY?
YEAH. YEAH, THAT'S WHAT I WANT TO DO, TOO...
...
CONNER?

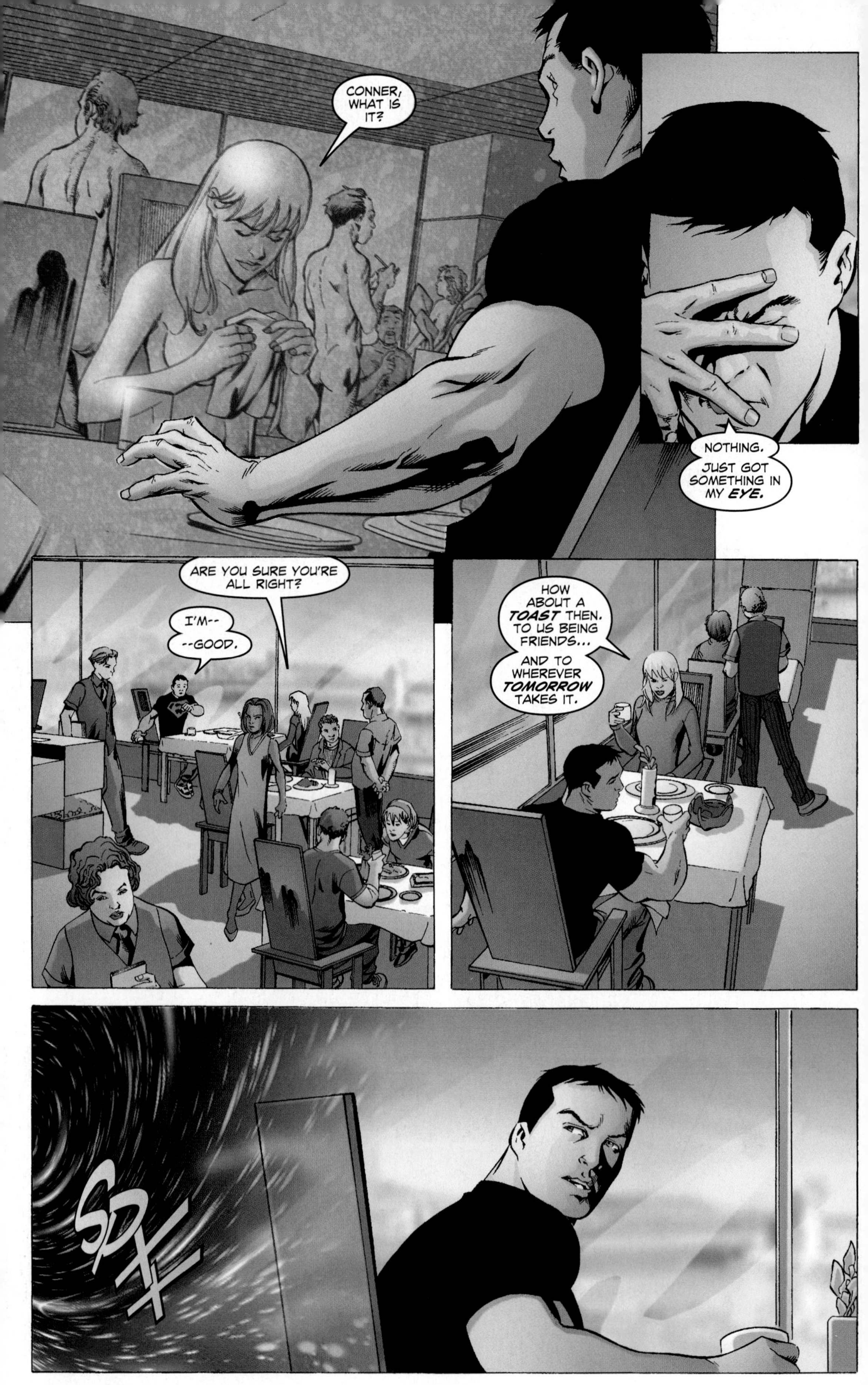
CONNER, WHAT IS IT?
NOTHING.
JUST GOT SOMETHING IN MY EYE.
ARE YOU SURE YOU'RE ALL RIGHT?
I'M--
--GOOD.
HOW ABOUT A TOAST THEN. TO US BEING FRIENDS...
AND TO WHEREVER TOMORROW TAKES IT.
SPXX

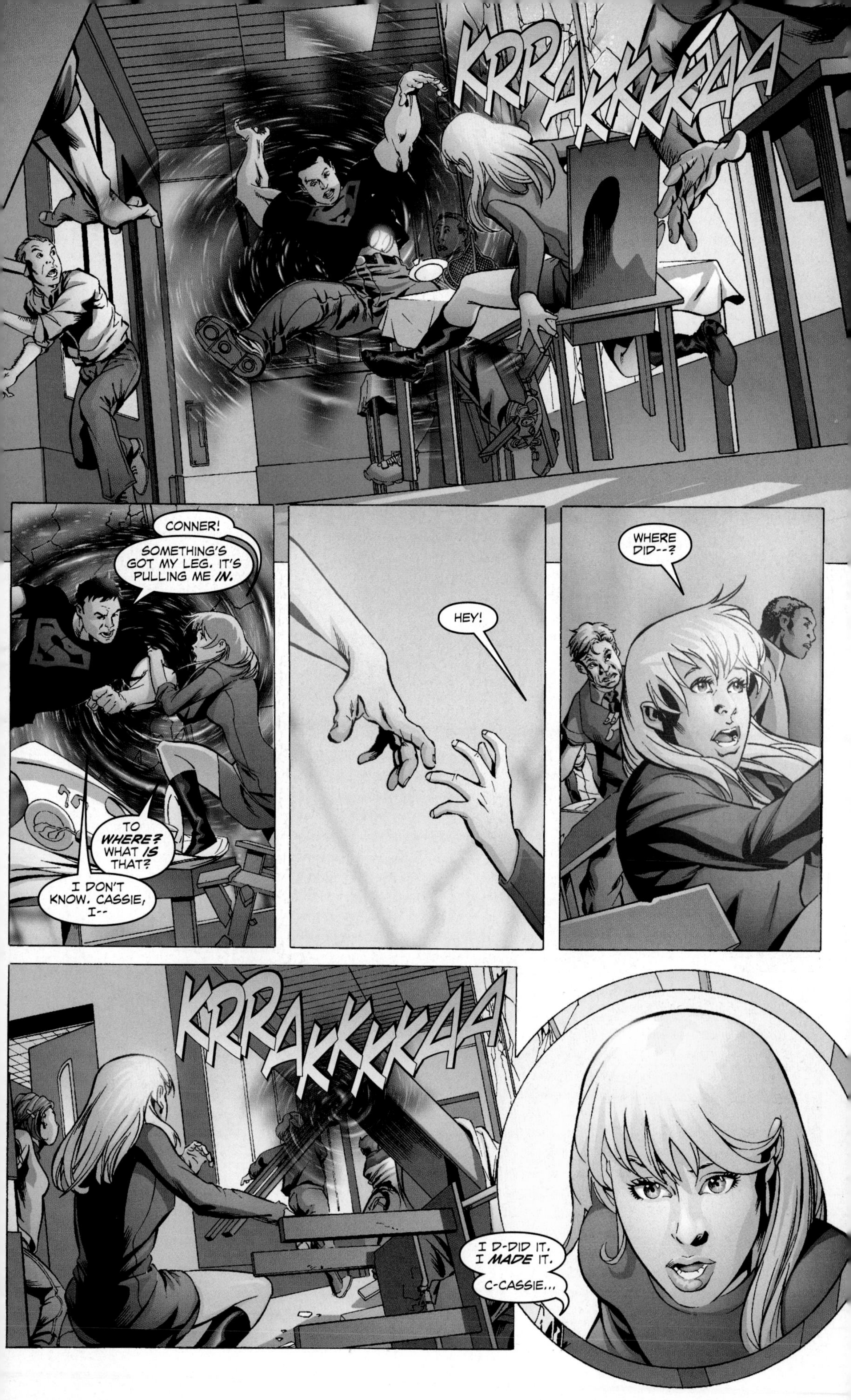
KRRAKKKKAA
CONNER!
SOMETHING'S GOT MY LEG. IT'S PULLING ME IN.
TO WHERE? WHAT IS THAT?
I DON'T KNOW. CASSIE, I--
HEY!
WHERE DID--?
KRRAKKKKAA
I D-DID IT. I MADE IT.
C-CASSIE...

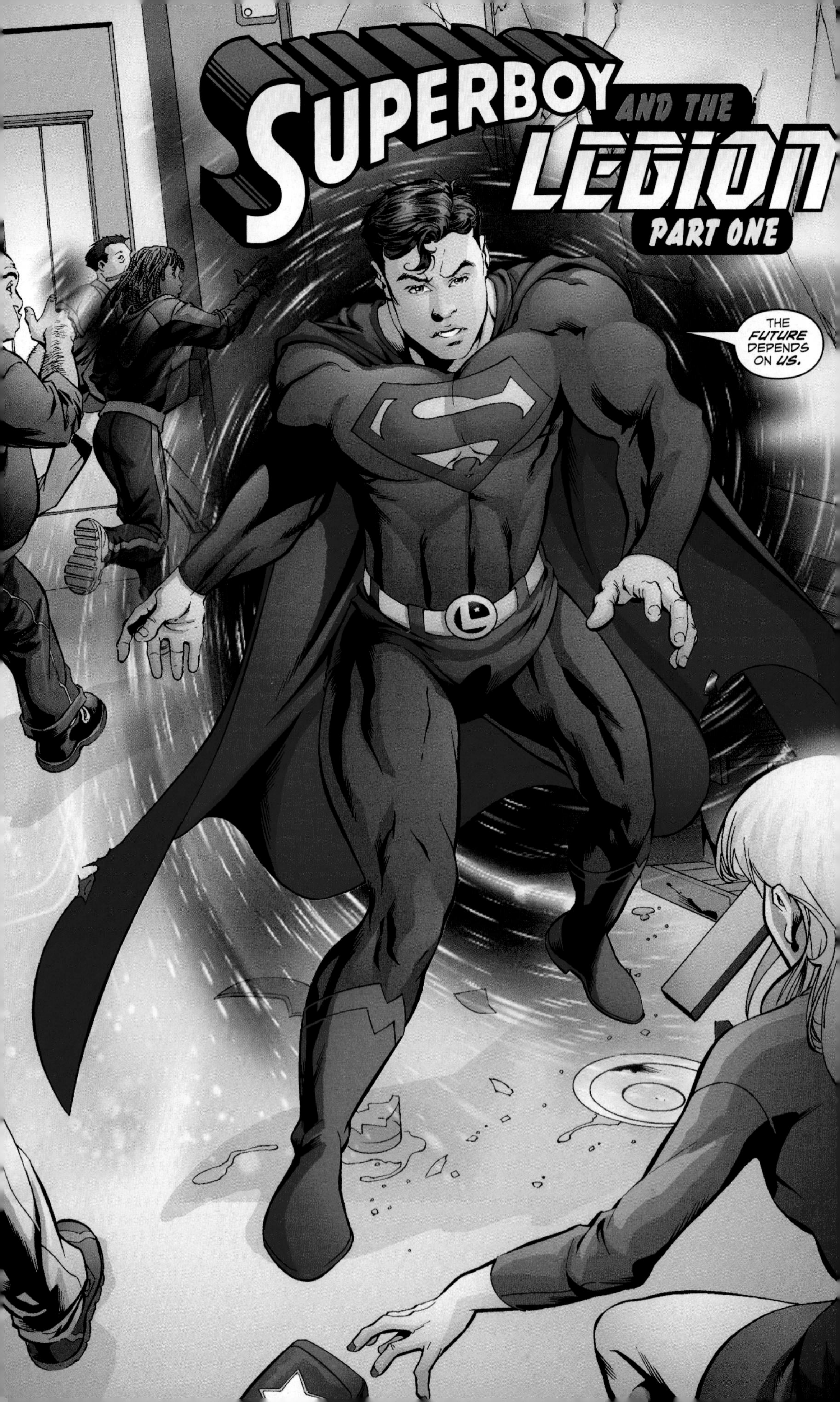
SUPERBOY AND THE LEGION
PART ONE
THE FUTURE DEPENDS ON US.

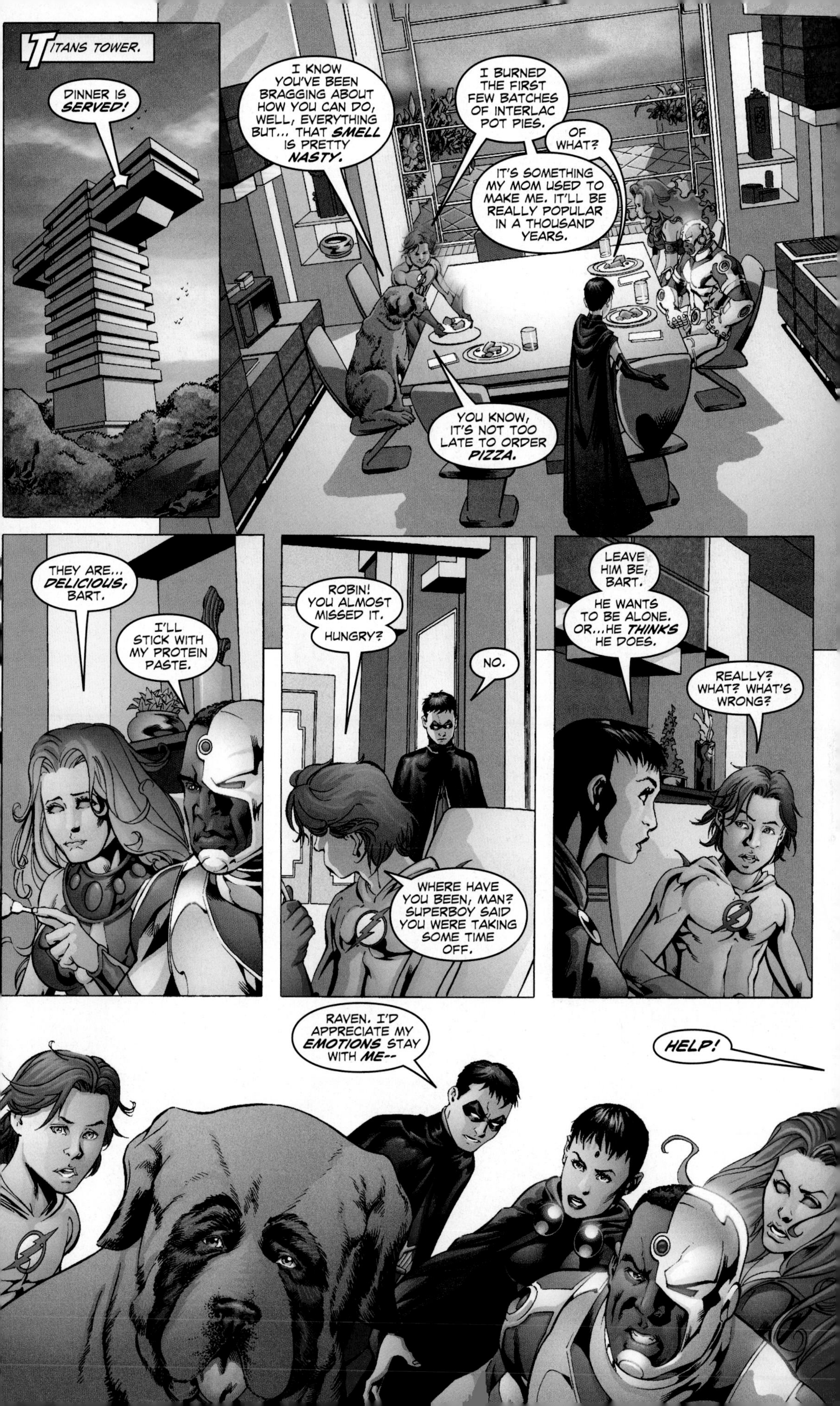
TITANS TOWER.
DINNER IS SERVED!
I KNOW YOU'VE BEEN BRAGGING ABOUT HOW YOU CAN DO, WELL, EVERYTHING BUT... THAT SMELL IS PRETTY NASTY.
I BURNED THE FIRST FEW BATCHES OF INTERLAC POT PIES.
OF WHAT?
IT'S SOMETHING MY MOM USED TO MAKE ME. IT'LL BE REALLY POPULAR IN A THOUSAND YEARS.
YOU KNOW, IT'S NOT TOO LATE TO ORDER PIZZA.
THEY ARE... DELICIOUS, BART.
I'LL STICK WITH MY PROTEIN PASTE.
ROBIN! YOU ALMOST MISSED IT.
HUNGRY?
NO.
WHERE HAVE YOU BEEN, MAN? SUPERBOY SAID YOU WERE TAKING SOME TIME OFF.
LEAVE HIM BE, BART.
HE WANTS TO BE ALONE. OR...HE THINKS HE DOES.
REALLY? WHAT? WHAT'S WRONG?
RAVEN. I'D APPRECIATE MY EMOTIONS STAY WITH ME--
HELP!

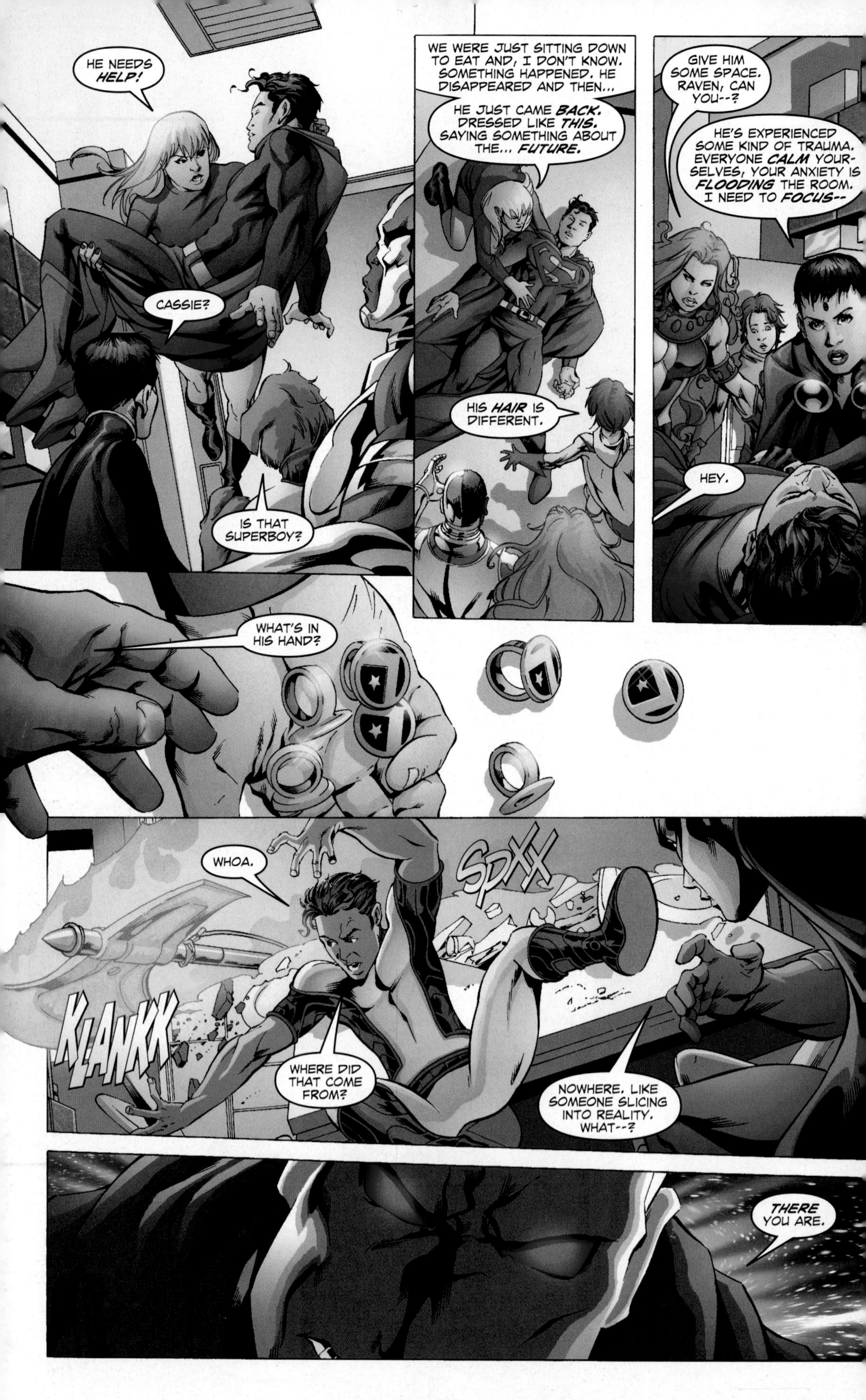
HE NEEDS HELP!
CASSIE?
IS THAT SUPERBOY?
WE WERE JUST SITTING DOWN TO EAT AND, I DON'T KNOW. SOMETHING HAPPENED. HE DISAPPEARED AND THEN...
HE JUST CAME BACK. DRESSED LIKE THIS. SAYING SOMETHING ABOUT THE... FUTURE.
HIS HAIR IS DIFFERENT.
GIVE HIM SOME SPACE. RAVEN, CAN YOU--?
HE'S EXPERIENCED SOME KIND OF TRAUMA. EVERYONE CALM YOURSELVES, YOUR ANXIETY IS FLOODING THE ROOM. I NEED TO FOCUS--
HEY.
WHAT'S IN HIS HAND?
WHOA.
SPXX
KLANKK
WHERE DID THAT COME FROM?
NOWHERE. LIKE SOMEONE SLICING INTO REALITY. WHAT--?
THERE YOU ARE.

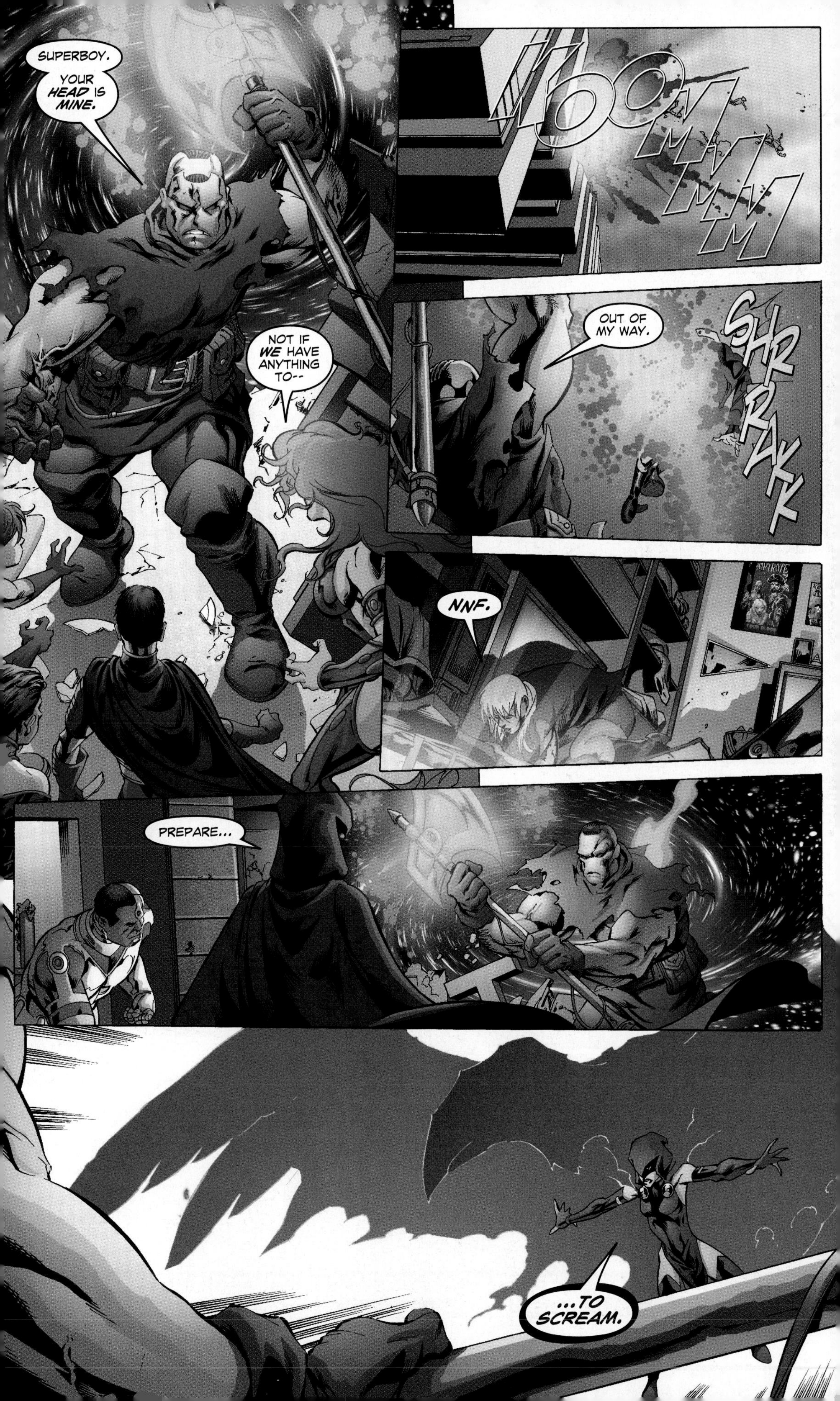
SUPERBOY. YOUR HEAD IS MINE.
VOOOMMMM
NOT IF WE HAVE ANYTHING TO--
OUT OF MY WAY.
SHRRAKK
NNF.
PREPARE...
...TO SCREAM.

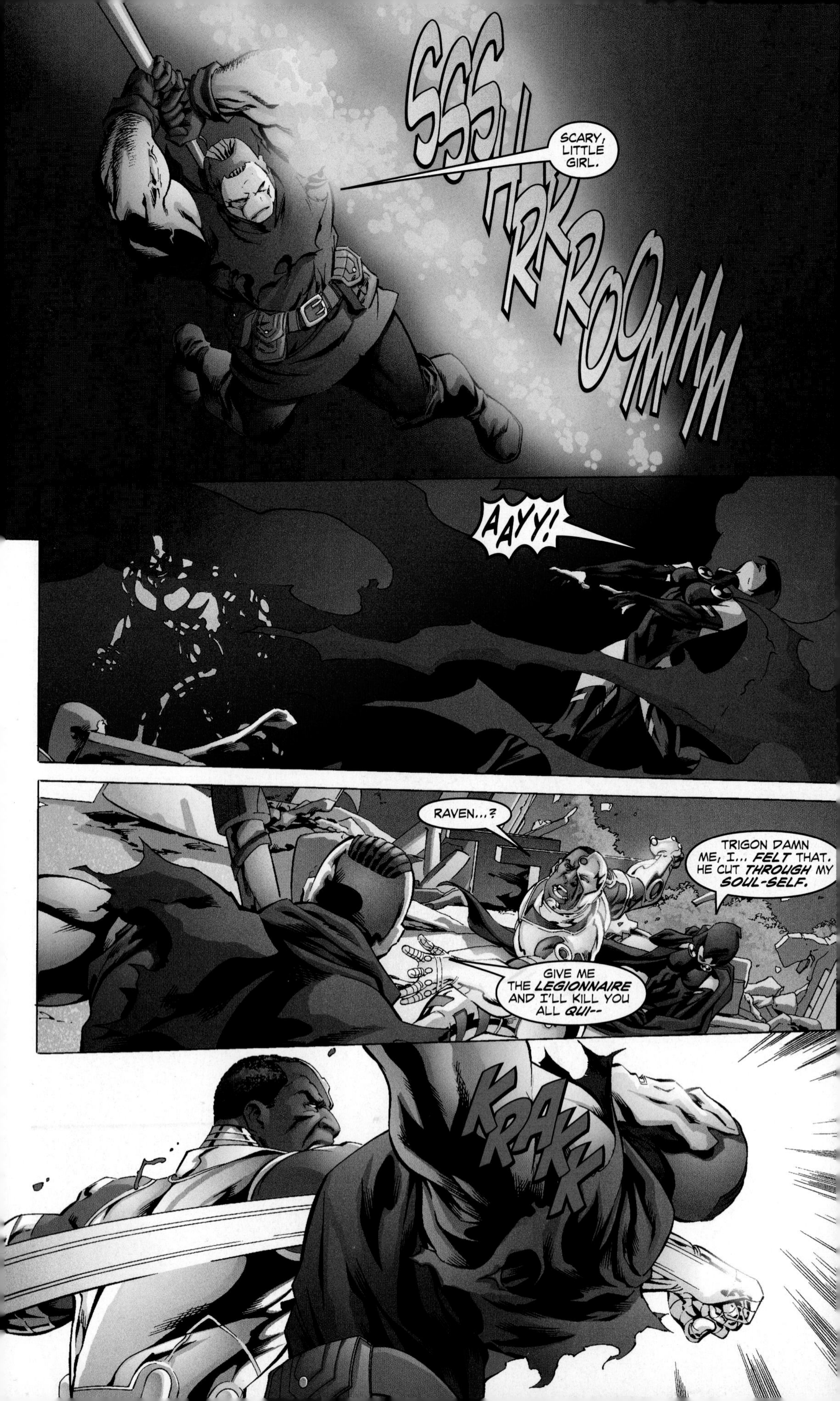
SSSHTRKROOMMM
SCARY, LITTLE GIRL.
AAYY!
RAVEN...?
TRIGON DAMN ME, I... FELT THAT. HE CUT THROUGH MY SOUL-SELF.
GIVE ME THE LEGIONNAIRE AND I'LL KILL YOU ALL QUI--
KRAKK

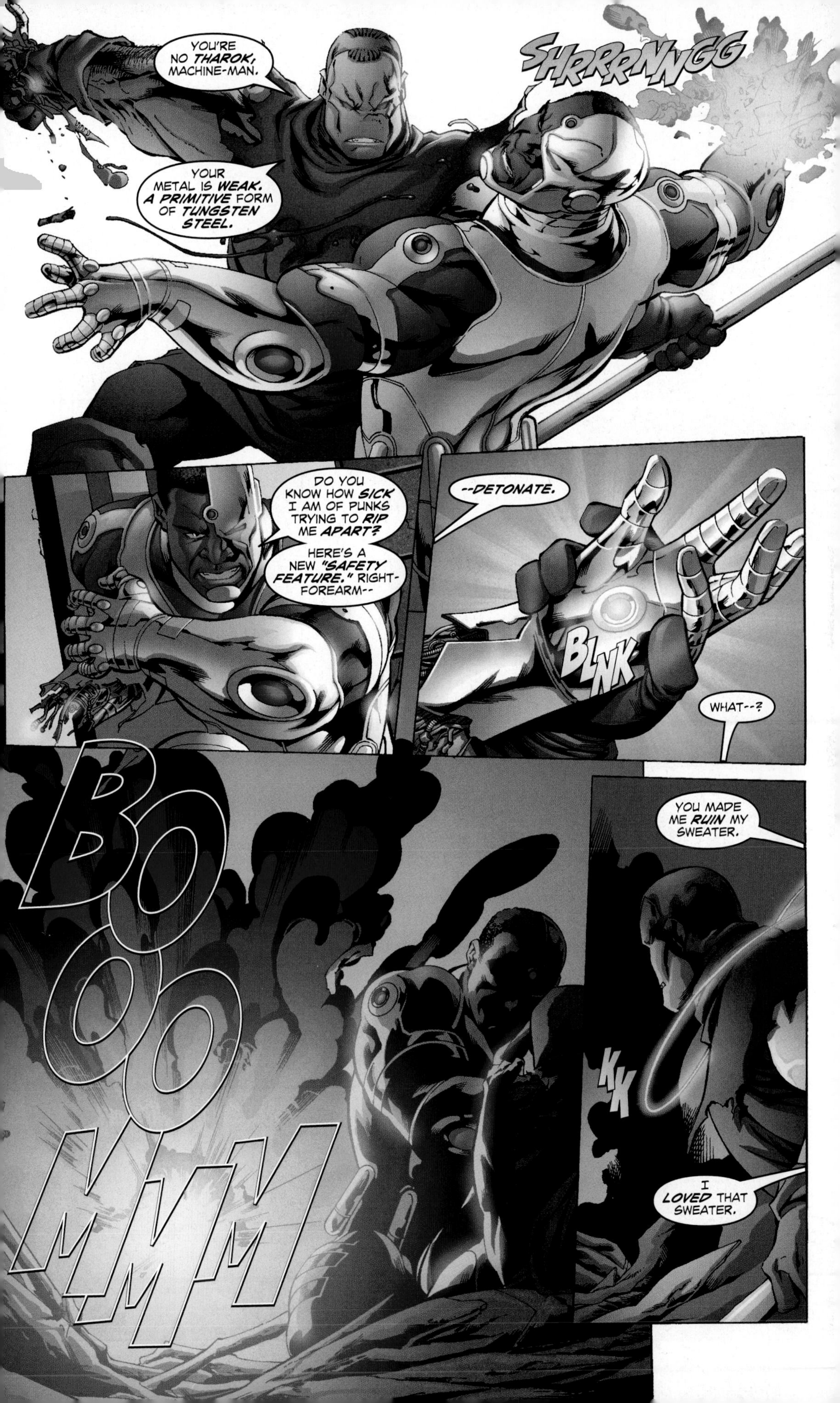

YOU'RE NO THAROK, MACHINE-MAN.
YOUR METAL IS WEAK. A PRIMITIVE FORM OF TUNGSTEN STEEL.
SHRRRNNGG
DO YOU KNOW HOW SICK I AM OF PUNKS TRYING TO RIP ME APART?
HERE'S A NEW "SAFETY FEATURE." RIGHT-FOREARM--
--DETONATE.
BLNK
WHAT--?
BOOOMMMM
YOU MADE ME RUIN MY SWEATER.
KK
I LOVED THAT SWEATER.

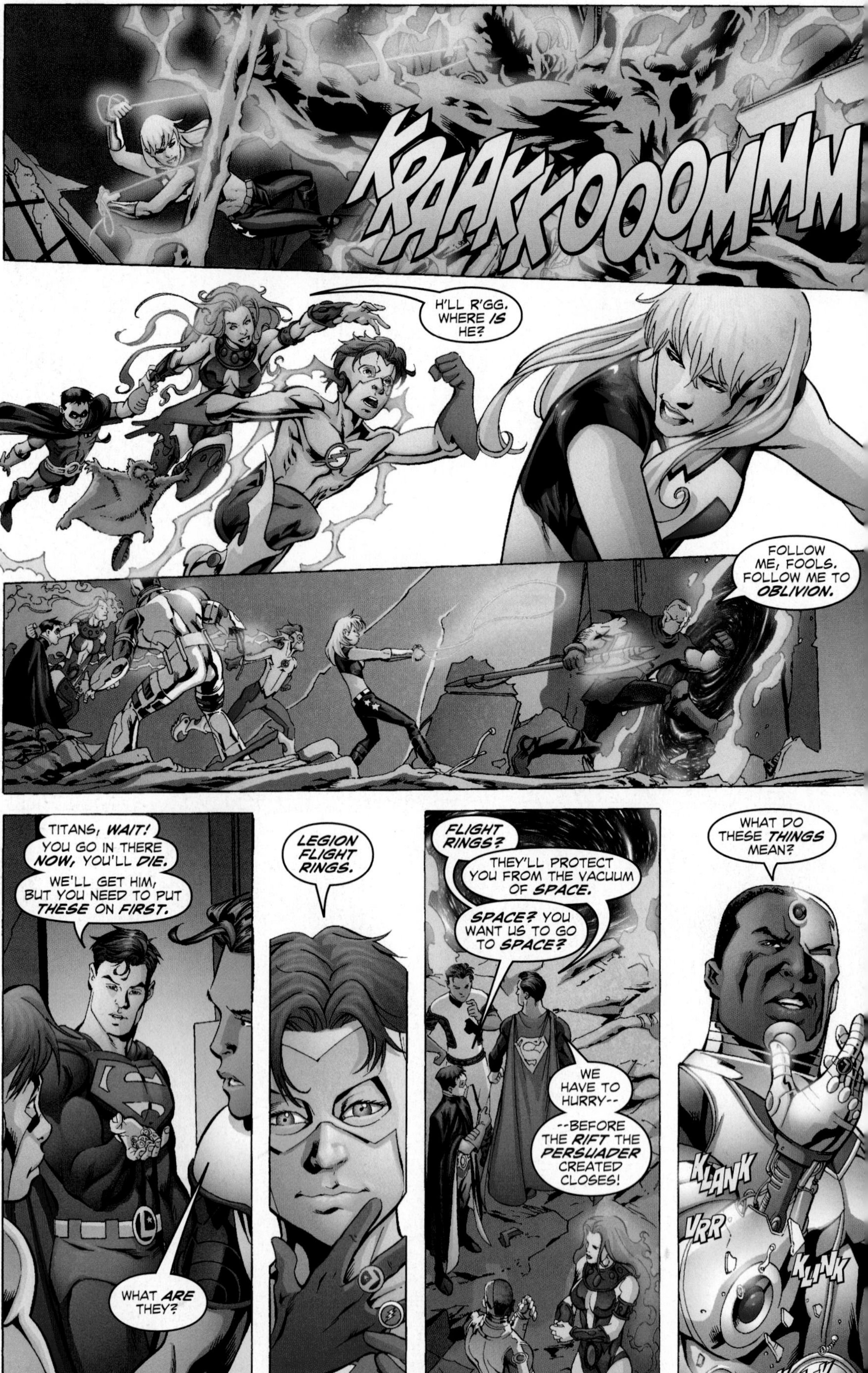

KRAAKOOOMMM
H'LL R'GG. WHERE IS HE?
FOLLOW ME, FOOLS. FOLLOW ME TO OBLIVION.
TITANS, WAIT! YOU GO IN THERE NOW, YOU'LL DIE.
WE'LL GET HIM, BUT YOU NEED TO PUT THESE ON FIRST.
WHAT ARE THEY?
LEGION FLIGHT RINGS.
FLIGHT RINGS?
THEY'LL PROTECT YOU FROM THE VACUUM OF SPACE.
SPACE? YOU WANT US TO GO TO SPACE?
WE HAVE TO HURRY--
--BEFORE THE RIFT THE PERSUADER CREATED CLOSES!
WHAT DO THESE THINGS MEAN?
KLANK
URR
KLINK
KLANK

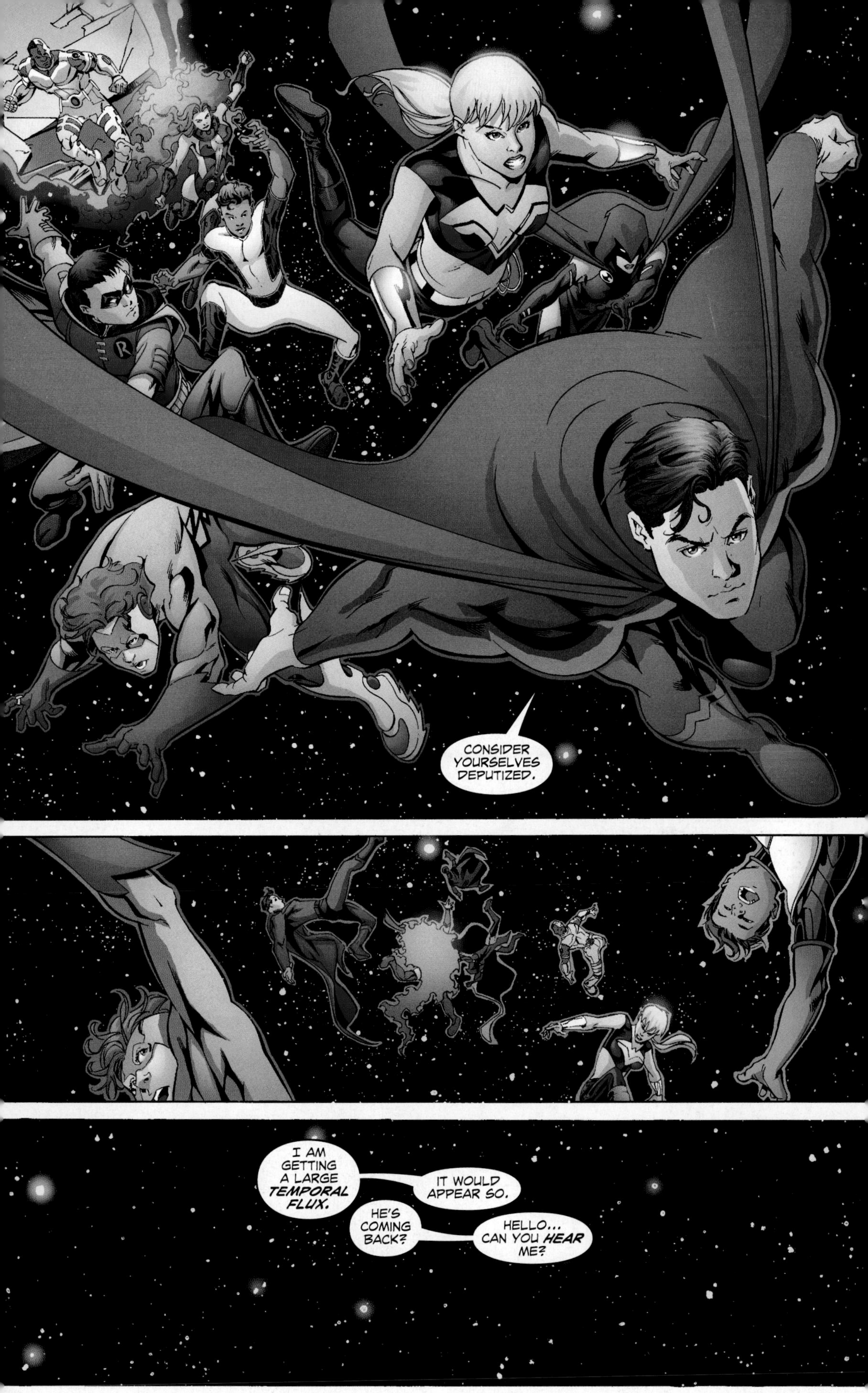
CONSIDER YOURSELVES DEPUTIZED.
I AM GETTING A LARGE *TEMPORAL FLUX.*
IT WOULD APPEAR SO.
HE'S COMING BACK?
HELLO... CAN YOU *HEAR* ME?

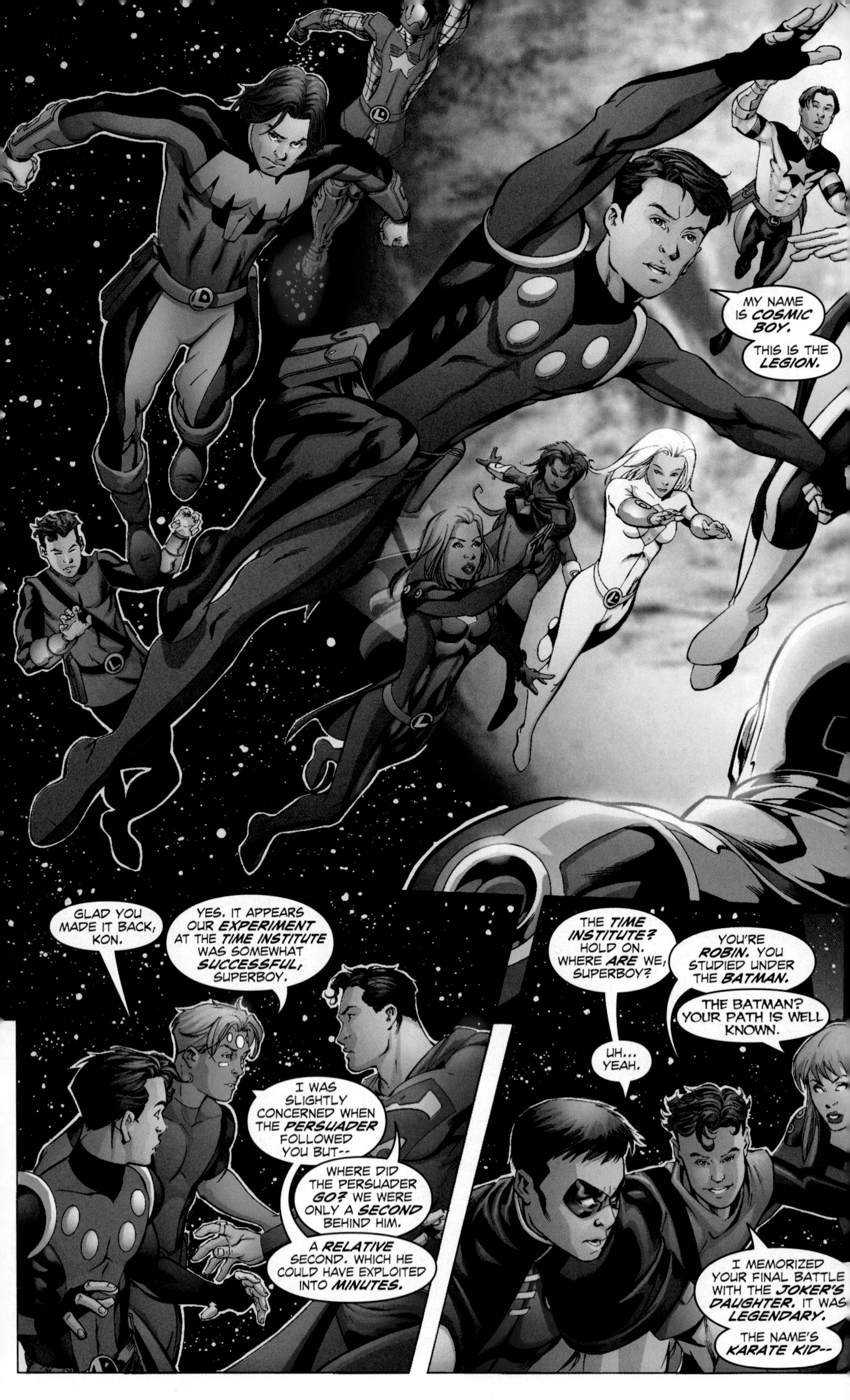
MY NAME IS COSMIC BOY.
THIS IS THE LEGION.
GLAD YOU MADE IT BACK, KON.
YES. IT APPEARS OUR EXPERIMENT AT THE TIME INSTITUTE WAS SOMEWHAT SUCCESSFUL, SUPERBOY.
I WAS SLIGHTLY CONCERNED WHEN THE PERSUADER FOLLOWED YOU BUT--
WHERE DID THE PERSUADER GO? WE WERE ONLY A SECOND BEHIND HIM.
A RELATIVE SECOND. WHICH HE COULD HAVE EXPLOITED INTO MINUTES.
THE TIME INSTITUTE? HOLD ON. WHERE ARE WE, SUPERBOY?
UH... YEAH.
YOU'RE ROBIN. YOU STUDIED UNDER THE BATMAN.
THE BATMAN? YOUR PATH IS WELL KNOWN.
I MEMORIZED YOUR FINAL BATTLE WITH THE JOKER'S DAUGHTER. IT WAS LEGENDARY.
THE NAME'S KARATE KID--

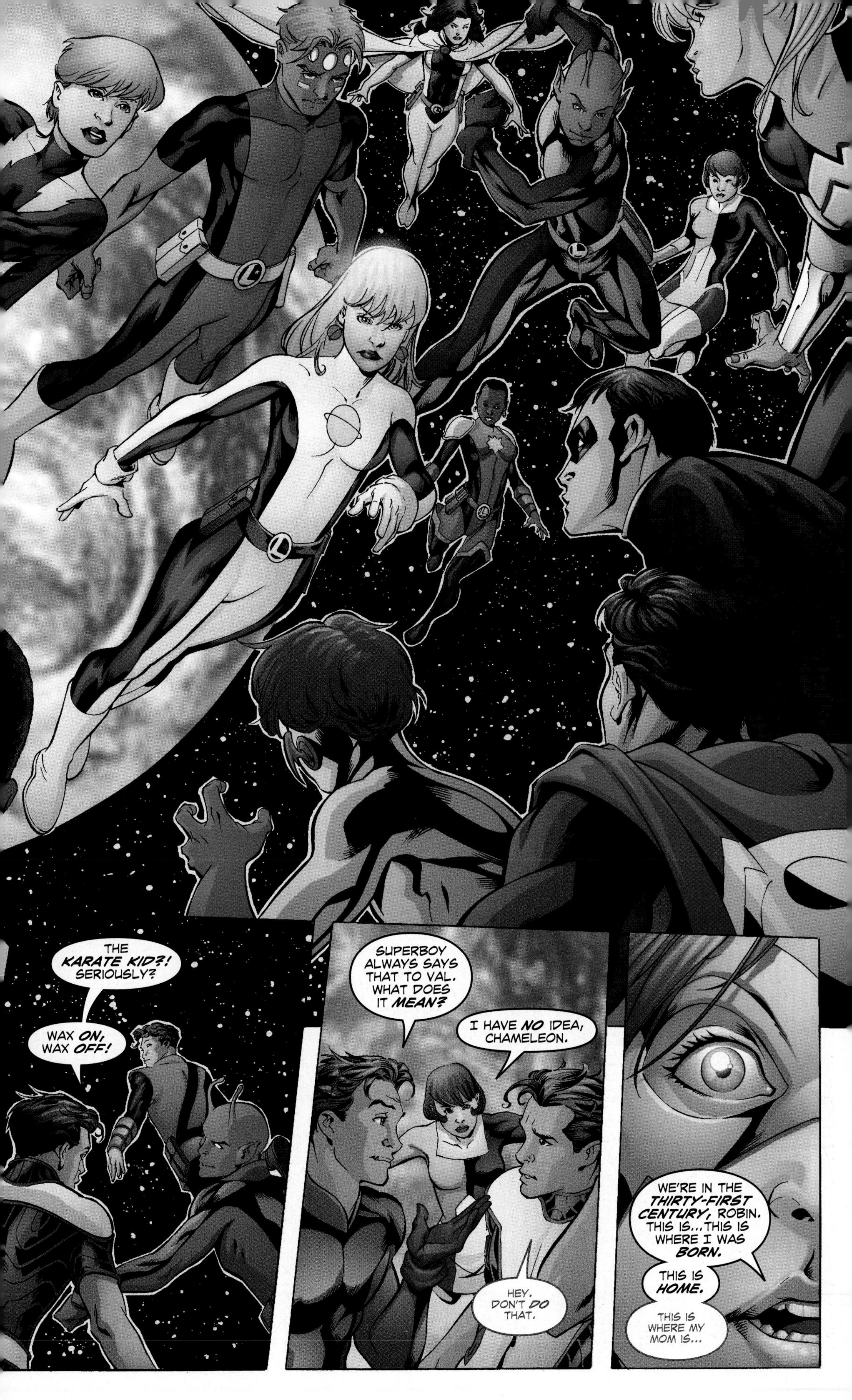
THE KARATE KID?! SERIOUSLY?
WAX ON, WAX OFF!
SUPERBOY ALWAYS SAYS THAT TO VAL. WHAT DOES IT MEAN?
I HAVE NO IDEA, CHAMELEON.
HEY. DON'T DO THAT.
WE'RE IN THE THIRTY-FIRST CENTURY, ROBIN. THIS IS... THIS IS WHERE I WAS BORN.
THIS IS HOME.
THIS IS WHERE MY MOM IS...

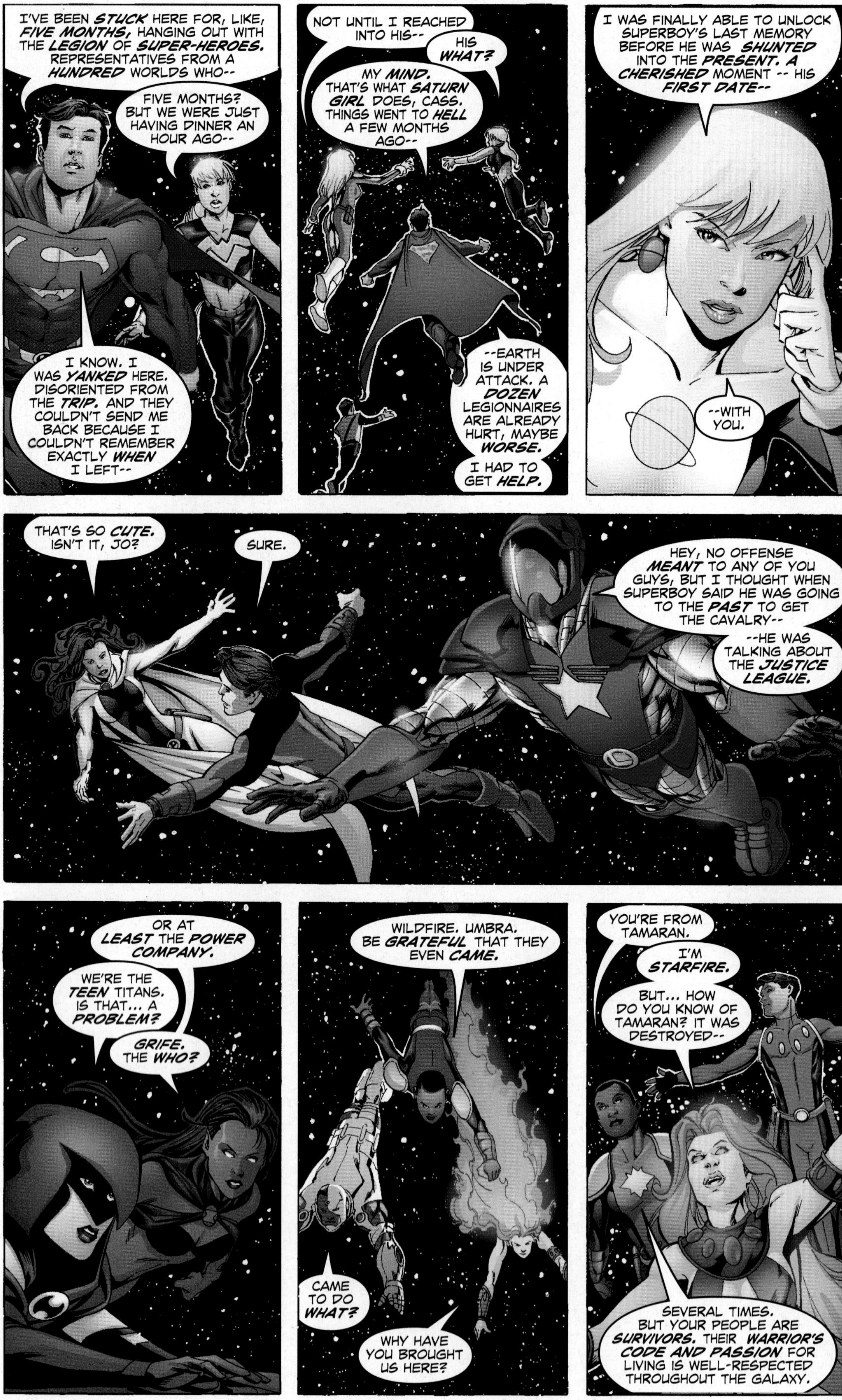
I'VE BEEN STUCK HERE FOR, LIKE, FIVE MONTHS, HANGING OUT WITH THE LEGION OF SUPER-HEROES. REPRESENTATIVES FROM A HUNDRED WORLDS WHO--
FIVE MONTHS? BUT WE WERE JUST HAVING DINNER AN HOUR AGO--
I KNOW. I WAS YANKED HERE. DISORIENTED FROM THE TRIP. AND THEY COULDN'T SEND ME BACK BECAUSE I COULDN'T REMEMBER EXACTLY WHEN I LEFT--
NOT UNTIL I REACHED INTO HIS--
HIS WHAT?
MY MIND. THAT'S WHAT SATURN GIRL DOES, CASS. THINGS WENT TO HELL A FEW MONTHS AGO--
--EARTH IS UNDER ATTACK. A DOZEN LEGIONNAIRES ARE ALREADY HURT, MAYBE WORSE.
I HAD TO GET HELP.
I WAS FINALLY ABLE TO UNLOCK SUPERBOY'S LAST MEMORY BEFORE HE WAS SHUNTED INTO THE PRESENT. A CHERISHED MOMENT -- HIS FIRST DATE--
--WITH YOU.
THAT'S SO CUTE. ISN'T IT, JO?
SURE.
HEY, NO OFFENSE MEANT TO ANY OF YOU GUYS, BUT I THOUGHT WHEN SUPERBOY SAID HE WAS GOING TO THE PAST TO GET THE CAVALRY--
--HE WAS TALKING ABOUT THE JUSTICE LEAGUE.
OR AT LEAST THE POWER COMPANY.
WE'RE THE TEEN TITANS. IS THAT... A PROBLEM?
GRIFE. THE WHO?
WILDFIRE. UMBRA. BE GRATEFUL THAT THEY EVEN CAME.
CAME TO DO WHAT?
WHY HAVE YOU BROUGHT US HERE?
YOU'RE FROM TAMARAN.
I'M STARFIRE.
BUT... HOW DO YOU KNOW OF TAMARAN? IT WAS DESTROYED--
SEVERAL TIMES. BUT YOUR PEOPLE ARE SURVIVORS. THEIR WARRIOR'S CODE AND PASSION FOR LIVING IS WELL-RESPECTED THROUGHOUT THE GALAXY.

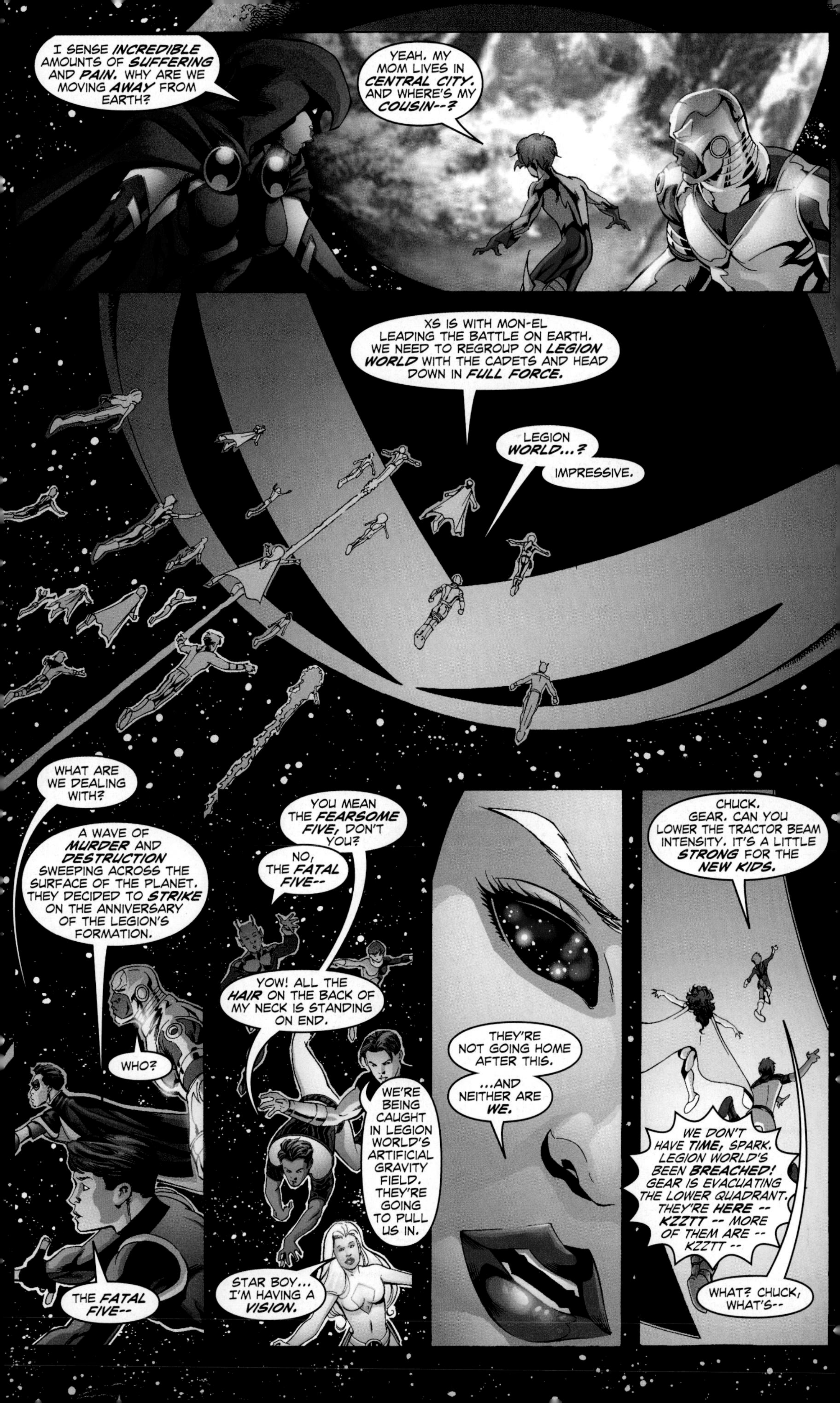

I SENSE INCREDIBLE AMOUNTS OF SUFFERING AND PAIN. WHY ARE WE MOVING AWAY FROM EARTH?
YEAH. MY MOM LIVES IN CENTRAL CITY. AND WHERE'S MY COUSIN--?
XS IS WITH MON-EL LEADING THE BATTLE ON EARTH. WE NEED TO REGROUP ON LEGION WORLD WITH THE CADETS AND HEAD DOWN IN FULL FORCE.
LEGION WORLD...?
IMPRESSIVE.
WHAT ARE WE DEALING WITH?
A WAVE OF MURDER AND DESTRUCTION SWEEPING ACROSS THE SURFACE OF THE PLANET. THEY DECIDED TO STRIKE ON THE ANNIVERSARY OF THE LEGION'S FORMATION.
WHO?
THE FATAL FIVE--
YOU MEAN THE FEARSOME FIVE, DON'T YOU?
NO, THE FATAL FIVE--
YOW! ALL THE HAIR ON THE BACK OF MY NECK IS STANDING ON END.
WE'RE BEING CAUGHT IN LEGION WORLD'S ARTIFICIAL GRAVITY FIELD. THEY'RE GOING TO PULL US IN.
STAR BOY... I'M HAVING A VISION.
THEY'RE NOT GOING HOME AFTER THIS.
...AND NEITHER ARE WE.
CHUCK. GEAR. CAN YOU LOWER THE TRACTOR BEAM INTENSITY. IT'S A LITTLE STRONG FOR THE NEW KIDS.
WE DON'T HAVE TIME, SPARK. LEGION WORLD'S BEEN BREACHED! GEAR IS EVACUATING THE LOWER QUADRANT. THEY'RE HERE -- KZZTT -- MORE OF THEM ARE -- KZZTT --
WHAT? CHUCK, WHAT'S--

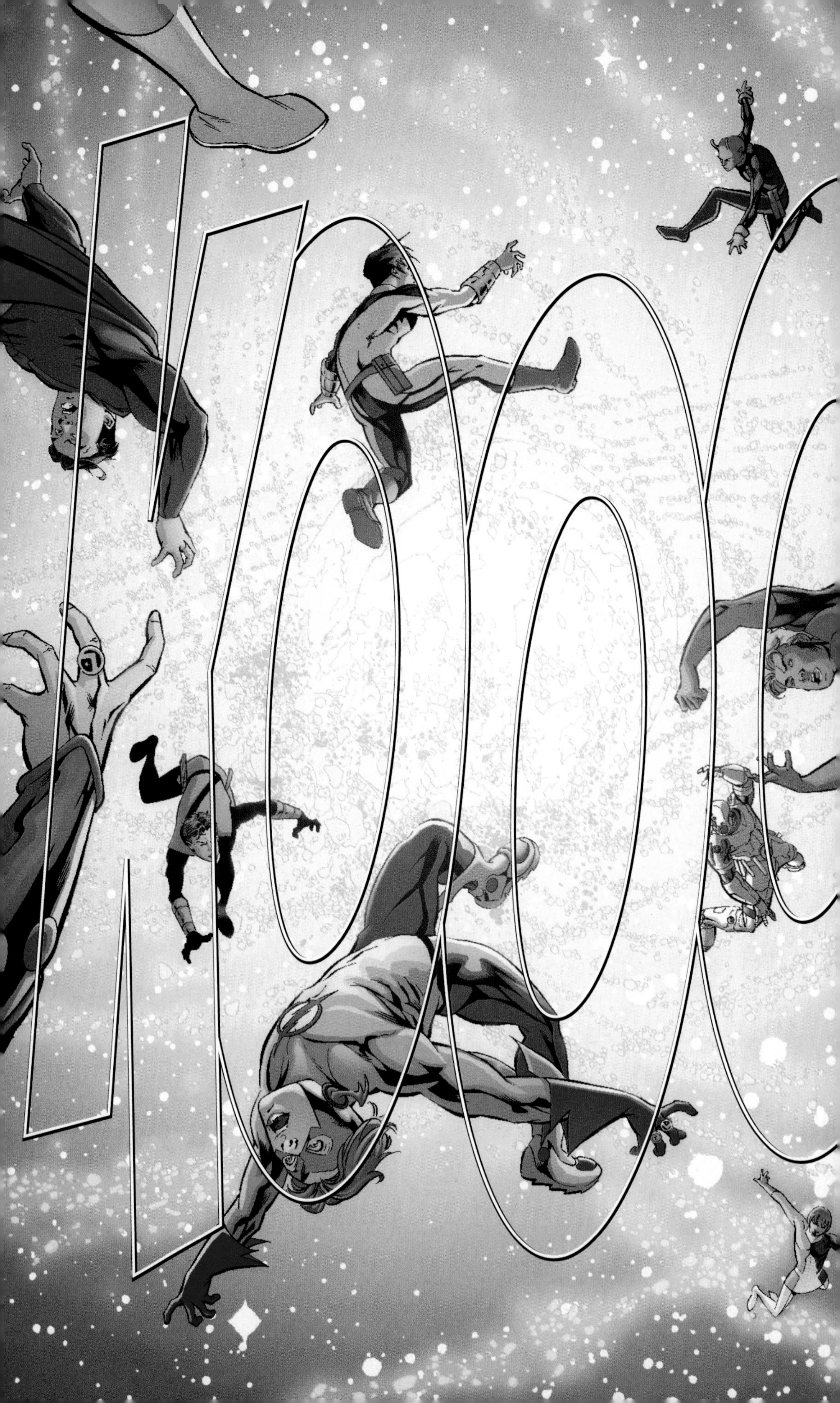
WOOO

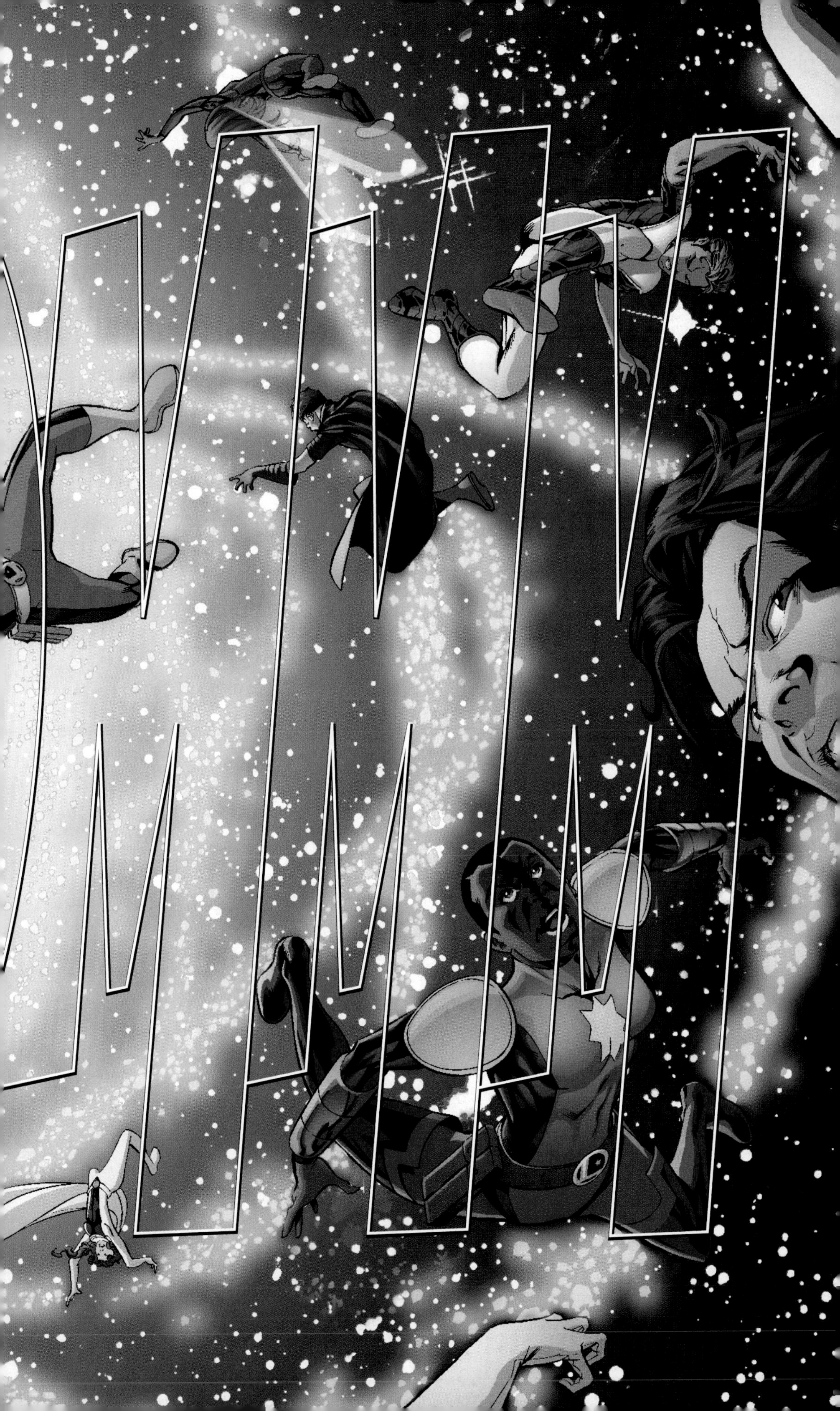

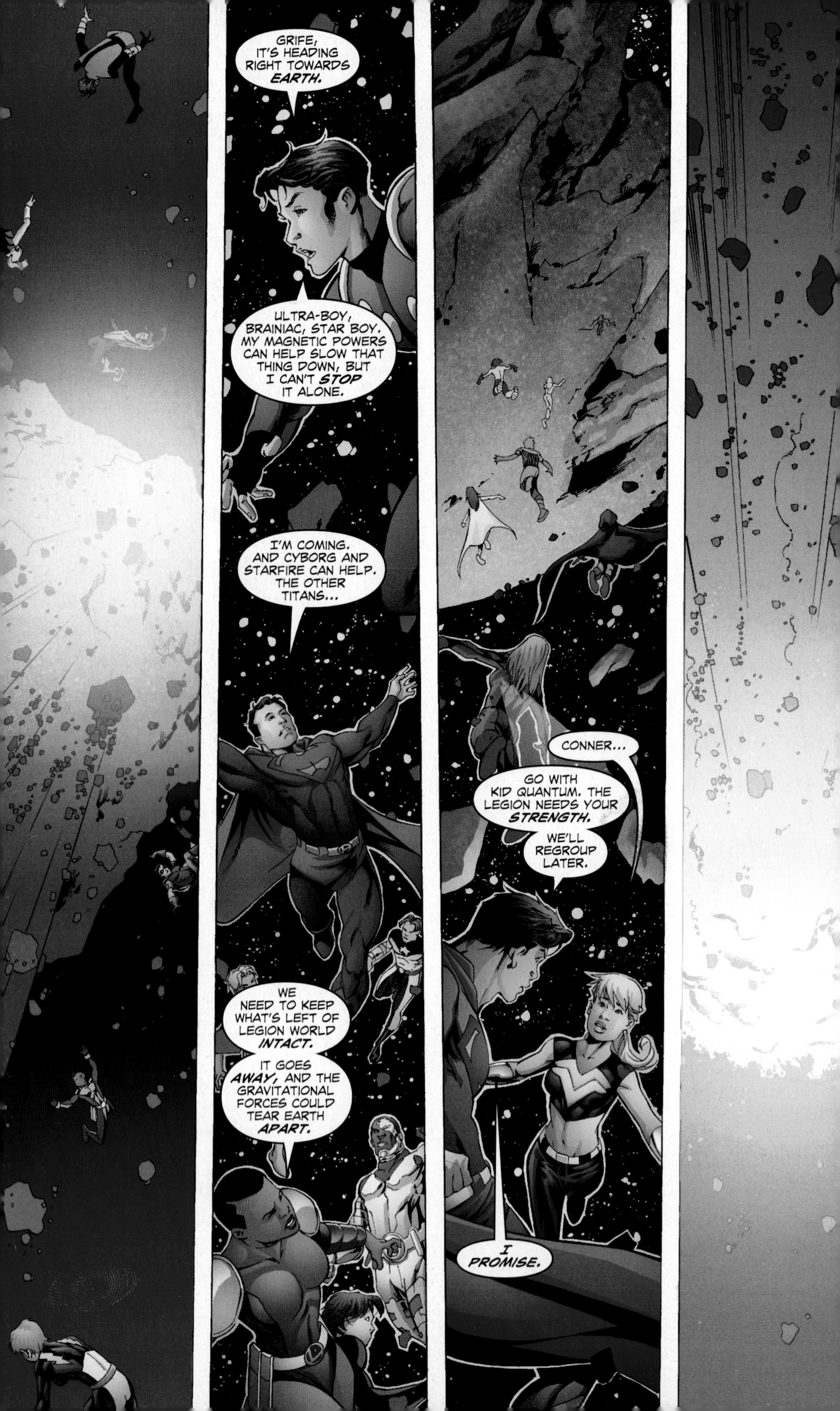
GRIFE, IT'S HEADING RIGHT TOWARDS EARTH.
ULTRA-BOY, BRAINIAC, STAR BOY. MY MAGNETIC POWERS CAN HELP SLOW THAT THING DOWN, BUT I CAN'T STOP IT ALONE.
I'M COMING. AND CYBORG AND STARFIRE CAN HELP. THE OTHER TITANS...
WE NEED TO KEEP WHAT'S LEFT OF LEGION WORLD INTACT.
IT GOES AWAY, AND THE GRAVITATIONAL FORCES COULD TEAR EARTH APART.
CONNER...
GO WITH KID QUANTUM. THE LEGION NEEDS YOUR STRENGTH.
WE'LL REGROUP LATER.
I PROMISE.

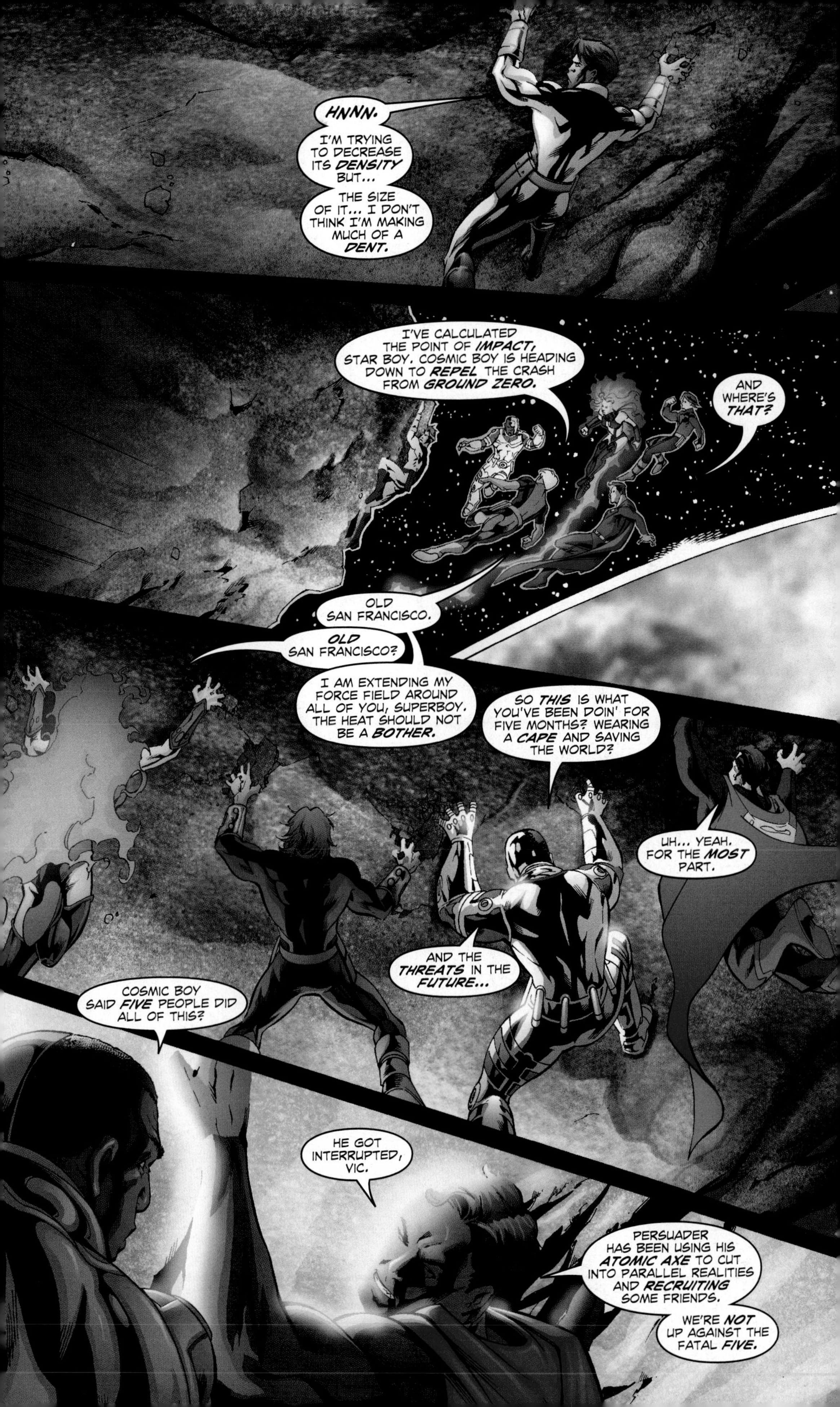

HNNN.
I'M TRYING TO DECREASE ITS DENSITY BUT...
THE SIZE OF IT... I DON'T THINK I'M MAKING MUCH OF A DENT.
I'VE CALCULATED THE POINT OF IMPACT, STAR BOY. COSMIC BOY IS HEADING DOWN TO REPEL THE CRASH FROM GROUND ZERO.
AND WHERE'S THAT?
OLD SAN FRANCISCO.
OLD SAN FRANCISCO?
I AM EXTENDING MY FORCE FIELD AROUND ALL OF YOU, SUPERBOY. THE HEAT SHOULD NOT BE A BOTHER.
SO THIS IS WHAT YOU'VE BEEN DOIN' FOR FIVE MONTHS? WEARING A CAPE AND SAVING THE WORLD?
UH... YEAH. FOR THE MOST PART.
AND THE THREATS IN THE FUTURE...
COSMIC BOY SAID FIVE PEOPLE DID ALL OF THIS?
HE GOT INTERRUPTED, VIC.
PERSUADER HAS BEEN USING HIS ATOMIC AXE TO CUT INTO PARALLEL REALITIES AND RECRUITING SOME FRIENDS.
WE'RE NOT UP AGAINST THE FATAL FIVE.

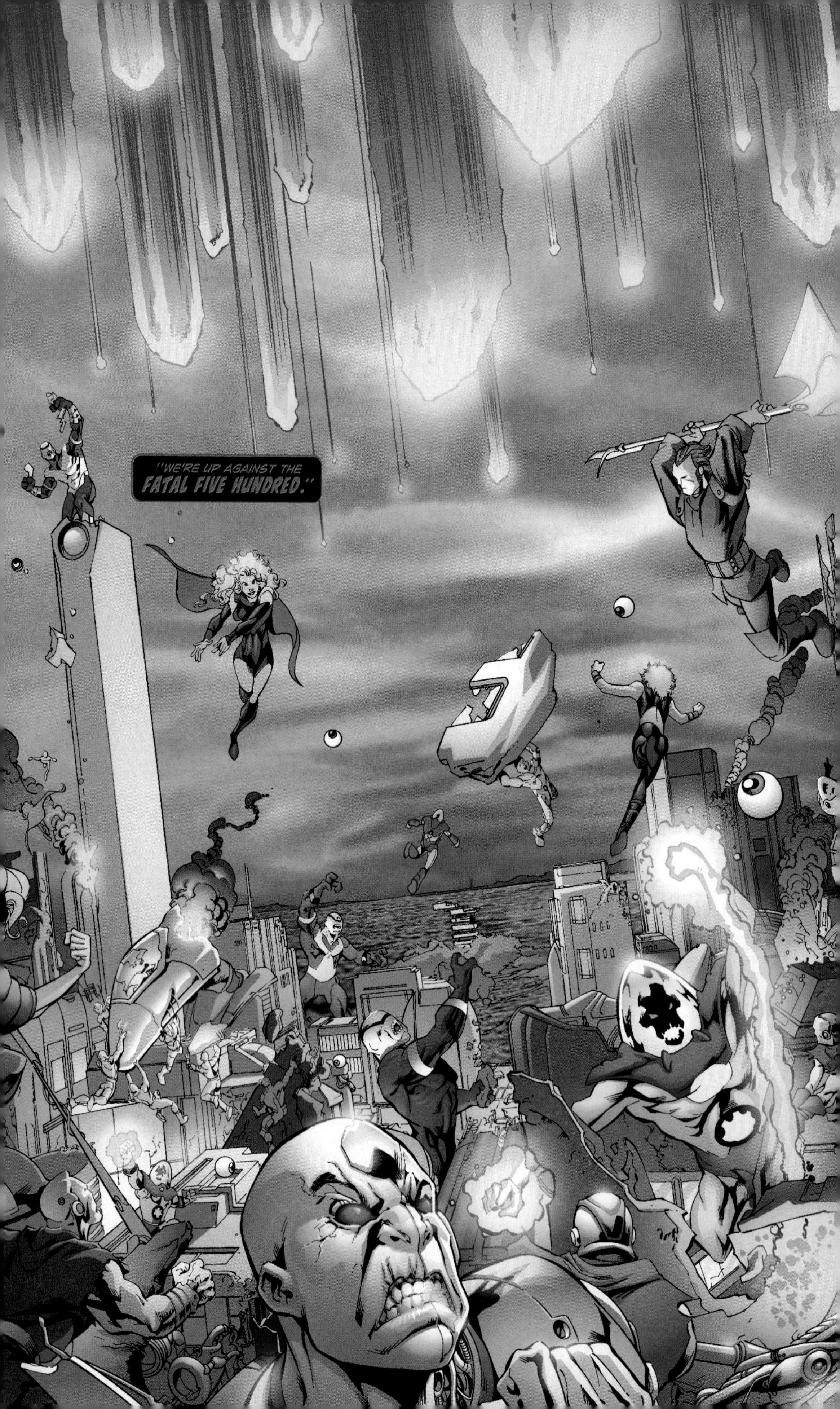
"WE'RE UP AGAINST THE FATAL FIVE HUNDRED."

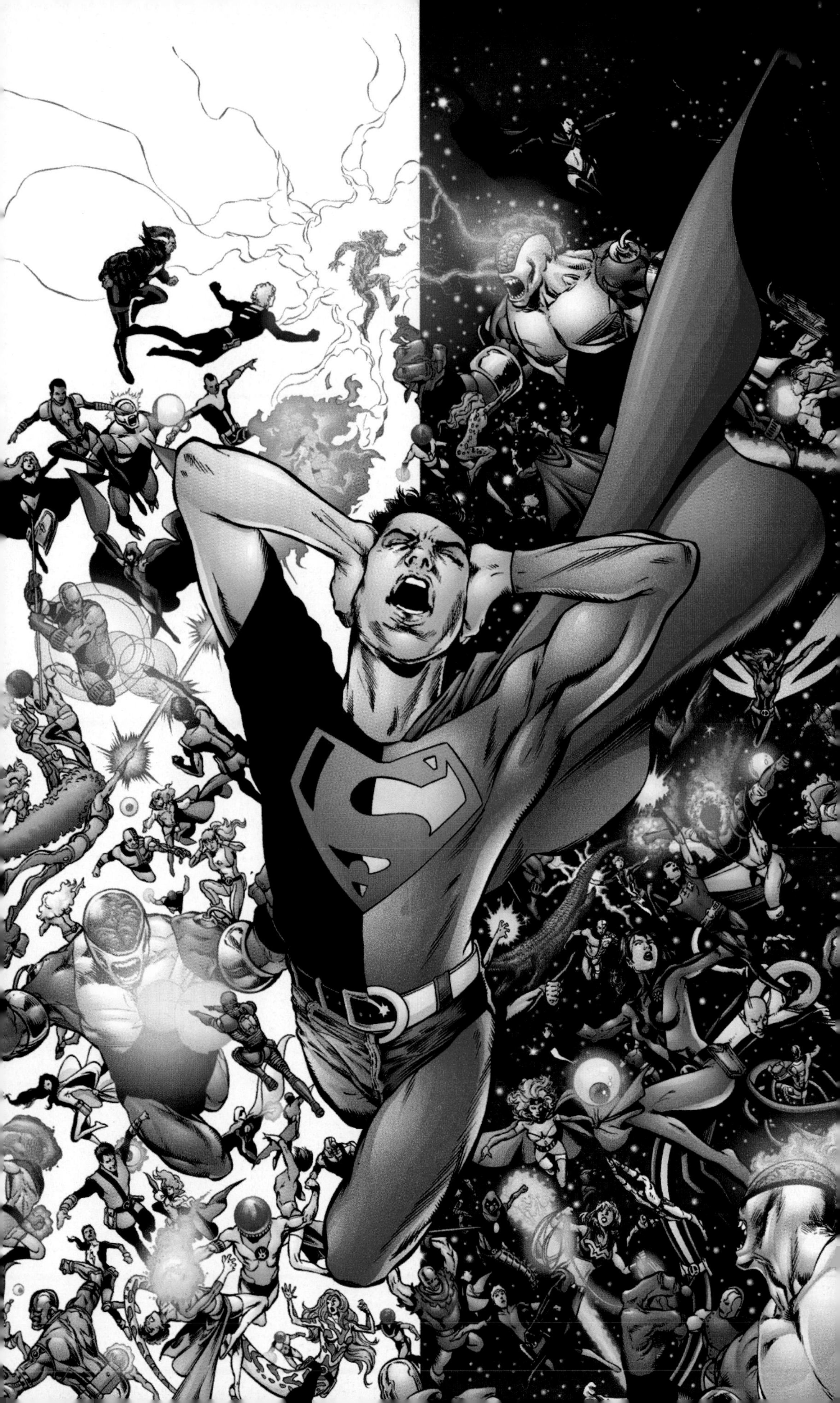

TEEN TITANS/LEGION OF SUPER-HEROES SPECIAL #1

GEOFF JOHNS
MARK WAID
Writers

IVAN REIS
JOE PRADO
Pencillers

MARC CAMPOS
Inker

SNO-CONE
Colorist

ROB LEIGH
Letterer

PHIL JIMENEZ, ANDY LANNING
and TANYA & RICHARD HORIE
Cover Artists

31ST-CENTURY EARTH IS PROTECTED BY THE **LEGION OF SUPER-HEROES,** A BAND OF TEENAGE CHAMPIONS CULLED FROM THE DIVERSE WORLDS OF THE **UNITED PLANETS.**

NORMALLY, THEY DO A BETTER JOB THAN THIS.

NORMALLY, HOWEVER, THE ODDS ARE GREATLY IN THEIR **FAVOR** AGAINST THE XENO-TERRORIST GROUP KNOWN AS THE **FATAL FIVE.**

SOMEHOW, THE FATAL FIVE HAS MULTIPLIED ITS MEMBERSHIP A **HUNDREDFOLD--**

--NOW, EVEN AFTER HAVING RECRUITED THE 21ST-CENTURY'S **TEEN TITANS** TO THEIR SIDE--

--THE LEGIONNAIRES ARE FIGHTING A **LOSING BATTLE** TO DEFEND THEIR ADOPTED WORLD AGAINST AN ARMY OF A **HALF-THOUSAND** VILLAINS.

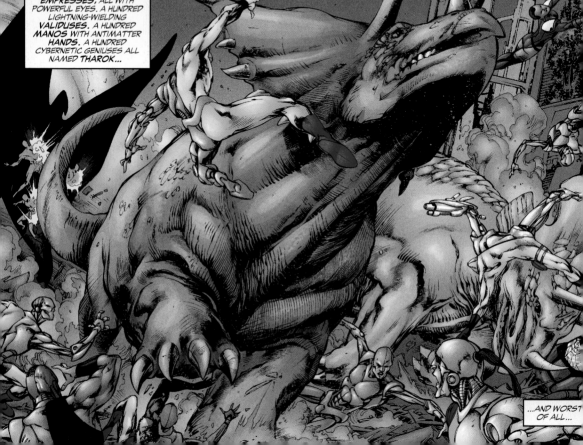

A HUNDRED **EMERALD EMPRESSES**, ALL WITH POWERFUL EYES. A HUNDRED LIGHTNING-WIELDING **VALIDUSES**. A HUNDRED **MANOS** WITH ANTIMATTER HANDS. A HUNDRED CYBERNETIC GENIUSES ALL NAMED **THAROK**...

...AND WORST OF ALL...

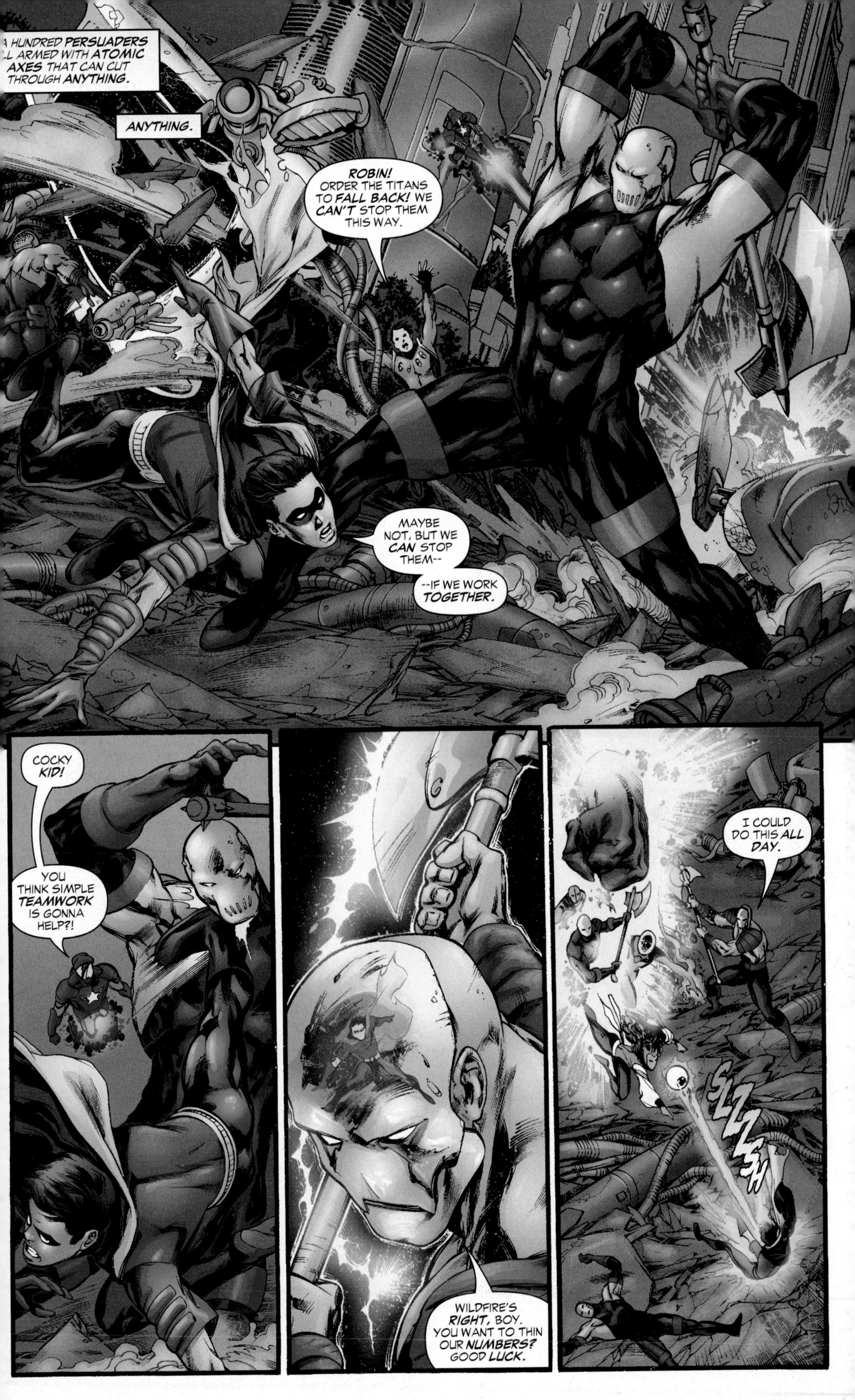
A HUNDRED PERSUADERS ALL ARMED WITH ATOMIC AXES THAT CAN CUT THROUGH ANYTHING.
ANYTHING.
ROBIN! ORDER THE TITANS TO FALL BACK! WE CAN'T STOP THEM THIS WAY.
MAYBE NOT, BUT WE CAN STOP THEM--
--IF WE WORK TOGETHER.
COCKY KID!
YOU THINK SIMPLE TEAMWORK IS GONNA HELP?!
WILDFIRE'S RIGHT, BOY. YOU WANT TO THIN OUR NUMBERS? GOOD LUCK.
I COULD DO THIS ALL DAY.
SLZZZSH

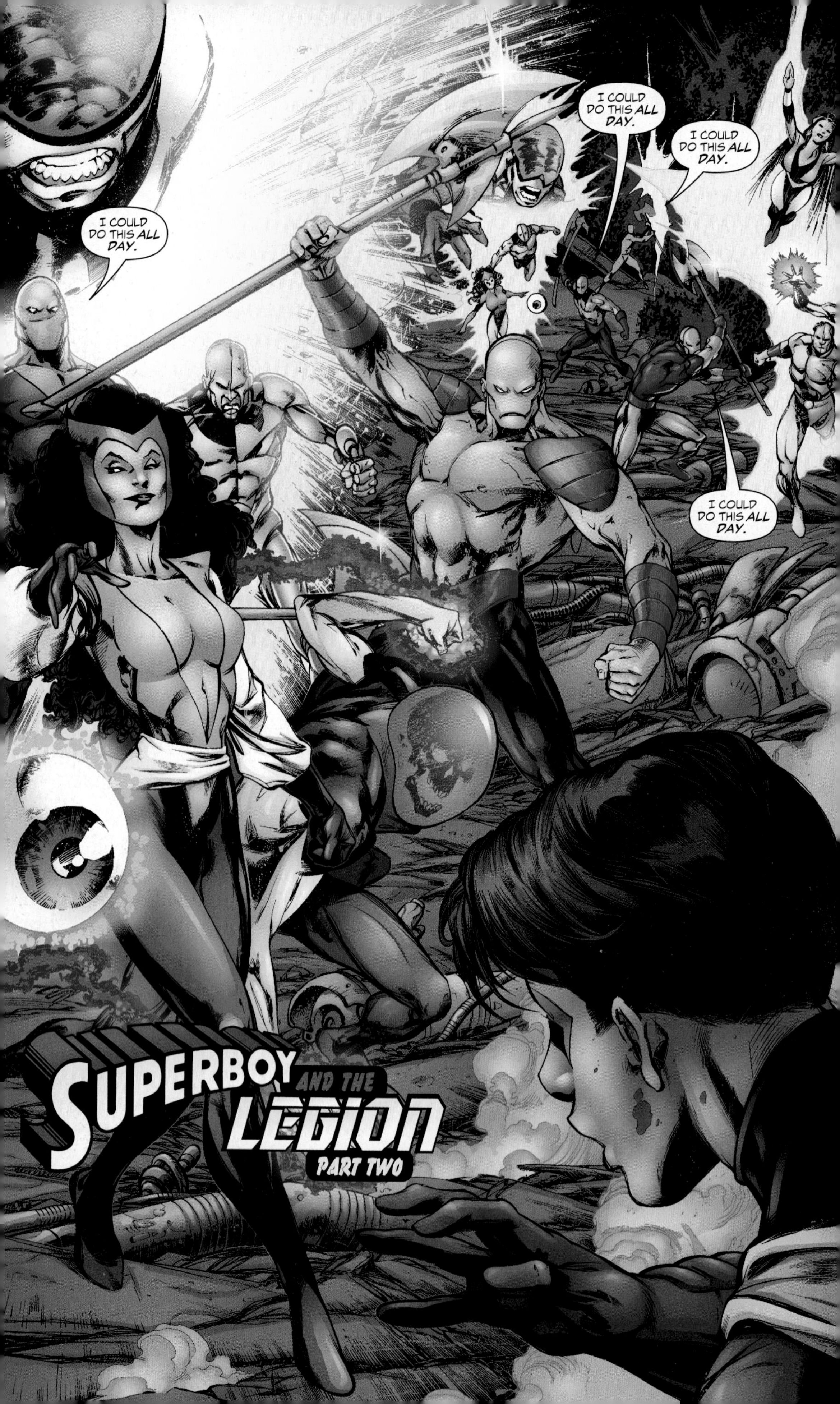

I COULD DO THIS ALL DAY.
I COULD DO THIS ALL DAY.
I COULD DO THIS ALL DAY.
I COULD DO THIS ALL DAY.
SUPERBOY AND THE LEGION
PART TWO

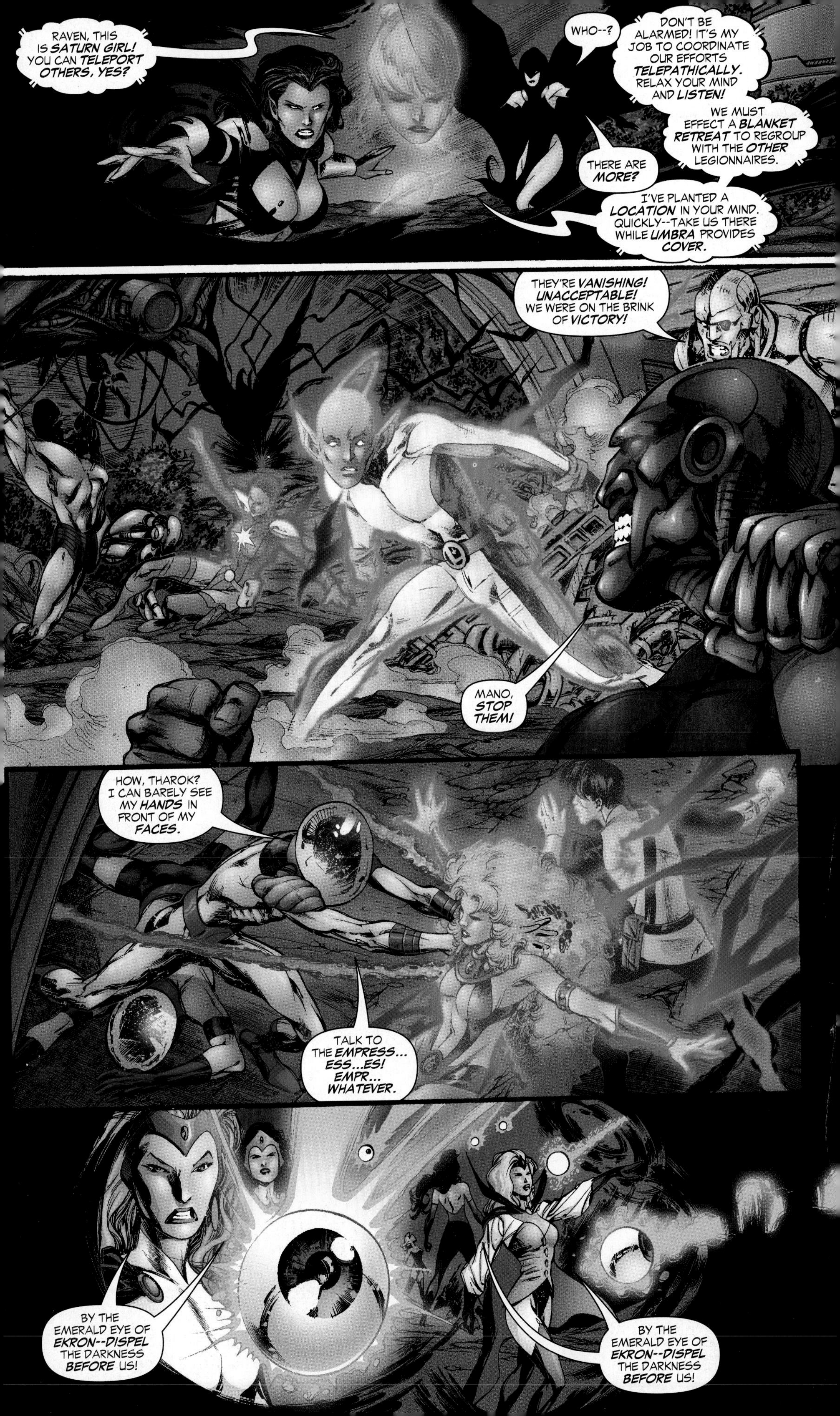
RAVEN, THIS IS SATURN GIRL! YOU CAN TELEPORT OTHERS, YES?
WHO--?
DON'T BE ALARMED! IT'S MY JOB TO COORDINATE OUR EFFORTS TELEPATHICALLY. RELAX YOUR MIND AND LISTEN!
WE MUST EFFECT A BLANKET RETREAT TO REGROUP WITH THE OTHER LEGIONNAIRES.
THERE ARE MORE?
I'VE PLANTED A LOCATION IN YOUR MIND. QUICKLY--TAKE US THERE WHILE UMBRA PROVIDES COVER.
THEY'RE VANISHING! UNACCEPTABLE! WE WERE ON THE BRINK OF VICTORY!
MANO, STOP THEM!
HOW, THAROK? I CAN BARELY SEE MY HANDS IN FRONT OF MY FACES.
TALK TO THE EMPRESS... ESS...ES! EMPR... WHATEVER.
BY THE EMERALD EYE OF EKRON--DISPEL THE DARKNESS BEFORE US!
BY THE EMERALD EYE OF EKRON--DISPEL THE DARKNESS BEFORE US!

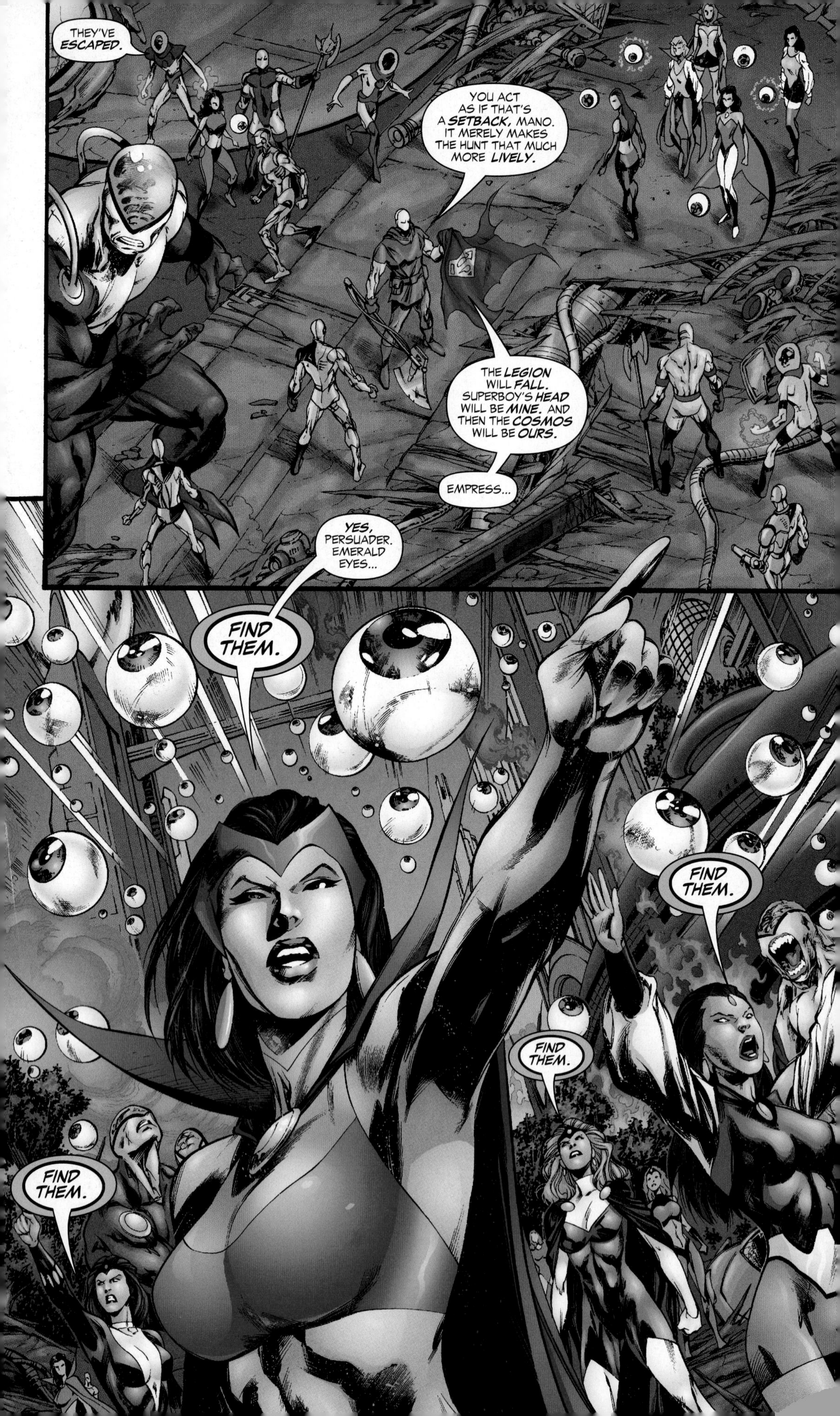
THEY'VE ESCAPED.
YOU ACT AS IF THAT'S A SETBACK, MANO. IT MERELY MAKES THE HUNT THAT MUCH MORE LIVELY.
THE LEGION WILL FALL. SUPERBOY'S HEAD WILL BE MINE. AND THEN THE COSMOS WILL BE OURS.
EMPRESS...
YES, PERSUADER. EMERALD EYES...
FIND THEM.
FIND THEM.
FIND THEM.
FIND THEM.

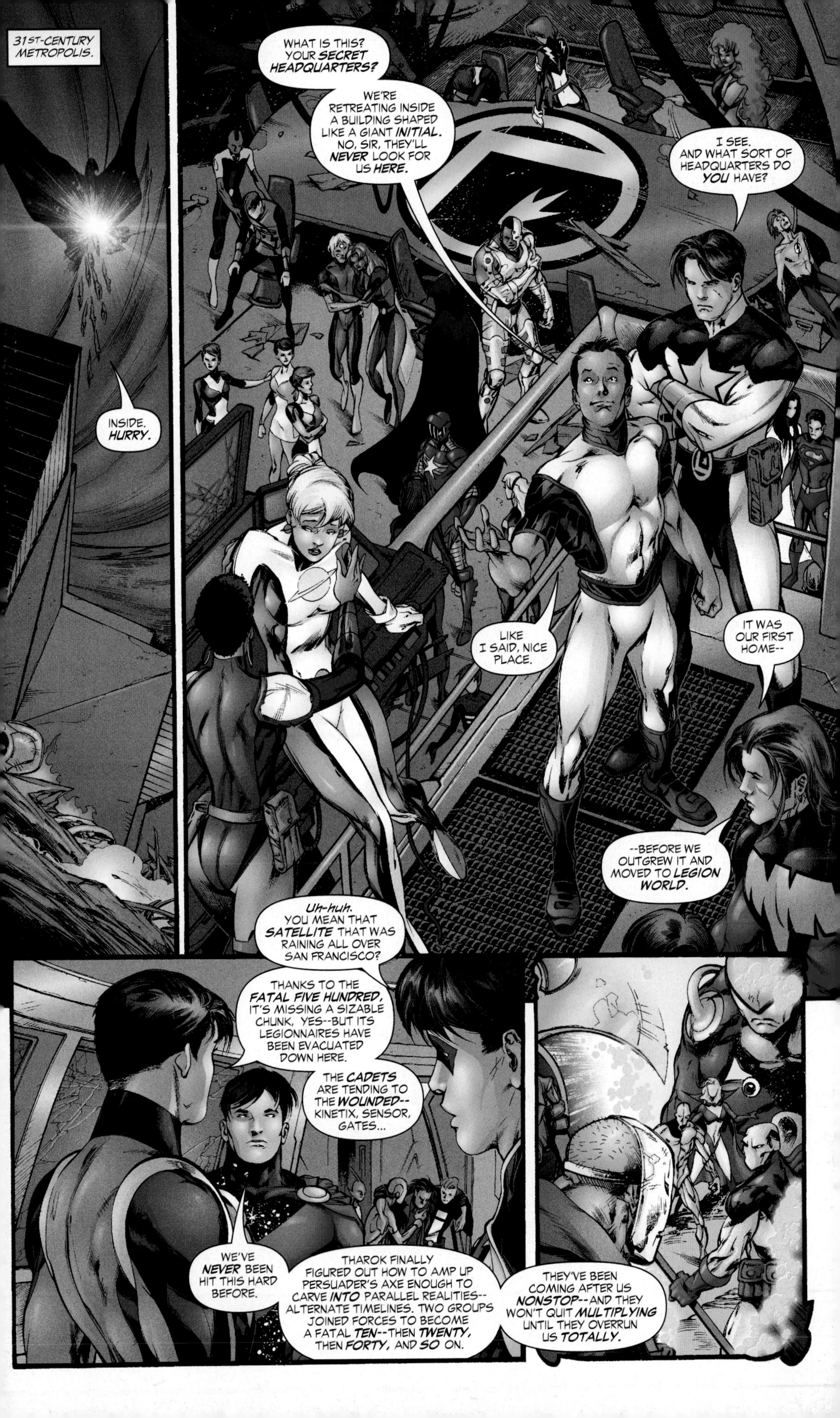
31ST-CENTURY METROPOLIS.
INSIDE. HURRY.
WHAT IS THIS? YOUR SECRET HEADQUARTERS?
WE'RE RETREATING INSIDE A BUILDING SHAPED LIKE A GIANT INITIAL. NO, SIR, THEY'LL NEVER LOOK FOR US HERE.
I SEE. AND WHAT SORT OF HEADQUARTERS DO YOU HAVE?
LIKE I SAID, NICE PLACE.
IT WAS OUR FIRST HOME--
--BEFORE WE OUTGREW IT AND MOVED TO LEGION WORLD.
Uh-huh. YOU MEAN THAT SATELLITE THAT WAS RAINING ALL OVER SAN FRANCISCO?
THANKS TO THE FATAL FIVE HUNDRED, IT'S MISSING A SIZABLE CHUNK, YES--BUT ITS LEGIONNAIRES HAVE BEEN EVACUATED DOWN HERE.
THE CADETS ARE TENDING TO THE WOUNDED-- KINETIX, SENSOR, GATES...
WE'VE NEVER BEEN HIT THIS HARD BEFORE.
THAROK FINALLY FIGURED OUT HOW TO AMP UP PERSUADER'S AXE ENOUGH TO CARVE INTO PARALLEL REALITIES-- ALTERNATE TIMELINES. TWO GROUPS JOINED FORCES TO BECOME A FATAL TEN--THEN TWENTY, THEN FORTY, AND SO ON.
THEY'VE BEEN COMING AFTER US NONSTOP--AND THEY WON'T QUIT MULTIPLYING UNTIL THEY OVERRUN US TOTALLY.

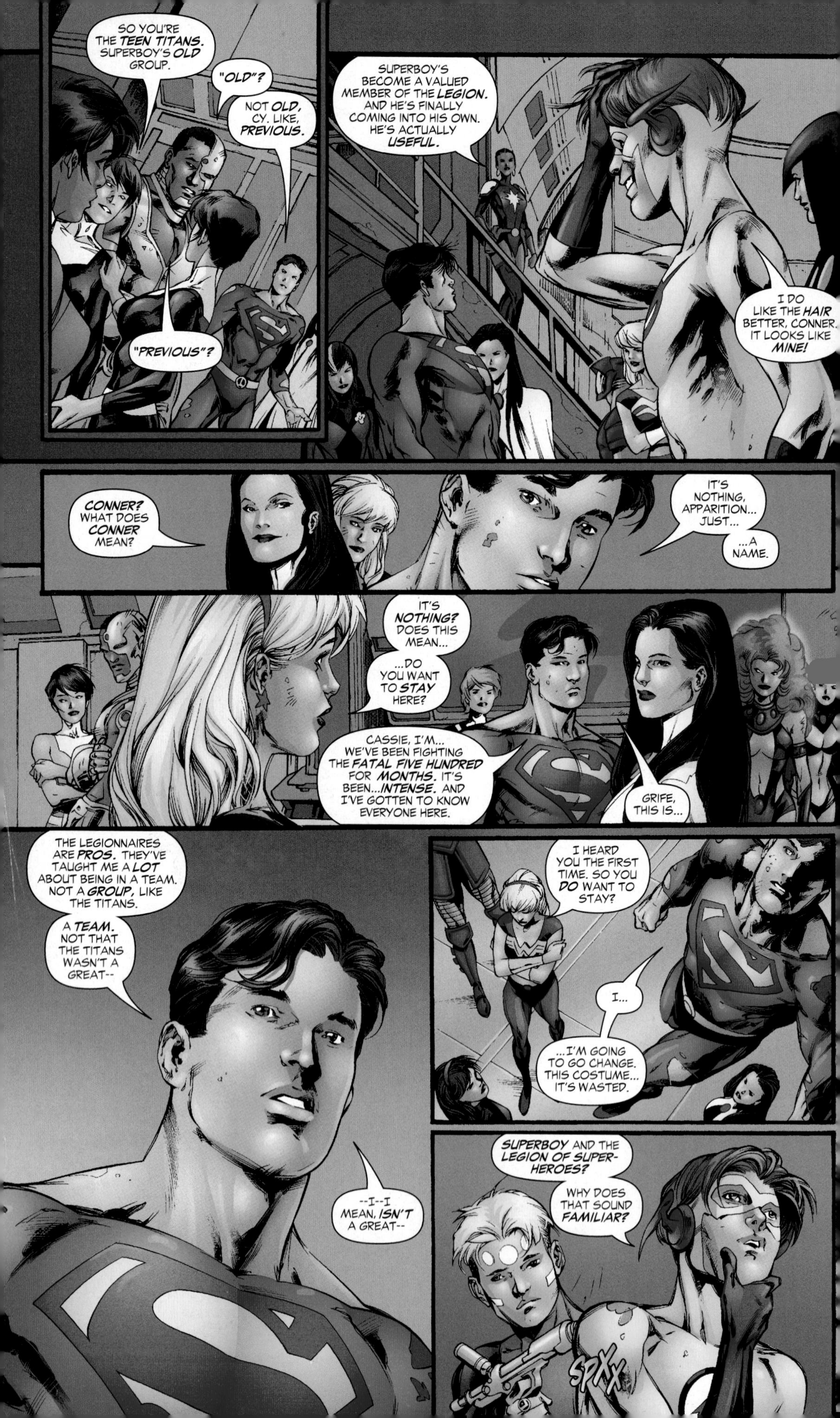
SO YOU'RE THE TEEN TITANS. SUPERBOY'S OLD GROUP.
"OLD"?
NOT OLD, CY. LIKE, PREVIOUS.
"PREVIOUS"?
SUPERBOY'S BECOME A VALUED MEMBER OF THE LEGION. AND HE'S FINALLY COMING INTO HIS OWN. HE'S ACTUALLY USEFUL.
I DO LIKE THE HAIR BETTER, CONNER. IT LOOKS LIKE MINE!
CONNER? WHAT DOES CONNER MEAN?
IT'S NOTHING, APPARITION... JUST...
...A NAME.
IT'S NOTHING? DOES THIS MEAN...
...DO YOU WANT TO STAY HERE?
CASSIE, I'M... WE'VE BEEN FIGHTING THE FATAL FIVE HUNDRED FOR MONTHS. IT'S BEEN...INTENSE. AND I'VE GOTTEN TO KNOW EVERYONE HERE.
GRIFE, THIS IS...
THE LEGIONNAIRES ARE PROS. THEY'VE TAUGHT ME A LOT ABOUT BEING IN A TEAM. NOT A GROUP, LIKE THE TITANS.
A TEAM. NOT THAT THE TITANS WASN'T A GREAT--
--I--I MEAN, ISN'T A GREAT--
I HEARD YOU THE FIRST TIME. SO YOU DO WANT TO STAY?
I...
...I'M GOING TO GO CHANGE. THIS COSTUME... IT'S WASTED.
SUPERBOY AND THE LEGION OF SUPER-HEROES?
WHY DOES THAT SOUND FAMILIAR?
SPXX

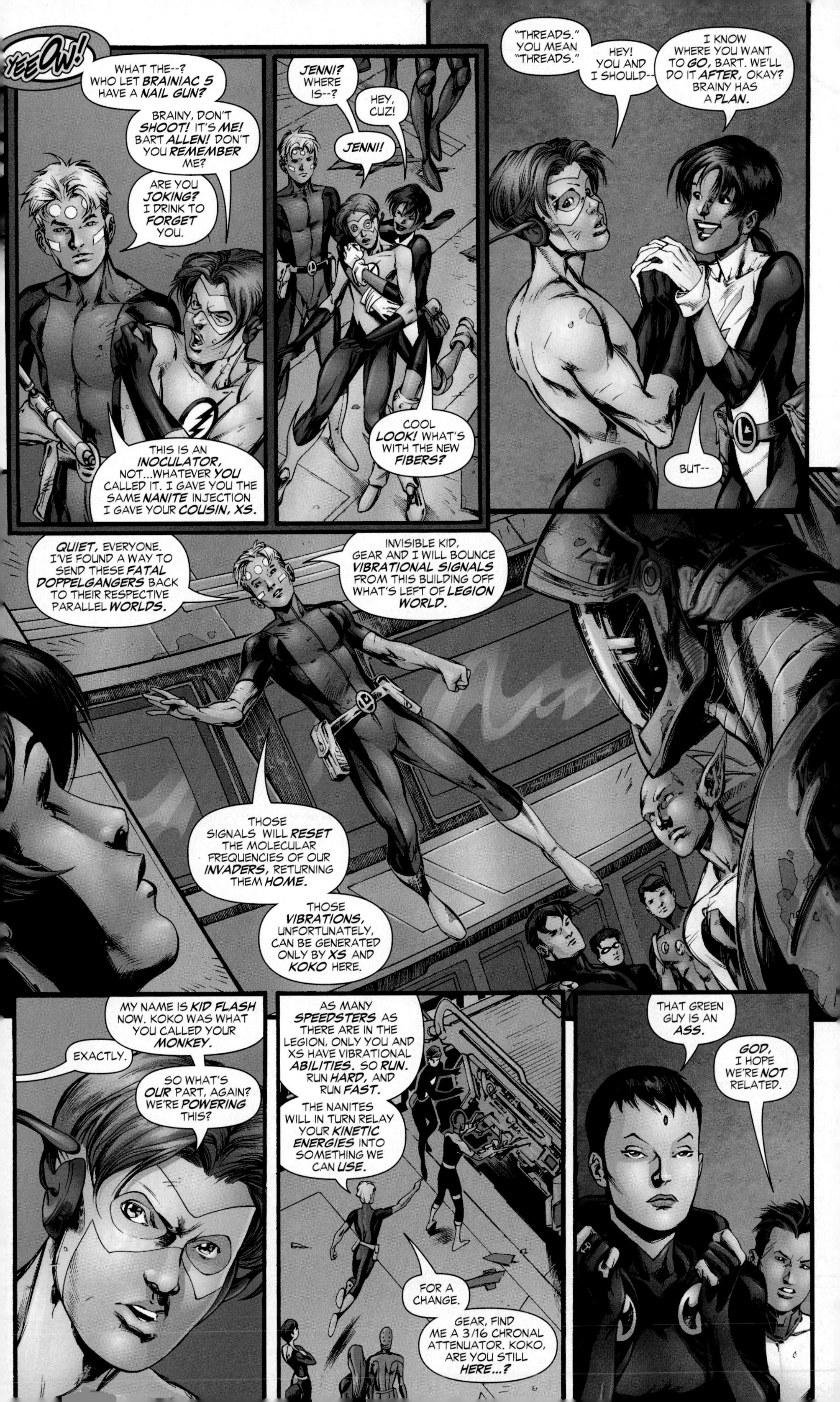

YEEOW!
WHAT THE--? WHO LET BRAINIAC 5 HAVE A NAIL GUN?
BRAINY, DON'T SHOOT! IT'S ME! BART ALLEN! DON'T YOU REMEMBER ME?
ARE YOU JOKING? I DRINK TO FORGET YOU.
THIS IS AN INOCULATOR, NOT...WHATEVER YOU CALLED IT. I GAVE YOU THE SAME NANITE INJECTION I GAVE YOUR COUSIN, XS.
JENNI? WHERE IS--?
HEY, CUZ!
JENNI!
COOL LOOK! WHAT'S WITH THE NEW FIBERS?
"THREADS." YOU MEAN "THREADS."
HEY! YOU AND I SHOULD--
I KNOW WHERE YOU WANT TO GO, BART. WE'LL DO IT AFTER, OKAY? BRAINY HAS A PLAN.
BUT--
QUIET, EVERYONE. I'VE FOUND A WAY TO SEND THESE FATAL DOPPELGANGERS BACK TO THEIR RESPECTIVE PARALLEL WORLDS.
INVISIBLE KID, GEAR AND I WILL BOUNCE VIBRATIONAL SIGNALS FROM THIS BUILDING OFF WHAT'S LEFT OF LEGION WORLD.
THOSE SIGNALS WILL RESET THE MOLECULAR FREQUENCIES OF OUR INVADERS, RETURNING THEM HOME.
THOSE VIBRATIONS, UNFORTUNATELY, CAN BE GENERATED ONLY BY XS AND KOKO HERE.
MY NAME IS KID FLASH NOW. KOKO WAS WHAT YOU CALLED YOUR MONKEY.
EXACTLY.
SO WHAT'S OUR PART, AGAIN? WE'RE POWERING THIS?
AS MANY SPEEDSTERS AS THERE ARE IN THE LEGION, ONLY YOU AND XS HAVE VIBRATIONAL ABILITIES. SO RUN. RUN HARD, AND RUN FAST.
THE NANITES WILL IN TURN RELAY YOUR KINETIC ENERGIES INTO SOMETHING WE CAN USE.
FOR A CHANGE.
GEAR, FIND ME A 3/16 CHRONAL ATTENUATOR. KOKO, ARE YOU STILL HERE...?
THAT GREEN GUY IS AN ASS.
GOD, I HOPE WE'RE NOT RELATED.

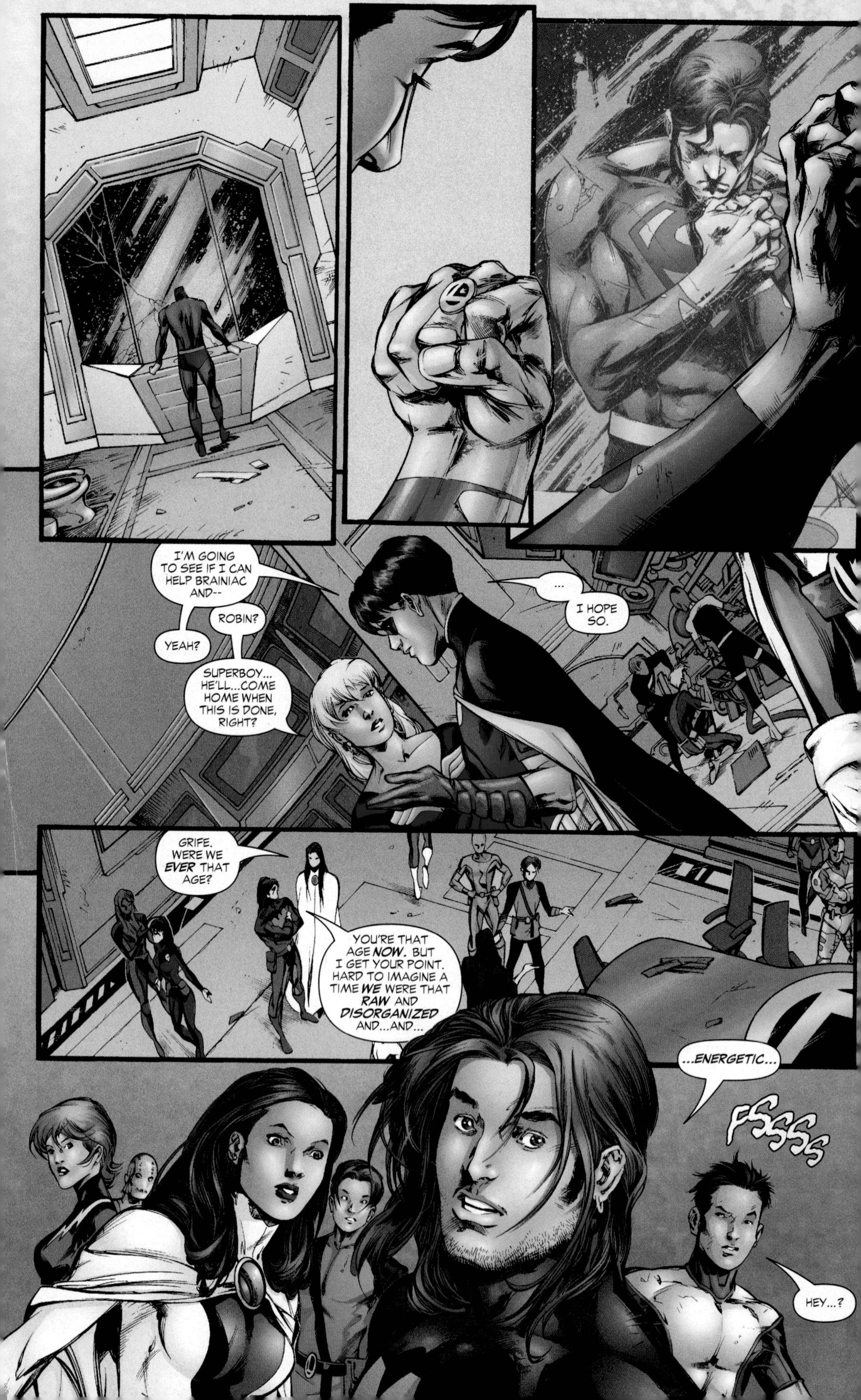

I'M GOING TO SEE IF I CAN HELP BRAINIAC AND--
ROBIN?
YEAH?
SUPERBOY... HE'LL...COME HOME WHEN THIS IS DONE, RIGHT?
...
I HOPE SO.
GRIFE. WERE WE EVER THAT AGE?
YOU'RE THAT AGE NOW. BUT I GET YOUR POINT. HARD TO IMAGINE A TIME WE WERE THAT RAW AND DISORGANIZED AND...AND...
...ENERGETIC...
FSSSS
HEY...?

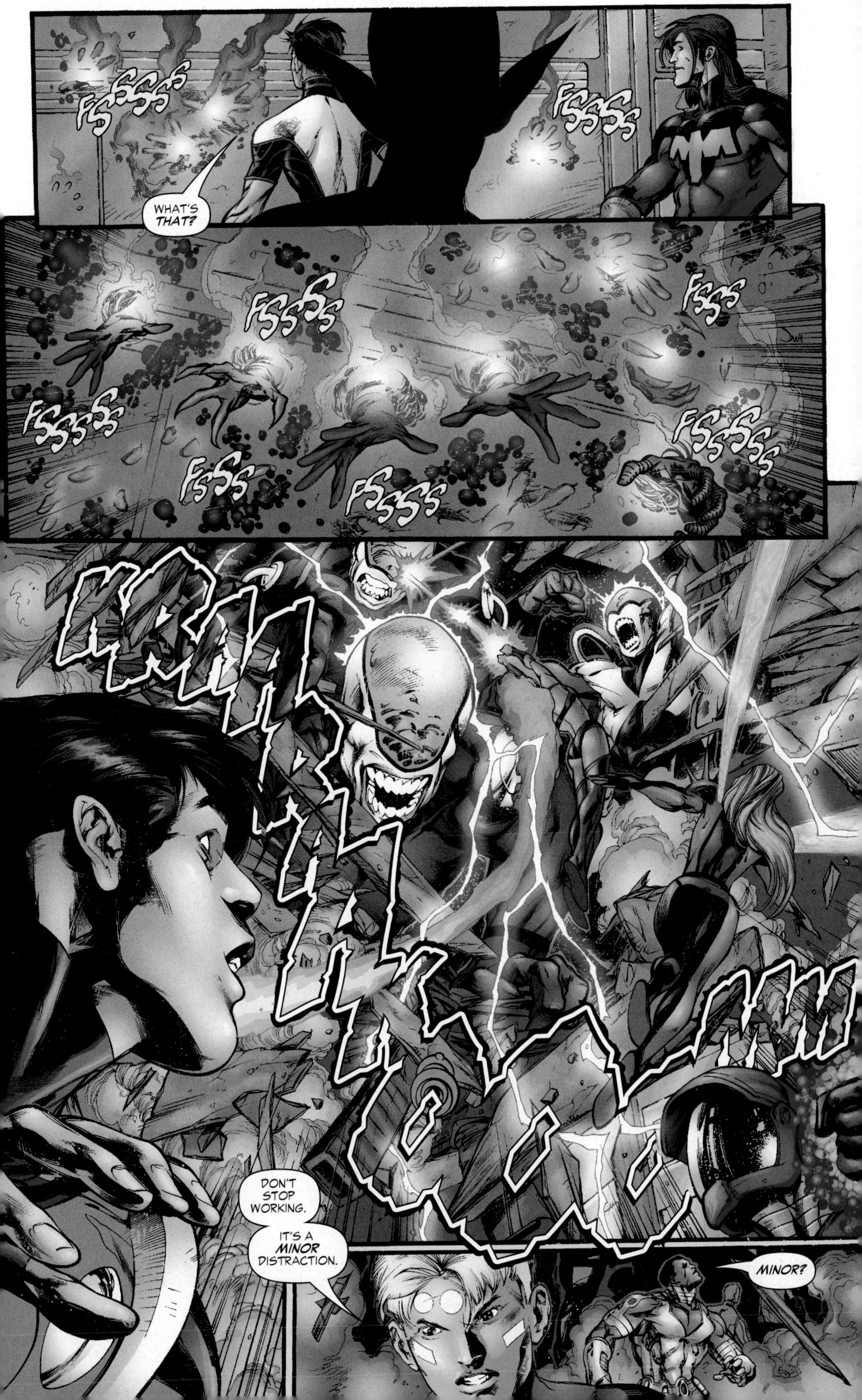
FSSSSSS
FSSSSS
WHAT'S *THAT?*
FSSSSS
FSSS
FSSSSS
FSSS
FSSSS
FSSSSSS
DON'T STOP WORKING.
IT'S A *MINOR* DISTRACTION.
MINOR?

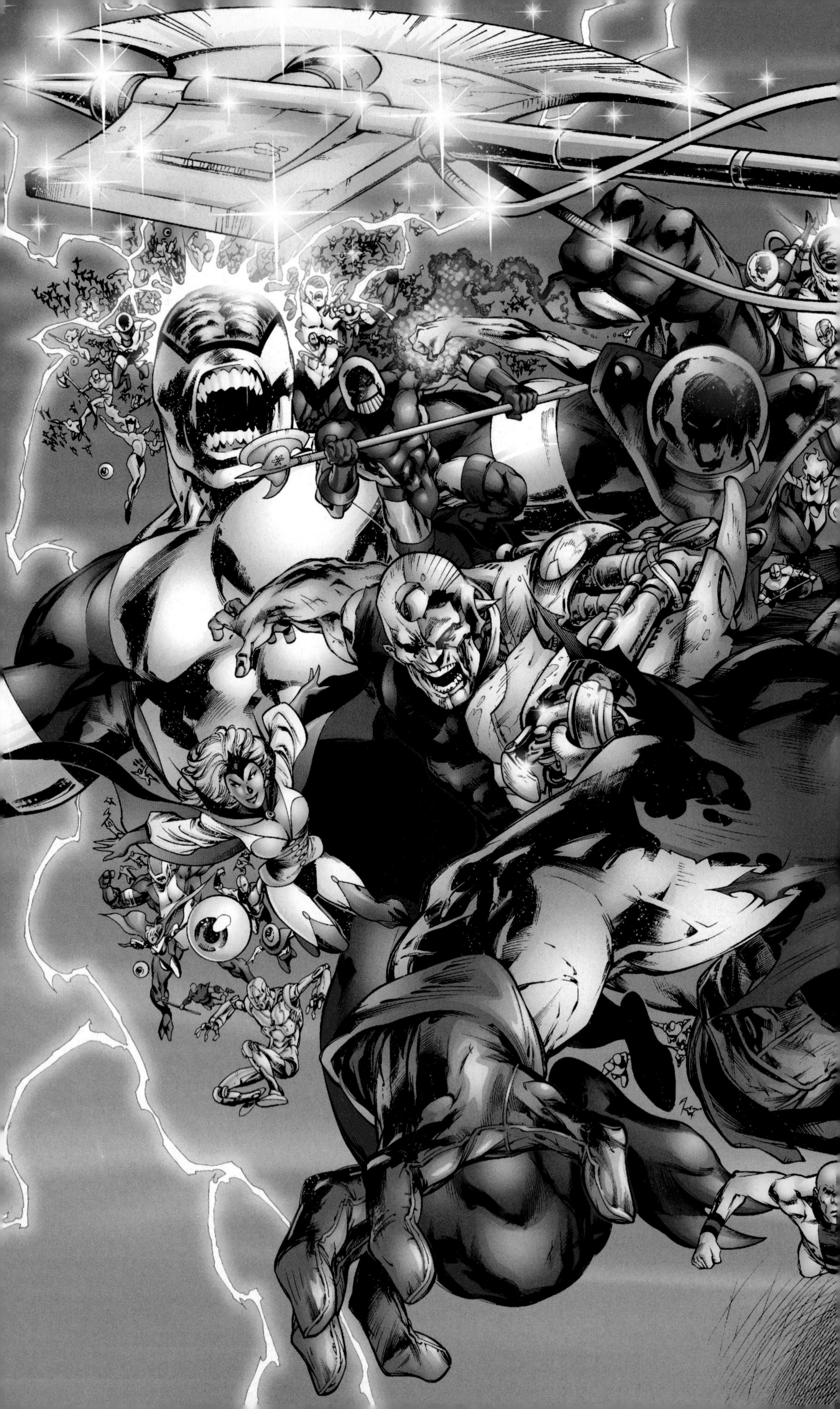

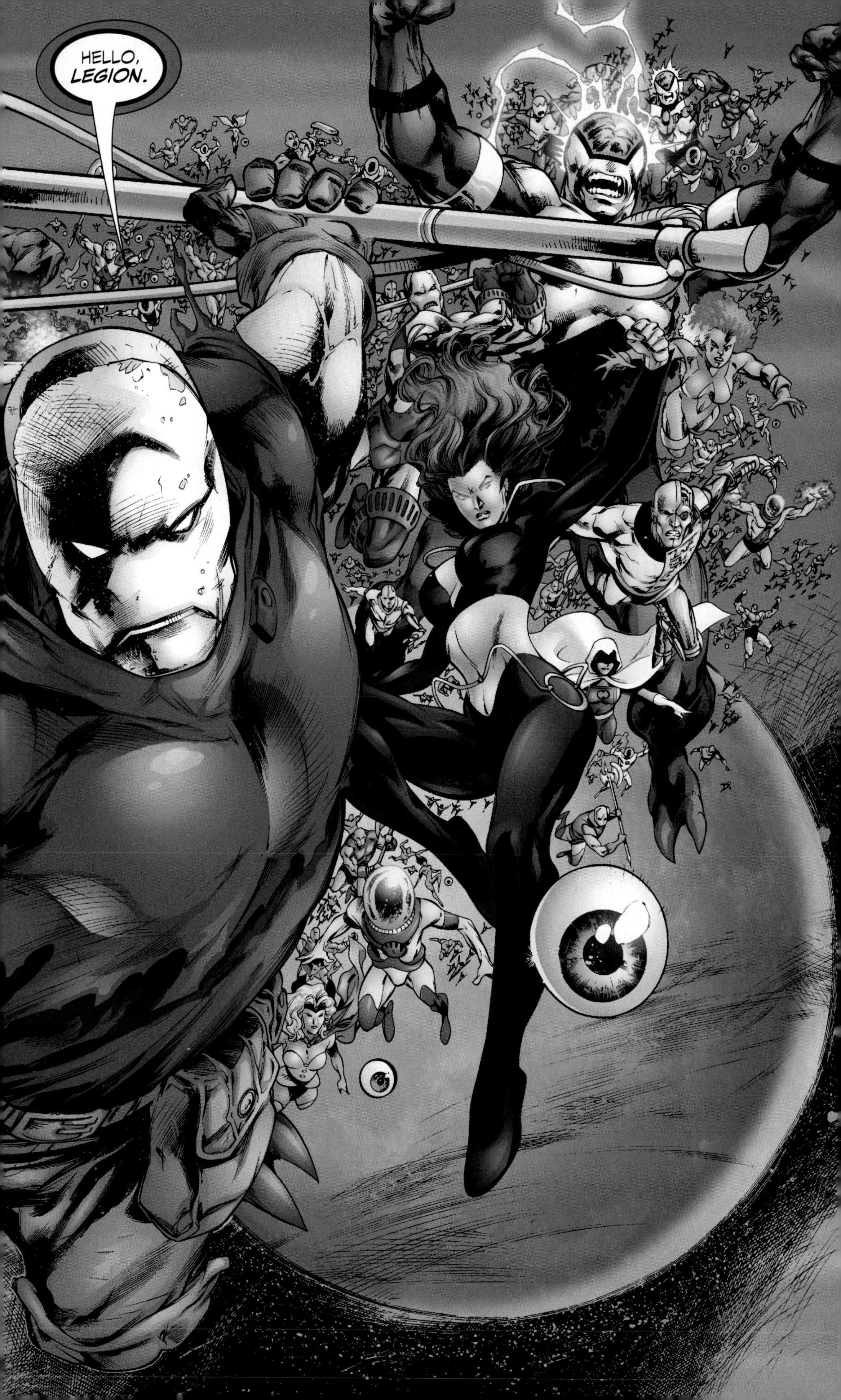
HELLO, LEGION.

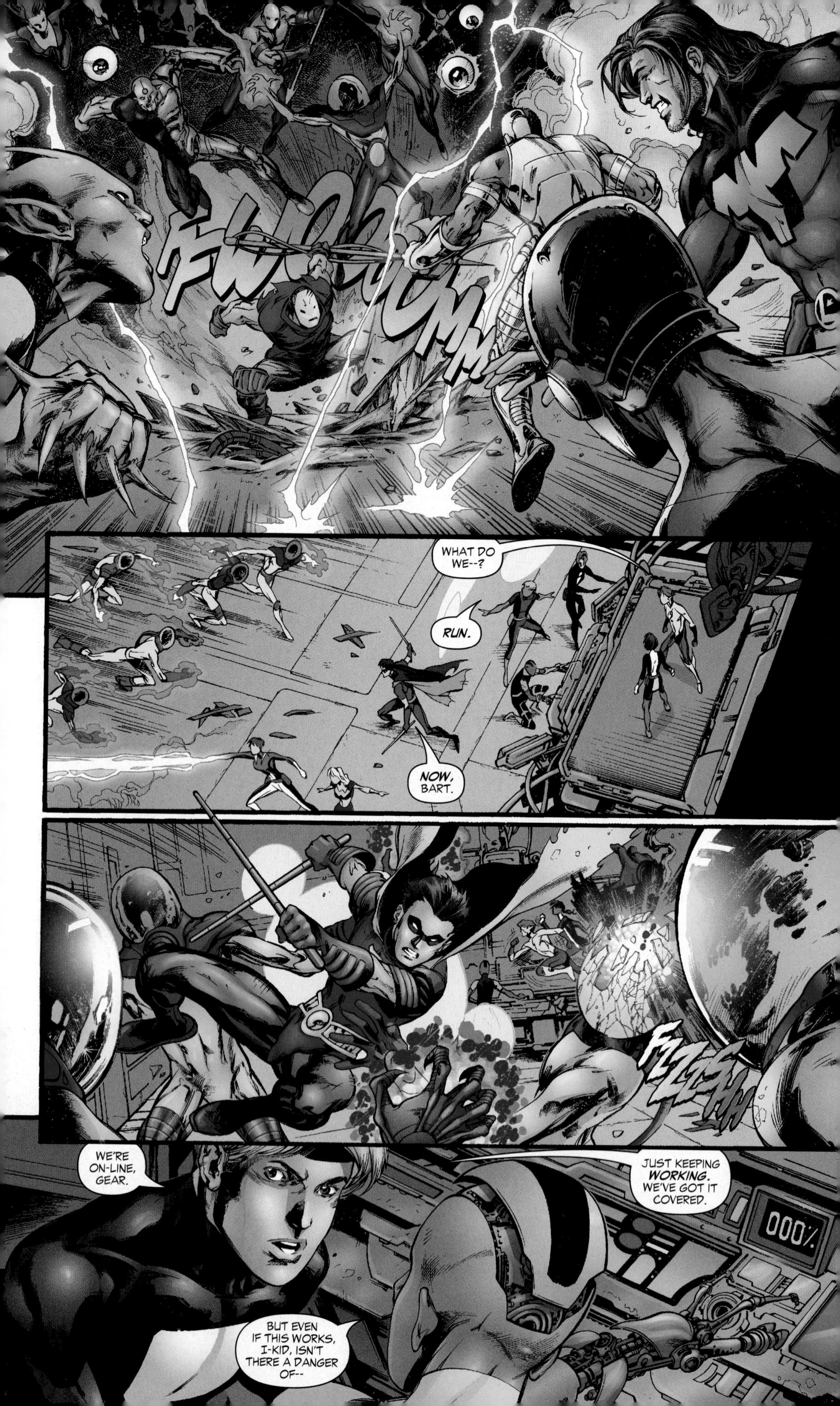
FWOOOOMM
WHAT DO WE--?
RUN.
NOW, BART.
FZZZZHH
WE'RE ON-LINE, GEAR.
JUST KEEPING WORKING. WE'VE GOT IT COVERED.
000%
BUT EVEN IF THIS WORKS, I-KID, ISN'T THERE A DANGER OF--

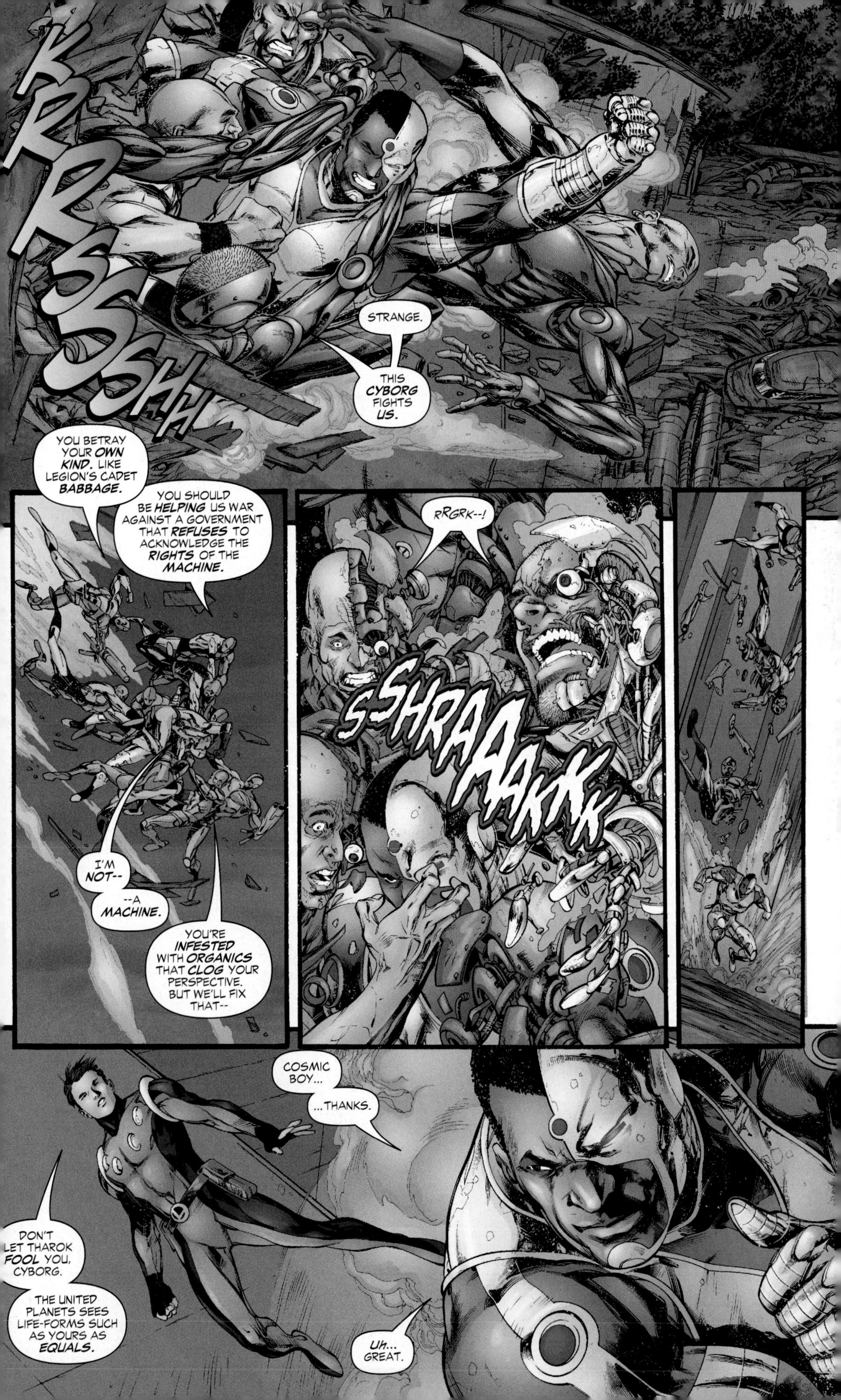

KRRSSSHH
STRANGE.
THIS CYBORG FIGHTS US.
YOU BETRAY YOUR OWN KIND. LIKE LEGION'S CADET BABBAGE.
YOU SHOULD BE HELPING US WAR AGAINST A GOVERNMENT THAT REFUSES TO ACKNOWLEDGE THE RIGHTS OF THE MACHINE.
I'M NOT--
--A MACHINE.
YOU'RE INFESTED WITH ORGANICS THAT CLOG YOUR PERSPECTIVE. BUT WE'LL FIX THAT--
RRGRK--!
S-SHRAAAKKK
COSMIC BOY...
...THANKS.
DON'T LET THAROK FOOL YOU, CYBORG.
THE UNITED PLANETS SEES LIFE-FORMS SUCH AS YOURS AS EQUALS.
Uh... GREAT.

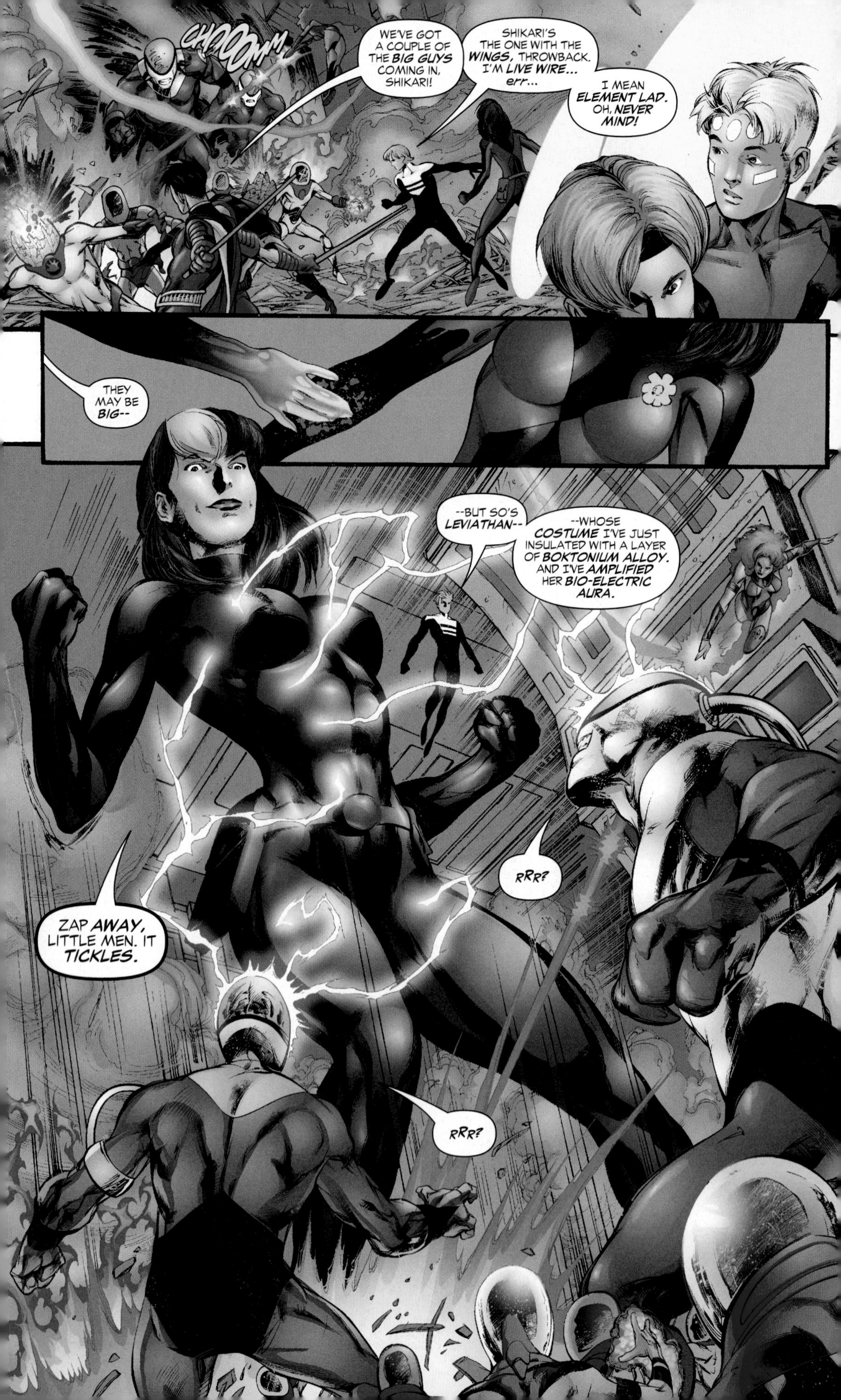
CHOOOMM
WE'VE GOT A COUPLE OF THE BIG GUYS COMING IN, SHIKARI!
SHIKARI'S THE ONE WITH THE WINGS, THROWBACK. I'M LIVE WIRE... err...
I MEAN ELEMENT LAD. OH, NEVER MIND!
THEY MAY BE BIG--
--BUT SO'S LEVIATHAN--
--WHOSE COSTUME I'VE JUST INSULATED WITH A LAYER OF BOKTONIUM ALLOY. AND I'VE AMPLIFIED HER BIO-ELECTRIC AURA.
RRR?
ZAP AWAY, LITTLE MEN. IT TICKLES.
RRR?

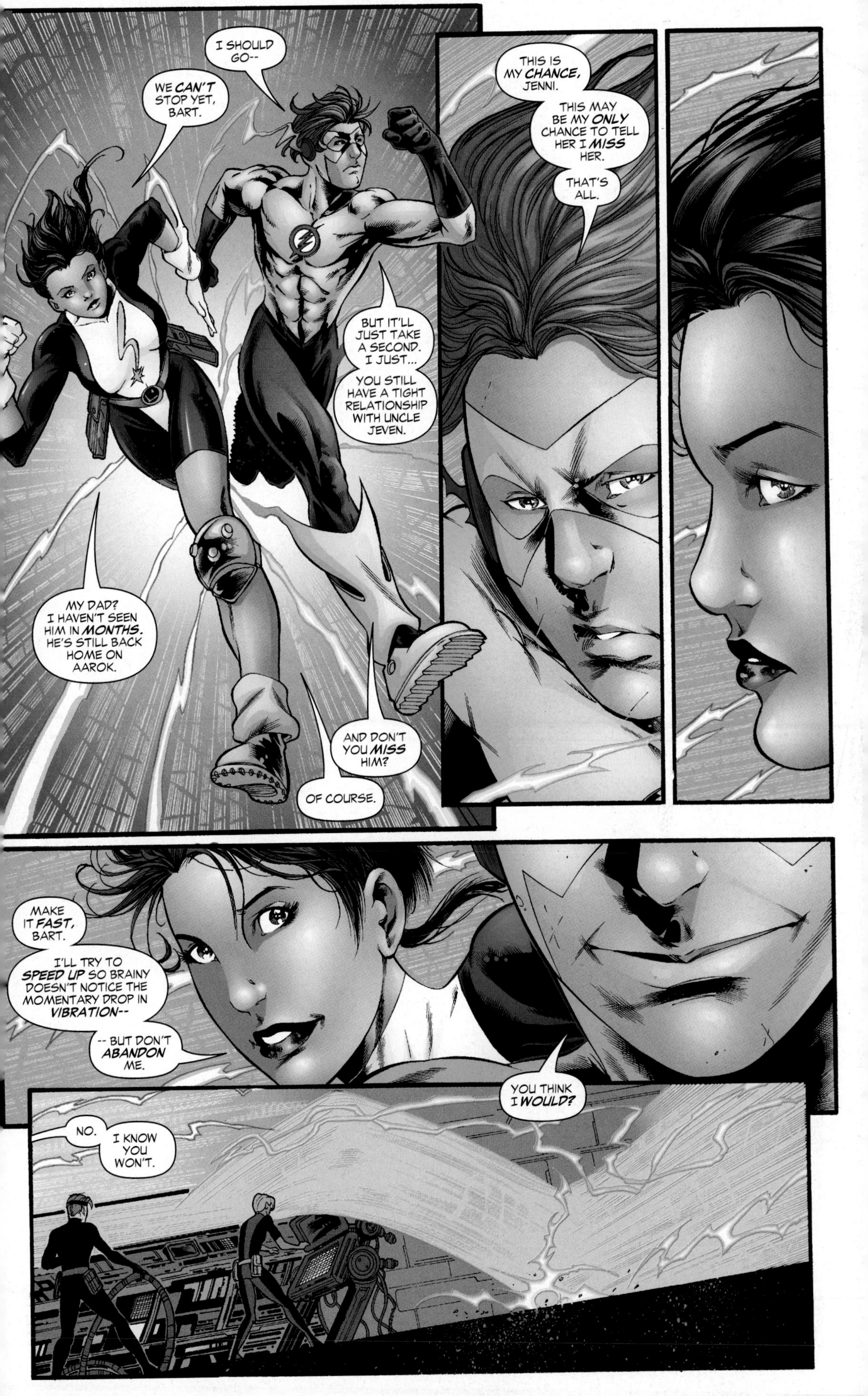
I SHOULD GO--
WE CAN'T STOP YET, BART.
BUT IT'LL JUST TAKE A SECOND. I JUST...
YOU STILL HAVE A TIGHT RELATIONSHIP WITH UNCLE JEVEN.
MY DAD? I HAVEN'T SEEN HIM IN MONTHS. HE'S STILL BACK HOME ON AAROK.
AND DON'T YOU MISS HIM?
OF COURSE.
THIS IS MY CHANCE, JENNI.
THIS MAY BE MY ONLY CHANCE TO TELL HER I MISS HER.
THAT'S ALL.
MAKE IT FAST, BART.
I'LL TRY TO SPEED UP SO BRAINY DOESN'T NOTICE THE MOMENTARY DROP IN VIBRATION--
-- BUT DON'T ABANDON ME.
YOU THINK I WOULD?
NO.
I KNOW YOU WON'T.

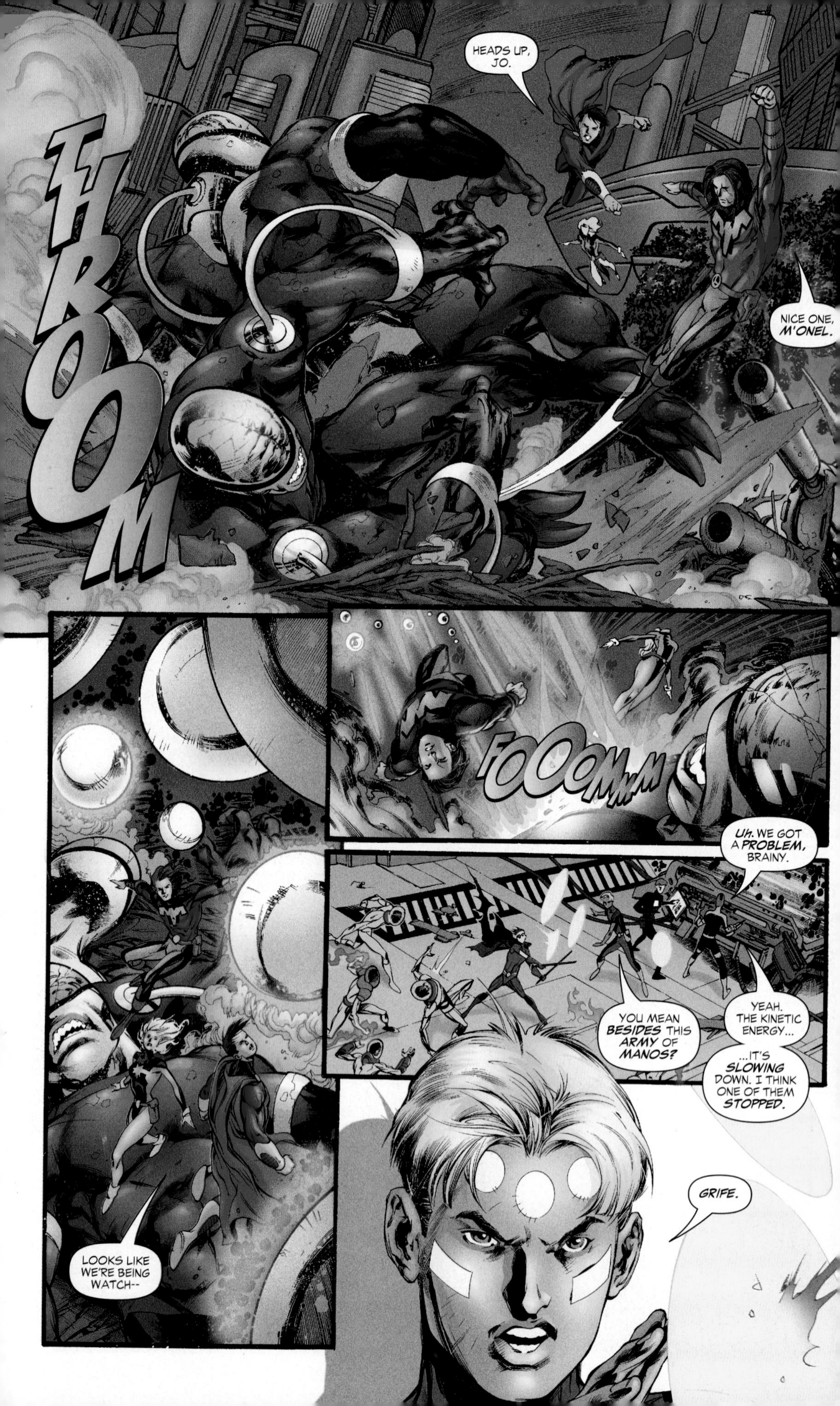
THROOOM
HEADS UP, JO.
NICE ONE, M'ONEL.
FOOOMMM
LOOKS LIKE WE'RE BEING WATCH--
UH. WE GOT A PROBLEM, BRAINY.
YOU MEAN BESIDES THIS ARMY OF MANOS?
YEAH. THE KINETIC ENERGY...
...IT'S SLOWING DOWN. I THINK ONE OF THEM STOPPED.
GRIFE.

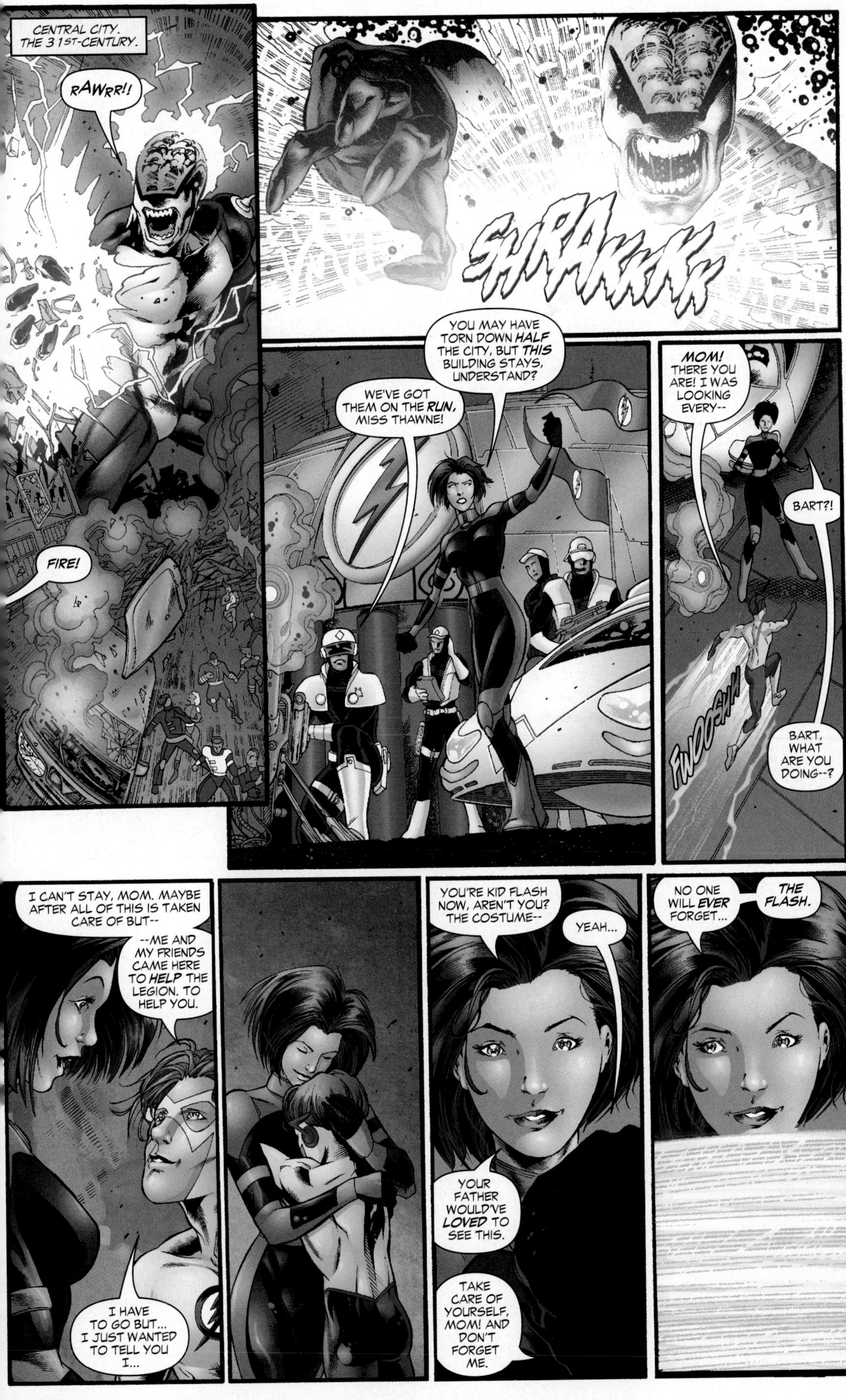
CENTRAL CITY. THE 31ST-CENTURY.
RAWRR!!
FIRE!
SHRAKKKK
YOU MAY HAVE TORN DOWN HALF THE CITY, BUT THIS BUILDING STAYS, UNDERSTAND?
WE'VE GOT THEM ON THE RUN, MISS THAWNE!
MOM! THERE YOU ARE! I WAS LOOKING EVERY--
BART?!
FWOOSHH
BART, WHAT ARE YOU DOING--?
I CAN'T STAY, MOM. MAYBE AFTER ALL OF THIS IS TAKEN CARE OF BUT--
--ME AND MY FRIENDS CAME HERE TO HELP THE LEGION. TO HELP YOU.
I HAVE TO GO BUT... I JUST WANTED TO TELL YOU I...
YOU'RE KID FLASH NOW, AREN'T YOU? THE COSTUME--
YEAH...
YOUR FATHER WOULD'VE LOVED TO SEE THIS.
TAKE CARE OF YOURSELF, MOM! AND DON'T FORGET ME.
NO ONE WILL EVER FORGET...
THE FLASH.

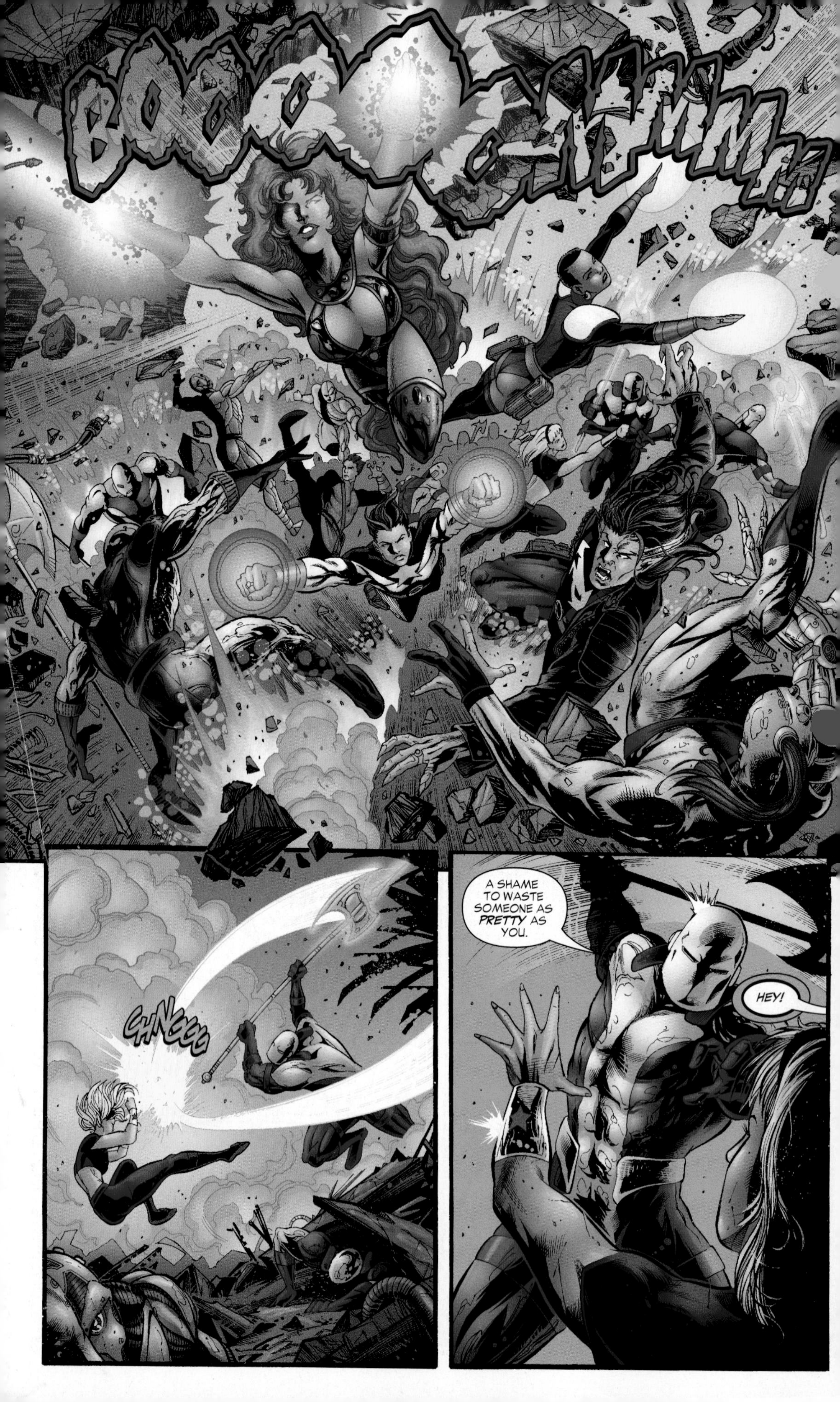
BOOOOM
A SHAME TO WASTE SOMEONE AS PRETTY AS YOU.
HEY!

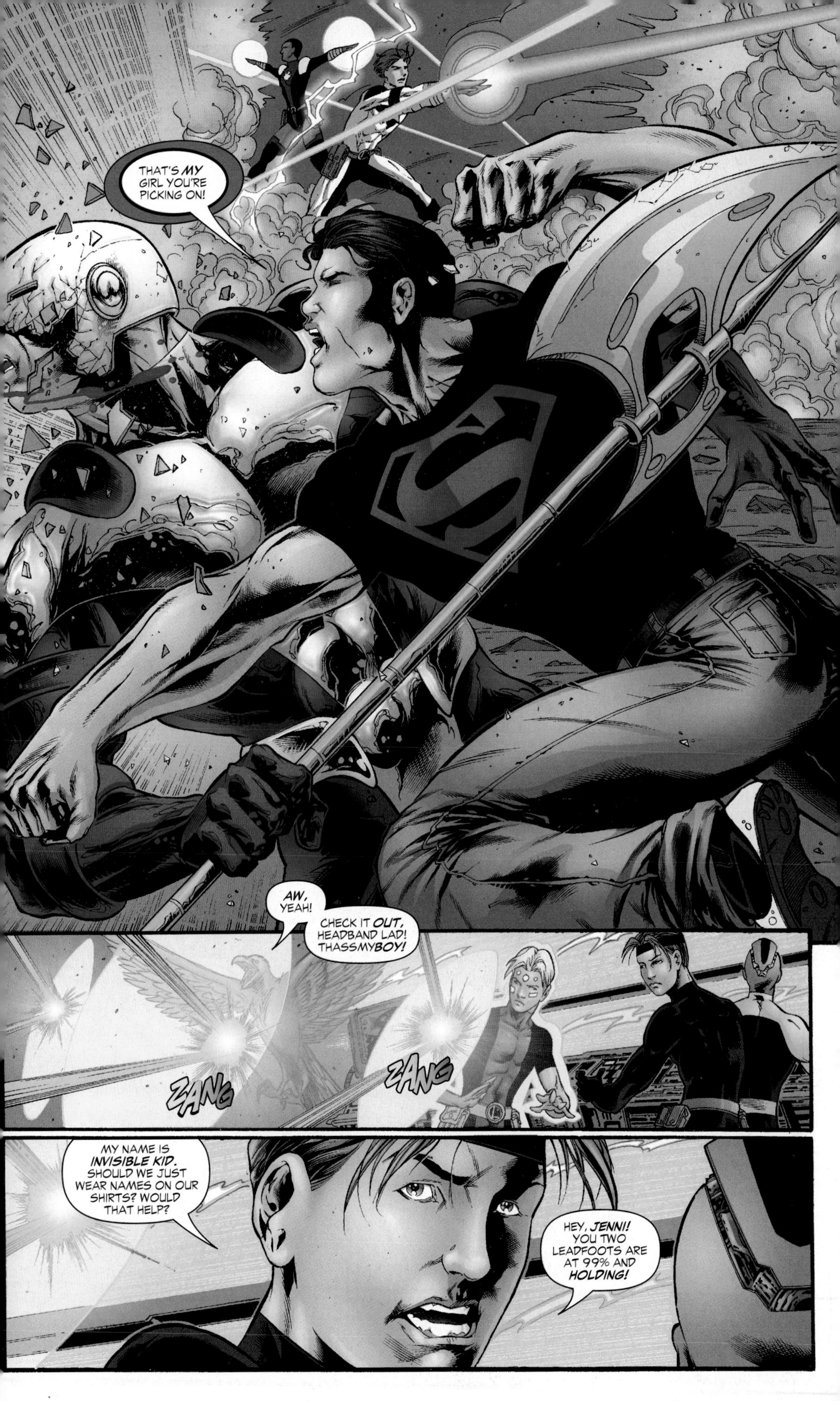
THAT'S MY GIRL YOU'RE PICKING ON!
AW, YEAH!
CHECK IT OUT, HEADBAND LAD! THASSMYBOY!
ZANG
ZANG
MY NAME IS INVISIBLE KID. SHOULD WE JUST WEAR NAMES ON OUR SHIRTS? WOULD THAT HELP?
HEY, JENNI! YOU TWO LEADFOOTS ARE AT 99% AND HOLDING!

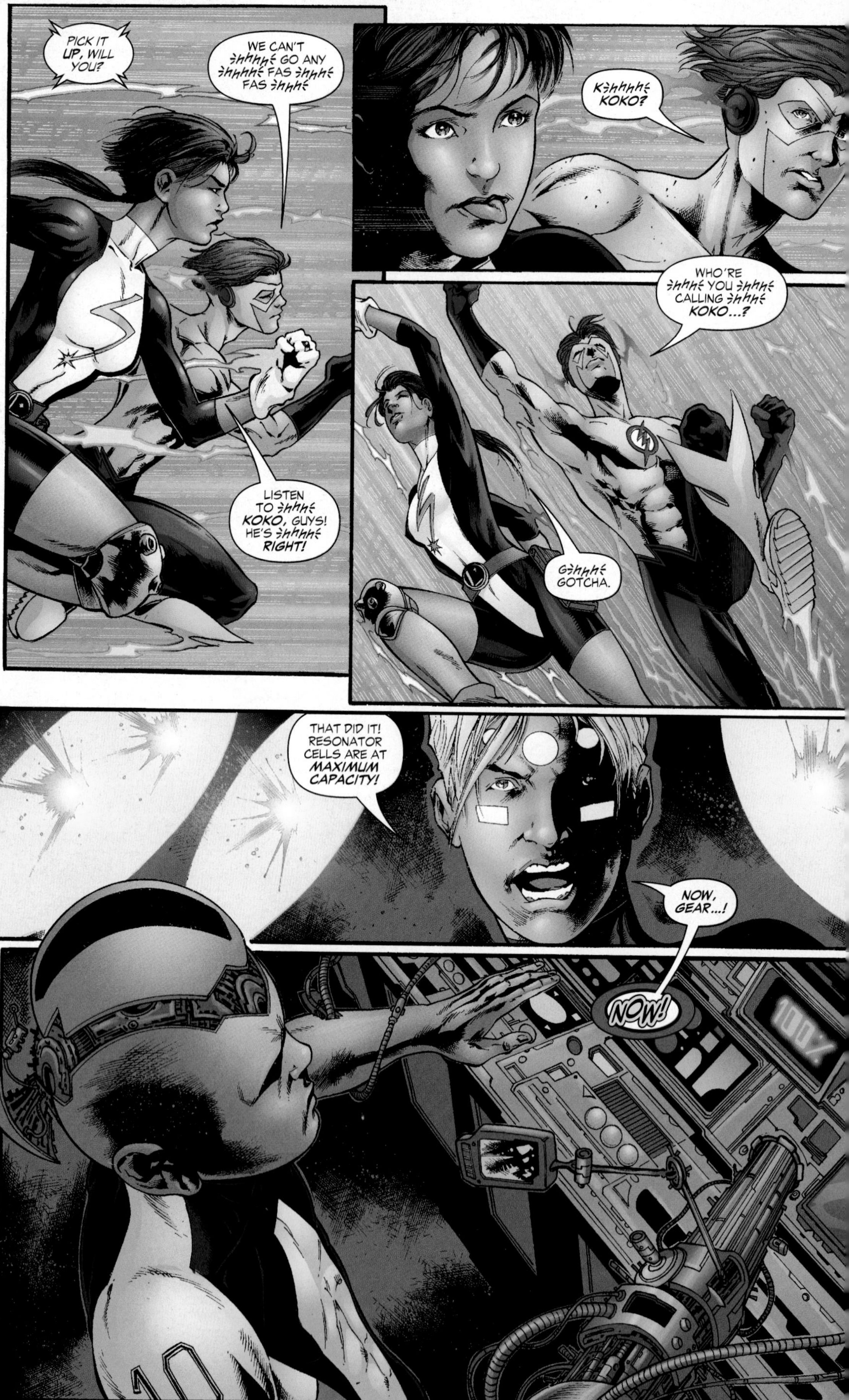
PICK IT UP, WILL YOU?
WE CAN'T ≡hhhh≡ GO ANY ≡hhhh≡ FAS ≡hhh≡ FAS ≡hhh≡
LISTEN TO ≡hhh≡ KOKO, GUYS! HE'S ≡hhhh≡ RIGHT!
K≡hhhh≡ KOKO?
WHO'RE ≡hhh≡ YOU ≡hhh≡ CALLING ≡hhh≡ KOKO...?
G≡hhh≡ GOTCHA.
THAT DID IT! RESONATOR CELLS ARE AT MAXIMUM CAPACITY!
NOW, GEAR...!
NOW!
100%

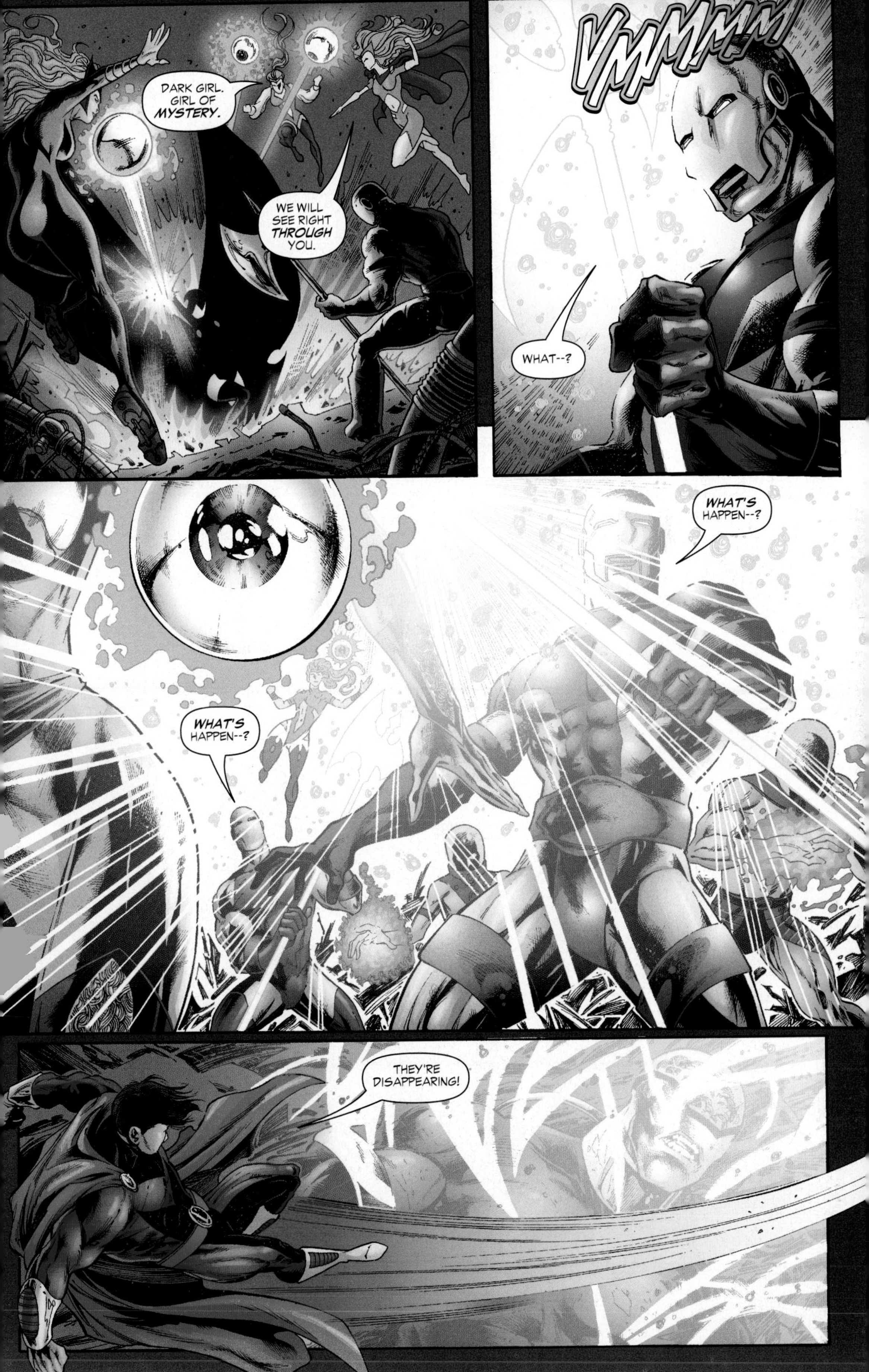
DARK GIRL. GIRL OF MYSTERY.
WE WILL SEE RIGHT THROUGH YOU.
VMMMMM
WHAT--?
WHAT'S HAPPEN--?
WHAT'S HAPPEN--?
THEY'RE DISAPPEARING!

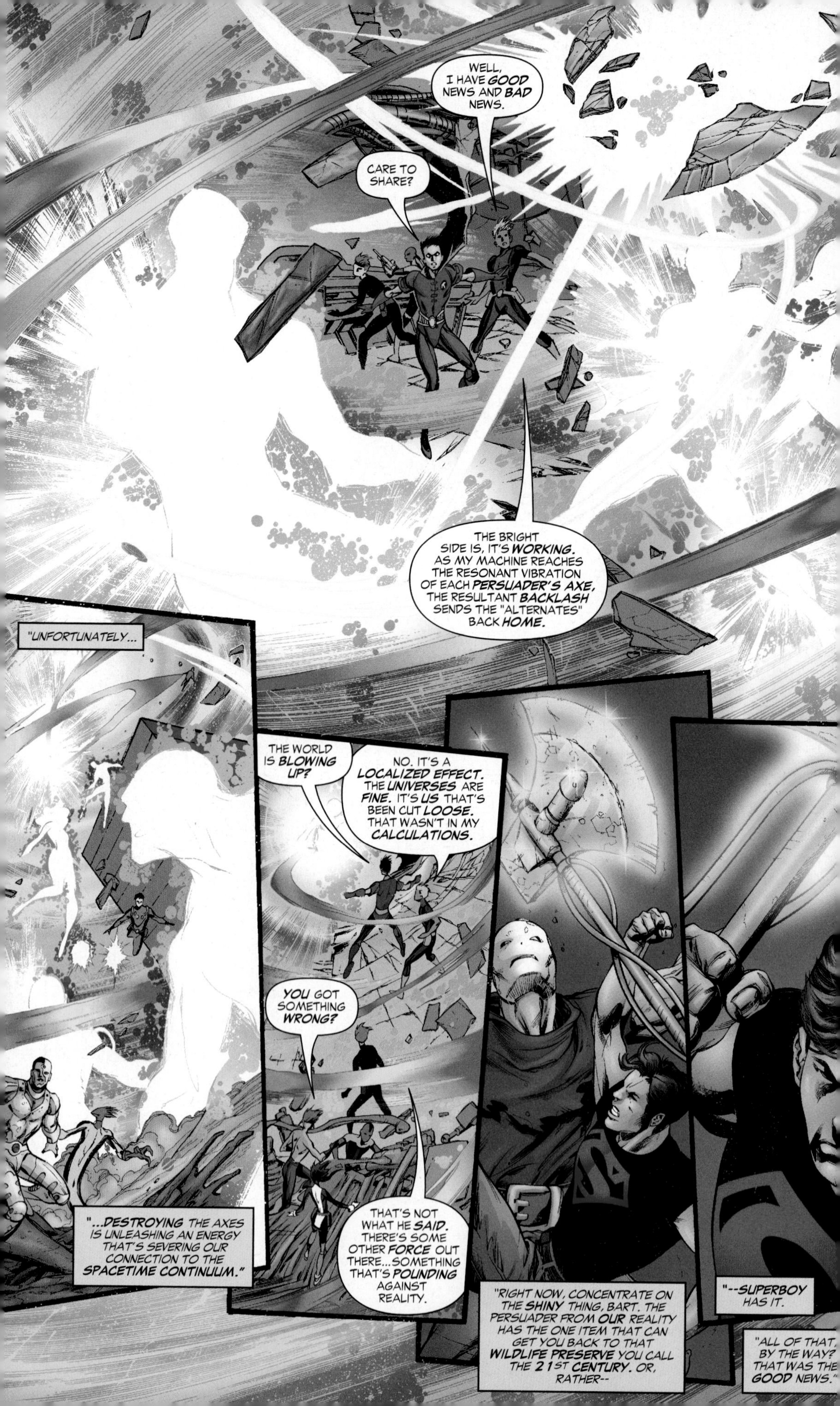

WELL, I HAVE GOOD NEWS AND BAD NEWS.
CARE TO SHARE?
THE BRIGHT SIDE IS, IT'S WORKING. AS MY MACHINE REACHES THE RESONANT VIBRATION OF EACH PERSUADER'S AXE, THE RESULTANT BACKLASH SENDS THE "ALTERNATES" BACK HOME.
"UNFORTUNATELY...
"...DESTROYING THE AXES IS UNLEASHING AN ENERGY THAT'S SEVERING OUR CONNECTION TO THE SPACETIME CONTINUUM."
THE WORLD IS BLOWING UP?
NO. IT'S A LOCALIZED EFFECT. THE UNIVERSES ARE FINE. IT'S US THAT'S BEEN CUT LOOSE. THAT WASN'T IN MY CALCULATIONS.
YOU GOT SOMETHING WRONG?
THAT'S NOT WHAT HE SAID. THERE'S SOME OTHER FORCE OUT THERE...SOMETHING THAT'S POUNDING AGAINST REALITY.
"RIGHT NOW, CONCENTRATE ON THE SHINY THING, BART. THE PERSUADER FROM OUR REALITY HAS THE ONE ITEM THAT CAN GET YOU BACK TO THAT WILDLIFE PRESERVE YOU CALL THE 21ST CENTURY. OR, RATHER--
"--SUPERBOY HAS IT.
"ALL OF THAT, BY THE WAY? THAT WAS THE GOOD NEWS."

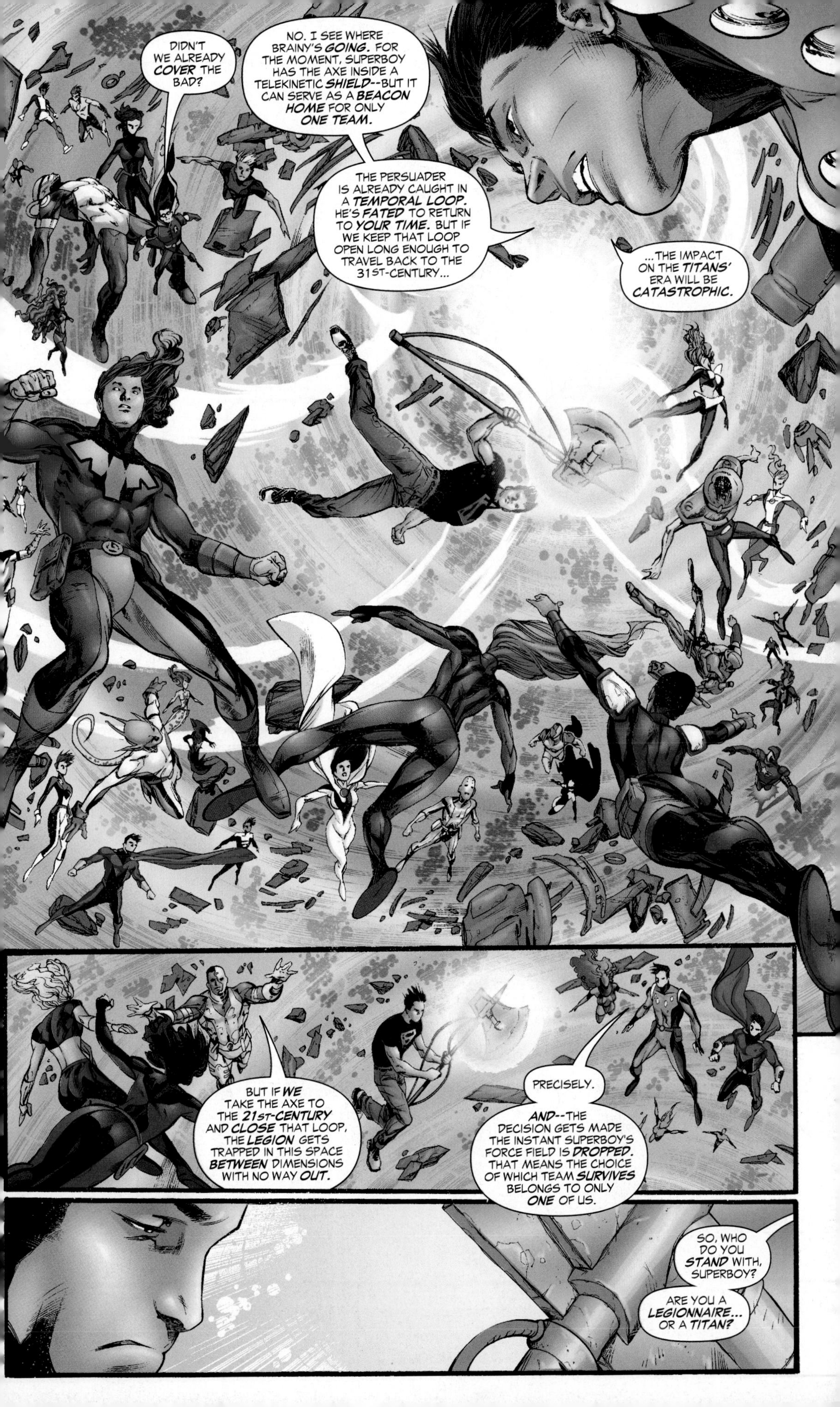

DIDN'T WE ALREADY COVER THE BAD?
NO. I SEE WHERE BRAINY'S GOING. FOR THE MOMENT, SUPERBOY HAS THE AXE INSIDE A TELEKINETIC SHIELD--BUT IT CAN SERVE AS A BEACON HOME FOR ONLY ONE TEAM.
THE PERSUADER IS ALREADY CAUGHT IN A TEMPORAL LOOP. HE'S FATED TO RETURN TO YOUR TIME. BUT IF WE KEEP THAT LOOP OPEN LONG ENOUGH TO TRAVEL BACK TO THE 31ST-CENTURY...
...THE IMPACT ON THE TITANS' ERA WILL BE CATASTROPHIC.
BUT IF WE TAKE THE AXE TO THE 21ST-CENTURY AND CLOSE THAT LOOP, THE LEGION GETS TRAPPED IN THIS SPACE BETWEEN DIMENSIONS WITH NO WAY OUT.
PRECISELY.
AND--THE DECISION GETS MADE THE INSTANT SUPERBOY'S FORCE FIELD IS DROPPED. THAT MEANS THE CHOICE OF WHICH TEAM SURVIVES BELONGS TO ONLY ONE OF US.
SO, WHO DO YOU STAND WITH, SUPERBOY?
ARE YOU A LEGIONNAIRE... OR A TITAN?

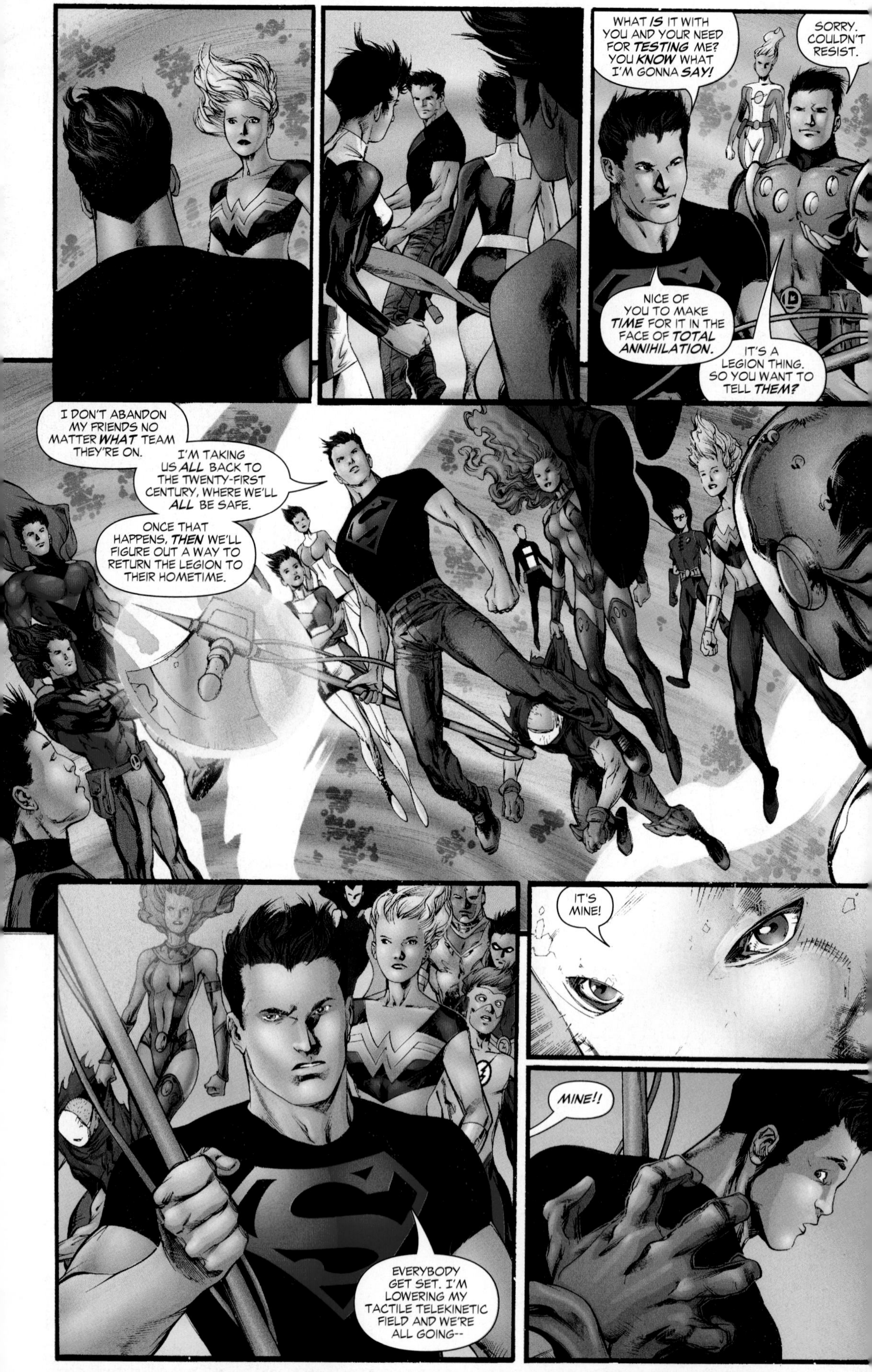
WHAT IS IT WITH YOU AND YOUR NEED FOR TESTING ME? YOU KNOW WHAT I'M GONNA SAY!
SORRY. COULDN'T RESIST.
NICE OF YOU TO MAKE TIME FOR IT IN THE FACE OF TOTAL ANNIHILATION.
IT'S A LEGION THING. SO YOU WANT TO TELL THEM?
I DON'T ABANDON MY FRIENDS NO MATTER WHAT TEAM THEY'RE ON.
I'M TAKING US ALL BACK TO THE TWENTY-FIRST CENTURY, WHERE WE'LL ALL BE SAFE.
ONCE THAT HAPPENS, THEN WE'LL FIGURE OUT A WAY TO RETURN THE LEGION TO THEIR HOMETIME.
EVERYBODY GET SET. I'M LOWERING MY TACTILE TELEKINETIC FIELD AND WE'RE ALL GOING--
IT'S MINE!
MINE!!

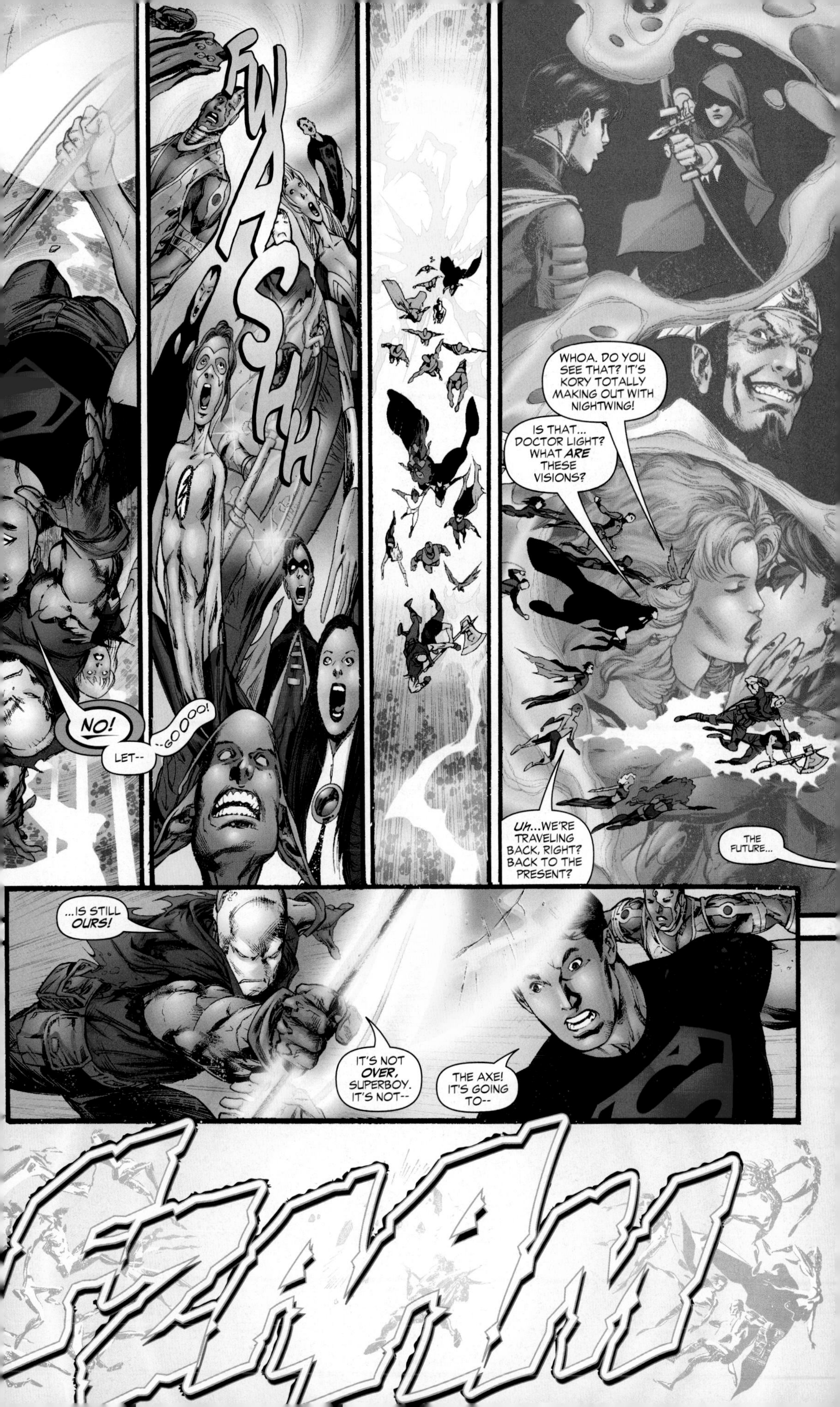
FWASHH
NO!
LET--
--GOOOO!
WHOA. DO YOU SEE THAT? IT'S KORY TOTALLY MAKING OUT WITH NIGHTWING!
IS THAT... DOCTOR LIGHT? WHAT ARE THESE VISIONS?
UH...WE'RE TRAVELING BACK, RIGHT? BACK TO THE PRESENT?
THE FUTURE...
...IS STILL OURS!
IT'S NOT OVER, SUPERBOY. IT'S NOT--
THE AXE! IT'S GOING TO--

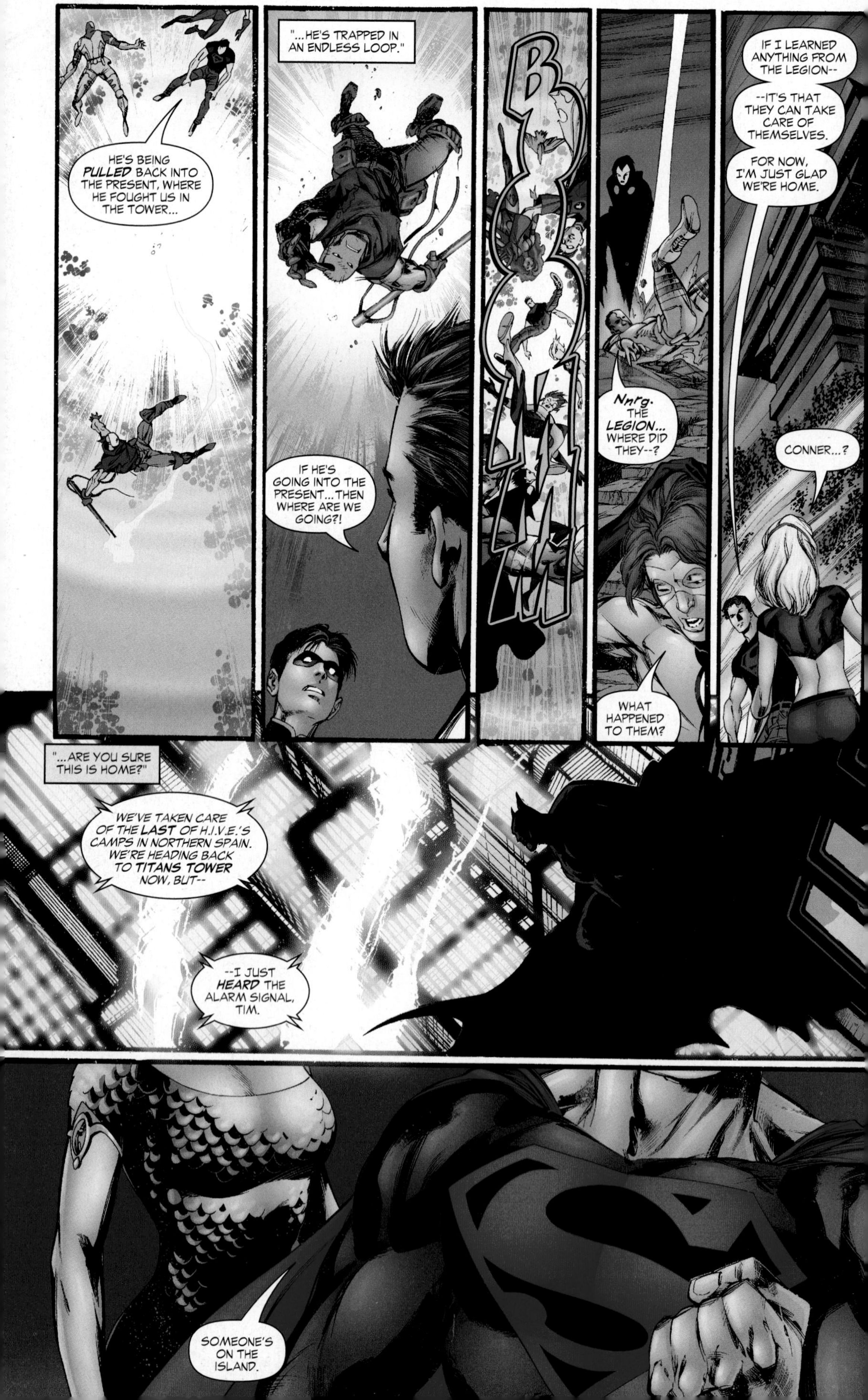

HE'S BEING PULLED BACK INTO THE PRESENT, WHERE HE FOUGHT US IN THE TOWER...
"...HE'S TRAPPED IN AN ENDLESS LOOP."
IF HE'S GOING INTO THE PRESENT...THEN WHERE ARE WE GOING?!
BOOM
Nnrg. THE LEGION... WHERE DID THEY--?
WHAT HAPPENED TO THEM?
IF I LEARNED ANYTHING FROM THE LEGION--
--IT'S THAT THEY CAN TAKE CARE OF THEMSELVES.
FOR NOW, I'M JUST GLAD WE'RE HOME.
CONNER...?
"...ARE YOU SURE THIS IS HOME?"
WE'VE TAKEN CARE OF THE LAST OF H.I.V.E.'S CAMPS IN NORTHERN SPAIN. WE'RE HEADING BACK TO TITANS TOWER NOW, BUT--
--I JUST HEARD THE ALARM SIGNAL, TIM.
SOMEONE'S ON THE ISLAND.

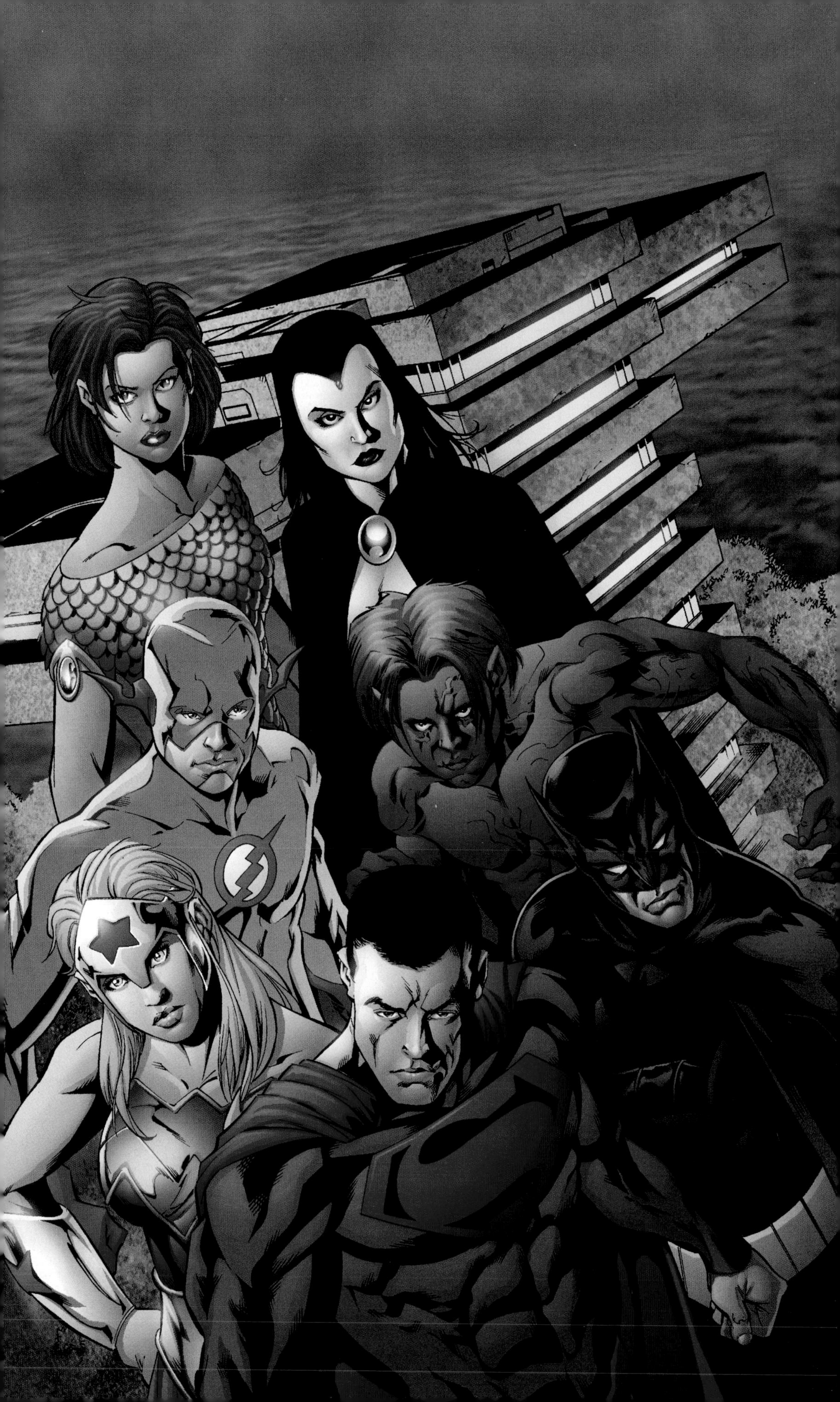

TEEN TITANS #17

GEOFF JOHNS
Writer

MIKE McKONE
Penciller

MARLO ALQUIZA
Inker

JEROMY COX
Colorist

COMICRAFT
Letterer

**MIKE McKONE, MARLO ALQUIZA
& JEROMY COX**
Cover Artists

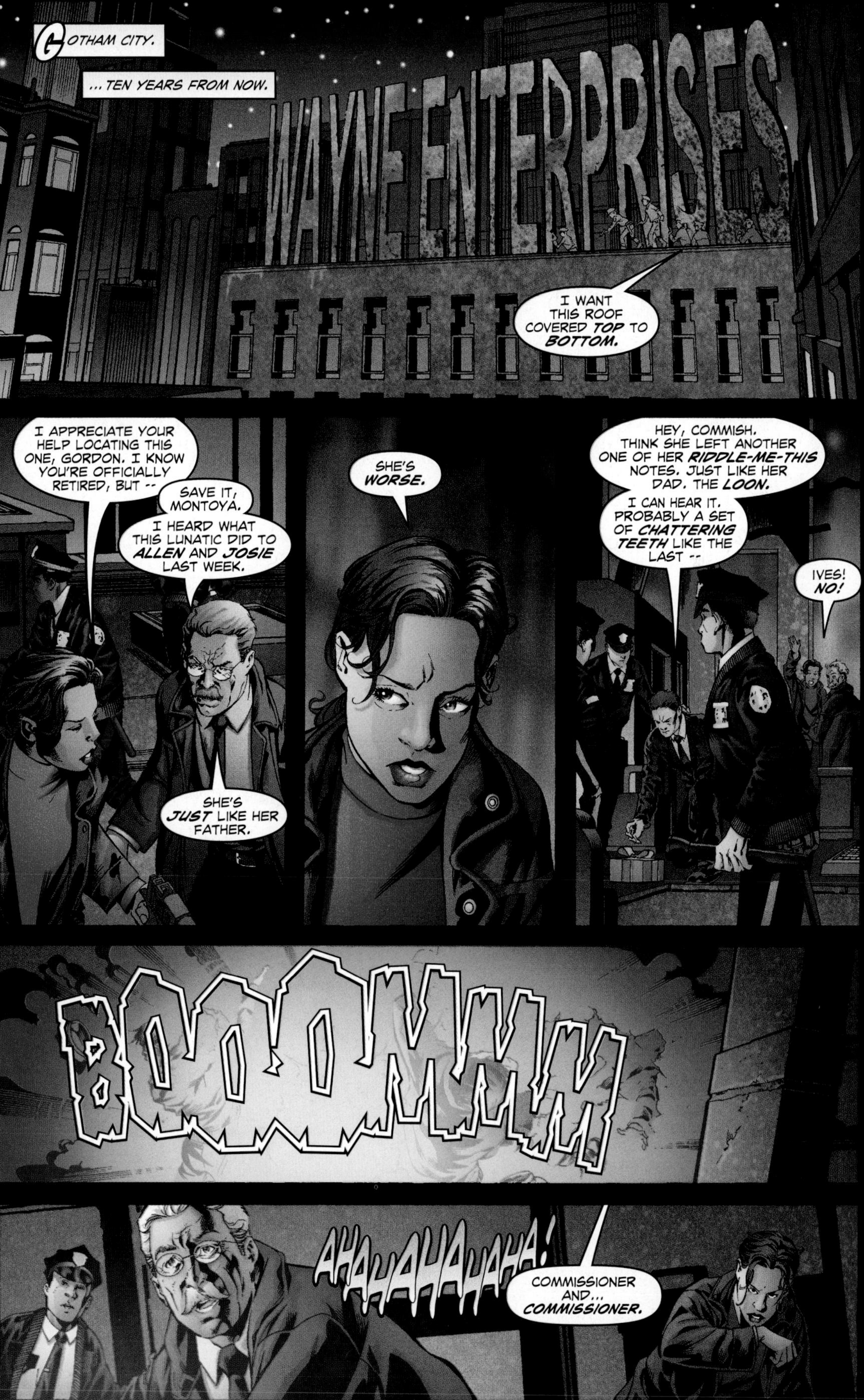
GOTHAM CITY.
...TEN YEARS FROM NOW.
WAYNE ENTERPRISES
I WANT THIS ROOF COVERED TOP TO BOTTOM.
I APPRECIATE YOUR HELP LOCATING THIS ONE, GORDON. I KNOW YOU'RE OFFICIALLY RETIRED, BUT --
SAVE IT, MONTOYA.
I HEARD WHAT THIS LUNATIC DID TO ALLEN AND JOSIE LAST WEEK.
SHE'S JUST LIKE HER FATHER.
SHE'S WORSE.
HEY, COMMISH. THINK SHE LEFT ANOTHER ONE OF HER RIDDLE-ME-THIS NOTES. JUST LIKE HER DAD. THE LOON.
I CAN HEAR IT. PROBABLY A SET OF CHATTERING TEETH LIKE THE LAST --
IVES! NO!
BOOOMMMM
AHAHAHAHAHAHA!
COMMISSIONER AND... COMMISSIONER.

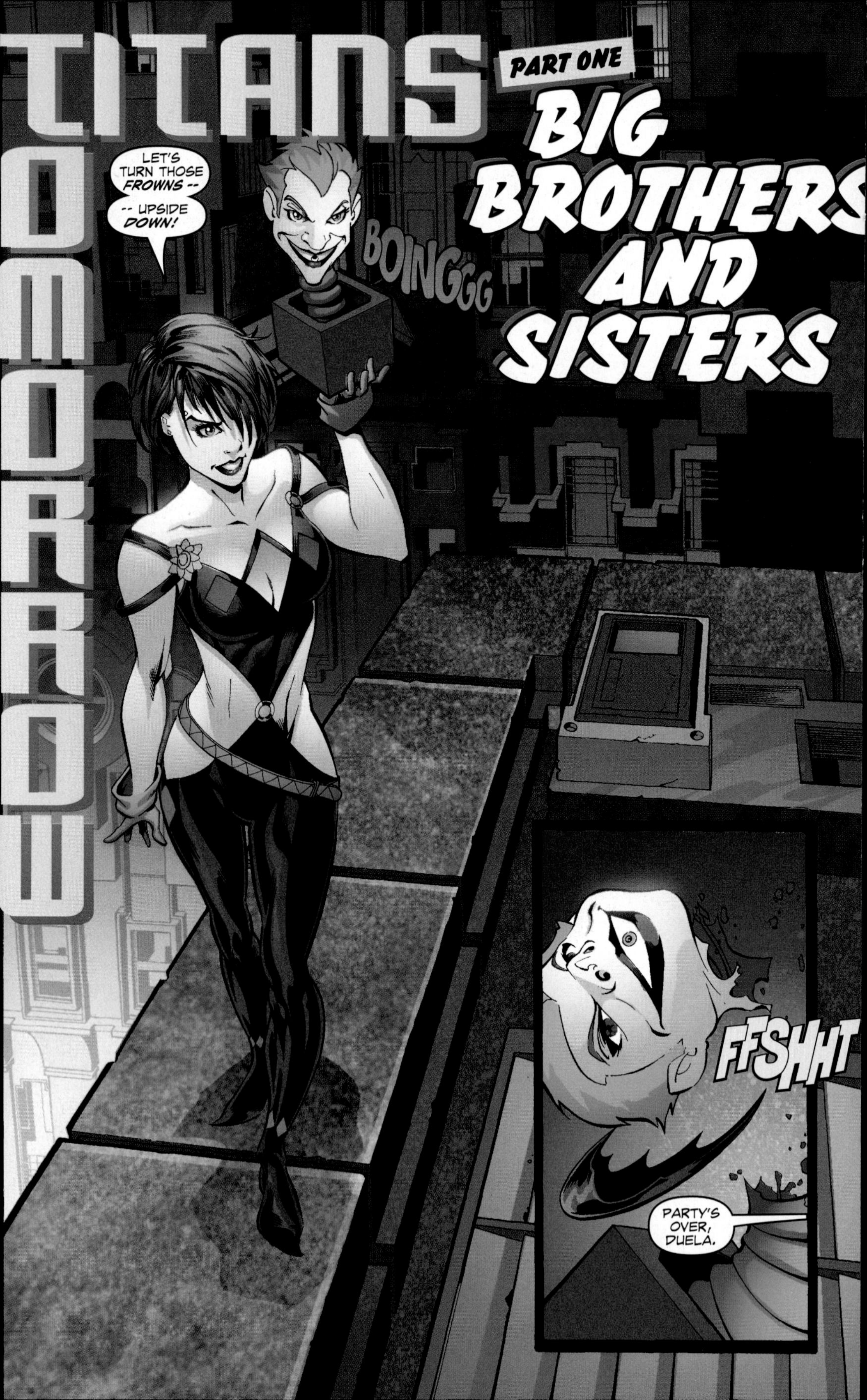
TITANS TOMORROW
PART ONE
BIG BROTHERS AND SISTERS
LET'S TURN THOSE FROWNS --
-- UPSIDE DOWN!
BOINGGG
FFSHHT
PARTY'S OVER, DUELA.

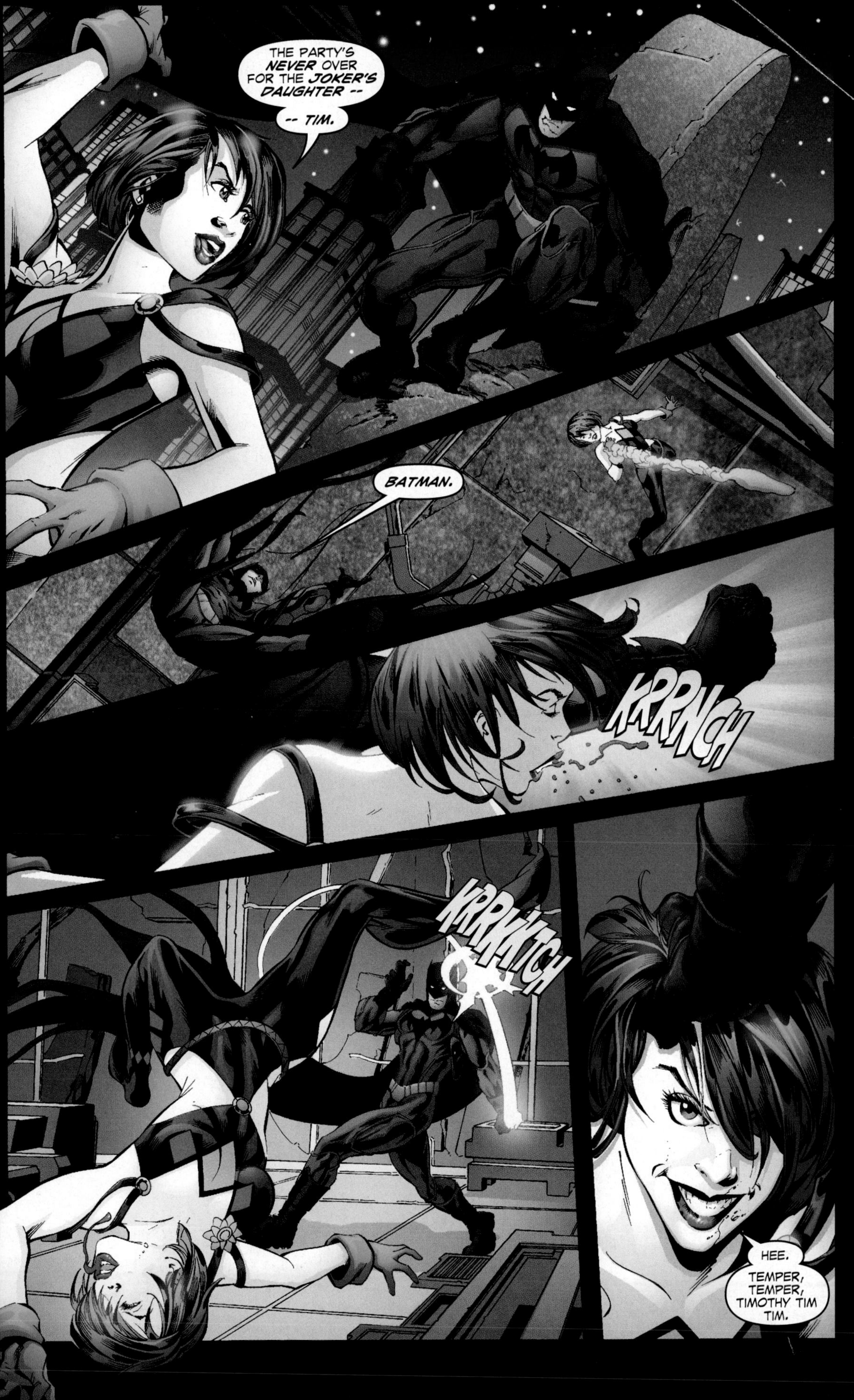
THE PARTY'S NEVER OVER FOR THE JOKER'S DAUGHTER --
-- TIM.
BATMAN.
KRRNCH
KRRKKTCH
HEE.
TEMPER, TEMPER, TIMOTHY TIM TIM.

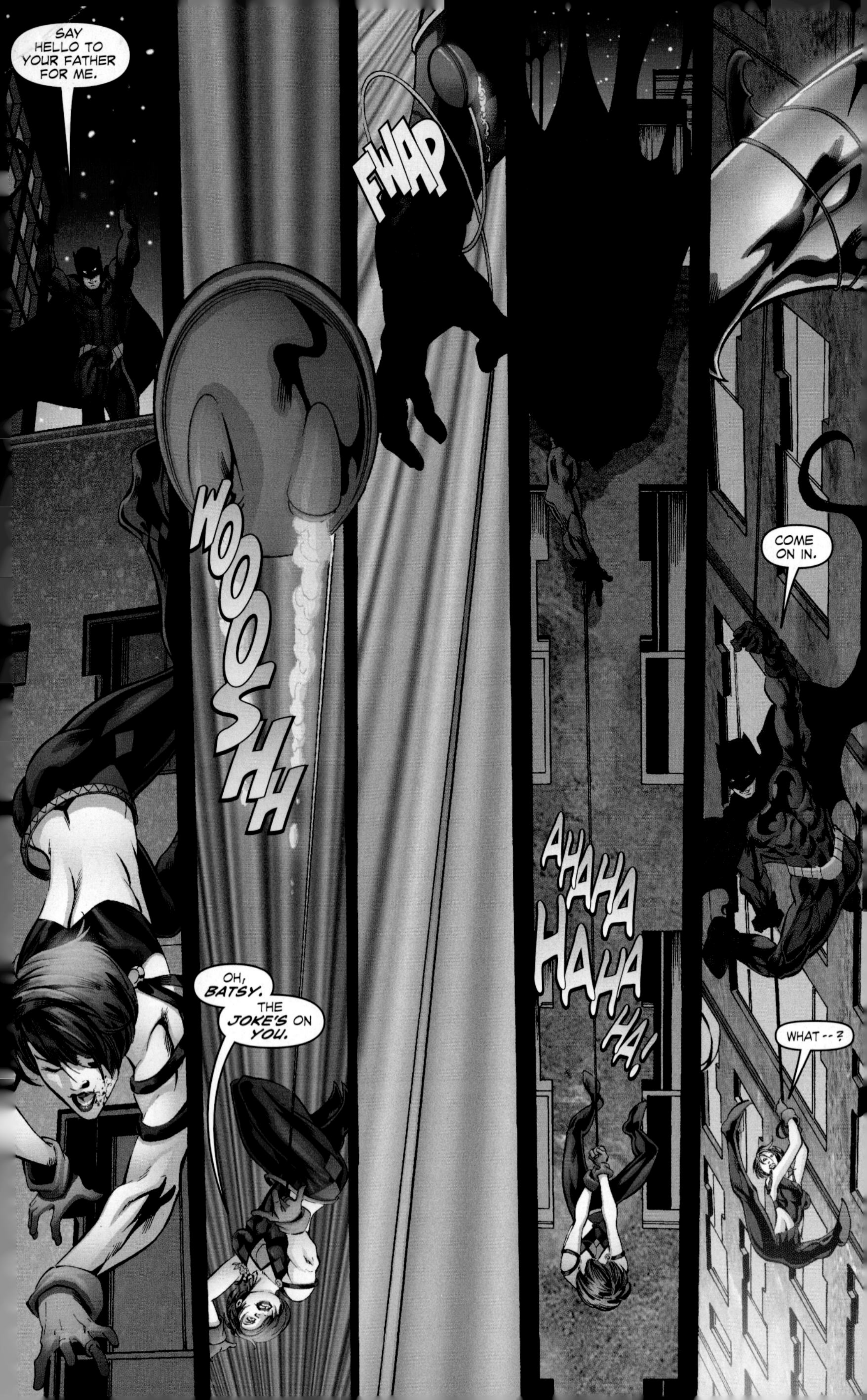
SAY HELLO TO YOUR FATHER FOR ME.
WOOOOOSHHH
OH, BATSY. THE JOKE'S ON YOU.
FWAP
AHAHA HAHAHA!
COME ON IN.
WHAT -- ?

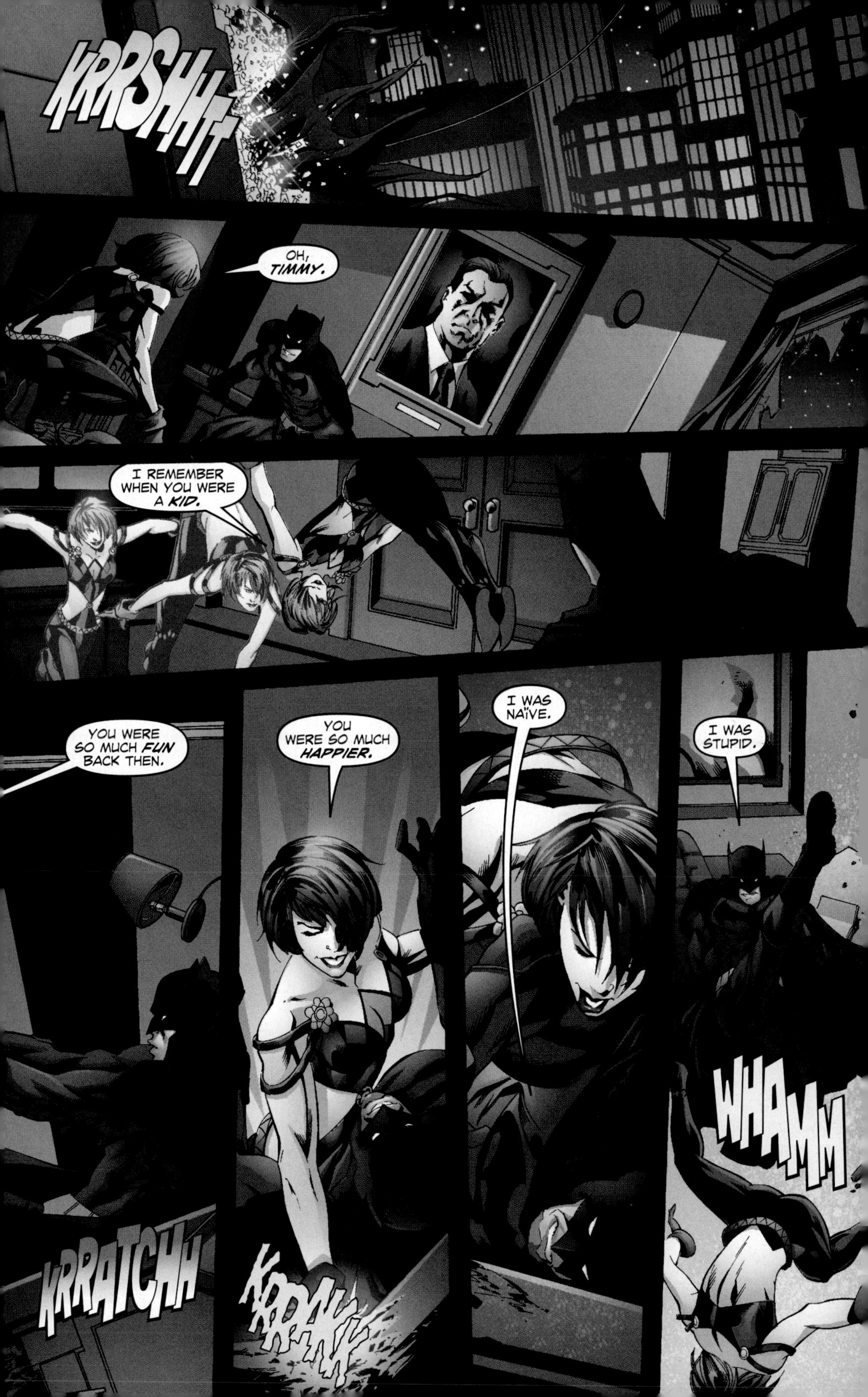
KRRSHHT
OH, TIMMY.
I REMEMBER WHEN YOU WERE A KID.
YOU WERE SO MUCH FUN BACK THEN.
KRRATCHH
YOU WERE SO MUCH HAPPIER.
I WAS NAÏVE.
I WAS STUPID.
WHAMM

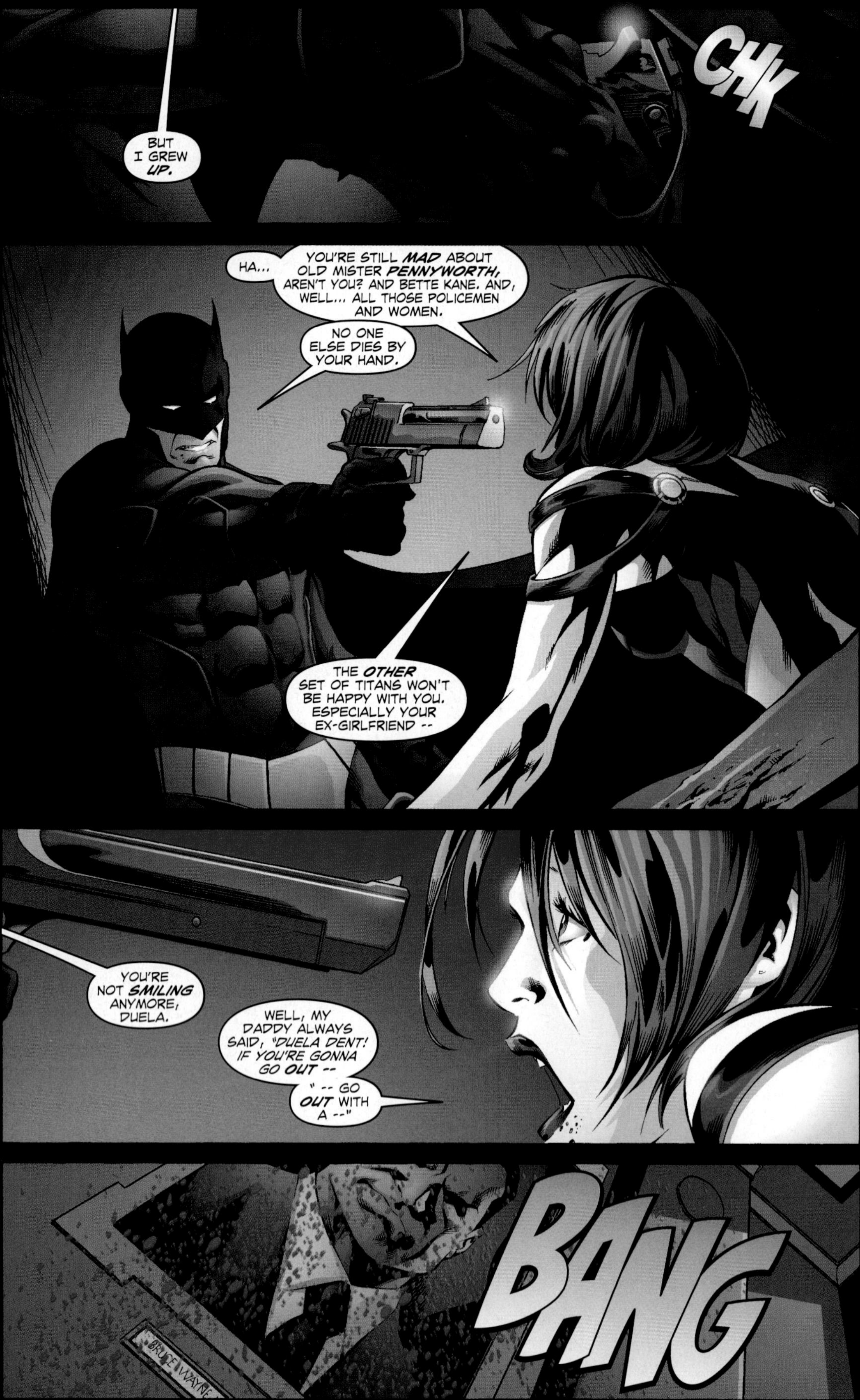
BUT I GREW *UP.*
CHK
HA...
YOU'RE STILL ***MAD*** ABOUT OLD MISTER ***PENNYWORTH,*** AREN'T YOU? AND BETTE KANE. AND, WELL... ALL THOSE POLICEMEN AND WOMEN.
NO ONE ELSE DIES BY YOUR HAND.
THE ***OTHER*** SET OF TITANS WON'T BE HAPPY WITH YOU. ESPECIALLY YOUR EX-GIRLFRIEND --
YOU'RE NOT ***SMILING*** ANYMORE, DUELA.
WELL, MY DADDY ALWAYS SAID, *"DUELA DENT! IF YOU'RE GONNA GO* ***OUT*** *--*
" -- GO ***OUT*** WITH A --"
BANG
BRUCE WAYNE

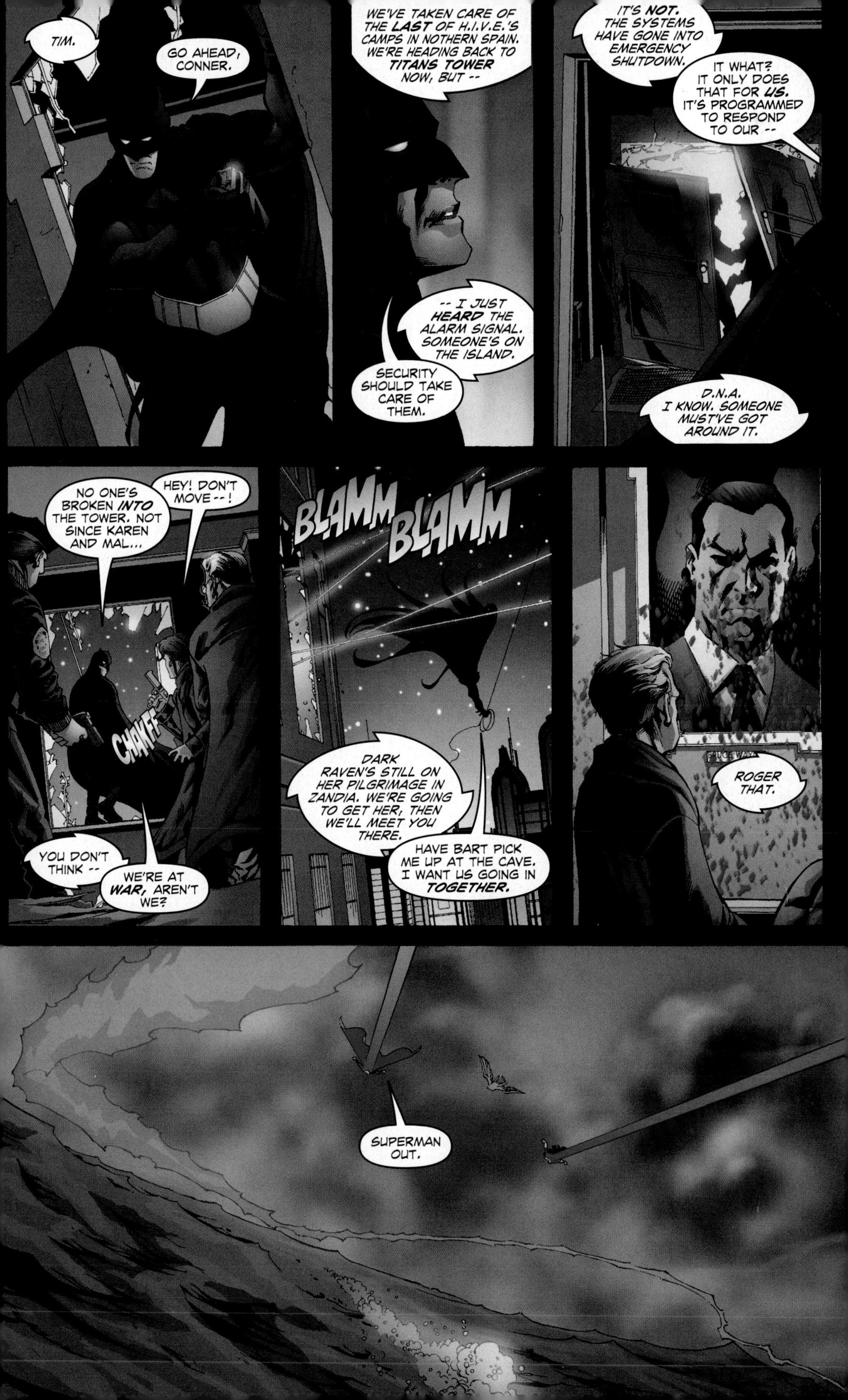
TIM.
GO AHEAD, CONNER.
WE'VE TAKEN CARE OF THE LAST OF H.I.V.E.'S CAMPS IN NOTHERN SPAIN. WE'RE HEADING BACK TO TITANS TOWER NOW, BUT --
-- I JUST HEARD THE ALARM SIGNAL. SOMEONE'S ON THE ISLAND.
SECURITY SHOULD TAKE CARE OF THEM.
IT'S NOT. THE SYSTEMS HAVE GONE INTO EMERGENCY SHUTDOWN.
IT WHAT? IT ONLY DOES THAT FOR US. IT'S PROGRAMMED TO RESPOND TO OUR --
D.N.A. I KNOW. SOMEONE MUST'VE GOT AROUND IT.
NO ONE'S BROKEN INTO THE TOWER. NOT SINCE KAREN AND MAL...
HEY! DON'T MOVE --!
CHAKFF
YOU DON'T THINK --
WE'RE AT WAR, AREN'T WE?
BLAMM BLAMM
DARK RAVEN'S STILL ON HER PILGRIMAGE IN ZANDIA. WE'RE GOING TO GET HER, THEN WE'LL MEET YOU THERE.
HAVE BART PICK ME UP AT THE CAVE. I WANT US GOING IN TOGETHER.
ROGER THAT.
SUPERMAN OUT.

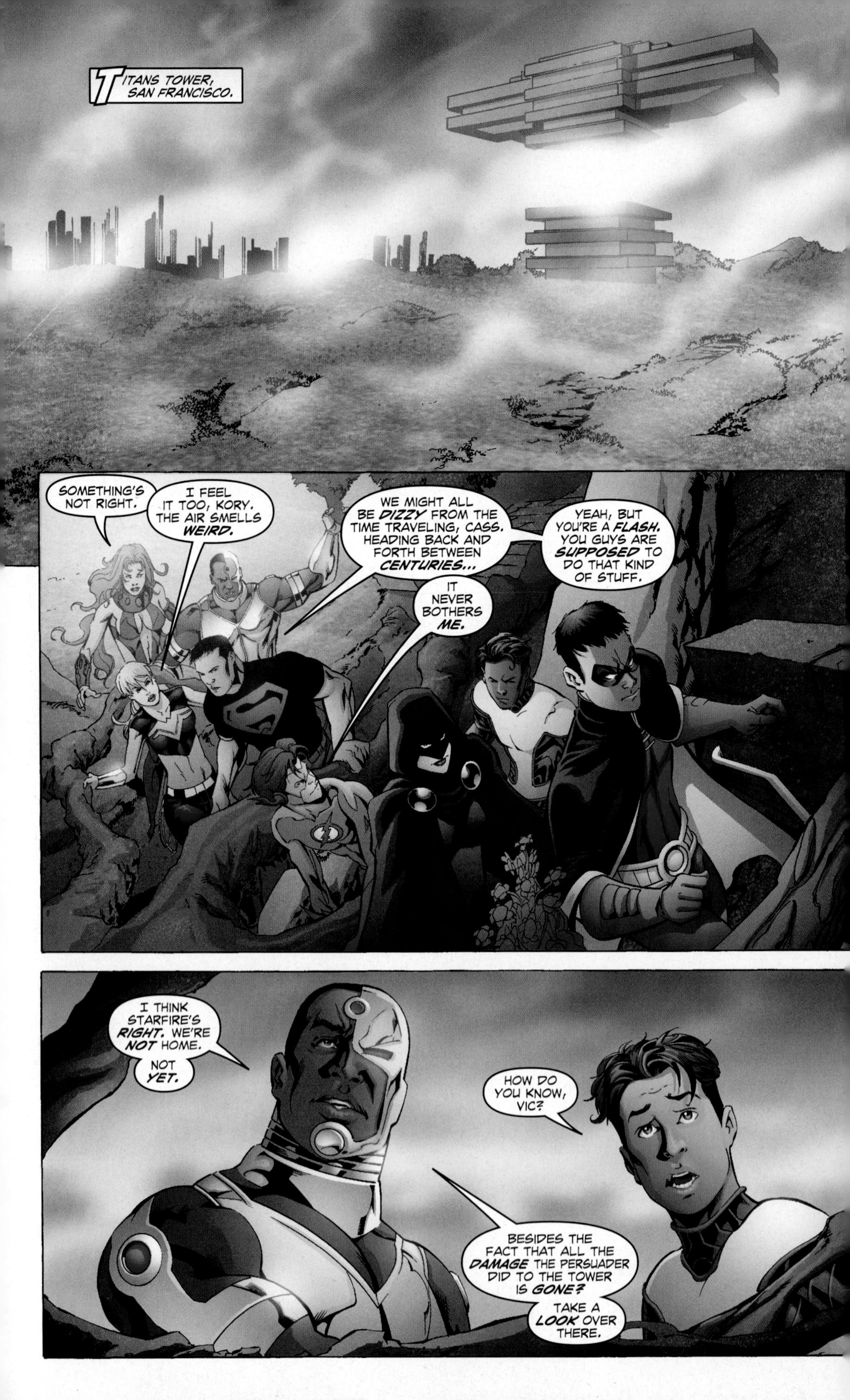
TITANS TOWER, SAN FRANCISCO.
SOMETHING'S NOT RIGHT.
I FEEL IT TOO, KORY. THE AIR SMELLS WEIRD.
WE MIGHT ALL BE DIZZY FROM THE TIME TRAVELING, CASS. HEADING BACK AND FORTH BETWEEN CENTURIES...
YEAH, BUT YOU'RE A FLASH. YOU GUYS ARE SUPPOSED TO DO THAT KIND OF STUFF.
IT NEVER BOTHERS ME.
I THINK STARFIRE'S RIGHT. WE'RE NOT HOME.
NOT YET.
HOW DO YOU KNOW, VIC?
BESIDES THE FACT THAT ALL THE DAMAGE THE PERSUADER DID TO THE TOWER IS GONE?
TAKE A LOOK OVER THERE.

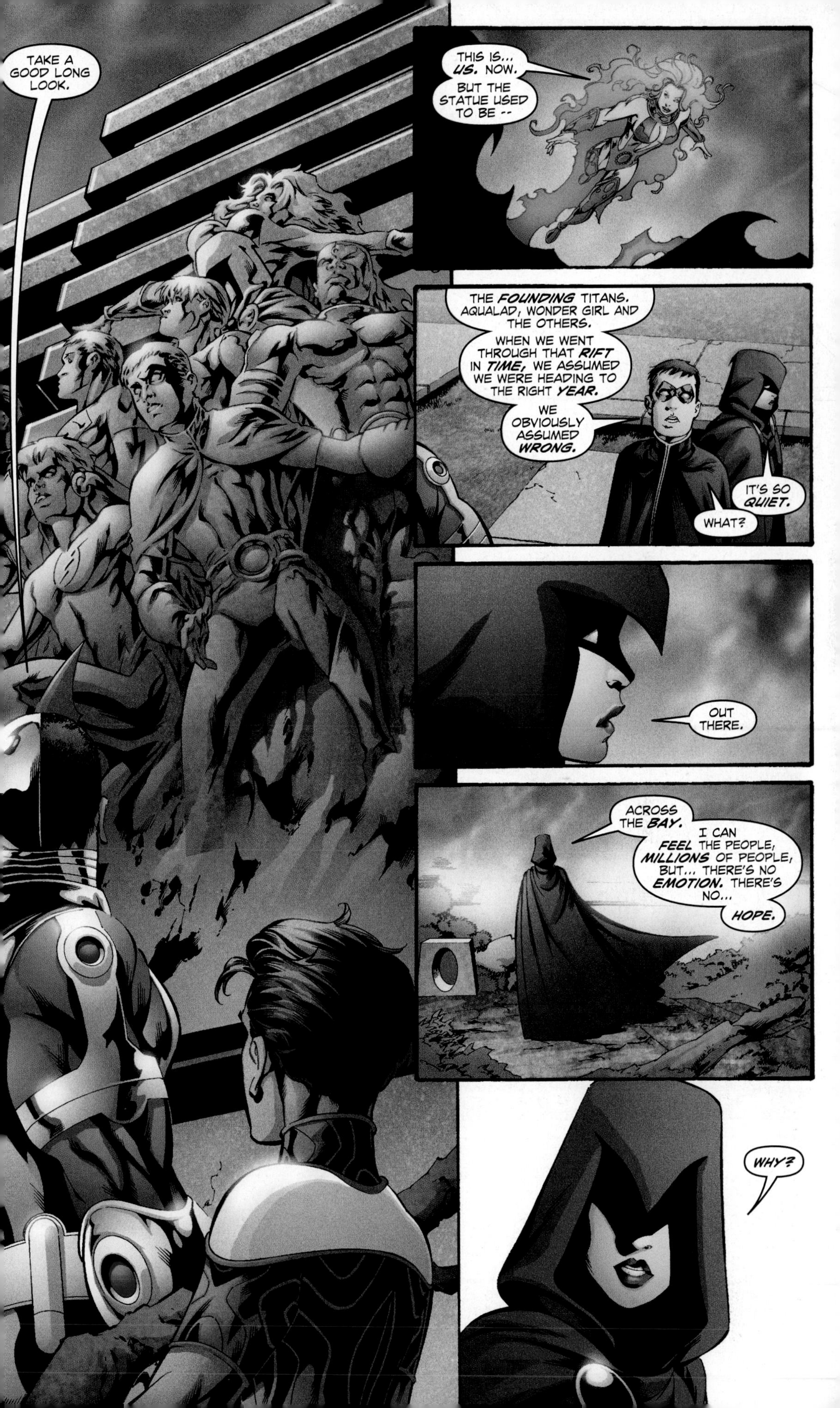

TAKE A GOOD LONG LOOK.
THIS IS... *US.* NOW.
BUT THE STATUE USED TO BE --
THE *FOUNDING* TITANS. AQUALAD, WONDER GIRL AND THE OTHERS.
WHEN WE WENT THROUGH THAT *RIFT* IN *TIME,* WE ASSUMED WE WERE HEADING TO THE RIGHT *YEAR.*
WE OBVIOUSLY ASSUMED *WRONG.*
IT'S SO *QUIET.*
WHAT?
OUT THERE.
ACROSS THE *BAY.*
I CAN *FEEL* THE PEOPLE, *MILLIONS* OF PEOPLE, BUT... THERE'S NO *EMOTION.* THERE'S NO...
HOPE.
WHY?

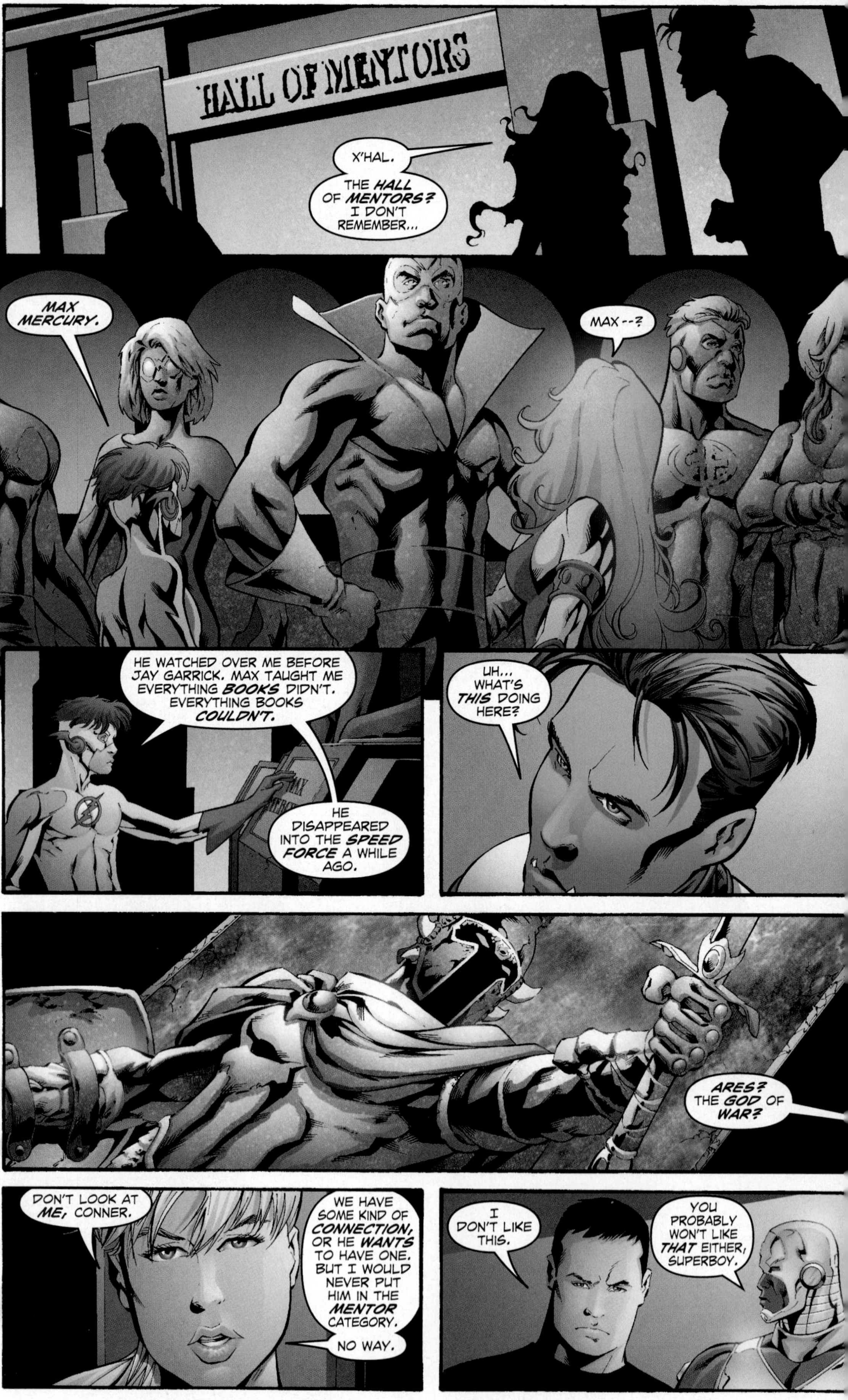
HALL OF MENTORS
X'HAL.
THE HALL OF MENTORS? I DON'T REMEMBER...
MAX MERCURY.
MAX--?
HE WATCHED OVER ME BEFORE JAY GARRICK. MAX TAUGHT ME EVERYTHING BOOKS DIDN'T. EVERYTHING BOOKS COULDN'T.
HE DISAPPEARED INTO THE SPEED FORCE A WHILE AGO.
UH... WHAT'S THIS DOING HERE?
ARES? THE GOD OF WAR?
DON'T LOOK AT ME, CONNER.
WE HAVE SOME KIND OF CONNECTION, OR HE WANTS TO HAVE ONE. BUT I WOULD NEVER PUT HIM IN THE MENTOR CATEGORY.
NO WAY.
I DON'T LIKE THIS.
YOU PROBABLY WON'T LIKE THAT EITHER, SUPERBOY.

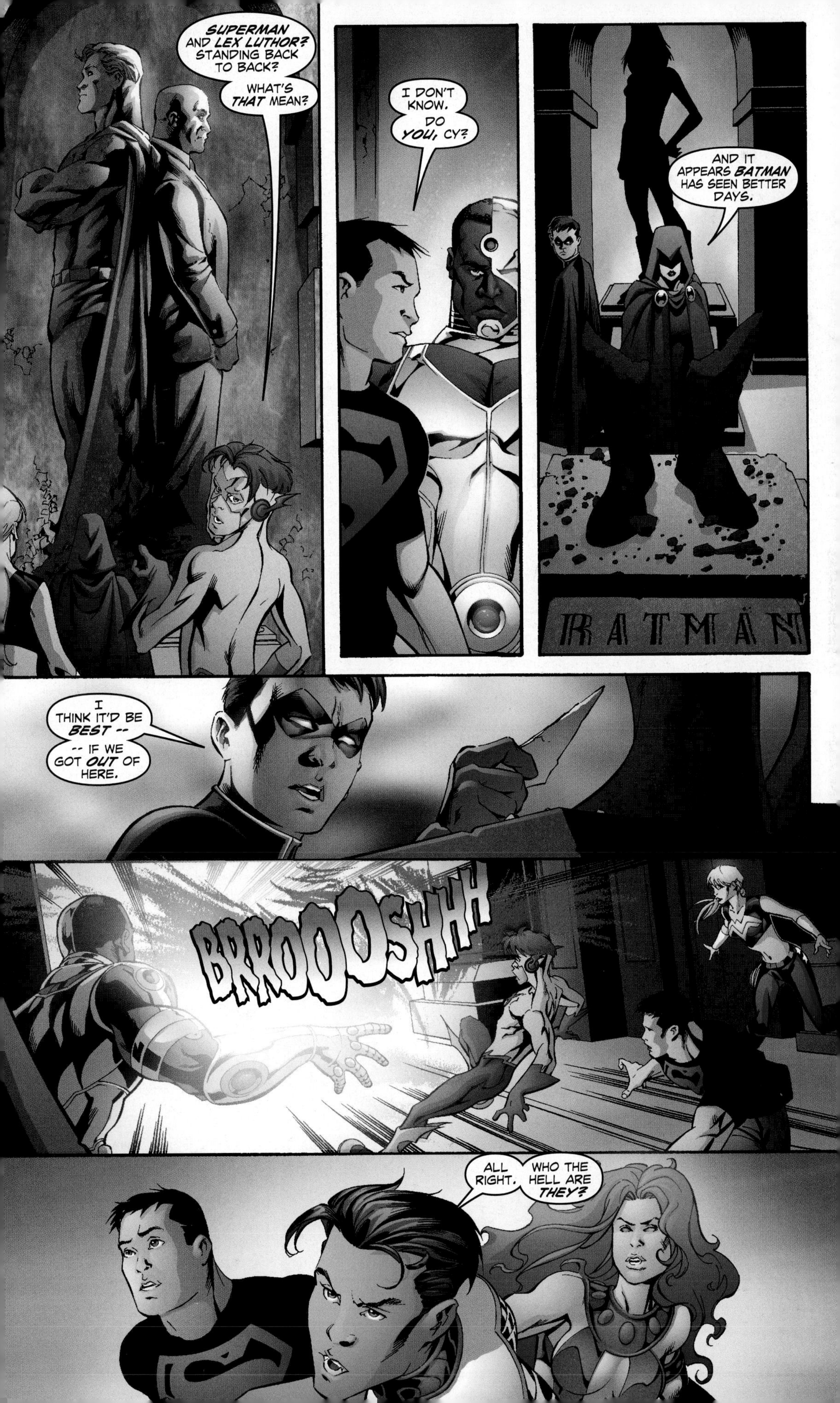
SUPERMAN AND LEX LUTHOR? STANDING BACK TO BACK?
WHAT'S THAT MEAN?
I DON'T KNOW.
DO YOU, CY?
AND IT APPEARS BATMAN HAS SEEN BETTER DAYS.
BATMAN
I THINK IT'D BE BEST --
-- IF WE GOT OUT OF HERE.
BRROOOSHHH
ALL RIGHT.
WHO THE HELL ARE THEY?

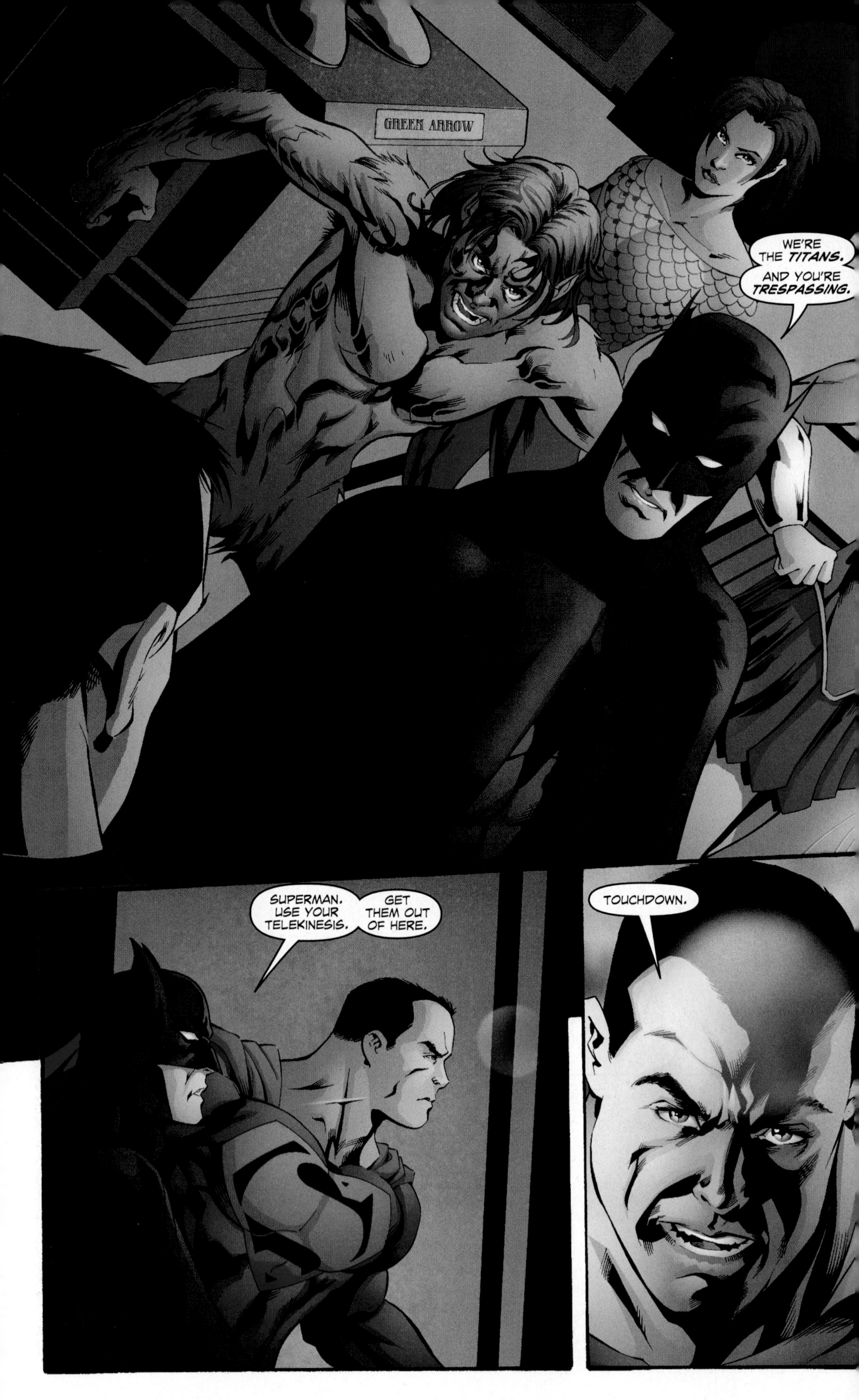
GREEN ARROW
WE'RE THE *TITANS.*
AND YOU'RE *TRESPASSING.*
SUPERMAN. USE YOUR TELEKINESIS.
GET THEM OUT OF HERE.
TOUCHDOWN.

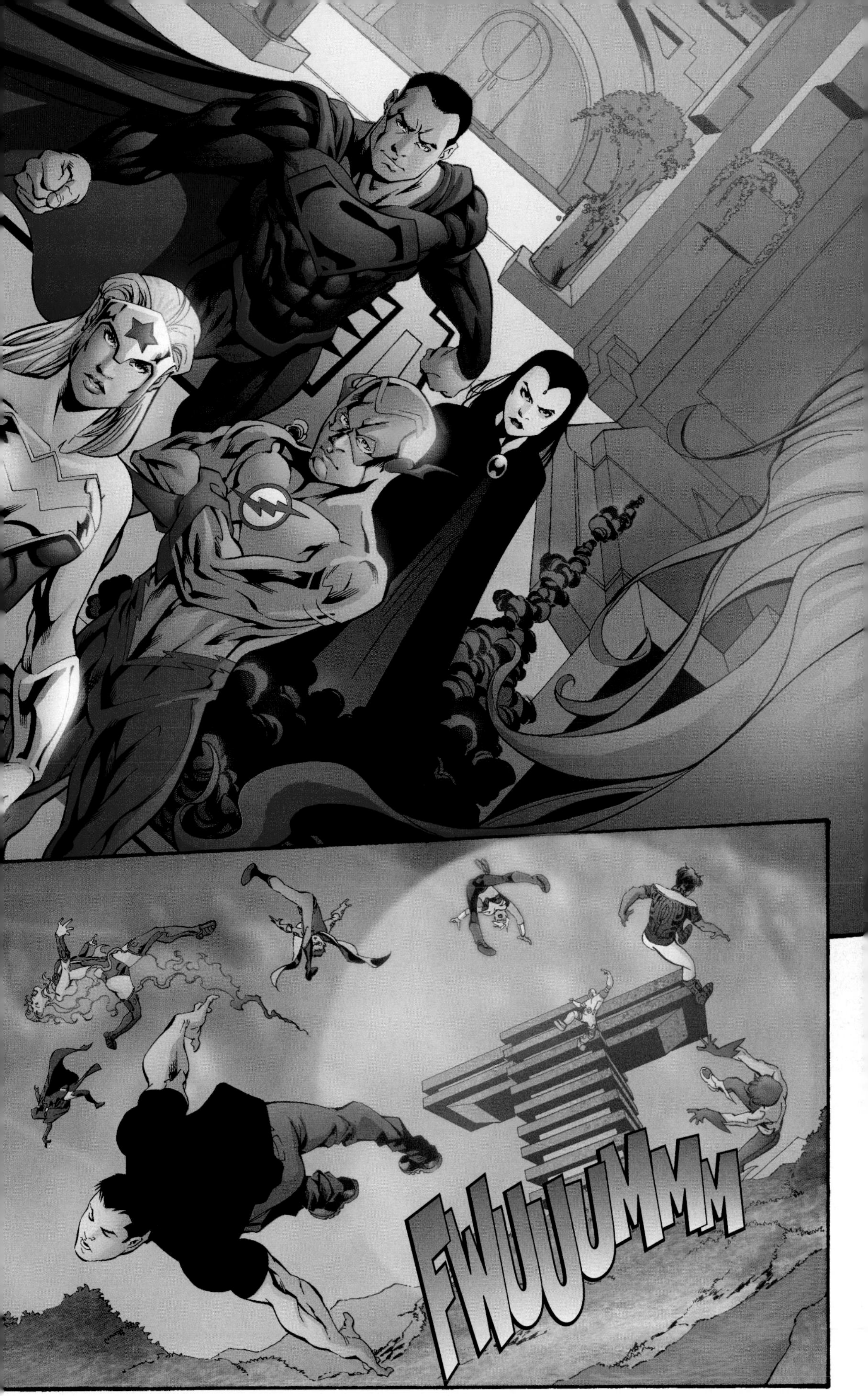
FWUUUMMM

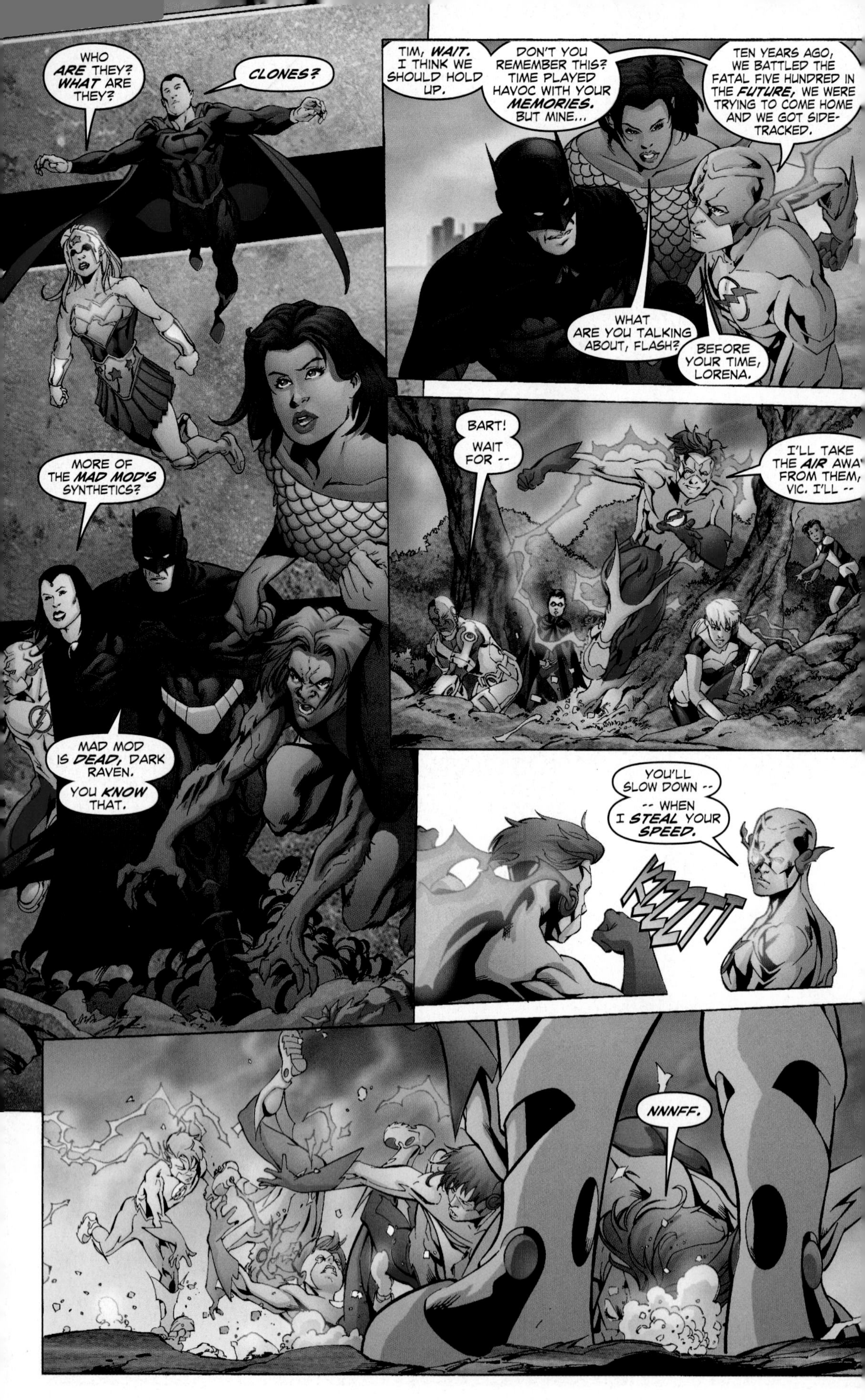
WHO ARE THEY? WHAT ARE THEY?
CLONES?
TIM, WAIT. I THINK WE SHOULD HOLD UP.
DON'T YOU REMEMBER THIS? TIME PLAYED HAVOC WITH YOUR MEMORIES. BUT MINE...
TEN YEARS AGO, WE BATTLED THE FATAL FIVE HUNDRED IN THE FUTURE, WE WERE TRYING TO COME HOME AND WE GOT SIDE-TRACKED.
WHAT ARE YOU TALKING ABOUT, FLASH?
BEFORE YOUR TIME, LORENA.
MORE OF THE MAD MOD'S SYNTHETICS?
MAD MOD IS DEAD, DARK RAVEN.
YOU KNOW THAT.
BART! WAIT FOR --
I'LL TAKE THE AIR AWA FROM THEM, VIC. I'LL --
YOU'LL SLOW DOWN --
-- WHEN I STEAL YOUR SPEED.
KZZZTT
NNNFF.

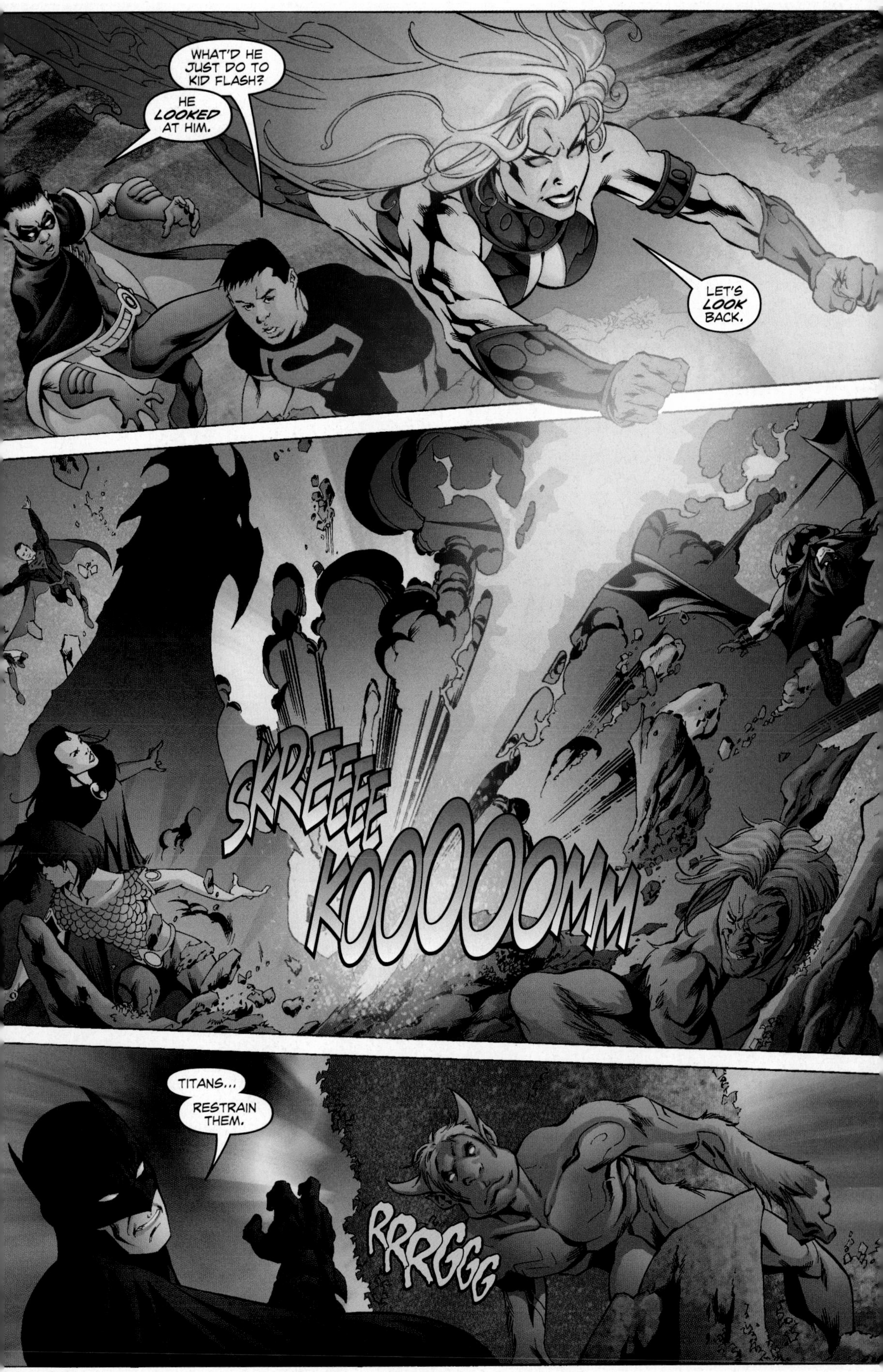

WHAT'D HE JUST DO TO KID FLASH?
HE LOOKED AT HIM.
LET'S LOOK BACK.
SKREEEE
KOOOOOMM
TITANS... RESTRAIN THEM.
RRRGGG

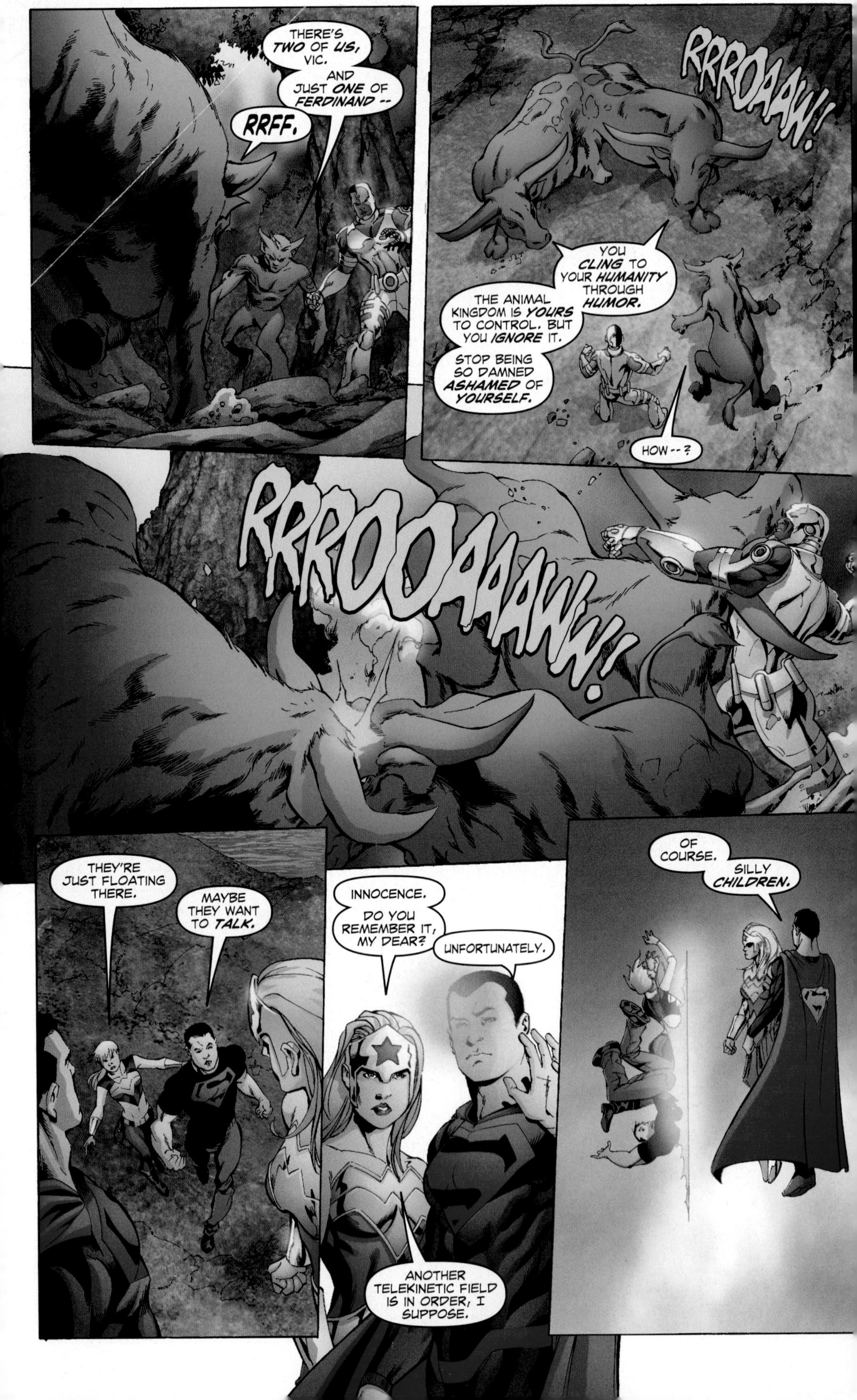

THERE'S TWO OF US, VIC.
AND JUST ONE OF FERDINAND --
RRFF.
RRROAAAW!!
YOU CLING TO YOUR HUMANITY THROUGH HUMOR.
THE ANIMAL KINGDOM IS YOURS TO CONTROL. BUT YOU IGNORE IT.
STOP BEING SO DAMNED ASHAMED OF YOURSELF.
HOW -- ?
RRROOAAAAWW!!
THEY'RE JUST FLOATING THERE.
MAYBE THEY WANT TO TALK.
INNOCENCE.
DO YOU REMEMBER IT, MY DEAR?
UNFORTUNATELY.
ANOTHER TELEKINETIC FIELD IS IN ORDER, I SUPPOSE.
OF COURSE.
SILLY CHILDREN.

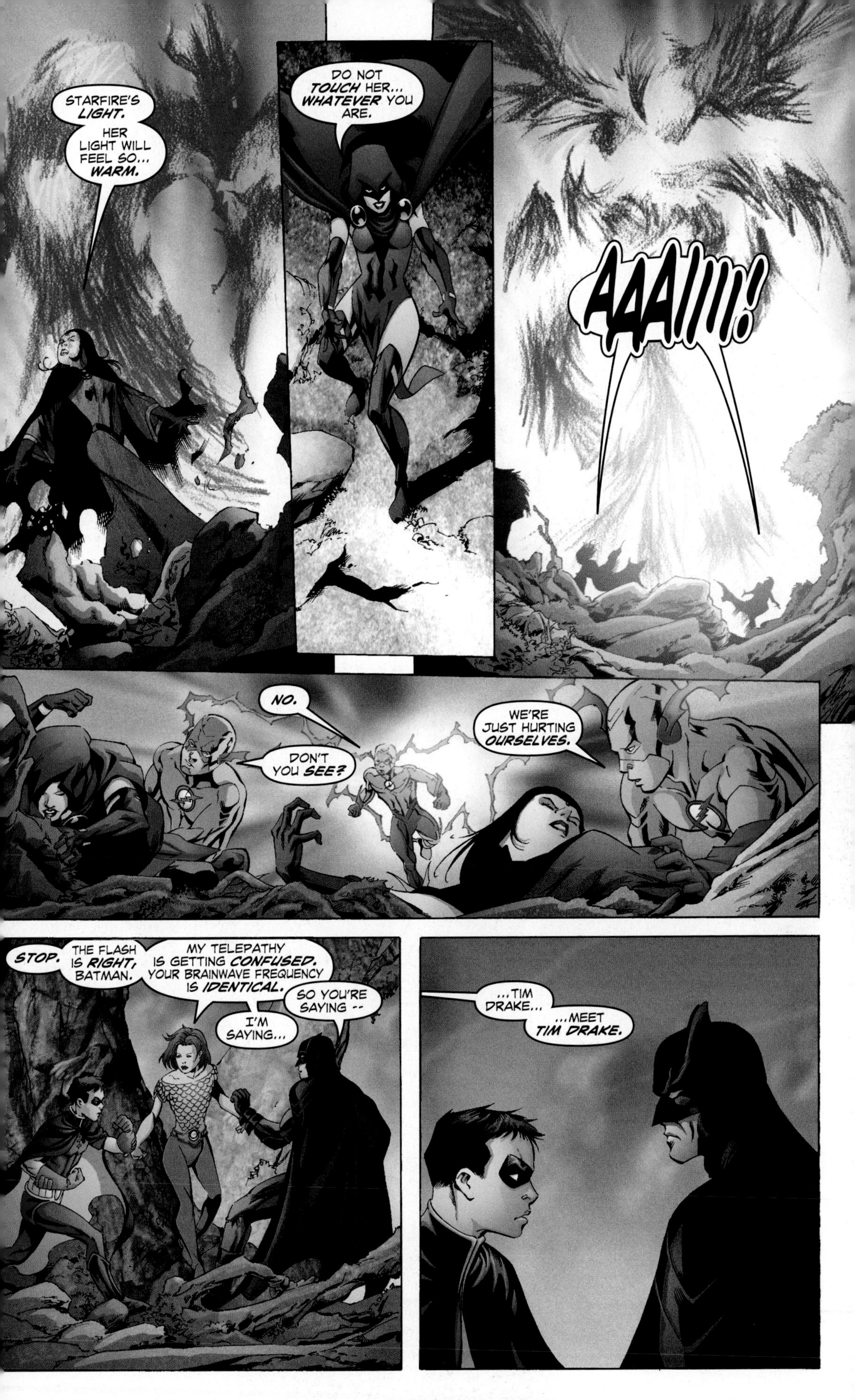

STARFIRE'S LIGHT.
HER LIGHT WILL FEEL SO... WARM.
DO NOT TOUCH HER... WHATEVER YOU ARE.
AAAIIIII!
NO.
DON'T YOU SEE?
WE'RE JUST HURTING OURSELVES.
STOP.
THE FLASH IS RIGHT, BATMAN.
MY TELEPATHY IS GETTING CONFUSED. YOUR BRAINWAVE FREQUENCY IS IDENTICAL.
SO YOU'RE SAYING --
I'M SAYING...
...TIM DRAKE...
...MEET TIM DRAKE.

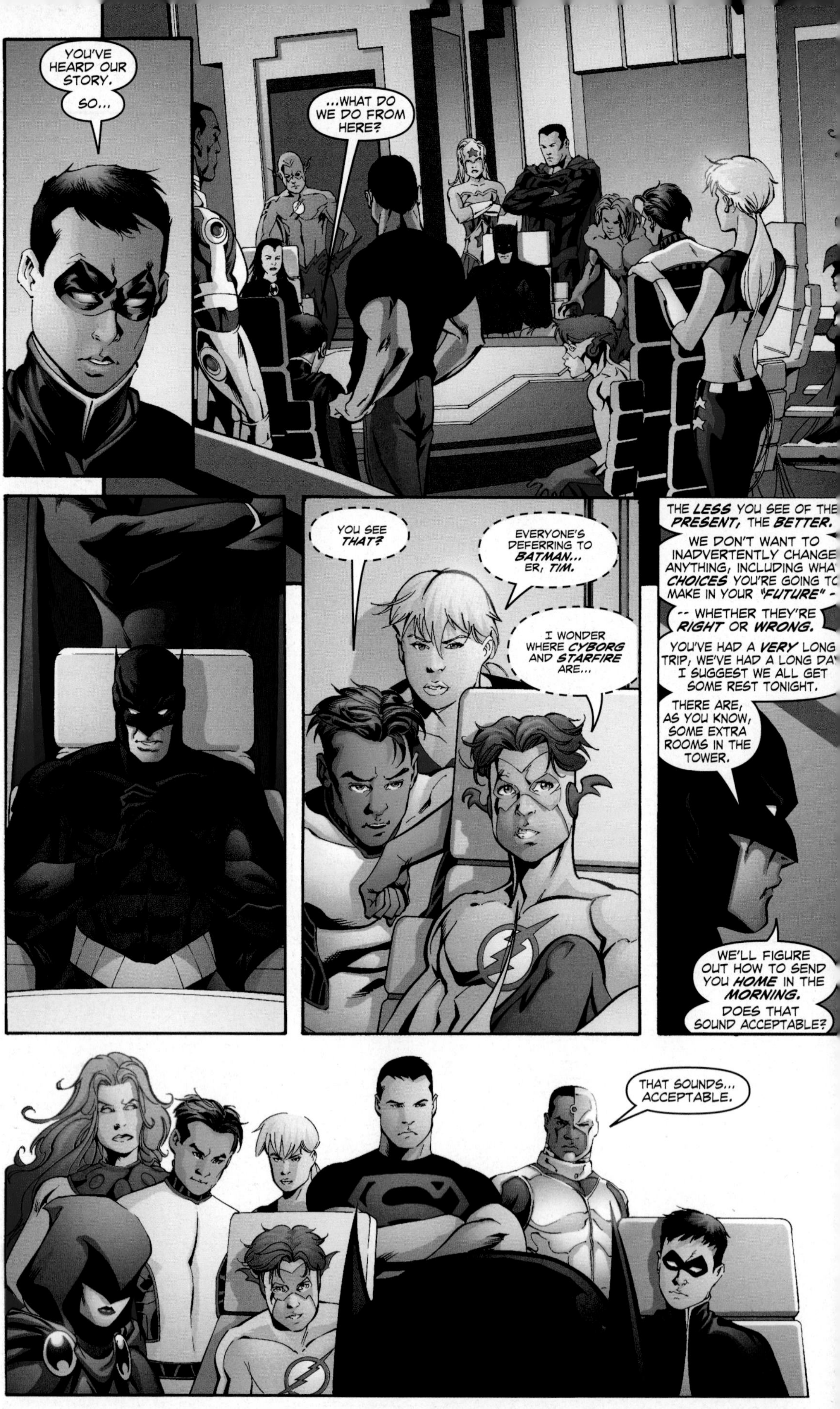
YOU'VE HEARD OUR STORY.
SO...
...WHAT DO WE DO FROM HERE?
YOU SEE THAT?
EVERYONE'S DEFERRING TO BATMAN... ER, TIM.
I WONDER WHERE CYBORG AND STARFIRE ARE...
THE LESS YOU SEE OF THE PRESENT, THE BETTER.
WE DON'T WANT TO INADVERTENTLY CHANGE ANYTHING, INCLUDING WHAT CHOICES YOU'RE GOING TO MAKE IN YOUR "FUTURE" --
-- WHETHER THEY'RE RIGHT OR WRONG.
YOU'VE HAD A VERY LONG TRIP, WE'VE HAD A LONG DAY. I SUGGEST WE ALL GET SOME REST TONIGHT.
THERE ARE, AS YOU KNOW, SOME EXTRA ROOMS IN THE TOWER.
WE'LL FIGURE OUT HOW TO SEND YOU HOME IN THE MORNING.
DOES THAT SOUND ACCEPTABLE?
THAT SOUNDS... ACCEPTABLE.

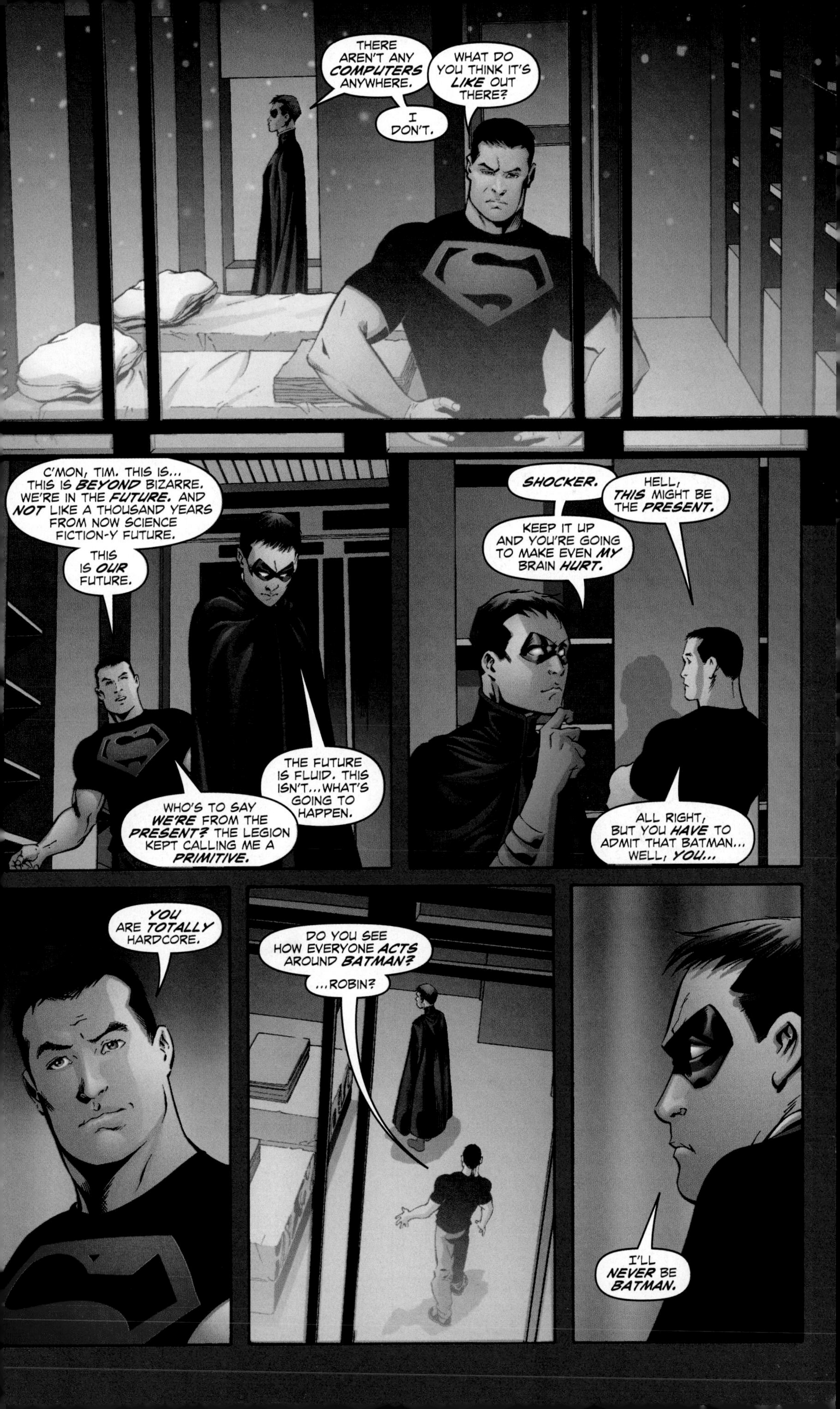
THERE AREN'T ANY COMPUTERS ANYWHERE.
WHAT DO YOU THINK IT'S LIKE OUT THERE?
I DON'T.
C'MON, TIM. THIS IS... THIS IS BEYOND BIZARRE. WE'RE IN THE FUTURE. AND NOT LIKE A THOUSAND YEARS FROM NOW SCIENCE FICTION-Y FUTURE.
THIS IS OUR FUTURE.
THE FUTURE IS FLUID. THIS ISN'T...WHAT'S GOING TO HAPPEN.
WHO'S TO SAY WE'RE FROM THE PRESENT? THE LEGION KEPT CALLING ME A PRIMITIVE.
SHOCKER.
HELL, THIS MIGHT BE THE PRESENT.
KEEP IT UP AND YOU'RE GOING TO MAKE EVEN MY BRAIN HURT.
ALL RIGHT, BUT YOU HAVE TO ADMIT THAT BATMAN... WELL, YOU...
YOU ARE TOTALLY HARDCORE.
DO YOU SEE HOW EVERYONE ACTS AROUND BATMAN?
...ROBIN?
I'LL NEVER BE BATMAN.

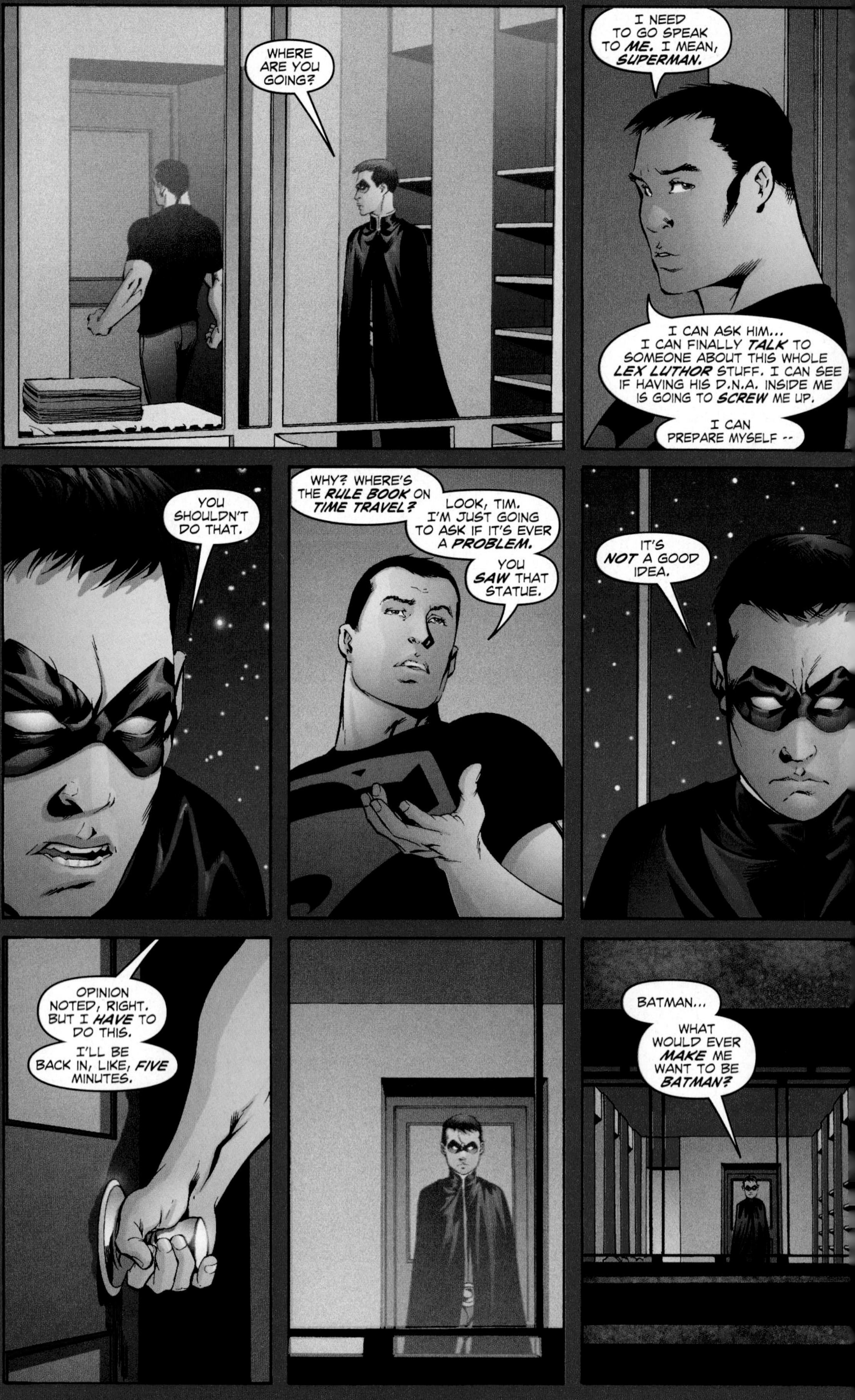
WHERE ARE YOU GOING?
I NEED TO GO SPEAK TO ME. I MEAN, SUPERMAN.
I CAN ASK HIM... I CAN FINALLY TALK TO SOMEONE ABOUT THIS WHOLE LEX LUTHOR STUFF. I CAN SEE IF HAVING HIS D.N.A. INSIDE ME IS GOING TO SCREW ME UP.
I CAN PREPARE MYSELF --
YOU SHOULDN'T DO THAT.
WHY? WHERE'S THE RULE BOOK ON TIME TRAVEL?
LOOK, TIM. I'M JUST GOING TO ASK IF IT'S EVER A PROBLEM.
YOU SAW THAT STATUE.
IT'S NOT A GOOD IDEA.
OPINION NOTED, RIGHT. BUT I HAVE TO DO THIS.
I'LL BE BACK IN, LIKE, FIVE MINUTES.
BATMAN...
WHAT WOULD EVER MAKE ME WANT TO BE BATMAN?

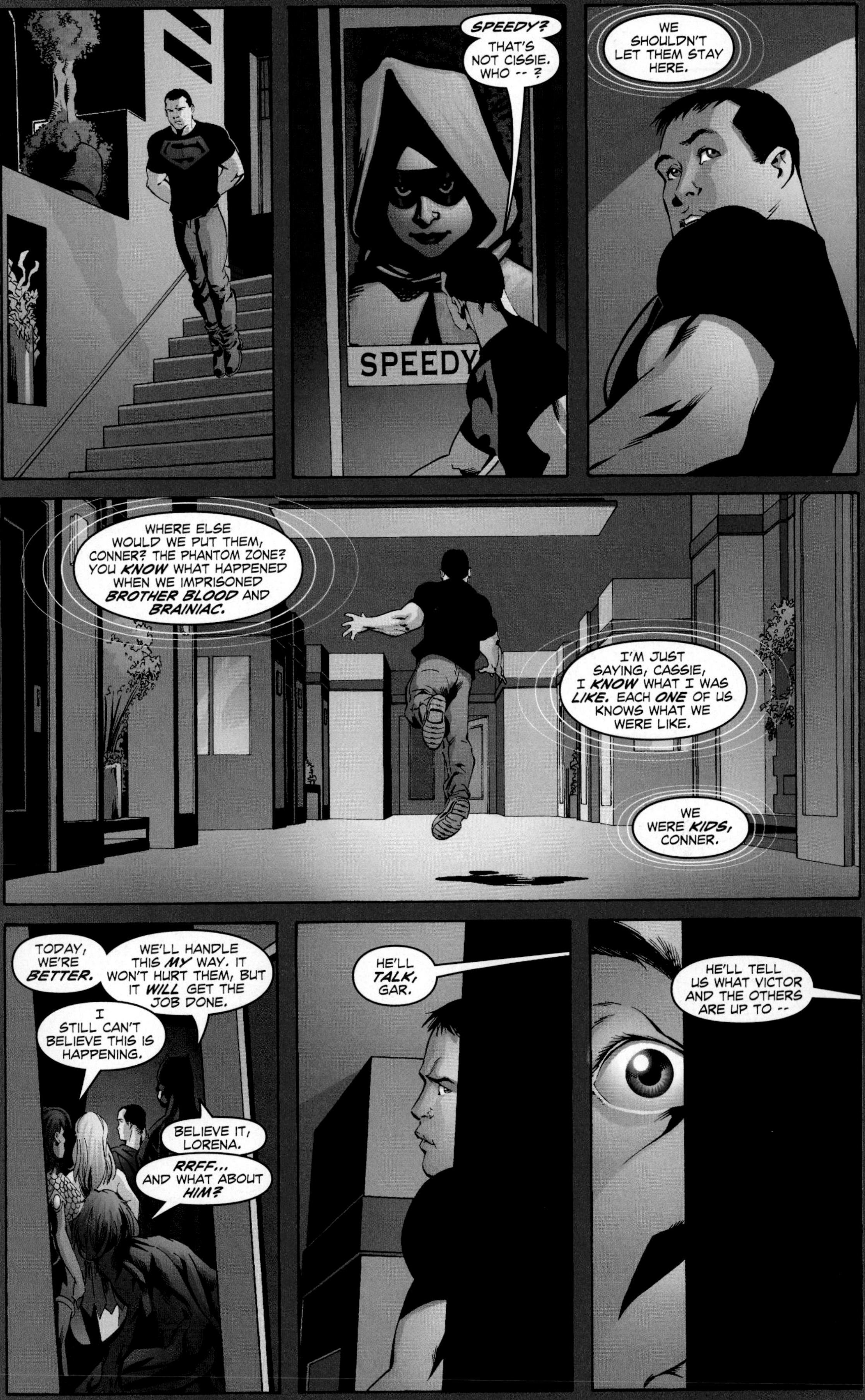
SPEEDY? THAT'S NOT CISSIE. WHO -- ?
SPEEDY
WE SHOULDN'T LET THEM STAY HERE.
WHERE ELSE WOULD WE PUT THEM, CONNER? THE PHANTOM ZONE? YOU KNOW WHAT HAPPENED WHEN WE IMPRISONED BROTHER BLOOD AND BRAINIAC.
I'M JUST SAYING, CASSIE, I KNOW WHAT I WAS LIKE. EACH ONE OF US KNOWS WHAT WE WERE LIKE.
WE WERE KIDS, CONNER.
TODAY, WE'RE BETTER.
WE'LL HANDLE THIS MY WAY. IT WON'T HURT THEM, BUT IT WILL GET THE JOB DONE.
I STILL CAN'T BELIEVE THIS IS HAPPENING.
BELIEVE IT, LORENA.
RRFF... AND WHAT ABOUT HIM?
HE'LL TALK, GAR.
HE'LL TELL US WHAT VICTOR AND THE OTHERS ARE UP TO --

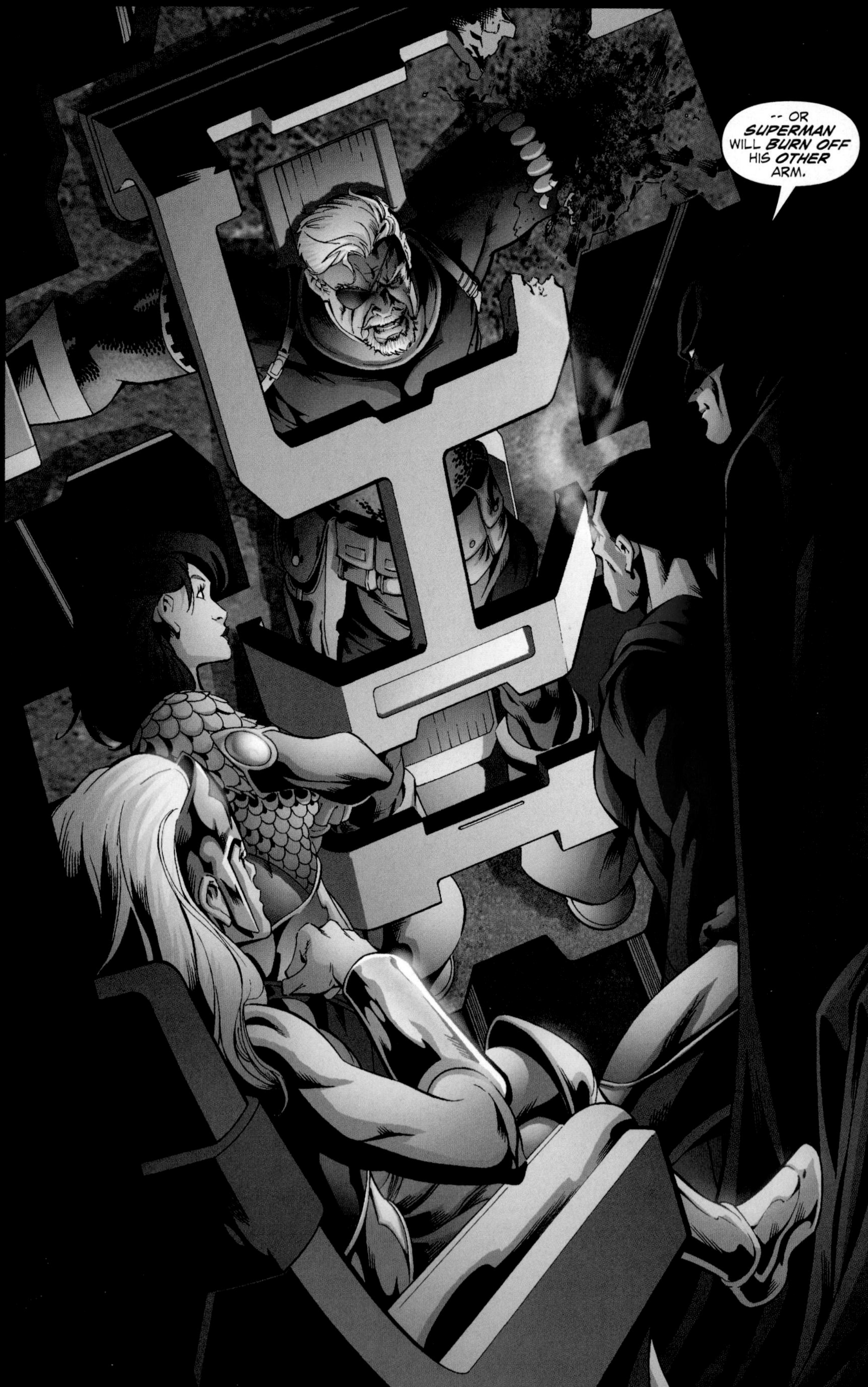
-- OR *SUPERMAN* WILL *BURN OFF* HIS *OTHER* ARM.

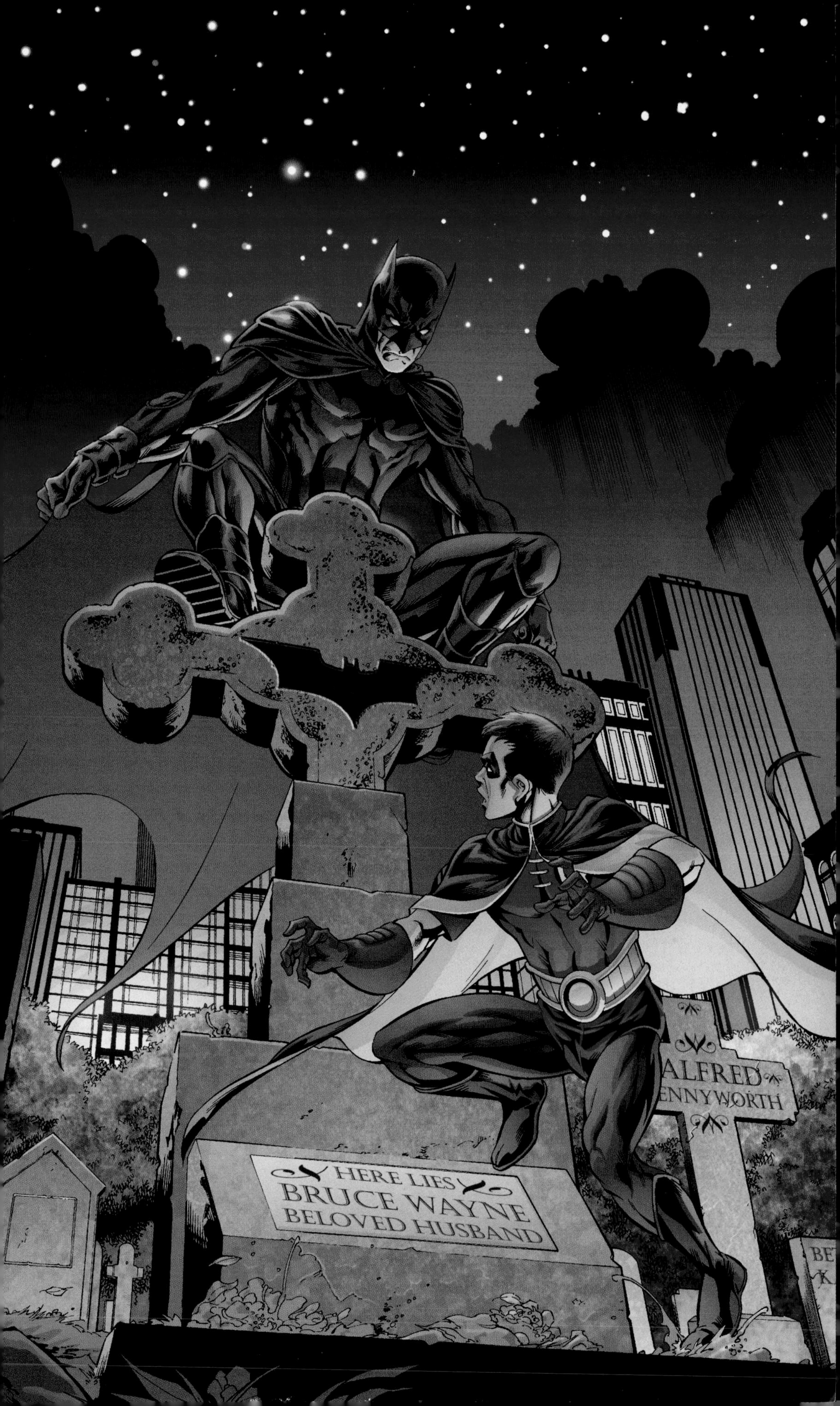
HERE LIES
BRUCE WAYNE
BELOVED HUSBAND
ALFRED
ENNYWORTH

TEEN TITANS #18

GEOFF JOHNS
Writer

MIKE McKONE
Penciller

MARLO ALQUIZA
Inker

JEROMY COX
Colorist

COMICRAFT
Letterer

**MIKE McKONE, MARLO ALQUIZA
& JEROMY COX**
Cover Artists

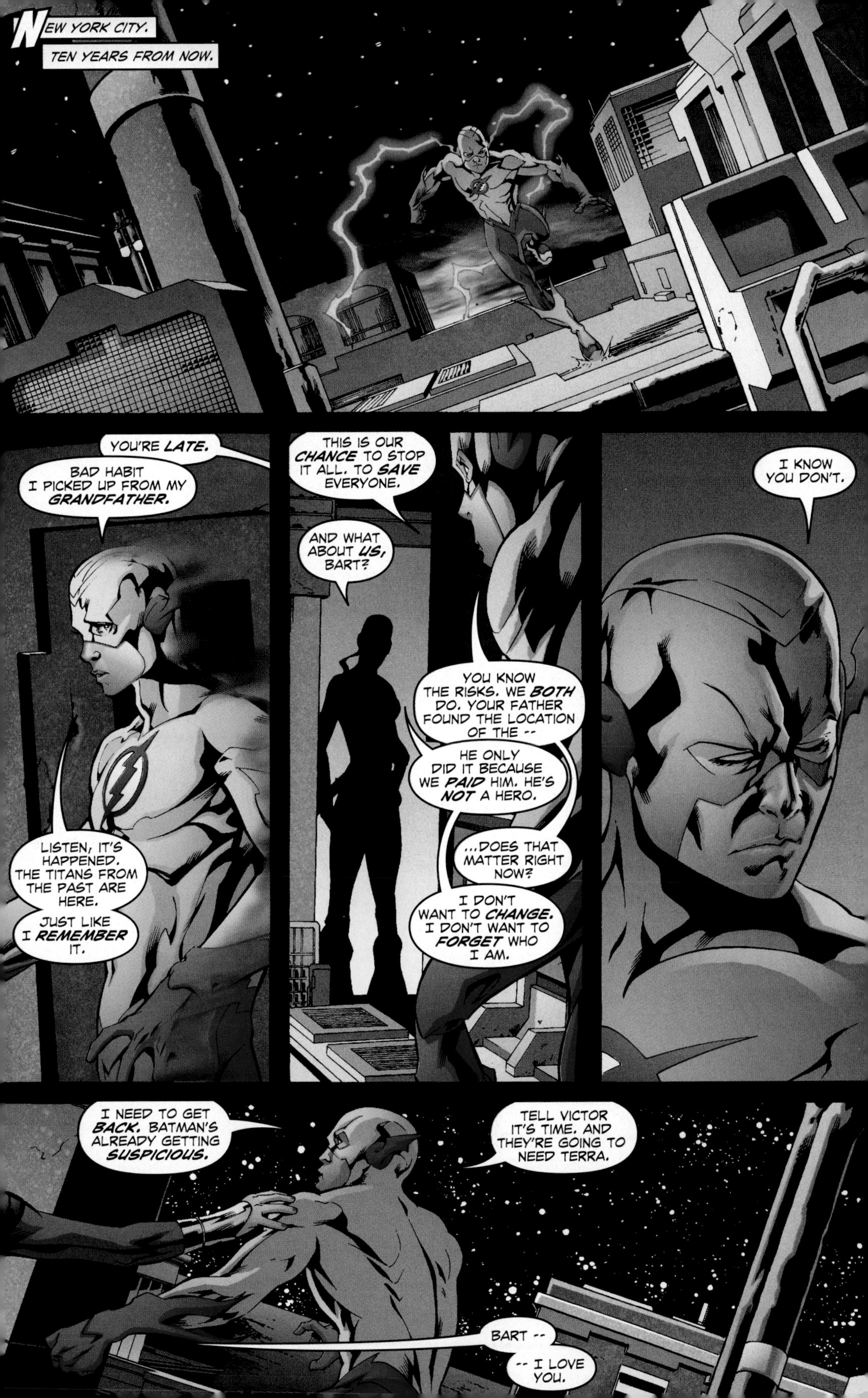
NEW YORK CITY.
TEN YEARS FROM NOW.
YOU'RE LATE.
BAD HABIT I PICKED UP FROM MY GRANDFATHER.
LISTEN, IT'S HAPPENED. THE TITANS FROM THE PAST ARE HERE.
JUST LIKE I REMEMBER IT.
THIS IS OUR CHANCE TO STOP IT ALL. TO SAVE EVERYONE.
AND WHAT ABOUT US, BART?
YOU KNOW THE RISKS. WE BOTH DO. YOUR FATHER FOUND THE LOCATION OF THE --
HE ONLY DID IT BECAUSE WE PAID HIM. HE'S NOT A HERO.
...DOES THAT MATTER RIGHT NOW?
I DON'T WANT TO CHANGE. I DON'T WANT TO FORGET WHO I AM.
I KNOW YOU DON'T.
I NEED TO GET BACK. BATMAN'S ALREADY GETTING SUSPICIOUS.
TELL VICTOR IT'S TIME. AND THEY'RE GOING TO NEED TERRA.
BART --
-- I LOVE YOU.

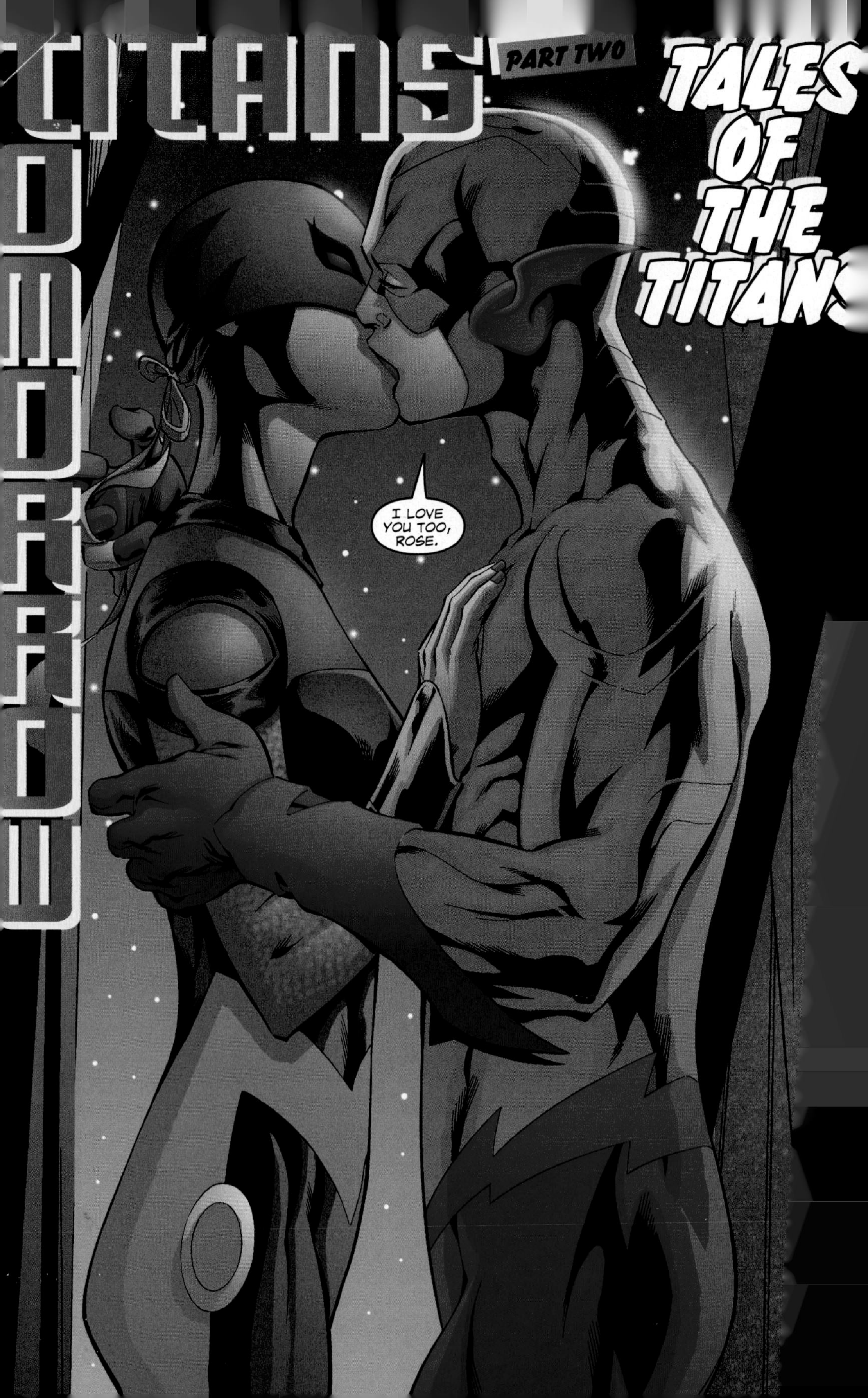
TITANS TOMORROW
PART TWO
TALES OF THE TITANS
I LOVE YOU TOO, ROSE.

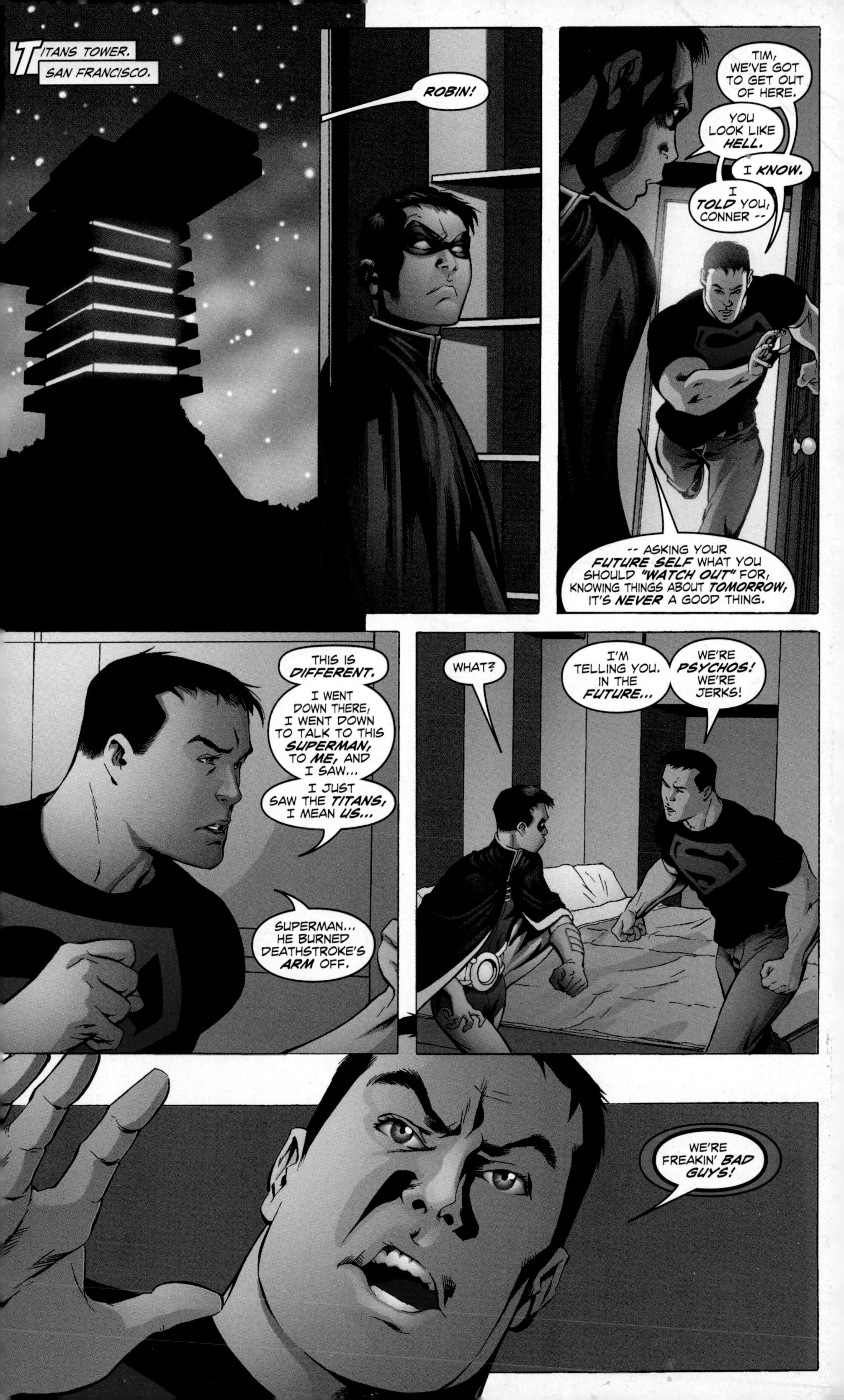
TITANS TOWER.
SAN FRANCISCO.
ROBIN!
TIM, WE'VE GOT TO GET OUT OF HERE.
YOU LOOK LIKE HELL.
I KNOW.
I TOLD YOU, CONNER --
-- ASKING YOUR FUTURE SELF WHAT YOU SHOULD "WATCH OUT" FOR, KNOWING THINGS ABOUT TOMORROW, IT'S NEVER A GOOD THING.
THIS IS DIFFERENT.
I WENT DOWN THERE, I WENT DOWN TO TALK TO THIS SUPERMAN, TO ME, AND I SAW...
I JUST SAW THE TITANS, I MEAN US...
SUPERMAN... HE BURNED DEATHSTROKE'S ARM OFF.
WHAT?
I'M TELLING YOU. IN THE FUTURE...
WE'RE PSYCHOS! WE'RE JERKS!
WE'RE FREAKIN' BAD GUYS!

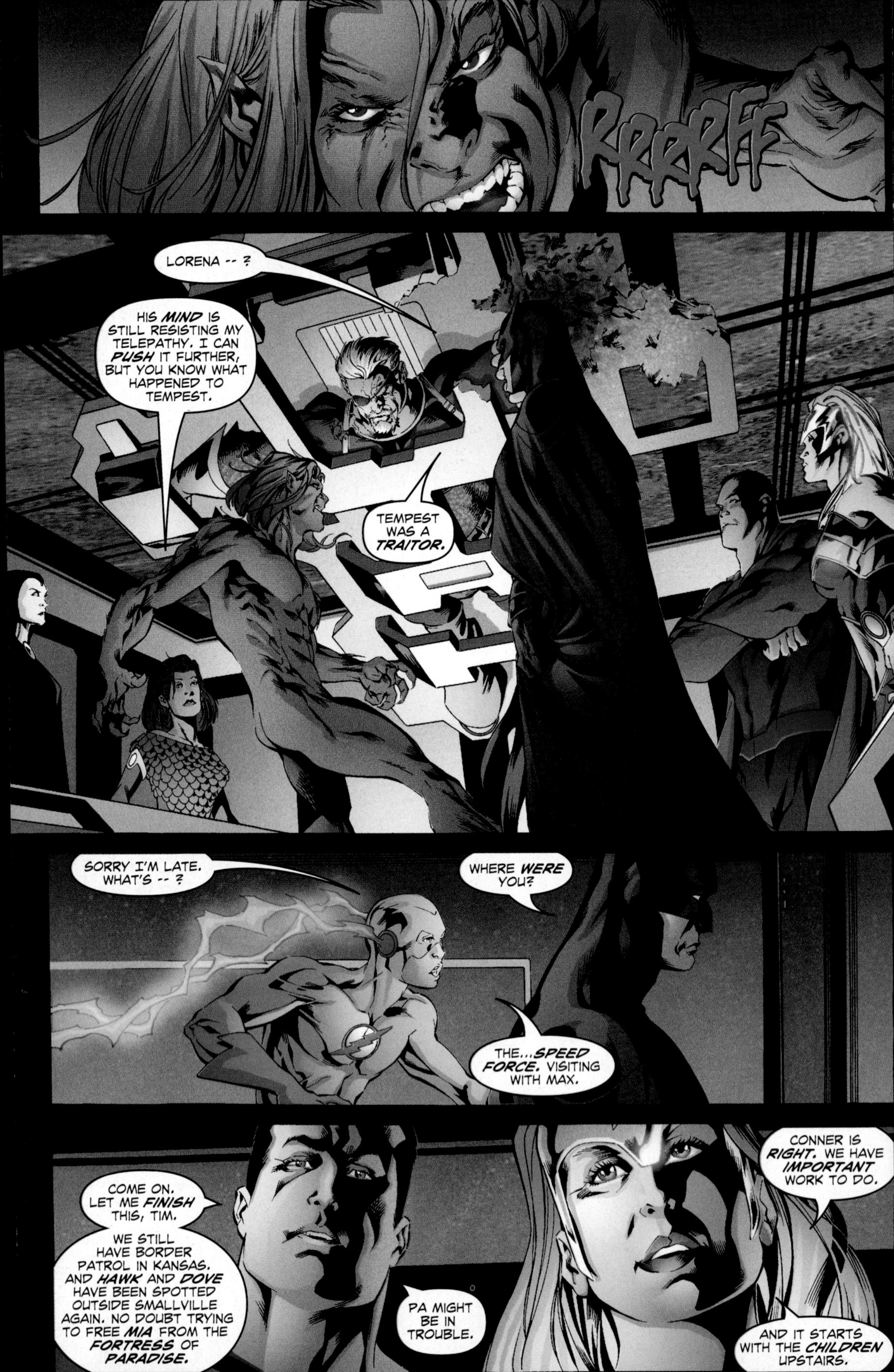
RRRRFF
LORENA -- ?
HIS MIND IS STILL RESISTING MY TELEPATHY. I CAN PUSH IT FURTHER, BUT YOU KNOW WHAT HAPPENED TO TEMPEST.
TEMPEST WAS A TRAITOR.
SORRY I'M LATE. WHAT'S -- ?
WHERE WERE YOU?
THE... SPEED FORCE. VISITING WITH MAX.
COME ON. LET ME FINISH THIS, TIM.
WE STILL HAVE BORDER PATROL IN KANSAS. AND HAWK AND DOVE HAVE BEEN SPOTTED OUTSIDE SMALLVILLE AGAIN. NO DOUBT TRYING TO FREE MIA FROM THE FORTRESS OF PARADISE.
PA MIGHT BE IN TROUBLE.
CONNER IS RIGHT. WE HAVE IMPORTANT WORK TO DO.
AND IT STARTS WITH THE CHILDREN UPSTAIRS.

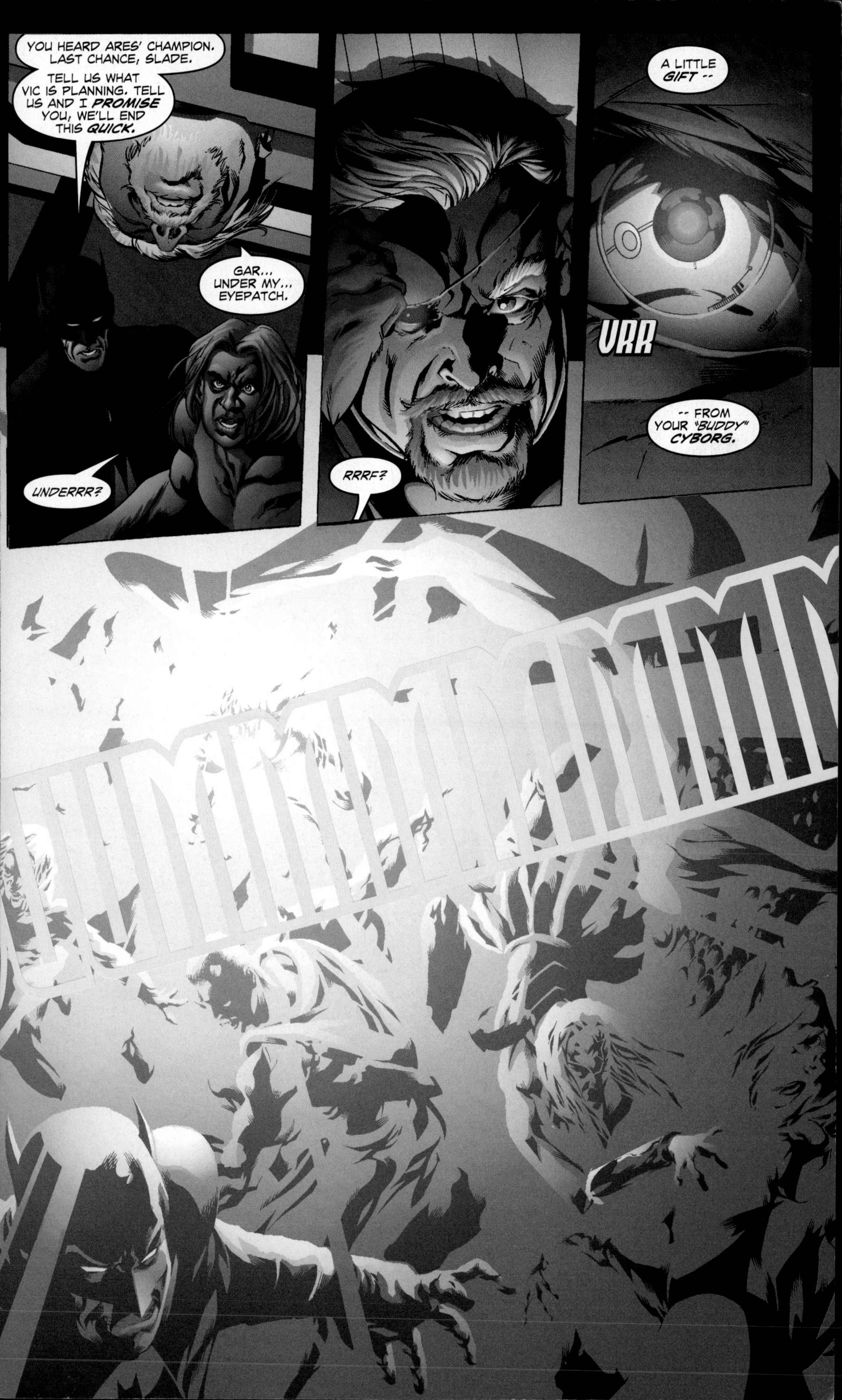

YOU HEARD ARES' CHAMPION. LAST CHANCE, SLADE.
TELL US WHAT VIC IS PLANNING. TELL US AND I *PROMISE* YOU, WE'LL END THIS *QUICK.*
GAR... UNDER MY... EYEPATCH.
UNDERRR?
RRRF?
A LITTLE *GIFT* --
VRR
-- FROM YOUR "BUDDY" CYBORG.

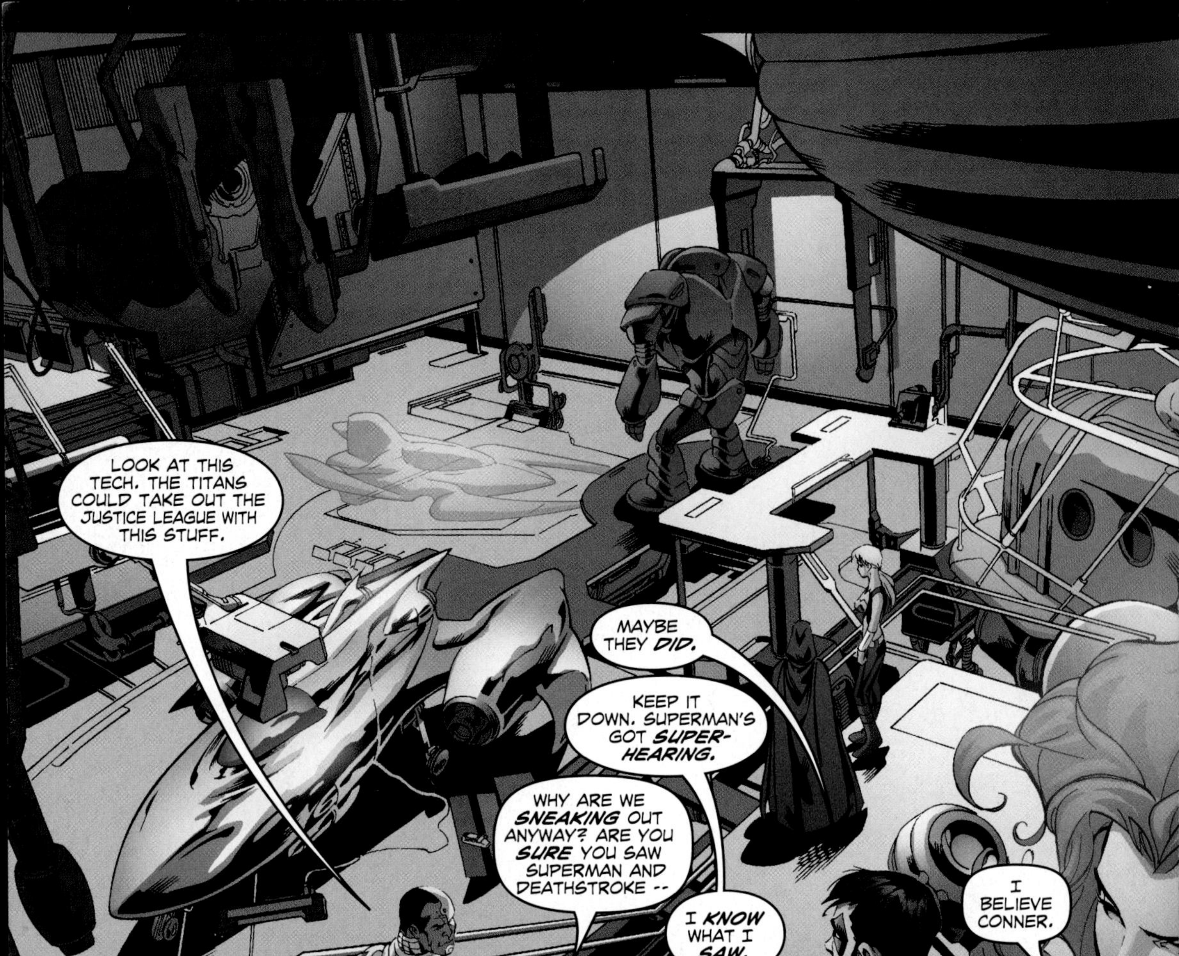
LOOK AT THIS TECH. THE TITANS COULD TAKE OUT THE JUSTICE LEAGUE WITH THIS STUFF.
MAYBE THEY DID.
KEEP IT DOWN. SUPERMAN'S GOT SUPER-HEARING.
WHY ARE WE SNEAKING OUT ANYWAY? ARE YOU SURE YOU SAW SUPERMAN AND DEATHSTROKE --
I KNOW WHAT I SAW.
I BELIEVE CONNER.

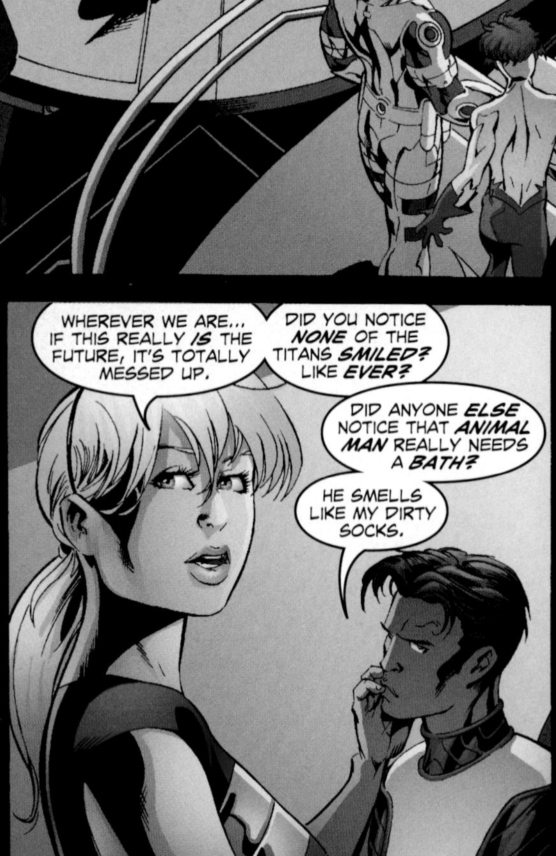
WHEREVER WE ARE... IF THIS REALLY IS THE FUTURE, IT'S TOTALLY MESSED UP.
DID YOU NOTICE NONE OF THE TITANS SMILED? LIKE EVER?
DID ANYONE ELSE NOTICE THAT ANIMAL MAN REALLY NEEDS A BATH?
HE SMELLS LIKE MY DIRTY SOCKS.

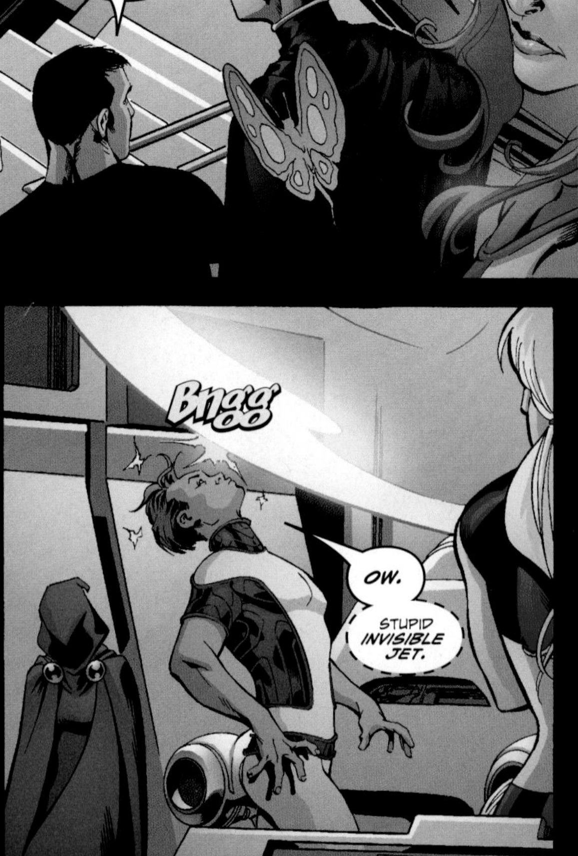
Bngg
OW.
STUPID INVISIBLE JET.

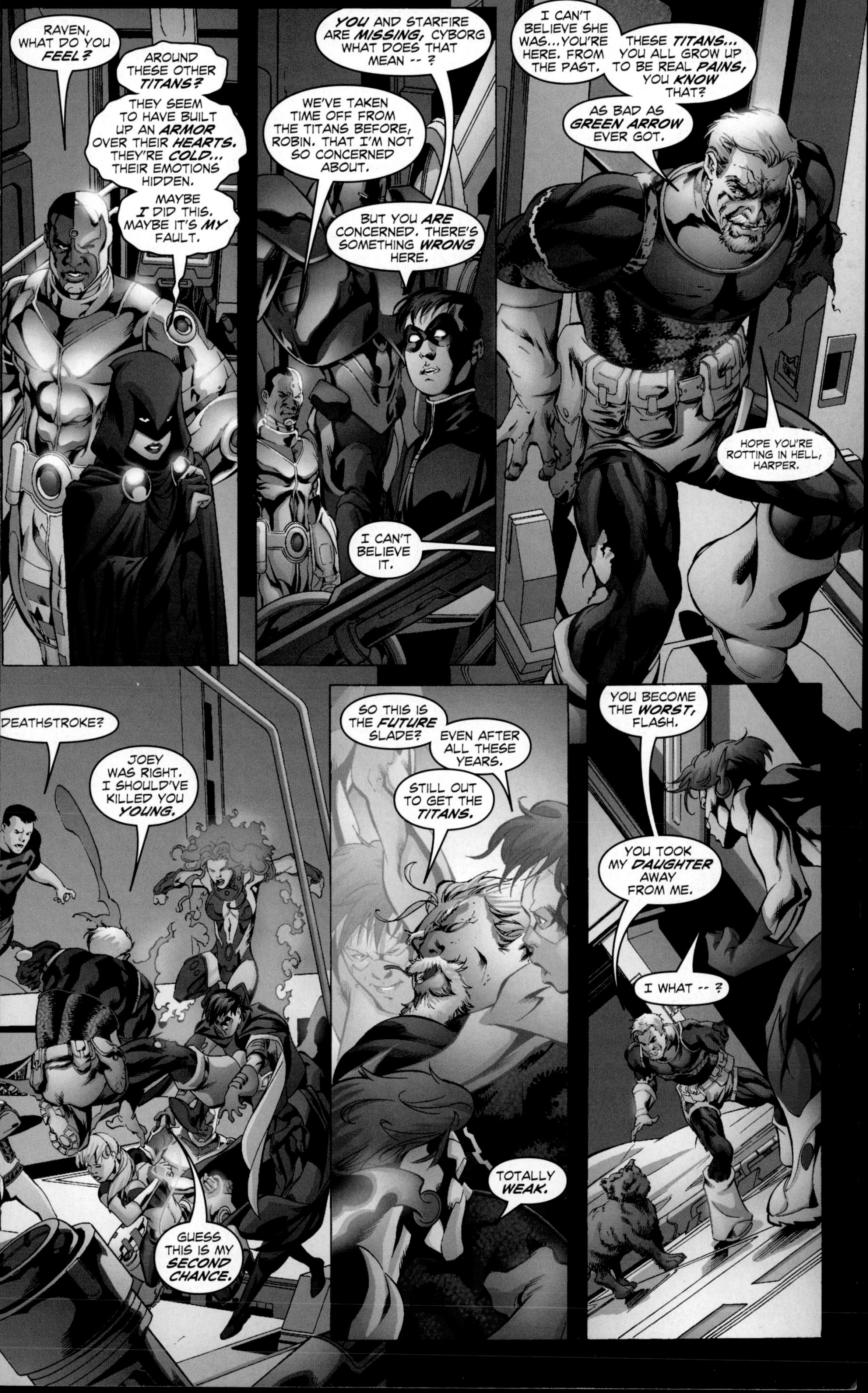
RAVEN, WHAT DO YOU FEEL?
AROUND THESE OTHER TITANS?
THEY SEEM TO HAVE BUILT UP AN ARMOR OVER THEIR HEARTS. THEY'RE COLD... THEIR EMOTIONS HIDDEN.
MAYBE I DID THIS. MAYBE IT'S MY FAULT.
YOU AND STARFIRE ARE MISSING, CYBORG WHAT DOES THAT MEAN -- ?
WE'VE TAKEN TIME OFF FROM THE TITANS BEFORE, ROBIN. THAT I'M NOT SO CONCERNED ABOUT.
BUT YOU ARE CONCERNED. THERE'S SOMETHING WRONG HERE.
I CAN'T BELIEVE IT.
I CAN'T BELIEVE SHE WAS...YOU'RE HERE. FROM THE PAST.
THESE TITANS... YOU ALL GROW UP TO BE REAL PAINS, YOU KNOW THAT?
AS BAD AS GREEN ARROW EVER GOT.
HOPE YOU'RE ROTTING IN HELL, HARPER.
DEATHSTROKE?
JOEY WAS RIGHT. I SHOULD'VE KILLED YOU YOUNG.
GUESS THIS IS MY SECOND CHANCE.
SO THIS IS THE FUTURE SLADE?
EVEN AFTER ALL THESE YEARS.
STILL OUT TO GET THE TITANS.
TOTALLY WEAK.
YOU BECOME THE WORST, FLASH.
YOU TOOK MY DAUGHTER AWAY FROM ME.
I WHAT -- ?

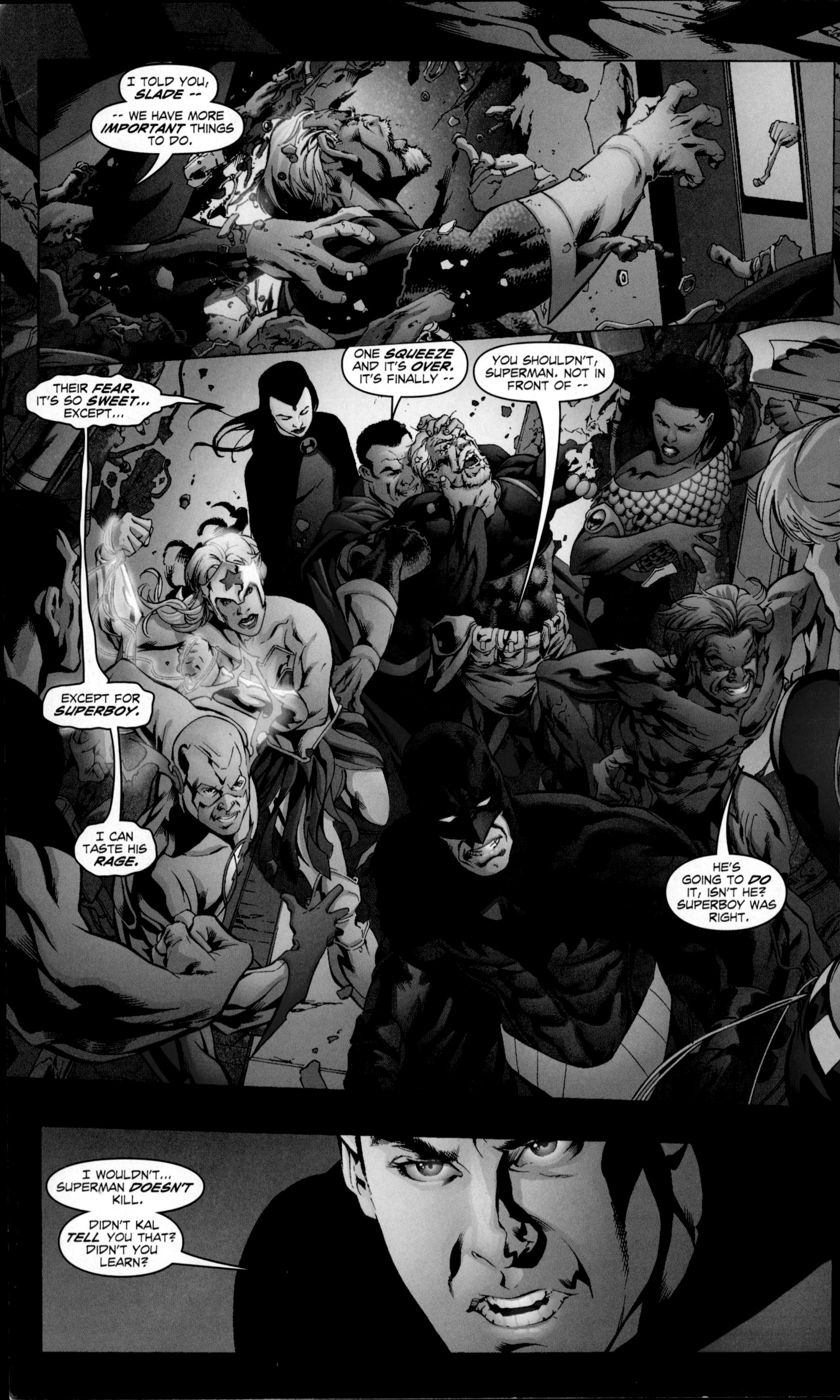
I TOLD YOU, SLADE --
-- WE HAVE MORE IMPORTANT THINGS TO DO.
THEIR FEAR. IT'S SO SWEET... EXCEPT...
ONE SQUEEZE AND IT'S OVER. IT'S FINALLY --
YOU SHOULDN'T, SUPERMAN. NOT IN FRONT OF --
EXCEPT FOR SUPERBOY.
I CAN TASTE HIS RAGE.
HE'S GOING TO DO IT, ISN'T HE? SUPERBOY WAS RIGHT.
I WOULDN'T... SUPERMAN DOESN'T KILL.
DIDN'T KAL TELL YOU THAT? DIDN'T YOU LEARN?

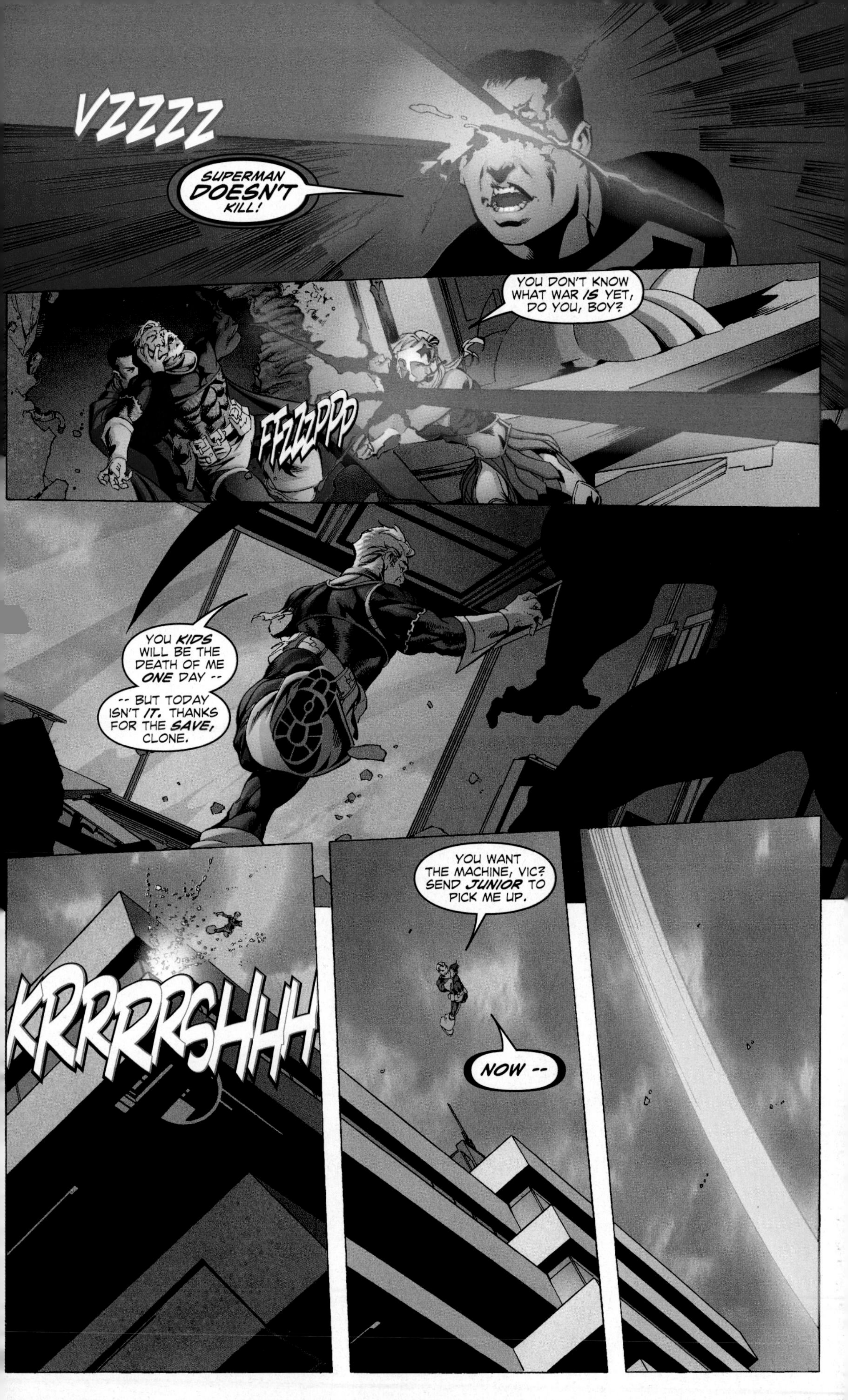
VZZZZ
SUPERMAN DOESN'T KILL!
YOU DON'T KNOW WHAT WAR IS YET, DO YOU, BOY?
FFZZZPPP
YOU KIDS WILL BE THE DEATH OF ME ONE DAY --
-- BUT TODAY ISN'T IT. THANKS FOR THE SAVE, CLONE.
KRRRRSHHH
YOU WANT THE MACHINE, VIC? SEND JUNIOR TO PICK ME UP.
NOW --

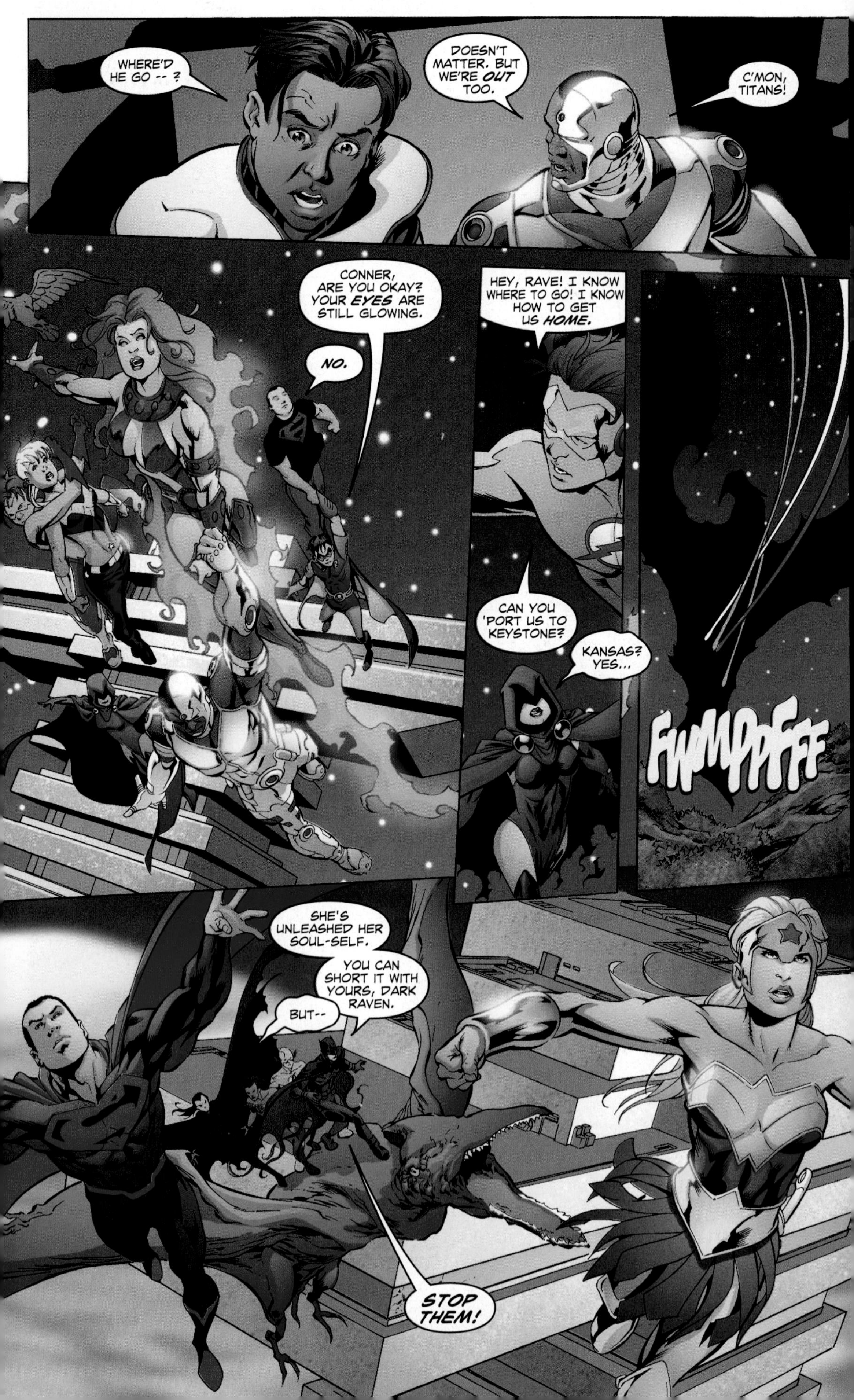
WHERE'D HE GO -- ?
DOESN'T MATTER. BUT WE'RE OUT TOO.
C'MON, TITANS!
CONNER, ARE YOU OKAY? YOUR EYES ARE STILL GLOWING.
NO.
HEY, RAVE! I KNOW WHERE TO GO! I KNOW HOW TO GET US HOME.
CAN YOU 'PORT US TO KEYSTONE?
KANSAS? YES...
FWMPDFFF
SHE'S UNLEASHED HER SOUL-SELF.
YOU CAN SHORT IT WITH YOURS, DARK RAVEN.
BUT--
STOP THEM!

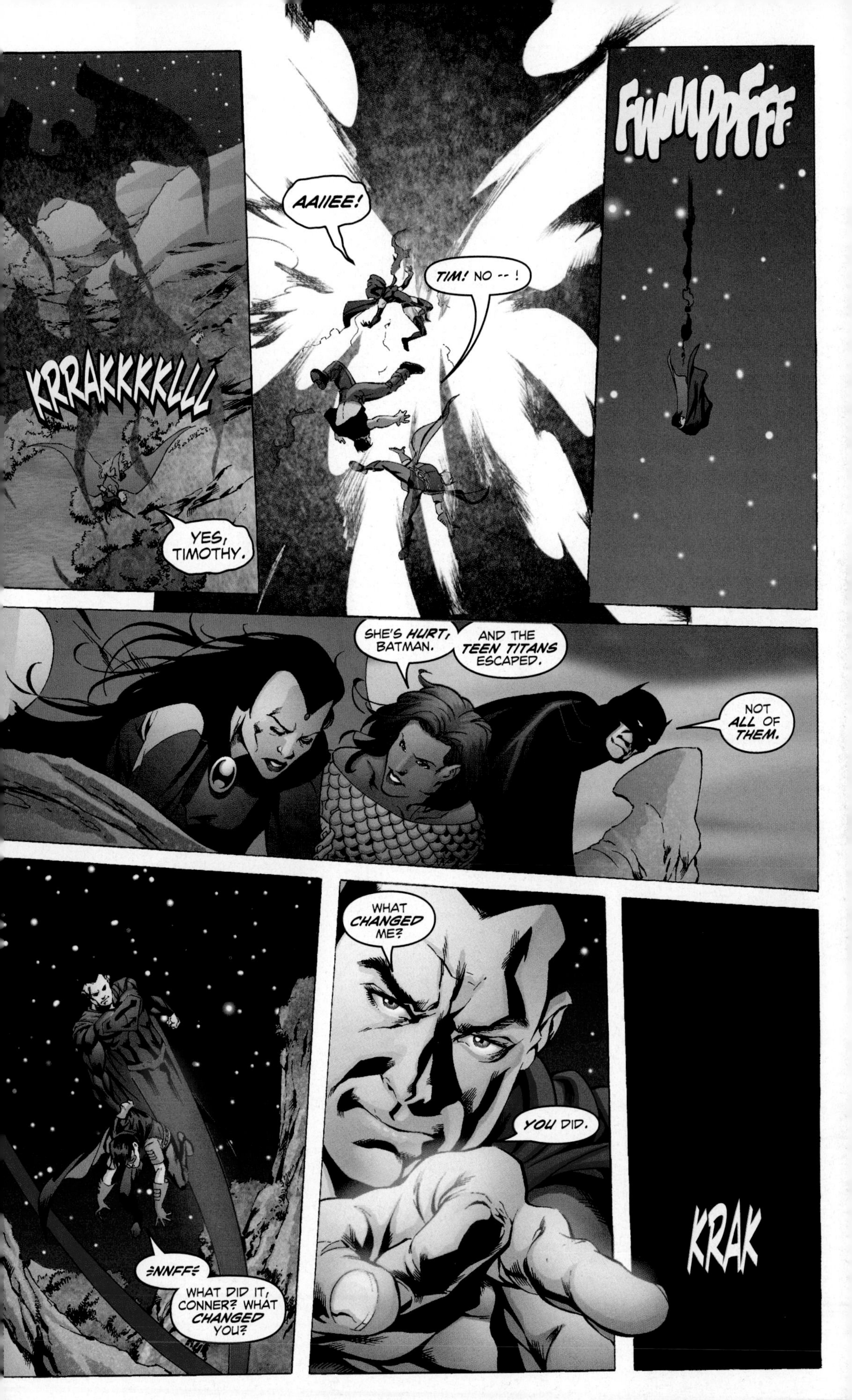
KRRAKKKKLLL
YES, TIMOTHY.
AAIIEE!
TIM! NO -- !
FWMPDFFF
SHE'S HURT, BATMAN.
AND THE TEEN TITANS ESCAPED.
NOT ALL OF THEM.
=NNFF=
WHAT DID IT, CONNER? WHAT CHANGED YOU?
WHAT CHANGED ME?
YOU DID.
KRAK

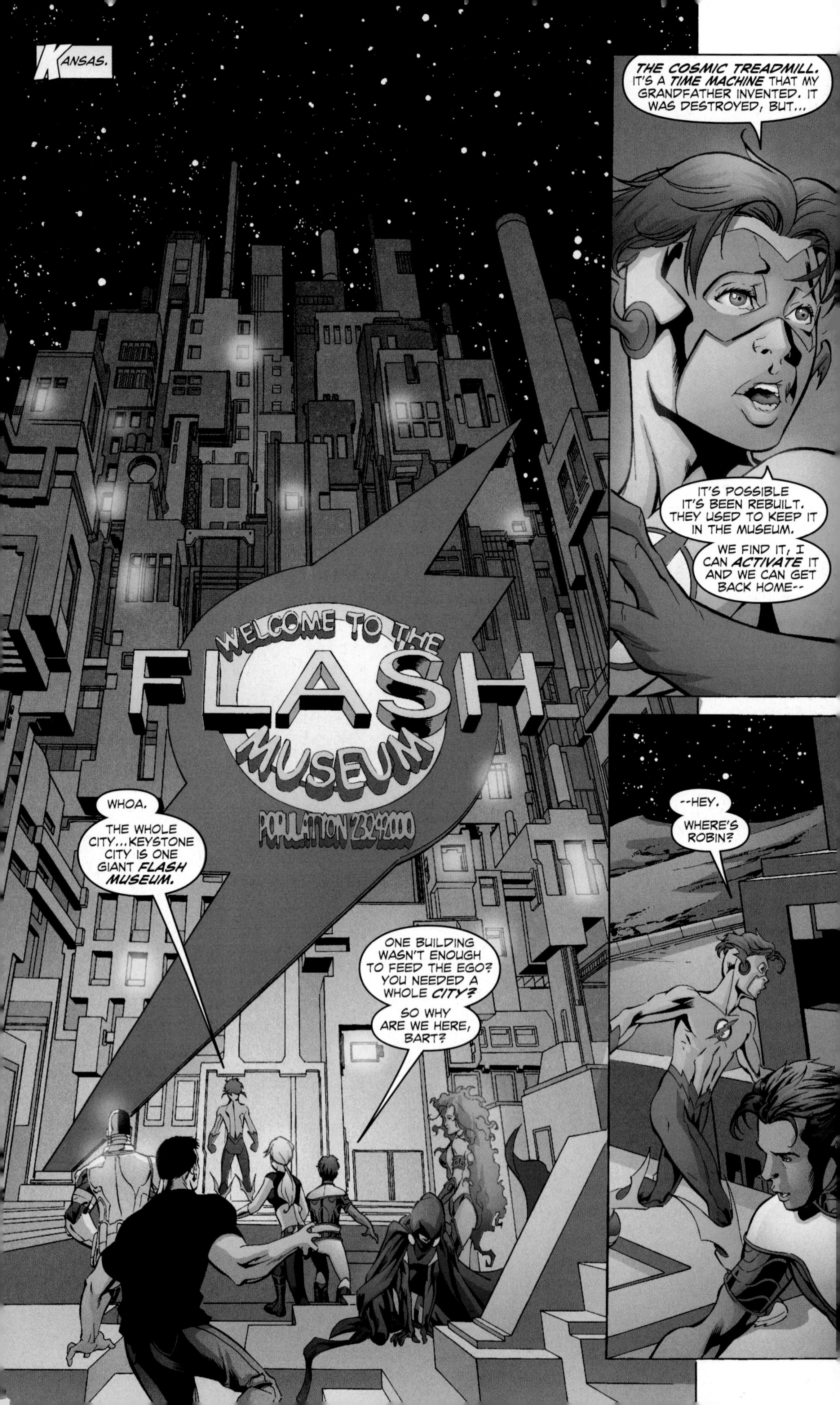
KANSAS.
WELCOME TO THE
FLASH
MUSEUM
POPULATION 23242000
WHOA.
THE WHOLE CITY... KEYSTONE CITY IS ONE GIANT FLASH MUSEUM.
ONE BUILDING WASN'T ENOUGH TO FEED THE EGO? YOU NEEDED A WHOLE CITY?
SO WHY ARE WE HERE, BART?
THE COSMIC TREADMILL. IT'S A TIME MACHINE THAT MY GRANDFATHER INVENTED. IT WAS DESTROYED, BUT...
IT'S POSSIBLE IT'S BEEN REBUILT. THEY USED TO KEEP IT IN THE MUSEUM.
WE FIND IT, I CAN ACTIVATE IT AND WE CAN GET BACK HOME--
--HEY.
WHERE'S ROBIN?

WHEN RAVEN'S SOUL-SELVES INTEGRATED, ROBIN WAS THROWN *CLEAR.*

WE NEED TO GO BACK. WE NEED TO GO BACK AND GET TIM. YOU SAW WHAT THEY DID TO DEATHSTROKE--

I... I CAN'T TELEPORT, CONNER. I NEED TO... REST. JUST GIVE ME A MINUTE TO...

LET HER REST. THEY *CAN'T* HURT ROBIN WITHOUT HURTING *BATMAN.* WE GET THE TIME MACHINE THEN WE HEAD BACK TO THE TOWER--

I'LL GO BY *MYSELF* IF I HAVE --

WE DON'T STAND A CHANCE UNLESS WE DO THIS TOGETHER.

VIC--

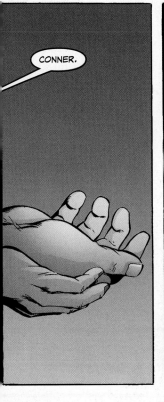

CONNER.

CYBORG'S RIGHT.

WE HAVE TO DO THIS *TOGETHER.*

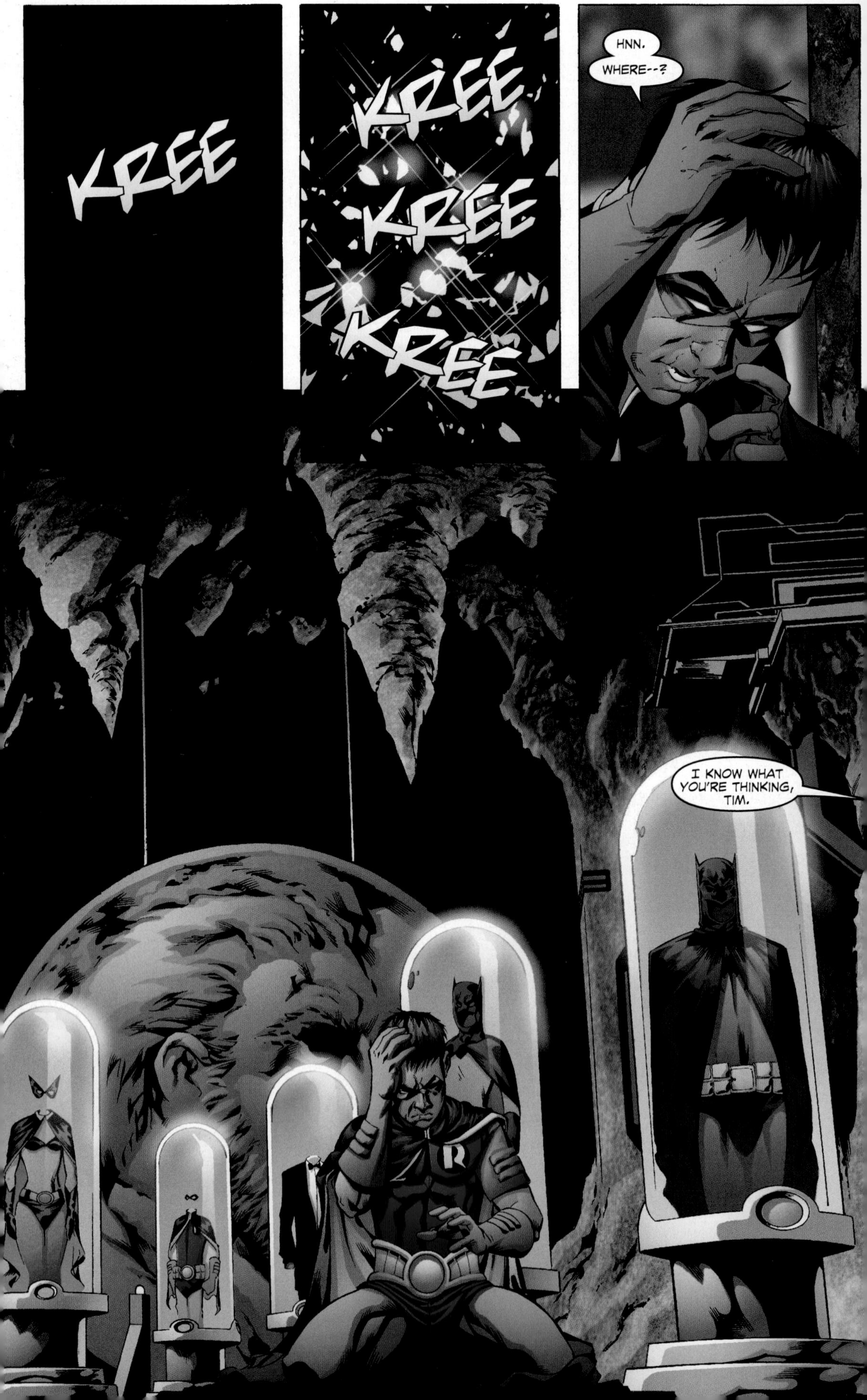
KREE
KREE
KREE
KREE
HNN. WHERE--?
I KNOW WHAT YOU'RE THINKING, TIM.

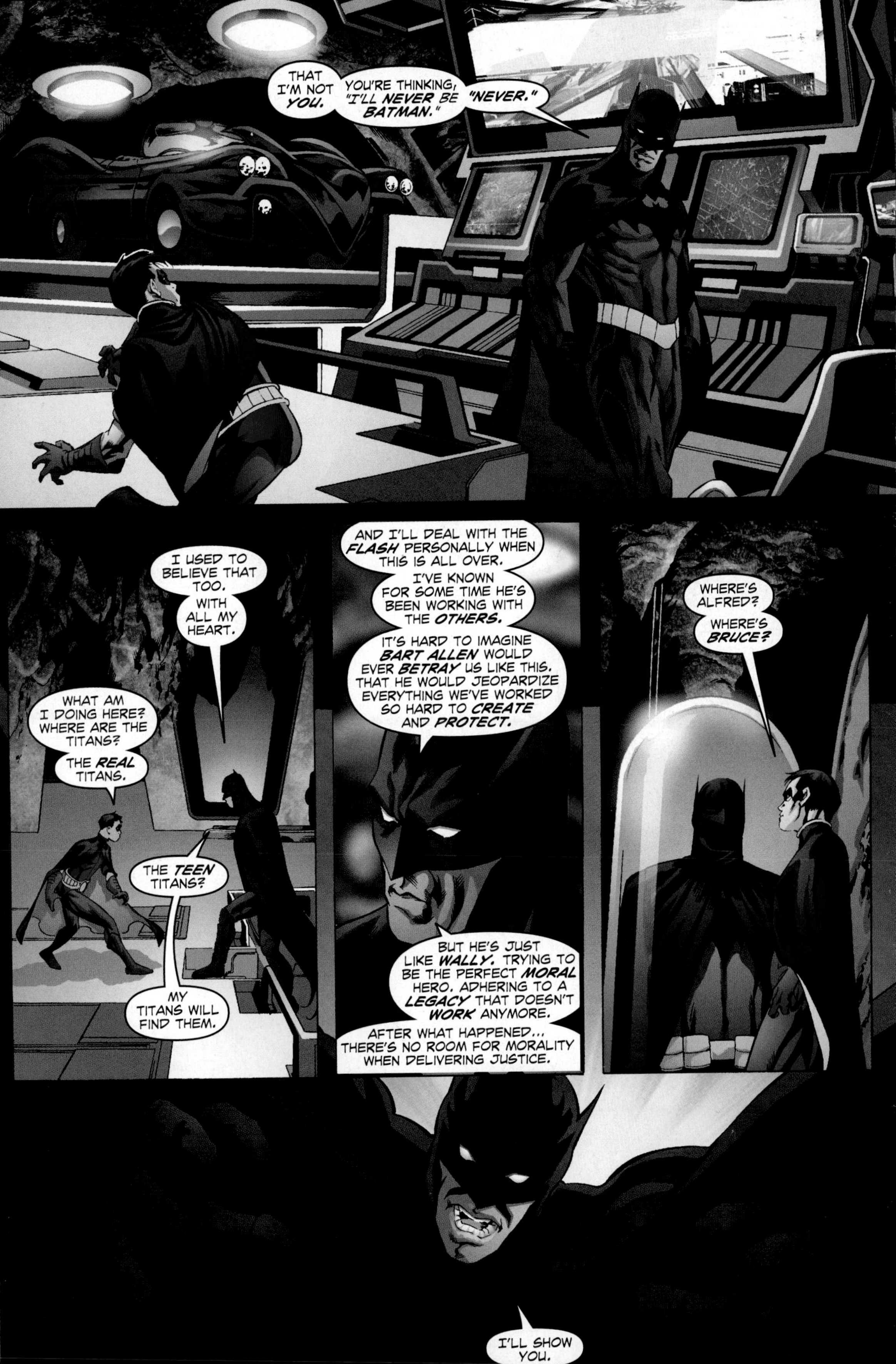

THAT I'M NOT YOU.
YOU'RE THINKING, "I'LL NEVER BE BATMAN."
"NEVER."
I USED TO BELIEVE THAT TOO.
WITH ALL MY HEART.
WHAT AM I DOING HERE? WHERE ARE THE TITANS?
THE REAL TITANS.
THE TEEN TITANS?
MY TITANS WILL FIND THEM.
AND I'LL DEAL WITH THE FLASH PERSONALLY WHEN THIS IS ALL OVER.
I'VE KNOWN FOR SOME TIME HE'S BEEN WORKING WITH THE OTHERS.
IT'S HARD TO IMAGINE BART ALLEN WOULD EVER BETRAY US LIKE THIS. THAT HE WOULD JEOPARDIZE EVERYTHING WE'VE WORKED SO HARD TO CREATE AND PROTECT.
BUT HE'S JUST LIKE WALLY. TRYING TO BE THE PERFECT MORAL HERO. ADHERING TO A LEGACY THAT DOESN'T WORK ANYMORE.
AFTER WHAT HAPPENED... THERE'S NO ROOM FOR MORALITY WHEN DELIVERING JUSTICE.
WHERE'S ALFRED?
WHERE'S BRUCE?
I'LL SHOW YOU.

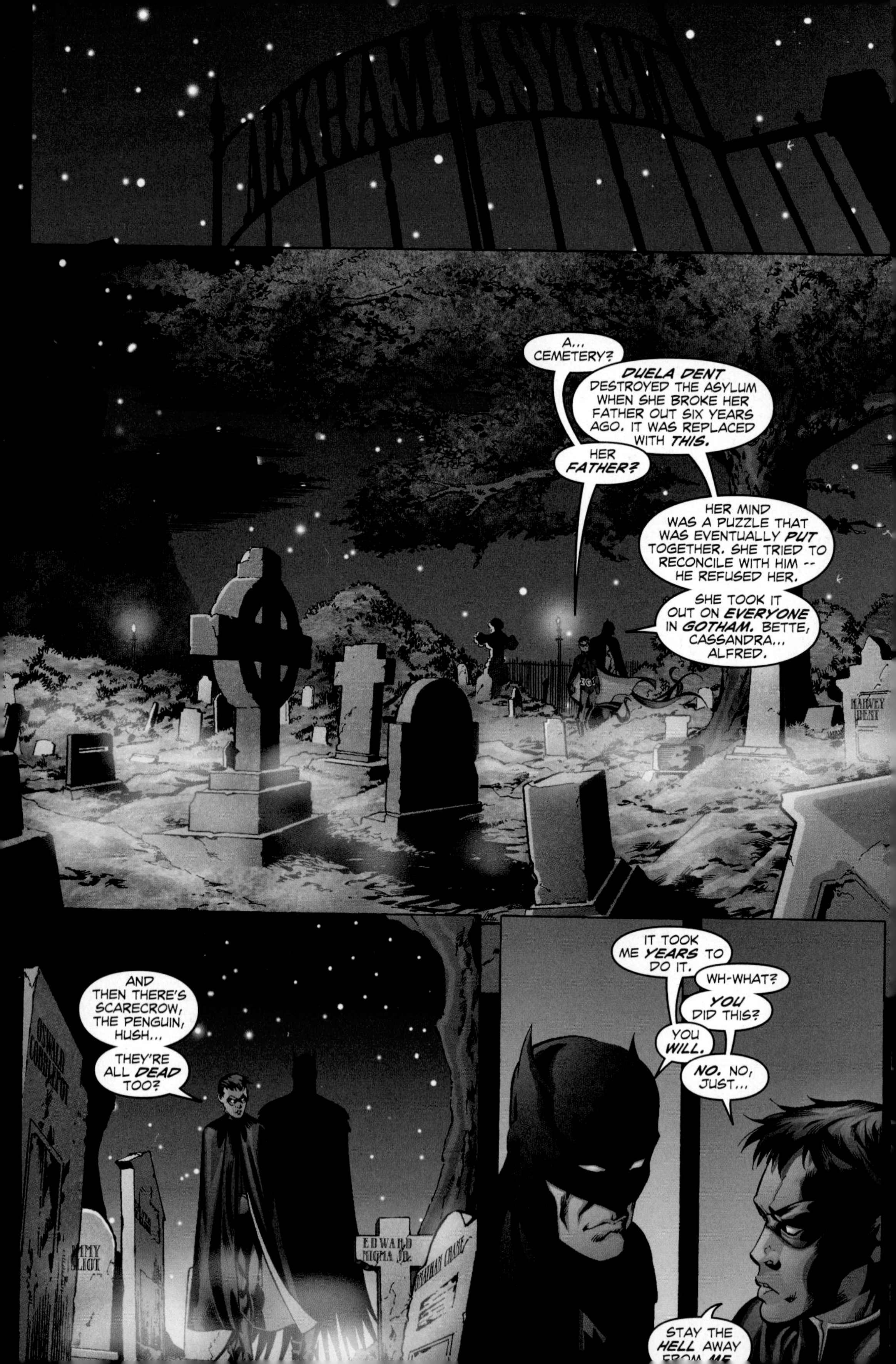
ARKHAM ASYLUM
A... CEMETERY?
DUELA DENT DESTROYED THE ASYLUM WHEN SHE BROKE HER FATHER OUT SIX YEARS AGO. IT WAS REPLACED WITH THIS.
HER FATHER?
HER MIND WAS A PUZZLE THAT WAS EVENTUALLY PUT TOGETHER. SHE TRIED TO RECONCILE WITH HIM -- HE REFUSED HER.
SHE TOOK IT OUT ON EVERYONE IN GOTHAM. BETTE, CASSANDRA... ALFRED.
HARVEY DENT
AND THEN THERE'S SCARECROW, THE PENGUIN, HUSH...
THEY'RE ALL DEAD TOO?
EDWARD NIGMA JR.
IT TOOK ME YEARS TO DO IT.
WH-WHAT?
YOU DID THIS?
YOU WILL.
NO. NO, JUST...
STAY THE HELL AWAY

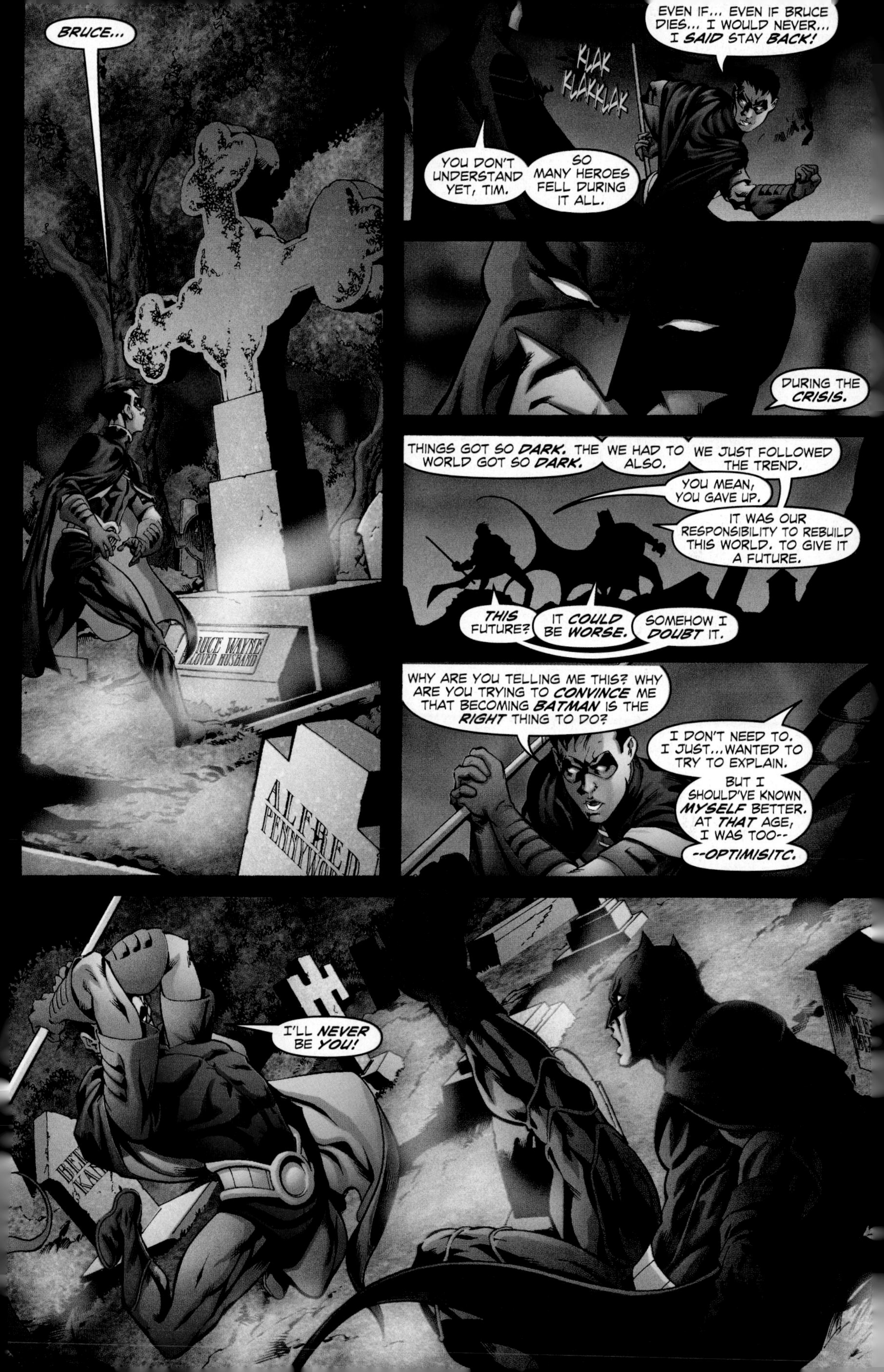
BRUCE...
EVEN IF... EVEN IF BRUCE DIES... I WOULD NEVER... I SAID STAY BACK!
KLAK KLAKKLAK
YOU DON'T UNDERSTAND YET, TIM.
SO MANY HEROES FELL DURING IT ALL.
DURING THE CRISIS.
THINGS GOT SO DARK. THE WORLD GOT SO DARK.
WE HAD TO ALSO.
WE JUST FOLLOWED THE TREND.
YOU MEAN, YOU GAVE UP.
IT WAS OUR RESPONSIBILITY TO REBUILD THIS WORLD. TO GIVE IT A FUTURE.
THIS FUTURE?
IT COULD BE WORSE.
SOMEHOW I DOUBT IT.
WHY ARE YOU TELLING ME THIS? WHY ARE YOU TRYING TO CONVINCE ME THAT BECOMING BATMAN IS THE RIGHT THING TO DO?
I DON'T NEED TO. I JUST...WANTED TO TRY TO EXPLAIN.
BUT I SHOULD'VE KNOWN MYSELF BETTER. AT THAT AGE, I WAS TOO--
--OPTIMISITC.
I'LL NEVER BE YOU!
RUCE WAYNE
BELOVED HUSBAND
ALFRED PENNYWO

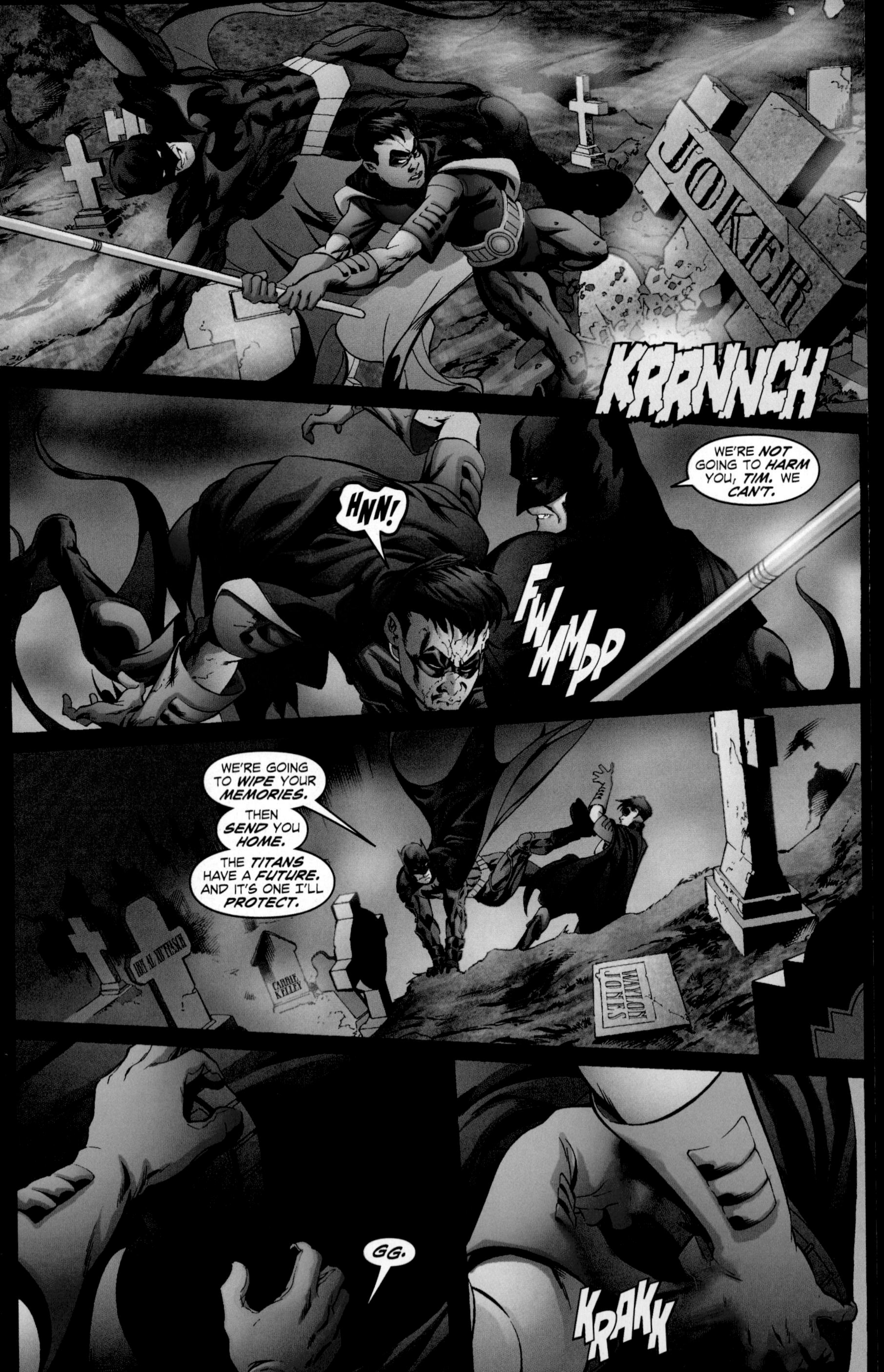
JOKER
KRANNCH
WE'RE NOT GOING TO HARM YOU, TIM. WE CAN'T.
HNN!
FWMMPP
WE'RE GOING TO WIPE YOUR MEMORIES.
THEN SEND YOU HOME.
THE TITANS HAVE A FUTURE. AND IT'S ONE I'LL PROTECT.
CARRIE KELLEY
WAYLON JONES
GG.
KRAKK

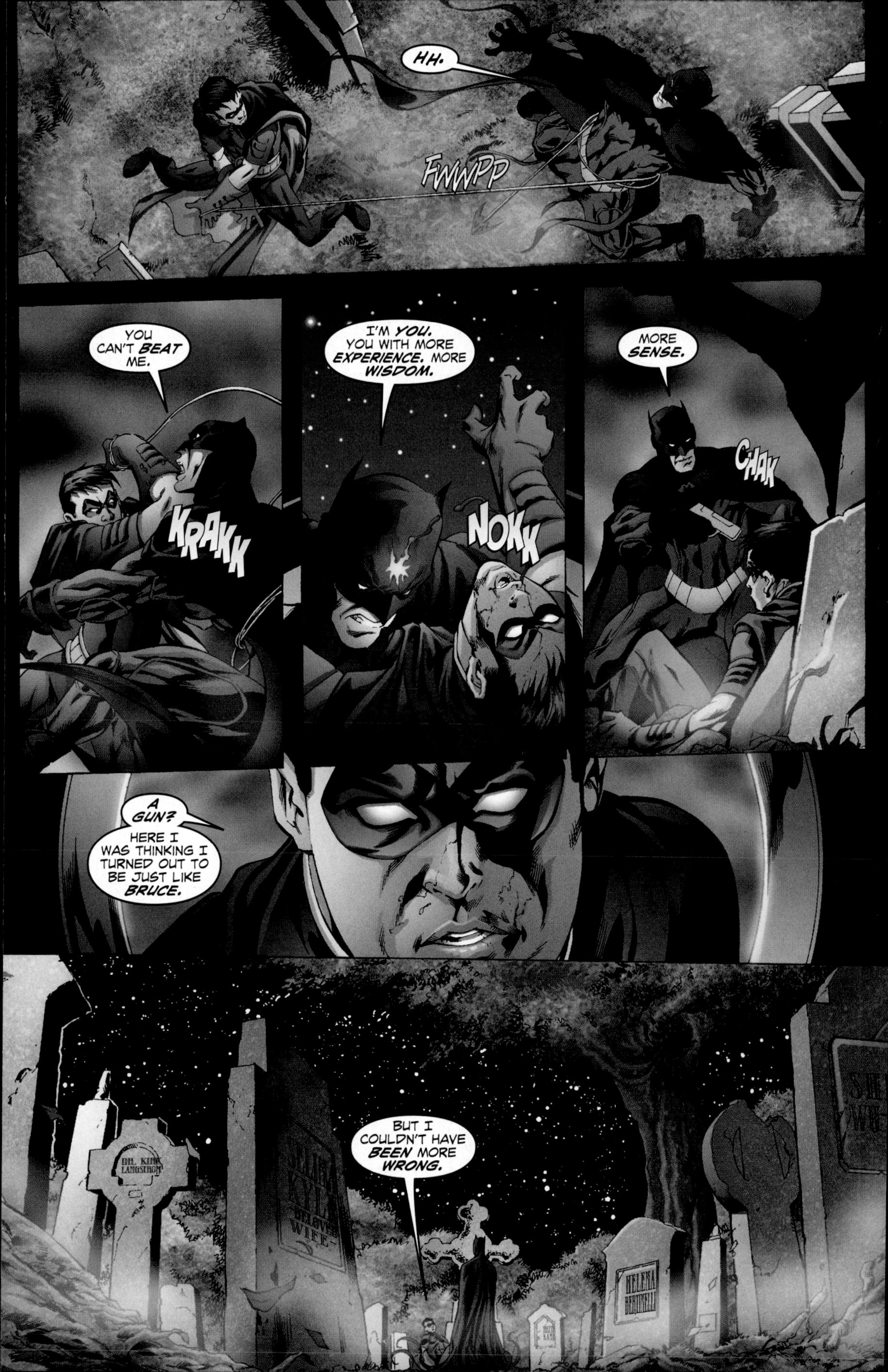
HH.
FWWPP
YOU CAN'T BEAT ME.
KRAKK
I'M YOU. YOU WITH MORE EXPERIENCE. MORE WISDOM.
NOKK
MORE SENSE.
CHAK
A GUN? HERE I WAS THINKING I TURNED OUT TO BE JUST LIKE BRUCE.
BUT I COULDN'T HAVE BEEN MORE WRONG.

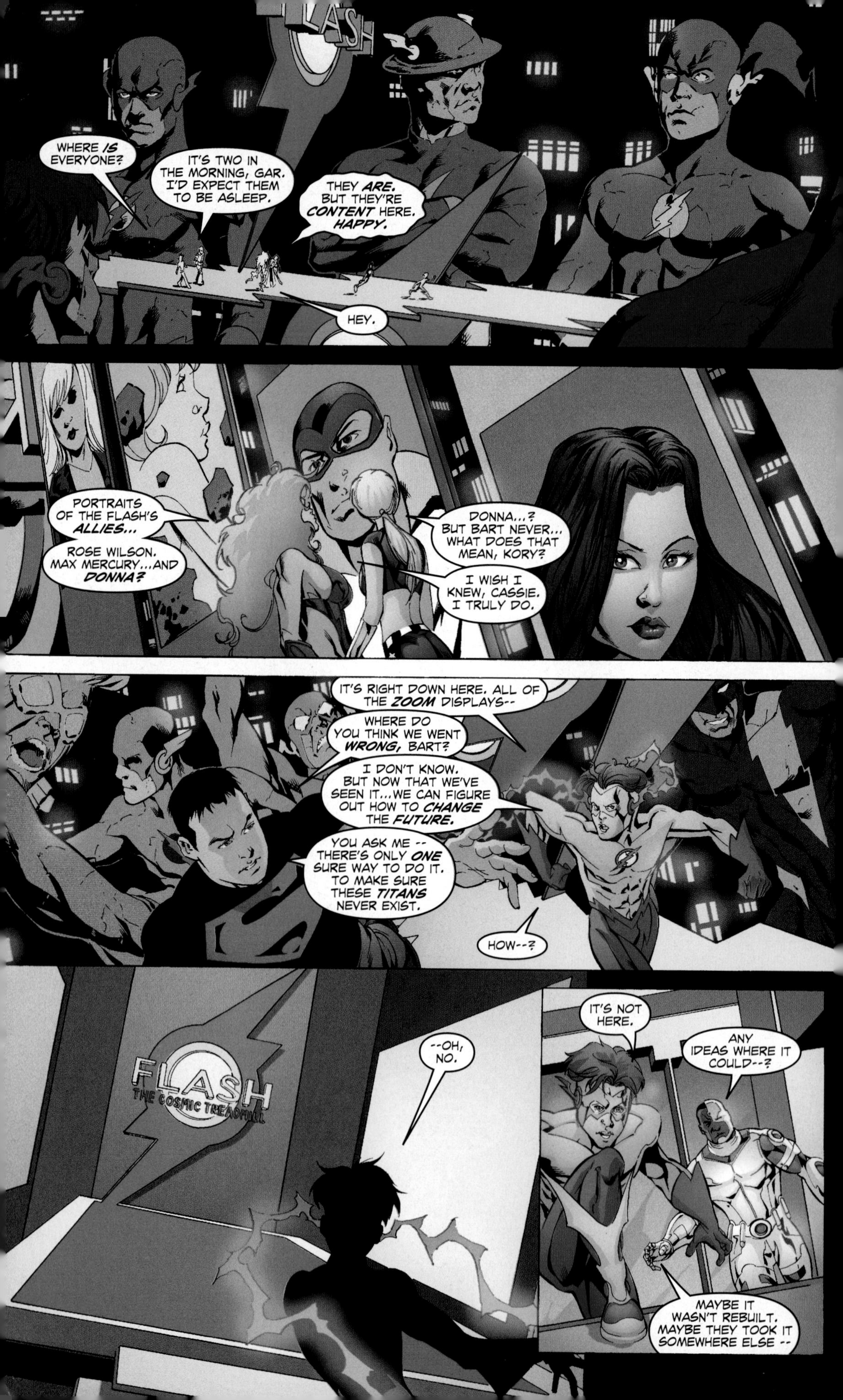
FLASH
WHERE IS EVERYONE?
IT'S TWO IN THE MORNING, GAR. I'D EXPECT THEM TO BE ASLEEP.
THEY ARE. BUT THEY'RE CONTENT HERE. HAPPY.
HEY.
PORTRAITS OF THE FLASH'S ALLIES...
ROSE WILSON. MAX MERCURY...AND DONNA?
DONNA...? BUT BART NEVER... WHAT DOES THAT MEAN, KORY?
I WISH I KNEW, CASSIE. I TRULY DO.
IT'S RIGHT DOWN HERE. ALL OF THE ZOOM DISPLAYS--
WHERE DO YOU THINK WE WENT WRONG, BART?
I DON'T KNOW. BUT NOW THAT WE'VE SEEN IT...WE CAN FIGURE OUT HOW TO CHANGE THE FUTURE.
YOU ASK ME -- THERE'S ONLY ONE SURE WAY TO DO IT. TO MAKE SURE THESE TITANS NEVER EXIST.
HOW--?
FLASH THE COSMIC TREADMILL
--OH, NO.
IT'S NOT HERE.
ANY IDEAS WHERE IT COULD--?
MAYBE IT WASN'T REBUILT. MAYBE THEY TOOK IT SOMEWHERE ELSE --

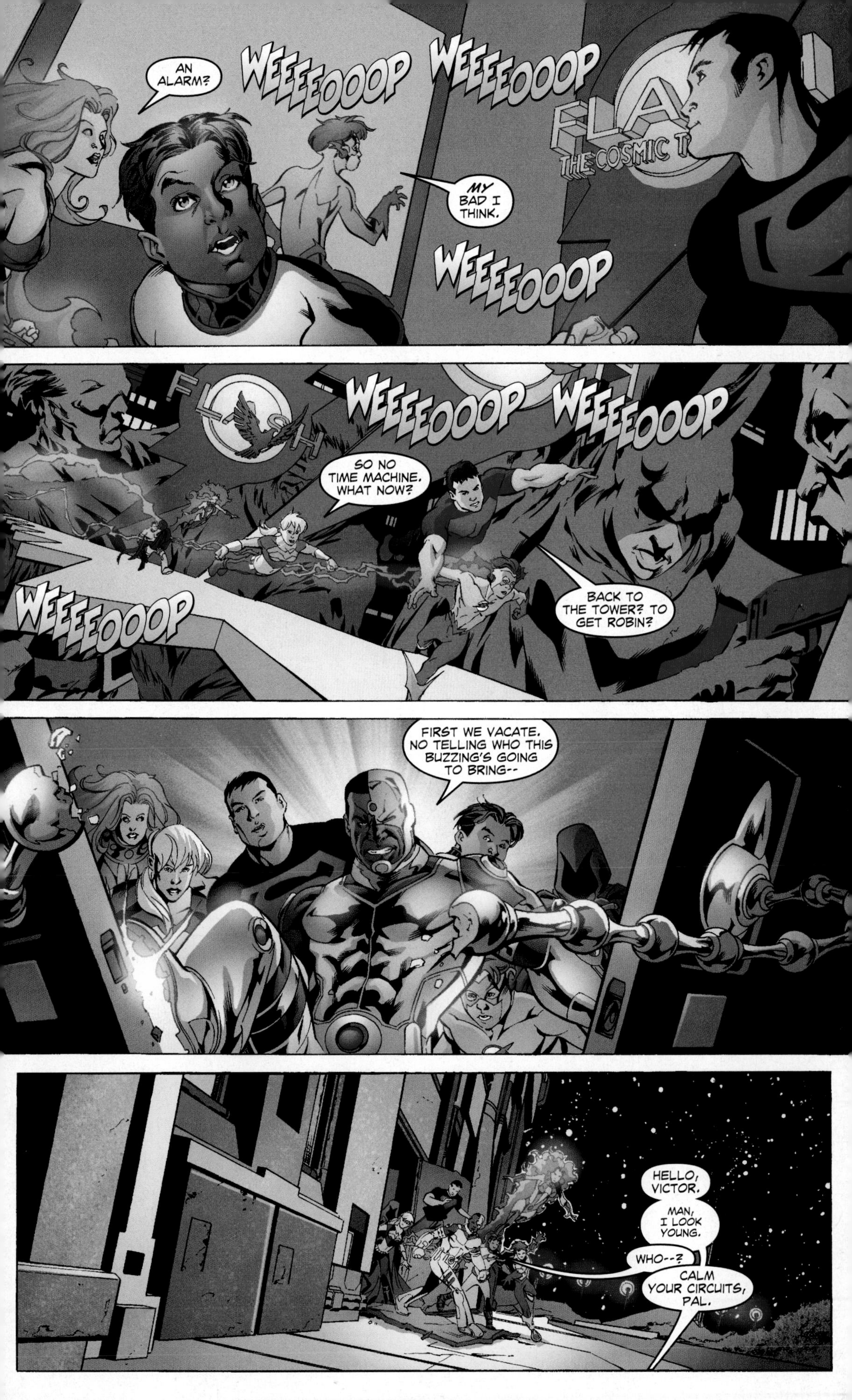
AN ALARM?
WEEEEOOOP WEEEEOOOP
FLA
THE COSMIC T
MY BAD I THINK.
WEEEEOOOP
FLASH
WEEEEOOOP WEEEEOOOP
SO NO TIME MACHINE. WHAT NOW?
WEEEEOOOP
BACK TO THE TOWER? TO GET ROBIN?
FIRST WE VACATE. NO TELLING WHO THIS BUZZING'S GOING TO BRING--
HELLO, VICTOR.
MAN, I LOOK YOUNG.
WHO--?
CALM YOUR CIRCUITS, PAL.

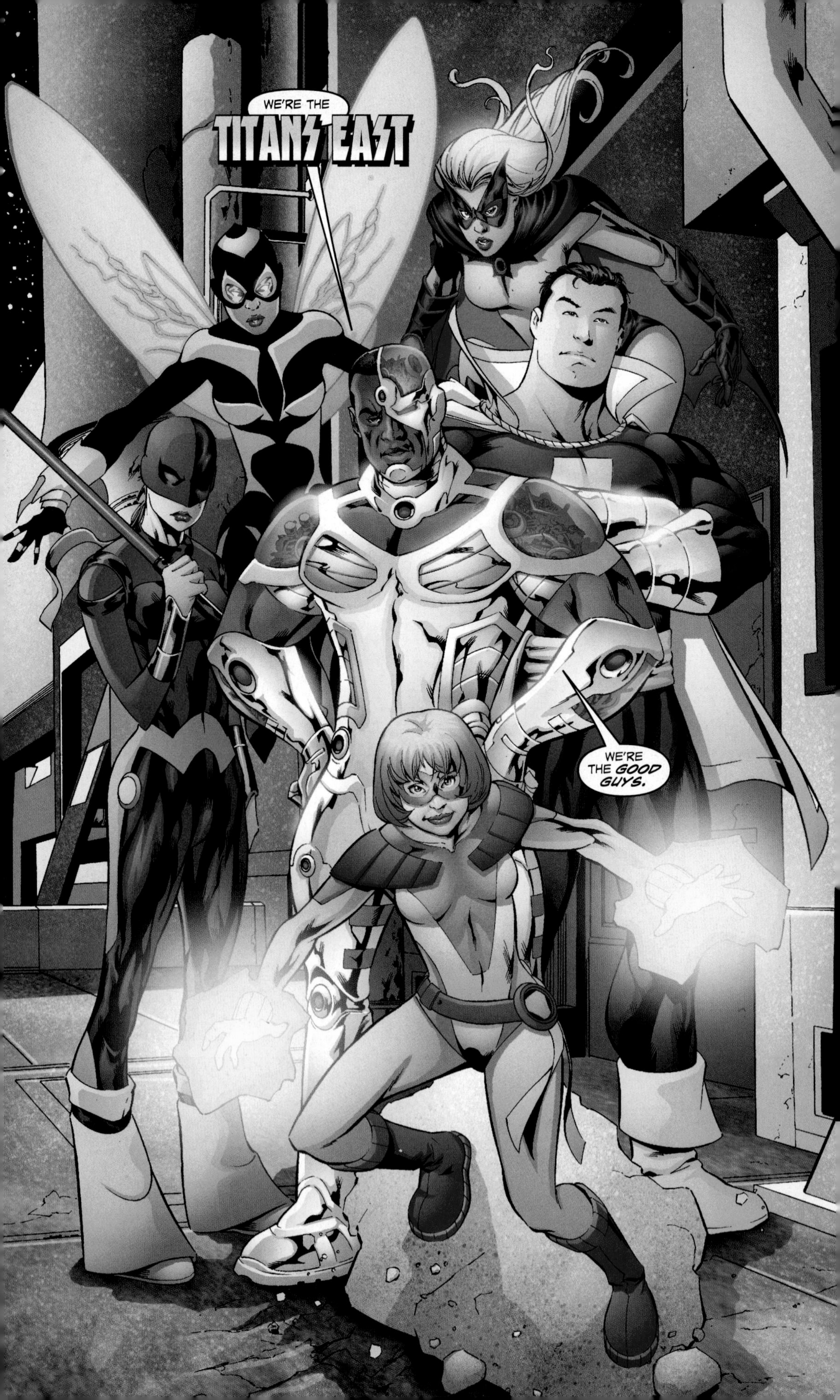
WE'RE THE TITANS EAST
WE'RE THE GOOD GUYS.

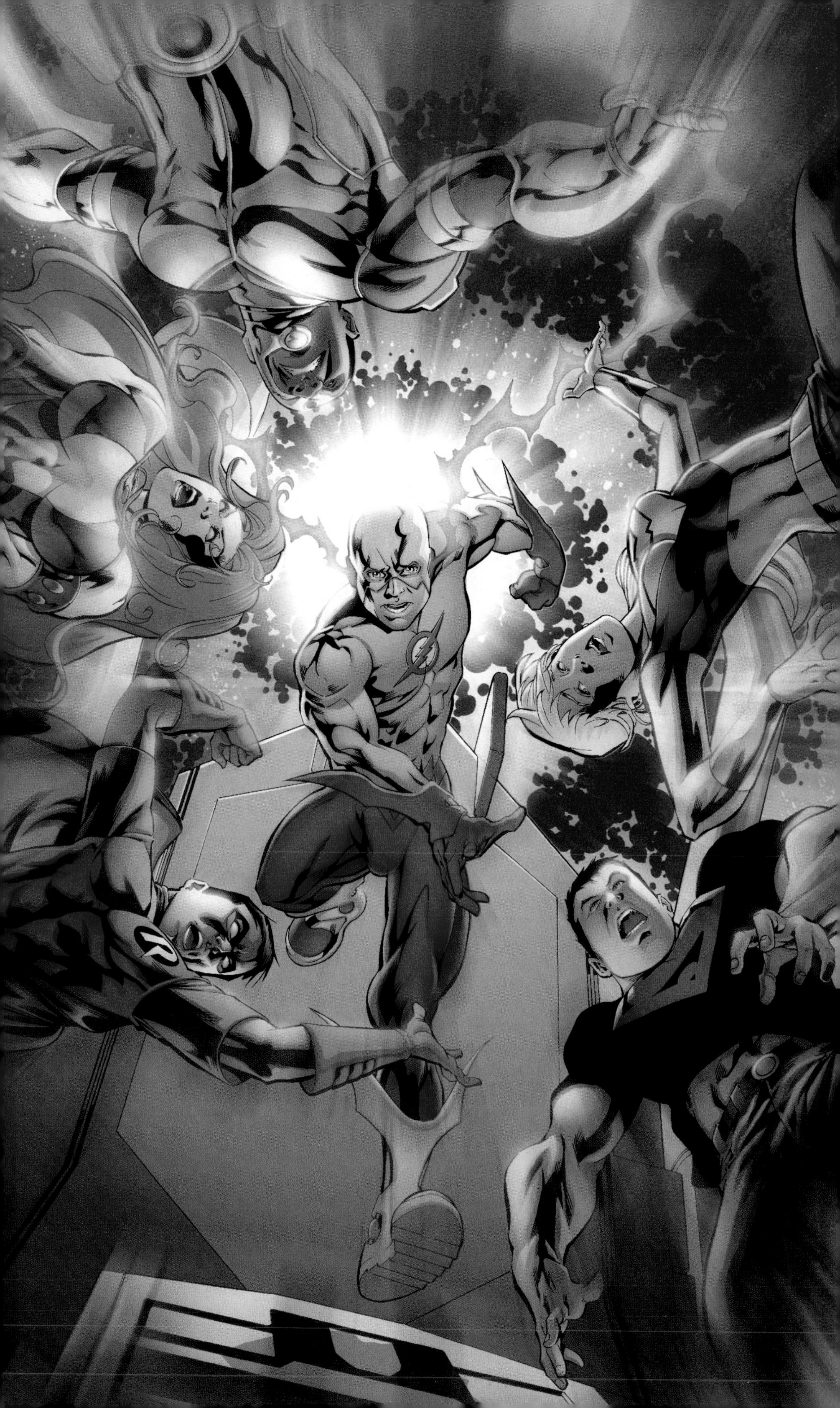

TEEN TITANS #19

GEOFF JOHNS
Writer

MIKE McKONE
Penciller

MARLO ALQUIZA
Inker

JEROMY COX
Colorist

COMICRAFT
Letterer

**MIKE McKONE, MARLO ALQUIZA
& JEROMY COX**
Cover Artists

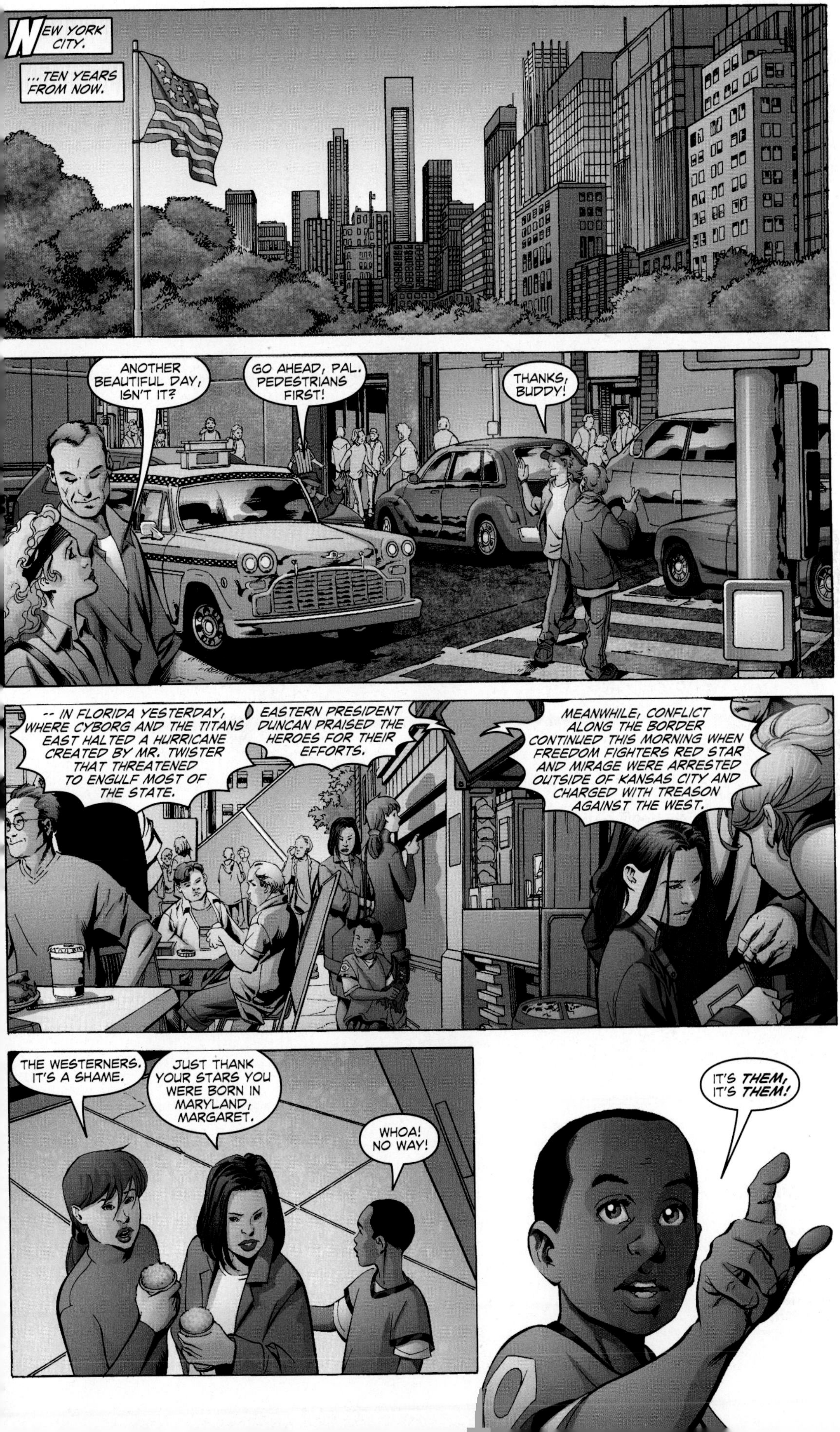
NEW YORK CITY.
...TEN YEARS FROM NOW.
ANOTHER BEAUTIFUL DAY, ISN'T IT?
GO AHEAD, PAL. PEDESTRIANS FIRST!
THANKS, BUDDY!
-- IN FLORIDA YESTERDAY, WHERE CYBORG AND THE TITANS EAST HALTED A HURRICANE CREATED BY MR. TWISTER THAT THREATENED TO ENGULF MOST OF THE STATE.
EASTERN PRESIDENT DUNCAN PRAISED THE HEROES FOR THEIR EFFORTS.
MEANWHILE, CONFLICT ALONG THE BORDER CONTINUED THIS MORNING WHEN FREEDOM FIGHTERS RED STAR AND MIRAGE WERE ARRESTED OUTSIDE OF KANSAS CITY AND CHARGED WITH TREASON AGAINST THE WEST.
THE WESTERNERS. IT'S A SHAME.
JUST THANK YOUR STARS YOU WERE BORN IN MARYLAND, MARGARET.
WHOA! NO WAY!
IT'S THEM, IT'S THEM!

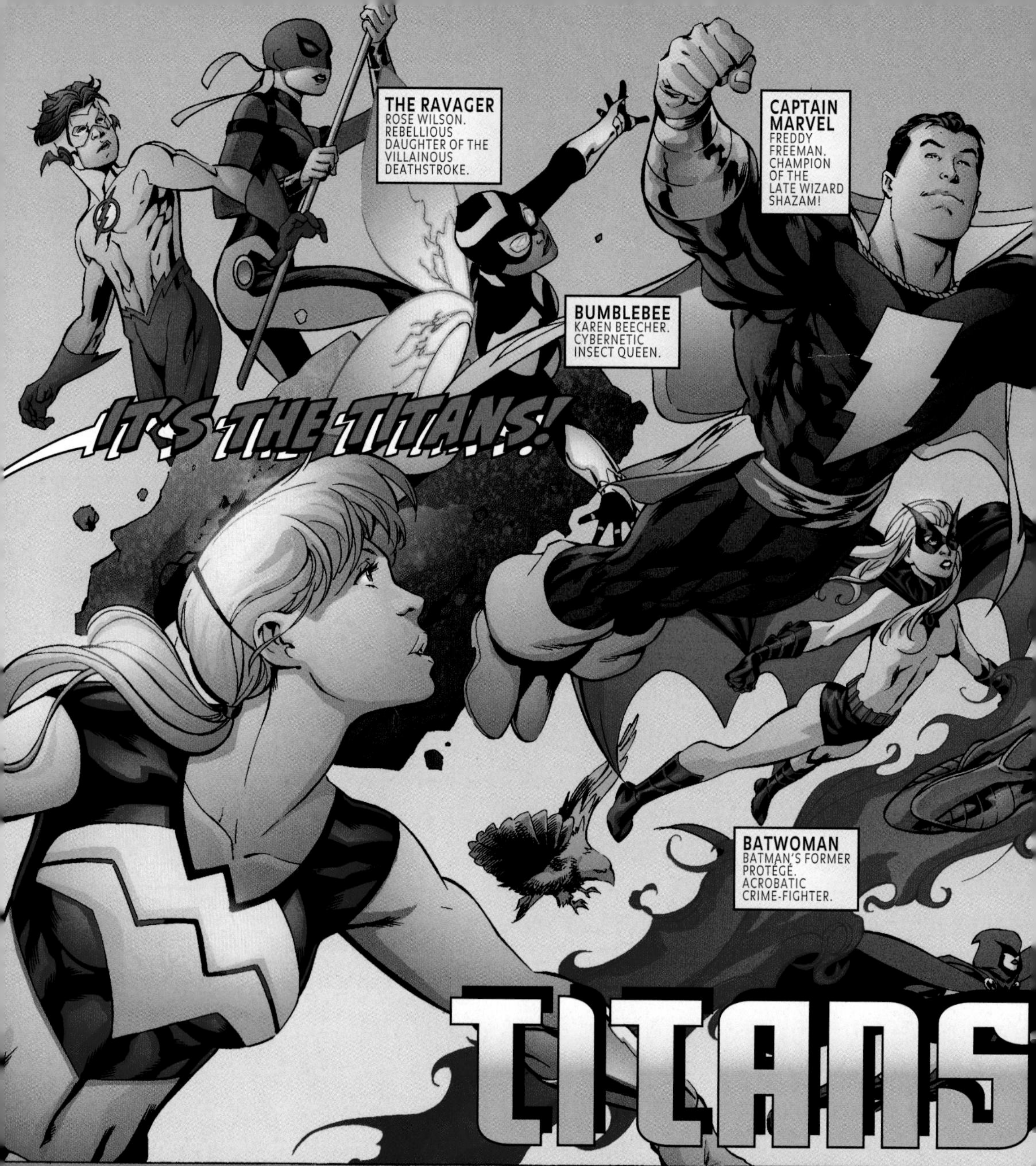
THE RAVAGER
ROSE WILSON. REBELLIOUS DAUGHTER OF THE VILLAINOUS DEATHSTROKE.
CAPTAIN MARVEL
FREDDY FREEMAN. CHAMPION OF THE LATE WIZARD SHAZAM!
BUMBLEBEE
KAREN BEECHER. CYBERNETIC INSECT QUEEN.
IT'S THE TITANS!
BATWOMAN
BATMAN'S FORMER PROTÉGÉ. ACROBATIC CRIME-FIGHTER.
TITANS

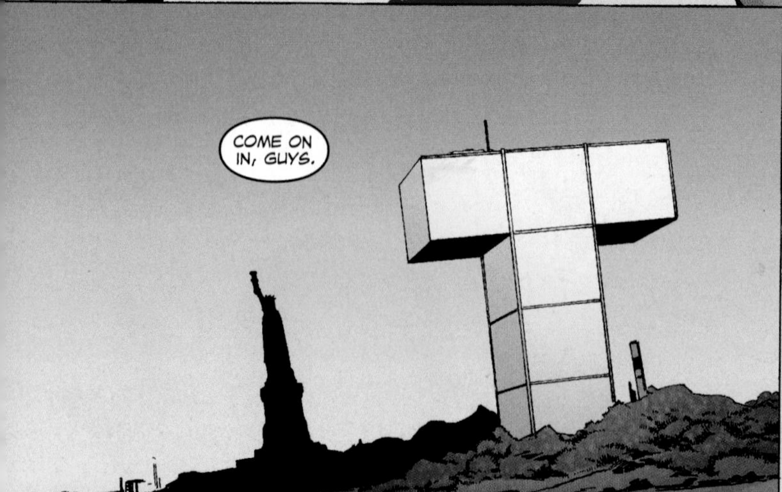
COME ON IN, GUYS.

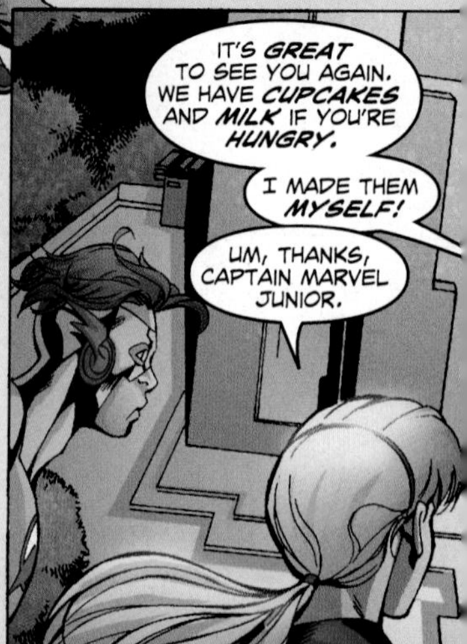
IT'S GREAT TO SEE YOU AGAIN. WE HAVE CUPCAKES AND MILK IF YOU'RE HUNGRY.
I MADE THEM MYSELF!
UM, THANKS, CAPTAIN MARVEL JUNIOR.

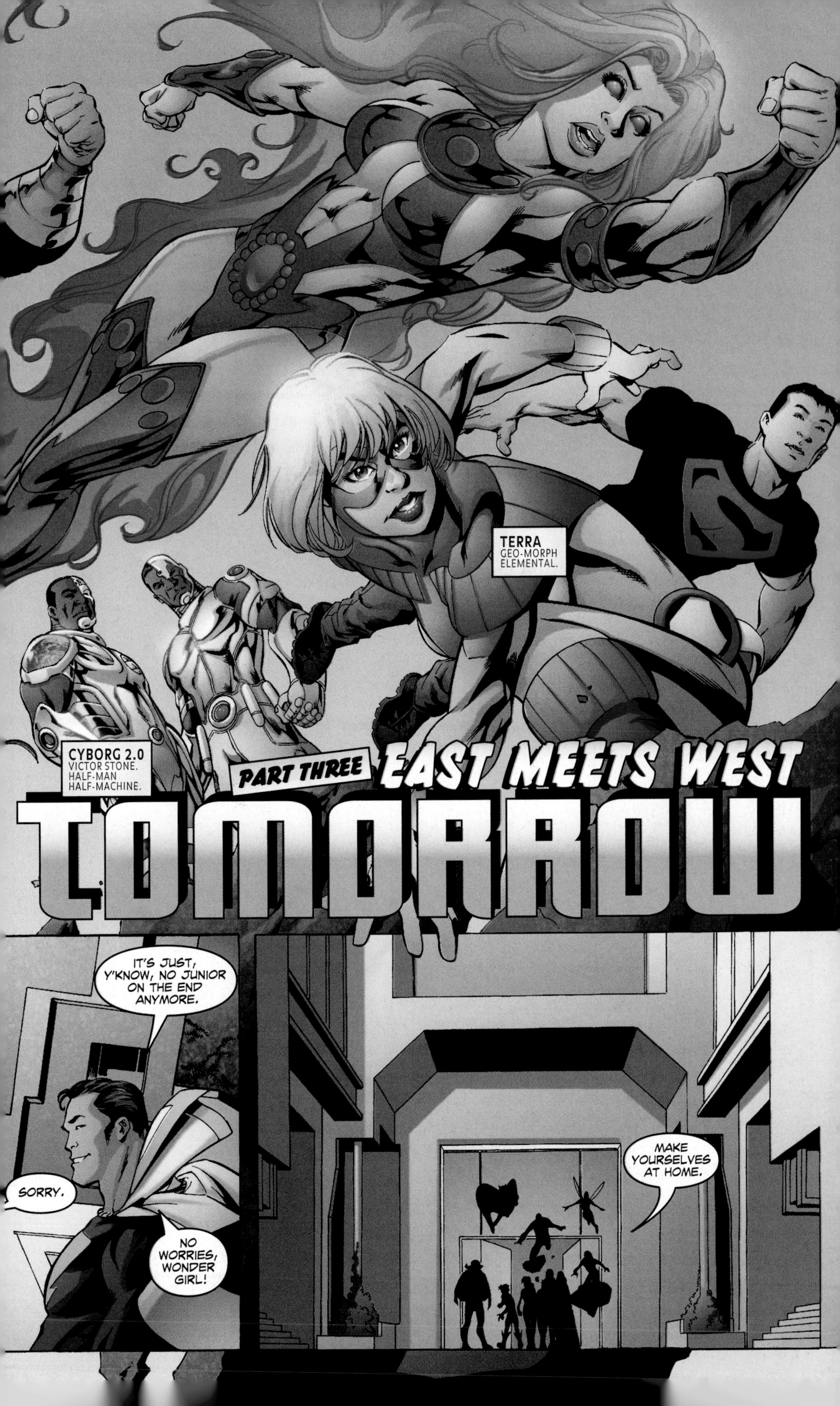

TERRA GEO-MORPH ELEMENTAL.
CYBORG 2.0 VICTOR STONE. HALF-MAN HALF-MACHINE.
PART THREE
EAST MEETS WEST
TOMORROW
IT'S JUST, Y'KNOW, NO JUNIOR ON THE END ANYMORE.
SORRY.
NO WORRIES, WONDER GIRL!
MAKE YOURSELVES AT HOME.

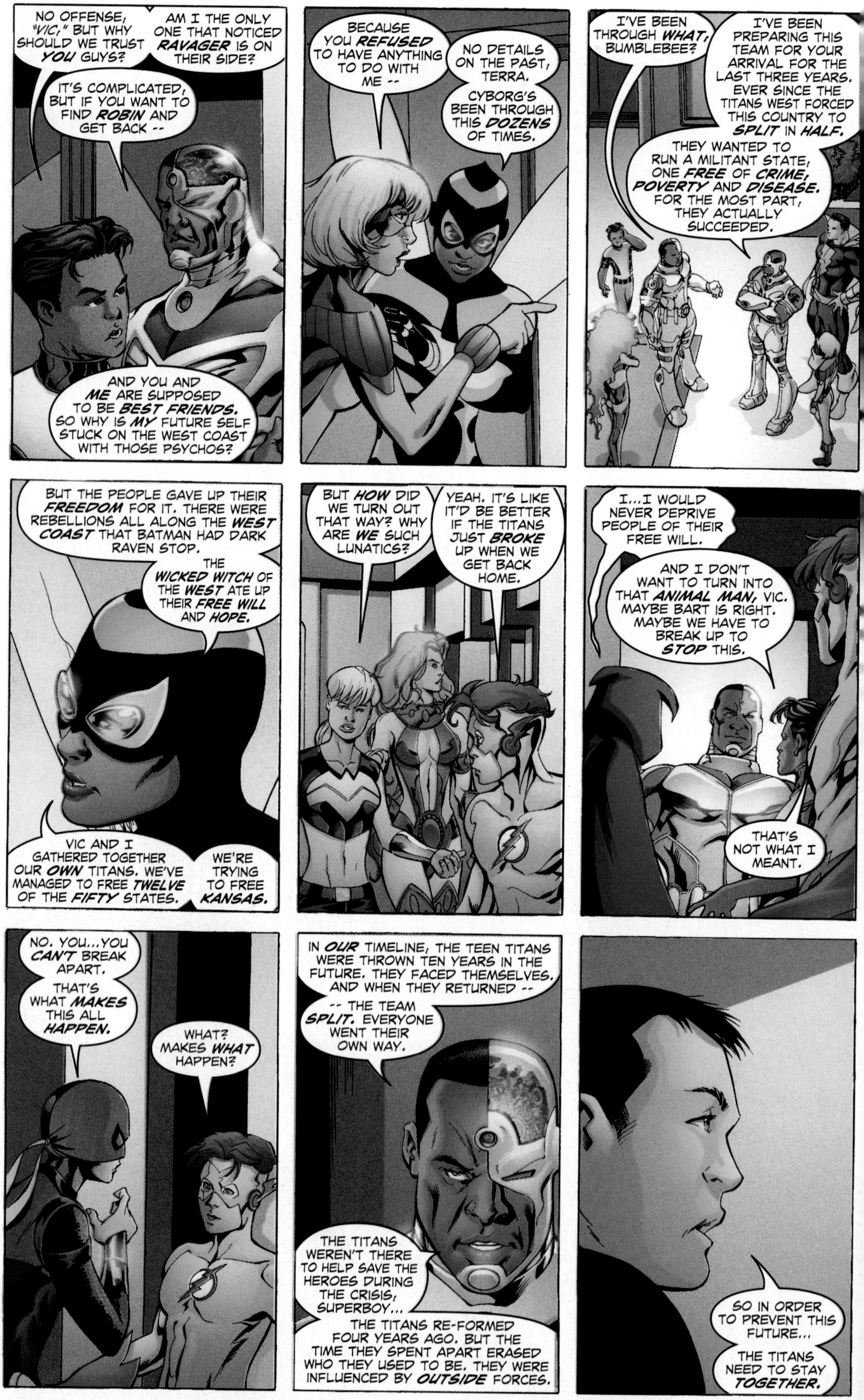

NO OFFENSE, "VIC," BUT WHY SHOULD WE TRUST YOU GUYS?
AM I THE ONLY ONE THAT NOTICED RAVAGER IS ON THEIR SIDE?
IT'S COMPLICATED, BUT IF YOU WANT TO FIND ROBIN AND GET BACK --
AND YOU AND ME ARE SUPPOSED TO BE BEST FRIENDS. SO WHY IS MY FUTURE SELF STUCK ON THE WEST COAST WITH THOSE PSYCHOS?
BECAUSE YOU REFUSED TO HAVE ANYTHING TO DO WITH ME --
NO DETAILS ON THE PAST, TERRA.
CYBORG'S BEEN THROUGH THIS DOZENS OF TIMES.
I'VE BEEN THROUGH WHAT, BUMBLEBEE?
I'VE BEEN PREPARING THIS TEAM FOR YOUR ARRIVAL FOR THE LAST THREE YEARS. EVER SINCE THE TITANS WEST FORCED THIS COUNTRY TO SPLIT IN HALF.
THEY WANTED TO RUN A MILITANT STATE, ONE FREE OF CRIME, POVERTY AND DISEASE. FOR THE MOST PART, THEY ACTUALLY SUCCEEDED.
BUT THE PEOPLE GAVE UP THEIR FREEDOM FOR IT. THERE WERE REBELLIONS ALL ALONG THE WEST COAST THAT BATMAN HAD DARK RAVEN STOP.
THE WICKED WITCH OF THE WEST ATE UP THEIR FREE WILL AND HOPE.
VIC AND I GATHERED TOGETHER OUR OWN TITANS. WE'VE MANAGED TO FREE TWELVE OF THE FIFTY STATES.
WE'RE TRYING TO FREE KANSAS.
BUT HOW DID WE TURN OUT THAT WAY? WHY ARE WE SUCH LUNATICS?
YEAH. IT'S LIKE IT'D BE BETTER IF THE TITANS JUST BROKE UP WHEN WE GET BACK HOME.
I...I WOULD NEVER DEPRIVE PEOPLE OF THEIR FREE WILL.
AND I DON'T WANT TO TURN INTO THAT ANIMAL MAN, VIC. MAYBE BART IS RIGHT. MAYBE WE HAVE TO BREAK UP TO STOP THIS.
THAT'S NOT WHAT I MEANT.
NO. YOU...YOU CAN'T BREAK APART.
THAT'S WHAT MAKES THIS ALL HAPPEN.
WHAT? MAKES WHAT HAPPEN?
IN OUR TIMELINE, THE TEEN TITANS WERE THROWN TEN YEARS IN THE FUTURE. THEY FACED THEMSELVES. AND WHEN THEY RETURNED --
-- THE TEAM SPLIT. EVERYONE WENT THEIR OWN WAY.
THE TITANS WEREN'T THERE TO HELP SAVE THE HEROES DURING THE CRISIS, SUPERBOY...
THE TITANS RE-FORMED FOUR YEARS AGO. BUT THE TIME THEY SPENT APART ERASED WHO THEY USED TO BE. THEY WERE INFLUENCED BY OUTSIDE FORCES.
SO IN ORDER TO PREVENT THIS FUTURE...
THE TITANS NEED TO STAY TOGETHER.

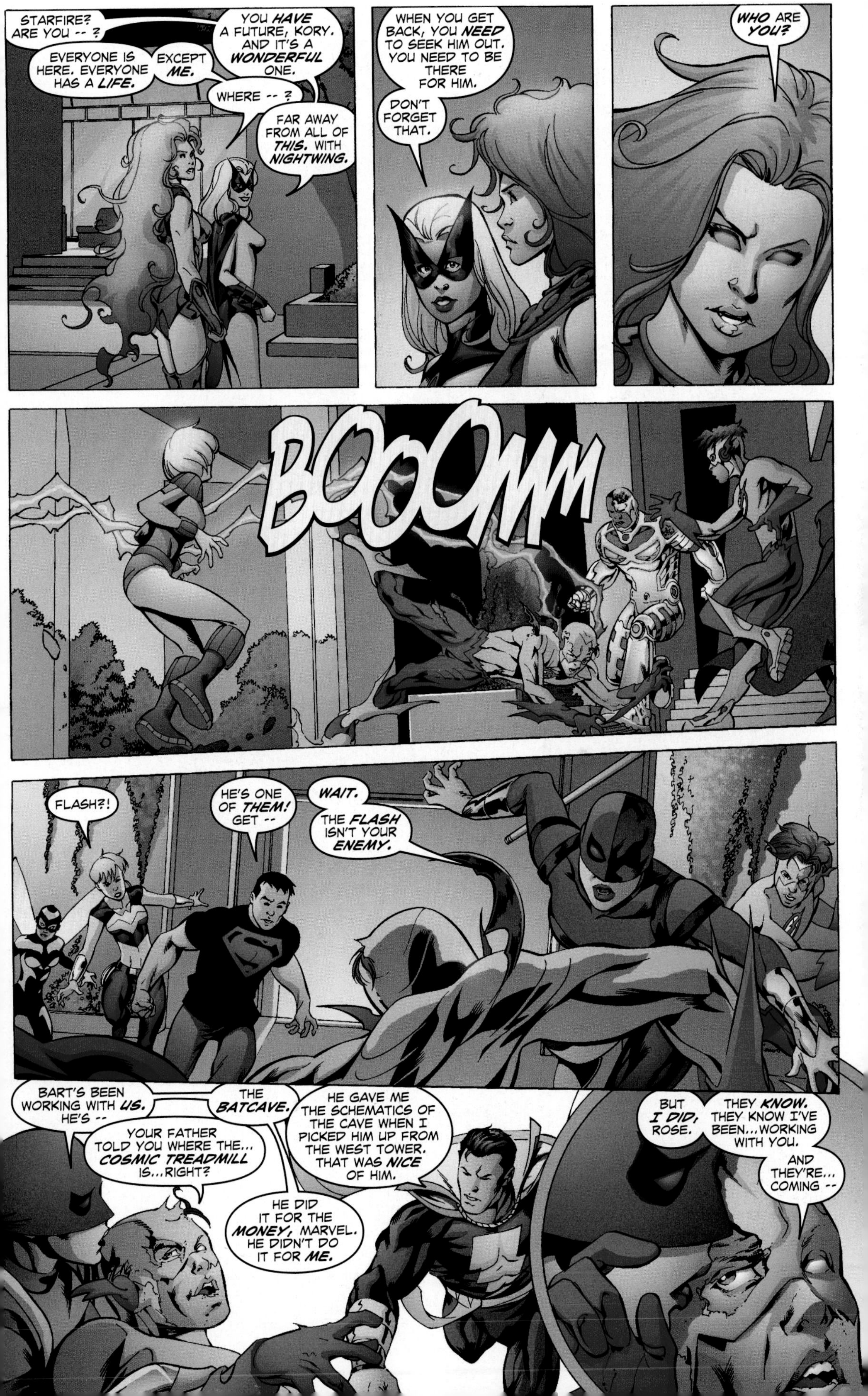
STARFIRE? ARE YOU -- ?
EVERYONE IS HERE. EVERYONE HAS A LIFE.
EXCEPT ME.
YOU HAVE A FUTURE, KORY. AND IT'S A WONDERFUL ONE.
WHERE -- ?
FAR AWAY FROM ALL OF THIS. WITH NIGHTWING.
WHEN YOU GET BACK, YOU NEED TO SEEK HIM OUT. YOU NEED TO BE THERE FOR HIM.
DON'T FORGET THAT.
WHO ARE YOU?
BOOOMM
FLASH?!
HE'S ONE OF THEM! GET --
WAIT.
THE FLASH ISN'T YOUR ENEMY.
BART'S BEEN WORKING WITH US. HE'S --
YOUR FATHER TOLD YOU WHERE THE... COSMIC TREADMILL IS...RIGHT?
THE BATCAVE.
HE GAVE ME THE SCHEMATICS OF THE CAVE WHEN I PICKED HIM UP FROM THE WEST TOWER. THAT WAS NICE OF HIM.
HE DID IT FOR THE MONEY, MARVEL. HE DIDN'T DO IT FOR ME.
BUT I DID, ROSE.
THEY KNOW. THEY KNOW I'VE BEEN...WORKING WITH YOU.
AND THEY'RE... COMING --

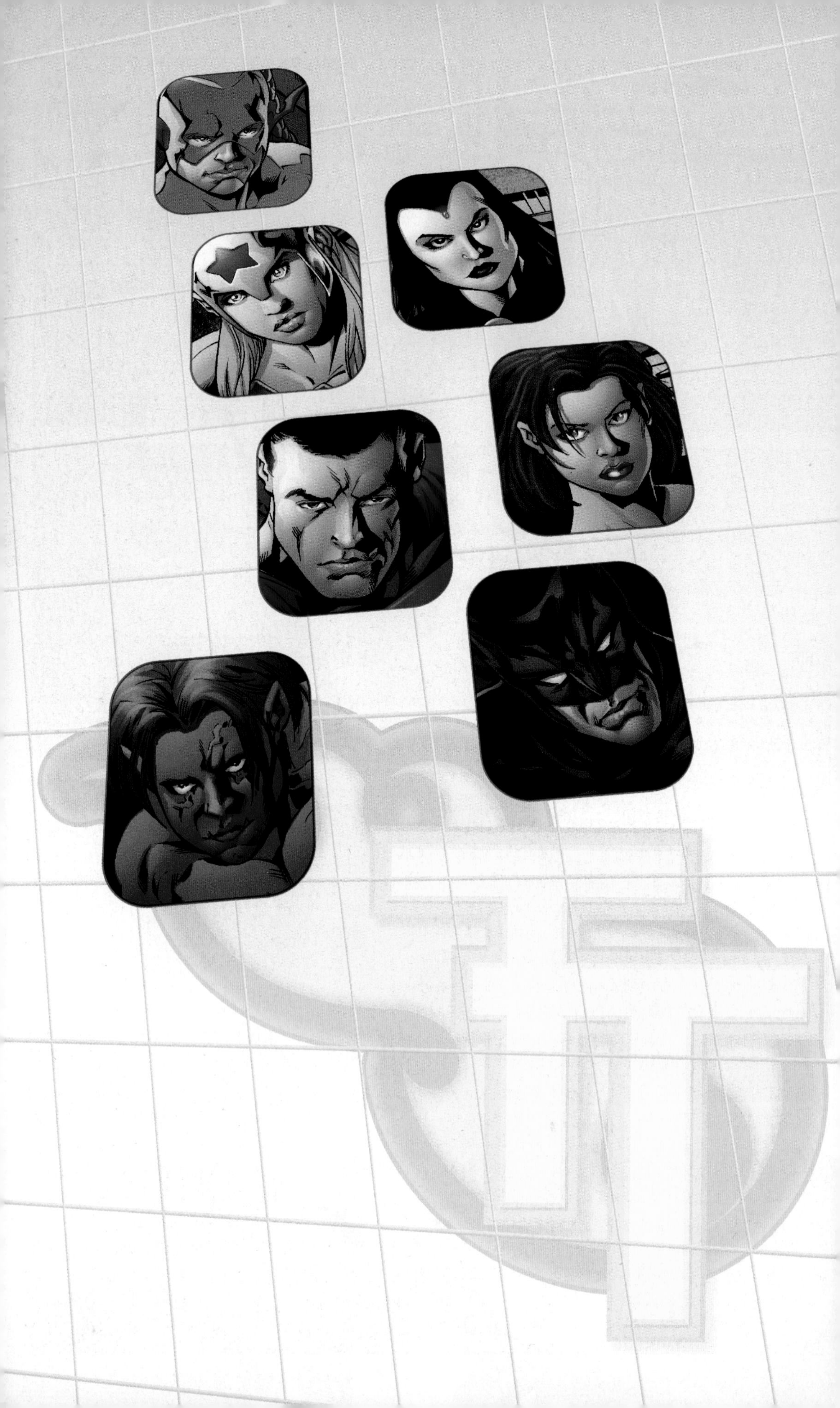

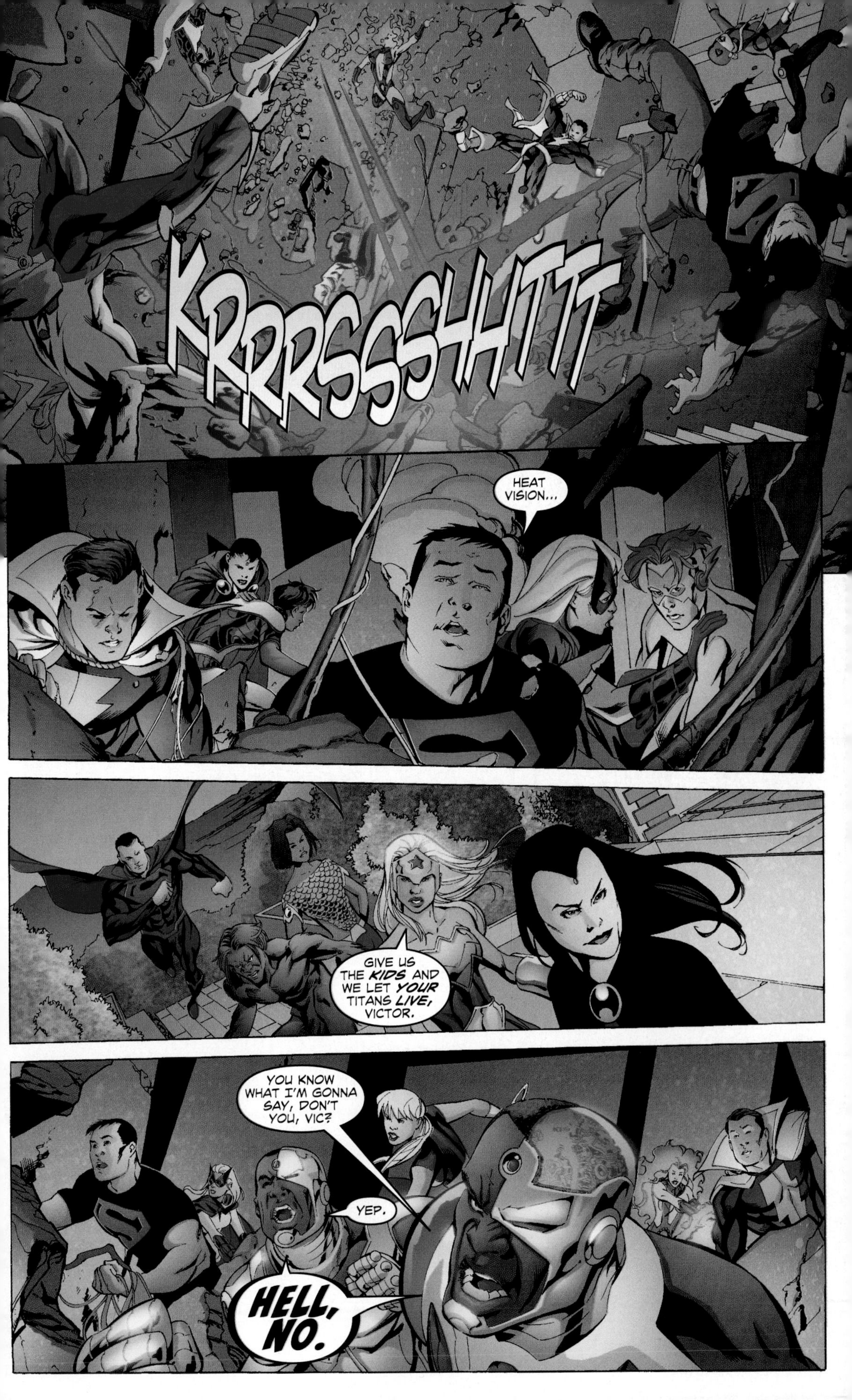

KRRRSSSHTTT
HEAT VISION...
GIVE US THE KIDS AND WE LET YOUR TITANS LIVE, VICTOR.
YOU KNOW WHAT I'M GONNA SAY, DON'T YOU, VIC?
YEP.
HELL, NO.

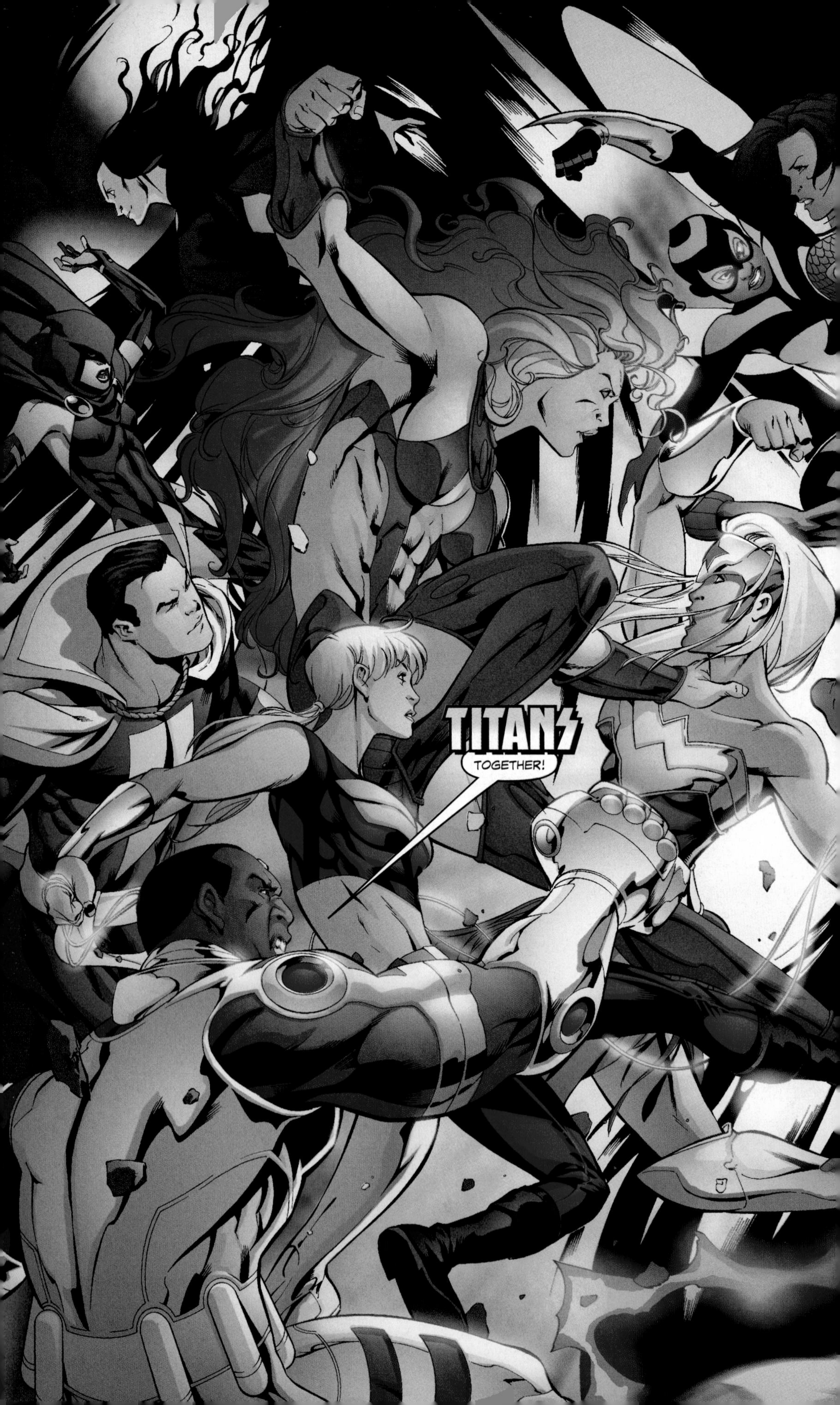
TITANS
TOGETHER!

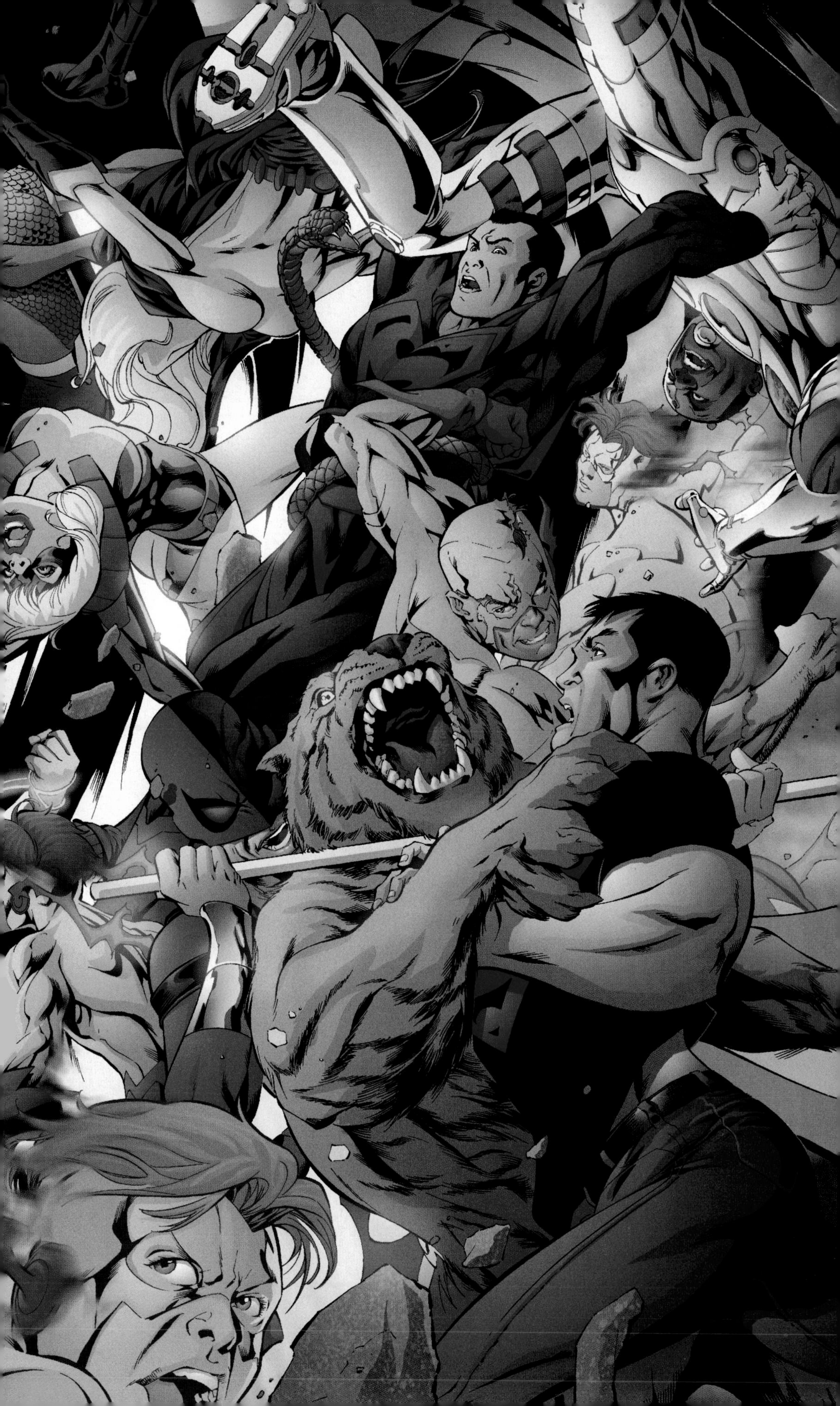

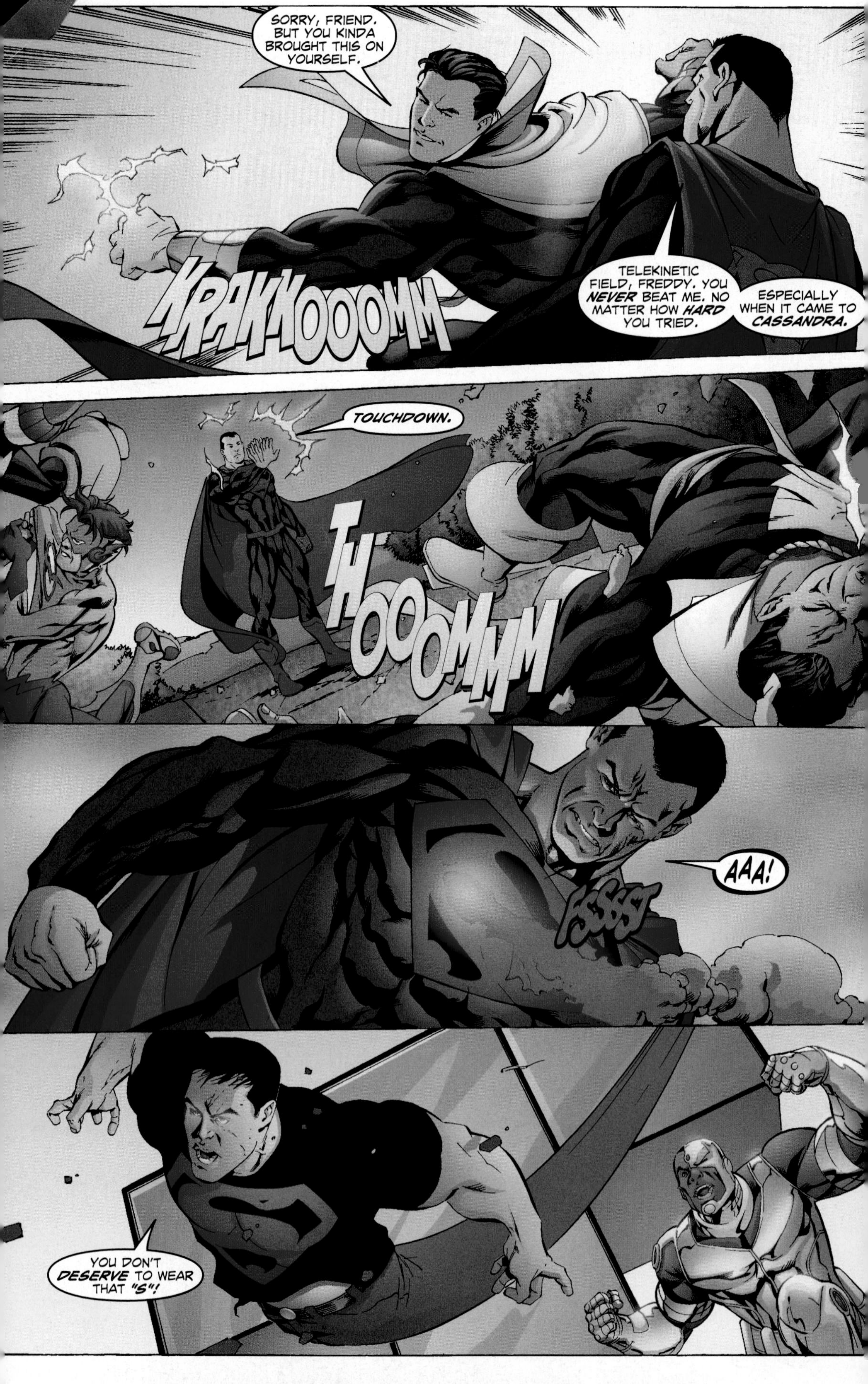
SORRY, FRIEND. BUT YOU KINDA BROUGHT THIS ON YOURSELF.
KRAKKOOOMM
TELEKINETIC FIELD, FREDDY. YOU NEVER BEAT ME. NO MATTER HOW HARD YOU TRIED.
ESPECIALLY WHEN IT CAME TO CASSANDRA.
TOUCHDOWN.
THOOOMMM
AAA!
FSSSST
YOU DON'T DESERVE TO WEAR THAT "S"!

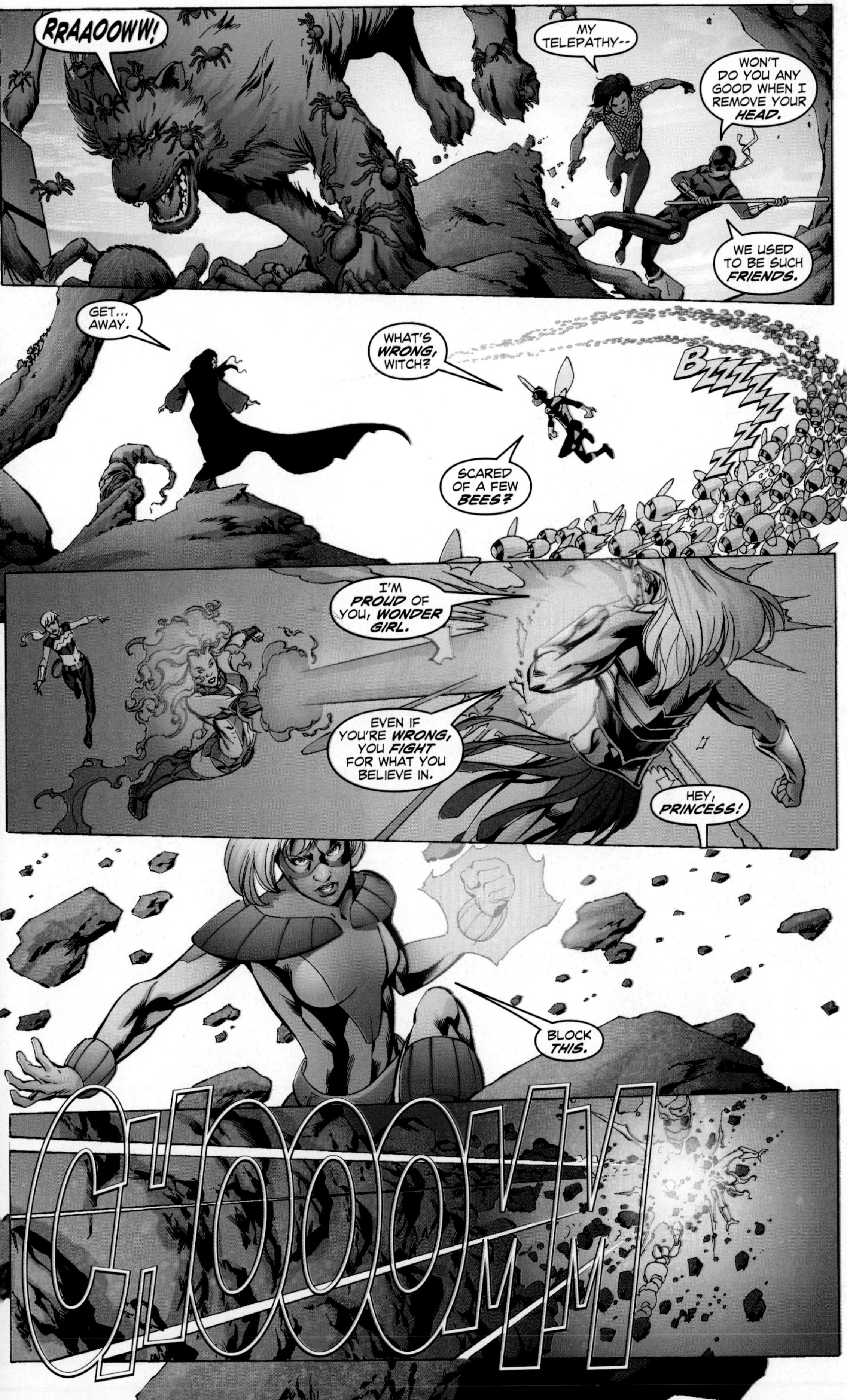

RRAAOOWW!
MY TELEPATHY--
WON'T DO YOU ANY GOOD WHEN I REMOVE YOUR HEAD.
WE USED TO BE SUCH FRIENDS.
GET... AWAY.
WHAT'S WRONG, WITCH?
SCARED OF A FEW BEES?
BZZZZZZ
I'M PROUD OF YOU, WONDER GIRL.
EVEN IF YOU'RE WRONG, YOU FIGHT FOR WHAT YOU BELIEVE IN.
HEY, PRINCESS!
BLOCK THIS.
CHOOOOMMM

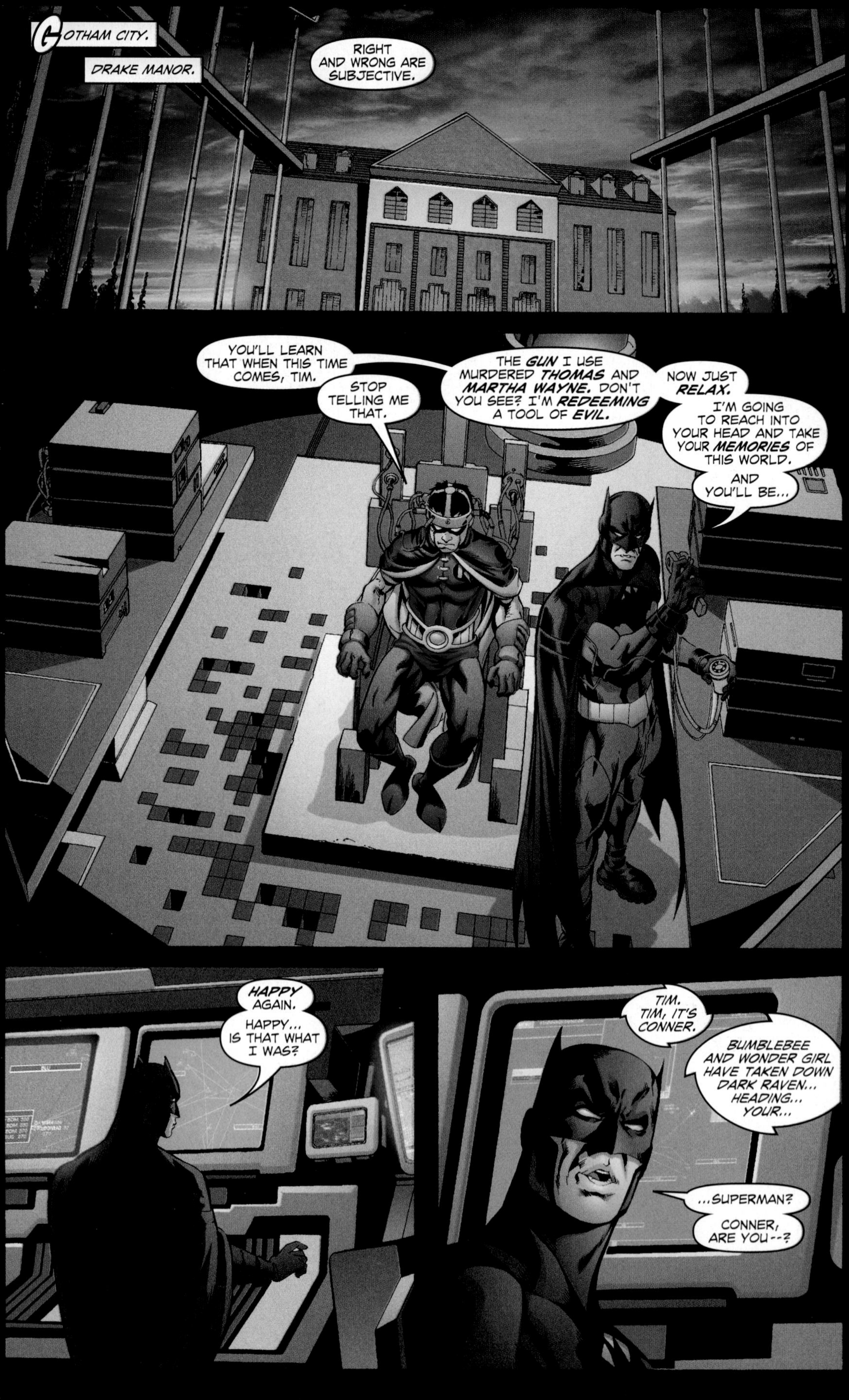
GOTHAM CITY.
DRAKE MANOR.
RIGHT AND WRONG ARE SUBJECTIVE.
YOU'LL LEARN THAT WHEN THIS TIME COMES, TIM.
STOP TELLING ME THAT.
THE GUN I USE MURDERED THOMAS AND MARTHA WAYNE. DON'T YOU SEE? I'M REDEEMING A TOOL OF EVIL.
NOW JUST RELAX.
I'M GOING TO REACH INTO YOUR HEAD AND TAKE YOUR MEMORIES OF THIS WORLD.
AND YOU'LL BE...
HAPPY AGAIN.
HAPPY... IS THAT WHAT I WAS?
TIM. TIM, IT'S CONNER.
BUMBLEBEE AND WONDER GIRL HAVE TAKEN DOWN DARK RAVEN... HEADING... YOUR...
...SUPERMAN?
CONNER, ARE YOU--?

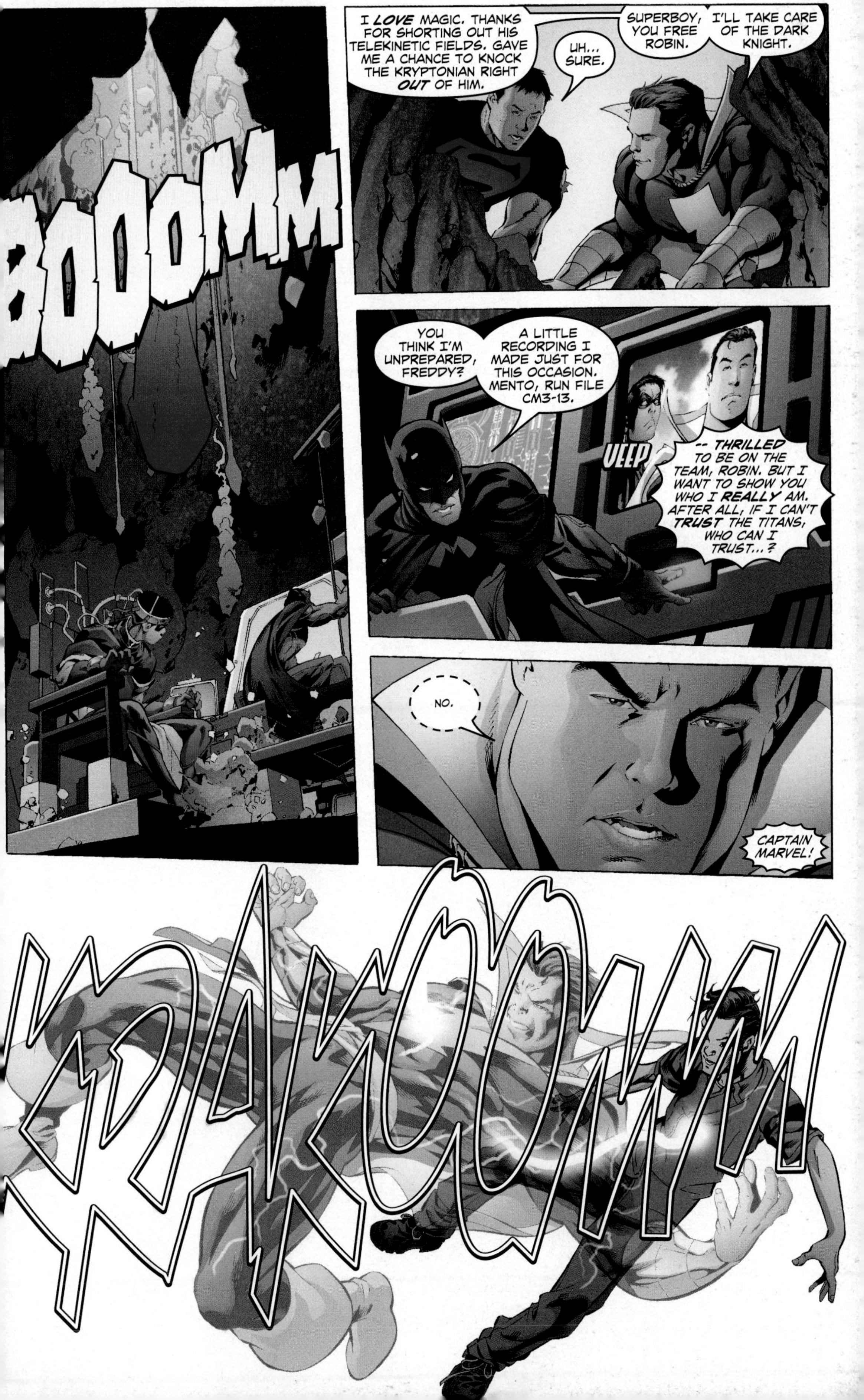
BOOOMM
I LOVE MAGIC. THANKS FOR SHORTING OUT HIS TELEKINETIC FIELDS. GAVE ME A CHANCE TO KNOCK THE KRYPTONIAN RIGHT OUT OF HIM.
UH... SURE.
SUPERBOY, YOU FREE ROBIN.
I'LL TAKE CARE OF THE DARK KNIGHT.
YOU THINK I'M UNPREPARED, FREDDY?
A LITTLE RECORDING I MADE JUST FOR THIS OCCASION. MENTO, RUN FILE CM3-13.
VEEP
-- THRILLED TO BE ON THE TEAM, ROBIN. BUT I WANT TO SHOW YOU WHO I REALLY AM. AFTER ALL, IF I CAN'T TRUST THE TITANS, WHO CAN I TRUST...?
NO.
CAPTAIN MARVEL!
KRAKOOOM

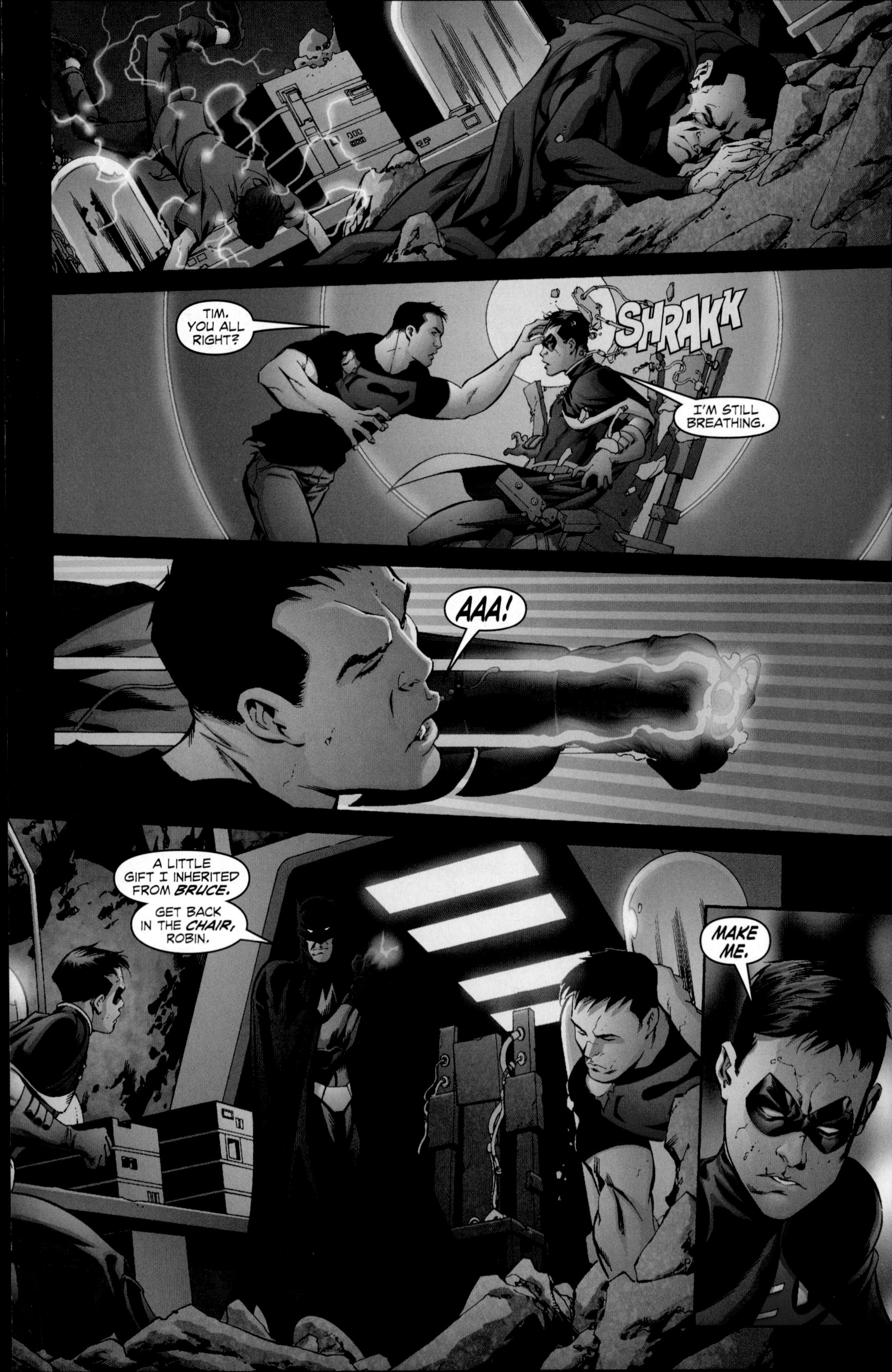
TIM. YOU ALL RIGHT?
SHRAKK
I'M STILL BREATHING.
AAA!
A LITTLE GIFT I INHERITED FROM BRUCE.
GET BACK IN THE CHAIR, ROBIN.
MAKE ME.

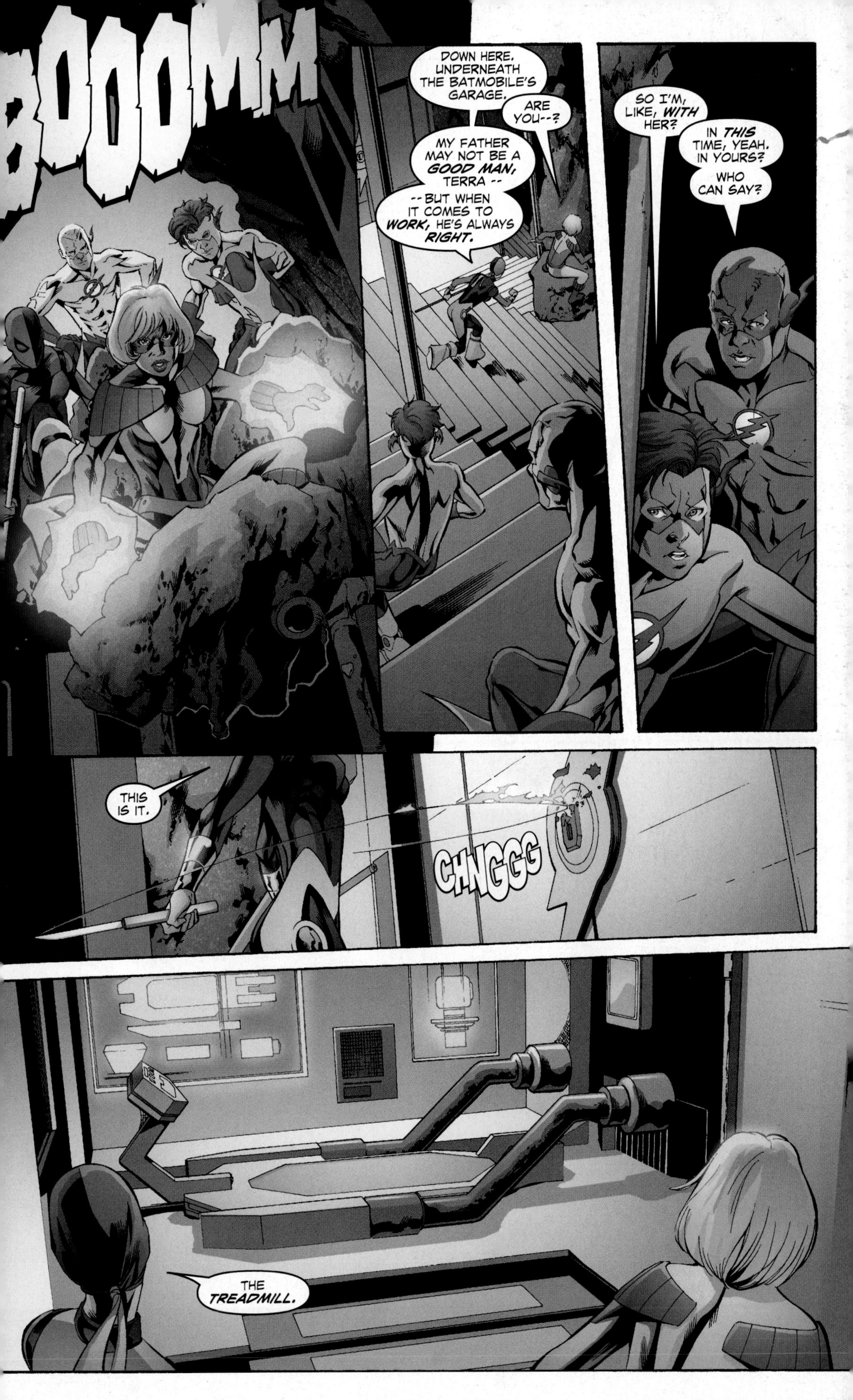
BOOOMM
DOWN HERE. UNDERNEATH THE BATMOBILE'S GARAGE.
ARE YOU--?
MY FATHER MAY NOT BE A GOOD MAN, TERRA --
-- BUT WHEN IT COMES TO WORK, HE'S ALWAYS RIGHT.
SO I'M, LIKE, WITH HER?
IN THIS TIME, YEAH. IN YOURS?
WHO CAN SAY?
THIS IS IT.
CHNGGG
THE TREADMILL.

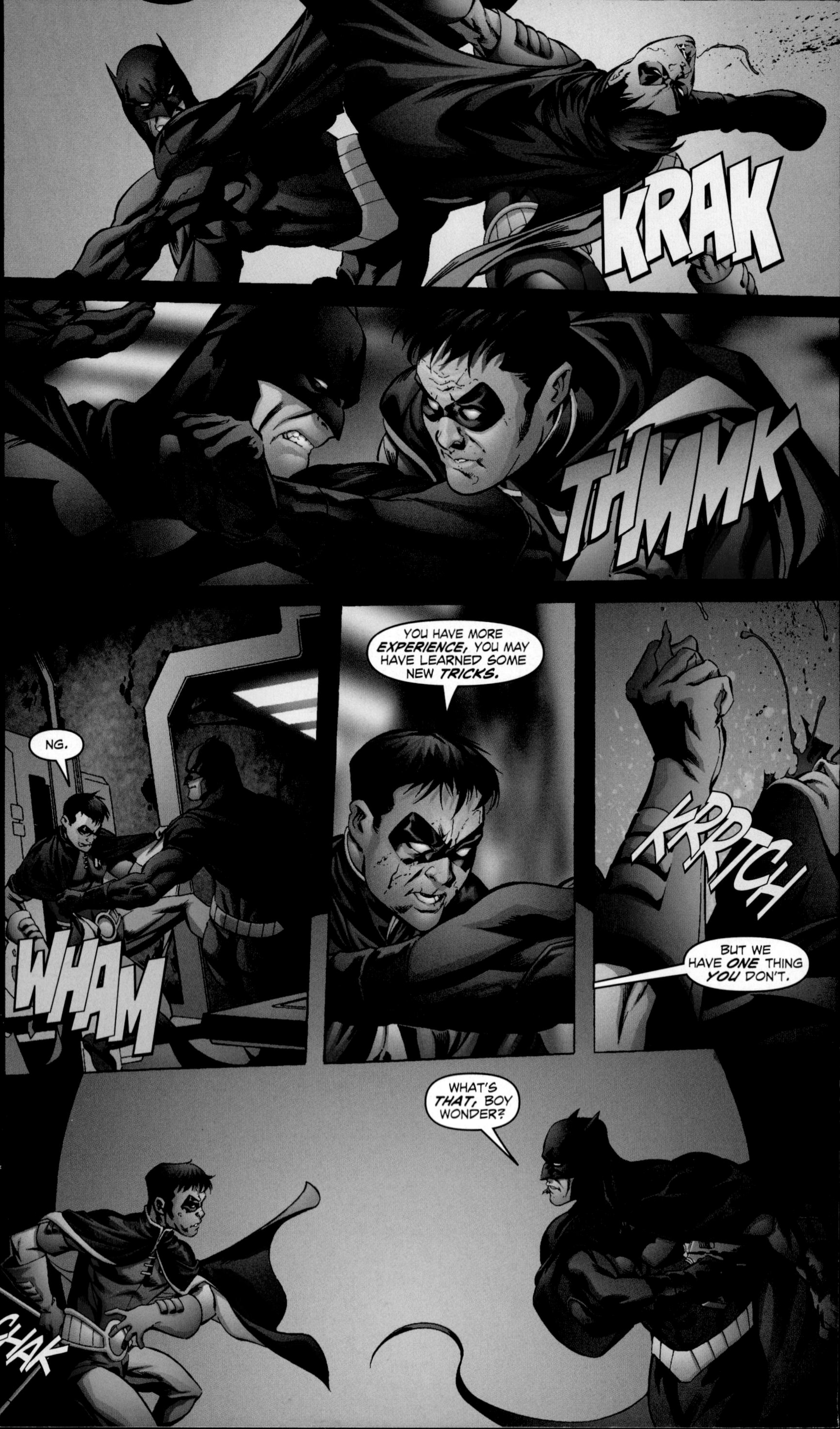
KRAK
THMMK
NG.
WHAM
YOU HAVE MORE EXPERIENCE, YOU MAY HAVE LEARNED SOME NEW TRICKS.
KRRTCH
BUT WE HAVE ONE THING YOU DON'T.
WHAT'S THAT, BOY WONDER?
CHAK

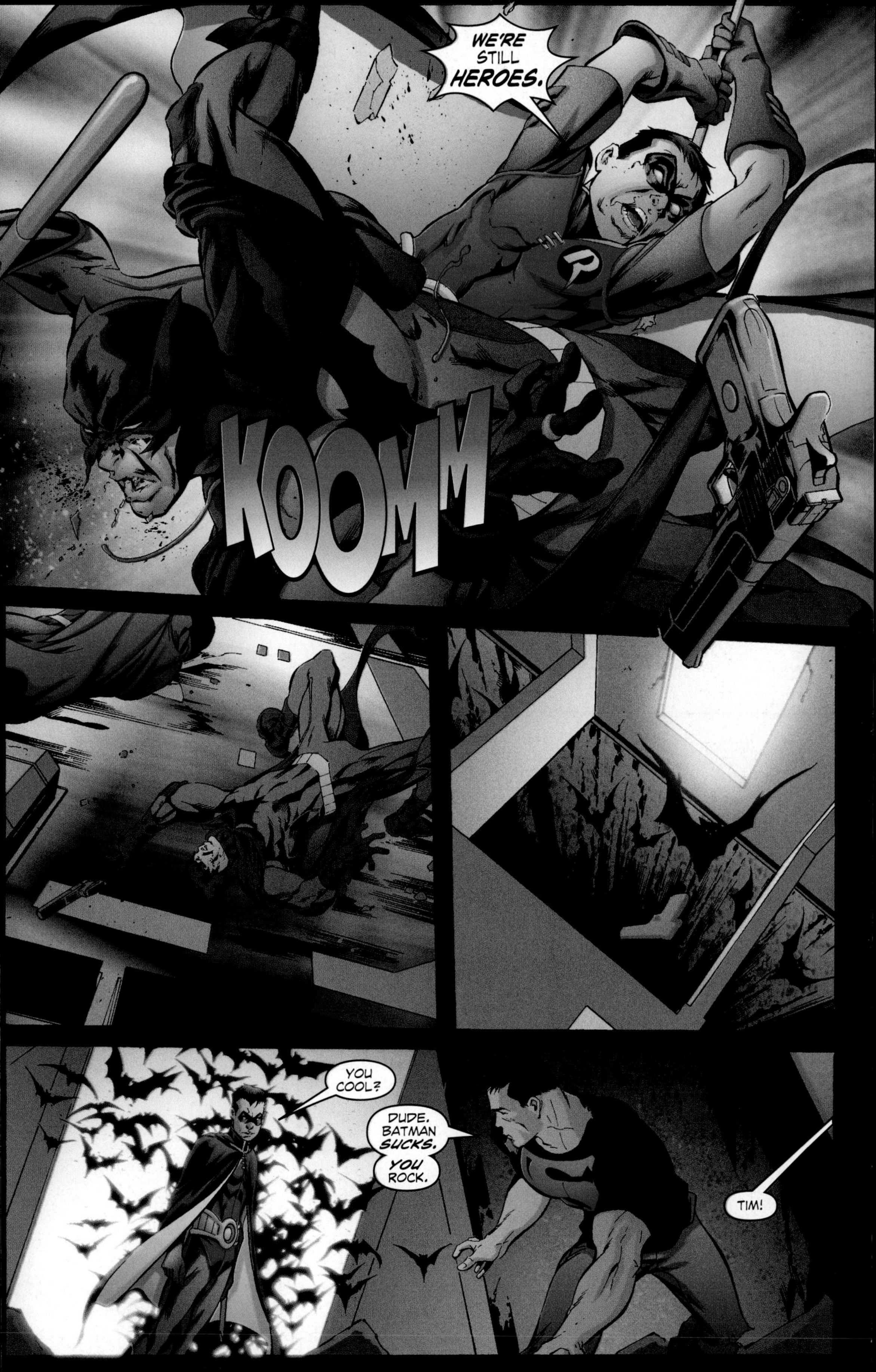

WE'RE STILL HEROES.
KOOMM
YOU COOL?
DUDE. BATMAN SUCKS.
YOU ROCK.
TIM!

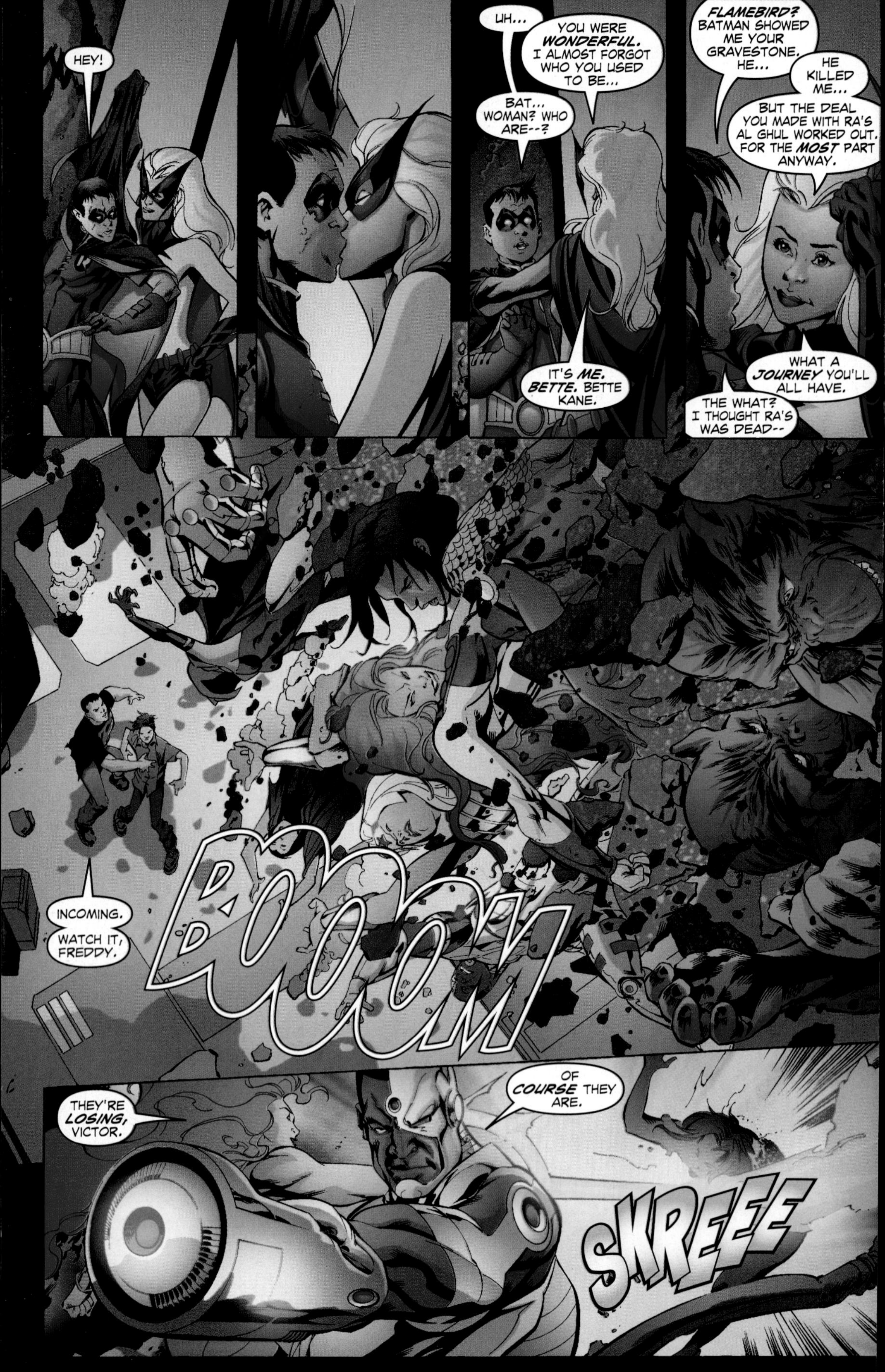
HEY!
UH...
YOU WERE WONDERFUL. I ALMOST FORGOT WHO YOU USED TO BE...
BAT... WOMAN? WHO ARE--?
IT'S ME. BETTE. BETTE KANE.
FLAMEBIRD? BATMAN SHOWED ME YOUR GRAVESTONE. HE...
HE KILLED ME...
BUT THE DEAL YOU MADE WITH RA'S AL GHUL WORKED OUT. FOR THE MOST PART ANYWAY.
WHAT A JOURNEY YOU'LL ALL HAVE.
THE WHAT? I THOUGHT RA'S WAS DEAD--
INCOMING.
WATCH IT, FREDDY.
BOOOM
THEY'RE LOSING, VICTOR.
OF COURSE THEY ARE.
SKREEE

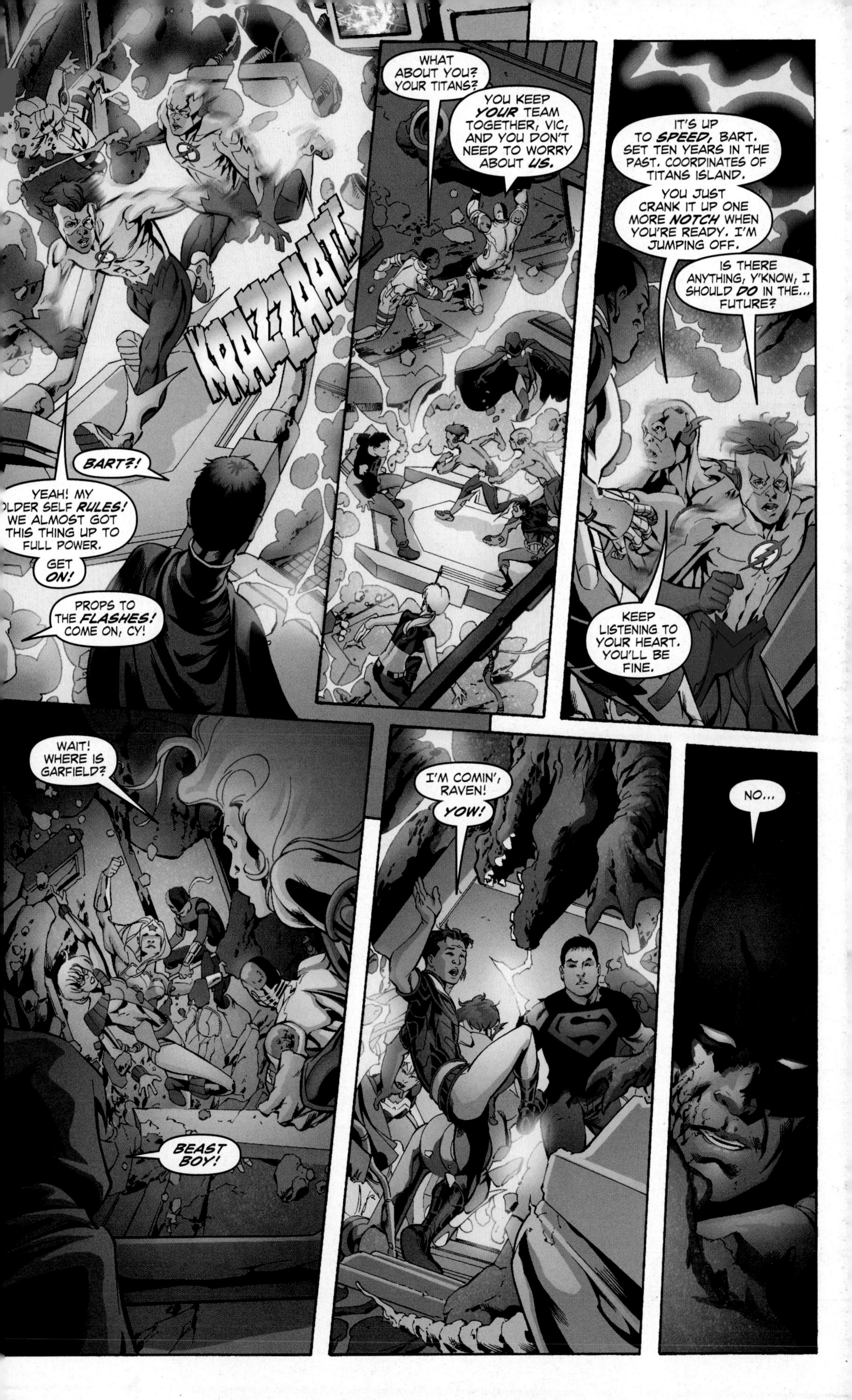
KRAZZZATT!
BART?!
YEAH! MY OLDER SELF RULES! WE ALMOST GOT THIS THING UP TO FULL POWER.
GET ON!
PROPS TO THE FLASHES! COME ON, CY!
WHAT ABOUT YOU? YOUR TITANS?
YOU KEEP YOUR TEAM TOGETHER, VIC, AND YOU DON'T NEED TO WORRY ABOUT US.
IT'S UP TO SPEED, BART. SET TEN YEARS IN THE PAST. COORDINATES OF TITANS ISLAND.
YOU JUST CRANK IT UP ONE MORE NOTCH WHEN YOU'RE READY. I'M JUMPING OFF.
IS THERE ANYTHING, Y'KNOW, I SHOULD DO IN THE... FUTURE?
KEEP LISTENING TO YOUR HEART. YOU'LL BE FINE.
WAIT! WHERE IS GARFIELD?
BEAST BOY!
I'M COMIN', RAVEN!
YOW!
NO...

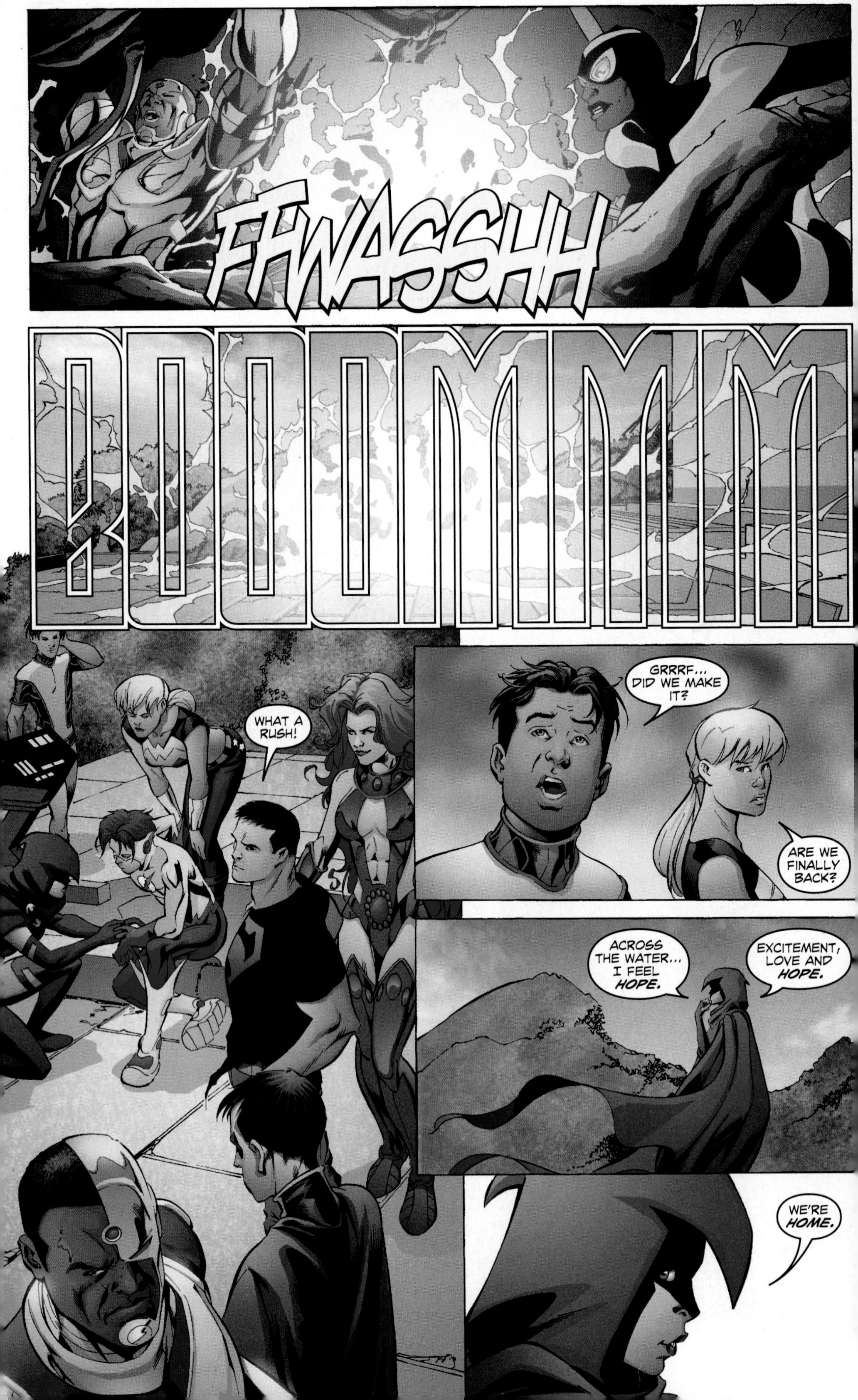
FFWASSHH
BOOOMMMM
WHAT A RUSH!
GRRRF... DID WE MAKE IT?
ARE WE FINALLY BACK?
ACROSS THE WATER... I FEEL *HOPE.*
EXCITEMENT, LOVE AND *HOPE.*
WE'RE *HOME.*

TITANS TOWER.

SAN FRANCISCO.

SATURDAY, 4:45 P.M.

HEY, MAN.

HEY.

CAN I BORROW A SHIRT? I DON'T HAVE ANYTHING HERE WITHOUT AN "S" ON IT.

BART IS MAKING US GO TO DAVE AND BUSTERS. PLAY SOME GAMES. HAVE SOME FUN.

SOMETIMES I THINK WE *FORGOT* HOW TO DO THAT.

IF WHAT WE JUST SAW TAUGHT US *ANYTHING*, TIM--

-- IT'S THAT WE NEED TO *LIGHTEN* UP.

AND WE NEED TO STICK *TOGETHER*.

NO MATTER *WHAT*.

NO MATTER *WHAT*, CONNER.

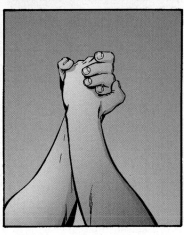

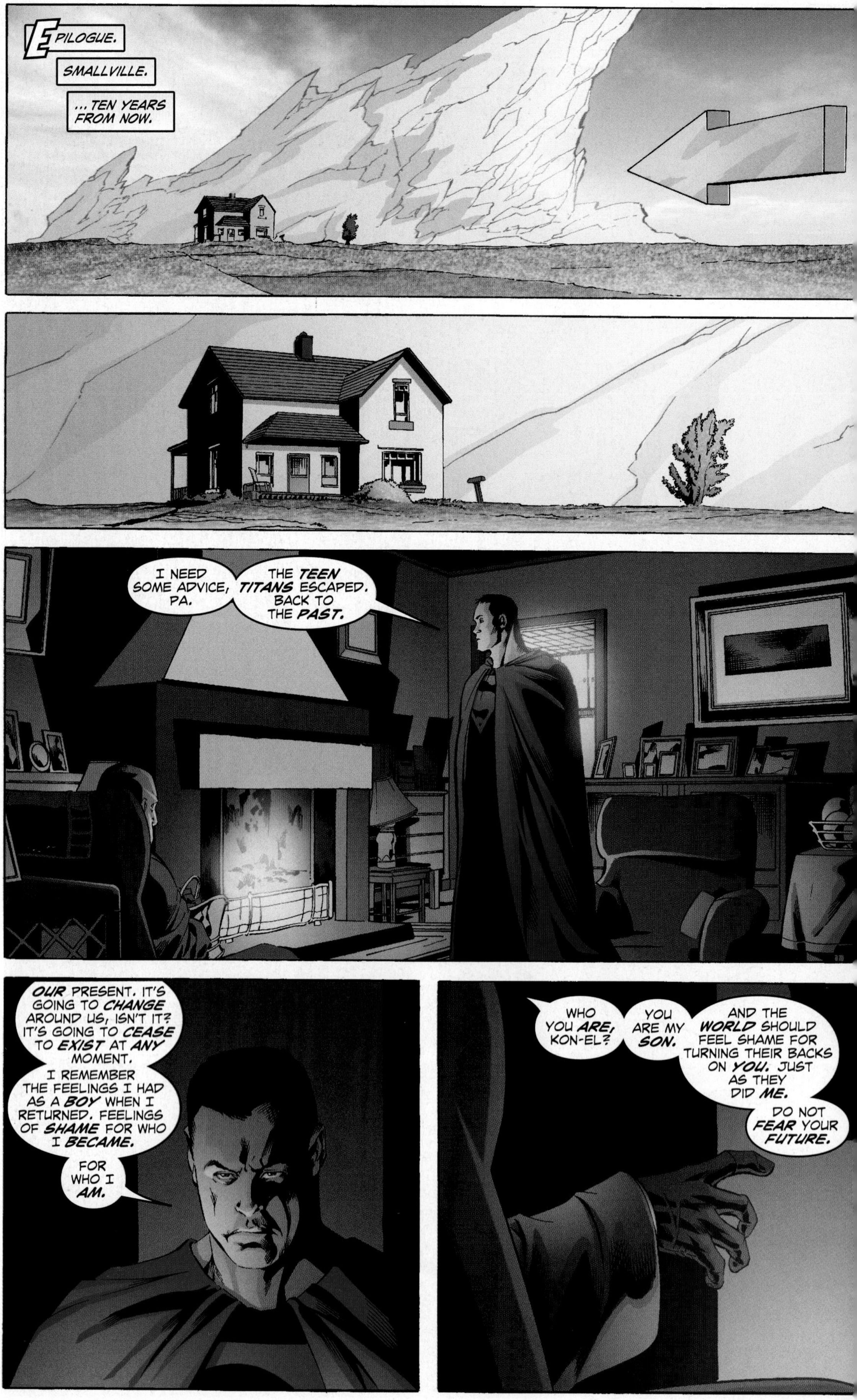
EPILOGUE.
SMALLVILLE.
...TEN YEARS FROM NOW.
I NEED SOME ADVICE, PA.
THE TEEN TITANS ESCAPED. BACK TO THE PAST.
OUR PRESENT. IT'S GOING TO CHANGE AROUND US, ISN'T IT? IT'S GOING TO CEASE TO EXIST AT ANY MOMENT.
I REMEMBER THE FEELINGS I HAD AS A BOY WHEN I RETURNED. FEELINGS OF SHAME FOR WHO I BECAME.
FOR WHO I AM.
WHO YOU ARE, KON-EL?
YOU ARE MY SON.
AND THE WORLD SHOULD FEEL SHAME FOR TURNING THEIR BACKS ON YOU. JUST AS THEY DID ME.
DO NOT FEAR YOUR FUTURE.

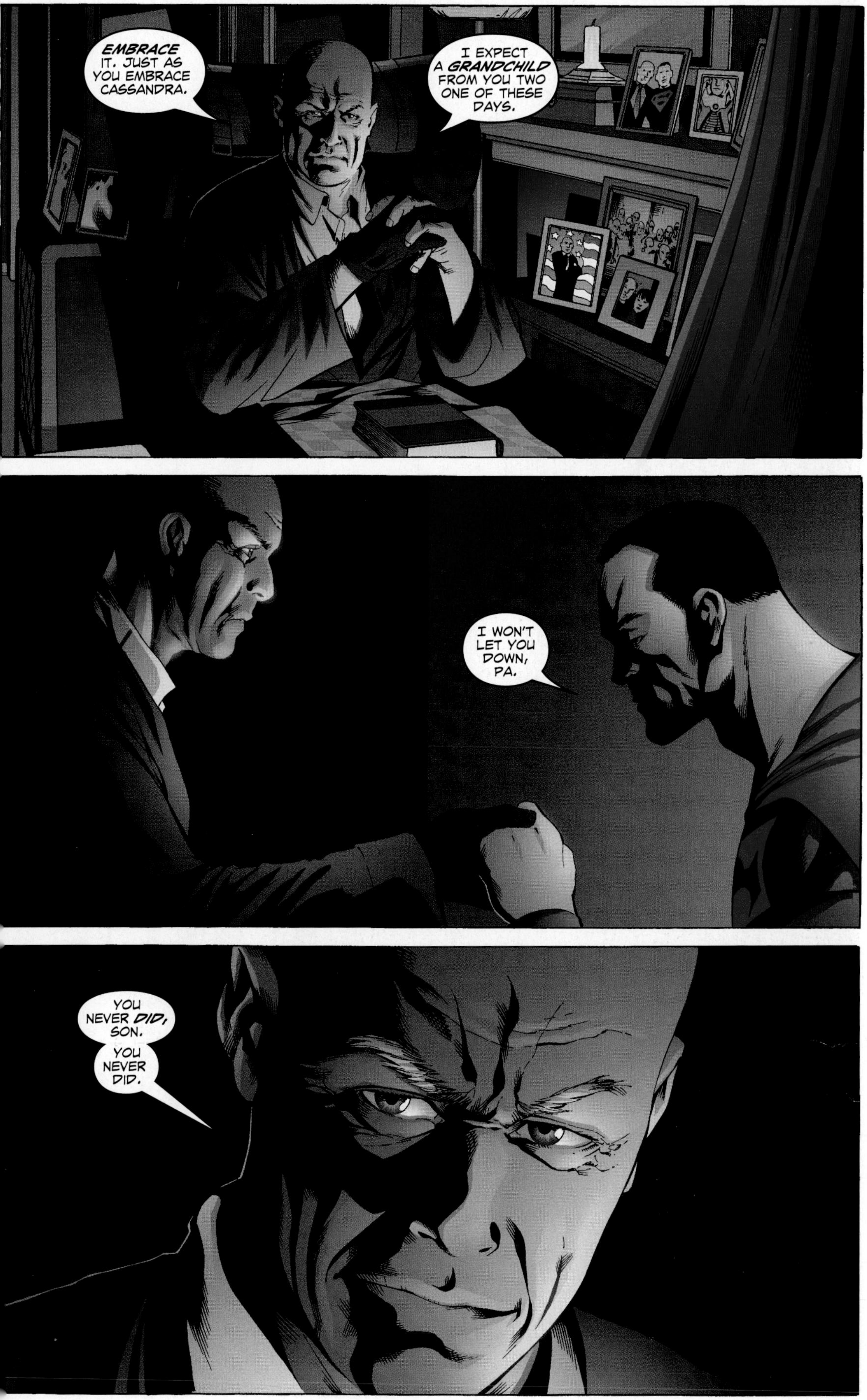
EMBRACE IT. JUST AS YOU EMBRACE CASSANDRA.
I EXPECT A GRANDCHILD FROM YOU TWO ONE OF THESE DAYS.
I WON'T LET YOU DOWN, PA.
YOU NEVER DID, SON.
YOU NEVER DID.

DESIGNING THE FUTURE

Mike McKone got a rare chance to redesign the Teen Titans for a new generation,
one ten years in the future. He relished the opportunity and proved both prolific and creative.
From his files, here are some of the designs he envisioned for the team.

Left: Robin becomes Batman, keeping the cape and cowl, but also retaining elements from his own uniform.
Sleek and made for acrobatic battle, the outfit is more for a darker world than just the streets of Gotham.
Right: Superboy in an outfit that's familiar but more militaristic.

Left: Aquagirl joins the team at some point in the future and is seen here in a modified chain-mail outfit.
Right: Kid Flash, honoring the Flash legacy.

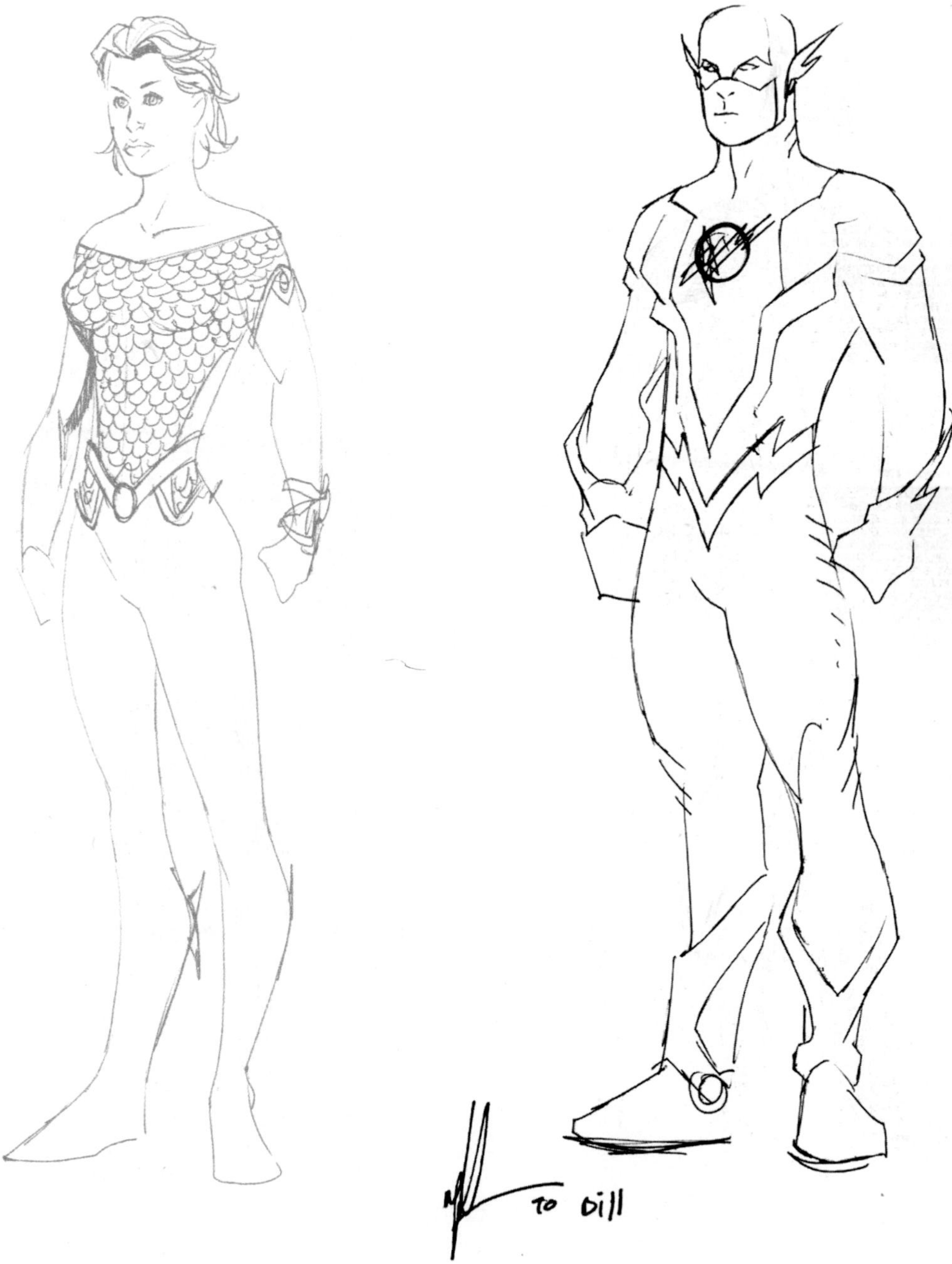

Cassie in full Amazon armor.

Left: Gar Logan as a more amorphous figure. Right: Raven, dark and moody as ever.

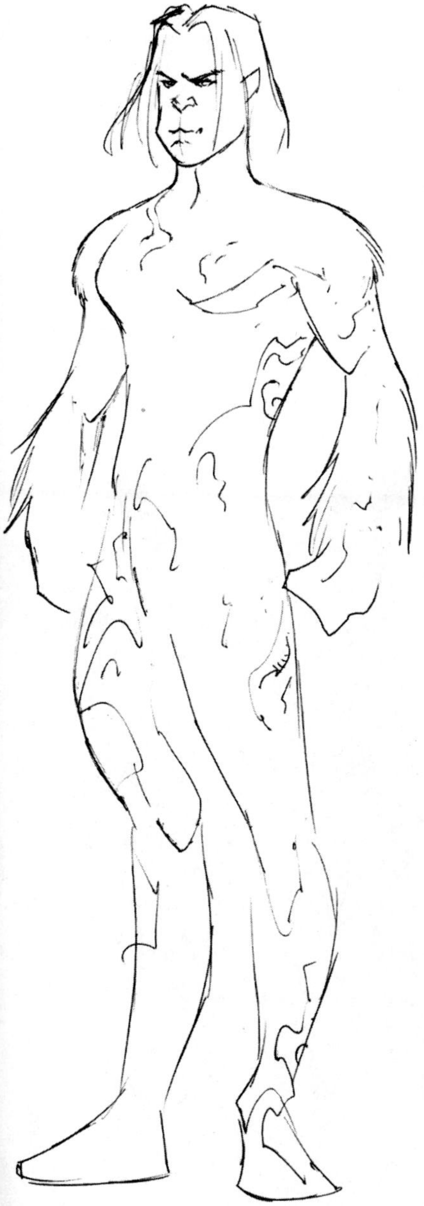

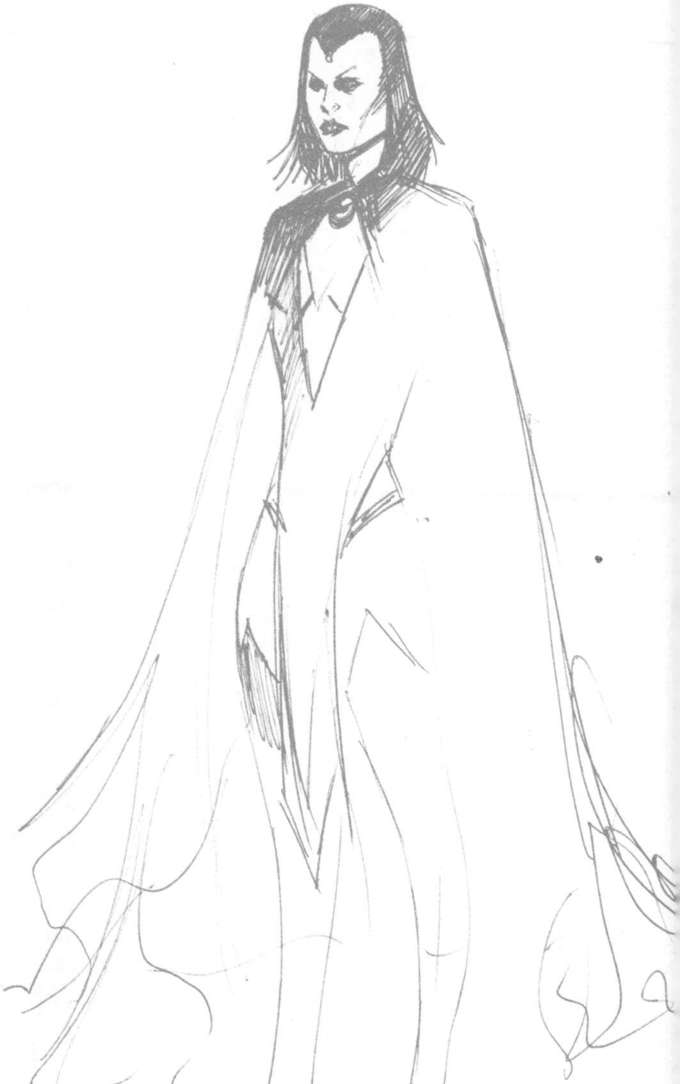

Left: A very rough composition for the future's Titans West. Right: The revised final line art.

> "This is comic book storytelling at its absolute finest."
> —IGN

> "If you've read a superhero comic book published by DC Comics within the last few years, and were completely blown away by it, there's a good chance that it was something written by Geoff Johns." —WASHINGTON EXAMINER

FROM THE WRITER OF
JUSTICE LEAGUE AND *THE FLASH*

GEOFF JOHNS
GREEN LANTERN: REBIRTH

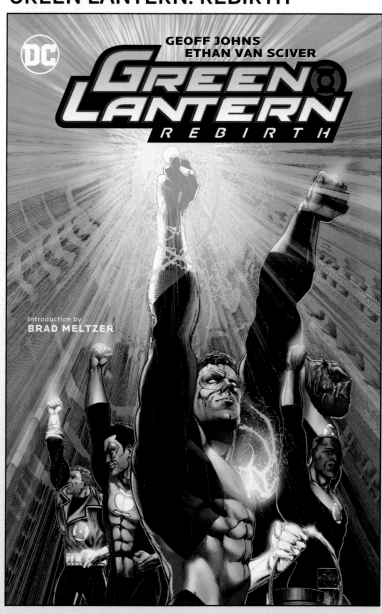

GEOFF JOHNS
ETHAN VAN SCIVER

Green Lantern
REBIRTH

Introduction by
BRAD MELTZER

Get more DC graphic novels wherever comics and books are sold!

"Impressive."
– **MTV SPLASH PAGE**

"The Flash couldn't be in better hands."
– **NEWSARAMA**

"Geoff Johns on THE FLASH has been a true boon for the Scarlet Speedster, putting him right up there in popularity with the likes of Batman, Superman and Green Lantern."
– **USA TODAY**

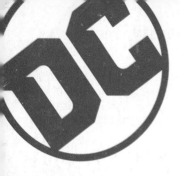

FROM THE WRITER OF *JUSTICE LEAGUE* AND *GREEN LANTERN*

GEOFF JOHNS

with ETHAN VAN SCIVER

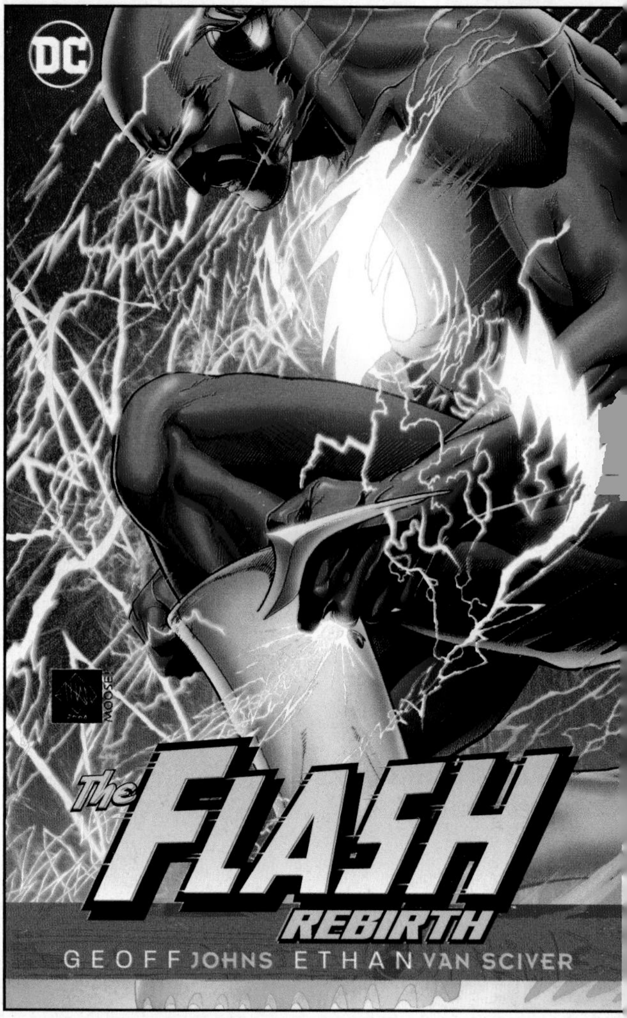
The FLASH
REBIRTH
GEOFF JOHNS ETHAN VAN SCIVER

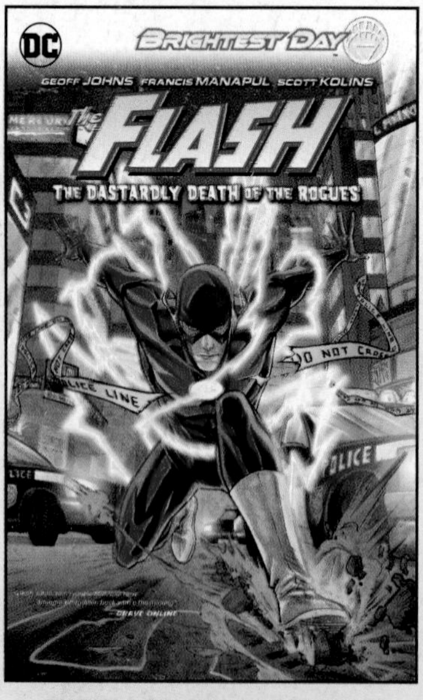
BRIGHTEST DAY
GEOFF JOHNS FRANCIS MANAPUL SCOTT KOLINS
The FLASH
THE DASTARDLY DEATH OF THE ROGUES

THE FLASH: THE DASTARDLY DEATH OF THE ROGUES! with FRANCIS MANAPUL

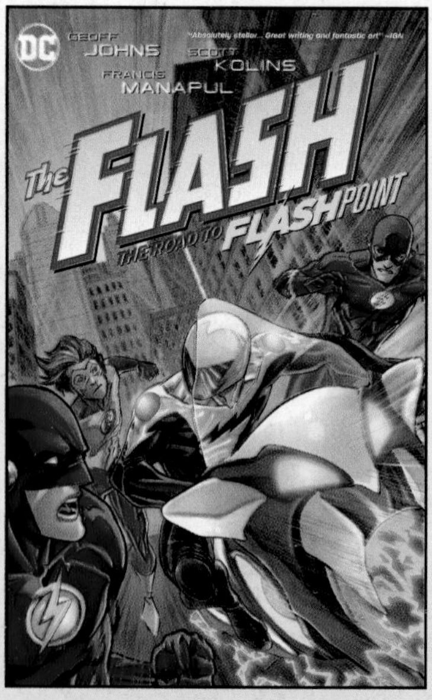
GEOFF JOHNS
SCOTT KOLINS
FRANCIS MANAPUL
The FLASH
THE ROAD TO FLASHPOINT

THE FLASH: THE ROAD TO FLASHPOINT with FRANCIS MANAPUL and SCOTT KOLINS

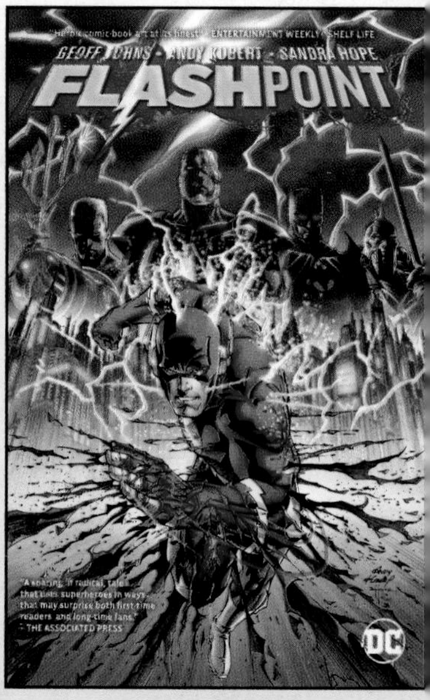
GEOFF JOHNS · ANDY KUBERT · SANDRA HOPE
FLASHPOINT

FLASHPOINT: with ANDY KUBERT

Get more DC graphic novels wherever comics and books are sold!